Emotions as Bio-cultural Processes

Birgitt Röttger-Rössler · Hans J. Markowitsch
Editors

Emotions as Bio-cultural Processes

Springer

Universität Bielefeld
ZiF

Editors
Birgitt Röttger-Rössler
Max Planck Institute for
Social Anthropology
Halle, Germany
roettger@eth.mpg.de

Hans J. Markowitsch
University of Bielefeld
Germany
hjmarkowitsch@uni-bielefeld.de

ISBN: 978-0-387-74134-5 e-ISBN: 978-0-387-09546-2
DOI 10.1007/978-0-387-09546-2

Library of Congress Control Number: 2008937455

Printed on acid-free paper

springer.com

In memory of Dr. Johannes Roggenhofer
(1962–2008)

Preface

The present volume emerged from discussions in the research group "Emotions as Bio-cultural Processes" (April 1, 2004 to March 31, 2005), which was generously funded and hosted by the Center for Interdisciplinary Research (ZIF), Bielefeld University.

A central figure in the ZiF organization was Johannes Roggenhofer, the exceptionally skilful and tactful executive secretary of the Center. His calmly objective style combined with kind and warm-hearted humor and the way he always had a sympathetic ear for the major and minor troubles of colleagues and research fellows decisively shaped the harmonious atmosphere that we have come to appreciate so much at the ZiF. His sudden death on January 24, 2008 at the age of 45 was a shock for all of us and left a great gap in the lives of many. We dedicate this volume to his memory.

Our special thanks go to the permanent fellows of this research group and simultaneously contributors to this volume with whom we shared an exciting year of stimulating and fruitful discussions, workshops, and conferences. Owing to both their profound interest in this research topic and their enthusiasm for interdisciplinary communication, the year became a highly rewarding experience for us as organizers—not only scientifically but in interpersonal terms. One person of utmost importance for the smooth running of all research group affairs was our special assistant, Henrik Bollermann, to whom we owe many thanks.

The task of translating the German and/or correcting the English of contributions written by nonnative speakers has been accomplished meticulously by Jonathan Harrow, who displayed not only an outstanding sensitivity to the various disciplinary languages but also extraordinary patience with the sometimes chaotic text and time management of several contributors. Especially with regard to this last aspect, the book would still be unfinished without the unflinching commitment of Mo Tschache, who undertook the painstaking labor of formatting and finishing the text, fitting in new versions, and entering more corrections. She always knew exactly where things stood and never failed to exert her rigorous charm when chasing up authors for their mistakes and omissions.

We highly appreciate the readiness of Springer Science+Business Media to publish such a broadly interdisciplinary work.

Halle, Germany Birgitt Röttger-Rössler
Bielefeld, Germany Hans J. Markowitsch

Contents

Contributors

Michael J. Casimir
Department of Social and Cultural Anthropology, University of Cologne, Cologne, Germany; michael.casimir@uni-koeln.de

Irene Daum
Department of Neuropsychology, Institute of Cognitive Neuroscience, Ruhr University Bochum, Bochum, Germany; irene.daum@rub.de

Eva-Maria Engelen
Department of Philosophy, Faculty of Philosophy, University of Konstanz, Konstanz, Germany; eva-maria.engelen@uni-konstanz.de

Manfred Holodynski
Psychology and Sport Studies, University of Münster, Münster, Germany; manfred.holodynski@uni-muenster.de

Sven Ismer
Department of Movement Science, University of Hamburg, Hamburg, Germany; sven.ismer@uni-hamburg.de

Susanne Jung
Independent Consultant, Göttingen, Germany; susa_jung@web.de

Stefanie Kronast
Independent Consultant, Bielefeld, Germany; steffkro@gmx.de

Margot L. Lyon
School of Archaeology and Anthropology, The Australian National University, Canberra, ACT, Australia; margot.lyon@anu.edu.au

Hans J. Markowitsch
Department of Physiological Psychology, University of Bielefeld, Bielefeld, Germany; hjmarkowitsch@uni-bielefeld.de

Sighard Neckel
University of Vienna, Institute of Sociology, Vienna, Austria
e-mail: sighard.neckel@univie.ac.at

Birgitt Röttger-Rössler
Max Planck Institute for Social Anthropology, Department I – Integration and Conflict, Halle, Germany; roettger@eth.mpg.de

Christian von Scheve
University of Vienna, Institute of Sociology, Vienna, Austria
e-mail: christian.von.scheve@univie.ac.at

Achim Stephan
Institute of Cognitive Science, University of Osnabrück, Osnabrück, Germany; acstepha@uos.de

Thomas Stodulka
PhD candidate in social anthropology, Germany; tstodulka@hotmail.com

Marie Vandekerckhove
PhD, Department of Cognitive & Biological Psychology, Faculty of Psychology and Educational Sciences, Vrije Universiteit Brussel, Belgium; e-mail: marie.vandekerckhove@vub.ac.be

Prologue

Introduction

Birgitt Röttger-Rössler and Hans J. Markowitsch

Gut feelings, or intuitions, are considered to be more dominant than rational thought (Gigerenzer, 2007); and particularly in situations not totally under our control and with unpredictable outcome, it is our emotional self that guides our behavior. Antonio Damasio (1999), in the subtitle of his book *The Feeling of What Happens*, stated that body and emotion make up our consciousness. We are bound to our body; and when it comes to our brain, we are bound much more closely to those parts that are phylogenetically old and guide our emotions—the limbic system—than the recent additions so important for organization and planning—the frontal lobes.

This book follows quite divergent perspectives—from philosophy, psychology, physiology and the neurosciences, ethnology, and sociology—to pursue the common goal of elucidating why emotions function as a bridge between our social and cognitive beings. In contrast to the usual, more limited approaches, it encompasses views extending from our evolutionary history to our cultural present—from the isolated emotional outbursts of an individual to the similarly uncontrolled emotional eruptions of social communities as described by Sigmund Freud (1921/1951).

The articles collected here are an outcome of the work of a research group organized jointly by the editors and running for a full year from April 2004 to March 2005 at a well known German institute of advanced study, the Center of Interdisciplinary Research, located at the University of Bielefeld. Throughout that fruitful year, the contributors to this book worked together to promote our understanding of emotions from their biological background to their cultural refinements. Despite many discipline-specific differences, the fellows of the research group agreed from the outset that the emotions felt by an individual in a given situation depend on several factors: the particular social context and the corresponding cultural models of interpretation and behavior, the biography and psychological structures of the single individual, and innate physiological

B. Röttger-Rössler (✉)
Max Planck Institute for Social Anthropology, Department I – Integration and Conflict, Halle, Germany
e-mail: roettger@eth.mpg.de

B. Röttger-Rössler, H.J. Markowitsch (eds.), *Emotions as Bio-cultural Processes*,
DOI 10.1007/978-0-387-09546-2_1, © Springer Science+Business Media, LLC 2009

processes anchored in human biology ("bodily reactions") and their subjective perception ("feeling"). The latter, in turn, is partly shaped by culture, just as the expression of emotions is molded by culture-specific display rules. In short, the researchers shared the view that emotions should be conceptualized as highly complex bio-cultural interaction systems that develop and change over the course of time. Thus, the main goal of the group was to lay down the foundations for the development of an interdisciplinary model of emotions while paying special attention to the bio-cultural dialectics of emotional processes.

Nonetheless, while pursuing this goal, we were immediately confronted by the enormous heterogeneity of underlying assumptions, theoretical approaches, specialized terminologies, and research methods applied by the representatives of the various disciplines. To overcome these differences so that a truly interdisciplinary dialogue could emerge, our first task was to develop a common language, including a common terminology—not the easiest endeavor with scientists from such different backgrounds who are used to working with their discipline-specific methodologies and concepts.

It took several months to build a framework that satisfied all of us. On the one hand, this framework provided a basis for distinguishing between emotions common to us as humans and our relatives from the animal kingdom, those emotions apparently found only in our own species, and finally those few complex emotions that may not be universal to humankind but perhaps limited to certain cultures. On the other hand, it provided the parameters for consistently conceiving emotions as bio-cultural processes while simultaneously taking account of their dynamic nature—their continuous development and change over and within time.

During the course of these conceptual discussions and gatherings, the need emerged to apply our theoretical considerations and models in an exemplary analysis of prototypical emotions. Therefore, a subgroup was set up to specialize in a refined analysis of two emotions that seem to appear in the human species alone: shame and pride. These emotions, often referred to in the literature as the higher, or "social," emotions, are considered to reflect the complex shaping processes inherent in our existence as social beings dependent on the recognition and judgments of our fellows.

In line with these specializations and divisions of labor, the book is organized into two sections. The first part is oriented primarily toward theoretical issues, and the second is oriented primarily toward empirical applications in concrete case studies of pride and shame as well as honor and dishonor.

Before presenting the contents and goals of each part, as well as the individual chapters in more detail, we emphasize once again the unusual context in which this book emerged. The individual chapters were preceded by discussions undertaken by a research group of unparalleled scientific heterogeneity. The discussions served two purposes: (1) to gain an understanding across disciplines, that is, to outline and explain discipline-specific concepts, findings, and assumptions; and (2) to formulate interdisciplinary research questions, postulates, and interfaces. To come to the point, the goal of this book is to inform the reader about the variety of disciplinary perspectives and then go on to develop new perspectives that go beyond the borders of these disciplines. It is of a highly explorative nature; it offers food for thought and triggers questions that we hope will stimulate interdisciplinary cooperation. Our goal is no more than this but also no less.

This introduction is immediately followed by a consideration of emotions from the philosophical perspective: What are human beings? What distinguishes them from other living creatures, and what do they have in common with them? What is specifically human, and how can it be defined? The cognitive philosopher Achim Stephan considered the major attempts to define what is human that have evolved and continue to dominate the history of ideas in the Western world. He shows that emotionality has not been treated as an ability that is particularly human. Even in modern philosophy, it is not one of the generally recognized "topologies of being human." Stephan drew on findings from modern brain research that show how strongly rational action and social interactions depend on and are controlled by emotional evaluation processes, and he called for a reformulation of our view of the human being for an understanding of *Homo sapiens* as an *animal emotionale*.

The first part of the main book then starts off with "Emotions as Bio-cultural Processes: Disciplinary Debates and an Interdisciplinary Outlook," a chapter written jointly by several members of the research group, with the philosopher Eva-Maria Engelen at the helm. This chapter is the outcome of joint discussions among the fellows on the classic question "What are emotions?" aimed at formulating a common terminology and an interdisciplinary understanding of emotion. It can be understood as the key not just to Part I but to the entire book.

In one way or another, all subsequent chapters illuminate various aspects addressed or problematized here. For example, in the next chapter, "On the Origin and Evolution of Affective Capacities in Lower Vertebrates," social anthropologist and biologist Michael Casimir sets out the fundamentals of emotional developmental from a phylogenetic perspective. He emphasizes how certain basic forms of emotions can be seen in animals such as reptiles that evolved long before the first mammal appeared on earth. Based on the notion that emotions are elicited through sensing or perceiving specific environmental stimuli, he shows how increasingly complex emotional capacities have evolved in line with the growing complexity of the neural structures intertwined with the various senses.

Carrying on from here, the physiological psychologist and brain researcher Hans Markowitsch focuses on the brain—but this time with an emphasis on higher animals, including humans, and on the interdependence of emotion and intellect at both the behavioral and neural levels.

Irene Daum, Hans Markowitsch, and Marie Vandekerckhove then stress how the brain controls and guides our emotional behavior. In doing so, they specify the brain regions and circuits important for the expression of emotions. Furthermore, they refer to common errors in relating emotions to the brain und emphasize the roles of the amygdala, septum, and diencephalic nuclei in emotional processing by providing case examples that give a particularly clear demonstration of the contribution of individual brain structures to emotional processing. They also address the involvement of the "expanded limbic system" in emotional-cognitive control, the brain's biochemistry (transmitter systems), and laterality effects.

Whereas these chapters are generally committed to an evolutionary time scale, the next three contributions address the formation and change of emotions during the individual's life course and try to grasp the social and cultural modeling of emotional development processes. The chapter "Milestones and Mechanisms of Emotional Development" by developmental psychologist Manfred Holodynski takes us from the evolutionary to the individual perspective by studying the development of emotions during the course of childhood. He describes interactions between the child and the caregiver as the decisive mediators in the process "through which culture enters into emotion."

Social anthropologist Birgitt Röttger-Rössler then focuses attention on the problem of how the social and cultural emotional code has changed historically. Macrosocial changes frequently confront individuals with life situations of such novelty that they can no longer cope with them appropriately on the basis of given conventional feeling rules. It then becomes necessary for the members of a society to reformulate the feeling rules that have lost their validity. Röttger-Rössler analyzes such reformulation processes in terms of the changed meaning of pregnancy loss in contemporary Germany, and she describes the significant role of social communication and verbalization processes in the modification of handed-down social feeling rules.

The concept of social feeling rules (Hochschild, 1983), which are modified constantly within the context of macrosocietal processes of change, is the focus of the next chapter. Sociologist Sighard Neckel addresses the continuous growth of various programs for emotional self-management since the 1990s in Western societies, which have appeared in the form of advice books and training courses offering strategies for successful emotional self-regulation and optimizing the emotional experience and performance. He works out how these advice books and training programs relate to the principles and demands of a modern market society characterized by flexible "network capitalism," and he shows how these discourses treat emotions as goods, or "marketable products." They are seen as important strategic instruments for realizing goals that are subject to the rational calculation of how to increase one's own skills, well-being, and effectiveness.

The chapter by social anthropologist Margot Lyon focuses on the search for meaningful theoretical approaches to the complex interactions between the bodily and the sociocultural dimensions of emotional processes. In this context, she points to a number of early approaches in German philosophical anthropology (e.g., Plessner, 1928; Gehlen, 1957/1980). These approaches have received little attention in recent emotion research even though they strove explicitly to (1) incorporate natural science explanations into the understanding of society and human nature and (2) include important ideas on the relation between social life and bodily processes. Lyon uses this work along with some older sociological approaches to develop a "social emotions" approach that aims at a deeper understanding of emotion's central place in the mediation of bodily and sociocultural domains.

At the end of Part 1, Achim Stephan pursues the philosophical tradition of the thought experiment and asks whether artificial feelings can exist and, if so, what they would have to look like to distinguish them from "natural feelings." From the perspective of classic philosophy, he reiterates the criteria for defining the various feelings, thereby not only improving our understanding of emotions but also furthering the Western traditions of thought that continue to shape both the popular and the scientific understanding of emotions—that is, are part of the cultural knowledge that also influences the approaches of modern emotion research.

As already mentioned, the second part of the book focuses on the specific emotions pride and shame. The social significance assigned to these emotions not only varies considerably among cultures; it reveals different emphases within a single society as well as over the course of ontogenesis. It should be stressed here that pride and shame are not viewed antagonistically but as interconnected emotional domains closely linked to processes of social inclusion and exclusion.

We start off with a comprehensive study from Michael Casimir in cooperation with Susanne Jung. This chapter focuses on the theoretically significant relation between the social emotions pride and shame as immediate, short-term, bodily felt phenomena versus the highly complex social and symbolic categories of honor and dishonor/shame. It also asks whether—and, if so, how far—the socially and culturally formulated honor and shame codes found in many societies shape the individual experience of pride and shame; in other words, how far these pan-human emotional dimensions are shaped by specific cultures. The first part of Casimir and Jung's detailed analysis is a comprehensive anthropological overview of the facets of various "honor societies." This provides the necessary introductory framework within which to address the interaction between cultural value systems, emotion models, and the emotional episodes of individual actors.

The next chapter, from Birgitt Röttger-Rössler, addresses change in culture-specific honor codes within a Southeast Asian context. The central issue is how cultural models of emotions, and thereby emotions themselves, are transformed within the context of changing societal conditions. Röttger-Rössler draws on empirical material from her field research in Indonesia and uses a micro level analysis of a social conflict to plot how individual actors modify the social structures and emotional codes of their society through their own emotionally motivated behaviors and decisions. In this context, she details the translocal and global connections and the potential orientations that play a role in these processes.

This analysis is followed by another chapter that focuses on empirical anthropological research in Indonesia: Thomas Stodulka's analysis of the life situation of male street youths in the Javanese city of Yogyakarta. Stodulka is interested in the sociopsychological processes and strategies that groups on the fringe of society apply to cope with their marginalization. He postulates that one decisive determinant of whether such youths are able to cope with social exclusion and the hardships of living on the street is how far they succeed in developing a collective identity and manage to transform their individual shame at being a society dropout into a collective pride in being a member of a street gang.

The next chapter, by Sven Ismer, deals with the development of emotions and emotion regulation during adolescence, a life phase confronting youths with a multitude of new challenges and an increasing shift in their social focus—at least in Western societies—away from the family and toward school and peer relationships. An important issue in this context is the role of "youth cultures" and the extent to which they offer ways for adolescents to cope with their specific emotional problems. Ismer uses the example of hip-hop to address this domain, showing how this youth movement particularly enables marginalized adolescents to experience social recognition and compensate for the social devaluation and shaming processes to which they are exposed in mainstream society.

The contribution from developmental psychologist Manfred Holodynski and the educational scientist Stefanie Kronast focuses on the role of shame and pride in the school learning context. They show how fundamentally adapting to school achievement standards and norms is linked to the triggering of feelings of shame and pride. Students who do not meet the academic standard are excluded through a variety of subtle shaming processes, whereas successful students frequently experience pride through praise and social recognition. The authors analyze how harmful the "spiral of shaming and discouragement" is to learning motivation because once a certain stage has been reached any willingness to achieve is suffocated by self-protective measures. They criticize the insufficient consideration given to these emotional processes in the literature on learning theory and school psychology.

This book both starts and ends with philosophy, the latter being a chapter with an analysis of anger, shame, and justice in the ancient and modern worlds by Eva-Maria Engelen. She asks about the significance of anger and shame for the individual in a social context and the role these emotions play in the recognition of social order and the rules of living together in communities; in other words, she examines the social regulatory and evaluative functions of shame and anger. She not only analyzes how closely social norms and values, laws, and justice are interwoven with these emotions, she addresses the central question on what distinguishes shame from guilt. She finds the answer in the two-sided nature of shame, that is, in the fact that individuals feel shame not only when failing to meet social standards through their own actions but also when others fail to treat them according to accepted social and moral standards, thereby "devaluing" them in a fundamental way. This form of shame persists; unlike guilt, it cannot be confessed, recompensed, or forgiven in the Christian sense. It marks a substantial social devaluation that remains branded on the mind and body of the individual.

In summary, the chapters in this second part of the book show how significant the emotional dimensions of pride and shame are for human social behavior and what a crucial role they play in processes of social conformity. Both emotions—whether the shame accompanied by fear of social exclusion or the pride when embodying central social values through one's own achievements or features—motivate individuals to orient their behavior toward the standards of the society to which they are attached.

As the editors, we close here with what we consider to be justifiable pride in this volume. We believe that it offers the reader deep and thorough insights into mechanisms of human action that, though based on our animal heritage, have developed in accordance with our being as a *zoon politikon*—a social animal who is oriented toward and forms communities.

References

Damasio, A. (1999). *The feeling of what happens: Body and emotion in the making of consciousness*. San Diego, CA: Harcourt.

Freud, S. (1951). *Group psychology and the analysis of the ego* (E. Jones, Ed., J. Strachey, Trans.). New York: Liveright Publishing. (Original work published 1921)

Gehlen, A. (1980). *Man in the age of technology* (P. Lipscomb, Trans; Foreword by P. L. Berger). New York: Columbia University Press. (Original work published 1957)

Gigerenzer, G. (2007). *Gut feelings*. New York: Random House.

Hochschild, A. (1983). *The managed heart: Commercialization of human feeling*. Berkeley, CA: University of California Press.

Plessner, H. (1928). *Die Stufen des Organischen und der Mensch* [The levels of the organic and the human being]. Berlin: de Gruyter.

Homo Sapiens—The Emotional Animal

Achim Stephan

Abstract Traditionally, in attempts to define what comprises being human, philosophers have referred to features such as rationality, language, culture, free will, creativity, or political structures to distinguish humans from other living beings. In the long run, these attempts to separate humans sharply from the animal kingdom have all failed. Emotions have been largely ignored on the grounds that humans share them with many other animals. As a result of this neglect, it has been overlooked how essential emotions are for what it means to be human.

Looking back over the last 2000 to 3000 years in the history of ideas, we find a series of proposals for defining what makes human beings human and thereby different from all other animals. Immanuel Kant (1724–1804) analyzed this central issue in anthropology—the nature of man—in a transparent and effective way in the introduction of his *Logik* (edited by Gottlob Jäsche). After defining philosophy as the "science of the ultimate objects of human reason," he formulated four fundamental questions for philosophical study (that have now become almost common property), also stipulating where their answers should be sought.

- What can I know?
- What ought I do?
- What may I hope for?
- What is man?

The first question is the concern of metaphysics, the second of ethics, the third of religion, and the fourth of anthropology. Basically, according to Kant, one can assign all topics associated with these questions to anthropology (AA IX, pp. 24–25).

A. Stephan (✉)
Institute of Cognitive Science, University of Osnabrück, Osnabrück, Germany
e-mail: acstepha@uos.de

B. Röttger-Rössler, H.J. Markowitsch (eds.), *Emotions as Bio-cultural Processes*,
DOI 10.1007/978-0-387-09546-2_2, © Springer Science+Business Media, LLC 2009

In 2004, the German Wissenschaftliche Buchgesellschaft commenced a seven-volume series entitled *Topologien des Menschlichen* [Human Taxonomies] (edited by Heinrich Schmidinger and Clemens Sedmak). One of the goals of the series was to examine the old Kantian question: "What is man?" by particularly considering findings from the natural sciences and the humanities. Titles of this series, starting with the first volume, are (in translation) *Man—A Rational Animal?*, with the subtitle, *Reason–Cognition–Intelligence*, followed by *Man—A Free Being?*, *Man—A "Zoon Politikon?"*, *Man—An "Animal Symbolicum?"*, *Man—A Creative Being?*, *Man—A Deficient Being?*, and *Man—Image of God?*

Without exception, these titles refer directly to the traditional attempts to define what humans essentially are. As a rule, it means distinguishing humans from the animal world. Many of these attempts draw on the classical theory of definition, according to which every concept is defined as a subclass of a more general concept. This general concept is called the *genus proximum*. Each subclass of the genus proximum is characterized by special features called the *differentiae specificae*. Hence, there is consensus regarding the more comprehensive, more general concept: Humans are living beings. According to traditional proposals, they differ from other living beings through (1) their reasoning skills, (2) their efforts to form state-like communities, (3) their ability to use symbols, (4) their possession of free will, and/or (5) their ability to be creative. Humans are also viewed as (6) "deficient beings" or (7) an image of God. In contrast, emotions, passions, affects, feelings, and sensations have never played any role whatsoever in all these attempted definitions. The idea of conceiving humans also, and in particular, as an *animal emotionale* was (and is) not considered in this context.

Many of the above-mentioned attempts at definition go back a long way historically. Classic Greek philosophy, Judaism, and Christianity have provided a stockpile of definitions of humans that continue to characterize philosophy to this day. It is particularly interesting to see that the premise of a biologically deficient endowment and its compensation through higher mental abilities reflects a motive that can already be found in a mythical form in Hesiod's Theogony (~ 700 BC) and has been handed down to us by Plato (~ 428–348 BC) as Protagoras's myth on the emergence of culture.

Protagoras tells his visitors that after the gods had decided to create mortal beings and had fashioned them from earth and fire the gods then ordered Prometheus and Epimetheus to equip them with properties. Epimetheus asked Prometheus to grant him the right to distribute the abilities and features, and he tried to proceed in a balanced way so that no species could be made extinct by another. That is why he gave some strength without swiftness, and the weaker were made swift. Epimetheus also clothed the mortal beings with thick hair and tough skins so they could withstand cold and heat. Particularly, he made predators to be far less prolific than their prey. However, despite all his efforts, Epimetheus was not very wise, because he

> didn't notice that he had used up all the powers on the non-rational creatures; so last of all he was left with human kind, quite unprovided for, and he was at a loss what to do. As he was racking his brains Prometheus came to inspect the distribution, and saw the other creatures well provided for in every way, while man was naked and unshod, without any covering for his bed or any fangs or claws; and already the appointed day was at hand, on which man too had to come out of the earth to the light of day. (321c; translated by Taylor)

Nonetheless, Prometheus had an idea. He stole from Hephaestus and Athene their technical skill along with the use of fire, and that was what he gave to humans. This is the way, according to the myth, in which humans came to have "a share of the divine attributes" (322a) and went on to take their place between the [other] animals and the gods.

The idea emerging here of the human as a creation with little endowment from the gods or from nature recurs much later with Johann Gottfried Herder (1744–1803) in, for example, his *Abhandlung über den Ursprung der Sprache* (Essay on the Origin of Language) in which he describes the human as "naked and bare, weak and in need, shy and unarmed, and—to make the sum of its misery complete—deprived of all guides of life" (1772/1966, p. 107).

Nowadays, the definition of the human as a deficient being is associated particularly with Arnold Gehlen (1904–1976), who presented the human inadequacies described by Protagoras and Herder more scientifically in his book *Der Mensch. Seine Natur und seine Stellung in der Welt* [Man: His Nature and Place in the World].

> In terms of morphology, man is, in contrast to all other higher mammals, primarily characterized by deficiencies, which, in an exact, biological sense, qualify as a lack of adaptation, lack of specialization, primitive states, and failure to develop, and which are therefore essentially negative features. Humans have no natural protection against inclement weather; we have no natural organs for defense and attack but yet neither are our bodies designed for flight. Most animals surpass man as far as acuity of the senses is concerned. Man has what could even be termed a dangerous lack of true instincts and needs an unusually long period of protection and care during his infancy and childhood. In other words, under natural conditions, among dangerous predators, man would long ago have died out. (1940/1988, p. 26)

In his introduction to a later edition, Gehlen added:

> If, in comparison to animals, man appears as a "deficient being," then this designation expresses a comparative relationship. . . . In this respect, this concept attempts precisely what H. Freyer criticizes it for: "One envisions man fictitiously as animal only to discover that he makes an imperfect and indeed impossible animal." (1940/1988, p. 13)

Gehlen willingly admitted that characterizing humans as deficient beings is in no way a complete definition. Nonetheless, it does serve to point out our "special position" from a morphological perspective.

In the following, I pick up the threads of these old myths again and look at one of the positive definitions of the human being. The most well known is naturally the premise probably going back to the Greek physician and philosopher Alcmaeon ($\sim$ 500 BC) that human beings differ particularly from all other animals through being the only ones who can comprehend and think; that is, they possess understanding, reason, awareness-a mind. This perspective can be seen in definitions of the human being as *zoon logon echon*, as *animal rationale*, or as *Homo sapiens*. The valuation assigned to the ability to think or the activity of thinking is simultaneously the standard for measuring the valuation assigned to humans.. This applies to Socrates and Plato just as much as to Descartes and Kant. For René Descartes (1596–1650), reason was the defining property that discriminates true human beings from possible artificial imitations, and it does so in principle. In a famous passage from his *Discours de la Méthode*, he stated:

> [I]f there were machines bearing the image of our bodies, and capable of imitating our actions as far as it is morally possible, there would still remain two most certain tests whereby to know that they were not therefore really men. Of these the first is that they could never use words or other signs arranged in such a manner as is competent to us in order to declare our thoughts to others ... The second test is, that although such machines might execute many things with equal or perhaps greater perfection than any of us, they would, without doubt, fail in certain others from which it could be discovered that they did not act from knowledge, but solely from the disposition of their organs: for while reason is an universal instrument that is alike available on every occasion, these organs, on the contrary, need a particular arrangement for each particular action. (§ 5.10)

In general, many authors, particularly during the Middle Ages, agreed unanimously that humans are the image of God precisely because they possess reason, free will, and self-regulation (Grawe & Hügli, 1980, p. 1072). The strongest expression of this idea can be found in the bible when the Book of Genesis addresses the origins of creation:

> Then God said, Let us make man in our image, in our likeness, and let them rule over the fish of the sea and the birds of the air, over the livestock, over all the earth, and over all the creatures that move along the ground. So God created man in his own image, in the image of God he created him; male and female he created them. (Genesis, I, 26–27)

The idea of humans as free and creative beings is expressed most impressively in Pico della Mirandola's (1463–1494) *De Hominis Dignitate Oratio*—which Jacob Burckhardt (1818–1897) called one of the "most noble legacies of the Renaissance" (Burckhardt, 1952, p. 330). Pico della Mirandola let "God the father," the greatest architect of the world, speak to Adam after releasing him into the world:

> All other things have a limited and fixed nature prescribed and bounded by Our laws. You, with no limit or no bound, may *choose for yourself the limits and bounds of your nature*. We have placed you at the world's center so that you may survey everything else in the world. We have made you neither of heavenly nor of earthly stuff, neither mortal nor immortal, so that *with free choice and dignity*, you may fashion yourself into whatever form you choose. To you is granted the power of degrading yourself into the lower forms of life, the beasts, and to you is granted the power, contained in your intellect and judgment, to be reborn into the higher forms, the divine. (pp. 5–7)

Nowadays, Kant's thesis presented in *The Critique of Pure Reason* under "The antinomy of pure reason third conflict of the transcendental ideas" provides a more suitable focus for the modern and contemporary debate on human freedom. He stated:

> Thesis: Causality in accordance with laws of nature is not the only causality from which the appearances of the world can one and all be derived. To explain these appearances it is necessary to assume that there is also *another causality, that of freedom.* (AA III, p. 308)

In his commentary on this thesis, he remarked:

> If, for instance, I at this moment arise from my chair, *in complete freedom*, without being necessarily determined thereto by the influence of natural causes, a new series, with all its natural consequences in infinitum, has its absolute beginning in this event.... For this resolution and act of mine do not form part of the succession of purely natural effects, and are not a mere continuation of them.... (AA III, p. 312)

The definition of the human being as a *zoon politikon*, that is, as a being that forms states, is arguably first found in such a form in Aristotle's (384–322 BC) *Politics*. In Book One, Aristotle addresses the relations between individuals, households, villages, and states. A polis (city-state) is accordingly the final association, formed of several villages. It has become substantial enough to reach self-sufficiency. This led Aristotle to the conclusion that:

> When several villages are united in a single complete community, large enough to be nearly or quite self-sufficing, the state comes into existence.... Hence it is evident that the state is a creation of nature, and that *man is by nature a political animal....* The proof that the state is a creation of nature and prior to the individual is that the individual, when isolated, is not self-sufficing; and therefore he is like a part in relation to the whole. But he who is unable to live in society, or who has no need because he is sufficient for himself, must be either a beast or a god: He is no part of a state. (1252b–1253a)

However, humans are by their nature "state-forming"-that is, animals that create social order-and they do this to a far greater extent "than bees or any other gregarious animal" (1253a).

At the time, a new proposal for defining the human being was formulated by Ernst Cassirer (1874–1945) in his *Essay on Man.* In his introduction to a philosophy of human culture, Cassirer started by using Jakob Johann von Uexküll's (1864–1944) terminology to demarcate humans as such from all other animals.

> The functional circle [i.e., the cooperation of a certain *Merknetz* (a receptor system) and a certain *Wirknetz* (an effector system)] of man is not only quantitatively enlarged; it has also undergone a qualitative change. Man has, as it were, discovered a new method of adapting himself to his environment. Between the receptor system and the effector system, which are to be found in all animal species, we find in man a third link which we may describe as the symbolic system. This new acquisition transforms the whole of human life. (1944, p. 24)

Hence, humans no longer live in a merely natural universe but also in a symbolic one. Language, myth, art, and religion are parts of this universe. In Cassirer's words, they are the "varied threads which weave the symbolic net, the tangled web of human experience" (p. 25). Taking these aspects into account, Cassirer proposed a correction and extension to the classic definition of the human being. He wrote:

> The great thinkers who have defined man as an *animal rationale* were not empiricists, nor did they ever intend to give an empirical account of human nature.... Reason is a very inadequate term with which to comprehend the forms of man's cultural life in all their richness and variety. But all these forms are *symbolic* forms. Hence, instead of defining man as an *animal rationale*, we should define him as an *animal symbolicum*. By so doing we can designate his specific difference, and we can understand the new way open to man-the way to civilization. (1944, pp. 25–26)

If we now stand back and reconsider these attempts to define the human being, it becomes conspicuous that one central human property is never used to define human beings: our emotionality. There seem to be several reasons for this: First, emotional behavior is not conceived as one of our valuable properties but more as a weakness that needs to be restrained by reason—a passion to which we seem exposed rather than an active behavior. Moreover, naturally, our ability to react emotionally to events in the world was not viewed as a *differentia specifica* of humans because emotions were readily attributed to animals as well. Thus, Aristotle, for example, emphasized in his *Politics* that "man is the only animal whom ... [nature] has endowed with the gift of speech ... whereas mere voice is but an indication of pleasure or pain, and is therefore found in other animals (for their nature attains to the perception of pleasure and pain and the intimation of them to one another)" (1253 a).

Indeed, there are a number of ways in which the expression of emotions corresponds between humans and at least our closest relatives, the great apes. As a result, emotions could not and cannot be considered a potential species-forming difference between humans and animals.

Nonetheless, none of the other definitions proposed so far provide convincingly real definitions of humans. The definition as an image of God is not only based on strong theological assumptions that one is in no way obliged to share and that cannot form the basis for a philosophical definition, it is also not free from a certain degree of hubris. The definition of humans as possessing free will who, in strict Kantian terms, should be able to initiate chains of causality as it were outside the laws of nature carries implausibly strong connotations of substance dualism. There is little to indicate that we possess freedom in this sense. Turning to the other definitions as an *animal rationale* or a *zoon politikon*, Cassirer and Gehlen have already presented justified objections to them. Gehlen, for example, pointed out that once one starts to examine single features or properties one can no longer find anything specifically human.

> Human beings do indeed have a very unusual physical structure but the anthropoids (great apes) have one quite similar. In addition, there are many animals, from ants to

> beavers, that form living quarters or artificial dwellings or that are social. Like man, elephants are also clever, and acoustical communication similar to our language definitely exists in many species.... If, in addition to such specific observations we add into account evolutionary theory, then anthropology would seem at best to be the last chapter in zoology. (1988, p. 7)

Since then, careful studies of chimpanzees and above all bonobos have shown that the use of symbols and cultural achievements are also not exclusively human if we understand culture as meaning that knowledge and customs are acquired from others and are not innate or acquired by chance. A good example of the cultural life of animals can be found in Frans de Waal's book *The Ape and the Sushi Master* (2001). He showed how chimpanzees, for example, acquired the use of tools to crack nuts from other members of a group. Furthermore, highly impressive forms of the use of symbols are shown, for example, by the two bonobos Kanzi and Panbanisha who learned to comprehend detailed phonetic messages. They can communicate with keyboards, thereby handling symbols in a quite creative way.

Because I also see no particular attraction in justifying a special status for humans specifically in terms of their deficiencies, I consider that all previously proposed definitions of the human being have, in the last analysis, been failures.

Naturally, this is not to imply that there are no major differences between humans and other primates in those dimensions on which a species-forming difference had been sought: Even in the future, bonobos will not compose requiems, write poetry, produce barrique wines, develop computer viruses, or wage war for supposed ideals. Nor will they, or any other more highly developed animal, ever ask themselves who they are, what they can know, what they ought to do, or what they may hope for. The same applies to their emotional life: They will not have hopes for a better future; they will not feel either insulted or dishonored by others; they will not experience nostalgia like we do when we think back to happier days; they will not perceive national pride when standing before a flag; nor will they sense the hate and disrespect humans sometimes feel for their fellows that turns them into beasts more vicious than any to be found in the animal world. In other words, emotions also distinguish human beings in a completely special way. They are those animals who have developed the finest nuances and the greatest cultural variety of emotional states of mind.

Any description and explanation of cultural differences in emotional reactions must analyze the dominant beliefs and values within a culture. For humans, even so-called primary emotional states such as fear, anger, sorrow, joy, pride, and disgust are embedded in the totality of their other intentional attitudes. Therefore—unlike the animals—they do not have just a biological basis; they always have a sociocultural basis as well.

Furthermore, emotions have culturally defined conditions of adequacy. In contrast to the emotional behavior of animals, emotional reactions of humans (and the strength of their expression) are open to criticism. Moreover, these reactions can be reevaluated almost immediately after they are expressed. Therefore, one should be cautious about attributing sweeping generalizations to humans based on insights gained from so-called affect programs identified in animals. Any description and explanation of human emotions requires not only a biological but also a folk psychological approach to gain an appropriate conceptualization of culturally mediated preferences and attitudes.

Because emotions have never been a suitable candidate in the continuingly unsuccessful search for a species-specific difference between humans and animals, they were never classified as essential properties of the human being. Their central significance for the rest of our mental life was neglected. However, studies in neuroscience, as popularized particularly by Antonio Damasio (1994), confirm how strongly rational and goal-oriented behavior depends on intact emotional evaluation processes. Without emotions, much would leave us indifferent; even our own future would seem uninteresting and trivial. Without emotions, we would be unable to make the decisions that guide our actions; we would have no evaluative basis for more long-term rational judgments and decisions. Without emotions, we would be incapable of a social and cultural life in a close community with many other persons. Therefore, it is time for us to recognize the full significance of emotions for our thinking and acting:[1] Humans are emotional beings in a crucial sense—not in the sense that they differ fundamentally from other living beings through their emotionality but in the sense that without their emotionality many of the properties formerly proposed as species-forming differences such as our ability to act rationally (*animal rationale*) or our ability to form and sustain social communities (*zoon politikon*) would not exist either.

In closing, even Protagoras was well aware of the significance of emotions for humans. In Plato's report of his myth on the emergence of culture mentioned above, he told about Zeus's concern that the human race would be wholly wiped out if it were to weaken itself through continuous strife and prove unable to form communities. Therefore, he "sent Hermes unto mankind with justice (*dikē*) and a sense of shame (*aidōs*), to bring order to their cities and common bonds of amity" (322a; translated by Hubbard & Karnofsky, 1982).

Shame, love, affection, worry, sadness, joy, hope, and many other emotions make an essential contribution to what was and continues to be the self—concept of humans—a being capable of rational action and social community. At the same time, they constitute what humans should also be according to their own self-concept: emotional beings.

Notes

1 In recent years, such insights have exerted an increasing influence on research into artificial intelligence and robotics. There are now several research programs designed to equip artificial systems with emotion-like behavior programs. This should be highly relevant not only for human–machine communication but also—and even more decisively—for the development of so-called autonomous agents.

References

Aristotle. *Politics*. Translated by Benjamin Jowett (1885).

Bible. Retrieved November 5, 2006 from www.bibleserver.com (International Bible Society).

Burckhardt, J. (1952). *Die Kultur der Renaissance in Italien*. Durchgesehen von W. Goetz. Stuttgart, Germany: Kröner.

Cassirer, E. (1944). *An essay on man. An introduction to a philosophy of human culture*. New Haven, CT: Yale University Press.

Damasio, A. R. (1994). *Descartes' error. Emotion, reason, and the human brain*. New York: Putnam's Sons.

Descartes, R. (1637). *Discours de la Méthode*. Translated as *Discours on the Method*. In The Philosophical Writings of Descartes (Vol. I). Cambridge: Cambridge University Press, 1985.

Gehlen, A. (1940). *Der Mensch. Seine Natur und seine Stellung in der Welt*. Translated as *Man: His Nature and Place in the World*. New York: Columbia University Press 1988.

Grawe, Chr., & Hügli, A. (1980). Mensch. III. Die anthropologischen Hauptstränge. In J. Ritter & K. Gründer (Eds.) *Historisches Wörterbuch der Philosophie* (Vol. 5, pp. 1071–1074). Basel, Switzerland/Stuttgart, Germany: Schwabe.

Herder, J. G. (1772). *Abhandlung über den Ursprung der Sprache*. Translation: Essay on the origin of language. In J. H. Moran & A. Gode (Eds.), *On the Origin of Language* (pp. 87–166). New York: Frederick Ungar, 1966.

Hubbard, B. A. F., & Karnofsky, E. S. (1982) *Plato's Protagoras. A Socratic commentary*. London: Duckworth.

Kant, I. (1787). *Kritik der reinen Vernunft*. (*Akademie Textausgabe* Bd. III). Translated by Norman Kemp Smith as *The Critique of Pure Reason*. Retrieved November 15, 2006 from humanum.arts.cuhk.edu.hk/Philosophy/Kant/cpr/

Kant, I. (1800). *Logik*. Herausgegeben von Gottlob Benjamin Jäsche unter dem Titel *Immanuel Kant's Logik. Ein Handbuch zu Vorlesungen*. Königsberg. (*Akademie Textausgabe* Bd. IX).

Pico della Mirandola, G. (~1485). *Oration on the Dignity of Man*. Translated from the Latin by Richard Hooker. Retrieved November 15, 2006 fromhttp://www.wsu.edu:8080/~dee/REN/ORATION.HTM

Plato. *Protagoras*. Translation: C. C. W. Taylor (Clarendon Plato Series). Oxford, UK: Clarendon Press, 1991, revised edition.

Schmidinger, H., & Sedmak, C. (2004 ff.). (Eds.). *Topologien des Menschlichen*. 7 Bde. Darmstadt, Germany: Wissenschaftliche Buchgesellschaft.

Waal, Frans B. M. de (2001). *The ape and the sushi master: Cultural reflections by a primatologist*. New York: Basic Books.

Part I
Concepts and Approaches

Emotions as Bio-cultural Processes: Disciplinary Debates and an Interdisciplinary Outlook

Eva-Maria Engelen, Hans J. Markowitsch, Christian von Scheve, Birgitt Röttger-Rössler, Achim Stephan, Manfred Holodynski, and Marie Vandekerckhove

Abstract This chapter develops a theoretical framework that is capable of integrating the biological foundations of emotions with their cultural and semantic formation. It starts by investigating two leading scientific theories about emotions: one that is dominant in biology and a second one that is dominant in psychology. In biology, we consider the theory of basic emotions that focuses on innate biological emotional mechanisms. Using this approach, we can take physiological states into account. In psychology, we take a closer look at theories focusing on appraisals—the so-called appraisal theories—because these can be brought in to explain the cultural and semantic modification of biological emotional processes. Our examination of the major factors and elements of appraisal processes, which is also an examination of the internal processing of an emotional episode, discriminates unconscious from conscious processes and mental from nonmental processes. The next step is to integrate the two theories—the theory of basic emotions and appraisal theory—to couple emotional sensations with emotional concepts (semanticization). We clarify how basic innate emotional processes and complex learned ones are related to each other. We assume that cognition, feeling, and consciousness gradually become more differentiated in single species and organisms (phylogeny). Correspondingly, one possible hypothesis is that this differentiation process runs parallel on all levels, meaning that these domains can be assumed to be closely linked or even interdependent.

When asked to give typical examples of emotions, people may think of fear, love, hate, anger, jealousy, shame, pride, joy or disgust; perhaps, after some pause for thought, they add surprise, offended honor, or melancholy. Such lists are easy to extend. However, scientific studies, not being satisfied with lists of this kind, introduce criteria to categorize the phenomenal domain. By allying

E.-M. Engelen (✉)
Department of Philosophy, Faculty of Philosophy, University of Konstanz, Konstanz, Germany
email: eva-maria.engelen@uni-konstanz.de

B. Röttger-Rössler, H.J. Markowitsch (eds.), *Emotions as Bio-cultural Processes*,
DOI 10.1007/978-0-387-09546-2_3, © Springer Science+Business Media, LLC 2009

structural and comparative analyses, the phenomenal domain of the emotions can be studied from completely different perspectives.

To start with, we have to ask what exactly are emotions. Are they a set of entities that can be distinguished clearly not only from other mental or cognitive processes and states such as thoughts, conclusions, judgments, or perceptions but also from actions? Or do they form a specific subgroup of one or several of these other entities?

As soon as we move away from everyday psychological categories, scientific categories and criteria emerge to take their place. Emotions could then be a specific group of physiological processes that come about at a certain developmental stage in evolution and are further refined in the hierarchy of vertebrates and in particular mammals—before finally appearing in a certain variety of forms in human beings. This variety does not just refer to the range of single emotions but also to their many cultural and individual variations, such as the strength of emotional expression. The questions that then arise are directed toward how emotions come about exactly, what forms them, and how decisive are the biological and cultural influences. When formulating a model of the emotions that may be capable of answering these questions, it is necessary to take into account both the biological and cultural aspects of emotional processes.

Conceptually, there are various theoretical approaches to studying emotions. Two major approaches, which have generated intensive discussion in recent years, are represented by two groups of scientists: those who assume that emotions can be broken down into so-called basic emotions and complex emotions versus those who concentrate on the evaluation or appraisal aspect common to all emotional events. It should be noted that *appraisal theories* proceed from our so-called everyday understanding of emotions, whereas *physiological theories*, which are primarily oriented toward "basic emotions," concentrate particularly on the physiological changes involved in emotional processes.

For our research group, the decisive question was how to integrate the different conceptual perspectives so that both physiological and cultural aspects of emotions could be taken into account. A good way to get closer to answering this question is to start by inspecting the two dominant research directions and examine what the supporters of basic theories and appraisal theories have to tell us. This should help us to work out an approach with which we can consider not only the biological foundations but also the cultural and semantic shaping and refinement of emotions and other affective states. The theories that assume the existence of basic emotional dimensions (basic emotions) and thereby of innate physiological mechanisms offer a suitable starting point for a physiological approach to the research topic. In contrast, the theories that focus on the appraisal character as a function of emotions can be related successfully to explanatory approaches to how they are shaped and refined by culture and semantics.

In the following, we show how a biological-physiological approach and a cultural-semantic approach can be related to each other to form a greater whole. We also clarify how we can use the relation between complex, nonbasic, noninnate emotions and physiologically determined innate emotions to explain emotions as a bio-cultural process.

The research tradition that focuses on basic emotions emphasizes both the communicative function of emotional expression and the action-guiding aspect of emotions. It also assumes that all humans are born with basic emotional abilities in a physiological form, and that we even share several "affect programs" with other animals—from nonhuman primates to other mammals, birds, and reptiles. Dividing emotions into basic emotions and nonbasic, or complex, emotions is nonetheless only one way to categorize them (see, for overviews, e.g., Ekman & Davidson, 1994, pp. 5–47; Ortony & Turner, 1990).

From a scientific point of view, it may well seem like a good idea to start by examining emotions that seem to be universal for all humans as well as, perhaps, some of the other primates. Then, by drawing on examples and counterexamples from other disciplines, we can move toward a concept that is no longer founded exclusively on the so-called basic emotions.

It should be noted here that the various approaches follow different research questions and epistemological interests. Whereas, as mentioned above, the theoretical approaches favoring basic emotions focus their research on the communicative function of emotional expression and the action-guiding aspect of emotions, appraisal theories concentrate on the cognitive function of emotions, that is, the appraisal or evaluation process.

Nonetheless, all emotions are assumed to possess an appraisal or evaluation function regardless of whether they are built on an innate basic emotional ability. The question of a fundamental biological or physiological "emotional tool kit," as posed since Charles Darwin (1872/1904), William James (1884), and William McDougall (1908/1960), cannot be restricted to a few specific (basic) emotions.

Criteria for Basic Emotional Processes

When scientists are asked to name emotions, they generally list fear, anger, joy, disgust, and sadness in the sense of loss.[1] These are held to be universal because it would seem inconceivable for persons not to feel pain and sorrow at the loss of a loved one or not to feel fear when threatened by a wild animal.

The question is: How do things look when we move on to other emotional states that do not belong to this set of basic emotions? Are they assembled from this limited set of basic emotions that cannot be broken down any further (e.g., Johnson-Laird & Oatley, 1992)? Theories supporting this assumption divide emotional states or processes into innate basic emotions and acquired complex emotions. Nonetheless, it must be noted that this classification is the outcome of an evolutionary approach to emotions that concentrates on the emergence of psychological and psychophysiological mechanisms. In this perspective, the mechanisms underlying the basic emotions are an outcome of natural selection and have a corresponding adaptive function. The differential criterion in this case is phylogenetic continuity. This hypothesis is supported by, for example, the presence of several specific emotions in nonhuman primates as well as in humans (e.g., Cosmides & Tooby, 2000; see also Ortony & Turner, 1990; Reisenzein, 2000).

However, even innate mechanisms, also known as innate affect programs, are not necessarily conceived as unmodifiable mechanisms. Jaak Panksepp (1998), for example, argued that basal emotional processes emerge through "homologous" brain mechanisms in mammals. These mechanisms, or affect programs, are then shaped by an organism's further development and the experiences it goes through. The human ability to think then becomes one way of influencing these universal affect programs.

The most convincing empirical evidence for the existence of basic emotional mechanisms is that discrete emotional behaviors and states can be elicited in mammals through electrical and chemical stimulation. Bejjani et al. (1999), for example, induced a sudden depressive reaction through electrical stimulation of the medial diencephalon close to the subthalamic nuclei of the brain.[2]

Nonetheless, such reductionist theories are confronted with a problem. They must report what constitutes the specific sensation of a basic emotion such as joy or fear. How can we tell whether a mechanism in a human being is basic; and if so, which one is it? We cannot perform experiments on humans comparable to those on animals. Moreover, it is only through analogies based on expressive behavior that we can deduce that certain basal mechanisms ascertained in the rat are similar to those we label joy in humans.

Hence, it is still uncertain how far the theoretical discrimination between basic and nonbasic emotions has any general validity. For example, we still do not know whether there is any meaning in making such a distinction in animals. Initially, it seems that some emotional reactions in humans are similar to those in animals, whereas others are too subtle ever to be found in the animal domain. In any case, at least some emotional components of simpler emotions can be diagnosed in animals.

We compiled a list of criteria that an emotion (an emotional process) must meet to be called basic.

1. It has to be irreducible or "pure"; that is, no other emotion is involved.
2. It has to be universal; that is, it must be impossible to find any social group that does not exhibit this emotion.
3. It has to have a distinct facial and postural expression that is easy for others to interpret.
4. It has to be based on an innate affect program.
5. It has to be accompanied by immediate and significant bodily changes that are also assumed to be universal.

6. It has to emerge very early in ontogenesis and disappear very late in cases of degeneration of the brain.
7. It can be induced without the involvement of consciousness (e.g., propositional processes and without the presence of a self-concept).
8. No thoughts are required for it to occur.
9. Arousal has to be of short duration.

These criteria are based on an understanding of basic emotional processes as (still) nonsemanticized (noncognitive) fundamental emotional abilities. We now consider these criteria in more detail.

- *Irreducibility*. This postulate states that no other emotions can be perceived in the irreducible emotion. For example, joy always seems to be only joy compared with the emotion of love, for example, that may well contain joy.[3]
- *Universality*. This criterion means that there is no known social grouping that does not exhibit this basic emotional pattern. The universal basic pattern is then shaped culture-specifically; that is, it does not develop in all cultures in the same way or to the same degree and intensity.[4]
- *Distinctive (facial) expression readable by others*. Paul Ekman and his colleagues (e.g., Ekman, 1972, 1993, 2004; Ekman & Friesen, 1975) focused particularly on this criterion in their research. Nonetheless, even Ekman himself admitted that no data were available on how many forms of expression are universal for one emotion. They also have no one-to-one relation, that is, there is no single specific form of facial expression for each emotion.
- *Innate affect program*. The discovery of such an innate affect program has been claimed by, for example, Joseph LeDoux (1996, 2000) and Jaak Panksepp (1998, 2004). They pointed out that the human species shares this innate affect program with other animals and postulated that this program [i.e., the (discrete) emotions that belong to it] is determined phylogenetically. With this approach, the supporters of affect programs provide us with a central concept of biologically determined basic emotions (although these research approaches have been subject to some criticism from, among others, Paul Griffiths, 1997).
- *Immediate and significant, automatic bodily change*. This is assumed to manifest universally. These changes are attributed to emotions that are assumed to be universal or, otherwise, the outcome of an innate affect program. An example is breaking out in a cold sweat when frightened.[5]
- *Early emergence*. Basic emotions appear very early in ontogenesis and disappear very late during the course of brain degeneration (e.g., during the course of Alzheimer's disease).[6]

These first six criteria are all found frequently in the literature. The next three criteria were formulated by our research group.

- *No necessity for a self-image*. In line with the argument that universal, basic emotions or affect programs can be induced without the involvement of consciousness (e.g., propositional processes), we assume that affect programs can be activated without any need for the presence of a self-image. Strictly speaking, this is not an additional criterion for defining basic emotions. Any emotion requiring a self-image cannot be a basic emotion. The nonnecessity for a self-image can be seen by looking at neonates, adults suffering from senile dementia, and even other mammals. They all display emotional expressions without possessing a self-image. This is not the case with complex emotions. Persons have to possess a self-image that they can relate to the "images" of other persons to be able to have complex emotions. The self-image locates persons within a (what may well be imaginary) social space or set of relationships. As Ben-Ze'ev and Oatley (1996) stated:

> Emotions that are not basic, but are complex, are those requiring second-order intentionality. They depend on reference to a conception of the self and a social comparison of the present situation of the self with imagined alternatives of the self or others. (p. 89)

A series of emotions, including all those commonly regarded as basic such as fear, anger, joy, disgust, or sorrow (over a loss), do not require a self-image in this sense. However, these emotional processes may arise in a qualitatively different form when a person does possess a self-image. Anger over a perceived insult or disgust as an aversion to persons or ideas are examples of this. For example, before I can be insulted and become angry, I have to be able to relate the insult to myself.

- *No thoughts necessary*. This criterion is also an outcome of analyzing emotional events in babies, nonhuman mammals, and adults with senile dementia. Strictly speaking, although it indicates that no higher cognitions such as deduction, planning, decision-making, or evaluation are necessary, we assume that at least some cognitive processes such as stimulus processing or perception are involved in basic emotions—this position is relatively noncontroversial in the literature (e.g., Clore & Ortony, 2000; Ellsworth, 1994; Frijda, 1994).
- *Short duration of arousal*. This is a further general criterion for a basic emotion, but how far it applies in the same way to all emotions requires further analysis. Someone who feels joy shows it with a smile. Once the cause for this joy has disappeared, the emotion may persist for a short time—but generally no longer than a few minutes and hardly ever for hours (the research literature frequently reveals the claim that an emotion may persist for less than 1 minute). Whether it may also last for days or even weeks is questionable because then it is no longer the immediate first reaction that is typical when, for example, we meet a good friend on the street by chance.

The question whether one can assume that something like basic emotions actually exists relates to the question on how to classify emotions. We consider it important to point out that any consideration of basic emotions is always subject to certain constraints. Even emotions such as joy or fear, which are attributed with universality, are shaped by culture; and once they are also shaped by language, they are accompanied by higher cognitive processes. As Prinz (2004) expressed it:

> [E]very emotion that we have a word for bears the mark of both nature and nurture. Each is built up from a biologically basic emotion, but its conditions of elicitation, and hence its content, is influenced by learning. No lexicalized emotion is biologically basic. But there is a sense in which all lexicalized emotions are psychologically basic. No emotion contains [insofar] other emotions as component parts. (p. 85)

It should also be considered that during the complex everyday life of a healthy adult human an emotion occurs rarely—if at all—in a basic or "pure" form. It mostly contains elements of other emotional dimensions determined by what is going on in the specific social context. For example, test anxiety (i.e., the mental idea that one will not be able to cope with a future task) is also linked to aspects of shame and the fear of failure; in contrast, the anxiety for a loved person who embarks on a dangerous journey alternates with elements of worry. Likewise, the prospective fear that one feels when one knows one is going to have to walk through a dangerous part of town at night involves earlier experiences of violence and pain. To which basic pattern should this variety be reduced? Are these all forms of fear? Or are we dealing with what is only a culture-specific terminology that lumps together various emotional phenomena? In view of such justified reservations, how can we assess basic emotional processes empirically in the real social world?

Moreover, we find that those who favor a theory of basic emotions significantly (though not exclusively) base their classification into basic emotions and complex emotions according to characteristic signs of an emotional sensation that "break through to the surface." These are, particularly, facial expressions, prosody, gestures, and action readiness. Concentrating on external signs when classifying emotional processes broadly ignores factors such as sensing or implicitly evaluating an event through an emotional process; however, just because such factors do not take on any role on the physiological level of explanation, they do not become irrelevant for the classification of emotions.

Estimation, Evaluation, Appraisal

Categorizing emotions is linked closely to how meaningful or useful it is to distinguish basic from complex emotions, and, in turn, to whether one should start by assuming the existence of so-called innate, physiological basic emotions or focus on an appraisal theory founded mostly on a cognitive model of the emotions. It is important to start by distinguishing clearly between these two levels. Whereas appraisal theories proceed from our so-called everyday understanding of emotions—i.e., are embedded in (everyday) psychology—physiological theories of the emotions address the aspects of emotional processes embedded in physiology. This raises two issues: The first is whether these levels really can be separated from each other completely. Which physiological mechanisms would physiologists look for if they had no prior understanding (everyday knowledge) of the "object" they wanted to study? Second, the specific social and cultural aspects of emotional processes cannot be understood if one remains on a physiological level of explanation. Persons act and feel on the basis of their everyday psychological understanding of situations. It is important to emphasize once again that physiological processes are shaped by experiences and that these experiences are shaped by culture. We shall return to this later and consider how far it actually is the case.

Appraisal theories provide clearer contours for the cultural modeling of emotions. Focusing exclusively on so-called basic emotions makes it impossible to grasp the total cultural breadth of emotional processes and explain their various cultural specifics. Therefore, we now take a closer look at appraisal theories.

It has already been pointed out that theories restricted to studying basic emotional abilities and forms of expression focus particularly on the communication function and the aspect of action readiness to which emotions contribute. It has also been pointed out that appraisal theories have shifted attention to the cognitive function of emotions. This is significant in the following discussion insofar as cognitive function is important when it comes to explaining complex emotions.

The *appraisal theories* of emotions, which have grown into an important field of emotion research over the last two decades, pay less attention to the ontological status of specific emotions and far more to how emotions arise in general. Their central assumption is that emotions are triggered by the subjective appraisal or evaluation of situations and events in terms of the significance of what is perceived for the organism (e.g., Roseman & Evdokas, 2004; Roseman & Smith, 2001; Scherer, 1988; Schorr, 2001). A further assumption is that different emotions are accompanied by different patterns of appraisal; that is, each discrete emotion is triggered by a correspondingly discrete pattern of appraisal. Hence, the "character of an emotion" (i.e., how it is perceived or felt) is determined by its specific pattern of appraisal. This leads to a further assumption: Appraisals precede an emotion and *trigger* emotions. They are not, for example, a phenomenon that accompanies an emotion and is stored in memory after an actual emotion has occurred, nor are they an appendage to physiological reactions (Roseman & Smith, 2001). They *may* be part of an emotion, but they do not *have* to be because not every appraisal is also followed by an emotion. By making us "aware" of the appraisal (Roseman & Smith, 2001), an emotion additionally possesses an evaluative function when it is the consequence of an appraisal. However, because appraisals trigger emotions, this does not mean that they cannot also be part of or even the consequence of an emotion.

Hence, appraisal theories are confronted with two types of problems when explaining how emotions are triggered: first, regarding assumptions about the appraisal process; and second, regarding assumptions about the structure of the appraisal. Assumptions on the process point to the sequence of mental and nonmental processes as well as how these processes relate to and possibly influence each other. Assumptions on the structure of emotional processes refer to the appraisal *dimensions* and the appraisal *patterns* (i.e., what is appraised in relation to what in each case and which specific emotions correspond with which patterns of appraisal).

We start with assumptions on the structure of emotional processes. Many critics of appraisal theories equate appraisals exclusively with *cognitive* and largely conscious evaluation processes that grasp the significance of events and situations by comparing the qualities of these events with the mental structures of the persons perceiving them. This turns opinions, intentions, wishes, goals, and beliefs into matrices for depicting and appraising situations and events. Although most appraisal theories also take into account automatic and nonconscious appraisal processes, they develop a clear concept on the participation of (higher) cognitions in the genesis of emotions. Such concepts generally contain more or less detailed considerations of the various object domains that are appraised, such as actions, events, and objects (e.g., Ortony, Clore, & Collins, 1988; Parkinson & Manstead, 1992). Furthermore, they report which properties of the object domains are appraised—e.g., their valence (positive–negative) or, depending on the level of cognitive development, the probability of occurrence, the "coping" potential, or the attribution of responsibility or causality (e.g., Scherer, 2001). Propositional attitudes often play an important role, thus requiring the presence of verbal structures (particularly marked in, e.g., Solomon, 1976 but also in Oatley, 1992 and Oatley & Johnson-Laird, 1987).

Although most appraisal theories expressly permit nonconscious and automatic appraisals, this level of the genesis of emotions was long neglected. Recent work has attempted to explain how automatic appraisal processes (what Ekman, 2004, called "auto-appraisers") can be related to more cognitive appraisal processes and, above all, how these levels can still be taken into account while avoiding the assumption of pure determinism and pure automatism (which is precisely the appraisal theorists' criticism of the basic emotions approach). It has already been mentioned that most appraisal theories consider that the cognitive components of the genesis of emotions reveal highly depictable links to social and cultural spheres (Manstead & Fischer, 2001; Mesquita & Ellsworth, 2001).

These studies relating auto-appraisers to more cognitive appraisal processes should form the basis for the development of more advanced models capable of forging even stronger links to automatic physiological and, in particular, neurological processes in the genesis of emotions. Furthermore, it may be possible to bring these two forms of theory closer together, even though appraisal theories are psychological theories whereas physiological theories are applied on another level of explanation.

However, as soon as one tries to form such links, one is compelled to analyze the *process assumptions* in appraisal theories in more detail. As mentioned above, any interpretation of the (supposed) focus of appraisal theories on conscious estimations leads to a strongly cognitivist or mentalistic perspective that broadly ignores the autonomic and physiological processes as triggers of emotions (or as chronologically first elements). Particularly LeDoux (1996), Öhman (1986), and Zajonc (1980, 1984) have emerged as opponents of such purportedly purely cognitivist appraisal theories. These authors introduce the results of subliminal priming studies or conditioning studies as arguments supporting the possibility of *affective* reactions before cognitive activities become involved. In contrast, other findings—particularly those from the neurosciences—also indicate that emotional or affective reactions can emerge without the involvement of (higher) cognitive activity. Moreover, under some circumstances, they even have to do so if one wishes to pay heed to the arguments in evolution theory that the speed of subcortical processing particularly serves adaptive behavior in critical situations (Berridge, 2003; Cosmides & Tooby, 2000; LeDoux, 1996; Öhman, Flykt, & Lundqvist, 2001). Admittedly, even what were originally conscious processes can become so automatic that they are carried out at great speed. One has only to think of the reactions of competitive athletes or acrobats. There are also purely neuroanatomical justifications for the existence of systems that may trigger emotions (or affect programs) independently from those systems responsible for higher cognition (Gray, 1994; Panksepp, 1998).

Even the founders of appraisal theories such as Magda Arnold (1960) or Richard Lazarus (1966) paid explicit attention to the possibility of nonconscious, automatic appraisal processes. Accordingly, "Appraisal is not the result of reflection. It is immediate and indeliberate" (Arnold, 1960, p. 172, cited in Kappas, 2002, p. 86). Hence, how can we coordinate these two ways in which emotions emerge? It is necessary to bring together higher cognitive processes on the one side and subcortical processes on the other because they are able to both assess the significance of events in the environment in relation to the organism and trigger affect programs or emotions.

Without wanting to go any further into the well known debates on what cognition contributes to the emergence of emotion, we point to integrative approaches that view the process of the emergence of emotions as a hierarchical and modular, but not necessarily parallel, system. These approaches assume different levels of information processing that are generally distinguished in terms of the degree of (conscious) cognitive involvement.

From a process perspective, an example of the integration of different forms of emotional processing is Scherer's component-process model. This discriminates, in principle, three possible forms of information processing: sensorimotor, schematic, and conceptual (Leventhal & Scherer, 1987; Scherer, 1994).

Sensorimotor processing is the lowest stage of potential emotion-initiating processes, comparable with, for example, the innate subcortical affect programs postulated in neuroscientific models that function in a manner similar to that of stimulus–reaction mechanisms. As Leventhal and Scherer (1987) stated:

> The sensory motor level of processing consists of multiple components, including a set of innate expressive-motor programmes and cerebral activating systems which are

> stimulated automatically, that is, without volitional effort, by a variety of external stimuli and by internal changes of state. (p. 8)

Damasio's (1994) discussion of innate emotional reactions to certain *properties* of stimuli (not to their conceptual content) can be viewed as such a sensorimotor case.

The next level in the hierarchy is the *schematic* processing level on which learned emotional reactions acquired during the course of socialization occur. This level integrates sensorimotor processes with picture-like prototypes of emotional situations. Leventhal and Scherer (1987), once again, stated:

> Schemata are created in emotional encounters with the environment and are conceptualised as memories of emotional experience: They are concrete representations in memory of specific perceptual, motor (expressive, approach–avoidance tendencies and autonomic reactions), and subjective feelings each of which were components of the reaction during specific emotional episodes. (p. 10)

LeDoux's (1996, 2000) studies on the conditioning of fear are a good example of schematic processes. Another is the uneasiness one feels when returning after a long time to a place associated with a number of "bad memories."

Finally, the *conceptual* level of information processing integrates reflective, abstract, and deliberative activities (Leventhal & Scherer, 1987, p. 11). Anxiety about a future test would be a typical process for this.

Proceeding from this model of information processing and the theory of stimulus evaluation checks (SECs) (Leventhal & Scherer, 1987; Scherer, 1993), Scherer has argued in favor of a concept of "modal" emotions (see also Scherer, 1984) because all of the possible combinations of SECs can result in an almost infinite number of emotions that differ not only in kind but also intensity. Scherer pointed to correspondences regarding certain problems confronting organisms in their ontogenesis. He called emotions that appear regularly because of frequently occurring SEC combinations "modal emotions," and argued:

> Modal emotions are therefore characterized by a prototypical pattern of appraisals and the corresponding patterning of expression, autonomic arousal, action tendencies, and feeling states (Scherer, 1994, p. 30).

We use the explanation of the following scheme for the internal processing of an emotional episode worked out by part of our research group to continue our examination of the major factors and elements of appraisal processes.

Course of an Emotional Episode

Internal Processing of an Emotional Episode

The following scheme covers the mental and nonmental states, events, and processes involved in emotional processing. It does not represent a purely temporal sequence but is predominantly the outcome of analysis. Entries printed with a gray background in the scheme indicate a conscious process.

Sensation (*Sinnesreizverarbeitung*)	Unconscious, automatic, physiological Sensational phenomenal experience (*Sinnesempfindung*)
Perception (*Wahrnehmung*)	Interpretation of the sensation:[1] (1) The whole process is unconscious, or (2) one becomes conscious of that which is perceived ("perceived as"), or (3) conscious reflection on what is perceived as something: Perceptual phenomenal experience (*bewusste Wahrnehmung*)
Appraisal (*Einschätzung*)	Interpretation of the perceived in relation to its significance for the organism/the self: (1) the whole process is nonconscious, *or* (2) the outcome of the appraisal process becomes conscious to varying degrees: -Sensational experience of an emotional state (feeling) -Conceptualized emotional experience
Evaluation/reappraisal (*Bewertung*)	Conscious, evaluative reflections about the perceived or the appraised (or other contents of consciousness) in relation with its significance for the self

We introduce three examples to make the scheme easier to understand: (1) Assume that you are walking along the street in the dark. You see a man approaching you with a baseball bat, and you react with fear. Here is another, different kind of example: (2) You are reading a crime story late in the afternoon just as dusk is falling. You have just arrived at the passage describing how the victim is murdered. When you finish reading it, you draw the curtains, make sure your front door really is locked, and phone a friend for a chat. Finally, (3) You come into a room, shake hands with everybody there except one. When you ask yourself afterward how you could have been so rude as to leave somebody out, you explain it to yourself by thinking that you did not greet this person properly because you spontaneously found him or her unpleasant.

How can we describe these episodes in detail? Each begins with a *sensation* that initially remains nonconscious and proceeds automatically on the physiological level. This means that you do not perceive the "gestalt" in the dark as a man or even as a gestalt; you do not perceive the letters on the page of your crime story as letters or the meaning of these letters as a meaning. When entering the room full of persons, you initially do not perceive the room as such or the persons as persons, and so forth. Your senses are initially stimulated unspecifically. This is a purely physiological or neurophysiological level of description. In philosophical terms, this is the level of sensation that, in contrast to the purely physiological, is accompanied by consciousness.

The next stage of *perception* (i.e., conscious reflection on that which is perceived to be something) is of particular interest in, for example, philosophical deliberations over consciousness. It also relates to the concept of intentionality. I relate myself to something as being something—for example, to the man as being a man with a baseball bat—and the first thing I ask myself is whether he intends to attack me. At this stage of perception, one can say that we are already dealing with a "semanticized" perception, that is, the meaning of the term "man" is already linked to the perception. Naturally, this is a conscious perception.

The second example, in which the reaction of fear follows the description of a murder in a crime story, differs from the first example because the fear is not elicited by a concretely experienced situation but by the description of a situation that captures the imagination (Holodynski & Friedelmeier, 2005, p. 49). Although this is not conscious perception of a situation, it is nonetheless conscious imagining.

Finally, in the last example, in which one enters a room and greets everybody present except one person, all the persons in the room have been perceived consciously, but their appraisal or evaluation—exhibited in the failure to greet one of them—initially remains subconscious. Nonetheless, it can be made conscious through later reflection on one's own behavior and is therefore not inaccessible to consciousness.

This brings us to the next component in the emotional process: the *appraisal*. Here as well, a distinction is made between consciously perceived and not consciously perceived. A common definition for appraisal is interpretation of the perceived in terms of its significance for the organism, or the self. This process may proceed completely without consciousness (as in the failure to greet one person in the room), or one becomes conscious of the outcome of the appraisal process in various stages (when we see the man coming toward us on the street with the baseball bat and interpret what we perceive as a threat to the self).

Conscious appraisal is accompanied only by a sensational experience of an emotional state so long as it is neither conceptualized nor semanticized: that is, the sensation is not linked to the concept "fear" or to another concept such as "joy." However, when we are dealing with a conceptualized sensation, as is mostly the case in humans, we call it a conceptualized emotional experience because a sensation is perceived as a specific emotion, such as fear. This is because humans acquire concepts about the use of words in situations in which, in the case of emotions, there is a sensational experience of an emotional state.

The coupling of sensation and concept (semanticization) can be clarified as follows: The startle reflex of an infant is assigned the term fear by repeatedly pairing a sound with a sensation. For this word to become a concept for the developing child, she or he will also learn when she or he is entitled to have this sensation and when not (e.g., "You don't have to be afraid of. . . ."). A facial expression is perceived in another member of the species that is given the name "fear." The other is consoled and protected. The word "fear" becomes embedded in action contexts and accompanies specific forms of sensation and expression. It is only then that it can be called a *concept*. In addition, the ways of regulating emotion are also learned conceptually (i.e., together with the concept or in the sense that they belong to the complete meaning of the concept).

However, successful regulation of emotion or the lack thereof also influences the strength of sensation. Eventually, the sensational experience and the concept of an emotional state can no longer be separated. Nonsemanticized body sensations cease to exist.

The process scheme of an emotion described above requires further explanation. The conceptualized emotional experience can lead to a conscious *evaluation* or *reappraisal*. Such consciously evaluative thoughts (reflections) on what is perceived or appraised (or other contents of our minds) are made with reference to the significance of what is perceived for the self. An interesting case here is our example in which one person was not greeted. This "failure to greet" is also perceived, but it is only later that it becomes subject to a reappraisal with the conclusion that the person who has not been greeted is an unpleasant person with whom one does not want to have anything to do.

What is special about this case is certainly that there is initially no conscious appraisal and also no sensational conscious experience of an emotional state or conceptualized emotional experience. The usual cases of reappraisal are certainly those in which we reconsider a conscious conceptualized emotional experience along with the appraisal linked to it. In the crime story example, it would be typical for an adult who has just drawn the curtains and made sure the front door is locked to reassure himself or herself that these acts were merely anxious reactions due to reading the story, in other words, a fiction that is not pertinent to the current real-life situation. The reader would then decide that he or she should not exaggerate, and there is no need to feel any more afraid than in a comparable situation in which reading a crime story had not made such an impression.

We could have placed the aspect "evaluation or reappraisal" under the heading "appraisal." However, it is helpful to distinguish it conceptually when analyzing examples such as the one in which a person enters a room and greets all but one person.

The appraisal accompanying an emotion is an interpretation of that which is perceived in terms of its significance for the organism, or the self. Referring to the examples: What is the significance of the baseball bat in a man's hand on a street at night? Phrased in this way, it seems that appraisal always has to be a conscious process. This is also not the case. The entire process can proceed unconsciously, or the outcome of the appraisal process can become conscious to varying degrees. Conscious appraisals or evaluations require the ability to engage in conscious reflection, whereas unconscious appraisals proceed almost automatically. Of course, a conscious decision does not have to trigger an emotion. One can arrive at the conscious appraisal that children in Africa are living in terrible conditions and that it is absolutely necessary to help them without having to trigger the emotion "compassion."

The fear in the first example is generated from the simultaneous nonconscious processing of the three schemes "man," "baseball bat," and "nighttime"—a combination that forms a prototypical mental model of fear in Western culture. If, for example, the Makassar (an ethnic group in Indonesia) were to go for a walk at dusk, they would probably have to simultaneously perceive the hoot of an owl and a certain whistling of the wind through the trees to trigger fear because they take this as indicating the presence of certain dangerous spirit beings (the "owl wind"). Interpreting these perceptions as antecedents of danger is something that is learned culturally.

Naturally, one can ask whether this type of quasi-automatic appraisal is in any way an evaluation. If this type of appraisal, and thereby the emotional process, is disengagement of the stimulus–reaction mechanism, it should mean that although the person does not have freedom of action in the sense of reflection on which is the better alternative the reaction is based on an unconscious appraisal (i.e., on a largely habitualized appraisal or interpretation), not just on the triggered stimulus. Hence, what we call "appraisal" can also be a learned reaction to pleasant or unpleasant experiences; it does not necessarily have to be the outcome of conscious reflection on these experiences. With a stimulus–reaction mechanism, however, the reaction always follows the stimulus, even in circumstances in which this mechanism may damage the organism or not lead to success (Damasio, 1994; LeDoux, 1996; Scherer, 1994).

One generally talks about emotions when the appraisal emerges from a pleasant or unpleasant feeling of which one is conscious. There are no unconscious feelings. Appraisal and feeling coincide. This is not a conscious cognitive appraisal, but an "intuitive" one, a sensational experience of an emotional state. It may well be that the Makassar feel the owl wind rather than perceive it consciously. They register a sudden feeling of fear. Alarmed by this, they focus attention on their environment and then perceive the hooting owl and the specific wind.

It can be assumed that cognition, feeling, and consciousness gradually become more differentiated in single species and organisms (phylogeny). Correspondingly, one hypothesis is that this differentiation process runs parallel on all levels, meaning that these domains can be assumed to be closely linked or interdependent.

There have been comprehensive debates on the proportion of cognition and consciousness in this process. When it is stated in the literature that the "nature and intensity of the emotion are predominantly determined by the subjective evaluation of the meaning and consequences of an event for the individual concerned" (Scherer, 2004, p. 140), it implies that emotions accompany conscious experiences.

The process scheme presented above should tell us which mental and nonmental states, events, and processes are involved in emotional episodes. Usually, one starts such processes with sensations and perceptions that are appraised or evaluated by the individual experiencing them. We have seen that most of these stages can be accompanied by phenomenal experiences.

Body-Related Aspects of the Processing of an Emotional Episode

When asking which mental and nonmental states and processes are involved in emotional episodes, it is also necessary to take into account the body-related aspects. These aspects permit distinction between "internal" bodily changes (internal events during an emotional episode) and "external" bodily changes (expressive and bodily reactions as "external" changes during an emotional episode). The internal changes are "steered" by the regions of the brain responsible for nonmotor changes, including autonomic bodily changes that we (generally) are unable to modify voluntarily such as neuroendocrine changes, that is, hormonal and (para-)sympathic changes (e.g., changes in blood pressure, heart rate, skin conduction; hair raising; goose pimples).

Externally observable bodily reactions that accompany emotional behavior are mostly controlled automatically, particularly by subcortical brain regions. Such reactions include facial expression, prosody or tone of voice, gestures, and body language. The latter is expressed through how persons stand, sit down, incline their head, or hold their hands defensively in front of the chest or reach out in a greeting of welcome. Empirical emotion research has focused particularly on facial expression and prosody—the former because it is extremely differentiated and is viewed as a universal means of expression and communication. Although these bodily reactions are largely automatic, their occurrence and strength can be influenced consciously.

Not only body language but also facial expression and prosody provide our interaction partners with information on our emotional state. They tell them something about what situation we are in and how we "appraise" it. In this sense, we communicate something to our interaction partner. This communication can have an "objective" and a "subjective" character. If we display a face distorted by fear, it implicitly communicates a warning to our partner. She or he then automatically looks around to locate the source of this fear and, if need be, protects herself or himself as well. If we meet a happily smiling girlfriend in the local bar, we tend to conclude that the smile reflects her subjective mood rather than her evaluation of the bar as such a great place. In the first case the communication provides information on the objective situation in our environment and in the second on the subjective well-being of our girlfriend.

Within an evolutionary or natural history framework, the informative or communicative character of emotional expression seems to have a central function. Even when an organism communicates only subjective well-being, we still know that its display of contentment and relaxation does not threaten danger. Things are different when we have to deal with a young person who is grimacing aggressively. The signs of the subjective mood are also elements of a situation that involves us and to which we can and must adapt our behavior.

The externally observable bodily reactions that not only help to form but also accompany emotional behavior include action readiness as well as actions or movements. Escape behavior is a typical example: We, or our bodies, react to a situation that arouses fear by tensing our muscles and "readying" the movements that will enable us to run away. In some circumstances, however, we hear only one suspicious noise, and our muscles tense; but when this noise is not followed by any further unsettling events, our body relaxes again. In this case, the readiness to flee is not followed by flight; we do not jump up and run out of the house. Our heart rate subsides, and we do not break out in a sweat.

Moreover, there are bodily changes that we can attribute precisely to certain bodily zones, although we can generally describe them only metaphorically. These could be labeled gestalt bodily changes. Many of them are well-known sayings, typically found in utterances such as: "Those pictures of starving children in Africa brought a lump to my throat." "I was so in love. Even just seeing him or thinking about him sent tingles up and down my spine." "When he stressed that the only reason Mr. Jones had commended me was because he was in a good mood today, I felt my hackles rise." These bodily sensations are subjective representations of expressive and bodily reactions. Along with the appraisal, the actual expression, and bodily reactions, they are a further component of an emotion.

Whereas the gestalt bodily changes represent conscious perceptions of our own bodily changes, other bodily changes remain completely nonconscious.[8]

Relation Between Basic Emotions and Appraisal Processes

We assume the existence of basic emotions in the sense of basic emotional abilities that have evolved adaptively to promote survival. These specific basic emotional dimensions (e.g., sorrow, disgust, joy, fear) are, to a certain degree, innate and emerge very early in phylogenesis in all known cultures as well as in some of the higher mammals, particularly the nonhuman primates. They are triggered by appraisal processes whose course must also be innate in a rudimentary form; that is, there are certain basic appraisal processes as well. These appraisal processes are less accessible to modification than those for other emotions; that is, they are less susceptible not only to cultural influence and shaping but also to being shaped by personal experiences. Nonetheless, they can still be modified over the course of the personal biography (e.g., the lion trainer who displays no fear or flight when approaching lions) and through growing up in a particular society and culture. However, there are stereotype trigger mechanisms for certain emotions. An example is the aggressive behavior of mothers when their offspring are threatened. These emotions do not have only *one* specific trigger mechanism; aggressive behavior can also be triggered by other situations.

It is not just stereotype trigger mechanisms that can be shaped by culturally molded experience; this is even truer for nonstereotype trigger mechanisms. Moreover, appraisal processes may be acquired that are culturally shaped (i.e., not innate) and are therefore assigned to the so-called complex emotions—the next topic in this chapter.

Complex Emotions/Nonbasic Emotional Events

We start by listing a series of nonbasic, "complex" emotions and then name criteria to show how far the content of this list is justified and what elements these examples have in common.

- Anxiety
- Trust
- Shame
- Pride
- Agape
- Eros
- Hate
- Compassion
- Malicious joy (gloating)
- Test anxiety
- Enjoyment
- Envy
- Jealousy

Despite its arbitrariness, this list presents a highly characteristic selection of nonbasic or complex emotions. By and large, what all these emotional states have in common is the need for higher cognitive abilities than basic emotions and the fact that they are generally accompanied by a simultaneous decline in the elements of bodily arousal.

This finding can be specified further and in no way indicates that it is impossible to apply the scheme introduced above (sensation, sensational phenomenal experience, perception, appraisal/evaluation, emotional sensation, emotional perception). Just as we listed criteria for the attribution of basic states above, we can now give additional criteria for nonbasic states:

For more complex emotions to emerge, it is necessary for an organism to have an image of the self. In our work group, this is one of the most important preconditions for the presence of a complex emotion. In contrast, this is not necessary for a basic emotion such as fear to emerge. However, for an organism to feel shame, it must become aware that it has done something wrong and has not met a social expectation; it has to relate the violation to itself—sanctions from a group that prescribes rules are not sufficient.

It is also frequently possible to identify basic emotions as components of complex emotions. Shame, for example, can be the fear of having done something wrong and being sanctioned for this in whatever form, even if this means that one has "only" failed to live up to one's self-image. Gloating contains joy at somebody else's misfortune; even pride contains joy as a basic emotion.[9]

We can also see that more complex emotions are shaped to a far greater extent by culture than basic ones. An extreme is malicious joy (gloating) because it does not seem to exist in the form we know it in some cultures—or at least, a number of cultures reveal no word and no mental concept of gloating. Moreover, different forms of jealousy or envy are an almost paradigmatic example for the study of cultural differences. The cultural differences within human emotionality also seem to be based partly on the fact that basic emotions fuse to form more complex emotional schemes in completely different ways. For example, among the Ilongot, an ethnic group of (former) headhunters living in the Philippines, sorrow and anger are conceived as one emotional unit. Sorrow over the death of a relative is always accompanied by anger at the painful loss, and this generates a readiness to injure others, making it a frequent trigger for headhunting excursions in earlier times (Rosaldo, 1993).

A further central aspect is that complex emotions emerge later in ontogenesis than basic emotions and disappear earlier in forms of dementia. The opposite is a defining characteristic for basic emotions (they emerge early in ontogenesis and disappear late).

Moreover, we assume that the bodily changes at the beginning of an emotional episode are less significant and less immediate in complex emotions (e.g., love, anxiety, and trust). For some complex emotions, it is even conceivable that they are marginal. Hence, one of our group's hypotheses is that highly cognitive emotions (e.g., *Weltschmerz*) are rarely associated with strong bodily changes; they are mostly weak changes. However, because *Weltschmerz* is still a phenomenal experience (i.e., it is still "felt"), one has to ask what is felt when no clear bodily changes can be ascertained.

In contrast, there is no question that these emotional episodes call for and involve higher, more complex cognitive processes such as associative processes or propositional abilities. It has already been pointed out that having an image of the self is also a major precondition for the emergence of complex emotions.

We qualified the definition of complex emotions above by stating that the bodily changes at the beginning of an emotional episode are less significant and less immediate. This qualification comes from the "observation" that, at least in the highly cognitive emotions, a disturbance of the emotional balance (as one could call it in everyday language) can lead to significant bodily changes. This can even be introduced as a defining criterion for this form of emotion. (The observation that the intensity of an emotion declines as a function of the cognitive ability to anticipate it is, in contrast, a different aspect.)

A good example of this is enduring love compared with falling in love (even at first sight). The love between long-term partners cannot be confirmed bodily in the same way as that between partners who have just fallen in love. In the latter, "hearts beat faster" when they see each other or think about each other, and their hormone levels fluctuate rapidly. These intensive psychophysiological "arousal states" generally smooth out over the course of a relationship, giving way to a "calmer" emotional attachment. It could be that enduring love is experienced as being less emotional because a level of homeostasis (including, for example, strengthening of the immune system) has become established. In contrast, a disturbance to this level of homeostasis through, for example, the death of one partner, triggers major emotional reactions such as shock, deep sorrow, and depression. The love, the intensity of the attachment between long-term partners, can then frequently be traced in physiologically intensive ways through feelings of sorrow and the pain of loss. In this context, it seems worth mentioning the ethnographic finding that there are cultures, such as the Ifaluk in Micronesia, that make no conceptual distinction between sorrow and love. They are both described with the same term, *fago*. These connotations may be explained by the frequent experiences of loss facing these inhabitants of atolls so frequently devastated by typhoons. Each loving attachment is accompanied by the—in this context, very real—possibility of loss, making sadness and sorrow a basic element of love (Lutz, 1988, pp. 119–149).

Beyond the emergence of emotions when the level of homeostasis is disrupted in enduring affective states, the relation between these states and the accompanying emotions that emerge parallel to them can be conceptualized in a further important way: Enduring love is not an emotion like falling in love. It is a far more permanent (i.e., dispositional) affective state. Persons have to accept this state for themselves; that is, they have to find themselves in this state and feel it as such. It is not enough for them to have knowledge of such states in the form of social or symbolic categories.

However, both an affective disposition and knowledge about socially relevant states involve forms of self-appraisal that may be accompanied by the corresponding emotions or form the backdrop against which these emotions are staged.

The relation between emotions (e.g., falling in love, shame, pride) and the enduring (dispositional) states (i.e., love, disgrace, honor) related to them can be analyzed and conceptualized as follows: The enduring states are a kind of background feeling, background disposition (love), or in some cases background knowledge (honor, disgrace) that provide a framework within which emotions such as an acute feeling of love, pride, or shame are staged. Although these background states are shaped strongly by social and symbolic categories, they also have natural biological foundations such as the phylogenetically given attachment behavior to be observed in many species in the animal domain in the case of love, the display pattern or posturing in the case of victorious superiority (pride), or signs of shame, that is, bodily hunching and ducking in the case of defeat or rule-breaching behavior.

Hence, from the perspective of a theory of emotion, pride and shame (just like love) can be labeled as internalized social and symbolic categories that (may) include an affective disposition facilitating the context-dependent occurrence of specific emotions. Therefore, a person who loves a partner is predisposed in a special way to feel fear and anxiety when this partner is in trouble without even considering that a long-term "calm" love can "flare up" intensively again and again in certain contexts. Individuals who have an inferior status in their social environment-perhaps the "black sheep" of the family or a school dropout with a failed career in a community of educated and respected "high achievers"—are particularly predisposed to frequent experiences of shame (e.g., when their successful brothers and sisters receive praise and recognition).

Differential Criteria for Specific Emotions

When considering how to distinguish between specific emotions, it is useful to draw on the concept of the "formal object" in philosophy. This concept makes it possible to characterize an emotional process as a specific process. Because sweat is perspired, the heart beats faster, fists are clenched, tears are shed, and so forth during more than one emotion, bodily processes (outside the brain) do not suffice to explain the finely graded distinctions in our emotional sensations.

Ronald de Sousa's (2003) explanation for the concept of the "formal object" is particularly helpful because it refers directly to emotions.

> . . . every emotion has a *formal object* if it has any object. A formal object is a property implicitly ascribed by the emotion to its target, focus, or propositional object, in virtue of which the emotion can be seen as intelligible. My fear of a dog, for example, construes a number of the dog's features (its salivating maw, its ferocious bark) as being frightening, and it is my perception of the dog as frightening that makes my emotion fear, rather than some other emotion. The formal object associated with a given emotion is essential to the definition of that particular emotion. It is also, in part, what allows us to speak of emotions being appropriate or inappropriate. If the dog obstructing my path is a shitzu, my fear is mistaken: the target of my fear fails to fit fear's formal object. (3)

The core of this definition is the statement that a formal object is a property (being frightening) that implicitly attributes an emotion (fear) to its target (the dog) and through which the emotion may also be appropriate or inappropriate.

To clarify once again what de Sousa meant: Imagine that you are walking past a farmyard when a dog rushes toward you barking angrily. You enter a state of fear and try to flee. This emotion can be called appropriate because it can be assumed that the dog could cause major injury. However, if somebody calls out that the dog no longer has any teeth, the fear, were it to continue, could be called inappropriate because you now know that under these circumstances the dog can no longer do you any harm.

In this case, the action tendency that accompanies fear (i.e., to flee) could also specify the emotion "fear." Nonetheless, in many cases, emotions or feelings are not specified unequivocally by such action tendencies. For example, a major property of yearning is that the person, object, or location we yearn for is not to be found in our proximity because otherwise we would be unable to attribute the emotional state of yearning.

Universal and Culture-Specific Emotions

A large part of early and more recent debates on a theory of emotion have focused on how far emotions are shaped by culture. We have turned this question around: Can we find any emotions at all in humans that can be confirmed as not being subject to the shaping of culture? We believe that every emotion can be shaped by culture in social situations. Admittedly, we assume that some emotions are far more indifferent to culture than others and, in this sense, also less socially and culturally modeled. However, these basic emotions are difficult to study empirically because we encounter emotions only in their socially and culturally conveyed forms. It is only very early and very late in life—when cultural and social influences have either not yet (in infants) or are no longer (in persons with senile dementia) formed completely—that we can come close to the postulated basic emotions. Nonetheless, even here they always occur within a cultural context.

Universal Emotions

Emotions are termed universal in terms of their expression, the ability to recognize them, the stereotyped bodily reaction(s) they produce, and their underlying affect programs. Nonetheless, we can identify cultural variations even with this type of emotion (e.g., the intensity of their occurrence, the motor reactions incurred, their potential for being copied, and the trigger situations and regulation styles that are always highly socially defined).

Culture-Specific Emotions

Some examples of culture-specific emotions are *Weltschmerz*, nostalgia, *amae* (form of love), or *amok* (form of frenzy).

In the literature, the Japanese love concept of *amae* is frequently discussed as an example of a culture-specific emotion. Japanese psychoanalyst Takeo Doi (1973, 1986) has defined it as a form of passive love that he understands as the cultural elaboration of childhood attachments and their mental correlates. *Amae* is a need for dependence—a strong desire to be surrounded by, cared for, spoilt by, and protected by others in a manner similar to the childhood experience of loving parents. Passive love in the sense of being "cared for and looked after lovingly" by others is, according to Doi, a universal pattern of experience during infancy that Japanese culture raises to the emotional prototype for love attachments between adults as well (couples as well as close relatives). Doi stated that even in adult love relationships the Japanese seek and cultivate forms of infantile attachment behavior that are inconceivable in love relationships in the European-American context. The *amae* concept, with its emphasis on the aspect of dependence, relates closely to the social and familial structures of Japanese society that do not anticipate reciprocity within the internal family context.[10] Hence, *amae* is the culture-specific manifestation, emphasis, and conceptual elevation of a universal (basic) affective attachment experience but does not represent a completely cultural construct.

The Malaysian phenomenon of *amok*, a term that has also entered many European languages, can be conceived as being somewhat more culture-specific. In the context of traditional Malaysian cultures, two forms of *amok* can be distinguished (from a Western perspective): the collective "martial *amok*" and the individual "solitary *amok*" (Spores, 1988; Winzeler, 1990). The former used to be (and still is) practiced in martial conflicts. A group of males would use ritualized spiritual and physical techniques to bring themselves into a state of fearless, highly aggressive frenzy that would enable them to attack their enemies without fear of death. This is the *amok*—of a sacred spiritual and heroic nature from the Malaysian perspective—with which Europeans came into contact particularly in the context of anticolonial uprisings and struggles. This form of spiritually based collective heroic *amok*, found in numerous Southeast Asian societies, continues to play a significant role in resistance movements as well as in the context of the Islamic *perang sabil* (Holy War) movements.

Amok is part of a complex set of culturally shaped physical techniques, particularly including diverse martial arts (*silat*) with a general emphasis on extreme physical self-control. The ability to build up and focus one's own aggressive potential purposefully so it can be unleashed in battle in a concentrated form is a major element of these physical techniques. In this sense, the Malaysian *amok* is exactly the opposite of its Western interpretation as a "blind frenzy" arising from a confused mental state. To some extent, the same applies to the forms of solitary or also "secular *amok*" (Winzeler, 1990, p. 120) in which individuals deliberately induce an *amok* state in themselves for personal reasons before attacking their surroundings with mortal intent, taking into account that these attacks will probably bring about their own death. Winzeler (1990) pointed out that Malays themselves make no conceptual distinction between collective and solitary forms of *amok*:

> The evident fact that the two forms were either the same or closely related in Malay culture helps to explain what often appalled or puzzled later European observers about individual amok—which was that death sought or achieved through an attack upon innocents could have a positive, even heroic, meaning. (p. 100)

Because *amok* also refers to the conscious elicitation of an emotional state, it is questionable whether it is a culture-specific emotion or more of a culture-specific form of emotion regulation.

Interdisciplinary Outlook

During the course of this chapter, we have mapped out and considered central problem areas and discussion fields for the emotions. We here summarize the outcome of these ideas, and, once again, outline the interdisciplinary nature of our cooperation in detail.

We start with a brief summary of the central problem areas in this chapter: differential criteria and the justification for distinguishing between basic and nonbasic, or complex, emotions; the cultural shaping of the processes of emotion; the relation between physiological processes (basic emotions, affect programs) and appraisal processes; the relation between emotions and enduring dispositional emotional states; and finally the specificity of emotions.

Although we have repeatedly questioned the theoretical validity of distinguishing between basic and nonbasic emotions in this chapter, we have decided to retain it. At the end of the day, it does make it possible to work out and classify the effects and functions of physiology, semantics, and culture. We can summarize this again in few sentences.

On the whole, there are two main reservations about assuming the existence of basic processes of emotion. First, an emotion hardly ever occurs in a basic form in a healthy adult embedded in the complexity of daily life. For example, which proportions of other emotional dimensions may "fear" still contain to be identified as such? This varies greatly as a function of culture-specific habitualization and terminology. Even emotions that are held to be universal, such as joy or fear, are shaped by culture; that is, they are habitualized and semanticized (i.e., conceptualized) in different ways in each culture. As soon as they become shaped by language, higher cognitive processes accompany them.

Nonetheless, it is still possible to ascertain basic emotional abilities, which are defined as emotional processes that are, to a certain degree, innate and appear very early in phylogenesis in all known cultures as well as in higher mammals and primates. These emotions are triggered by innate appraisal processes.

We then define nonbasic emotions as those in which the accompanying appraisal process is either not innate but acquired or in which basic emotions are fused in culturally different ways to form more complex emotional schemes. However, this appraisal also involves the acquisition of processes that are likewise shaped by culture (i.e., are not innate). Therefore, we assign these to the group of so-called complex, or nonbasic, emotions.

We made further statements on the cultural shaping of emotion processes. We recalled, for example, that even the circumstance that certain perceptions are interpreted as antecedents of risk is something that has been learned culturally. Furthermore, we pointed out once more that unconscious appraisals may also be shaped culturally insofar as they can become to a large extent habitualized and are no longer elicited solely in response to a stimulus. Because cultural shaping can extend to acquired patterns of behavior, these can also remain nonconscious as a result of habitualization.

We then turned to the relation between physiological processes (basic emotions, affect programs) and appraisal processes: Although most appraisal theories also include automatic and nonconscious appraisal processes, their main focus has been on formulating a concept for the involvement of (higher, conscious) cognitions in the genesis of emotions. Hence, we have to ask how automatic physiological emotion processes relate to the appraisal processes that trigger an emotion process and belong to it. We have confirmed that even automatized physiological processes and their attendant automatized appraisal processes are not only influenced and shaped by culture but are also shaped by personal experience. However, this applies to a much smaller extent than it does in those emotional processes linked to higher cognition and accompanied by a higher degree of consciousness. Whereas conscious appraisals or evaluations require the ability to engage in cognitive reflection, it is not necessary for nonconscious appraisals, which occur almost automatically. In fact, we noted that formerly conscious processes can become so automatic that they can be performed at great speed.

This finding fits in with the ideas of appraisal theorists who depict the process by which emotions emerge as a hierarchical and modular system. They assume different levels of information processing that can generally be distinguished in terms of the degree of (conscious) cognitive involvement (this final point should also have become clear in our scheme for the internal emotional process). Sensorimotor processing, which is comparable with the innate subcortical affect programs postulated in neuroscientific models, represents the lowest level of possible emotion-initiating processes. The hierarchically higher level is that of schematic processing on which learned emotional reactions are initiated that have been acquired during the course of socialization and are strongly shaped by culture.

Our scheme, which has subjected the functions and degrees of consciousness in emotional events to a more precise analysis, reveals that if conscious appraisal is not conceptualized or semanticized it is accompanied by a sensational experience of an emotional state. However, when (as is mostly the case in humans) we are dealing with a conceptualized sensation, we call it a conceptualized emotional experience because the sensation is perceived as a specific emotion. Appraisal and feeling are then congruent, so this is not a conscious cognitive appraisal but a sensational experience of an emotional state. It is not only the outcome of the appraisal process that differs in the degree to which it is conscious; the entire process leading up to the outcome can run automatically and nonconsciously.

Therefore, we assume a slow, gradual separation of cognition, feeling, and consciousness over the course of evolution. We also assume that these domains can be closely linked or interdependent.

The relation between cognition and physiological processes is a special case. What all nonbasic emotional processes have in common is the need for greater cognitive ability than is required for basic emotional processes. The more an emotion process is shaped cognitively (as in *Weltschmerz*), the greater the decline in the physiological processes involved. Nonetheless, because *Weltschmerz* is also a phenomenal experience (i.e., it is "felt"), our research group performed a theoretical analysis of what happens when the bodily arousal components decline. Even in what are called highly cognitive emotions, we find significant bodily changes when the emotional balance is disturbed (disturbance of the homeostatic level). Emotional processes can therefore be distinguished not only from other mental or cognitive processes or states (e.g., thoughts, conclusions, judgments, perceptions) but from actions as well through the presence of an element of appraising or evaluative phenomenal experience.

We have ascertained that emotions (e.g., falling in love, shame, pride) and enduring (dispositional) states (e.g., love, shame, honor) are frequently interrelated. When this is the case, their relation can be analyzed and conceptualized as follows: The enduring states provide a kind of background feeling, background disposition, or in some cases even a background knowledge that serves as a framework in which acute emotions are actualized. Although these background states are shaped by social and symbolic categories, they nonetheless have natural, biological foundations.

To explain the specificity of an emotion, we have fallen back on the concept of the "formal object" in philosophy. This views a formal object as a property that an emotion implicitly attributes to its goal object. We explained this with an example.

We hope that these interdisciplinary considerations and analyses will provide a suitable framework for defining the phenomenal domain of emotions in more precise scientific terms. Taking various interdisciplinary perspectives should simultaneously make this framework more comprehensive.

Notes

[1] These typical forms of emotion, which frequently correspond to classifications into basic emotions, are almost exactly the same as the common—modern Western—understanding of emotion. When US-American college students were asked to give typical examples of the category "emotions," they most frequently named happiness (152) followed by anger (149), sadness (136), love (124), fear (96), hate (89), and joy (82) (Fehr & Russell, 1984; see, also, Johnson-Laird & Oatley, 1989).

[2] The automatic way in which this emotion arises is supported and made understandable by LeDoux's (1996) hypothesis. This assumes the existence of two neural circuits for the activation of emotions, one subcortical (thalamoamygdala) and one involving the neocortex. The subcortical circuit evaluates the emotional significance of events via rapid and automatic processing of sensory data. For instance, according to LeDoux (1996), neurons in the thalamus projecting to the amygdala are distinct from those that provide the major inputs to the auditory cortex (after having reached the thalamus). The direct connections from the thalamus to the amygdala respond to a much wider range of stimuli and are broadly tuned. An acoustic stimulus that reaches the amygdala via the thalamus needs much less time than a stimulus reaching the amygdala via the cortical pathway. According to LeDoux (1996), the amygdala can be activated without cortical interference within a period of about 12 ms (for a review of research on the amygdala, see Markowitsch 1998/1999). In

other words, the direct thalamic shortcut to the amygdala bypasses the cortex. It cannot inform the amygdala on what is being perceived but can induce a fast signal that, for instance, warns that something dangerous may be there. The cortical pathway, on the other hand, allows detailed recognition. By the time the cortex has evaluated the meaning of the sound, the amygdala has already started to react.

3 This does not, and cannot, answer the question whether complex emotions can also be traced back to basic emotional abilities and, if so, how. It also does not state to what basic emotions they, in turn, can be reduced. A strong hypothesis is that the basic emotions reveal a monadic character and thereby an "intrinsic affectivity" (Reisenzein, 2000, p. 211). The weak hypothesis is that basic emotions also possess nonaffective components such as cognitions. Diametrically opposed perspectives would be, for example, the early positions of Robert Solomon (1976) and Dietrich Dörner (1993), which reduce the emotions completely to nonemotional cognitions.

4 In contrast to universality, certain complex emotions are unknown in some cultures, not only in terms of their phenomenology, the subjective sensation (the feeling), but also in terms of whether there is a word to describe them. Robert Solomon (2002, p. 138) commented on the ambiguity arising from this criterion by asking: "Is an emotion basic because it is found to be universal, or is an emotion necessarily universal because it is basic?"

5 Meta-analyses of the available findings provide far more support for the idea that specific activity in the autonomic nervous system (ANS) does not correspond to discrete emotions but could be more in line with a dimensional concept along a positive–negative or "approach–avoidance" continuum (Cacioppo, Berntson, Klein, & Poehlmann, 1997; Cacioppo, Berntson, Larsen, Poehlmann, & Ito, 2000; Davidson, 1994). Cacioppo and colleagues go further and point out that bodily changes are not a necessary condition for the appearance of discrete emotions because there are significant indications for emotional states without differentiated ANS changes (Cacioppo et al., 2000; see Davidson, 1994, p. 240).

6 As explained above, LeDoux's (1996) hypothesis that subcortical processing or thalamus–amygdala interaction bypasses the neocortex at a first level of processing helps us to understand why human infants smile at a face as soon as they are capable of detecting its contours and why children, according to Trevarthen (2004) and Trevarthen, Aitken, Vandekerckhove, Delafield-Butt, and Nagy (2006), first interact with their environment on an affective–procedural level.

On a global level, the subcortical interaction may be sufficient for generating emotional feelings. Subcortical regions mature relatively early, whereas higher cortical areas, including the memory-processing hippocampus, mature later. The cortical circuit participates in the deeper processing of faces and in all higher-order cognitive antecedents of emotion, such as appraisal or attribution. These underlying pathways are genetically predetermined and designed to respond unconditionally to stimuli arising from life-challenging circumstances (Panksepp, 1998). In line with Panksepp, after birth a great deal of neural unfolding remains to be completed in every species. The maturation of specific neural systems establishes essential conditions for certain forms of emotionality to unfold. The interaction between environmental events and genetic events in the brain is dynamic. Only the basic blueprints for brain connectivities are encoded in genes. Primary emotional tendencies related to attachment, fear, anger, and separation distress emerge very early in development to help organisms cope in situations that compromise their survival. Other emotional tendencies, such as sexual lust and maternal devotion, may emerge later to promote reproductive processes. Social emotions, such as play and dominance-seeking, appear later in development to help promote the establishment of social structures (Panksepp, 1998).

7 The term "interpretation" is not being used here in the cultural or humanistic tradition but in the sense of categorical interpretation. An example is the perception of another person and his or her classification as female or male. Hence, this does not concern the meaning of the perception for the perceiver.

[8] Whether gestalt bodily changes are perceived consciously also depends on social and cultural factors. To a great extent, bodily perceptions are learned socially and culturally. The history of medicine provides a multitude of examples. As soon as syndromes become named and classified as specific diseases, there are always people who start to perceive them in themselves and suffer from them consciously. The "burnout syndrome" is a good example.

[9] This raises the question of the relation between basic and complex emotions. Is it similar to that between primary and mixed colors? That is, are basic emotions like primary colors that can be mixed together to produce a multitude of shades (Plutchik, 1984, p. 217)? Or is a more appropriate model one based on analogies with chemical compounds, so basic emotions can be combined similarly to chemical elements to form new "matter" in which the constituent elements can no longer be recognized (e.g., water, in which the elements of hydrogen and oxygen become unrecognizable (Röttger-Rössler, 2004, p. 11).

[10] A full account of *amae* cannot be given here. For more details, see Doi (1973, 1974, 1986) and Hinton (1999).

References

Arnold, M. B. (1960). *Emotion and personality* (Vols. 1–2). New York: Columbia University Press.

Bejjani, B. P., Damier, P., Arnulf, I., Thivard, L., Bonnet, A. M., Dormont, D., Cornu, P., et al. (1999). Transient acute depression induced by high-frequency deep brain stimulation. *New England Journal of Medicine, 340*, 1476–1480.

Ben-Ze'ev, A., & Oatley, K. (1996). The intentional and social nature of human emotions: Reconsideration of the distinctions between basic and non-basic emotions. *Journal for the Theory of Social Behaviour, 26*(1), 81–94.

Berridge, K. C. (2003). Comparing the emotional brains of humans and other animals. In R. J. Davidson, K. R. Scherer, & H. H. Goldsmith (Eds.), *Handbook of affective sciences* (pp. 25–51). New York: Oxford University Press.

Cacioppo, J. T., Berntson, G. G., Klein, D. J., & Poehlmann, K. M. (1997). Psychophysiology of emotion across the lifespan. *Annual Review of Gerontology and Geriatrics, 17*, 27–74.

Cacioppo, J. T., Berntson, G. G., Larsen, J. T., Poehlmann, K. M., & Ito, T. A. (2000). The psychophysiology of emotion. In R. Lewis & J. M. Haviland-Jones (Eds.), *Handbook of emotions* (2nd ed., pp. 173–191). New York: Guilford Press.

Clore, G. L., & Ortony, A. (2000). Cognition in emotion: Always, sometimes, or never? In R. D. Lane & L. Nadel (Eds.), *Cognitive neuroscience of emotion* (pp. 24–61). New York: Oxford University Press.

Cosmides, L., & Tooby, J. (2000). Evolutionary psychology and the emotions. In R. Lewis & J. M. Haviland-Jones (Eds.), *Handbook of emotions* (2nd ed., pp. 91–115). New York: Guilford Press.

Damasio, A. R. (1994). *Descartes' error: Emotion, reason and the human brain*. New York: HarperCollins.

Darwin, C. (1904). *The expression of the emotions in man and animals*. London: John Murray. (Original work published 1872)

Davidson, R. J. (1994). Complexities in the search for emotion-specific physiology. In P. Ekman & R. J. Davidson (Eds.), *The nature of emotion* (pp. 237–242). New York: Oxford University Press.

Doi, T. (1973). *The anatomy of dependency*. Tokyo: Kodansha International.

Doi, T. (1974). *Amae*: A key concept for understanding Japanese personality structure. In R. Levine (Ed.), *Culture and personality: Contemporary readings* (pp. 307–314). Chicago, IL: Aldine.

Doi, T. (1986). *The anatomy of self: Self versus society*. Tokyo: Kodansha International.
Dörner, D. (1993). Wissen, Emotionen und Handlungsregulation oder die Vernunft der Gefühle. [Knowledge, emotions, and the control of action. Or: The rationality of feelings] *Zeitschrift für Psychologie, 201*(2), 167–202.
Ekman, P. (1972). Universals and cultural differences in facial expressions of emotions. In J. K. Cole (Ed.), *Nebraska symposium on motivation 1972* (pp. 207–285). Lincoln, NE: University of Nebraska Press.
Ekman, P. (1993). Facial expression and emotion. *American Psychologist, 48*, 384–392.
Ekman, P. (2004). What we become emotional about. In A. S. Manstead, N. H. Frijda, & A. Fischer (Eds.), *Feelings and emotions. The Amsterdam symposium* (pp. 119–135). New York: Oxford University Press.
Ekman, P., & Davidson, R. J. (1994). *The nature of emotion*. New York: Oxford University Press.
Ekman, P., & Friesen, W. (1975). *Unmasking the face*. Englewood Cliffs, NJ: Prentice Hall.
Ellsworth, P. C. (1994). Levels of thought and levels of emotion. In P. Ekman & R. J. Davidson (Eds.), *The nature of emotion* (pp. 192–196). New York: Oxford University Press.
Fehr, B., & Russell, J. A. (1984). Concept of emotion viewed from a prototype perspective. *Journal of Experimental Psychology: General, 113*, 464–486.
Frijda, N. H. (1994). Emotions require cognitions, even if simple ones. In P. Ekman & R. J. Davidson (Eds.), *The nature of emotion* (pp. 197–202). New York: Oxford University Press.
Gray, J. A. (1994). Three fundamental emotion systems. In P. Ekman & R. J. Davidson, (Eds.), *The nature of emotion* (pp. 243–247). New York: Oxford University Press.
Griffiths, P. E. (1997). *What emotions really are*. Chicago, IL: University of Chicago Press.
Hinton, A. L. (1999). Outline of a bioculturally based "processual" approach to the emotions. In A. L. Hinton (Ed.), *Biocultural approaches to the emotions* (pp. 299–328). Cambridge, UK: Cambridge University Press.
Holodynski, M., & Friedlmeier, W. (2005). *Development of emotions and emotion regulation*. Boston, New York: Springer (Kluwer International Series in Outreach Scholarship).
James, W. (1884). What is an emotion? *Mind, 9*, 188–205.
Johnson-Laird, P. N., & Oatley, K. (1989). The language of emotions: An analysis of a semantic field. *Cognition and Emotion, 3*(2), 81–123.
Johnson-Laird, P. N., & Oatley, K. (1992). Basic emotions, rationality, and folk theory. *Cognition and Emotion, 6*, 201–223.
Kappas, A. (2002). The science of emotion as a multidisciplinary research paradigm. *Behavioural Processes, 60*, 85–98.
Lazarus, R. S. (1966). *Psychological stress and the coping process*. New York: MacGraw Hill.
Lazarus, R. S., & Folkman, S. (1984). *Stress, appraisal, and coping*. New York: Springer.
LeDoux, J. E. (1996). *The emotional brain*. New York: Touchstone.
LeDoux, J. E. (2000). Emotion circuits in the brain. *Annual Review of Neuroscience, 23*, 155–184.
Leventhal, H., & Scherer, K. R. (1987). The relationship of emotion to cognition: A functional approach to a semantic controversy. *Cognition and Emotion, 1*, 3–28.
Lutz, C. (1988). *Unnatural emotions. Everyday sentiments on a Micronesian atoll and their challenge to western theory*. Chicago, IL: University of Chicago Press.
Manstead, A. S., & Fischer, A. H. (2001). Social appraisal: The social world as object of and influence on appraisal processes. In K. R. Scherer, A. Schorr, & T. Johnstone (Eds.), *Appraisal processes in emotion* (pp. 221–232). Oxford, UK: Oxford University Press.
Markowitsch, H. J. (1998/1999). Differential contribution of the right and left amygdala to affective information processing. *Behavioural Neurology, 11*, 233–244.
McDougall, W. (1960). *An introduction to social psychology*. London: Methuen. (Original work published 1908)

Mesquita, B., & Ellsworth, P. C. (2001). The role of culture in appraisal. In K. R. Scherer, A. Schorr, & T. Johnstone (Eds.), *Appraisal processes in emotion* (pp. 233–248). Oxford, UK: Oxford University Press.

Oatley, K. (1992). *Best laid schemes.* New York: Cambridge University Press.

Oatley, K., & Johnson-Laird, P. N. (1987). Towards a cognitive theory of emotions. *Cognition and Emotion, 1*, 29–50.

Öhman, A. (1986). Face the beast and fear the face: Animal and social fears as prototypes for evolutionary analyses of emotion. *Psychophysiology, 23*, 123–145.

Öhman, A., Flykt, A., & Lundqvist, D. (2000). Unconscious emotion: Evolutionary perspectives, psychophysiological data and neuropsychological mechanism. In R. D. Lane & L. Nadel (Eds.), *Cognitive neuroscience of emotion* (pp. 96–327). New York: Oxford University Press.

Ortony, A., Clore, G. L., & Collins, A. (1988). *The cognitive structure of emotions.* New York: Cambridge University Press.

Ortony, A., & Turner, T. J. (1990). What's basic about basic emotions? *Psychological Review, 97*, 315–331.

Panksepp, J. (1998). *Affective neuroscience. The foundations of human and animal emotions.* New York: Oxford University Press.

Panksepp, J. (2004). Basic affects and the instinctual emotional systems of the brain. In A. S. Manstead, N. H. Frijda, & A. Fischer (Eds.), *Feelings and emotions. The Amsterdam symposium* (pp. 174–193). New York: Oxford University Press.

Parkinson, B., & Manstead, A. S. (1992). Appraisal as a cause of emotion. In M. S. Clark (Ed.), *Review of personality and social psychology: Emotion* (Vol. 13, pp. 122–149). Newbury Park, CA: Sage.

Plutchik, R. (1984). A general psychoevolutionary theory. In K. R. Scherer & P. Ekman (Eds.), *Approaches to emotion* (pp. 197–220). Hillsdale, NJ: Erlbaum.

Prinz, J. (2004). Which emotions are basic? In D. Evans & P. Cruse (Eds.), *Emotion, evolution, and rationality* (pp. 69–87). New York: Oxford University Press.

Reisenzein, R. (2000). Worum geht es in der Debatte um die Basisemotionen [What is the debate on basic emotions all about]? In F. Försterling & J. Stiensmeier-Pelster (Eds.), *Kognitive Aspekte von Motivation und Emotion* (pp. 205–237). Göttingen, Germany: Hogrefe.

Röttger-Rössler, B. (2004). *Die kulturelle Modellierung des Gefühls. Ein Beitrag zur Theorie und Methodikum ethnologischer Emotionsforschung anhand indonesischer Fallstudien* [The cultural modeling of feeling: A contribution to the theory and methods of ethnological emotion research based on Indonesian case studies.] Münster, Germany: LIT.

Rosaldo, R. (1993). Der Kummer und die Wut des Kopfjägers. Über die kulturelle Intensität von Emotionen [The sorrow and anger of the headhunter: The cultural intensity of emotions]. In E. Berg & M. Fuchs (Eds.), *Kultur, soziale Praxis, Text. Die Krise der ethnographischen Repräsentation* (pp. 375–401). Frankfurt am Main, Germany: Suhrkamp.

Roseman, I. J., & Evdokas, A. (2004). Appraisals cause experienced emotions: Experimental evidence. *Cognition and Emotion, 18*, 1–28.

Roseman, I. J., & Smith, C. A. (2001). Appraisal theory: Overview, assumptions, varieties, controversies. In K. R. Scherer, A. Schorr, & T. Johnstone (Eds.), *Appraisal processes in emotion* (pp. 3–19). Oxford, UK: Oxford University Press.

Scherer, K. R. (1984). On the nature and function of emotion: A component process approach. In K. R. Scherer & P. Ekman (Eds.), *Approaches to emotion* (pp. 293–318). Hillsdale, NJ: Erlbaum.

Scherer, K. R. (Ed.). (1988). *Facets of emotion. Recent research.* Hillsdale, NJ: Erlbaum.

Scherer, K. R. (1993). Neuroscience projections to current debates in emotion psychology. *Cognition and Emotion, 7*, 1–41.

Scherer, K. R. (1994). Toward a concept of modal emotions. In P. Ekman & R. J. Davidson (Eds.), *The nature of emotion* (pp. 25–31). New York: Oxford University Press.
Scherer, K. (2001). Appraisal considered as a process of multilevel sequential checking. In K. R. Scherer, A. Schorr, & T. Johnstone (Eds.), *Appraisal processes in emotion* (pp. 92–120). New York: Oxford University Press.
Scherer, K. R. (2004). Feelings integrate the central representation of appraisal-driven response organization in emotion. In A. S. R. Manstead, N. H. Frijda, & A. H. Fischer (Eds.), *Feelings and emotions: The Amsterdam symposium* (pp. 136–157). Cambridge, UK: Cambridge University Press.
Schorr, A. (2001). Appraisal: The evolution of an idea. In K. R. Scherer, A. Schorr, & T. Johnstone (Eds.), *Appraisal processes in emotion* (pp. 20–34). Oxford, UK: Oxford University Press.
Solomon, R. C. (1976). *The passions*. New York: Doubleday-Anchor.
Solomon, R. (2002). Back to basics: On the very idea of "basic emotions." *Journal for the Theory of Social Behaviour, 32*, 115–144.
Sousa, R. de (2003). Emotion. In E. N. Zalta (Ed.), *Stanford Encyclopedia of Philosophy* (3). Retrieved December 30, 2005, from http://plato.stanford.edu/archives/spr2003/entries/emotion/
Spores, J. (1988). Running amok. A historical inquiry. *Ohio University Monographs in International Studies; Southeast Asian Series No. 82*. Athens, OH: Ohio University Center for International Studies.
Trevarthen, C. (2004). Infancy, mind in. In R. L. Gregory (Ed.), *The Oxford companion to the mind* (2nd ed., pp. 455–464). Oxford, UK: Oxford University Press.
Trevarthen, C., Aitken, K. J., Vandekerckhove, M., Delafield-Butt, J., & Nagy, E. (2006). Collaborative regulations of vitality in early childhood: Stress in intimate relationships and postnatal psychopathology. In D. Cicchetti & D. J. Cohen (Eds.), *Developmental psychopathology* (2nd ed., pp. 65–126). New York: Wiley.
Winzeler, R. (1990). Amok: Historical, psychological, and cultural perspectives. In W. J. Karim (Ed.), *Emotions of culture. A Malay perspective* (pp. 96–122). Singapore: Oxford University Press.
Zajonc, R. (1980). Feeling and thinking: Preferences need no inferences. *American Psychologist, 35*, 151–75.
Zajonc, R. (1984). On primacy of affect. In K. R. Scherer & P. Ekman (Eds.), *Approaches to emotion* (pp. 259–270). Hillsdale, NJ: Erlbaum.

On the Origin and Evolution of Affective Capacities in Lower Vertebrates

Michael J. Casimir

Abstract The relation between nociception, related neuromorphological structures and neurophysiological processes, and the learning abilities in some members of various invertebrate and lower vertebrate taxa are described in this chapter. They may stand for the long-extinct members of the taxa that followed each other on the "scale of evolution." Based on the definition of fear as the emotion that emerges if danger is expected, the specific sensory and neuromorphological structures and capacities that are a sine qua non for the ability to "experience" fright and fear are described. This area concerns mainly (1) the capacity to sense a noxious, tissue-damaging event through nociceptors, and (2) the memorising and recollection of nox-related cues/stimuli. By recollecting such stimuli when and if they recur, a lurking danger can be foreseen and thus avoided. The observable behavioural reactions (flight or attack) can then be related to the basic emotions "fear" and "rage," respectively.

Introduction: Emotions, Feelings, and Darwinean Theory

> Men ought to know that from the brain, and from the brain only, arise our pleasures, joys, laughter and jests, as well as our sorrows, pains, grief, and tears. Through it, in particular, we think, see, hear, and distinguish the ugly from the beautiful, the bad from the good, the pleasant from the unpleasant. (Attributed to Hippocrates, as cited in Kandel, Schwartz, & Jessell, 2002)

In this chapter, I try to answer the question of how more and more complex emotional and feeling capacities have evolved during the course of evolution in line with the growing complexity and differentiation of neural structures intertwined with the different senses. At the root of this endeavour lies the notion that emotions and feelings are related to, and are elicited through, the sensing/perception of specific cues/stimuli in the natural and social environment. The related subconscious or conscious appraisals (related to embodied values) of these agencies then

M.J. Casimir (✉)
Department Social and Cultural Anthropology, University of Cologne, Cologne, Germany
e-mail: michael.casimir@uni-koeln.de

B. Röttger-Rössler, H.J. Markowitsch (eds.), *Emotions as Bio-cultural Processes*,
DOI 10.1007/978-0-387-09546-2_4,

lead, by means of neural processing, to emotions or on the highest levels of complexity to conscious feelings as observed in our own species and possibly in some other higher mammals.

To avoid terminological misunderstandings, I shall—with the help of Damasio (1994, pp.127–164) and LeDoux (1996, p.329, footnote 3, LeDoux & Armony, 1999)—differentiate between "emotions" and "feelings." Paraphrasing the two, one can say, like Dolan (2003, p.893), that: "Emotion refers to the external consequences of processing an emotion-eliciting object; feelings to a private internal experience engendered by an emotional occurrence" or "Feelings are defined as mental representations of physiological changes that characterize and are consequent upon processing emotion-eliciting objects or states" (Dolan, 2002, p.1193; for a critical discussion of the "emotion/feeling problem," see Panksepp, 2003).

In the framework of the Darwinian paradigm, we understand the interrelated functioning of the individual parts of the body as a means of maximising life sustainability, enabling the organism to optimise the intake of energy and nutrients and avoid life-threatening dangers. This involves all morphological structures and physiological processes including the sense organs and neural "data processing." Generalising, it can be stated that those that are "better equipped" with these faculties have a differentially higher reproduction rate and more probably can pass on their "better" genes to a next generation. Although terms such as "better equipped" connote here only the individual's differential capacity to "solve problems" relevant to its survival when competing for fitness with others of the same species, they can also connote such capacities and related behavioural patterns of a whole taxon competing with another one. The various environmental factors and forces acting on the individual can thus be understood as prime movers that positively select those that are well equipped for finding food and recognising dangers while negatively selecting those who are less well equipped and thus less successful.

Every morphological structure and every behavioural pattern derives from less complex phylogenetic predecessors; and thus at each level of evolution it should, in theory, be possible to trace morphological structures and physiological processes back to phylogenetically earlier ones from which they have evolved. In an evolutionary quest for the emergence of such phenomena as emotions and feelings, which are grounded in the evolution of the various perceptive capacities and the related neural processing of sensory information, we can try to analyse the interplay of the relevant sensory and neural structures and the resulting behavioural functioning that enables individuals of given species to cope with environmental hazards at the various evolutionary "levels." Only an analysis and comparison of these capacities and functions in species of different taxa living today can shed some light on the phylogeny of emotional capacities. By such a comparison, I hope to find sensory-cum-neural precursors (and the related behavioural patterns) from which the more complex affective processes and capacities have evolved. Here, it should be noted that when the terms "higher," "lower," and "primitive" are used they refer only to differences in complexity. Bullock (1990) noted that "complex" means:

> having more parts, processes, interrelations, aspects and details.... *Higher animals* can be defined as those that are more complex than the lower species ... [they are] not necessarily better adapted or more perfect but simply using more parts, processes, and interrelationships ... [these terms] carry no automatic connotations of value or anthropocentricity. (p. 247)

Basic Needs, Basic Dangers, Basic Emotions

Organisms can be defined as living systems capable of extracting energy and nutrients from the environment. Owing to their metabolic capacities, they are able to synthesise their species-specific tissues to maintain themselves, grow, and multiply. In contrast to green plants, which obtain energy through sunlight and utilise soil nutrients, all animals have to prey—as herbivores on plants, carnivores on other animals, or omnivores on both. All animals can become victims of environmental dangers such as extreme temperature differences; and (with few exceptions) they are prey and predators at the same time.

Each animal in its specific ecological niche has the "problem" of constantly having to detect and differentiate between the manifold factors that preserve its life and those that endanger it. Basically, such factors can be of a chemical or a physical nature. The first class of indicators or cues involve a plethora of molecules and compounds that can, if the adequate chemical sense organs are developed, inform the individual specifically about food, the presence of a sexual partner, and the presence of an enemy and generally about, for example, the changing quality of the medium (e.g., water) in which it lives. The second class involves characteristics of the physical environment (e.g., changes in temperature, light intensity, and currents) or a mechanical impediment, but it can also concern the social environment, signalling the presence of a sex partner, a rival, or a predator. Here, in the various families, genera, and species of the animal kingdom, senses have been developed (e.g., eyes, mechanoreceptors, electric receptors) that individually or in combination can detect relevant positive or negative cues. Success in approaching or avoiding these situations, respectively, has a positive effect on the animal's "well-being" and thus finally on its fitness.

Nociception, Conditioning, and the Evolution of Emotions

> All animals have at least one power of sensation, that of touch; but that which has sensation has also pleasure and pain and is affected by pleasurable and painful objects, and, if so it has *desire* also, since *desire* is a desire for the pleasurable. (Aristotle, *On the Soul* [*De Anima*], Book B, p. 23)

On Being Touchy and on Being in Pain

On Nociception and Pain

As Aristotle observed, all animals have the ability to perceive and react to the mechanical stimulus "touch"; even protozoa such as the paramecium or the flagellates (as well as some plants, e.g., the mimosa and some of the carnivorous plants) and all of the invertebrates are equipped with special structures that are sensitive to certain mechanical, chemical, or thermal stimuli. Many of these receptors are found in the epidermis of most invertebrates and vertebrates, but they are also found in the inner organs, the viscera (Kavaliers, 1988; for an overview, see Kandel et al., 2002, pp. 472–479). These sensory cells inform the animal not only about deviations from the species-specific optimal environmental parameters (e.g., light, temperature) or the presence of a predator but also about a positive "value" such as the vicinity of food or a sex partner or deviations from optimal physiological states.

However, among these receptors, it is mainly the nociceptors (from the Latin term *nox*, meaning pain), which sense noxious, tissue-damaging stimuli, that are of special interest for our enquiry. They are characterised by free nerve endings not only in the animal's epidermis or the cuticule (the hard outer covering of insects for example) but also in the viscera. Four types can be differentiated: (1) thermo nociceptors, which react to tissue damage evoked by temperatures higher than 45°C or lower than 5°C; (2) chemo nociceptors, which are sensitive to noxious chemical substances; (3) mechano nociceptors, which sense noxious pressure; and (4) polymodal nociceptors, which react to more than one or all of the stimuli mentioned.[1] When a noxious, tissue-damaging event occurs, all of these receptors communicate that information along the afferent neural pathway to a more or less complex neural centre (or centres) where, after processing, specific peripheral organs such as muscles are activated through the efferent pathways and various behaviours (as well as facial expressions) are obtained.

The term "pain," however, implies more than the processing of the somatosensory information and the release of specific behavioural patterns. Following the IASP (1986, p. 217), pain is usually defined as: "An unpleasant sensory or emotional *experience* [italics added] which we primarily associate with tissue damage or describe in terms of tissue damage, or both." Here, then, in addition to the physiological process of nociception, is a *subjective appraisal* (an unpleasant sensory or emotional experience) that runs parallel to or follows nociception and leads to feelings that humans can express through language.

There is still debate on whether, in a tissue-damaging situation, we can speak of "pain" (often not differentiated from suffering) in animals other than humans. Some argue that animals can be expected to feel pain prop only if they possess consciousness or even self-consciousness (see Smith & Boyd, 1991, p. 59). However, it is difficult, if not impossible, to show and conclude experimentally that an animal possesses such faculties. To circumvent this problem, some authors have suggested and argued that if an animal is endowed with nociceptors connected to specific areas of the central nervous system (CNS) supposed to be homologous to the ones active in the human brain when we feel pain (see Neugebauer, Li, Bird, & Han, 2004), the animal can also be expected to experience pain and suffering (see Kavaliers, 1988, p. 924; Zimmerman, 1986). Even when such morphological-cum-physiological requirements are not met, however, some authors claim that it is legitimate to deduce pain when an animal's behaviour following an obviously noxious event is comparable to the behavioural patterns observed in humans under similar and thus comparable circumstances (Sneddon, 2004, p. 127; see also Smith & Boyd, 1991, Table 4.2, p. 62; for a comprehensive discussion, see Dawkins, 2000; Grandin & Deesing, 2003).To avoid the problems that arise in conjunction with the various discussions about "consciousness" and "self-consciousness," I subscribe here to the latter chain of arguments and suspect and speak of pain in animals when, after a tissue-damaging event, some of their more complex behavioural patterns (e.g., pain guarding) are comparable to those observed in humans.

Hence, it seems safe to say that nociception lies at the evolutionary base of affective capacities. To give the following a solid framework, I describe this evolution according to the hypothesis that affective capacities in animals presuppose the following concomitance: An organism must be capable of (1) sensing a noxious (e.g., tissue-damaging event); (2) associating, for example, environmental cues with this noxious experience; (3) storing this association for some period of time; and (4) recalling the negative experience when it encounters and perceives cues that are the same as, or similar to, those associated with the earlier aversive experience. It is only when equipped with these four faculties that it becomes possible for an organism to anticipate a lurking danger, and we can observe the behaviours it elicits—namely, flight (related to the emotion "fear") or attack (related to the emotion "rage").

In the following section, I delineate and relate a noxious event to the animal's most basic behaviours to minimise an aversive effect and then, in a second step, describe the animal's ability to evade a future dangerous situation before it occurs. If this capacity to discover a lurking danger can be assumed through the observance of an avoidance behaviour, we can hazard the guess that in such situations the most basic of all the emotions is emerging—i.e., "fear."

"Once Bitten Twice Shy": From Fright to Fear

As many have assumed (e.g., Fessler, 2002, p. 207; McNally & Westbrook, 2006; Öhman, 1986), the first affective capacities to evolve in phylogeny pertain to the perception of either "positive" cues/stimuli (especially those linked to food or a sex partner) or "negative" ones linked to environmental dangers in the broadest sense (especially predators). The former "motivates" the individual to approach the source of the stimulus, whereas the latter leads to flight or fight reactions. It has been generally accepted that "fear" and/or its evolutionary precursors are emotions that can be observed in most animals. Many of the positive capacities mentioned above are more complex and are mainly activated through physiological changes. For instance, the decrement in blood sugar concentration leads to hunger, and the variance in the discharge of certain hormones leads to sexual arousal. Appetence behaviour is then activated, and the animal seeks to satisfy its "drive."

Here I deal mainly with the functioning and evolution of one of the "basic" emotions, "fear," of which, from the evolutionary point of view, Schulkin (1998) has noted:

> Motivational states like fear prepare us for action in the presence of *uncertainty* [italics added] ... which functionally serves to avoid harm. The mechanisms that orchestrate fear are those linked to the readiness to be active, for example, to perceive an event or to generate the requisite motor behavior. (p. 56)

In 2005, Schulkin, Morgan, and Rosen (p. 629) defined fear as "an adaptive response of a *potentially* [italics added] dangerous event." In both cases, the words "uncertainty" and "potentially" refer to a danger that might occur, not to one that has just struck. In the quest for the phylogeny of what can be assumed to be the earliest emotional capacity to have emerged in the animal kingdom, we have to look for the interrelatedness between the negative stimuli affecting an animal and its behaviour that can minimise or avoid a noxious situation. Two mechanisms or capacities can be observed here. The first, most basic one comprises an instant, reflex-like reaction to a detected noxious or aversive stimulus. The second comprises a situation in which an animal can memorise and recall attributes of, for example, a predator and/or other specific stimuli/cues in the environment in which the noxious event took place, so a lurking danger can be "foreseen" in future and thus avoided.

Often, however, the literature does not differentiate the emotion(s) elicited in different noxious or dangerous situations, simply calling them all "fear." However, a sudden, unexpected attack, for instance, does not lead immediately to fear; the emotion that emerges first is a shock-like "fright" that may then be followed by fear, especially if the danger is still lurking. For this phylogenetic enquiry, it is therefore helpful to differentiate between fright and two types of fear and to differentiate between them and some other affects/emotions. It is important to note here, once more, that in the case of nonhuman animals, terms such as fright and fear do not imply consciousness. They stand only for the same or similar (and possibly homologous) physiological processes and behavioural reactions that emerge in humans in comparable situations.

For methodological reasons, it therefore seems appropriate to differentiate clearly between some terms, especially between fright and fear.

- *Fright*: This term describes an animal's emotion coinciding with or immediately following a sudden shock-like aversive event, especially a noxious event. It may lead to a freeze response or to startle, a quick reflex-like flight movement. There is some evidence that together with or immediately thereafter the following three events occur.
- *Unconditioned (post-shock) fear*. It has been suggested (Cardinal, Parkinson, Hall, & Everitt, 2002, p. 330; Holahan & White, 2004), however, that rather than being a reflexive response to the shock presentation freezing is the expression of the conditioned pairing formed between the shock and a context (conditioned freezing). Whatever the exact behavioural-cum-neurophysiological processes might be, this type of fear should again be differentiated from unconditioned fear.

- *Unconditioned fear*. This fear emerges with the perception of an unconditioned stimulus (US) that is innately "preprogrammed" (Davey, 1995; see also Ewert, 1981). This type of fear is classified as "unconditioned" because the cue/stimulus has not been memorised by conditioning but releases fear behaviour innately (e.g., "freezing" or the "startle reflex"). For instance, it has been shown experimentally that typical fear and flight reactions can be elicited in laboratory mice and rats confronted with the odour of fox faeces or the odour of a snake (e.g., Campeau & Davis, 1995; Dell'Omo & Alleva, 1993; Fendt, Endres, & Apfelbach, 2003; Wallace & Rosen, 2001).
- *Conditioned fear* (proper). This fear emerges when a neutral stimulus (a tone or light) coincides with a noxious experience in the past. Here, specific information has been memorised through associative learning whereby the neutral stimulus has acquired aversive properties by virtue of its association with the aversive, unconditioned stimulus (US), thus becoming the conditioned stimulus (CS)-note that in the following "CS" stands for "conditional" as well as for "conditioned" stimulus (Fig. 1A). The recalling of the conditioned stimulus, if approached again, warns the animal of a possible danger (see also Flood & Overmier, 1981), which then leads to either vigilance and cautious behaviour (which might be tagged to the more vague emotion of apprehension or dread) or fear and immediate flight.
- *Aversion learning*. Next to imprinting (see Hess, 1973), aversion learning is the quickest of all learning processes and can be observed in all taxa (LeDoux, 1994). The specific taste or smell of an ingested toxic foodstuff is paired with an ensuing malaise, which can be understood as a specific type of conditioning. Here, specific smell/taste is memorised (often for a long time), and its occurrence leads to "fear" and hinders any tendency in the animal to digest it again[2] (Fig. 1B).
- *Rage*. When it is associated with fear, rage often occurs in the presence of a predator or rival as a last resort when escape is not possible (Siegel & Brutus, 1990, p. 135). The emotion that emerges in such a situation leads to an attack. Using the term "rage" is justified in such situations because the physiological processes and behaviours are comparable to those observed in our own species in similar situations.[3]

In contrast to experimental situations, under normal conditions one of the multitude of environmental cues can serve as a CS. To acquire this function, it has to be paired selectively with a noxious US. It can even be part of the noxious event itself (e.g., the colour or shape of a predator). Alternatively, it may be an ostentatious pattern in the environment (e.g., a dark hole or another salient landmark). In the moment at which the aversive experience occurs, this pattern becomes a stimulus acquiring the value of a CS. With the capacity to memorise and recall such CSs, a possible danger can then be anticipated and thus avoided (for details, see LeDoux, 1996, pp. 141–148, 2000a; LeDoux & Armony, 1999). Hence, according to our definition, "fear" (excluding here the innate mechanisms) can emerge in an animal only if a noxious event-related cue/stimulus has

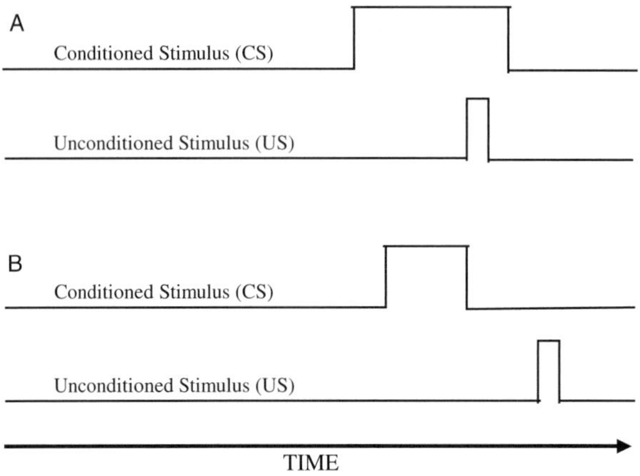

Fig. 1 With fear conditioning, the unconditioned stimulus (*US*) (e.g., a noxious or aversive event) is presented at the end of the presentation of a neutral, conditioning one (*CS*) (e.g., a tone or a light) (**A**). With fear conditioning due to a food-induced aversion, the unconditioned stimulus (e.g., sickness due to the food's toxicity), which is experienced some time after ingestion of the food item, is paired with a memorised food-specific cue (e.g., its smell or taste) (**B**). In both cases, after conditioning the animal shows fear reactions (behavioural and physiological) if the CS is encountered and sensed again

been paired and memorised and is recalled when this cue/stimulus is experienced again independent from the real source of danger. This requires the capacity to memorise and store for a short period of time (short-term memory) or for a longer time (long-term memory) cues/stimuli or even, as in the case of mental maps, complex and coherent environmental information.

To determine on which evolutionary level these intertwined capacities have emerged, I examine, first, how various animals sense aversive stimuli and how they react to them and, second, on which level of complexity the animals are able to memorise cues related to a detected noxious stimulus. In the next step, I align these observations with the respective morphological-cum-functional areas of the CNS. It is suggested that with the evolution of an increasingly complex CNS, certain areas became more specialised in processing and interrelating the afferent information with the conditioned, memorised stimuli.

Invertebrates

Noxious Events, Reflexive Behaviour, Fright and Fear in Invertebrates

In most invertebrates, the aversive stimuli causing avoidance reactions can be differentiated into three broad categories.

1. Negative noxious effect due to changes in the physical or chemical "external environment"-e.g., a rise in temperature, a sudden change in light intensity, or the occurrence of a noxious chemical compound
2. Mainly tissue-damaging encounters with, for example, a predator or competitor
3. Aversive effect due to intake of food containing noxious (e.g., toxic) compounds

In the first case, the animal usually tries to escape from the location to avoid adverse stimuli. In the second case, if a tissue-damaging stimulus affects an invertebrate, generally only a simple learning ability can be observed. When a touch stimulus is applied, the animal withdraws the part of the body inflicted; and if the stimulus is repeated, one can observe not only a spontaneous increment of a behaviour (sensitisation) but also a spontaneous decrement of this behaviour (habituation). If the stimulus is not presented for a period of time, the behavioural responses can be induced again (dishabituation). Furthermore, in some species, agonistic behaviours can also be observed in the threatened animal in menacing conflicting situations with predators or rivals (Fig. 2).

Most invertebrates (excluding insects[4]) have only short-term memory (STM), although in some species a relatively long-term memory (LTM) lasting for more than 24 hours has been observed. For instance, an associative memory has been shown through experiments using classical as well as operant conditioning in the sea hare *Aplysia* (Sharma et al., 2003; Sutton, Bagnall, Sharma,

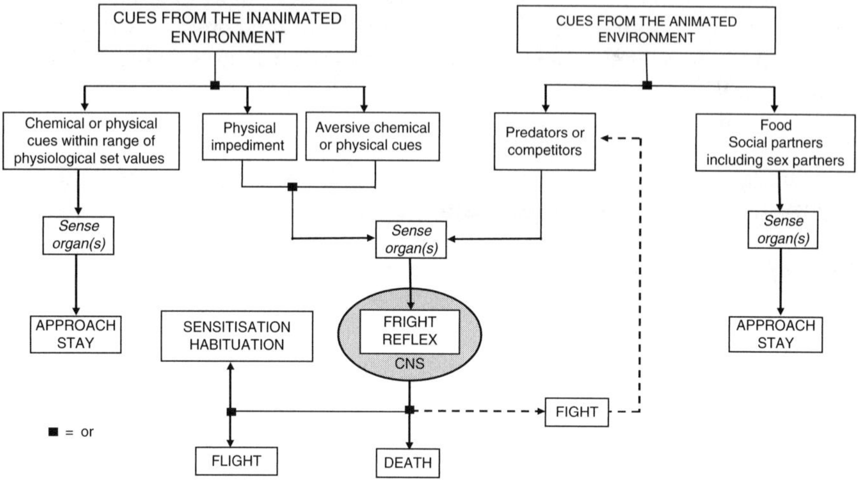

Fig. 2 Relation between environmental factors and the aversive or noxious stimuli that induce, via more or less specific sense organs, a reflex-like fright behaviour followed by flight or fight reactions in some invertebrates and lower vertebrates. *Dotted line* indicates that defence or fight behaviour has been observed in some of the invertebrates. *CNS*, central nervous system

Shobe, & Carew, 2004), the terrestrial slug *Limax valentianus* (Kasai, Watanabe, Kirino, & Matsuo, 2006), the nematode *Caenorhabditis elegans* (Bargmann, 2006; Quinn, 2005; Zhang, Lu, & Bargmann, 2005), and the flatworm *Planaria*. Nonetheless, it is still not clear if implicit memory storage can be recalled after a longer period of time in any of these animals (see Brembs, 2003a,b; Brembs, Lorenzetti, Baxter, & Byrne, 2002, Nolen, Marcus, & Carew, 1987). Until now, experimental evidence suggesting not only intermediate-term memory (> 90 minutes) but also LTM (> 24 hours) has been demonstrated only in the pond snail *Lymnaea* (Alexander, Audesirk, & Audesirk, 1984; Fulton, Kemenes, Andrew, & Benjamin, 2005; Lukowiak, Adatia, Krygier, & Syed, 2000; Lukowiak et al., 2003) and *Aplysia* (Brembs et al., 2002; Sutton et al., 2004). However, it has been reported that the most highly developed invertebrates, the *cephalopods* (octopus, squids), can store different kinds of sensory information in certain upper lobes of the brain for a longer period of time and react to their own advantage in situations similar or equal to those in which the information has been stored (Hochner, Brown, Langella, Shomrat, & Fiorito, 2003; Hochner, Shomrat, & Fiorito, 2006; Purchon, 1968, pp. 427–437; Young, 1995; see also Agin, Chicheri, Dickel,, & Chicheri, 2006)[5]. Figure 2 shows the environmental factors in relation to the aversive stimuli, the sense organs involved, the CNS, and the induced behaviours in some invertebrates and lower vertebrates.

The few examples given above have shown that some invertebrate taxa reveal simple capacities and behavioural patterns that, in an anthropomorphic analogy, can be described as "fright." In these taxa, avoidance behaviour based on LTM and recalling the CS in the appropriate situation (which would then be described as fear) seems to be rare. In the following sections, I comment on the possible ancestry of the vertebrates (chordates) and then describe the somatosensory abilities, related behaviours, and the neural structures involved in some of these animals.

Emotions and the Evolving Brain

Possible Ancestry and the Phylogeny of the Vertebrates

Recent data provided through the analysis of the molecular architecture of an annelide's nerve cord (Denes et al. 2007) now strongly support Dohrn's 1875 hypothesis of the homology of the ventral invertebrate and the dorsal vertebrate CNS. The evolutionary conservation of the molecular mediolateral architecture shared by the annelide *Platynereis* and the vertebrates point to early centralisation of the nervous system in the last common bilaterian ancestor, leading to the evolutionary lines of the insects (e.g., *Drosophila*), nematodes (e.g., *Caenorhabditis*), enteropneust (*Saccoglossus*), and vertebrates.

It is still controversial whether the sea squirts (*tunicates, urodeuterostomia*) or an enteropneust, the acorn worms (*hemichordata*), are more closely related to the lancelet, *Amphioxus* (*cephalochordata*), supposed to be the last surviving ancestor of the fish and thus of all the vertebrates. The larvae of tunicates show a nerve cord (notochord), a cerebral vesicle, gills, and an eyespot; and they share more genetic and morphological patterns with the lancelet than the acorn worms. Therefore, it has been supposed that they are more closely related to the *chordata* and that the acorn worm belongs to a sister group of the ancestral evolutionary line (see Holland & Garcia-Fernandez, 1996; Holland & Holland, 2001; Lacalli, 2001; Shimeld & Holland, 2000, 2005). On the other hand, genetic expression of specific domains (involved in the patterning of structures in the nervous system) in the embryo of the acorn worm *Saccoglossus kowalevskii* may have been homologised with the ones expressed in the anterior and posterior brain regions of the chordata. Thus, the acorn worm is also a good, if not a better, candidate for the role of starting point in the evolution of the phylum (Lowe et al., 2003; Tautz, 2003).

The lancelet *Amphioxus*, without any doubt the most primitive *chordate* known, already shows many morphological patterns that can be homologised with those of the bony fishes. However, in contrast to them, no segmentation (*neuromeres*) of the "brain" is found. On the next level of the "phylogenetic scale" we find the simple eel-like parasitic fish, the lampreys and the hagfish (*cyclostomata*), which developed well before the end of the Devonian Period and have survived the subsequent 360 million years (Gess, Coates, & Rubidge, 2006).

If we look at the neuroanatomy of these primitive, jawless (*agnathan)* fish (e.g., the lamprey), we already find a relatively well developed dorsal nerve cord and a concentration of nerve cells (ganglion) forming a simple brain with a tripartite forebrain, the telencephalon (similar and thus possibly homologue to that of the *gnathostomata*, all the jawed vertebrates). Furthermore, it has been assumed that the pallial area (the evolutionary precedent of the telencephalon) of the lampreys can be homologised with that of the other vertebrates (Northcutt & Wicht, 1997). Based on the data at hand, it has been suggested that the segmental and compartment architecture of the vertebrate brain was already established before the divergence of ag*nathans* and *gnathostomes* (Murakami et al., 2002, p. 271; see also Sneddon, Braithwaite, & Gentle, 2003).

Figure 3 shows the hypothetical phylogenetic cladogram of the major lineages of vertebrates of interest here. The quite primitive *agnathans,* just described, are at the bottom. It is assumed that the *gnatostomes*, fish that already have jaws, have developed from their early ancestors. The more primitive *gnatostomes* nowadays are the cartilaginous fish without calcified backbones (e.g., sharks and rays), and the "higher" ones are the bony fishes (e.g., trout or carp). Certain fishes (ancestors of lungfishes or the Coelacanth *Latimeria,* which is regarded as a survivor of the extinct crossopterygians) are the link between fishes and amphibia. This was followed by the evolution of reptiles. Crocodiles and birds branched off at an early stage; but what is of interest here is that the more primitive mammals, the marsupials, followed in a direct line from reptile stock (e.g., the platypus that lays eggs but also suckles its young

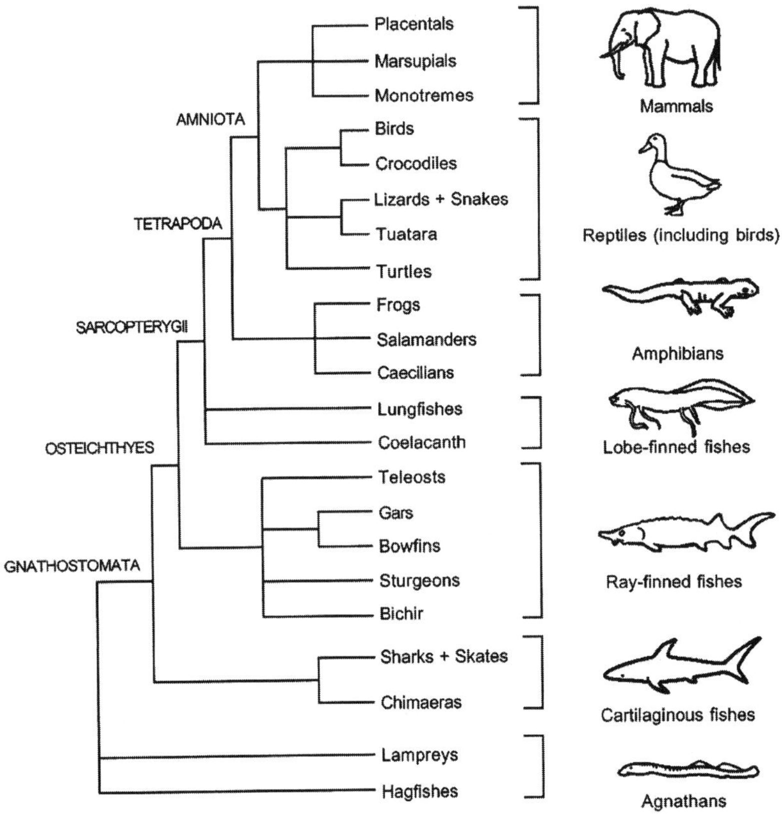

Fig. 3 Phylogenetic hypothesis for the major lineages of vertebrates based on morphological, paleontological, and molecular evidence. Disputed relationships are depicted as polytomies (i.e., where more than two branches originate from a knot). (Adapted from Meyer & Zardoya, 2003, Fig. 1, p. 312)

and the many species of kangaroo that give birth to an embryo that is then reared outside the body in a pouch). The mammals proper are those with placenta (placentals) that give birth to relatively well developed young that are suckled.

Sensory Organs, Nociception, and Memory in the Lower Chordates

As outlined above, the first emotions to evolve were "fear" and "rage." Fear can be experienced only when information on an aversive stimulus is transmitted (1) from somatosensory receptors (especially nociceptors) to (2) a nervous centre where (3) pairing of the US with a CS takes place so that in future detection of the CS alone leads to the physiological processes enabling the behavioural reactions flight or attack, which are then our indicators of fear. In the following sections, I examine the level of complexity these somatosensory-cum-neural preconditions must attain before release of the emotions fear and possibly rage can be expected, starting with the most primitive fishes.

Lancelets, Lampreys (Cephalochordata and Cyclostomata), Sharks, and Rays (Elasmobranchii)

A variety of ectodermal sensory cells have been identified in the lancelet (A*mphioxus*), most of which are probably mechanoreceptors that react in response to pressure (Lacalli, 2002a,b, 2004; Lacalli & Kelly, 2003). According to Holland and Yu (as cited in Lacalli, 2004, p. 153), the young larvae of *Amphioxus* respond most noticeably to touch at either end of the body, which releases a bout of escape swimming or a shorter startling escape response. This escape response in the young larvae may be related to the earliest epithelial sensory cells clustered at the tip of the rostrum and tail that send long, unbranched fibres into the cord. Propagation of the signal, possibly initiated by these cells along the cord, seems to depend, as in the adult *Amphioxus*, on local circuits resulting in this reflex (Lacalli, 2002a, p. 234). However, it can be presumed that even a rudimentary learning ability is absent in this animal.

The brains of lampreys and hagfishes have been well described by various authors, and Northcutt and Wicht (1997) have shown that the telencephalic pallium (the part of the brain forming the cortical structures in mammals) of the lamprey is homologous to that of the other vertebrates. The bulk of the telencephalon in the lamprey is composed of an olfactory bulb directly innervated by the bipolar receptor cells of the nasal mucosa (for details, see Aronson, 1981, pp. 39–40; Nieuwenhuys, 1967). Recent studies have indicated that this olfactory system in the lamprey has many similarities to the olfactory system of the bony fishes and mammals (Laframboise, Ren, Chang, Dubuc, & Zielinski, 2007). However, both lamprey and bony fish lack the distinct vomeronasal organ found in the larvae of some amphibians and some aquatic salamanders (Eisthen, 1992, 2000). It is fully developed in most reptiles and mammals, in most of which it shows, as we shall see, pronounced afferent connections via the bulbus olfactorius and the accessory bulbus olfactorius to the amygdaloid complex.

Experiments have shown that a startle reflex can be induced in the larvae of the lamprey by vibrations, making them withdraw deeper into the sandy or muddy burrows in which they live. In response to a vibration stimulus, specific anterior and posterior mechanoreceptors activate the central pattern generator of the CNS, which initiates the startle response and activates the musculature on both sides of the animal's body to produce the rapid withdrawal movements into their burrow (Currie & Carlsen, 1987; Einum & Buchanan, 2006; Kleerekoper, 1972; McClellan & Jang, 1993; Rovainen, 1982, pp. 69–72;

Rovainen & Yan, 2004). However, whether lamprey larvae have specialised nociceptors is still questionable; and Christenson, Bohman, Lagerback, and Grillner (1988; see also Sneddon et al., 2003, p. 1115), who described specific sensory neurons in the spinal cord of the lamprey's larvae that react on touch and pressure, noted that nociceptors proper have not been found. In the adult lamprey, however, Rovainen (1982, p. 70) noted that Martin and Wickelgren (1971) and Birnberger and Rovainen (1971) described cells in the skin of the adult *Petromyzon marinus* that respond to touch, pressure and nociception. Rovainen and Yan (2004) reported having found not only 15 pressure-sensitive cells that respond to mechanical stimulation of the dorsolateral skin of the head, but also two cells they classified as nociceptive. In the case of the *Amphioxus*, to the best of my knowledge, no conditioning experiments or observations are available that indicate either shorter or longer memory in the cyclostomata.

Among the rays, Sneddon et al. (2003) assumed that there were nociceptive abilities in one of the elsmobranchs, the cartilaginous fish in which the spinal cord is not protected by bones. Various articles have reported only that some of the neural prerequisites (mainly the trigeminal nerve tract) and some of the physiological processes can be equated morphologically and/or functionally with the ones that allow nociception in higher vertebrates. However, "true" nociceptors have not been found in these species; and because of the difficulty in homologising brain regions across species (Striedter, 2002; for details, see the next section), it seems too soon to conclude that these primitive vertebrates have nociceptive capacities. Among the elasmobranchs, however, unlike the "simple" chordates mentioned before, an elementary memory has been demonstrated in classic (Malyukova, Rakich, & Kovachevich, 1983) and instrumental (Clark, 1959; O'Gower, 1995) conditioning experiments, which have even provided some evidence for a space memory (as one aspect of the semantic memory, the memory of facts) in the Port Jackson Shark.

Evolution and the Brain in Vertebrates

On the basis of comparative analyses of the anatomy and morphology of the vertebrate brain, especially the telencephalon (Laming, 1981a; see also Butler, 2000), it has been supposed that the modern teleosts have developed from a hypothetical primitive ancestor of the holosteans (a group of archaic bony fish) and that the amphibians and finally the reptiles also evolved from the same forbearers via archaic cyclostomes and cross-opterygians (see genus *Coelacanthus*, with the surviving species *Latimeria chalumnae*). Before trying to identify the somatosensory receptors and the neural pathways to the higher nervous centres, I discuss their ability to memorise conditioned stimuli. I then describe the related behavioural patterns that indicate emotional capacities in the various taxa (fishes, amphibians, reptiles) and describe some morphological patterns involved in the generation of emotions in the most complex representatives of the phylum (i.e., mammals). Such a top-down approach is essential if we want to know what we are looking for when trying to homologise neural structures, their functioning, and the related behavioural patterns in the lower vertebrates.

The brains of all higher and lower vertebrates have a common structural organisation that can be subdivided into major parts: telencephalon, diencephalon, mesencephalon, metencephalon, and myelencephalon. In mammals, the telencephalon contains the cerebral cortex along with the basal ganglia and portions of the limbic system. The latter consists of the amygdaloid complex and parts of the cerebral cortex, such as the olfactory bulb, the hippocampal formation, and (in mammals) the surrounding cortex (peri- and entorhinal cortex, parahippocampal gyrus) and the cingulate and retrosplenial cortex. Portions of the frontal lobe, such as the orbifrontal cortex, are also sometimes regarded as part of the limbic cortex. The diencephalon with thalamus and hypothalamus contains some limbic nuclei as well. The septal nuclei, as a subpallial area, should also be mentioned. Caudal to these regions, we find the brainstem (mesencephalon, metencephalon, spinal cord). The upper brainstem nuclei receive much of the somatosensory information via the spinal cord—especially information on noxious stimuli, which is of special interest here (for further details, see Figures 4 and 5).

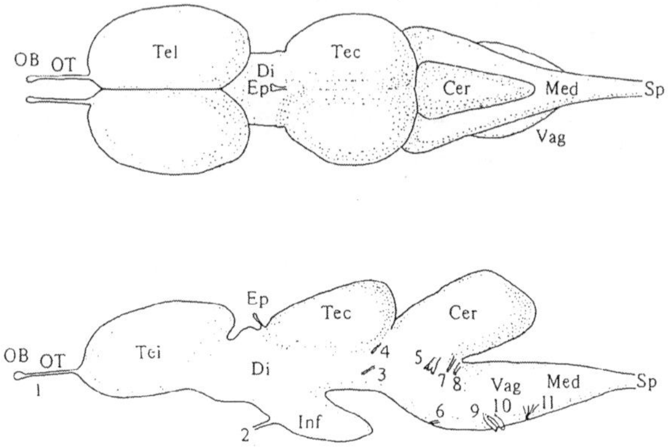

Fig. 4 Dorsal and lateral view of a generalised lower vertebrate brain showing the main superficial features of interest here. *Cer*, cerebellum; *Di*, diencephalon; *Inf*, inferior lobe of the hypothalamus; *Med*, medulla oblongata; *OB*, olfactory bulb; *Sp*, spinal cord; *Tec*, tectum opticum; *Vag*, vagal lobes; *Tel*, telencephalon; *1–11*, cranial nerves. (Adapted from Laming, 1981b, Fig. 1, p. 8)

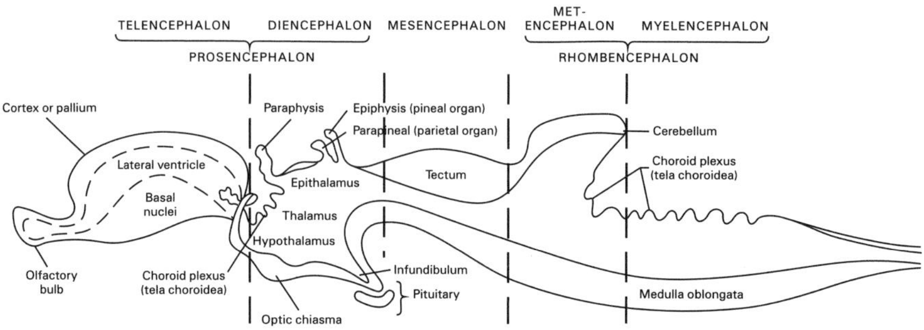

Fig. 5 Median section of a generalised mature vertebrate brain illustrating some of the principal divisions and structures. (Adapted from Abercrombie, Hickman, Johnson, & Thain, 1992, p. 71)

Emotions, the Limbic System of Mammals and the Problem of Homology

For the emergence of the emotion "fear" as defined here, two abilities must exist: (1) to sense an aversive incident and (2) to memorise the cues/stimuli in conjunction with this event. The first ability requires the existence of sensory cells, especially nociceptors; the second is the existence of specific neural structures, especially the hippocampal formation or some forerunner with comparable memory efficiency. In recent decades, a multitude of physiological and morphological studies combined with functional and psychological studies have shown that the most important neural structure for generating and processing emotions is the limbic system (the "emotional brain") and in particular the amygdaloid (from the Greek word *amygdala*, meaning almond) complex. Recently, the usefulness of the unifying concept of the "limbic system" (see LeDoux, 2000a) and that of a morphological and anatomical unity of the amygdala has been questioned (Swanson & Petrovich, 1998) and discussed widely (e.g., Laberge et al. 2006, pp. 177–178).

The following remarks adopt the traditional concept of the limbic system as a functional unit composed of heavily interconnected telencephalic and diencephalic structures. The latter include the hippocampal formation and the amygdaloid complex, hypothalamic nuclei, and (aside from the cingulated/retrosplenial and parahippocampal areas) structures in the ventral frontal lobe, in particular the nucleus accumbens and orbifrontal cortex. The amygdaloid complex is usually differentiated into three main units: the central nucleus (CeA) in which emotions are "generated," the lateral nucleus (LA), and the basolateral nucleus of the amygdala (BLA). The CeA receives and processes the incoming nociceptive information via the spinal cord and the brainstem. The information from the polymodal somatosensory cells reaches the LA from the thalamus and the cortex from which they are also transmitted via the BLA to the

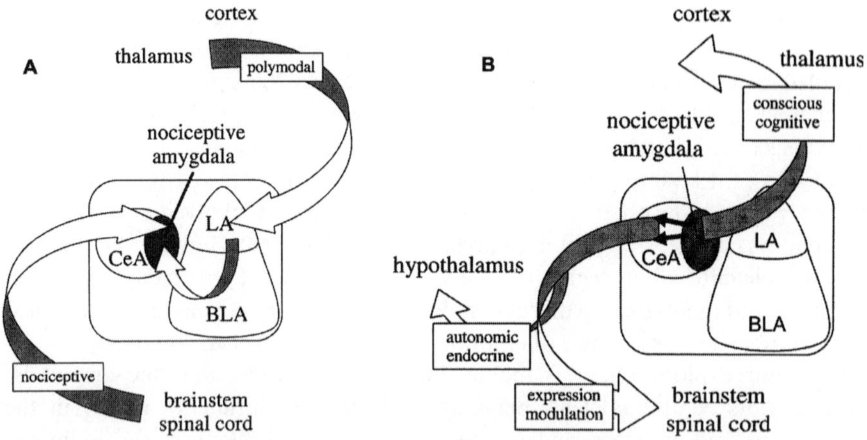

Fig. 6 Major sensory (especially nociceptive and polymodal) and sensosomatic inputs to the amygdala. **A** The central nucleus amygdala (more precisely the laterocapsular area of the central nucleus of the amygdala, or *CeA*) receives and processes incoming nociceptive information via the spinal cord and the brainstem. The information from the polymodal cells reaches the lateral nucleus of the amygdala (*LA*) via the cortex and the thalamus from where it is projected via the basolateral nucleus of the amygdala (*BLA*) to the CeA. **B** From the CeA, efferent fibres lead to the hypothalamus and trigger the autonomic endocrine processes and to the brainstem and the spinal cord, effecting the modulation of expressions. From the CeA, information also goes back to the thalamus and the cortex, where the information about the noxious event is recognised consciously in humans. (Adapted from Neugebauer et al., 2004, Fig. 2, p. 223)

CeA (Fig. 6A). Recapitulating and generalizing, it can be said (Campeau & Davis, 1995) that:

> The central nucleus of the amygdala might be the target of inputs from the basolateral complex, either directly or through multisynaptic intra- or extra-amygdaloid connections. These nuclei are part of a neural circuit necessary in the mediation of fear conditioning to auditory *and* visual conditioned stimuli, and probably to other sensory modalities as well. (p. 2305)

Efferent fibres lead from the CeA to the hypothalamus and elicit the autonomic endocrine processes and to the brainstem and spinal cord and elicit the modulation of expressions. Information from the CeA reaches the thalamus and the cortex (Fig. 6B), where "pain" is felt consciously in humans.

In the context of fear conditioning, it has been shown that not only the amygdala (McNally & Westbrook, 2006; Schafe, Doyère, & LeDoux, 2005; Schroeder & Shinnick-Gallagher, 2004) but also the lateral bed nucleus of the stria terminalis (a bundle of efferent fibres of the amygdala innervating nuclei of the basal forebrain and the hypothalamus) and the hippocampus are of special importance: After ablation of the amygdala, fear conditioning is impossible although explicit memory still functions. After lesions of the hippocampus, conditioning is still possible but explicit knowledge cannot be recalled; and if both centres are damaged, both abilities are impaired (for a comprehensive account, see Day, 2003; Iversen, Kupfermann, & Kandel, 2002; Schulkin et al., 2005). However, in a detailed review and analysis of recent findings, Davis (2000, pp. 255–256; see also Bucherelli, Baldi, Mariottini, Passani, & Blandina, 2006; Cahill & McGaugh, 1998) has noted that it is still not clear whether the amygdala actually stores fear memories or it is simply an essential part of the neural pathway that relays fear memory from some other structure to the brainstem sites involved in fear-related behaviours (startle, freezing). Lamprecht and Dudai (2000) showed that it is also still not clear to what degree the CeA and the BLA are involved in aversion learning, and there is also a discussion on whether the human amygdala is critical for the subjective experience of emotion (Anderson & Phelps, 2002).

For our exploration, it is mainly important to know that the amygdala, especially its central nucleus, plays an important multifunctional role in the production and/or processing of emotions (Fig. 7). Therefore, the following material examines whether not only the various nuclei of the amygdaloid complex (or their forerunners) but also some other emotion-significant structures can be found in the "lower" taxa—bony fishes, amphibians, reptiles—and if they serve the same or comparable functions as those observed in mammals.

If we try to analyse the morphological and functional changes that have taken place in the brain over the course of evolution, the main problem arises in the homologisation of the various areas in the different vertebrates. It has to be decided whether a given area or nucleus in the primitive pallial structures of the telencephalon of fishes is the one that can be localised again in the amphibian and reptile brain and whether it serves the same functions.

In the context of neuronal structures, Striedter (2002, p. 239) noted that "efforts to homologise brain regions across species are often motivated by the

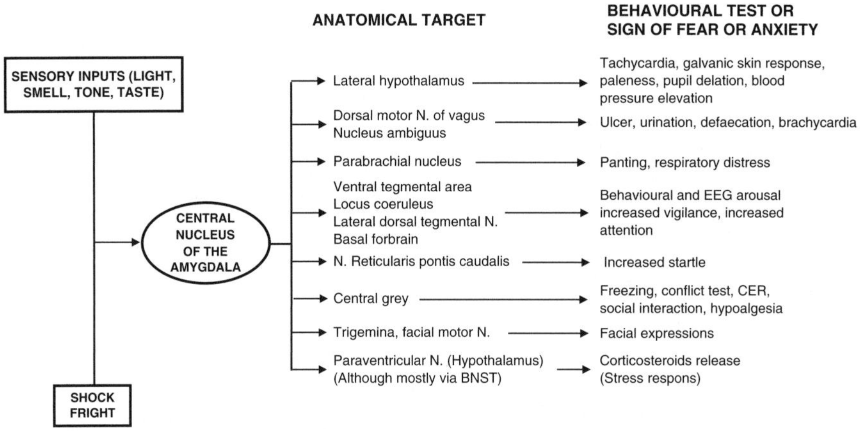

Fig. 7 Anatomical connections of the central nucleus of the amygdala and how they relate to behavioural tests or signs of fear and anxiety. *BNST*, bed nucleus of the stria terminalis; *N*, nerve; *EEG*, electroencephalography; *CER*, conditioned emotional response (adapted from Davis, 2000, Fig. 6.1, p. 215)

expectation that 'functional homology' can be deduced from structural homology" (see also Aronson, 1981; Northcutt, 2003). Homologue brain structures may have changed all or some of their function during the course of evolution, and/or other parts have taken over some of them. Striedter (2002) went on to remark that "most evolutionary morphologists have agreed ... that homology need not imply functional similarity." He therefore suggested that "there are three types of evolutionary changes in neural structures that are each associated with different kinds of functional change ... [that] of course ... may occur in various combinations with one another." He noted:

> First, one might have evolutionary changes in the internal organization of a brain region, e.g., changes in cytoarchitecture, neuron shape, and/or membrane properties. Such internal structure changes would likely alter what one might call the region's computational (or transfer) function, but it is unlikely to change the region's behavioural function....
>
> Second, a brain area might change its overall size and/or the strength of its neuronal connections. In such a case, the region's computational function might remain relatively unchanged, but its role within a neuronal circuit and in some specific behaviors would probably change significantly.
>
> Third, a brain region may during the course of evolution, add or lose neuronal connections. In that case, the region's computational function is also unlikely to change, but the region is likely to become involved in different sets of behavioural functions. (p. 241)

These problems are particularly important when we try to relate brain structures to the evolutionary process and examine how the basic nociceptive capacities in the lower taxa and the more complex neural connections in the brain (especially the telencephalon with its subregions) of lower vertebrates with the emergence of the capacity to learn are related to the affective system found in the highest mammals.

During the last decades, the new techniques applied in neurophysiology and genetics have enabled more precise localisation and homologisation of emotion-related neural structures across the vertebrate taxa. In the following section, I summarise some results from such studies, beginning with the bony fish followed by the amphibians and the reptiles (for the situation in mammals, see Markowitsch, Emotions: The shared heritage of animals and humans, this volume).

Bony Fishes

Nociception and Fear Conditioning in the Teleosts

As we have seen, nociception proper has not been shown among the invertebrates and the lowest chordates; and fear conditioning (mainly food aversion learning) and long-term memory (LTM) have been demonstrated in only a few cases. However, the bony fish with their different, specialised somatosensory receptors and afferent nerve connections to various areas of a complex CNS

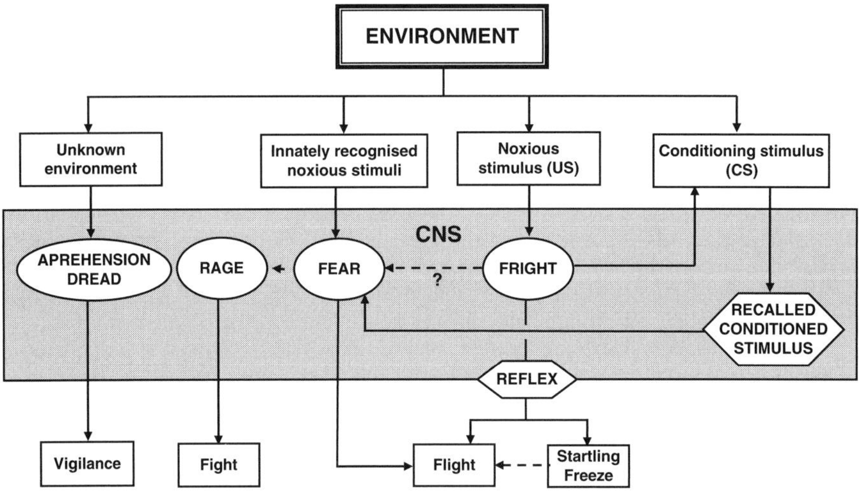

Fig. 8 "Fright-fear-rage system" in a lower vertebrate. This shows the environmental cues/ stimuli affecting the CNS (with its respective motive states), the respective behaviours elicited, and the fear-initiated memorising of a conditioning stimulus (the respectiv sensory organs are omitted)

(Figs. 4, 5) have reached a relatively highly developed level of neuro- and emotional functioning that manifests in agonistic behaviours (flight and fight) running parallel with the emotions "fear" and "rage," respectively. They also show behaviour patterns that, for instance, can be interpreted as vigilance (Fig. 8).

Like many lower vertebrates, the teleosts also respond to sudden frightening situations (e.g., a sudden noise, a shadow) with "freezing" or a "startle" (Laming, 1981b, pp. 204–206), and it is supposed that it is mainly the more dramatic noxious, tissue-damaging events, sensed through nociceptors, that lead to memorising a CS and to fear conditioning (Fig. 2). It is also believed that "an unexpected or surprising shock US is more effective in promoting learning than is an expected or unsurprising shock US" (McNally & Westbrook, 2006, p. 246). If, however, a shock is already predicted or unsurprising, a fear-related stimulus must have already been conditioned or the aversive prediction is based on an innate mechanism. In this situation, a fear-related behaviour such as vigilance or even flight should be observable. If the expected US "strikes" again, the threshold for fear-related behaviours should be lower in a future encounter with this CS.

Sneddon et al. (2003) reported finding 22 nociceptors located on the face of the rainbow trout that respond to mechanical pressure and 18, classified as polymodal nociceptors, that respond to chemical stimulation. They concluded that they are similar to those also found in amphibians, birds, and mammals. Whether they are "true" nociceptors (defined as being comprised of free nerve endings in the epidermis sensing tissue damage) might well be a matter of debate. However, the authors have shown that the sensory cells of the head send their information to the CNS mainly via the trigeminal nerve (cranial nerve V), and that the information of the somatosensory cells, distributed over different parts of the trout's body, reach their nucleus in the anterior medulla via cranial nerves VII, IX, and X (for details, see Laming, 1981b, pp. 17–20).[6]

Amygdaloid Complex, Learning, and Emotional Memory of Fishes

It is only in the bony fish that some of the emotion-related neural structures, efferent functioning, and elicited behaviours can be homologised with the structures and behaviour patterns observed in the higher taxa. Owing to the more complex organisation of the telencephalon, fish are able to pair a sensed noxious/aversive stimulus (US) with a CS; they can memorise the latter and recall it if the respective cue recurs. The results of classic conditioning experiments in teleost fish in which a noxious, aversive US is paired with a CS (e.g., a light or a tone) show striking similarity to those obtained in the higher vertebrates (Fig. 9).

Experimental physiological and psychological research mainly in mammals has shown that, next to other brain structures such as the cerebellum and the

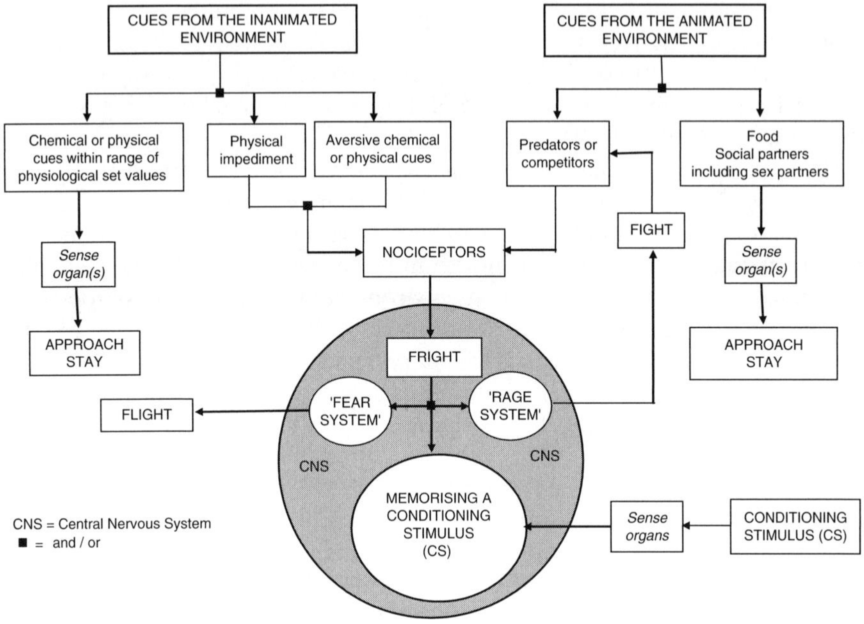

Fig. 9 Sensing a noxious or aversive event (US), the resulting fright experience, and its connection to the fear and/or rage system, the resulting flight or fight behaviour, the pairing with a CS, and its memorising (the possible appetitive conditioning is not included)

hippocampus, it is mainly the amygdala that plays a central role in emotional learning and emotional reactions (especially fear reactions) (see Aggleton, 2000; LeDoux, 1995, 2000b). Fishes do not have the vomeronasal organ with afferent connection to the amygdaloid complex found in most reptiles and mammals. The medial pallium in the fishes is thought to be homologous to the pallial amygdala; lesions of this area disrupt or disorganise various behaviours (aggressive, reproductive, parental), and focal electric stimulation elicits arousal, defensive, and escape responses (see Salas et al., 2006, p. 165). Compared to the mammalian brain, however, a relatively well circumscribed amygdala is not to be found in the various classes of teleost fishes. Nonetheless, Butler (2000) and Yoshimoto et al. (1998) have shown that specific telencephalic pallial regions can be homologised with specific parts of the mammalian amygdaloid complex; and several authors have recently reported strong evidence that the medial division of the fishes' pallium is comparable to the amygdala of tetrapodes[7] and that its lateral division is homologous to the hippocampus of the tetrapods (e.g., Braford, 1995; Broglio et al., 2005; Holmes & Northcutt, 2003; Northcutt, 2006; Portavella, Vargas, Torres, & Salas, 2002; Portavella, Torres, & Salas, 2004; Salas et al., 2006; Yoshimoto et al., 1998).[8] Emotional learning experiments (for a detailed discussion, see Salas et al., 2006, pp. 165–167) have shown that fear-induced behaviours can be invoked in the teleosts through fear conditioning and recalling the CS, as in mammals. Furthermore, lesions of the medial cephalic pallium in fishes have demonstrated that this region is functionally homologous with the amygdala in higher vertebrates. In both cases, deactivation of the respective regions mentioned, as well as a lesion of the cerebellum (Rodríguez et al., 2005), impairs the retention of conditioned avoidance behaviour (see also Overmier & Hollis, 1990; Portavella & Vargas, 2005; Portavella et al., 2002, 2004).

The next step in raising the probability of surviving a dangerous situation is to link the recalled CS, which warns before the danger occurs, with recall of a cognitive map that allows flight to a known hiding place. Spatial cognition, encompassing the capacity to memorise and recollect (e.g., landmarks), enables the animal to navigate optimally in its environment to find a source of food or a shelter. Such a cognitive map can, according to Salas et al. (2006, p. 158), be defined as "a map like "allocentric" memory representation of the environment, based on encoding the spatial relationships between multiple cues and sensory features, which enables the subject to locate the goal regardless of its own actual position and local view.

It should also be mentioned that pairing of a CS with a mental map enhances not only the ability to escape danger but also the probability of finding food or a sexual partner. If through appetitive conditioning a CS was paired with a positive US (e.g., food), and the CS is recalled and can be met with a recalled map-like representation of the environment, it raises the chance of achieving the consummatory act.

As in the amniotes (reptiles, birds, mammals), this higher-ordered cognitive relational and allocentric spatial memory in the teleost fish also depends, next to the cerebellum, on the forebrain and the hippocampal pallium. Moreover, there is strong evidence that especially the lateral telencephalic pallium, in all probability homologue to the hippocampus in mammals, is essential for their spatial and temporal memory and cognition (Lynch, 2004; Salas et al., 2006, p. 159).

These data corroborate the hypothesis that two memory systems exist in bony fishes and are located in two discrete telencephalic areas: The lateral telencephalic pallium is involved in the spatial, relational, and temporal memory system; and the medial telencephalic pallium is involved in the emotional memory system (Rodríguez et al., 2002a,b). Based on the bulk of data available, Salas et al. (2006) concluded that these areas

> show a remarkable parallelism between mammals and teleost fish concerning the role of different brain centers in learning and memory and cognitive processes. These [*sic*] evidence suggests that these separate memory systems could have appeared early during the evolution of vertebrates, having been conserved through phylogeny. (p. 157; see also Rodríguez et al., 2002a)

Amphibians

Nociception

Among the amphibians, especially frogs, various nociceptors with primary afferent fibres sensitive to chemical stimuli (acetic acid) have been identified; and the corresponding defence mechanism, especially the whipping response of the exposed skin, has been described (Hamamoto & Simone, 2003; see also Willenbring & Stevens, 1996). Kuffler, Lyfenko, Vyklický, and Vlachová (2002) analysed cellular mechanisms of nociceptive heat stimulation; and Chéry-Croze, Godinot, Jourdan, Bernard, and Chayvaille (2004) have shown, after measuring thermo- and nociceptive thresholds in the frog (*Rana esculenta*), that the nociceptive responses can be reduced via a subcutaneous injection of capsaicin.

Learning, Emotional Memory, and Amygdala Complex of Amphibians

Although only a few conditioning experiments have been undertaken in amphibians, they show, in principle, that members of this taxon are capable of learning. Instrumental conditioning was usually applied to detect, for instance, hearing thresholds in the clawed frog (*Xenopus laevis*) (see Elepfandt et al., 2000) or to study olfaction capacities in the tiger salamander (*Ambystoma tigrinum*) (see Mason, Stevens, & Rabin, 1980). In the newt (*Triturus alpestris*), it has been demonstrated that feeding behaviour can be modified by conditioning, so that, in contrast to their normal, innately "preprogrammed" fear-eliciting flight behaviour to escape from a predator dummy, they learn to raise their head in the expectancy of food (Wenz & Himsteadt, 1990). Moreover, Semlitsch and Reyer (1992) showed that the antipredatory behaviour of frogs (*Rana lessone* and *R. esculenta*) could be modified by environmental conditioning. A capacity to memorise specific, environment-related factors has also been shown. For instance, robust short-term spatial memory has been demonstrated in the frog (*Rana pipiens*). If threatened by a predator dummy (an innate US), the frog jumps in a direction that avoids collision with an obstacle. If this obstacle is then removed, memory of the object is retained for a short while and the then-threatened animal still takes refuge in the same direction as if the obstacle were still there (Ingle & Hoff, 1990). The authors supposed that this short-term memory ability in the frog depends on the striatum, a major part of the basal ganglia system, which seems to be homologous to the caudate nucleus (a telencephalic nucleus that is part of the basal ganglia) on which spatial memory function depends in mammals. The same authors have also shown that these frogs have specific long-term spatial memory involving the capacity to recollect (for about 12 hours) the direction in which they have to jump in order to take refuge in water (see also Jog, Kubota, Connolly, Hillegaart & Graybiel, 2008).

In a comparative analysis, Endepols, Roden, Luksch, Dicke, and Walkoviak (2004) delivered strong evidence that the anuran and urodele rostral striatum (the striatum is a major part of the basal ganglia system, a subcortical part of the telencephalon) is homologous to the mammalian striatum proper, that the amphibian caudal striatum is homologous to the mammalian globus pallidus, and that the intermedial striatum represents the transition between the two structures. Also, comparing the anuran's septal complex (a subpallial telencephalic area arising from the ventromedial wall of the cerebral hemispheres) with that of other vertebrates, Endepols, Mühlenbrock-Lenter, Roth, and Walkoviak (2006) showed that its lateral part has increased during the evolution from the anamniotes (fishes and amphibians) to the amniotes (reptiles and mammals), and that many septal functions (e.g., learning and memory) (see Font, Lanuza, Martinez-Marcos, Hoogland, & Martinez-Garcia, 1998, pp. 544–545) have persisted during the evolution of the vertebrates.

Despite the numerous studies carried out during the last decade and major progress in allocating and classifying the various units of the amphibian subpallial amygdala complex, many details of the morphological and functional homology with the amniotes are still controversial (see Laberge, Mühlenbrock-Lenter, Grunwald, & Roth, 2006; for details, see Brox, Ferreiro, Puelles, & Madina, 2002; Krug, Wicht, & Northcutt, 1993; Laberge & Roth, 2005; Marín, Smeets, Wilkelmus, & González, 1998; Moreno & González, 2004, 2005; Northcutt & Ronan, 1992; Papini, Muzio, & Segura, 1995; Roth, Mühlenbrock-Lenter, Grunwald, & Laberge, 2004; Westhoff & Roth, 2002). Eisthen (1992, 2000) has shown that a distinct vomeronasal organ, fully developed in the most reptiles and mammals, can be found in the larvae of some amphibians and some aquatic salamanders. This vomeronasal organ, as we shall see, shows pronounced afferent connections via the bulbus olfactorius and the accessory bulbus olfactorius to the amygdaloid complex in most reptiles (but not birds) and mammals. Based on the reports of Roth et al. (2004, p. 35) and Mühlenbrock-Lenter, Endepols, Roth, and Walkowiak (2005), it can be stated that the caudal mediolateral complex consisting of the extended central, vomeronasal, and olfactory amygdala of the anurans represents the ancestral condition of the amygdaloid complex. During the evolution of the mammalian telencephalon, this complex shifted medially and became involuted. The reptilian and mammalian basolateral amygdala is apparently a new structure in evolution, but the medial portion of the amygdaloid complex of anurans reveals hodological similarities with this structure and may serve similar functions. It has been shown that especially the medial amygdala, which integrates information from the main and the accessory olfactory system, modulates defence and different social behaviours. This part of the amygdaloid complex is also connected to brain areas known to be involved in emotion-related learning and memory, for instance, the circuitry mediating associative learning with an emotional component (for detailed analysis and discussion, see Moreno & González, 2003); thus, to a certain extent the hodological situation in amphibians (Neary, 1995; Scalia, Gallousis, & Roca, 1991) can also be understood as a forerunner of the situation in reptiles and finally, then, also in mammals.

Whereas detailed morphological and physiological-cum-functional data are available, as Ingle and Hoff (1990) have noted behavioural observations and experiments that might corroborate these findings are, unfortunately, largely missing.

Reptiles

Nociception

Nociceptive capacities in reptiles[9] have usually been taken for granted on the basis of the animal's behavioural reactions. Detailed morphological analyses of the nociceptors themselves and their hodology seem to be rare, and most research has been conducted to throw light on the interconnectivity of the different parts or centres of the CNS (e.g., Belekhova, 1990; Smeets, Lopez, & González, 2006; see also Kaplan, 2002).

Learning, Emotional Memory, and Amygdaloid Complex of Reptiles

Since Burghardt's (1977) comprehensive review article, we know that many species of the families, genera, and species of reptiles are capable of learning through conditioning. A number of such experiments used food as a reward; and in most cases a distinctive memory has been shown. As for the teleosts and amphibians, conditioning experiments in reptiles have also been applied mainly to study sensory and discriminatory abilities (e.g., to detect spectral sensitivity and wavelength discrimination) (for turtles, see Arnold & Neumeyer, 1987; Neumeyer & Jäger, 1985). Lepera (2000) reported that Nile crocodiles (*Crocodylus niloticus*) were trained successfully through operant conditioning by using a tone as a CA. In the small number of experiments in which an aversive stimulus (usually a light electrical stimulus) was paired with a CS, conditioning was usually completed after some 5 to 10 pairings, and fear reactions were measured and/or observed when the CS appeared. Stimulation of the amygdala in lizards showed flight reactions and behaviours comparable to those of mammals threatened by a predator (LeDoux, 1996, p. 171). As in many fishes, learning and recall of a CS (paired once with a noxious US) with the typical fear- or rage-related reactions could be observed (Fig. 10).

As in amphibians, many conditioning experiments have been conducted through appetitive conditioning to investigate the reptile's spatial memory. Rodríguez et al. (2002b) have shown that lesions of the medial cortex in turtles (like the lesions of the lateral pallium in goldfish and of the hippocampus in mammals) dramatically and selectively impair map-like memory representations of environmental space (for the retrieval of long-term memory and hippocampal-amygdala functioning, see Roozendaal, Hahn, Nathan, Quervain, & McGaugh, 2004).

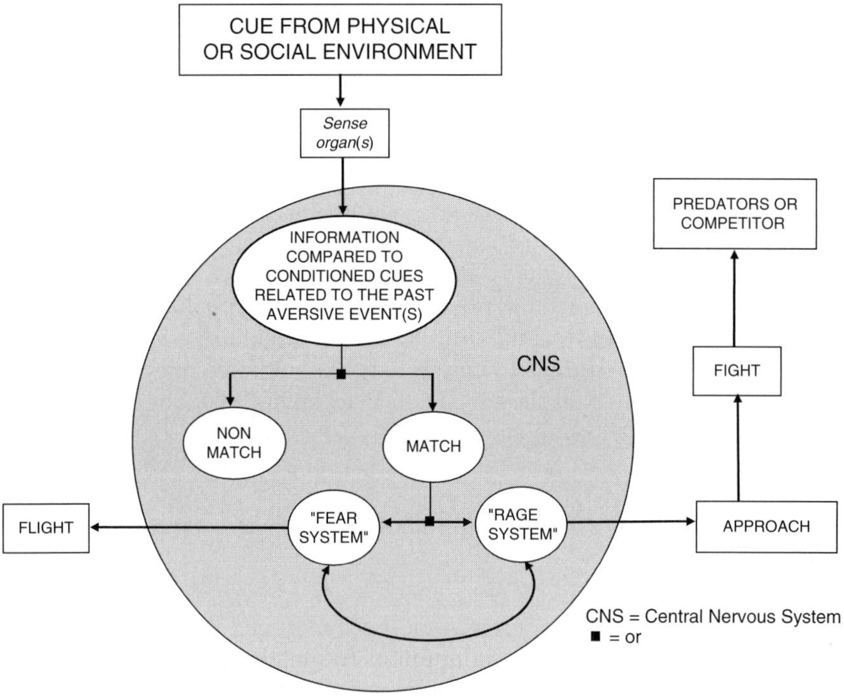

Fig. 10 Possible matching of an environmental cue/stimulus with a recollected CS memorised when paired with an aversive US in the past and the resulting emotions and behaviours elicited (see text for details)

Compared with fish and amphibian brains, a more differentiated amygdaloid complex can be seen in reptiles; in particular, as already mentioned, a basolateral nucleus has emerged that receives information (some possibly via the central nucleus) from all sensory modalities and relays it to the central nucleus. The strongest afferent connections comprise those from the vomeronasal organ via the olfactory and accessory olfactory bulbs to the various parts and nuclei of the amygdaloid complex. As Lanuza and Halpern (1997) have shown, the amygdalar nuclei reach different parts of the hypothalamus (medial, lateral, ventral) that monitor endocrine processes and the functioning of the autonomic nervous system. The latter causes the physiological processes that appear in parallel with "fear," such as an increased heart rate and breathing frequency (Davidson & Richardson, 1970). The hodological connectivity between the amygdalar nuclei, the hypothalamus, and the hippocampus of reptiles is largely comparable to that in mammals (e.g., Lanuza & Halpern, 1997).

It is well known that it is mainly the hippocampal formation of the limbic system together with some related structures that is involved in memorising spatial and temporal information—i.e., "facts" (declarative memory)—and that it receives inputs, besides other areas, from the amygdaloid complex involved in the processing of emotions. It can, however, be supposed (Day, 2003) that the reptilian hippocampus, next to special information, also retains and relays other types of information related to conditioning given stimuli.

As a preliminary conclusion it can be stated that, in principle, the various capacities we are interested in can be observed in all the lower vertebrate taxa. However, because of the lack of experiments and observations across many genera and species, the breadth of variation in these capacities and patterns cannot be assessed. It is suspected, though, that there is wide variation because of specific ecological adaptations. In short, this would mean that when looking, for instance, at memory faculties, we may find extremely "clever" fish and extremely "stupid" reptiles.

Summary and Conclusion

I have described the relation between nociception, the related neuromorphological structures, and neurophysiological processees as well as the learning abilities in some members of invertebrate and vertebrate taxa. They may represent the long-extinct members of the taxa that followed each other on the "scale of evolution." I have described how the first of all emotions, "fear," and some related ones came into being and how they may have developed during evolution. Based on the definition of fear as the emotion that emerges if danger is expected, the various sensory and neuromorphological structures and capacities mentioned are understood to be a sine qua non for the ability to "experience" fright and fear. This concerns mainly (1) the capacity to sense a noxious, tissue-damaging event through nociceptors, and (2) the memorising and recollection of *nox*-related cues/stimuli. By recollecting such stimuli if they recur, a lurking danger can be foreseen and thus avoided.

With a top-down approach, I have described briefly how in higher vertebrates, especially humans, various entities of the limbic system—especially the amygdaloid complex and hippocampus—together with some other interconnected neural structures function as an emotion-processing unit. On this basis, and applying a bottom-up approach, I described how in fishes, amphibians, and reptiles the supposedly homologous neuromorphological structures became differentiated and how their functioning correlates with emotion-related behaviours.

Analysis of the data permits the assumption that danger-related fright-analogue reactions, as observed in invertebrates, emerged early in evolution but that implicit learning capacities seem to be limited to a short time. Normally, only habituation and/or sensitisation following an aversive stimulus can be observed here, and a longer-lasting memory and recalling of conditioned stimuli has been reported in only a few instances, especially in the case of aversion learning.

These fright-related behaviours (freezing, startle) have also been observed in "simple" vertebrates, such as *Amphioxus* and lampreys. However, the question whether these animals have nociceptors still has no satisfactory answer; and to the best of my knowledge, learning capacities have not been reported. Evidence for epidermal nociceptors with their pathways to neural centres has been provided only for the bony fish, and a substantial number of conditioning experiments have demonstrated long-term implicit memory. The respective behaviours were observed following fear conditioning and legitimately interpreted as expressions of "fear."

In fishes, amphibians, and reptiles, it is especially the medial and lateral nuclei of the pallium and their pathways (e.g., to the striatum), possibly the septal complex and the hippocampus, that are effective and especially active if danger/fear-related stimuli are inflicted or experimentally elicited via a CS. It is safe to say that many, if not most, of these areas and nuclei can plausibly be homologised with regions or nuclei found in the developed mammalian brain. Irrespective of location (due to either involution or invagination of pallial structures), the homology of the areas and nuclei in the vertebrate taxa has been shown (only the basolateral amygdalar nucleus has emerged newly in reptiles). Due to the interplay between the various neural structures, physiological processes are induced that finally activate behaviours via the efferent pathways and can be related to emotions of dread, fear, or rage.

Furthermore, it can be said that, unlike many other morphological, physiological, and behavioural differences in the taxa concerned, it seems that the neural centres that process and generate emotions as well as many of the afferent and efferent pathways have been conserved throughout the evolution of the vertebrates. However, it would be naive to expect that in all genera and species simple phylogenetic ranking of the taxa from the lower vertebrates along a "scale of evolution" would correlate with linear augmentation of sensory and neuromorphological structures corresponding with an increase in affective functioning. It is necessary to suggest that great differences in the sensory capacities and behavioural patterns can be seen in the various genera or even species of fishes, amphibians, and reptiles. According to the specific ecological niches they occupy, the sensory capacities and learning abilities of, for instance, a given corral fish in its extremely complex environment are much "better" than the capacities in, for instance, a reptile such as a mainly subterranean living snake (e.g., the sand boa, *Eryx*). In this regard, Bshary, Wickler, and Fricke (2002) have provided ample evidence that in many fish species, some (i.e., cognitive) capacities are observable that were thought to occur only in primates.

It is only with the evolution of mammals (see Markowitsch, this volume)—especially with the advent of the higher primates with their extremely enlarged neocortex and augmented cognitive capacities—that a new level of affective capacities has evolved. The parallel processing of many different sensory inputs in the various cortical areas and their more complex interconnection with the old, but now also "advanced," parts of the limbic system generates more complex (e.g., socially "derived") emotions. However, it seems that only we humans consciously feel them and can think about them. Furthermore, because of our language skills, we can name them and talk about them with our fellow species members.

Notes

[1] The "true" nociceptors of mammals with their free nerve endings in the epidermis connect with the central nervous system (CNS) predominantly through two classes of primary afferent fibres (Aδ or C fibres). Of these fibres, the slowly conducting, thinly myelinated fibres mediate thermal and mechanical nociception, whereas the unmyelinated, polymodal C fibres are activated by a variety of high-intensity mechanical, chemical, hot, and cold stimuli (for details, see, e.g., Cox et al., 2006; Gardner, Martin, & Jesell, 2000, pp. 430–450; Phillips, Bradford, & Currier, 2004). For a detailed description of the molecular mechanisms of nociception, see Julius and Basbaum (2001).

[2] Some authors understand "aversion learning" as "innately predisposed, prepared" (Lamprecht & Dudai, 2000), but I do not see any principal difference between food-related aversion learning mediated through specific visceral sensory organs that senses *nox* and is then paired with the smell or taste of the digested food versus the pairing of a skin-damaging event sensed through nociceptors and then paired with a specific conditioning cue (which can also be a smell).

[3] For the sake of completeness, another emotion that may be closely related to fear is *anxiety*, understood as an unspecific response to the unknown that relates to an animal's insecurity and awareness of environmental factors (Degrazia, 1996/2005). The emotion of *dread* is closely related to anxiety and does not simply arise from fear, as Berns et al. (2006, p. 754) have shown; the term relates specifically to the attention devoted to an expected noxious or aversive event. This may happen because the insecurity arising in an unknown environment causes vigilance and a behaviour indicating alertness. However, in many cases, a learning mechanism can also be expected in such situations by which specific cues paired with an experienced noxious or aversive encounter in the past are now recognised and recollected, leading to the emotion "dread." The emotional state *apprehension* can be understood as a generalised, mild form of dread that, for instance, also emerges in an animal exposed to an unfamiliar situation such as ranging beyond familiar territory.

[4] In many insects, a relatively highly developed capacity for learning (e.g., Chabaud, Devaud, Pham-Delegue, Preat, & Kaiser, 2006) has evolved through which pairing a noxious US with a CS leads to further avoidance of the US if the CS is sensed (e.g., Akalal et al. 2006; Brembs & Wiener, 2006; Brembs & Hempel de Iberra, 2006; Davis, 2006; Pascual & Préat, 2001; Préat, 1999; Xu et al., 2006; Zars, Fischer, Schulz, & Heisenberg, 2000). Especially among many social insects such as bees and ants, memorising and recalling environmental cues (e.g., landmarks, mental mapping) related to the memorised occurrence of food has been described widely.

[5] It seems that the octopus is even capable of imitational learning by observing an experimentally learned predation pattern from other octopi (Fiorito & Scotto, 1992; for a critical review, see Biederman et al. 1993.

[6] Because the nerve pathways from these nociceptors are comparable to those in the higher vertebrates (including humans) and because the behavioural effect of discomforting tissue-damaging experiments in these fish shows special nonreflexive behaviours, the authors have concluded that the existence of "pain" in fish has been demonstrated. Others, such as Rose (2002), who related "pain" to functioning of the higher brain regions in the cerebral cortex necessary for the "psychological experience of pain," concluded that it is untenable that fish can experience pain. In humans and higher vertebrates, the brain areas called the "pain matrix" comprise a network of regions that respond to noxious stimuli; and in humans, its elements have been associated variously with different aspects of pain experience. The somatosensory aspect of pain has usually been associated with activity in the primary somatosensory cortex (SI), the secondary somatosensory cortex (SII), and the posterior insula. The visceral and emotional aspect of pain has been associated with activity in the anterior insula, the rostral anterior cingulated cortex (ACC), and the amygdala (see Berns et al., 2006, p. 754).

[7] At first glance, it seems confusing that the lateral pallium of fishes should be homologous to the hippocampus, as in all other vertebrates hippocampus homologues are situated in the medial pallium. The situation in fishes arises because parts of the telencephalon are everted, shifting the hippocampus to a lateral position (Wulliman & Mueller, 2004).

[8] Yoshimoto et al. (1998) showed that some of the small fibre bundles of the gustatory system in the teleosts finally terminate in telencephalic regions (area ventralis pars intermedia, area dorsalis pars postereor, and pars medialis), and that the pathway from the primary gustatory areas (the facial glossopharyngial and vagal lobes of the medulla) to the two telencephalic areas corresponds with the gustatory pathway to the amygdala in mammals. Recent investigations by Butler (2000) also showed that some parts of the telencephalic pallium in the bony fish can, with some certainty, be homologised with those of the higher vertebrates. She showed that the suprastriatal pallium, including the olfactory cortex proper and the pallial amygdala, in amniotes (reptiles, birds, and mammals) is homologous to at least part of medial zone of the pallial zones in the area dorsalis of the telencephalon in ray-finned fish. Portavella and Vargas (2005, p. 2800) postulated recently that in the goldfish "the medial and lateral region of the telencephalic pallia (cerebral cortex) might be the homologous neural structures to the mammalian amygdala and hippocampus, respectively" (see also Braford, 1995; Broglio et al., 2005; Northcutt, 2006; Portavella et al., 2002, 2004; Rodríguez et al., 2002a,b; Salas et al., 2006). For a comprehensive compilation of recent findings, see Salas et al. (2006).

[9] This chapter has left out the birds, which branched off from a phylogenetically early reptile stock, because I followed only the "direct" phylogenetic line from fish to reptiles. It should be mentioned, however, that the anatomy and morphology of, in particular, the bird's "prefrontal cortex" reveal a pattern that is very different from that of reptiles and mammals (cf. ABNC, 2005; Güntürkün, 2005). It seems, for instance, that the amygdala in birds does not process emotions but cognitions, which are highly developed in some genera (e.g., ravens and parrots).

Acknowledgments My thanks for comments and criticism on an earlier draft of the paper are due to Konstantin Behrend, Heike Endepols, Hans Markowitsch, Christa Neumeyer, Julia Pauli, Hans Scharstein, and Michael Schnegg. All remaining errors and shortcomings are of my own making.

References

Abercrombie, M., Hickman, M., Johnson, M. L., & Thain, M. (1992). *Dictionary of biology* (8th ed.). London: Penguin.

ABNC. (2005). Avian brains and a new understanding of vertebrate brain evolution (The Avian Brain Nomenclature Consortium). *Nature Reviews Neuroscience, 6*, 151–159; see, also, avianbrain.org/nomen/2002NomenClatureTable.html.

Aggleton, J. P. (Ed.). (2000). *The amygdala: A functional analysis*. Oxford, UK: Oxford University Press.

Agin, V., Chicheri, R., Dickel, L., & Chicheri, M.-P. (2006). The "prawn-in-the-tube" procedure in the cuttlefish: Habituation or passive avoidance learning? *Learning & Memory, 13*(1), 97–101.

Akalal, D.-B. G., Wilson, C. F., Zong, L., Tanaka, N. K., Ito, K., et al. (2006). Roles for *Drosophila* mushroom body neurons in olfactory learning and memory. *Learning & Memory, 13*, 659–668.

Alexander, J., Audesirk, T. E., & Audesirk, G. J. (1984). One-trial reward learning in the snail *Lymnaea stagnalis. Journal of Neurobiology, 15*, 67–72.

Anderson, A. K., & Phelps, E. A. (2002). Is the human amygdala critical for the subjective experience of emotion? Evidence of intact dispositional affect in patients with amygdala lesion. *Journal of Cognitive Neuroscience, 14*(5), 709–720.

Aristotle (Trans. 1981). *On the soul*. Translation with commentaries and glossary by Hippocrates G. Apostle. Grindell, IA: The Peripatetic Press.

Arnold, K., & Neumeyer, Ch. (1987). Wavelength discrimination in the turtle *Pseudemys scipta elegans. Vision Research, 27*(9), 1501–1511.

Aronson, L. R. (1981). Evolution of telencephalic function in lower vertebrates. In P. R. Laming (Ed.), *Brain mechanisms of behaviour in lower vertebrates* (pp. 33–58). Cambridge, UK: Cambridge University Press.

Bargmann, C. I. (2006). Chemosensation in C. elegans (2006, October 25), *WormBook*, ed. The C. elegans research community, WormBook, doi/10.1895/wormbook. 1.123.1, www.wormbook.org.

Belekhova, M. G. (1990). Connections linking the maxillary complex and hypothalamotegmental area of the brain with the brainstem in lizards. *Neurophysiology, 22*(1), 95–102.

Berns, G. S., Chapellow, J., Ceki, M., Zink, C. F. Pagnoni, G., & Martin-Skurski, M. E. (2006). Neurobiological substrates of dread. *Science, 312*, 754–758.

Birnberger, K. L. & Rovainen, C. M. (1971). Behavioral and intracellular studies of habituating fin reflex in the sea lamprey. *Journal of Neurophysiology, 34*: 983–989.

Biederman, G. B., Davey, A., Suboski, M. D., Muird, D., Hall, D., & Fiorito, G. (1993). Social learning in invertebrates: Response. *Science, 259*, 1627–1628.

Braford, M. R. (1995). Comparative aspects of forebrain organisation in ray-finned fishes: Touchstones or not? *Brain, Behavior and Evolution, 46*, 259–272.

Brembs, B. (2003a). Operant conditioning in invertebrates. *Current Opinion in Neurobiology, 13*, 710–717.

Brembs, B. (2003b). Operant reward learning in *Aplysia. Current Directions in Psychological Science, 12*(6), 218–221.

Brembs, B., Lorenzetti F. D., Baxter, D. A., & Byrne, J. H. (2002). Operant reward learning in Aplysia: Neuronal correlates and mechanisms. *Science, 296*, 1624–1625.

Brembs, B., & Wiener, J. (2006). Context and occasion setting in Drosophila visual learning. *Learning & Memory, 13*(5), 618–628.

Brembs, B., & Hempel de Iberra, N. (2006). Different parameters support generalization and discrimination learning in *Drosophila* at the flight simulator. *Learning & Memory, 13*, 629–637.

Broglio, C., Gomez, A. Duran, E., Ocaña, F. M., Jimenez-Moya, F., Rodríguez, F., et al. (2005). Hallmarks of common forebrain in vertebrate plan: Specialized pallial areas for spatial, temporal and emotional memory in actinopterygian fish. *Brain Research Bulletin, 66*(4–6), 277–281.

Brox, A., Ferreiro, B., Puelles, L., & Madina, L. (2002). The telencephalon of the frog *Xenopus* based on calretinin immunostaining and gene expression patterns. *Brain Research Bulletin, 57*(3/4), 381–384.

Bshary, R., Wickler, W., & Fricke, H. (2002). Fish cognition: A primate's eye view. *Animal Cognition, 5*(1), 1–13.

Bucherelli, C., Baldi, E., Mariottini, C., Passani, M. B., & Blandina, P. (2006). Aversive memory reactivation engages in the amygdala only some neurotransmitters involved in consolidation. *Learning & Memory, 13*(4), 426–430.

Bullock, T. H. (1990). Goals of neuroethology: Roots, rules, and relevance go beyond stories of special adaptation. *BioScience, 40*(4), 244–248.

Burghardt, G. M. (1977). Learning processes of the reptiles. In C. Gans, & D. W. Tincle (Eds.), *Biology of reptiles* (Vol. 7, pp. 555–681), London: Academic Press.

Butler, A. B. (2000). Topography and topology of the teleost telencephalon: A paradox resolved. *Neuroscience Letters, 293*, 95–98.

Cahill, L., & McGaugh, J. L. (1998). Mechanisms of emotional arousal and lasting declarative memory. *Trends in Neurosciences, 21*(7), 294–299.

Chabaud, M. A., Devaud, J. M., Pham-Delegue, M. H., Preat, T., & Kaiser, L. (2006). Olfactory conditioning of proboscis activity in Drosophila melanogaster. *Journal of Comparative Physiology. A, Neuroethology, Sensory, Neural, and Behavioral Physiology, 192*(12), 1335–1348.

Campeau, S., & Davis, M. (1995). Involvement of the central nucleus and basolateral complex of the amygdala in fear conditioning measured with fear-potentiated startle in rats trained concurrently with auditory and visual conditioned stimuli. *Journal of Neuroscience, 15*(3): 2301–2311.

Cardinal, R. N., Parkinson, J. A., Hall, J. & Everitt, B. J. (2002). Emotion and motivation: The role of the amygdala, ventral striatum, and prefrontal cortex. *Neuroscience and Biobehavioral Reviews, 26*, 321–352.

Chéry-Croze, S., Godinot, F., Jourdan, G., Bernard, C., & Chayvialle, J. A. (2004). Capsaicine in adult frogs: Effects on nociceptive responses to cutaneous stimuli and on nervous tissue concentrations of immunoreactive substance P, somatostatin and cholecystokin. *Naunyn-Schmiedeberg's Archives of Pharmacology, 331*(2–3), 159–165.

Christenson, J., Bohman, A., Lagerback, P. A., & Grillner, S. (1988). The dorsal cell, one class of primary sensory neuron in the lamprey spinal cord. I. Touch but no nociception—a physiological study. *Brain Research, 440*(1), 1–8.

Clark, E. (1959). Instrumental conditioning of lemon sharks. *Science, 130*, 217–218.

Cox, J. J., Reimann, F., Nicholas, A. K., Thornton, G., Roberts, E., Springell, K., et al. (2006). An SCN9A channelopathy causes congenital inability to experience pain. *Nature, 444*, 831–832.

Currie, S. N., & Carlsen, R. C. (1987). Functional significance and neural basis of larval lamprey startle behaviour. *Journal of Experimental Biology, 133*, 121–135.

Damasio, A. (1994). *Descartes' error. Emotion, reason, and the human brain.* New York: Avon Books.

Davey, G. L. (1995). Preparedness and phobias: Specific evolved associations or a generalized expectancy bias. *Behavioral and Brain Sciences, 18*, 289–325.

Davidson, R. E., & Richardson, A. M. (1970). Classical conditioning of skeletal and autonomic responses in the lizard (*Crotaphytus collaris*). *Physiology and Behaviour, 5*, 589–594.

Davis, M. (2000). The role of the amygdala in conditioned and unconditioned fear and anxiety. In J. P. Aggleton, (Ed.), *The Amygdala. A functional analysis* (pp. 213–287). Oxford: Oxford University Press.
Davis, R. L. (2006). Olfactory memory formation in *Drosophila*: From molecular to systems neuroscience. *Annual Review of Neuroscience*, *28*, 275–302.
Dawkins, M. (2000). Animal minds and animal emotions. *American Zoologist*, *40*, 883–888.
Day, L. B. (2003). The importance of hippocampus-dependent non-spatial tasks in analysis homology and homoplasy. *Brain, Behavior and Evolution*, *62*, 96–107.
Dell'Omo, G., & Alleva, E. (1993). Snake odor alters behavior, but not pain sensitivity in mice. *Physiology and Behavior*, *55*, 125–128.
Degrazia, D. (1996/2005). Taking animals seriously: Mental life and moral status. Cambridge: University Press. Reprint of the Chapter '*Feelings in Nature' Critical Concepts in the Social Sciences*. Inglis, D., Bone, J., & Wilkie, R. (Eds.), pp. 97–128.
Denes, A. S., Jékels, G., Steinmetz, P. R. H., Raible, F., Snyman, H., Prud'homme, B., et al. (2007). Molecular architecture of annelide nerve cord supports common origin of nervous system centralization in bilateria. *Cell*, *129* 277–288.
Dohrn, A. (1875). *Der Ursprung der Wirbelthiere und das Prinzip des Funktionswechsels*. Leipzig: Wilhelm Engelmann.
Dolan, R. J. (2002). Emotion, cognition, and behaviour. *Science*, *298*, 1191–1194.
Dolan, R. J. (2003). Feeling emotional. What can a seventeenth-century philosopher possibly tell us about emotion? *Nature*, *421*, 893–894.
Einum, J. F., & Buchannan, J. T. (2006). Spinobulbar neurons in lamprey: Cellular properties and synaptic interactions. *Journal of Neurophysiology*, *96*, 2042–2055.
Eisthen, H. L. (1992). Phylogeny of the vomeronasal system and receptor cell types in the olfactory and vomeronasal epithelia of vertebrates. *Microscopic Reseach and Technique*, *23*, 1–21.
Eisthen, H. L. (2000). Presence of the vomeronasal system in aquatic salamanders. *Philosophical Transactions if the Royal Society London B, Biological Science*, *355*, 1209–1213.
Elepfandt, A., Eistetter, I., Fleig, A., Günther, E., Hainich, M. Hepperle, S., et al. (2000). Hearing threshold and frequency discrimination in the purely aquatic frog *Xenopus laevis* (Pipdae): measurement by meand of conditioning. *The Journal of Experimental Biology*, *203*, 3621–3629.
Endepols, H., Roden, K., Luksch, H., Dicke, U., & Walkowiak, W. (2004). Dorsal striatopallial system in anurans. *Journal of Comparative Neurology*, *468*(2), 299–310.
Endepols, H., Mühlenbrock-Lenter, S., Roth, G., & Walkowiak, W. (2006). The septal complex of the Fire-Bellied Toad *Bombina orientalis*: Chemoarchitecture. *Journal of Chemical Neuroanatomy*, *31*, 59–76.
Ewert, J.-P. (1981). Neural coding of 'worms' and 'antiworms' in the brain of toads: The question of hardwired and softwired systems. In P. R. Laming (Ed.), *Brain mechanisms of behaviour in lower vertebrates*(pp. 137–168). Cambridge: Cambridge University Press.
Fendt, M., Endres, Th., & Apfelbach, R. (2003). Temporary inactivation of the bed nucleus of the stria terminalis but not of the amygdala blocks freezing induced trimethylthiazoline, a component of fox faeces. *The Journal of Neuroscience*, *23*(1), 23–28.
Fessler, D. M. T. (2002). Emotions and cost-benefit assessment. The role of shame and self-esteem in risk taking. In G. Gigerenzer, & R. Selten (Eds.), *Bounded rationality. The adaptive toolbox* (pp. 191–214). Cambridge MA: The MIT Press.
Fiorito, G., & Scotto, P. (1992). Observational learning in Octopus vulgaris. *Science*, *256*, 545–547.
Flood, N. B., & Overmier, J. B. (1981). Learning in teleost fish: Role of the telencephalon. In P. R. Laming, (Ed.), *Brain mechanisms of behaviour in lower vertebrates* (pp. 259–279). Cambridge: Cambridge University Press.
Font, Ch., Lanuza, E., Martinez-Marcos, A., Hoogland, P. F., & Martinez-Garcia, F. (1998). Septal complex of the telencephalon in lizards: III. Efferent connections and general discussion. *The Journal of Comparative Neurology*, *401*, 525–548.

Fulton, D., Kemenes, I., Andrew, R. J., & Benjamin, P. R. (2005). A single time-window for protein synthesis-dependent long-term-memory formation after one-trial appetitive conditioning. *European Journal of Neuroscience, 21*, 1347–1358.

Gardner, E. P., Martin, J. H., & Jesell, Th. M. (2000). The bodily senses. In E. R. Kandel, J. H. Schwartz, & T. M. Jessell (Eds.), *Principles of Neural Science* (pp. 430–450). New York: McGraw-Hill.

Gess, R. W., Coates, M. I., & Rubidge, B. S. (2006). A lamprey from the Devonian period of South Africa. *Nature, 443*, 981–984.

Grandin, T., & Deesing, M. (2003). Distress in animals: Is it fear, pain or physical stress. www.grandin.com/wellfare/fear.pain.stress.html

Güntürkün, O. (2005). The avian 'prefrontal cortex' and cognition. *Current Opinion in Neurobiology, 15*(6), 686–693.

Hamamoto, D. T, & Simone, D. A. (2003). Characterisation of cutaneous primary afferent fibers exited by acetic acid in a model of nociception in frogs. *The Journal of Neurophysiology, 90*, 566–577.

Hess, E. H. (1973). *Imprinting. Early experiences and the developmental psychobiology of attachment*. New York: Van Norstrand Reinhold Comp.

Hochner, B., Brown, E. R., Langella M., Shomrat, T., & Fiorito, G. (2003). A learning and memory area in the octopus brain manifests a vertebrate-like long-term potentiation. *Journal of Neurophysiology, 90*(5), 3547–3554.

Hochner, B., Shomrat, T., & Fiorito, G. (2006). The octopus: A model for a comparative analysis of the evolution of learning and memory mechanisms. *Biological Bulletin, 210*, 308–317.

Holahan, M. R., & White, N. M. (2004). Intra-amygdala muscimol injections impair freezing and place avoidance in aversive contextual conditioning. *Learning & Memory, 11*, 436–446.

Holland, P. W., & Garcia-Fernandez, J. (1996). Hox genes and chordate evolution. *Developmental Biology, 173*, 382–394.

Holland, L. Z., & Holland, N. D. (2001). Evolution of neural crest and placodes: Amphioxus as model for the ancestral vertebrate. *Journal of Anatomy, 199*(1–2), 85–98.

Holmes, P. H., & Glenn Northcutt, R. (2003). Connections of the pallial telencephalon in the Senegal Bichir, Polypterus. *Brain, Behavior and Evolution, 61*, 113–147.

IASP. (International Association for the Study of Pain) (1986). Pain terms: A list with definitions and notes on usage. *Pain 1, 24*, 215–221.

Ingle, D. J., & Hoff, K. vS. (1990). Visually elicited evasive behavior in frogs. Giving memory research an ethological context. *BioScience, 40*(4), 284–291.

Iversen, S., Kupfermann, I., & Kandel, E. R. (2002). Emotions and feelings. In E. R. Kandel, J. H. Schwartz, & T. M. Jessell (Eds.), *Principles of Neural Science* (pp. 982–997). New York: McGraw-Hill, Ch. 50.

Jog, M. S., Kubota, Y., Connolly, C. I, Hillegaary, V., & Graybiel, A. G. (2008). Building neural representations of habits. *Science 26*, 1745–1749.

Julius, D., & Basbaum, A. I. (2001). Molecular mechanisms of nociception. *Nature, 413*, 203–210.

Kandel, E. R., Schwartz, J. H., & Jessell, T. M. (2002). *Principles of Neural Science*. New York: McGraw-Hill.

Kaplan, M. (2002). Melissa Kaplan's herp care collection. Bibliography of pain and analgesia in herps. (anapsid.org/herppainbiblio.html)

Kasai, Y., Watanabe, S., Kirino, Y., & Matsuo, R. (2006). The cerebrum is necessary for odor-aversion learning in the terrestrial slug *Limax valentianus*. *Learning & Memory, 13*(4), 482–488.

Kavaliers, M. (1988). Evolutionary and comparative aspects of nociception. *Brain Research Bulletin, 21*(6), 923–931.

Kleerekoper, H. (1972). The sense organs. In M. W. Hardesty, & I. C. Potter (Eds.), *The biology of Lampreys* (Vol. 2, pp. 373–404). London: Academic Press.

Krug, L. Wicht, H., & Northcutt, R. G. (1993). Afferent and efferent connections of the thalamic eminence in the Axolotl, Mblystoma mexicanum. *Neuroscience Letters, 149*(2), 145–148.

Kuffler, D. P., Lyfenko, L., Vyklický, L., & Vlachová, V. (2002). Cellular mechanisms of nociception in the frog. *The Journal of Neurophysiology, 88*, 1843–1850.

Laberge, F., & Roth, G. (2005). Connectivity and cytoarchitecture of the ventral telencephalon in the salamander Plethodon sharmani. *Journal of Comparative Neurology, 482*(2), 176–200.

Laberge, F., Mühlenbrock-Lenter, S., Grunwald, W., & Roth, G. (2006). Evolution of the amygdala: New insights from the studies in amphibians. *Brain, Behavior and Evolution, 67*(4), 177–187.

Laframboise, A. J., Ren, X., Chang, S., Dubuc, R., & Zielinski, B. S. (2007). Olfactory sensory neurons in the sea lamprey display polymorphisms. *Neuroscience Letter, 414*(3), 277–281.

Lacalli, T. C. (2001). New perspective on the evolution of protochordate sensory and locomotory systems, and origin of brains and head. *Philosophical Transactions of the Royal Society B., 356*(1414), 1565–1572.

Lacalli, T. C. (2002a). The dorsal compartment locomotory control system in Amphioxus larvae. *Journal of Morphology, 252*, 227–237.

Lacalli, T. C. (2002b). Sensory pathways in Amphioxus larvae I. Constituent fibres of the rostral and anterodorsal nerves, their targets and evolutionary significance. *Acta Zoologica, 83*, 149–166.

Lacalli, T. C. (2004). Sensory systems in Amphioxus: A window on the ancestral chordate condition. *Brain, Behavior and Evolution, 64*(3), 148–162.

Lacalli, T. C., & Kelly, S. J. (2003). Sensory pathways in Amphioxus larvae II. Dorsal tracts and translumenal cells. *Acta Zoologica, 84*, 1–13.

Laming, P. R. (1981a). An introduction to the functional anatomy of the brains of fish and amphibians (with comments on the reptiles). In P. R. Laming, (Ed.), *Brain mechanisms of behaviour in lower vertebrates* (pp. 7–32). Cambridge. Cambridge University Press.

Laming, P. R. (1981b). The physiological basis of alert behaviour in fish. In P. R. Laming, (Ed.), *Brain mechanisms of behaviour in lower vertebrates* (pp. 203–237). Cambridge: Cambridge University Press.

Lanuza, E., & Halpern, M. (1997). Afferent and efferent connections of the nucleus sphericus in the snake Thamophis sirtalis: Convergence of olfactory and vomeronasal information in the lateral cortex and the amygdala. *The Journal of Comparative Neurology, 385*, 627–640.

Lamprecht, R., & Dudai, Y. (2000). The amygdala in conditioned taste aversion: It's there but where? In J. P. Aggleton (Ed.), *The amygdala. A functional analysis* (pp. 331–351). Oxford: Oxford University Press.

LeDoux, J. E. (1994). Emotion, memory, and the brain. *Scientific American, 270*, 32–39.

LeDoux, J. E. (1995). Emotions: clues from the brain. *Annual Review of Psychology, 46*, 209–235.

LeDoux, J. E. (1996). *The emotional brain. The mysterious underpinnings of emotional life.* New York: Simon and Schuster.

LeDoux, J. E., & Armony, J. (1999). Can neurobiology tell us anything about human feelings? In D. Kahneman, E. Diener, & N. Schwarz (Eds.), *Well-being: The foundations of hedonic psychology* (pp. 489–499). New York: Russell Sage Foundation.

LeDoux, J. E. (2000a). Emotion circuits in the brain. *Annual Review of Neuroscience, 23*, 155–184.

LeDoux, J. E. (2000b). The amygdala and emotion: A view through fear. In J. P. Aggleton (Ed.), *The amygdala. A functional analysis* (pp. 289–310). Oxford: Oxford University Press.

Lepera, G. C. (2000). *Shifts, squeezes, tubes, and conditioning: techniques for managing mambas and crocodiles.* Abstracts from the 24th Annual Meeting of the International Herpetological Symposium, New Orleans, Lusiana July 19–22.

Lowe, C. J., Wu, M., Salic, A., Evens, L., Lander, E., Strange-Thomann, N., et al. (2003). Anteroposterior patterning in hemichordates and the origin of the chordate nervous system. *Cell, 113*, 853–865.

Lukowiak, K., Adatia, N., Krygier, D., & Syed, N. (2000). Operant conditioning in Lymnaea: Evidence for intermediate- and long-term memory. *Learning & Memory, 7*, 140–150.
Lukowiak, K., Sangha, S., McComb, C., Varshney, N., Rosenegger, D., Sadamoto, H., et al. (2003). Associative learning and memory in *Lymnaea stagnalis*: How well do they remember. *The Journal of Experimental Biology, 206*, 2097–2103.
Lynch, M. A. (2004). Long-term potentiation and memory. *Physiological Review, 84*, 87–136.
Malyukova, I. V., Rakich, L., & Kovachevich, N. (1983). Conditioned motor reactions in free-moving elasmobrancs and bony fish. *Neuroscience and Behavioral Physiology, 13*(6), 482–485.
Marín, O., Smeets, W. J., Wilkelmus, J. A. S., & González, A. (1998). Basal ganglia organization in amphibians: Chemoarchitecture. *The Journal of Comparative Neurology, 392*, 285–312.
Martin, A. R., & Wickelgren, Warren, O. (1971). Sensory cells in the spinal cord of the lamprey. *Journal of Physiology, 221(1)*, 65–83.
Mason, J. R., Stevens, D. A., & Rabin, M. D. (1980). Instrumental conditioned avoidance by tiger salamanders (*Ambystoma tigrinum*) to reagent grade odorants. *Chemical Senses, 5*(2), 99–105.
McClellan, A. D., & Jang, W. (1993). Mechanosensory inputs in the central pattern generators for locomotion in the Lamprey spinal cord: Resetting, entrainment, and computer modelling. *Journal of Neurophysiology, 70*(6), 2442–2454.
McNally, G. P., & Westbrook, R. F. (2006). Predicting danger: the nature, consequences, and neural mechanisms of predictive fear learning. *Learning & Memory, 13*(3), 245–253.
Meyer, A., & Zardoya, R. (2003). Recent advances in the (molecular) phylogeny of vertebrates. *Annual Review of Ecology and Systematics, 34*, 311–338.
Moreno, N., & González, A. (2003). Hodological characterization of the medial amygdala in anuran amphibians. *The Journal of Comparative Neurology, 466*, 389–408.
Moreno, N., & González, A. (2004). Localization and connectivity of the lateral amygdala in anuran amphibians. *The Journal of Comparative Neurology, 479*, 130–148.
Moreno, N., & González, A. (2005). Forebrain projections to the hypothalamus are topographically organized in anurans; Conservative traits as compared with amniotes. *European Journal of Neuroscience, 21*, 1895–1910.
Mühlenbrock-Lenter, S., Endepols, H., Roth, G., & Walkowiak, W. (2005). Immunohistological characterisazion of striatal and amygdalar structures in the telencephalon of the Fire-Bellied Toad *Bombina orientalis*. *Neuroscience, 134*, 705–719.
Murakami, Y., Ogasawara, M., Satoh, N., Sugahara, F., Myojin, M., Hirano, S., et al. (2002). Compartments in the lamprey embryonic brain as revealed by regulatory gene expression and the distribution of reticulospinal neurons. *Brain Research Bulletin, 57*(3/4), 271–275.
Neary, T. J. (1995). Afferent projections to the hypothalamus in ranid frogs. *Brain, Behavior and Evolution, 46*, 1–13.
Neugebauer, V., Li, W., Bird, G. C., & Han, J. S. (2004). The amygdala and persistent pain. *The Neuroscientist, 10*(3), 221–234.
Neumeyer, Ch., & Jäger, J. (1985). Spectral sensitivity of the freshwater turtle *Pseudemys scripta elegans*: Evidence for the filter-effect of colored oil droplets. *Vision Research, 25*(6), 833–838.
Nieuwenhuys, R. (1967). Comparative anatomy of olfactory centres and tracts. *Progress in Brain Research, 23*,1–64.
Nolen, T. G., Marcus, E. A., & Carew, T. J. (1987). Development of learning and memory in Aplysia. III. Central neuronal correlates. *Journal of Neuroscience, 7*, 155–153.
Northcutt, R. G. (2006). Connections of the lateral and medial divisions of the goldfish telencephalic pallium. *Journal of Comparative Neurology, 20, 494*(6), 903–943.
Northcutt, R. G., & Ronan, M. (1992). Afferent and efferent connections of the bullfrog medial pallium. *Brain, Behavior and Ecology, 40*(1), 1–16.
Northcutt, R. G., & Wicht, H. (1997). Afferent and efferent connections of the lateral and medial pallia of the Silver Lamprey. *Brain, Behavior and Evolution, 49*(1), 1–19.

Northcutt, R. G. (2003). The use and abuse of developmental data. Comment to Aboitiz, F., Morales, D., & Montiel, J. (2003), The evolutionary origin of the mammalian isocortex: towards an integrated developmental and functional approach, pp. 565–566. *Behavioral and Brain Sciences, 26*, 535–586.
O'Gower, A. K. (1995). Speculations on a spatial memory of the Port Jackson Shark (*Heterodontus portusjacksoni*). (Meyer) (Heterodontidae). *Marine and Freshwater Research, 46*(5), 861–871.
Öhman, A. (1986). Face the beast and fear the face: Animal and social fears as prototypes for evolutionary analyses of emotions. *Psychophysiology, 23*(2), 123–145.
Overmier, J. B., & Hollis, K. L. (1990). Fish in the think tank: Learning memory and integrated behavior. In R. P. Kesner, & D. S. Olton (Eds.), *Neurobiology of comparative cognition* (pp. 204–236). Hillsdale: Lawrence Erlbaum Associates.
Panksepp, J. (2003). Damasio's Error? *Consciousness & Emotion, 4*(1), 111–134.
Papini, M. R., Muzio, R. N., & Segura, E. T. (1995). Instrumental learning in toads (*Bufo arenarium*): Reinforcer magnitude and the medial pallium. *Brain, Behavior and Evolution, 46*(1), 61–71.
Pascual, A., & Préat, T. (2001). Localisation of long-term memory within the *Drosophila* mushroom body. *Science, 294*, 1115–1117.
Phillips, W. J., Bradford, L., & Currier, B. L. (2004). Analgesic pharmacology: I. Neurophysiology. *The American Academy of Orthopaedic Surgeons, 12*(4), 213–220.
Portavella, M., Vargas, J., Torres, B., & Salas, C. (2002). The Effect of telencephalic pallial leseions on spatial, temporal, and emotional learning in goldfish. *Brain Research Bulletin, 57*, (3/4), 397–399.
Portavella, M., Torres, B., & Salas, C. (2004). Avoidance response in goldfish: Emotional and temporal involvement of medial and lateral telencephalic pallium. *The Journal of Neuroscience, 24*(9), 2335–2342.
Portavella, M., & Vargas, J. (2005). Emotional and spatial learning in goldfish is dependent on differernt telencephalic pallial systems. *European Journal of Neuroscience, 21*(10), 1800–1806.
Préat, T. (1999). Testing associative learning in Drosophila. In W. E. Crusio, & R. T. Gerlai (Eds.), *Handbook of molocular genetic techniques for brain and behaviour research* (pp. 79–126). New York: Elsevier Science.
Purchon, R. D. (1968). *The biology of molusca*. Oxford: Oxford University Press.
Quinn, W. G. (2005). Nematodes learn: Now what? *Nature Neuroscience, 8*, 1639–1640.
Rodríguez, F., López, J. C., Vargas, J. P., Broglio, C., Gómez, Y., & Salas C. (2002a). Spatial memory and hippocampal palium through vertebrate evolution: Insight from reptiles and fish. *Brain Research Bulletin, 57*(3/4), 499–503.
Rodríguez, F., López, J. C., Vargas, J. P., Broglio, C., Gómez, Y., & Salas, C. (2002b). Conservation of spatial memory function in the pallial forbrain of reptiles and ray-finned fishes. *The Journal of Neurosciences, 22*(7), 2894–2903.
Rodríguez, F., Duran, E., Gomez, A., Ocana, F. M., Alvarez, E., Jimenez-Moya, F., et al. (2005). Cognitive and emotional functions of the teleost fish cerebellum. *Brain Research Bulletin, 66*(4–6), 365–370.
Roozendaal, B., Hahn, E. I., Nathan, S. V., Quervain, D. J.-F. de, & McGaugh, J. L. (2004). Glycocorticoid effects on memory retrieval require concurrent noradrenegic activity in the hippocampus and basal amygdala. *The Journal of Neuroscience, 24*(37), 8161–8169.
Rose, J. D. (2002). The neurobehavioral nature of fishes and the question of awareness and pain. *Reviews in Fisheries Science, 10*(1), 1–38.
Roth, G., Mühlenbrock-Lenter, S., Grunwald, W., & Laberge, F. (2004). Morphology and axonal projection pattern of neurons in the telencephalon of the Fire-Bellied Toad *Bombina orientalis*: An anterograde, retrograde, and intercellular biocytin labeling study. *The Journal of Comparative Neurology, 478*(1), 35–61.
Rovainen, C. M. (1982). Neurophysiology. In M. W. Hardesty, & I. C. Potter (Eds.), *The Biology of Lampreys* (Vol. 4A, pp. 1–136). London: Academic Press.

Rovainen, C. M., & Yan, Q. (2004). Sensory responses of dorsal cells in the lamprey brain. *Journal of Comparative Physiology A, 156*(2), 181–183.
Salas, C., Briglio, Ch., Durán, E., Gómez, A., Ocaña, F. M., Jiménez-Moya, F., et al. (2006). Neurophysiology of learning and memory in teleost fish. *Zebrafish, 3*(2), 157–171.
Scalia , F., Gallousis, G., & Roca, S. (1991). The differential projections of the main and accessory olfactory bulb in the frog. *Journal of Comparative Neurology, 161*, 31–56.
Schafe, G. E., Doyère, V., & LeDoux, J. E. (2005). Tracking the fear engramm: the lateral amygdala is an essential locus of fear memory storage. *The Journal of Neuroscience, 25*(43), 10010–10014.
Schroeder, B. W., & Shinnick-Gallagher, P. (2004). Fear memories induce switch in stimulus response and signaling mechanisms for long-term potentiation in the lateral amygdala. *European Journal of Neuroscience, 20*, 549–556.
Schulkin, J. (1998). Fear and its neuroendocrine basis. *Progress in Psychobiology and Psychological Psychology, 17*, 35–66.
Schulkin, J., Morgan, M. A., & Rosen, J. B. (2005). A neuroendocrine mechanism for sustaining fear. *Trends in Neurosciences, 28*(12), 629–635.
Semlitsch, R. D., & Reyer, H.-U. (1992). Modification of anti-predator behaviour in tadpoles by environmental conditioning. *The Journal of Animal Ecology, 61*(2), 353–360.
Sharma, S. K., Sherff, C. M., Shobe, J., Bagnall, M. W., Sutton, M. A., & Carew, T. J. (2003). Differential role of mitogen-activated protein kinase in three distinct phases of memory for sensitization in *Aplysia. The Journal of Neuroscience, 23*(9), 3899–3907.
Shimeld, S. M., & Holland, P. W. H. (2000). Vertebrate innovations. *PNAS, 97*(9), 4449–4452.
Shimeld, S. M., & Holland, N. D. (2005). Amphioxus molecular biology: Insights into vertebrate evolution and developmental mechanisms. *Canadian Journal of Zoology, 83*, 90–100.
Siegel, A., & Brutus, M. (1990). Neural substrates of aggression and rage in the cat. *Progress in Psychobiology and Physiological Psychology, 14*, 135–233.
Smeets, W. J., Lopez, J. M., & González, A. (2006). Distribution of neuropeptige FF-like immunoreactivity in the brain of the lizard Gekko gekko and its relation to catecholaminergic structures. *Journal of Comparative Neurology, 498*(1), 31–45.
Smith, J. A., & Boyd, K. M. (Eds.). (1991). *Lives in the balance. The ethics of using animals in biomedical research.* Oxford: Oxford University Press.
Sneddon, L. U. (2004). Evolution of nociception in vertebrates: Comparative analysis of lower vertebrates. *Brain Research Reviews, 46*, 123–130.
Sneddon, L. U., Braithwaite, V. A., & Gentle, M. J. (2003). Do fish have nociceptors? Evidence for the evolution of a vertebrate sensory system. *Proceedings of the Royal Societ B, 270*, 1115–1121.
Striedter, G. F. (2002). Brain homology and function: An uneasy alliance. *Brain Research Bulletin, 57*(3/4), 239–242.
Sutton, M. A., Bagnall, M. W., Sharma, S. K., Shobe, J., & Carew, T. J. (2004). Intermediate-term memory for site-specific sensitization in *Aplysia* is maintained by persistent activation of protein kinase C. *The Journal of Neuroscience, 24*(14), 3600–3609.
Swanson, L. W., & Petrovich, G. D. (1998). What is the amygdala? *Trends Neurosciences, 21*, 323–331.
Tautz, D. (2003). Chordate evolution in new light. *Cell, 113*(7), 812–813.
Wallace, K. J., & Rosen, J. B. (2001). Neurotoxic lesions of the lateral nucleus of the amygdala decreases conditioned fear but not unconditioned fear of a predator odor: Comparison with electrolytic lesions. *The Journal of Neuroscience, 21*(10), 3619–3627.
Wenz, E., & Himsteadt, W. (1990). Telencephalic Structures are involved in learning and memory in the newt *Triturus alpestris. Naturwissenschaften, 77*, 239–240.
Westhoff, G., & Roth, G. (2002). Morphology and projection pattern of medial and dorsal pallial neurons in the frog Discoglossus pictus and the salamander Plethodon jordani. *Journal of Comparative Neurology, 445*(2), 97–121.

Willenbring, S., & Stevens, C. W. (1996). Thermal, mechanical and chemical pripheral sensation in amphibians: Opioid and adrenergic effects. *LiveScience, 58*(2), 125–133.
Wulliman, M. F., & Mueller, T. (2004). Teleostian and mammalian forebrains contrasted: Evidence from genes to behaviour. *Journal of Comparative Neurology, 475*(2), 143–162.
Xu, S. Y., Cang, C. L., Liu, X. F., Peng, Y. Q., Ye, Y. Z., Zhao, Z. Q., et al. (2006). Thermal nociception in adult Drosophila: Behavioural characterization and the role of the painless gene. *Genes, Brain & Behavior, 5*(8), 602–613.
Young, J. Z. (1995). Multiple matrices in the memory system of *Octopus.* In N. J. Abbott, R. Williamson, & L. Maddock (Eds.), *Cephalopod Neurobiology* (pp. 431–443). Oxford: Oxford University Press.
Yoshimoto, M., Albert, J. S., Sawai, N., Shimizu, M., Yamamoto, N., & Ito, H. (1998). Telencephalic ascending gustatory system in a cichlid fish, Oreochromis (Tilapia) niloticus. *Journal of Comparative Neurology, 392*(2), 209–226.
Zars, T., Fischer, M., Schulz, R., & Heisenberg, M. (2000). Localisation of short-term memory in *Drosophila. Science, 288*, 672–675.
Zimmerman M. (1986). Behavioural investigations of pain in animals. In I. J. H. Duncan, & V. Molony (Eds.), *Assessing pain in farm animals* (pp. 30–35). Luxemburg: Commission of European Communities.
Zhang, Y., Lu, H., & Bargmann, C. I. (2005). Pathogenic bacteria induce aversive olfactory learning in Caenorhabditis elegans. *Nature, 438*, 179–184.

Emotions: The Shared Heritage of Animals and Humans

Hans J. Markowitsch

Abstract The development of mammals from simple to complexly organized species has been delineated, and it is assumed that the expansion of the cerebral cortex correlates in particular with the ability to perform complex behavioral acts. On the anatomical side, particular emphasis is laid on structures of the frontal lobes and the limbic system; and on the behavioral side, emotional and intellectual functions are highlighted.

Phylogenetic Brain Development in Mammals

The *Bauplan* (plan of construction) of the mammalian brain is largely similar across species (Fig. 1). All major structures can be found from the hedgehog to the whale—only their relative size may differ considerably, and there may be subdivisions, such as specific thalamic nuclei (pulvinar), in some but not in other mammalian species.

Despite this basic similarity, scientists have long tried (Markowitsch, 1992; Preuss & Kaas, 1999) to establish specific features and characteristics, raising humans above other animals. Aside from intellectual capacities, the brain was a major target of this endeavor (Cartwright, 2000).

On the mammalian level, an argument based on phylogenesis is usually aimed at comparing animals' anatomy or functions with those of humans. Nonbiologists, however, frequently tended to use hierarchies of mammals of different orders instead of adhering to the order depicted in Box 1 (cf. Bingham, 1992; Hodos, 1988; Hodos & Campbell, 1969, 1991). This was based on the animal species used most frequently in comparative and physiological psychology laboratories. Biologists, however, pointed to the various ecological adaptations and niches and, more importantly, to early diversification in the evolutionary tree that does not allow comparing species of different orders—demanding that they

H.J. Markowitsch (✉)
Department of Physiological Psychology, University of Bielefeld, Bielefeld, Germany
e-mail: hjmarkowitsch@uni-bielefeld.de

B. Röttger-Rössler, H.J. Markowitsch (eds.), *Emotions as Bio-cultural Processes*,
DOI 10.1007/978-0-387-09546-2_5, © Springer Science+Business Media, LLC 2009

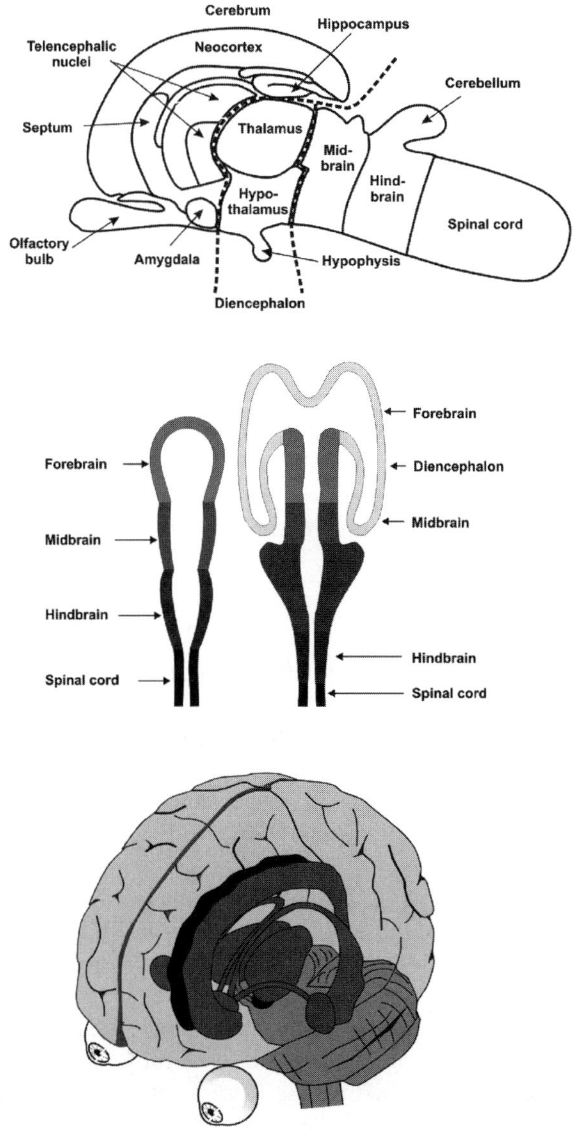

Fig. 1 Schematic Bauplan of the mammalian brain

represent a phylogenetic hierarchy or scale. Consequently, only species of one order should be compared phylogenetically (Fig. 2).

Within the human species there was an increase in brain size from the phylogenetically early *Australopithecus* to modern humans (Fig. 3). Brain volume and gyrification of the cerebral cortex were used as indices for establishing hierarchies, especially with the aim of relating anatomy and function

(Table 1, Fig. 4). This makes sense insofar as the cerebral cortex constitutes our "luxury" functions, which include those relevant for a fine-grain analysis of sensory input, fine-tuned motor output and (at least as important for us as humans) functions for associating, planning, monitoring, and abstract processing, including language processing. Indeed, the cerebral cortex expanded like a mushroom when considering the size, volume, and convolutions of the cerebral cortex (Fig. 5).

Box 1
Class: mammal
  Order: primate
    Suborder: anthropoid
      Superfamily: superhominoid
        Family: hominoid
          Genus: *Homo*
            Species: *Homo sapiens*

Especially the convolutions and gaps between the convolutions (i.e., sulci or fissures), fascinated scientists, especially as a crude comparison of mammalian

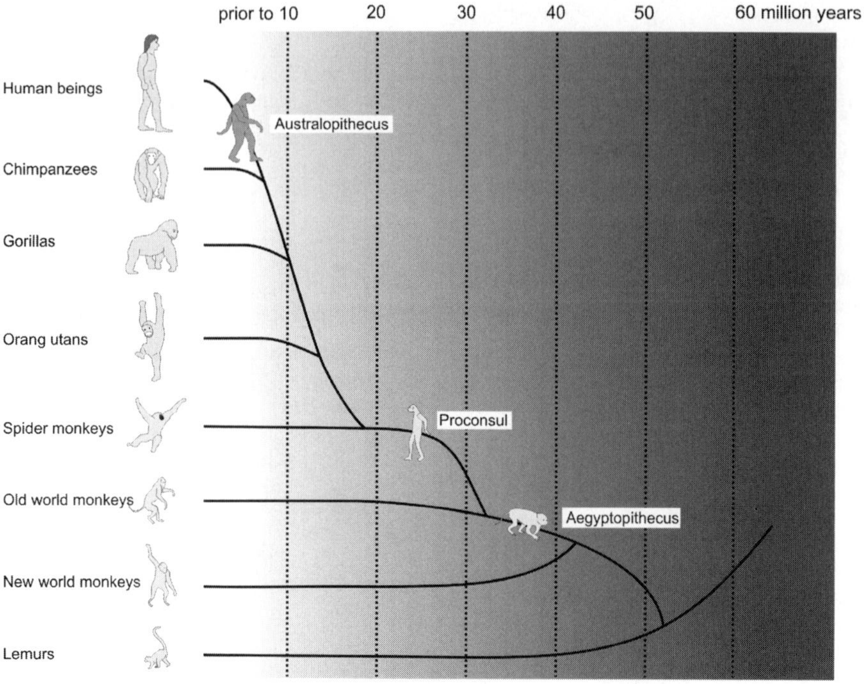

Fig. 2 A phylogenetic tree of primates

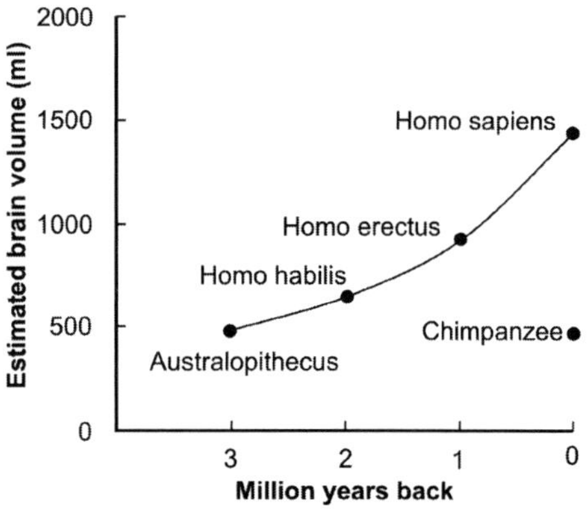

Fig. 3 Increase of human brain volume during evolution. The chimpanzee's brain volume is shown for comparison (after Fig. 3-3 from Grüsser, 1988)

Table 1 Brain volume and encephalization quotient of mammals

Mammal	Brain volume (ml)	Encephalization quotient[a]
Rat	2	0.4
Cat	25	1.0
Rhesus monkey	106	2.1
Gorilla	506	1.6
Orangutan	413	2.4
Chimpanzee	440/410	2.5/3.0[b]
Human	1350	7.3

[a] The encephalization quotient is defined as the factual brain volume divided by the predicted brain volume calculated by 0.12 times the body weight to the exponent of 2/3 (cf. Jerison, 1973)
[b] Various sources

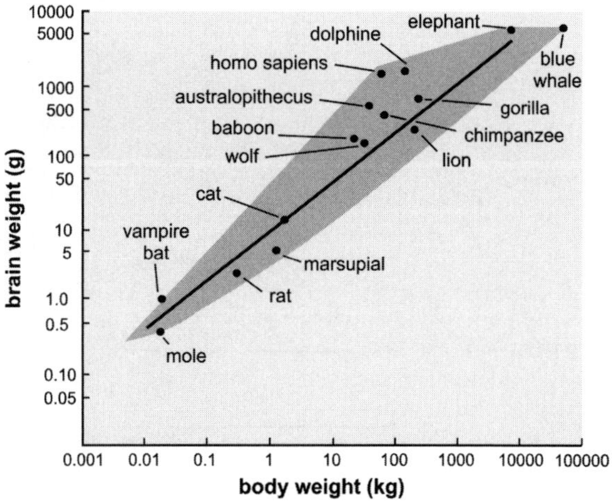

Fig. 4 Relation between brain weight and body weight in various mammalian species (so called double-logarithmic presentation). While most mammals adhere closely to the *straight line*, human beings and dolphins are considerably above it and therefore have an above average brain weight compared to their body weight

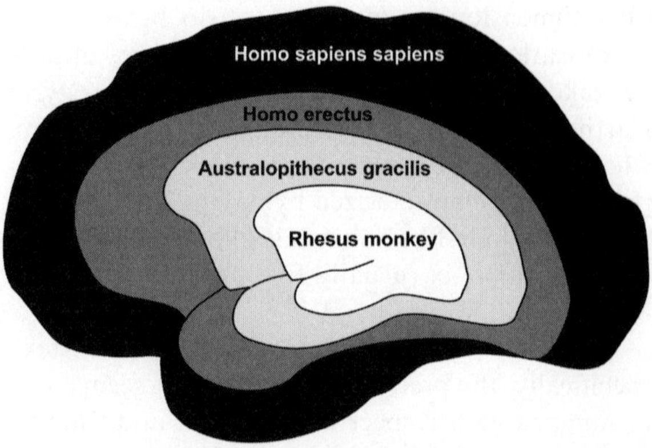

Fig. 5 Superimposed lateral views of cortex sizes of the rhesus monkey and three human species. (After Fig. 3-7 of Grüsser, 1988.)

species indicated that the dull and tiny ones (e.g., the hedgehog) had a flat brain, whereas humans and apes had a strongly "gyrificated" brain (Fig. 6). Furthermore, humans with a "flat brain," so-called lissencephalics, are of very low intelligence. Although higher gyrification seems generally to be of advantage (increasing the cortical surface, allowing a high level of interconnections), there are exceptions, such as the squirrel monkey, whales, and dolphins: Squirrel monkeys have a large head compared to their body size and a high encephalization quotient, indicating that they have a lot of brain compared to body size. The brains of most whale and dolphin species have much higher volumes than those of humans and show a higher degree of gyrification as well. However, these aquatic animals devote a considerable portion of their cortex to

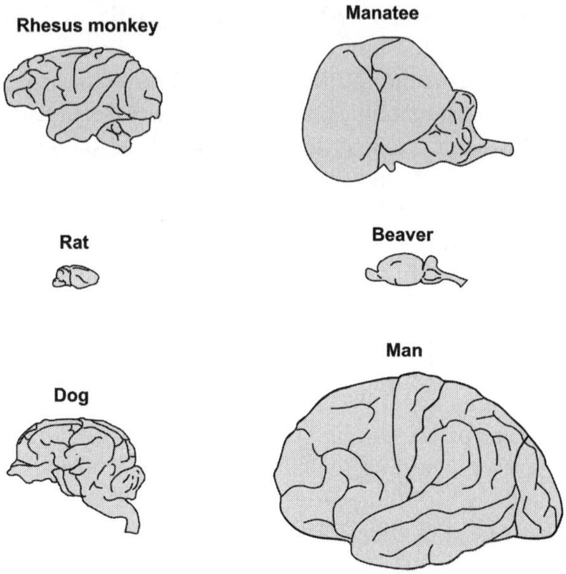

Fig. 6 Examples of lateral views of brains of different mammalian species. Of importance for comparative anatomists were both overall size and degree of gyrification (appearance or lack of sulci)

three-dimensional navigation (as do birds and bats) and for some kind of echolocation over high distances. Hence, these special functions must also be taken into account when comparing gyrification among mammals. Furthermore, and possibly at least as important, the cortical structure of whale-like species seems to be more "primitive" or old-fashioned: Whereas primates are characterized by having up to $\sim 90\%$ six-layered neocortex, the cortex of whale-like animals is allocortical to a large degree, being composed of fewer than six (usually five or four) nerve cell layers (Glezer, Jacobs, & Morgane, 1988).

There is also a structure of the cerebral cortex—the frontal lobe, or, more specifically, the prefrontal cortex—that seems to have evolved extraordinarily in humans with respect to structural and functional diversity (Fuster, 1997; Sanides, 1964; Stuss & Anderson, 2004; Stuss & Levine, 2002; Stuss, Gallup, & Alexander, 2001; Teuber, 1964, 1972). Based on the appearance of the skulls of human predecessors (e.g., *Homo erectus*) it is clear that the frontal lobes expanded during human evolution (Cartwright, 2000; Markowitsch, 1988).

In principle, therefore, the human brain seems to be exceptional compared to the brain of other mammals in regard to a number of features. This is all the more true when taking into account its lateralization (the functional and, in part, anatomical asymmetry of the two cerebral hemispheres), which if it exists in other species is of much less importance than in humans (see Evolution of Functions, below).

Limbic System—Basis of Emotions in Mammalian Brain

Along the whole vertebrate line, specific brain structures are of particular importance for controlling emotions. These structures are found from the brainstem to the telencephalon and have their center at the telo–diencephalic junction. In mammals, these regions were—since Broca (1878) subsumed under the heading "limbic system" ("le grand lobe limbic"), referring to the fact that they are situated around the the corpus callosum—the major fiber tract interconnecting the right and left halves of the cerebral cortex. Heath (1986) nevertheless pointed out that it would be short-sighted to limit the duties of the limbic system to emotions. In fact, one of the early circuits discovered in the limbic system, which Papez introduced in 1937 as "A proposed mechanism of emotions," is nowadays implicated in memory processing as well (Brand & Markowitsch, 2003; Markowitsch, 2000, 2005).

As LeDoux (1987, 1989) noted, there has been continuous expansion of the concept of the limbic system, starting from that of Broca (1878) and Cajal (1909), proceeding to Nauta (1958, 1962), MacLean (1970, 1972, 1990), and Damasio and Van Hoesen (1983), and continuing with Nauta (1979) and Nieuwenhuys (1996). Initially, the limbic system was largely equated with the "smell brain" (Herz & Engen, 1996; Markowitsch, 1999) (Fig. 7). As early as

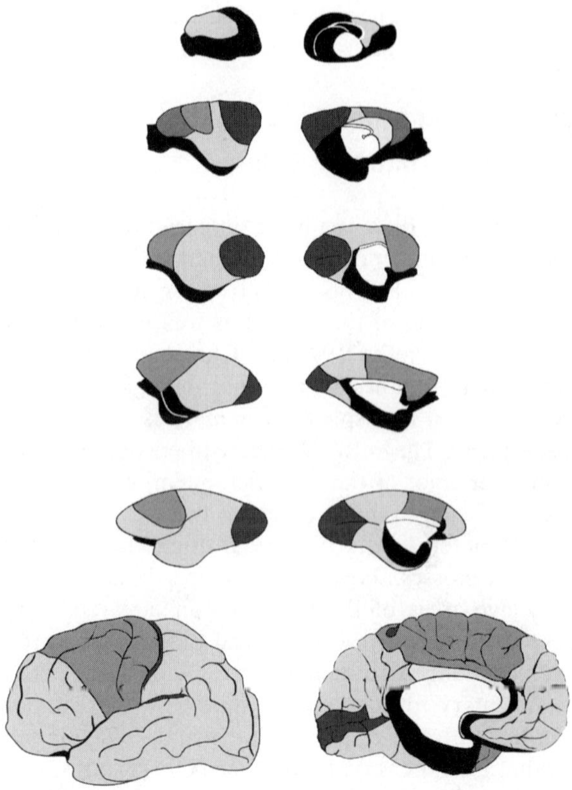

Fig. 7 Quasi-phylogenetic sequence in the primate species The *black areas represent* the phylogenetically old structures of the cerebral cortex ("smell brain") in the (top to bottom) elephant mouse, tupaia, two lemurs (tarsius, galago), a New World monkey (callithrix), and a human. (After Bonin & Bailey, 1961)

1982 Brodal suggested that we stop using the term limbic system (p. 539), and LeDoux (1987) suggested the less burdened term "limbic forebrain" (p. 425). Other researchers wrote of the limbic system and associated structures (Macchi, 1989), which then included the hypothalamus, rhinencephalon with hippocampus, amygdala, area olfactoria, and the septodiagonal area and limbic lobe (cingular and parahippocampal gyri). He furthermore mentioned the ventral striopallidum and the paralimbic cortical areas of the orbitofrontal and rostral temporal cortex and the insula, limbic thalamic nuclei, the habenular complex, and various brainstem nuclei as those structures associated with the limbic system (cf. also Fig. 5 in chapter 6, Daum et al., Neurobiological Basis of Emotions, this volume).

Although many of these structures exist in nonmammalian species as well, they have undergone considerable modification along the mammalian line, both structurally and functionally (Fig. 7). The amygdala, for instance, is constituted of a number of subnuclei, which again are combined into two or three complexes. For instance, the corticomedial amygdala is phylogenetically the oldest portion of the amygdala and is of inferior importance in humans, whereas the basolateral amygdala has expanded and is engaged in a number of functions in the human brain (Sarter & Markowitsch, 1985; Sims & Williams, 1990).

Further differences in limbic structures between mammalian species and especially between human and nonhuman species are discussed in the following section.

Evolution of Functions—Intellectual Changes during Phylogeny and Their Anatomical Bases

On one hand, there is a basic similarity of mammalians; but on the other hand, there are a number of details when individual regions are analyzed and compared among mammals. This holds true for morphological features (e.g., layer structure/lamination of the cortex) as well as for the distribution of neurochemical systems (see Preuss, 1995a,b). Characteristically, in humans especially, there is functional—and in part also morphological—asymmetry of the cerebrum. The right cerebral hemisphere of humans is slightly more voluminous than the left hemisphere. The ~ 100,000 nerve fibers of the pyramidal tract—the most important fiber tract of the motoric system, controlling the main fine-tuned movements—reach from the cortex to the lower brainstem (medulla oblongata); and in 87% of fetuses the pyramidar tract is larger in the left hemisphere than in the right. It crosses above the right fiber bundle (Nottebohm, 1981). The cortical language areas of the left cerebrum are represented as more complex (with respect to their gyral and sulcal pattern) and are more voluminous than the corresponding right-hemispheric regions (Fig. 8). This asymmetry, in a more rudimentary form, is seen in apes as well (Galaburda & Pandya, 1982; Galaburda, LeMay, Kemper, & Geschwind, 1978; Gannon, Holloway, Broadfield, & Braun, 1998; LeMay, 1976; Rubens, 1977) but seems to be much less determined functionally, as the larynx construction of apes prevents them from forming a greater number of tones. Lateral asymmetries of the hands or feet are found more universally (e.g., Hopkins, Wesley, Izard, & Hook, 2004).

As motor control and the perception and expression of language are modulated by feelings and emotions, these asymmetries and evolvements have implications for the phylogenetic importance of emotions and their anatomical bases.

Since the beginning of modern brain research, the frontal lobes have been regarded as specifically human and as processing the functions that distinguish humans from

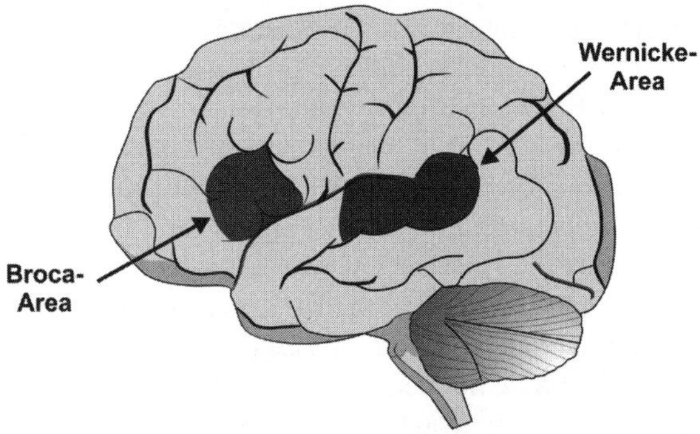

Fig. 8 Asymmetry of the human cerebrum with respect to the areas processing language

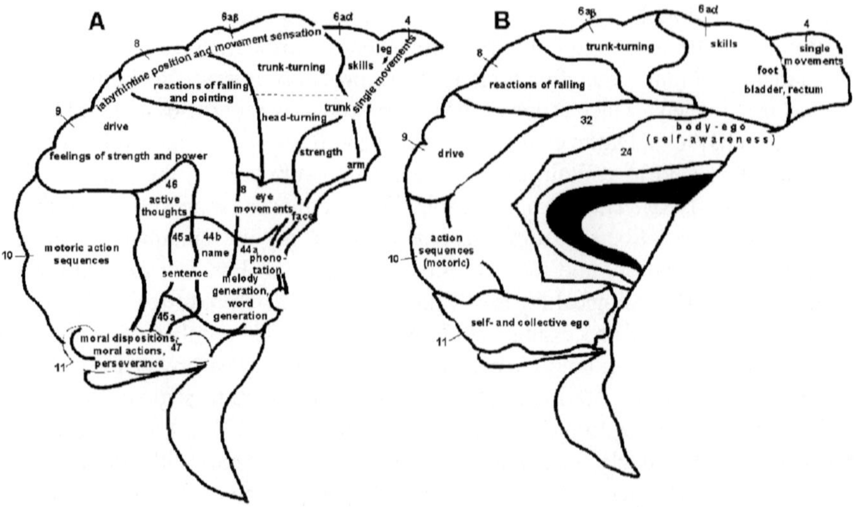

Fig. 9 The frontal lobes of the human brain. **A**: lateral, **B**: medial view. Number demarcations are according to Brodmann (1909), functional descriptions according to Kleist (1934). Portions of the orbitofrontal cortex are marked in *gray*

other animals (e.g., foresight, theory of mind functions, altruism, self-awareness, humor) (cf. Markowitsch, 1992) (Fig. 9). The advent of modern functional neuroimaging techniques (e.g., Keenan, Wheeler, Gallup, & Pascual-Leone, 2000) together with the results of sophisticated analyses on frontal lobe-damaged patients (Knight & Grabowecky, 2000; Stuss & Anderson, 2004) confirmed and underlined this view. It has been emphasized since the time of Flechsig (1896a,b) that portions of the prefrontal/orbitofrontal cortex develop and expand until the third decade of life; and up to this time they change their connectivity with other regions of the brain (Bourgeois, Goldman-Rakic, & Rakic, 2000). Moreover, the distribution of neurotransmitters changes and expands well beyond puberty (Benes, 2001). Recent tracing studies, based on magnetic resonance imaging spectroscopy, indicate that the fibers of the internal capsule (which arise mainly from the thalamus) are much more confined and bundled in the prefrontal cortex of normal humans compared to patients with schizophrenia (Buchsbaum, 2005). The continuing development of the prefrontal region is of special relevance as it also controls such functions as understanding wit and irony and being able to infer the moods of others; these abilities develop only late in childhood and are still expanding in youths.

The just mentioned findings of Buchsbaum on thalamocortical connections point to the importance of the thalamus as the gateway to the cortex. Certain nuclei (anterior and mediodorsal nuclei) in the thalamus expand, and others appear only in certain orders, among them primates (pulvinar) (Rapoport, 1990). The thalamus is seen as the “door to the cortex” (Dercum, 1925). The anterior and mediodorsal nuclei and probably even small portions of the pulvinar project to the prefrontal and orbitofrontal regions (Markowitsch, Emmans, Irle,

Streicher, & Preilowski, 1985). The pulvinar otherwise is found mainly in areas of the temporal, parietal, and occipital lobes—areas that control language perception and time judging, among other functions that are probably reserved to humans. The mediodorsal nucleus, which is one of the three cornerstones of the basolateral limbic circuit (see chapter 6, Daum et al., Neurobiological Basis of Emotions, this volume), for instance, is said to contain more than a dozen subnuclei in the human brain (Hassler, 1959, 1982). The so-called limbic thalamic nuclei—especially the anterior group, which send fibers to (and receive fibers from) the cingulate gyrus, the hippocampal formation, and the orbitofrontal cortex (cf. Fig. 5 in the chapter by Daum et al., Neurobiological Basis of Emotions) and therefore to regions centrally engaged in emotional processing—contain a much larger number of neurons in humans than are seen in apes (Armstrong, 1982, 1986; Armstrong & Falk, 1982). Moreover, these nuclei are much more complex in regard to structure and size, compared, for example, to those of the orang-utan (Hopf, 1956). Furthermore, the medial mammillary nuclei in the hypothalamus, which form part of the Papez circuit (cf. Fig. 2 in the chapter by Daum et al.), are larger in humans than in nonhuman primates (Armstrong, 1986).

On the functional side, research has revealed that animals demonstrate a number of quite astonishing abilities. Some birds can "fish" a worm out of a cylinder using a wire that they bend to lift a small bucket. Other birds can "remember" where older or fresher food is stored. A dog has been shown to react to words by bringing more than 200 of the so-named objects (Kaminski, Call, & Fischer, 2004). For primates, Tomasello (2000) summarized the cognitive abilities of nonhuman primates as follows.

- Nonhuman primates know what is where in their surroundings.
- They are able to follow visible and nonvisible movements of objects.
- They are able to categorize objects according to similarity.
- They can understand and compare the meaning of small numbers of objects.
- They are able to solve problems insightfully.

Furthermore, Tomasello listed a number of sociocultural abilities of nonhuman primates.

- They are able to recognize individuals in their social group.
- They can rank and accordingly treat other individuals based on consanguinity, friendship, and dominance hierarchy.
- They are able to predict the behavior of individuals on the basis of their emotional state and their movement direction.
- They can use various types of social and communicative strategies to trick group members with respect to precious resources.
- They can cooperate with other group members in problem solving tasks and in forming social coalitions and alliances.
- They can perform various forms of social learning, so they acquire important information and skills from their fellows.

However, in contrast to human children, apes and monkeys learn only changes in states, not the strategies that lead to such changes. Imitation learning by nonhuman primates is largely confined to those that live in the vicinity of humans. Despite their otherwise impressive abilities, nonhuman primates lack a central communicative ability: They are unable to orient themselves with respect to the actions of others and to imitate those actions effectively; that is, they are unable to figure out intentions. The theory of mind abilities, characteristic for adult humans, are generally absent in nonhuman primates. Because of this, they never point out anything to their fellows to draw attention to it.

Animals live in a total presence (i.e., they lack "episodic memory") (Tulving, 2005; Tulving & Markowitsch, 1998), focusing on drive reduction (Donald, 2001). Their planning horizon (e.g., when hunting) is short-lasting. They rarely use tools, whereas humans used stone tools and could handle fire two million years ago (Nelson, 2002). Furthermore, the ability to transfer and generalize tool use (e.g., to create art) is absent in animals. Rituals leading to social and cultural bonds and creations is absent in animals. Animals cannot represent themselves by thoughts (Donald, 2001).

Probably all of these additional abilities of humans required them to expand their brain, which was done not only by enlarging its volume (cf. Fig. 5) but also by forming an extraordinary state of cerebral lateralization. Grüsser (1988) was among those neuroscientists who has long recognized this point (Table 2).

Table 2 Functional asymmetry of the human cerebrum

Activity	Left hemisphere	Right hemisphere
Topographic planning	+	+ +
Elementary actions	+ +	+
Planning to create tools	+	+ +
Human nonverbal communication	+	+ +
Use of clothing	–	+
Verbal language	+ + +	(+)
Musical rhythm	+ +	–
Musical sensation for tones and harmony	–	+
Drawing, art painting	(+)	+ +
Forming gestalt	(+)	+ +
Calculating	+ +	–
Speaking poetically	+ +	+
Reading and writing	+ +	–
Segmentation of information with respect to time	+	–
Segmentation of information with respect to place	–	+
Intramodal[§] attention	+	–
Intermodal attention	–	+
Global, holistic processing of data	–	+
Detailed, serial processing of data	+	–
Emotional processing	–	+ +

–, no engagement of this hemisphere; +, engagement of this hemisphere; [§]intramodal, related to a sensory system; intermodal, interaction among various sensory systems; (+), engagement of this hemisphere in a minority of the population; + +, major engagement of this hemisphere; + + +, extraordinary engagement of this hemisphere.
After Table 3-3 of Grüsser, 1988 and Fig. 2-2 of Pritzel, Brand, & Markowitsch, 2003.)

Evolution points to both strong similarities among mammalian species (apes having only 1.5% genes that differ from those of humans) but also to important differences, which are attributable to the embeddedness of humans in society and culture. Humans are born at an intellectual level of other species, but most of them surpass their nonhuman relatives within the first years of life. On the other hand, we must accept that some humans remain at an intellectual level that is below that of intelligent apes, or they may lose most of their intellectual capacity (e.g., due to massive brain degeneration). Most importantly, the loss of intellectual capacity is paralleled by a loss of emotional diversification. Even basic emotions depend on a certain level of intellect. We therefore can conclude that, despite similarities in neuronal structure, the human environment created a multitude of specific human emotions.

References

Armstrong, E. (1982). Mosaic evolution in the primate brain: Differences and similarities in the hominoid thalamus. In E. Armstrong & D. Falk (Eds.), *Primate brain evolution* (pp. 131–161). New York: Plenum Press.

Armstrong, E. (1986). Enlarged limbic structures in the human brain: the anterior thalamus and medial mamillary body. *Brain Research, 362*, 394–397.

Armstrong, E., & Falk, D. (Eds.) (1982). *Primate brain evolution. Methods and concepts.* New York: Plenum Press.

Benes, F. M. (2001). The development of prefrontal cortex: the maturation of neurotransmitter systems and their interactions. In C. A. Nelson & M. Luciana (Eds.), *Handbook of developmental cognitive neuroscience* (pp. 79–92). Cambridge, MA: The MIT Press.

Bingham, V. P. (1992) The importance of comparative studies and ecological validity for understanding hippocampal structure and cognitive function. *Hippocampus, 2*, 213–220.

Bonin, G. von, & Bailey, P. (1961). Pattern of the cerebral isocortex. In H. Hofer, A. H. Schulz & D. Starck (Eds.), *Primatologia II* (2. Lieferung). Basel: Karger.

Bourgeois, J.-P., Goldman-Rakic, P. S., & Rakic, P. (2000). Formation, elimination, and stabilization of synapses in the primate cerebral cortex. In M. S. Gazzaniga (Ed.), *The new cognitive neurosciences* (2nd ed.) (pp. 45–53). Cambridge, MA: MIT Press.

Brand, M., & Markowitsch, H. J. (2003). The principle of bottleneck structures. In R. H. Kluwe, G. Lüer, & F. Rösler (Eds.), *Principles of learning and memory* (pp. 171–184). Basel: Birkhäuser.

Broca, P. (1878). Anatomie comparée des circonvolutions cérébrales. Le grand lobe limbique et la scissure limbique dans le série des mammifères. *Revue Anthropologique, 2*, 385–498.

Brodal, P. (1982). *Neurological anatomy in relation to clinical medicine* (2nd ed.). Oxford: Oxford University Press.

Brodmann, K. (1909). *Vergleichende Lokalisationslehre der Grosshirnrinde in ihren Prinzipien dargestellt auf Grund des Zellenbaues.* Leipzig: Barth.

Buchsbaum, M. (2005, September). *White matter volume and diffusion tensor imaging in the schizophrenia and bipolar affective disorder spectrum.* Paper presented at the second ECNS-ISNIP Joint Meeting, Munich.

Cajal, S. R. Y. (1909). *Histologie du systeme nerveux de l'homme et de vertébrès.* Paris: Maloine.

Cartwright, J. (2000). *Evolution and human behaviour.* New York: Palgrave.

Damasio, A. R., & Van Hoesen, G. W. (1983). Emotional disturbances associated with focal lesions of the limbic frontal lobe. In K. M. Heilman & P. Satz (Eds.), *Neuropsychology of human emotion* (pp. 85–109). New York: Guilford Press.

Dercum, F. X. (1925). The thalamus in the physiology and pathology of the mind. A.M.A. *Archives of Neurology and Psychiatry, 14*, 289–302.
Donald, M. (2001). *A mind so rare. The evolution of human consciousness*. New York: W. W. Norton.
Flechsig, P. (1896a). *Die Lokalisation der geistigen Vorgänge, insbesondere der Sinnesempfindungen des Menschen*. Leipzig: Veit.
Flechsig, P. (1896b). *Gehirn und Seele*. Leipzig: Veit.
Fuster, J. Q. (1997). *The prefrontal cortex. Anatomy, physiology and neuropsychology* (3rd ed.). New York: Raven Press.
Galaburda, A. M., LeMay, M., Kemper, T. L., & Geschwind, N. (1978). Right-left asymmetries in the brain. *Science, 199*, 852–856.
Galaburda, A. M., & Pandya, D. N. (1982). Role of architectonics and connections in the study of primate brain evolution. In E. Armstrong, & D. Falk (Eds.), *Primate brain evolution* (pp. 203–216). New York: Plenum Press.
Gannon, P. J., Holloway, R. L., Broadfield, D. C., & Braun, A. R. (1998). Asymmetry of chimpanzee planum temporale: Humanlike pattern of Wernicke's brain language area homolog. *Science, 279*, 220–222.
Glezer, I. L., Jacobs, M. S., & Morgane, P. J. (1988). Implications of the "initial brain" concept for brain evolution in Cetacea. *Behavioral and Brain Sciences, 11*, 75–116.
Grüsser, O.-J. (1988). Die phylogenetische Hirnentwicklung und die funktionelle Lateralisation der menschlichen Großhirnrinde. In G. Oepen (Ed.), *Psychiatrie des rechten und linken Gehirns: Neuropsychologische Ansätze zum Verständnis von "Persönlichkeit," "Depression" und "Schizophrenie"* (pp. 34–50). Köln: Deutscher Ärzte-Verlag.
Hassler, R. (1959). Anatomy of the thalamus. In G. Schaltenbrand & P. Bailey (Eds.), *Introduction to stereotaxis with an atlas of the human brain* (pp. 230–290). Stuttgart: Thieme.
Hassler, R. (1982). Architectonic organization of the thalamic nuclei. In G. Schaltenbrand, & A.E. Walker (Eds.), *Stereotaxy of the human brain* (pp. 140–180). Stuttgart: Thieme.
Heath, R. G. (1986). The neural substrate of emotion. In R. Plutchik, & H. Kellerman (Eds.), *Emotion. Theory, research, and experience* (pp. 3–35). Orlando, FL: Academic Press.
Herz, R. S., & Engen, T. (1996). Odor memory: Review and analysis. *Psychonomic Bulletin and Review, 3*, 300–313.
Hodos, W. (1988). Comparative neuroanatomy and the evolution of intelligence. In H. J. Jerison, & I. Jerison (Eds.), *Intelligence and evolutionary biology* (pp. 93–107). Berlin: Springer.
Hodos, W., & Campbell, C. B. G. (1969). Scala naturae: Why there is no theory in comparative psychology. *Psychological Review, 76*, 337–350.
Hodos, W., & Campbell, C. B. G. (1991). Evolutionary scales and comparative studies of animal cognition. In R. P. Kesner & D. S. Olton (Eds.), *Neurobiology of comparative cognition* (pp. 1–20). Hillsdale, NJ: Lawrence Erlbaum.
Hopf, A. (1956). Volumetrische Untersuchungen zur vergleichenden Anatomie des Thalamus. *Journal für Hirnforschung, 8*, 25–38.
Hopkins, W. D., Wesley, M. J., Izard, M. K., & Hook, M. (2004). Chimpanzees (*Pan troglodytes*) are predominantly right-handed: replication in three populations of apes. *Behavioral Neuroscience, 118*, 659–663.
Jerison, H. J. (1973). *The evolution of the brain and intelligence*. New York: Academic Press.
Kaminski, J., Call, J., & Fischer, J. (2004). Word learning in a domestic dog: evidence for "fast mapping". *Science, 304*, 1682–1683.
Keenan, J. P., Wheeler, M., Gallup, Jr G. G., & Pascual-Leone, A. (2000). Self-recognition and the right prefrontal cortex. *Trends in Cognitive Sciences, 4*, 338–344.
Kleist, K. (1934). *Gehirnpathologie*. Leipzig: Barth.
Knight R. T., & Grabowecky M. (2000). Prefrontal cortex, time, and consciousness. In M. S. Gazzaniga (Ed.), *The new cognitive neurosciences*, (2nd ed.) (pp. 1319–1339). Cambridge, MA: MIT Press.

LeDoux, J. E. (1987). Emotion. In F. Plum (Ed.), *Handbook of physiology: Section 1. The nervous system: Vol. V. Higher functions of the brain* (pp. 419–460). Bethesda: American Physiological Society.
LeDoux, J. E. (1989). Cognitive-emotional interactions in the brain. *Cognition and Emotion, 3*, 267–289.
LeMay, M. (1976). Morphological cerebral asymmetries of modern man, fossil man, and nonhuman primate. *Annals of the New York Academy of Sciences, 280*, 349–366.
Macchi, G. (1989). Anatomical substrate of emotional reactions. In L. Squire, & G. Gainotti (Eds.), *Handbook of neuropsychology, Vol. 3* (pp. 283–304). Amsterdam: Elsevier.
MacLean, P. D. (1970). The triune brain, emotion, and the scientific bias. In F. O. Schmitt (Ed.), *The neurosciences: Second study program* (pp. 336–349). New York: Rockefeller University Press.
MacLean, P. D. (1972). Cerebral evolution and emotional processes. *Annals of the New York Academy of Sciences, 193*, 137–149.
MacLean, P. D. (1990). *The triune brain in evolution.* New York: Plenum Press.
Markowitsch, H. J. (1988). Anatomical and functional organization of the primate prefrontal cortical system. In H. D. Steklis & J. Erwin (Eds.), *Comparative primate biology, Vol. IV: Neurosciences* (pp. 99–153). New York: Alan R. Liss.
Markowitsch, H. J. (1992). *Intellectual functions and the brain. An historical perspective.* Toronto: Hogrefe & Huber.
Markowitsch H. J. (1999). The limbic system. In R. Wilson, & F. Keil (Eds.), *The MIT encyclopedia of cognitive science.* Cambridge, MA: MIT Press.
Markowitsch, H. J. (2000). Memory and amnesia. In M.-M. Mesulam (Ed.), *Principles of cognitive and behavioral neurology* (pp. 257–293). New York: Oxford University Press.
Markowitsch, H. J. (2005). The neuroanatomy of memory. In P. Halligan, & P. Wade (Eds.). *The effectiveness of rehabilitation for cognitive deficits* (pp. 105–114). Oxford: Oxford University Press.
Markowitsch, H. J., Emmans, D., Irle, E., Streicher, M., & Preilowski, B. (1985). Cortical and subcortical afferent connections of the primate's temporal pole: A study of rhesus monkeys, squirrel monkeys, and marmosets. *Journal of Comparative Neurology, 242*, 425–458.
Nauta, W. J. H. (1958). Hippocampal projections and related neural pathways to the mid-brain in the cat. *Brain, 81*, 319–341.
Nauta, W. J. H. (1962). Neural associations of the amygdaloid complex in the monkey. *Brain, 85*, 505–520.
Nauta, W. J. H. (1979). Expanding borders of the limbic system concept. In T. Rasmussen, & R. Marino (Eds.), *Functional neurosurgery* (pp. 7–23). New York: Raven Press.
Nelson, K. (2002). Entering a community of minds: An experimental approach to "Theory of Mind". *Human Development, 191*, 1–23.
Nieuwenhuys, R. (1996). The greater limbic system, the emotional motor system and the brain. In G. Holstege, R. Bandler, & C. B. Saper (Eds.), *The emotional motor system* (Progress in Brain Research, Vol. 107, pp. 551–580). Amsterdam: Elsevier.
Nottebohm, F. (1981). Origins and mechanisms in the establishment of cerebral dominance. In M. S. Gazzaniga (Ed.), *Handbook of behavioral neurology: Vol. 2. Neuropsychology* (pp. 295–344). New York: Plenum Press.
Papez, J. W. (1937). A proposed mechanism of emotion. *Archives of Neurology and Psychiatry, 38*, 725–743.
Preuss, T. M. (1995a). Do rats have prefrontal cortex? The Rose-Woolsey-Akert program reconsidered. *Journal of Cognitive Neuroscience, 7*, 1–24.
Preuss, T. M. (1995b). The argument from animals to humans in cognitive neuroscience. In M. S. Gazzaniga (Ed.), *The cognitive neurosciences* (pp. 1227–1241). Cambridge, MA: MIT Press.
Preuss, T. M., & Kaas, J. H. (1999). Human brain evolution. In M. J. Zigmond, F. E. Bloom, S. C. Landis, J. L. Roberts, & L. R. Squire (Eds.), *Fundamental neuroscience* (pp. 1283–1311). San Diego, CA: Academic Press.

Pritzel, M., Brand, M., & Markowitsch, H. J. (2003). *Gehirn und Verhalten*. Heidelberg: Spektrum Akademische Verlagsanstalt.
Rapoport, S. I. (1990). Integrated phylogeny of the primate brain, with special reference to humans and their diseases. *Brain Research Reviews, 15*, 267–294.
Rubens, A. B. (1977). Asymmetries of human cerebral cortex. In S. Harnad, R. W. Doty, L. Goldstein, J. Jaynes, & G. Krauthamer (Eds.), *Lateralization in the nervous system* (pp. 503–516). New York: Academic Press.
Sanides, F. (1964). The cyto-myeloarchitecture of the human frontal lobe and its relation to phylogenetic differentiation of the cerebral cortex. *Journal für Hirnforschung, 6*, 269–292.
Sarter, M., & Markowitsch, H. J. (1985). The involvement of the amygdala in learning and memory: A critical review with emphasis on anatomical relations. *Behavioral Neuroscience, 99*, 342–380.
Sims, K. S., & Williams, R. S. (1990). The human amygdaloid complex: a cytologic and histochemical atlas using Nissl, myelin, acetylcholinesterase and nicotinamide adenine dinucleotide phosphate diaphorase staining. *Neuroscience, 36*, 449–472.
Stuss, D. T., & Anderson, V. (2004). The frontal lobes and theory of mind: developmental concepts from adult focal lesion research. *Brain and Cognition, 55*, 69–83.
Stuss, D. T., & Levine, B. (2002). Adult clinical neuropsychology. Lessons from studies of the frontal lobes. *Annual Review of Psychology, 53*, 401–433.
Stuss, D. T., Gallup, Jr G. G., & Alexander, M. P. (2001). The frontal lobes are necessary for 'theory of mind'. *Brain, 124*, 279–286.
Teuber, H.-L. (1964). The riddle of the frontal lobe function in man. In J. M. Warren & K. Akert (Eds.), *The frontal granular cortex and behavior* (pp. 410–444). New York: McGraw Hill.
Teuber, H.-L. (1972). Unity and diversity of frontal lobe functions. *Acta Neurobiologiae Experimentalis, 32*, 615–656.
Tomasello, M. (2000). *The cultural origins of human cognition*. Cambridge, MA: Harvard University Press.
Tulving, E. (2005). Episodic memory and autonoesis: Uniquely human? In H. S. Terrace & J. Metcalfe (Eds.). *The missing link in cognition: Self-knowing consciousness in man and animals* (pp. 3–56). New York: Oxford University Press.
Tulving, E., & Markowitsch, H. J. (1998). Episodic and declarative memory: Role of the hippocampus. *Hippocampus, 8*, 198–204.

Neurobiological Basis of Emotions

Irene Daum, Hans J. Markowitsch, and Marie Vandekerckhove

Abstract Experiencing emotions, the ability to identify emotions in others, and the capacity to express emotions are dependent on the functional integrity of a set of neural systems, with the limbic system and the amygdala being the most prominent key structures. Damage to the amygdala and its interconnected cortical and subcortical regions leads to severe impairment of emotional processing. Dysfunction of these circuits has also been related to a range of behavioral and neuropsychiatric problems, with the orbitofrontal cortex being the focus of recent research interest. Whether distinct neural systems specialize in the processing of distinct emotions (e.g., fear, happiness, disgust) remains to be fully determined

Emotions: Mediated by "Body and Brain"

Emotions are embedded in neural networks. There are, however, a number of false beliefs about the interactions between the behavioral expression of emotions and the underlying neurobiological substrates. Davidson (2003) termed the most common ones the "seven sins" in the study of emotion.

1. Affect and cognition are subserved by separate, independent neural circuits.
2. Affect is subcortical.
3. Emotions are in the head.
4. Emotions can be studied from a purely psychological perspective.
5. Emotions are similar in structure across both age and species.
6. Specific emotions are instantiated in discrete locations in the brain.
7. Emotions are conscious feeling states.

Davidson provided convincing arguments against each of these statements, stressing the interdependence of brain, body, and emotions. Whereas we also

I. Daum (✉)
Department of Neuropsychology, Institute of Cognitive Neuroscience, Ruhr University Bochum, Bochum, Germany
e-mail: irene.daum@rub.de

B. Röttger-Rössler, H.J. Markowitsch (eds.), *Emotions as Bio-cultural Processes*,
DOI 10.1007/978-0-387-09546-2_6, © Springer Science+Business Media, LLC 2009

emphasize the interwoven relations of brain, body, and emotions, this contribution focuses on the brain mechanisms of emotion.

The relation between emotions and the brain has interested scientists for centuries and has generated numerous textbooks (e.g., Damasio, 1999; Izard, 1971; LeDoux, 1998a; MacLean, 1990; Panksepp, 1998). One major brain system comes to mind immediately when considering the neural basis of emotions: the limbic system (Lautin, 2001).

Limbic System: The Neural Basis of Emotions

The term "limbic system" was first used during the 19th century by Paul Broca (1878) when he described "*le grand lobe limbique*." He was referring to structures adjacent to the corpus callosum (Markowitsch, 1999a; Nieuwenhuys, Voogt, & van Huizen, 1988; Stephan, 1975) (see Fig. 1). Because of the diversity of its structures and connections, a number of pros and cons for using the term limbic system have been expressed (Mark, Daniels, Naidich, & Hendrix, 1995). However, as much research has highlighted its usefulness, we use the term in this chapter.

A milestone in research on the brain basis of emotion was Papez' (1937) proposed mechanism of emotion. Contrary to Broca, who had emphasized cortical areas, Papez stressed the functional relevance of subcortical regions. More recently, another circuit intimately related to emotional processing has

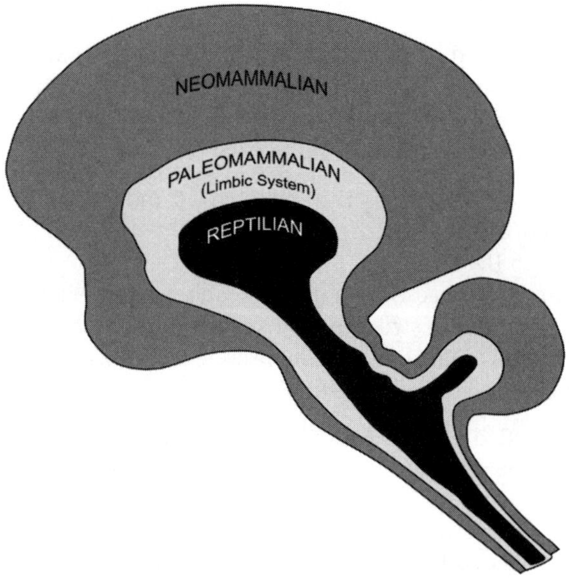

Fig. 1 Limbic system. (Adapted from MacLean, 1949, 1970, 1990)

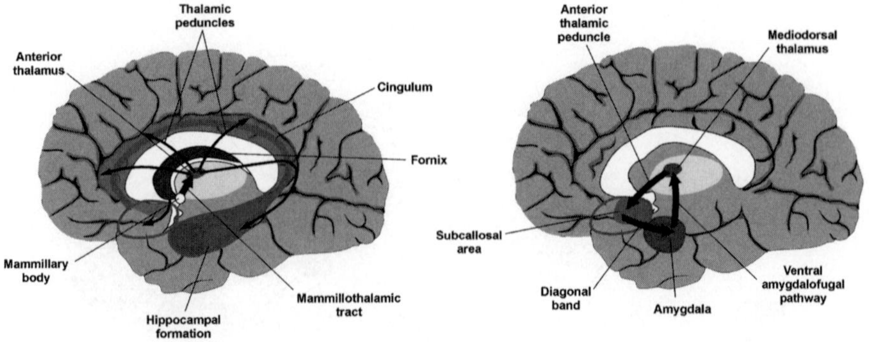

Fig. 2 Papez circuit and basolateral limbic circuit. The basolateral thalamic circuit, composed of the amygdala, mediodorsal thalamus, and subcallosal area, most likely supports the action of the Papez circuit by controlling and selecting information of major relevance to the organism. This loop may be interrupted after capsular genu infarcts, resulting in profound memory disturbances that have been interpreted as "contextual amnesia" (Schnider, Gutbrod, Hess, & Schroth, 1996)

been described: the basolateral limbic circuit (Livingston & Escobar, 1971; see also Irle & Markowitsch, 1982; Sarter & Markowitsch, 1985a,b). Both circuits are depicted in Fig. 2.

Individual structures of particular relevance are the amygdala—a conglomerate of nuclei forming two major subgroups: the phylogenetically old corticomedial and the phylogenetically young basolateral complexes (Sarter & Markowitsch, 1985a,b; see Fig. 3)—and the septal nuclei, formed by the medial and the lateral septal nucleus (Andy & Stephan, 1968). As LeDoux (1994, 1995) pointed out, the amygdala receives preprocessed sensory stimuli and allocates an emotional connotation ("interpretation") to them: Seeing a poisonous spider results in increased blood pressure, breathing frequency, heart rate, pulse rate, and skeletal muscle activity (see Fig. 3).

Amygdala

The amygdala is a complex nuclear mass that can be subdivided into a number of nuclei and nuclear complexes (Fig. 4). It integrates information about external stimuli conveyed by sensory cortices with somatic, visceral, and endocrine processes (Adolphs, 1999; Adolphs, Denburg, & Tranel, 2001; Zald & Pardo, 1997). In a threatening situation, the amygdala becomes active, leading to fear and a state of enhanced alertness that prepares the organism for flight or fight in the service of self-preservation. Amygdala activation may occur with a short latency of 12 ms, without the need for cortical input (LeDoux, 1996; Markowitsch, 1999a). Ascending projections from the amygdala to the cortex may influence subsequent cognitive processing associated with cortical

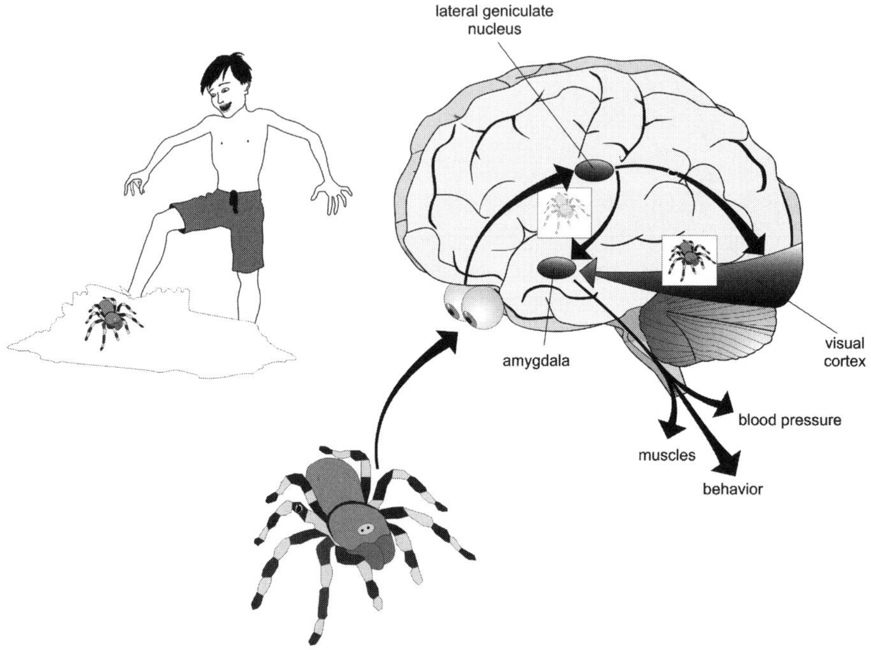

Fig. 3 Example of consequences triggered by the amygdala upon seeing a dangerous object (spider). (Adapted from LeDoux, 1994, 1996, 1998a, 1998b)

activation. Whereas the available evidence strongly indicates specific processing of negative stimuli, the amygdala has also been shown to be activated by certain classes of positive stimuli. Examples are the perception of erotic nude pictures (LaBar, Gatemby, Gore, LeDoux, & Phelps, 1998), perception of intensely pleasurable music (Blood & Zatorre, 2001), auditory perception of laughing (Sander & Scheich, 2001), and the retrieval of positively valued autobiographical memories (Piefke, Weiss, Zilles, Markowitsch, & Fink, 2003).

Both the right and the left amygdala are engaged in emotional processing and in associating emotional stimuli to memory (Alkire, 2001; Buchanan, Tranel, & Adolphs, 2003; Markowitsch, 1998/1999; Phelps et al., 1998). The right-hemispheric amygdala is preferentially involved in the processing of imagery-related and pictorial material; and it acts mainly in a fast, shallow, and implicit manner. The left-hemispheric amygdala is preferentially engaged in high-level processing or explicit, language-related in-depth evaluations. Global, rapid analysis of affective information is thus performed by the right amygdala; and detailed, deep information processing is done by the left amygdala. The feeling, or conscious representation, of affective meaning accompanied by arousal is probably mediated more by the left than the right amygdala. This view was supported by the results of a study by Najib, Lorberbaum, Kose, Bohning, and George (2004), who found a strong correlation between left

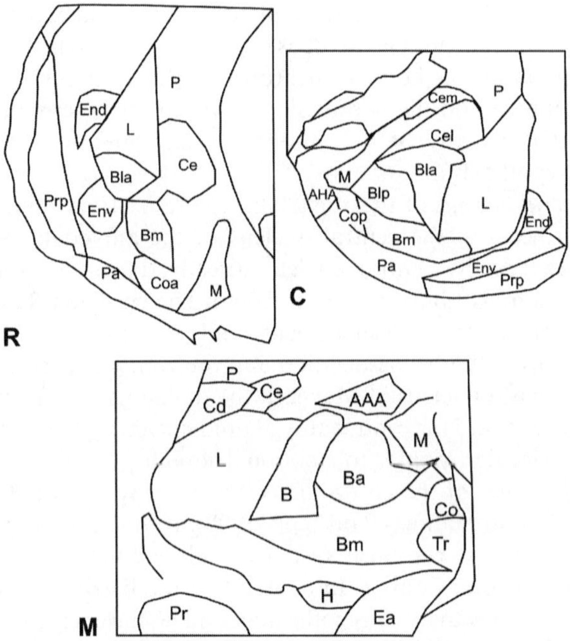

Fig. 4 Coronal sections of the amygdala of the rat (R), cat (C), and rhesus monkey (M). More detailed ways of subdividing some individual nuclei (magnocellular part and parvocellular part) have been omitted. Note that the drawings for the three species have not been made to the same scale. AAA, anterior amygdaloid area; AHA, amygdalo-hippocampal area; B, basal nucleus of the amygdala; Ba, basal accessory nucleus of the amygdala; Bla, anterior division of the basolateral nucleus of the amygdala; Blp, posterior division of the basolateral nucleus of the amygdala; Bm, basomedial nucleus of the amygdala; Cd, caudate nucleus; Ce, central nucleus of the amygdala; Cel, lateral division of the central nucleus; Cem, medial division of the central nucleus; Co, cortical nucleus of the amygdala; Coa, anterior division of the cortical nucleus; Cop, posterior division of the cortical nucleus; Ea, entorhinal cortex, anterior part; End, dorsal division of the endopiriform nucleus; Env, = ventral division of the endopiriform nucleus; H, hippocampal formation; L, lateral nucleus of the amygdala; M, medial nucleus of the amygdala; P, putamen; Pa, periamygdaloid cortex; Pr, prorhinal cortex; Prp, prepiriform cortex; Tr, transition area. (Adapted from Fig. 1 in Sarter & Markowitsch, 1985b)

amygdala activation and intensity of grief in women who had recently broken up a romantic relationship. The amygdala is also involved in the perceptual analysis of emotionally salient stimuli, such as facial expressions; and projections from the amygdala to the occipital cortex may serve to enhance the detailed visual processing of such stimuli (Adolphs, 2002).

The *corticomedial nucleus* of the amygdala receives input directly from the hypothalamus and the septal area and provides the main output for the basolateral complex of the amygdala. It plays an important role in the autonomic functions involved in emotional or sexual arousal. It is connected with olfactory structures and has efferent projections to (1) the hypothalamus for activation of the sympathetic nervous system; (2) the reticular nucleus for reflex modification; (3) the trigeminal and facial nerves for facial expressions of fear; and (4) the ventral tegmental area, locus coeruleus, and laterodorsal tegmental nucleus for activation of the main neurotransmitter systems. Other efferents reach the septal area and the hypothalamus via the stria terminalis. The stria terminalis mediates many of the autonomic correlates of emotional states processed by hypothalamus and amygdala.

The *basolateral nucleus* of the amygdala receives sensory inputs from many regions and projects to the central nucleus of the amygdala. Some sensory information reaches the central nucleus directly, bypassing the basolateral nucleus (Parkinson, Robbins, & Everitt, 2000). The basolateral nuclei (consisting of the lateral nucleus, basal nucleus, and accessory basal nucleus) also project to the cortex (limbic association and prefrontal cortices, hippocampal formation), the basal nucleus of Meynert, the thalamus (via the ventral amygdalofugal pathway), and the central amygdaloid nucleus, which is important for mediating behavioral responses to emotional stimuli.

The *central nucleus* of the amygdala is the major source of efferents to the brainstem and hypothalamus (Panksepp, 1998). It functions as a controller of brainstem arousal and response systems while subserving some forms of stimulus–response conditioning. In contrast to the basolateral nuclei, it has a well established connectivity to hypothalamic and brainstem regions (Swanson & Petrovich, 1998).

Amygdala–Septum Interactions

The amygdala and the septum have opposite functions: In healthy subjects, activation of the amygdala results in enhanced emotionality, whereas amygdala dysfunction leads to flattened emotional reactivity (Siebert, Markowitsch, & Bartel, 2003). Activation of the septum, on the other hand, lowers emotional processing, whereas dysfunction enhances affective awareness (Cramon, Markowitsch, & Schuri, 1993). The most well known disorder in this respect is the Klüver-Bucy syndrome, first described in monkeys that had undergone temporal lobe resection (Klüver & Bucy, 1937). The symptom complex includes agnosia, amnesia, hypersexuality, hyperorality, hyperphagia, tameness/placidity, and hypermetamorphosis (i.e., a tendency to attend and respond to all kinds of stimuli). Similar symptoms have been described in humans (e.g., Lilly, Cummings, Benson, & Frankel, 1983; Poeck, 1985). In summary, the amygdala is a key structure in a distributed neural system that connects stimuli and emotional responses.

Diencephalon: Thalamus and Hypothalamus

Within the diencephalon, the anterior and mediodorsal thalamic nuclei and the mammillary bodies are relevant for the integration and synchronization of emotions and memory. They process the biological and social significance of stimuli and thereby select information for long-term storage. The relevance of these diencephalic regions for memory processing has been documented in numerous case reports, particularly in patients suffering from Korsakoff's syndrome in whom chronic alcohol abuse has led to degeneration of the structures in question (see Brand et al., 2003; Markowitsch, Kessler, & Denzler, 1986; Victor, Adams, & Collins, 1989). Korsakoff patients frequently appear emotionally flat and detached, and they fail to sustain emotional involvement in ongoing events (see Ackermann & Daum, 1997). They also show impairments in identifying the affective status of voice intonations (affective prosody) in spoken sentences when semantic content is either neutral or incongruent (Snitz, Hellinger, & Daum, 2002). This deficit may contribute to their problems in appropriate emotional engagement with others. Because of the relatively diffuse nature of neuropathology in Korsakoff's syndrome, it remains unclear whether these emotional impairments are related to diencephalic pathology or damage to the basolateral circuit linking limbic, anterior temporal, and prefrontal structures, which are all thought to undergo degenerative changes in the presence of chronic alcoholism.

Patients with selective medial dorsal diencephalic damage may have major problems in encoding and consolidating emotional episodic memories, resulting in anterograde amnesia (Markowitsch, Cramon, & Schuri, 1993); they may also show impulsivity, poor control of affect, and inappropriate behavior in social situations (Daum & Ackermann, 1994).

Along with the amygdala and septal nuclei, the hypothalamus is considered a key region for emotional processes. It forms part of the diencephalon and controls the release of hormones by the pituitary gland. It is thus involved in temperature regulation; control of food and water intake, sexual behavior, and reproduction; and regulation of circadian rhythms. In summary, the hypothalamus controls and integrates autonomic, endocrine, and behavioral components of emotional responses (Adolphs, 2002).

Stimulation of hypothalamic nuclei in cats led to various forms of emotional expressions, such as aggression, threat, and fear (see Fig. 3) (Hess & Brügger, 1943). José Delgado (1969, 1987) demonstrated later that the behavior of a bull in a Spanish bull-fighting arena could be influenced telemetrically by hypothalamic stimulation: Behavior was aggressive or submissive depending on the stimulation site. More recent approaches view networks involving the periaqueductal gray, anterior and posterior portions of the cingulate cortex, amygdala, and septohippocampal system as the basis for the representation and control of these emotions (see also Gray, Braver, & Raichle, 2002).

Stimulation of other hypothalamic nuclei has been shown to affect interconnected emotion and motivation systems. The pioneering work of James Olds (1956) on intracranial self-stimulation in rats led to conceptualization of the lateral hypothalamic area as either reward and pleasure centers or lust centers (Olds & Milner, 1954). Figure 3 gives an overview of the hypothalamus and the mammillary bodies. Related to this work, neurosurgeon Penfield (1975) published a chapter "On Butterflies in the Brain." During electrical stimulation of the temporal lobe during surgery for drug-resistant epilepsy, patients frequently reported strange feelings, experiences, and sensory hallucinations, providing evidence of the involvement of these regions in emotions in human subjects as well.

Hippocampal Formation

The hippocampal formation is comprised of the hippocampus proper, the dentate gyrus, and the subiculum. It is highly interconnected with neocortical and allocortical (limbic) structures (e.g., entorhinal cortex, amygdala, septum) and all major neocortical association areas (Nieuwenhuys et al., 1988). The hippocampal formation is mainly involved in memory (for a summary, see Markowitsch, 1999b) and spatial functions (Maguire et al., 2000), but it may also contribute to the emotional modulation of memory via its involvement in neural networks (e.g., Driessen et al., 2004). The entorhinal cortex, for example, receives input from subcortical areas such as the amygdala and projects to the hippocampus. These pathways may explain why emotions facilitate remembering. The hippocampus is more involved in the explicit representation of details of an event, whereas the amygdala is more involved in its implicit or unconscious representation (e.g., Bechara et al., 1995; Brandt et al., 2005; LaBar, LeDoux, Spencer, & Phelps, 1995). The hippocampus is necessary for explicit knowledge about an emotional situation (e.g., its dangerous nature), whereas the amygdala mediates the fear response in appropriate situations (Funayama, Grillon, Davis, & Phelps, 2001). Activation of the amygdala facilitates the representation of events in the hippocampus and improves explicit memory (LeDoux & Phelps, 2000). This view is supported by clinical data indicating relatively good preservation of emotionally salient memories compared with neutral memories in patients suffering from retrograde amnesia (Daum, Flor, Brodbeck, & Birbaumer, 1996).

Expanded Limbic System

The complex nature of human emotions leads to a major involvement of neocortical regions; and within this context an "expanded" (Nauta, 1979), or "greater," limbic system (Nieuwenhuys, 1996) has been proposed. This system includes basal ganglia regions (ventral striatum, nucleus accumbens) as an interface between motor-related and emotional/motivational structures (Groenewegen, Wright, & Beijer, 1996) and between prefrontal/orbitofrontal und insular regions (e.g., Cardinal, Parkinson, Hall, & Everitt, 2002; Ikemoto & Panksepp, 1999). In addition, the brainstem and, in particular, the periaqueductal gray have been discussed as system components. Table 1 provides an

Table 1 Structures of the limbic system and their principal functional involvement

Structure	Functional involvement
Telencephalic cortical	
cingulate gyrus	Attention, drive, pain perception
Hippocampal formation	Memory, spatiotemporal integration
Entorhinal region	Memory
Telencephalic, subcortical	
amygdala	Emotional evaluation, motivations, olfaction
Basal forebrain	Emotional evaluation, memory
Ventral striatum, nucleus accumbens	Motor-related modulation of emotions
Diencephalic	
mammillary bodies	Memory, emotion?
anterior nucleus	Memory, emotion, attention
mediodorsal nucleus	Memory, consciousness?/sleep, emotion
nonspecific thalamic nuclei	Consciousness?
Associated regions ("paralimbic cortex," expanded limbic system; Nauta, 1979)	
medial and orbitofrontal cortex	Emotional evaluation, social behavior, initiative (initiation of retrieval)
insula	Sensory-motivational integration?
temporal pole (Brodmann Area 38)	Memory-related sensory integration, initiation of recall

overview of what are currently taken to be relevant limbic structures and their functional implications. Figure 5 illustrates the cortical paralimbic areas described originally by Mesulam (2000).

The mechanisms underlying the perception of emotional facial expressions exemplify the coordinated action of structures in the expanded limbic system—amygdala, insula, anterior cingulate cortex, and brainstem. The network is the substrate for integrating the visual perception of emotional facial expressions with differential cardiac responses, and it thereby serves as an interface for the selective generation of visceral reactions that are a critical embodied component of the emotional response. Problems in recognizing facial expressions among patients with limbic system damage are consistent with this view (Montagne, 2005).

Cingulate Cortex

The cingulate cortex, with its extensive connections to the amygdala, regulates attention, affect, and cognition (Devinsky, Morrell, & Vogt, 1995). It is subdivided into rostral and ventral Brodmann areas (BA24, BA25, BA32) primarily engaged in attention and emotion versus dorsal and posterior regions (BA23, BA29, BA30—the retrosplenial cortex) representing cognitive aspects of

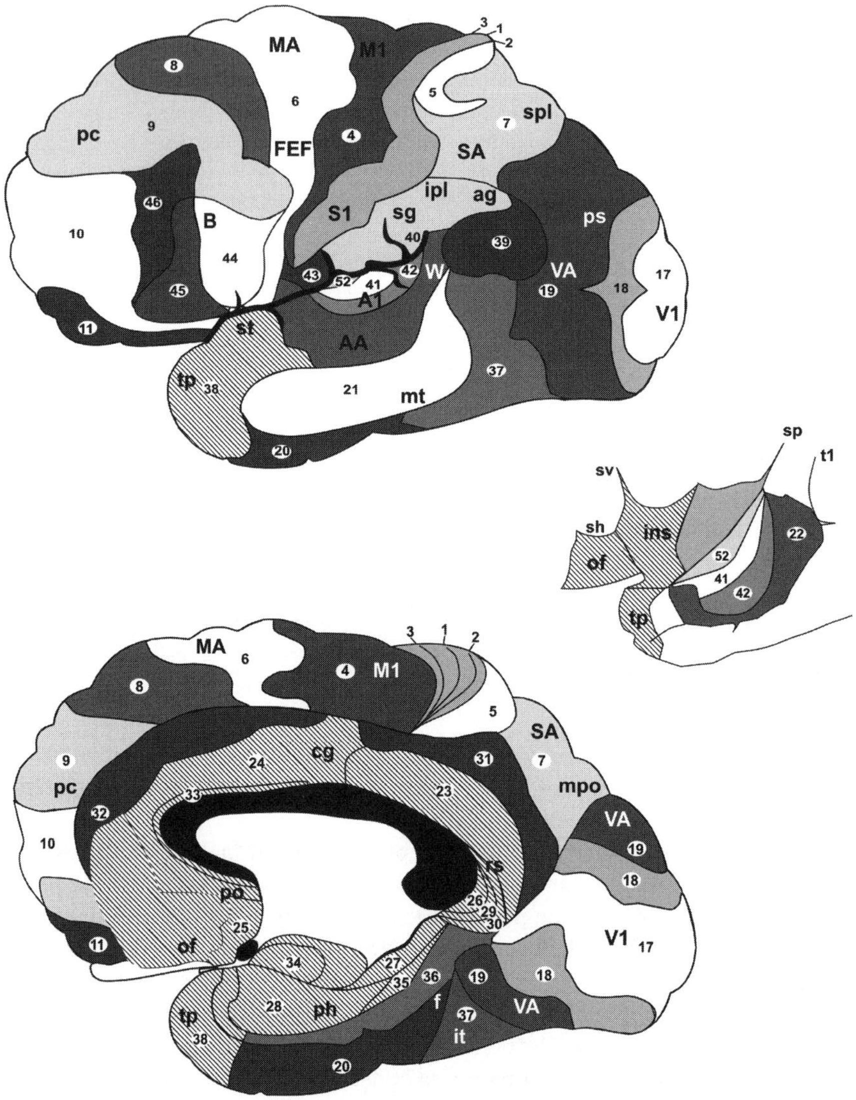

Fig. 5 Paralimbic regions according to Mesulam (2000). Numbers refer to Brodmann areas (BA). Other relevant abbreviations: cg, cingulate cortex; rs, retrosplenial cortex; ins, insula

information processing (Devinsky et al., 1995; Vogt, Nimchinsky, Vogt, & Hof, 1995) (see Fig. 5). The anterior cingulate cortex is connected extensively with the amygdala, periaqueductal gray, anterior and mediodorsal thalamic nuclei, nucleus accumbens, and ventral striatum; and it has been associated with autonomic and visceral functions as well as emotional behavior (Devinsky et al., 1995;

Paus, 2001). The rostral cingulate cortex is particularly important for the integration of visceral, attentional, and affective information.

Dorsal parts of the cingulate cortex are primarily involved in modulating attention and executive functions (Carter et al., 1998; Markowitsch, Vandekerckhove, Lanfermann, & Russ, 2003; Stuss et al., 2002). They are also involved in familiarity aspects of voices, faces, and objects (Sugiura, Shah, Zilles, & Fink, 2005) and in time and place orientation (Hirono et al., 1998).

Orbitofrontal Cortex

The orbitofrontal cortex is critically involved in the regulation of emotions and decision-making (Eslinger, 1999a,b; Knörlein, 1865; Rolls, 2004). It is connected reciprocally with the amygdala and serves to modulate behavioral responses as a function of the emotional significance of stimulus input. Both structures thus form part of a tightly linked circuit (Adolphs, 2002). In addition, the orbitofrontal cortex/basal forebrain area is relevant for the regulation of autonomic functions (Chapman, Livingston, & Livingston, 1949). The orbitofrontal cortex is referred to as the thinking part of the emotional brain. It is situated at the hierarchical apex of what is now termed the rostral limbic system or anterior limbic prefrontal network. The orbitofrontal cortices have a polymodal processing capacity. They receive input from different sensory modalities—directly from the respective neocortical sensory areas or indirectly via the amygdala. This region thus combines information from various external and internal sources and acts as an integrator of the inner and outer worlds. Caudal orbitofrontal areas, in particular, receive projections not only from visual, auditory, and somatosensory cortices but also from gustatory and primary olfactory cortices (Carmichael & Price, 1995). This area is responsible for our "gut reactions" to people and events—our earliest associations between experiences in the outside world and our internal physical responses or cognitive-affective sets. Lesions to the orbitofrontal area reduce behavioral control and impair the ability to translate judgments of events into appropriate feelings and behaviors (Borsutzky, Brand, & Fujiwara, 2000).

Insular Cortex

The insular cortex is critical for storing or retrieving the memory for incentive value in the absence of a reward. The insular area presumably codes the affective content of certain irritations, including vocalizations (Panksepp, 1998). The insula together with the ventral striatum has been found to be involved in the identification of the expression of disgust (for a review, see Phillips, Drevets, Rauch, & Lane, 2003).

Striatum

The striatum, especially the ventral striatum, receives input from a number of limbic areas. It has been termed one of the crossroads at which emotional and motor information can influence one another (Panksepp, 1998). The ventral striatum and the nucleus accumbens in particular have been viewed as an interface between motor-related and emotional/motivational structures (Groenewegen et al., 1996), and these regions are tightly linked with orbitofrontal regions critical for emotional processing. This involvement of striatal regions in emotional processing is documented by pronounced affective changes in patients suffering from striatal degeneration as in, for example, Parkinson's disease (see below).

Neurotransmitter Systems

In addition to the dopaminergic system, the cholinergic system of the basal forebrain has a major modulating influence on limbic structures through its widespread cholinergic efferents (Berntson, Sarter, & Cacioppo, 1998; Kaufer, Friedman, Seldman, & Soreq, 1998; Mesulam, 1995). Patients with damage to this system may show confabulations and emotional lability (Ptak & Schnider, 1999; Schnider, 2001), but there may also be motor system-related emotional changes.

The neurotransmitter system most directly related to emotion is the serotonin system, with serotonin neurons in brainstem raphe nuclei projecting to most brain areas. Apart from the well known involvement of the serotonin system in depression, low serotonin levels in both animals and humans are associated with aggression, impulsivity, and risk-taking. Moreover, raising serotonin levels pharmacologically reduces aggression and associated behaviors (for a summary, see Jokisch, Bellebaum, & Daum, 2005). In this context, adequate levels of serotonin have also been related to the modulation of emotion regulation (Krakowski, 2003). Anger or rage may intensify a tendency toward aggressive behavior, and reduced control of impulsive affect-driven behavior may relate to serotonergic dysfunction in the orbitofrontal cortex (see Jokisch et al., 2005). Regarding the interaction of cognition and emotion, diet-induced high serotonin levels in normal subjects lead to working memory deficits for emotional material, reflecting impairment of executive processes mediated mainly by the orbitofrontal cortex (Luciana, Burgund, Berman, & Hanson, 2001).

Emotional Changes in Patients Suffering from Brain Damage

It has long been known that temporal lobe or temporo-orbitofrontal damage may lead to pronounced emotional changes and changes in social behavior (e.g., Brand & Markowitsch, 2006; Markowitsch, 1992). Holländer (1900), for example, considered the basal part of the temporal lobe to be the seat of *folie furieuse* (raving madness). More recently, Damasio et al. (1985a,b) described related changes in emotional behavior as the result of diffuse brain damage due to hypoxia or encephalitis.

Amygdala

The study of patients with amygdala damage has consistently revealed deficits in adding an emotional flavor to memories and impairments in attending to relevant aspects of the environment (LeDoux, 1994, 1995). Such diverse functions are based on an anatomical agglomerate of phylogenetically old and young parts, either connected with sensory systems (e.g., olfaction) or related more intimately to interpretative aspects of information processing.

A good model for studying the effects of selective amygdala lesions is patients suffering from Urbach-Wiethe disease (lipoid proteinosis), a rare hereditary condition first described by Erich Urbach (1893–1946) and Camillo Wiethe (1888–1949). The disease is characterized initially by dermatological changes. For one-half to two-thirds of patients, disease progression leads to bilateral calcifications in the whole body of the amygdala (see Fig. 6).

An initial case report described changes in social behavior, including inappropriate behavior toward the examiner and problems with integrating memory and emotion (Tranel & Hyman, 1990). In an extensive neuropsychological assessment of another 39-year-old woman, poor performance on memory and

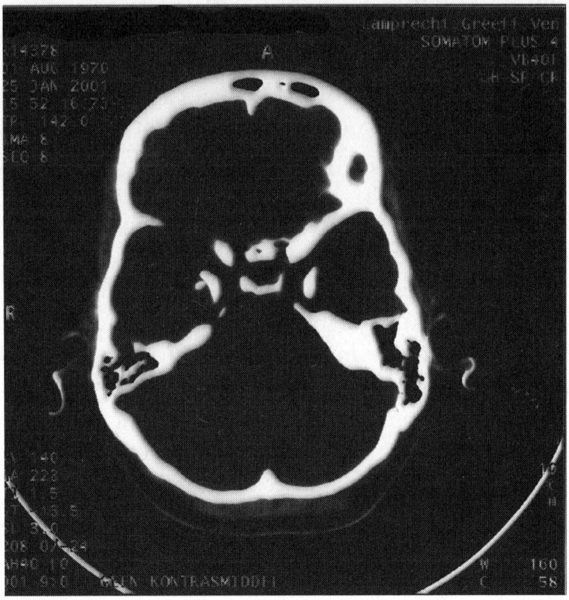

Fig. 6 Damage to the *left* and *right* amygdaloid body in a patient with Urbach-Wiethe disease (see Siebert et al., 2003)

odor discrimination tests as well as abnormal scores on personality questionnaires were observed together with problems in social adjustment and the evaluation of emotions (Babinsky et al., 1993). A subsequent study of this patient and her brother, who was also affected by the disease, yielded problems in evaluating emotional situations and deficits in remembering emotional aspects of a story (Cahill, Babinsky, Markowitsch, & McGaugh, 1995; Markowitsch et al., 1994). Hence, patients with bilateral amygdala damage may no longer be able to differentiate adequately between relevant and irrelevant information.

The detailed study of emotion perception in a larger patient group in South Africa (Siebert et al., 2003) yielded pronounced problems in identifying emotional expressions in faces (portraits of persons with a happy, surprised, sad, angry, disgusting, or fearful appearance; see Ekman & Friesen, 1975) and in performance on other tests of emotion recognition (e.g., Tübinger Affektbatterie; Breitenstein, Daum, Ackermann, Lütgehetmann, & Müller, 1996). Results showed disproportionate impairment in recognizing negative emotions but also considerable interindividual differences within the patient group, suggesting some degree of compensation by cognitive strategies or presumably also by other brain regions, given that amygdaloid calcification occurs gradually and starts at an early age (Diergaarde, 2004). Taken together, these and other patient studies highlight the central role of the amygdala in evaluating emotions in general and negative emotions in particular (Armony & LeDoux, 2000; LaBar et al., 1998).

The amygdala may also play a more general role in identifying human facial expressions. Autism, which is associated with hypoactivation in the amygdala and the fusiform gyrus, is frequently characterized by deficits in human face recognition, whereas identification of cartoon characters remains intact (Grelotti et al., 2005). Along similar lines, the "blindsight" ability of patients with primary visual cortex damage (i.e., evidence of some degree of recognition for facial expressions though not for affective pictures) is thought to be mediated by amygdala activation (de Gelder, Pourtois, & Weiskrantz, 2002; Morris, de Gelder, Weiskrantz, & Dolan, 2001). Many other studies have emphasized the contribution of the amygdala to socioemotional processing (e.g., Adolphs, 1999; Adolphs, Tranel, & Damasco, 1998).

Further evidence for the involvement of the amygdala in negative emotions comes from experimental work using fear conditioning or the fear-potentiated startle procedure. Fear conditioning, which can be studied in comparable animal and human learning studies, involves pairing a neutral stimulus with an aversive stimulus, which leads to a strong autonomic nervous system response (e.g., changes in skin conductance) thought to reflect fear. After a number of pairings, subjects exhibit an autonomic response to the neutral stimulus and therefore evidence of fear conditioning. Patients with amygdala lesions are impaired in regard to acquiring conditioned fear responses in such tasks (Bechara et al., 1995). Fear conditioning has also been associated with amygdala activations in several functional neuroimaging studies (e.g., Büchel, Morris, Dolan, & Friston, 1998).

The fear-potentiated startle response, which has also been used frequently in comparative research, refers to the increased amplitude of an eyeblink reflex to a loud tone when administered in the presence of an aversive stimulus but a reduced startle response in the presence of pleasant stimuli. The modulation of the startle reflex reflects the activation of aversive and appetitive motivational systems and thereby "emotional priming" (Lang, 1995). It has been considered a reliable indicator for the activation of emotion networks in the brain. Fear-potentiated startle, in particular, is thought to reflect fast identification of threat, interruption of ongoing action programs, and preparation for possible flight. In one study, patients with amygdala lesions did not show evidence of affect-related modulation of the startle reflex, consistent with a wealth of data derived from animal lesion studies (see Hamm, 2003).

Septal Nuclei

As described above, the septum works principally in opposition to the amygdala (Cramon & Markowitsch, 2000). Consistent with this idea, damage to septal nuclei and basal forebrain has been associated with grossly enhanced emotional reactivity to, for example, exaggeration of the emotional content of a story (Cramon et al., 1993). This septal lesion patient showed abnormal behavior on all tasks involving emotional (especially negative) stimuli. The septal area may serve as an interface contributing a specific combination of emotional flavor and evaluation to a larger (septo-hippocampal-amygdalar) memory and learning network.

Orbitofrontal Cortex

Orbitofrontal lesions in monkeys lead to emotional changes, including reduced aggression, changes in food-selection behavior, and learning problems (Meunier, Bachevalier, & Mishkin, 1997). The ventromedial prefrontal cortex has been implicated in the anticipation of future positive and negative affective consequences in decision-making (Bechara, Tranel, & Damasio, 2000; Fellows & Farah, 2005; Satish, Streufert, & Eslinger, 1999), preference judgments (Paulus & Frank, 2003), empathy (Shamay-Tsoory, Tomer, Berger, & Aharon-Peretz, 2003), and social conduct (Tranel, Bechara, & Denburg, 2002). Clinical data indicate that the orbitofrontal cortex has a more direct influence on social and emotional processing than any other cortical structure (Berlin, Rolls, & Kischka, 2004; Hornak et al., 2003; Séguin, 2004).

The case of Phineas Gage (known as the "crowbar case") is probably the most well known and best studied case of personality changes after orbitofrontal damage (Harlow, 1848, 1869). During a road accident, an iron rod passed through his frontal lobe behind the left eye, exiting at the right upper cranium. Harlow (1848) described the man as "Phineas P. Gage, a foreman, engaged in building the road, 25 years of age, of middle stature, vigorous physical organization, temperate habits, and . . . of considerable energy of character" (p. 20). Harlow observed an opening of about 8 cm in diameter as a result of the accident. Gage was in a semicomatose condition for more than 2 weeks but then improved during the next month.

About 3 months after the accident, Gage had lost vision in his left eye but was in good physical condition. His personality, however, had changed so radically that his friends said that he was "no longer Gage" (p. 14). In the years following the accident, he worked in a stable and then in Chile for nearly 8 years before returning to the United States. He died after several epileptic seizures 12 years after the accident.

This case demonstrated that after massive damage to the orbitofrontal cortex, a person can survive for years, earn a living, and therefore appear to be functioning on an adequate level. It also revealed, however, that orbitofrontal damage may result in personality changes and especially the loss of foresight and persistence in following through ideas or intentions. In Harlow's (1869) words:

> The equilibrium or balance, so to speak, between his intellectual faculties and animal propensities, seems to have been destroyed. He is fitful, irreverent, indulging at times in the grossest profanity (which was not previously his custom), manifesting but little deference for his fellows, impatient of restraint or advice when it conflicts with his desires, at times pertinaciously obstinate, yet capricious and vacillating, devising many plans of future operation, which are no sooner arranged than they are abandoned in turn for others appearing more feasible. (pp. 13–14)

Similar observations regarding the sequelae of frontal damage were published later by Welt (1888), Voegelin (1897), and Halpern (1930). Welt (1888) described a 37-year-old Swiss craftsman who fell from the fourth floor of a house and suffered left frontal damage (Case I). Before the accident, he had been a cheerful, relaxed man of good humor, but afterwards he became irritable, very critical, and annoying to his fellow patients. When reprimanded for this behavior, he blamed other patients and hospital staff while complaining about the quality of the hospital wine, boasting that he was used to drinking Chateau Lafite and other fine French wines. Welt (1888) wrote that character changes might go from better to worse, or vice versa; that is, someone who was originally taciturn might develop a lively and merry character. Comparing the effects of frontal lesions in 50 cases from the earlier literature, she stated that personality changes most likely followed damage to the (right) medial orbital surface of the frontal lobes. Recent accounts and interpretations of the relation between orbitofrontal damage and personality changes are given by Eslinger (1998, 1999a,b).

Bechara, Damasio, Damasio, and Anderson (1994) reported that lesions of the ventromedial cortex reduce the capacity for estimating future positive or negative consequences associated with risks. Only rewards and punishments immediately following actions influenced these patients' behavior. Electrodermal activity in anticipation of a risky choice was reduced in patients compared with that in control subjects, who exhibited such autonomic nervous system reactivity before they knew explicitly that the choice was risky (Bechara, Damasio, Tranel, & Damasio, 1997; Bechara, Damasio, Damasio, & Lee, 1999). These phenomena can explain the disinhibition following orbitofrontal damage that results from low levels of anxiety. This region is also implicated in mechanisms of impulse control or response inhibition (Rahman, Sahakian, Cardinal, Rogers, & Robbins, 2001).

Dysfunction of the orbitofrontal cortex has also been reported for a number of neuropsychiatric problems such as alcoholism and was found to lead to associated changes of emotional processing. Consistent with the idea that the prefrontal cortex is disproportionately vulnerable to the toxic effects of alcohol, alcoholics were found to be impaired in regard to decoding emotional facial expressions (Philippot et al., 1999) or understanding the meaning of the affective content of voice intonations (Monnot, Nixon, Lovallo, & Ross, 2001). The failure of prosodic identification was particularly pronounced in ambiguous situations, when affect and content of sentences were incongruent or when facial expression and vocal affect had to be matched (Uekermann, Daum, Schlebusch, & Trenckmann, 2005).

Other Regions

Other regions, such as the cingulate cortex, the insula (another paralimbic region) (Mesulam, 2000) (see Fig. 5), and the perirhinal area have more subtle, modulatory influences on the processing of emotions. This is due to their involvement in the control of nonemotional behavior, such as attention (cingulate area), memory (perirhinal cortex), and sensory-perceptual evaluations (insula) (Allman, Hakeem, Erwin, Nimchinsky, & Hof, 2001; Badgaiyan & Posner, 1998; Balmiou, Musiek, & Luxon, 2003; Brown & Bashir, 2002; Lane et al., 1998; Pritchard, Macaluso, & Eslinger, 1999).

The paralimbic cortical structures, in particular, the cingulate cortex, largely associate cognitive and emotive components of an experience (Allman et al., 2001) and process emotional-social interactions (Hadland, Rushworth, Gaffan, & Passingham, 2003). The cingulate cortex has also long been known to modulate pain perception (Hutchison, Davis, Lozano, Tasker, & Dostrovsky, 1999) and anxiety (Phan et al., 2005).

The insular cortex appears to be specialized in processing disgust (Wicker et al., 2003). The insula is engaged in integrating interoceptive and multimodal information and in processing taste information (e.g., Pritchard et al., 1999). It has been shown to be activated when affective states had to be generated in response to emotional stimuli (Phillips, Drevets, Rauch, & Lane, 2003), particularly to physical pain and disgust-related stimuli (Peyron, Laurent, & Garcia-Larrea, 2000).

Evidence for a role of the basal ganglia in emotional processing comes from lesion data showing that problems with perception of affect in cortical lesion patients were particularly pronounced when there was additional basal ganglia damage (Cancelliere & Kertesz, 1990). Degenerative disorders of the basal ganglia are frequently associated with changes in affect and the processing of emotions. Parkinson's disease (PD) patients frequently suffer from depression; and patients suffering from Huntington's disease (HD) show a wide range of affective changes, including depression, manic episodes, irritability, and a tendency toward aggressive behavior (Ackermann, 2003). HD patients manifest major problems in decoding emotions, particularly those in the negative spectrum (e.g., disgust) (see Sprengelmeyer, Rausch, Eysel, & Przuntek, 1998; Sprengelmeyer et al., 1999). PD patients in advanced stages of the disease have impaired facial expression and affective prosody recognition (Breitenstein, Daum, & Ackermann, 1998); their problems are presumably related to dysfunction of anatomical connections between the ventral striatum and the limbic system. It has also been suggested that damage to the basal ganglia interferes with the reproduction, or "simulation," of the autonomic or motor responses that help identify emotions in others (see Ackermann, 2003).

Laterality Effects: Right Hemisphere Hypothesis

It has long been suggested that the right hemisphere is preferentially involved in emotional processing, particularly nonverbal components of affect processing. Cortical circuits are involved in the detection of emotionally significant events such as emotional facial expressions, with cortical processing presumably following initial processing by the amygdala (see Eimer, Holmes, & McGlone, 2003). The right hemisphere is thought to act as an emotional processor analogous to the left hemisphere's role as a speech processor. Within this context, a further intrahemispheric specialization has been proposed, with anterior regions being involved in the expression of emotions and posterior regions in the perception of emotionally salient stimuli, but the supporting evidence for this distinction is sparse (for a discussion, see Breitenstein et al., 1998).

Right posterior cortical lesions are known to lead to deficits in experiencing emotions or emotional imagery (see Ackermann, 2003). There is also evidence to support right hemisphere dominance in the rapid perceptual analysis of emotionally salient external stimuli such as facial expressions or affective voice intonations. Recognition of facial affect was found to be disproportionately impaired after focal lesions to right hemisphere cortical regions (e.g., Adolphs, Tranel, & Denburg, 2000; Breitenstein et al., 1998). Particularly pronounced impairments were observed when damage involved the right somatosensory cortex; this pattern was interpreted in terms of impaired reconstruction of the somatosensory representations linked to the simulation of the "feeling" of an emotion in another person (Adolphs et al., 2000). Hence, the knowledge about the subjective feeling component of an emotion necessary to identify emotions in other people is related to the right somatosensory cortex. Dissociations of subjective experience and expression of emotions have also been reported after right hemisphere lesions. Such patients spoke in a monotonous voice and showed little facial affect when reporting, for example, a deep feeling of sadness after the death of a family member. Such problems have been linked to the right basal ganglia and the right frontal cortex (see Ackermann, 2003).

Identification and discrimination of vocal affect (affective prosody) in spoken sentences is frequently impaired after right cortical lesions, with pronounced impairment after right anterior damage, although prosody comprehension deficits may also occur after left anterior lesions (Breitenstein et al., 1998). Lesion data are consistent with findings reporting right prefrontal activation during identification of affective prosody in functional neuroimaging studies (e.g., Wildgruber, Pihan, & Ackermann, 2002).

Valence Hypothesis

Whether the right hemisphere acts as a central processor for all types of emotion or there is functional asymmetry—with the right hemisphere processing negative and the left hemisphere processing positive emotions—is an unresolved issue. The latter position has received some support from the observation of inappropriately euphoric mood states after right hemisphere damage and fearful or sad mood states after damage to the left hemisphere (Ackermann, 2003). However, the data are inconsistent regarding the perception of affective stimuli after unilateral brain damage. As most of these studies pooled data across negative and positive emotions, processing differences for single emotional categories may well have been overlooked.

Functional neuroimaging studies have provided recent evidence for distinct neural systems specializing in the processing of distinct emotions. They have shown support for disproportionate involvement of the amygdala in processing facial expressions of fear (and, less strongly, other arousing negative emotions), whereas the prefrontal cortex has been linked to the identification of angry facial expressions and the basal ganglia and the insula to the identification of disgust in facial expressions (for a summary, see Adolphs, 2002). The amygdala might be specialized for identification of stimuli that signal potential threat to the organism and therefore require immediate activation of processing resources (Adolphs, 1999). Comparison of facial and vocal affect perception in patients with cortical lesion has indicated that most of them had disproportionate problems in recognizing angry and fearful faces and sad and fearful intonations compared with their response to positive stimuli. The deficits thus appeared to be more extensive for emotions related to arousal and threat, but there was no clear association with lesion site (see Breitenstein et al., 1998). Because the emotional content of fear-related stimuli also appeared to be most difficult to recognize by healthy subjects in this study, differences in difficulty between emotion categories may thus partly affect the pattern of emotion-specific deficits in brain-damaged patients, and cognitive dysfunction may partly contribute to findings of impaired affect perception (see Breitenstein, van Lancker, Daum, & Waters, 2001). This issue has also been raised with respect to the preferential processing of disgust in the basal ganglia (see Ackermann, 2003). Consistent with this notion, the results from patients with mild brain dysfunction do not unequivocally support the valence hypothesis. Alcoholics did not show differential performance in identifying the affect categories (happy, angry, fearful, sad, neutral) (see Uekermann et al., 2005).

Electrophysiological studies in healthy humans did not provide support for the idea of distinct category-specific subsystems either because event-related potentials elicited in response to differential emotional facial expressions did not differ (Eimer et al., 2003). It is possible that early, predominantly subcortical processing of emotionally salient stimuli is associated with rapid detection and classification of affective stimuli, whereas later the cortical, in-depth processing is less specific with respect to various facial expressions and more related to attentional gating and the reduction of distractibility (see Eimer et al., 2003).

In conclusion, experiencing emotions, the ability to identify emotions in others, and the capacity to express emotions are dependent on the functional integrity of a set of neural systems, with the limbic system in general and the amygdala in particular being the most prominent key structures. Damage to the amygdala and its interconnected cortical and subcortical regions leads to severe impairment of emotional processing. Dysfunction of these circuits has also been related to a range of behavioral and neuropsychiatric problems, with the orbitofrontal cortex being the focus of recent research. Whether distinct neural systems specialize in the processing of distinct emotions (e.g., fear, happiness, disgust) remains to be fully determined.

References

Ackermann, H. (2003). Störungen des emotionalen Erlebens und Verhaltens [Disorders of emotional experience and behavior]. In H. O. Karnath, & P. Thier (Eds.), *Neuropsychologie* (pp. 581–588). Berlin: Springer.

Ackermann, H., & Daum, I. (1997). Wernicke-Enzephalopathie und Korsakow Syndrom [Wernicke's encephalopathy and Korsakoff's syndrome]. *Nervenheilkunde, 16*, 158–162.

Adolphs, R. (1999). The human amygdala and emotion. *Neuroscientist, 5*, 125–137.

Adolphs, R. (2002). Neural mechanisms for recognizing emotion. *Current Opinion in Neurobiology, 12*, 169–178.

Adolphs, R., Denburg, N. L., & Tranel, D. (2001). The amygdala's role in long-term declarative memory for gist and detail. *Behavioral Neuroscience, 115*, 983–992.

Adolphs, R., Tranel, D., & Damasco, A. R. (1998). The human amygdala in social judgment. *Nature, 393*, 470–474.
Adolphs, R., Tranel, D., & Denburg, N. (2000). Impaired emotional declarative memory following unilateral amygdala damage. *Learning & Memory, 7*, 180–186.
Alkire, M. T. (2001). Sex-related difference in amygdala activity during emotionally influenced memory storage *Neurobiology of Learning and Memory, 75*, 1–9.
Allman, J. M., Hakeem, A., Erwin, J. M., Nimchinsky, E., & Hof, P. (2001). The anterior cingulate cortex. The evolution of an interface between emotion and cognition. *Annals of the New York Academy of Sciences, 935*, 107–117.
Andy, O. J., & Stephan, H. (1968). The septum in the human brain. *Journal of Comparative Neurology, 133*, 383–410.
Armony, J. L., & LeDoux, J. E. (2000). How danger is encoded: Toward a systems, cellular, and computational understanding of cognitive-emotional interactions in fear. In M. S. Gazzaniga (Ed.), *The new cognitive neurosciences* (2nd ed., pp. 1067–1079). Cambridge, MA: MIT Press.
Babinsky, R., Calabrese, P., Durwen, H. F., Markowitsch, H. J., Brechtelsbauer, D., Heuser, L., & Gehlen, W. (1993). On the possible contribution of the amygdala in memory. *Behavioural Neurology, 6*, 167–170.
Badgaiyan, R. D., & Posner, M. I. (1998). Mapping the cingulate cortex in response selection and monitoring. *Neuroimage, 7*, 255–260.
Balmiou, D. E., Musiek, F. E., & Luxon, L. M. (2003). The insula (Island of Reil) and its role in auditory processing: Literature review. *Brain Research Reviews, 42*, 143–154.
Bechara, A., Damasio, A. R., Damasio, H., & Anderson, S. W. (1994). Insensitivity to future consequences following damage to human prefrontal cortex. *Cognition, 50*, 7–15.
Bechara, A., Damasio, H., Damasio, A. R., & Lee, G. P. (1999). Different contributions of the human amygdala and ventromedial prefrontal cortex to decision-making. *Journal of Neuroscience, 19*, 5473–5481.
Bechara, A., Damasio, H., Tranel, D., & Damasio, A. R. (1997). Deciding advantageously before knowing the advantageous strategy. *Science, 275*, 1293–1295.
Bechara, A., Tranel, D., & Damasio, H. (2000). Characterization of the decision-making deficit of patients with ventromedial prefrontal cortex lesions. *Brain, 123*, 2189–2202.
Bechara, A., Tranel, D., Damasio, H., Adolphs, R., Rockland, C., & Damasio, A. R. (1995). Double dissociation of conditioning and declarative knowledge relative to the amygdala and hippocampus in humans. *Science, 269*, 1115–1118.
Berlin, H. A., Rolls, E. T., & Kischka, U. (2004). Impulsivity, time perception, emotion and reinforcement sensitivity in patients with orbitofrontal cortex lesion. *Brain, 127*, 1108–1126.
Berntson, G. G., Sarter, M., & Cacioppo, J. T. (1998). Anxiety and cardiovascular reactivity: The basal forebrain cholinergic link. *Behavioural Brain Research, 94*, 225–248.
Blood, A. J., & Zatorre, R. J. (2001). Intensely pleasurable responses to music correlate with activity in brain regions implicated with reward and emotion. *Proceedings of the National Academy of Sciences of the USA, 98*, 11818–11823.
Borsutzky, S., Brand, M., & Fujiwara, E. (2000). Basal forebrain amnesia. *Neurocase, 6*, 377–391.
Brand, M., Fujiwara, E., Kalbe, E., Steingass, H.-P., Kessler, J., & Markowitsch, H. J. (2003). Cognitive estimation and affective judgments in alcoholic Korsakoff patients. *Journal of Clinical and Experimental Neuropsychology, 25*, 324–334.
Brand, M., & Markowitsch, H. J. (2006). Memory processes and the orbitofrontal cortex. In D. Zald, & S. Rauch (Eds.), *The orbitofrontal cortex* (pp. 285–306). Oxford, UK: Oxford University Press.
Brandt, T., Schautzer, F., Hamilton, D. A., Brüning, R., Markowitsch, H. J., Kalla, R., et al. (2005). Vestibular loss causes hippocampal atrophy and impaired spatial memory in humans. *Brain*, 128, 2732–2741.

Breitenstein, C., Daum, I., & Ackermann, H. (1998). Emotional processing following cortical and subcortical brain damage: Contributions of the fronto-striatal circuitry. *Behavioural Neurology, 11*, 1–14.

Breitenstein, C., Daum, I., Ackermann, H., Lütgehetmann, R., & Müller, E. (1996). Erfassung der Emotionswahrnehmung bei zentralnervösen Läsionen und Erkrankungen: Psychometrische Gütekriterien der "Tübinger Affekt Batterie" [Assessing the perception of emotions in lesions and disorders of the central nervous system]. *Neurologische Rehabilitation, 2*, 93–101.

Breitenstein, C., van Lancker, D., Daum, I., & Waters, C. H. (2001). Impaired perception of vocal emotions in Parkinson's disease: Influence of speech time processing and executive functioning. *Brain and Cognition, 45*, 277–314.

Broca, P. (1878). Anatomie comparée des circonvolutions cérébrales. Le grand lobe limbique et la scissure limbique dans la série des mammiféres [Comparative anatomy of the cerebral lobes. The grand limbic lobe and the limbic fissure throughout mammalian phylogeny]. *Revue Anthropologie, 2*, 385–498.

Brown, M. W., & Bashir, Z. I. (2002). Evidence concerning how neurons of the perirhinal cortex may effect familiarity discrimination. *Philosophical Transactions of the Royal Society of London B: Biological Sciences, 357*, 1083–1095.

Buchanan, T. W., Tranel, D., & Adolphs, R. (2003). A specific role for the human amygdala in olfactory memory. *Learning and Memory, 10*, 319–325.

Büchel, C., Morris, J., Dolan, R. J., & Friston, K. J. (1998). Brain systems mediating aversive conditioning: An event-related fMRI study. *Neuron, 20*, 947–957.

Cahill, L., Babinsky, R., Markowitsch, H. J., & McGaugh, J. L. (1995). Involvement of the amygdaloid complex in emotional memory. *Nature, 377*, 295–296.

Cancelliere, A. E., & Kertesz, A. (1990). Lesion localization in acquired deficits of emotional expression and comprehension. *Brain and Cognition, 13*, 133–147.

Cardinal, R. N., Parkinson, J. A., Hall, J., & Everitt, B. J. (2002). Emotion and motivation: The role of the amygdala, ventral striatum, and prefrontal cortex. *Neuroscience and Biobehavioral Reviews, 26*, 321–352.

Carmichael, S. T., & Price, J. L. (1995). Limbic connections of the orbital and medial prefrontal cortex in Macaque monkeys. *Journal of Comparative Neurology, 363*, 615–641.

Carter, C. S., Braver, T. S., Barch, D. M., Botvinick, M. M., Noll, D., & Cohen, J. D. (1998). Anterior cingulate cortex, error detection, and the online monitoring of performance. *Science, 280*, 747–749.

Chapman, W. P., Livingston, R. B., & Livingston, K. E. (1949). Frontal lobotomy and electrical stimulation of orbital surface and frontal lobes. A.M.A. *Archives of Neurology and Psychiatry, 62*, 701–716.

Cramon, D. Y. von, & Markowitsch, H. J. (2000). The septum and human memory. In R. Numan (Ed.), *The behavioral neuroscience of the septal region* (pp. 380–413). Berlin: Springer.

Cramon, D. Y. von, Markowitsch, H. J., & Schuri, U. (1993). The possible contribution of the septal region to memory. *Neuropsychologia, 31*, 1159–1180.

Damasio, A. R. (1999). *The feeling of what happens. Body and emotion in the making of consciousness*. New York: Harcourt Brace.

Damasio, A. R., Eslinger, P. J., Damasio, H., Van Hoesen, G. W., & Cornell, S. (1985a). Multimodal amnesic syndrome following bilateral temporal and basal forebrain damage. *Archives of Neurology, 42*, 263–271.

Damasio, A. R., Graff-Radford, N. R., Eslinger, P. J., Damasio, H., & Kassell, N. (1985b). Amnesia following basal forebrain lesions. *Archives of Neurology, 42*, 263–271.

Daum, I., & Ackermann, H. (1994). Frontal-type memory impairment associated with thalamic damage. *International Journal of Neuroscience, 77*, 187–198.

Daum, I., Flor, H., Brodbeck, S., & Birbaumer, N. (1996). Autobiographical memory for emotional events in amnesia. *Behavioural Neurology, 9*, 57–67.

Davidson, R. J. (2003). Seven sins in the study of emotion: Correctives from affective neuroscience. *Brain and Cognition, 52*, 129–132.
Delgado, J. M. R. (1969). *Physical control of the mind. Towards a psycho-civilized society.* New York: Harper & Row.
Delgado, J. M. R. (1987). Electrical stimulation of the brain. In G. Adelman (Ed.), *Encyclopedia of neuroscience* (Vol. 1, pp. 368–371). Boston, MA: Birkhäuser.
Devinsky, O., Morrell, M. J., & Vogt, B. A. (1995). Contributions of the anterior cingulate cortex to behaviour. *Brain, 118*, 279–306.
Diergaarde, L. (2004). *Social and cognitive dysfunction following neonatal amygdala damage.* Rotterdam, NL: Optima Grafische Communcate.
Driessen, M., Beblo, T., Mertens, M., Piefke, M., Rullkötter, N., Silva Saveedra, A., et al. (2004). Different fMRI activation patterns of traumatic memory in borderline personality disorder with and without additional posttraumatic stress disorder. *Biological Psychiatry, 55*, 603–611.
Eimer, M., Holmes, A., & McGlone, F. P. (2003). The role of spatial attention in the processing of facial expression: An ERP study of rapid brain responses to six basic emotions. *Cognitive, Affective and Behavioral Neuroscience, 3*, 97–110.
Ekman, P., & Friesen, W. (1975). *Unmasking the face.* Englewood Cliffs, NJ: Prentice Hall.
Eslinger, P. J. (1998). Neurological and neuropsychological bases of empathy. *European Neurology, 39*, 193–199.
Eslinger, P. J. (1999a). Orbital frontal cortex: Historical and contemporary views about its behavioral and physiological significance. An introduction to special topic papers: Part I. *Neurocase, 5*, 225–229.
Eslinger, P. J. (1999b). Orbital frontal cortex: Behavioral and physiological significance. An introduction to special topic papers: Part II. *Neurocase, 5*, 299–300.
Fellows, L. K., & Farah, M. J. (2005). Different underlying impairments in decision-making following ventromedial and dorsolateral frontal lobe damage in humans. *Cerebral Cortex, 15*, 58–63.
Funayama, E. S., Grillon, C., Davis, M., & Phelps, E. A. (2001). A double dissociation in the affective modulation of startle in humans: Effects of unilateral temporal lobectomy. *Journal of Cognitive Neuroscience, 13*, 721–729.
de Gelder, B., Pourtois, G., & Weiskrantz, L. (2002). Fear recognition in the voice is modulated by unconsciously recognized facial expressions but not by unconsciously recognized affective pictures. *Proceedings of the National Academy of Sciences of the USA, 99*, 4121–4126.
Gray, J. R., Braver, T. S., & Raichle, M. E. (2002). Integration of emotion and cognition in the lateral prefrontal cortex. *Proceedings of the National Academy of Sciences of the USA, 99*, 4115–4120.
Grelotti, D. J., Klin, A. J., Gauthier, I., Skudlarski, P., Cohen, D. J., Gore, J. C., et al. (2005). fMRI activation of the fusiform gyrus and amygdala to cartoon characters but not to faces in a boy with autism. *Neuropsychologia, 43*, 373–385.
Groenewegen, H. J., Wright, C. I., & Beijer, A. V. J. (1996). The nucleus accumbens: Gateway for limbic structures to reach the motor system? In G. Holstege, R. Bandler, & C. B. Saper (Eds.), *The emotional motor system: Progress in brain research* (Vol. 107, pp. 485–511). Amsterdam: Elsevier.
Hadland, K. A., Rushworth, M. F. S., Gaffan, D., & Passingham, R. E. (2003). The effect of cingulate lesions on social behaviour and emotion. *Neuropsychologia, 41*, 919–931.
Halpern, F. (1930). Kasuistischer Beitrag zur Funktion des Stirnhirns [Case reports on the function of the frontal lobe]. *Archiv für Psychiatrie und Nervenkrankheiten, 90*, 446–456.
Hamm, A. O. (2003). Psychologie der Emotionen [Psychology of the emotions]. In H. O. Karnath, & P. Thier (Eds.), *Neuropsychologie* (pp. 559–580). Berlin: Springer.
Harlow, J. M. (1848). Passage of an iron rod through the head. *Boston Medical and Surgical Journal, 39*, 389–393.

Harlow, J. M. (1869). *Recovery from the passage of an iron bar through the head.* Boston, MA: D. Clapp and Son.

Hess, W. R., & Brügger, M. (1943). Das subkortikale Zentrum der affektiven Abwehrreaktion [The subcortical area of affective defense reactions]. *Helvetica Physiologica Acta, 1*, 33–52.

Hirono, N., Mori, E., Ishii, K., Ikejiri, Y., Imamura, T., Shimomura, T., et al. (1998). Hypofunction in the posterior cingulate gyrus correlates with disorientation for time and place in Alzheimer's disease. *Journal of Neurology, Neurosurgery, and Psychiatry, 64*, 552–554.

Holländer, B. (1900). *Die Lokalisation der psychischen Thätigkeiten im Gehirn. Ergebnisse der Experimental-Physiologie, von Sectionsbefunden, von anatomischen und klinischen Beobachtungen, verwerthet für die Localisationslehre und Psychiatrie* [The localization of psychic functions in the brain. Results of experimental physiology, observations from sections, and anatomical and clinical observations, evaluated for the theory of localization and psychiatry]. Berlin: August Hirschwald.

Hornak, J., Bramham, J., Rolls, E. T., Morris, R. G., O'Doherty, J., Bullock, P. R., et al. (2003). Changes in emotion after circumscribed surgical lesions of the orbitofrontal and cingulate cortices. *Brain, 126*, 1691–1712.

Hutchison, W. D., Davis, K. D., Lozano, A. M., Tasker, R. R., & Dostrovsky, J. O. (1999). Pain-related neurons in the human cingulate cortex. *Nature Neuroscience, 2*, 403–405.

Ikemoto, S., & Panksepp, J. (1999). The role of nucleus accumbens dopamine in motivated behavior: A unifying interpretation with special reference to reward-seeking. *Brain Research Reviews, 31*, 6–41.

Irle, E., & Markowitsch, H. J. (1982). Connections of the hippocampal formation, mammillary bodies, anterior thalamus and cingulate cortex. A retrograde study using horseradish peroxidase in the cat. *Experimental Brain Research, 47*, 79–94.

Izard, C. E. (1971). *The face of emotion*. New York: Appleton-Century-Crofts.

Jokisch, D., Bellebaum, C., & Daum, I. (2005). Das serotonerge System und Kognition [The serotonergic system and cognition]. In H. Przuntek, & T. Müller (Eds.), *Das serotonerge System aus neurologischer und psychiatrischer Sicht* (pp. 39–53). Darmstadt, Germany: Steinkopf.

Kaufer, D., Friedman, A., Seldman, S., & Soreq, H. (1998). Acute stress facilitates long-lasting changes in cholinergic gene expression. *Nature, 393*, 373–377.

Klüver, H., & Bucy, P. C. (1937). "Psychic blindness" and other symptoms following bilateral lobectomy in rhesus monkeys. *American Journal of Physiology, 119*, 352–353.

Knörlein (no first name given) (1865). Krankengeschichte und Sectionsbefund eines basalen Hirntumors [Case history and autopsy of a basal brain tumor]. *Allgemeine Wiener Medicinische Zeitschrift, 15*, 250–252.

Krakowski, M. (2003). Violence and serotonin: Influence on impulse control, affect regulation and social functioning. *Journal of Neuropsychiatry and Clinical Neuroscience, 15*, 294–305.

LaBar, K. S., Gatemby, J. C., Gore, J. C., LeDoux, J. E., & Phelps, E. A. (1998). Human amygdala activation during conditioned fear acquisition and extinction: A mixed-trial fMRI study. *Neuron, 20*, 937–945.

LaBar, K. S., LeDoux, J. E., Spencer, D. D., & Phelps, E. A. (1995). Impaired fear conditioning following unilateral temporal lobectomy in humans. *Journal of Neuroscience, 15*, 6846–6855.

Lane, R. D., Reiman, E. M., Axelrod, B., Yun, L.-S., Holmes, A., & Schwartz, G. E. (1998). Neural correlated of levels of emotional awareness: Evidence of an interaction between emotion and attention in the anterior cingulate cortex. *Journal of Cognitive Neuroscience, 10*, 525–535.

Lang, P. J. (1995). The emotion probe. *American Psychologist, 50*, 372–385.

Lautin, A. (2001). *The limbic brain*. New York: Kluwer Academic/Plenum.

LeDoux, J. E. (1994). Emotion, memory and the brain. *Scientific American, 270*, 32–39.

LeDoux, J. E. (1995). Emotion: Clues from the brain. *Annual Review of Psychology, 46*, 209–235.
LeDoux, J. E. (1996). *The emotional brain: The mysterious underpinnings of emotional life*. New York: Simon and Schuster.
LeDoux, J. E. (1998a). *The emotional brain*. New York: Touchstone.
LeDoux J. E. (1998b). Fear and the brain: Where have we been, and where are we going? *Biological Psychiatry, 44*, 1229–1238.
LeDoux, J. E., & Phelps, E. (2000). Emotional networks in the brain. In M. Lewis, & J. M. Haviland (Eds.), *Handbook of emotions* (pp. 157–172). New York: Guilford Press.
Lilly, R., Cummings, J. L., Benson, D. F., & Frankel, M. (1983). The human Klüver-Bucy syndrome. *Neurology, 33*, 1141–1145.
Livingston, K. E., & Escobar, A. (1971). The anatomical bias of the limbic system concepts: A proposed reorientation. *Archives of Neurology, 24*, 90.
Luciana, M., Burgund, E. D., Berman, M., & Hanson, K. L. (2001). Effects of tryptophan loading on verbal, spatial and affective working memory functions in healthy adults. *Journal of Psychopharmacology, 15*, 219–230.
MacLean, P. D. (1949). Psychosomatic disease and the "visceral brain." *Psychosomatic Medicine, 11*, 338–353.
MacLean, P. D. (1970). The triune brain, emotion, and the scientific bias. In F. O. Schmitt (Ed.), *The neurosciences: Second study program* (pp. 336–349). New York: Rockefeller University Press.
MacLean, P. D. (1990). *The triune brain in evolution*. New York: Plenum Press.
Maguire, E. A., Gadian, D. G., Johnsrude, I. S., Good, C. D., Ashburner, J., Frackowiak, R. S. J., et al. (2000). Navigation-related structural change in the hippocampi of taxi drivers. *Proceedings of the National Academy of Sciences of the USA, 97*, 4398–4403.
Mark, L. P., Daniels, D. L., Naidich, T. P., & Hendrix, L. E. (1995). Limbic connections. *American Journal of Neuroradiology, 16*, 1303–1306.
Markowitsch, H. J. (1992). *Intellectual functions and the brain. An historical perspective*. Toronto: Hogrefe & Huber.
Markowitsch, H. J. (1998/99). Differential contribution of the right and left amygdala to affective information processing. *Behavioural Neurology, 11*, 233–244.
Markowitsch, H. J. (1999a). Limbic system. In R. Wilson, & F. Keil (Eds.), *The MIT encyclopedia of the cognitive sciences* (pp. 472–475). Cambridge, MA: MIT Press.
Markowitsch, H. J. (1999b). *Gedächtnisstörungen* [Memory disorders]. Stuttgart, Germany: Kohlhammer.
Markowitsch, H. J., Calabrese, P., Würker, M., Durwen, H. F., Kessler, J., Babinsky, R., et al. (1994). The amygdala's contribution to memory: A PET-study on two patients with Urbach-Wiethe disease. *NeuroReport, 5*, 1349–1352.
Markowitsch, H. J., Cramon, D. Y. von, & Schuri, U. (1993). Mnestic performance profile of a bilateral diencephalic infarct patient with preserved intelligence and severe amnesic disturbances. *Journal of Clinical and Experimental Neuropsychology, 15*, 627–652.
Markowitsch, H. J., Kessler, J., & Denzler, P. (1986). Recognition memory and psychophysiological responses towards stimuli with neutral or emotional content: A study of Korsakoff patients and recently detoxified and long-term abstinent alcoholics. *International Journal of Neuroscience, 29*, 1–35.
Markowitsch, H. J., Vandekerckhove, M. M. P., Lanfermann, H., & Russ, M. O. (2003). Brain circuits for the retrieval of sad and happy autobiographic episodes. *Cortex, 39*, 643–665.
Mesulam, M.-M. (1995). Cholinergic pathways and the ascending reticular activation system of the human brain. In L. G. Abood, & A. Lajtha (Eds.), *Functional diversity of interacting receptors. Annals of the New York Academy of Sciences* (Vol. 757, pp. 169–179). New York: Academy.

Mesulam, M.-M. (2000). Behavioral neuroanatomy. Large-scale networks, association cortex, frontal syndromes, the limbic system, and hemispheric specializations. In M.-M. Mesulam (Ed.), *Principles of cognitive and behavioral neurology* (pp. 1–120). New York: Oxford University Press.

Meunier, M., Bachevalier, J., & Mishkin, M. (1997). Effects of orbital frontal and anterior cingulated lesions on object and spatial memory in rhesus monkeys. *Neuropsychologia, 35*, 999–1015.

Monnot, M., Nixon, S., Lovallo, W., & Ross, E. (2001). Altered emotional perception in alcoholics: Deficits in affective prosody comprehension. *Alcoholism: Clinical and Experimental Research, 25*, 362–369.

Montagne, B. (2005). *Perception of facial expressions in psychiatric and neurological disorders.* Utrecht, NL: Febodruk.

Morris, J. S., de Gelder, B., Weiskrantz, L., & Dolan, R. J. (2001). Differential extrageniculostriate and amygdala responses to presentation of emotional faces in a cortically blind field. *Brain, 124*, 1241–1252.

Najib, A., Lorberbaum, J. P., Kose, S., Bohning, D. E., & George, M. S. (2004). Regional brain activity in women grieving a romantic relationship breakup. *American Journal of Psychiatry, 161*, 2245–2256.

Nauta, W. J. H. (1979). Expanding borders of the limbic system concept. In T. Rasmussen, & R. Marino (Eds.), *Functional neurosurgery* (pp. 7–23). New York: Raven Press.

Nieuwenhuys, R. (1996). The greater limbic system, the emotional motor system and the brain. In G. Holstege, R. Bandler, & C. B. Saper (Eds.), *The emotional motor system. Progress in Brain Research* (Vol. 107, pp. 551–580). Amsterdam: Elsevier.

Nieuwenhuys, R., Voogt, J., & van Huizen, C. (1988). *The human central nervous system. A synopsis and atlas* (3rd ed.). Berlin: Springer.

Olds, J. (1956). Pleasure centers in the brain. *Scientific American, 195*, 105–116.

Olds, J., & Milner, P. (1954). Positive reinforcement produced by electrical stimulation of septal area and other regions of the rat brain. *Journal of Comparative and Physiological Psychology, 47*, 419–427.

Panksepp, J. (1998). *Affective neuroscience.* New York: Oxford University Press.

Papez, J. W. (1937). A proposed mechanism of emotion. A.M.A. *Archives of Neurology and Psychiatry, 38*, 725–743.

Parkinson, J. A., Robbins, T. W., & Everitt, B. J. (2000). Dissociable roles of the central and basolateral amygdala in appetitive emotional learning. *European Journal of Neuroscience, 12*, 405–413.

Paulus, M. P., & Frank, L. R. (2003). Ventromedial prefrontal cortex activation is critical for preference judgments. *NeuroReport, 14*, 1311–1315.

Paus, T. (2001). Primate anterior cingulate cortex: Where motor control, drive and cognition interface. *Nature Reviews Neuroscience, 2*, 417–424.

Penfield, W. (1975). *The mystery of the mind.* Princeton, NJ: Princeton University Press.

Peyron, R., Laurent, B., & Garcia-Larrea, L. (2000). Functional imaging of brain responses to pain. A review and meta-analysis. *Neurophysiologie Clinique, 30*, 263–288.

Phan, K. L., Fitzgerald, D. A., Cortese, B. M., Seraji-Bozorgzad, N., Tancer, M. E., & Moore, G. J. (2005). Anterior cingulate neurochemistry in social anxiety disorder: ^{1}H-MRS at 4Tesla. *NeuroReport, 16*, 183–186.

Phelps, E. A., LaBar, K. S., Anderson, A. K., O'Connor, K. J., Fulbright, R. K., & Spencer, D. D. (1998). Specifying the contributions of the human amygdala to emotional memory: A case study. *Neurocase, 4*, 527–540.

Philippot, P., Kornreich, C., Blairy, S., Baert, I., Den Dulk, A., LeBon, O., et al. (1999). Alcoholics' deficits in the decoding of emotional facial expression. *Alcoholism: Clinical and Experimental Research, 23*, 1031–1038.

Phillips, M. L., Drevets, W. C., Rauch, S. L., & Lane, R. (2003). Neurobiology of emotion perception I: The neural basis of normal emotion perception. *Biological Psychiatry, 54*, 504–514.
Piefke, M., Weiss, P. H., Zilles, K., Markowitsch, H. J., & Fink, G. R. (2003). Differential remoteness and emotional tone modulate the neural correlates of autobiographical memory. *Brain, 126*, 850–868.
Poeck, K. (1985). The Klüver-Bucy syndrome in man. In J. A. M. Frederiks (Ed.), *Handbook of clinical neurology* (Vol. 1[45] Clinical neuropsychology, pp. 257–263). Amsterdam: Elsevier Science.
Pritchard, T. C., Macaluso, D. A., & Eslinger, P. J. (1999). Taste perception in patients with insular cortex lesions. *Behavioral Neuroscience, 113*, 663–671.
Ptak, R., & Schnider, A. (1999). Spontaneous confabulations after orbifrontal damage: The role of temporal context confusion and self-monitoring. *Neurocase, 5*, 243–250.
Rahman, S., Sahakian, B. J., Cardinal, R., Rogers, R., & Robbins, T. (2001). Decision making and neuropsychiatry. *Trends in Cognitive Science, 5*, 271–277.
Rolls, E. T. (2004). The functions of the orbitofrontal cortex. *Brain and Cognition, 55*, 11–29.
Sander, K., & Scheich, H. (2001). Auditory perception of laughing and crying activates human amygdala regardless of attentional state. *Cognitive Brain Research, 12*, 181–198.
Sarter, M., & Markowitsch, H. J. (1985a). The amygdala's role in human mnemonic processing. *Cortex, 21*, 7–24.
Sarter, M., & Markowitsch, H. J. (1985b). The involvement of the amygdala in learning and memory: A critical review with emphasis on anatomical relations. *Behavioral Neuroscience, 99*, 342–380.
Satish, U., Streufert, S., & Eslinger, P. J. (1999). Complex decision making after orbifrontal damage: Neuropsychological and strategic management simulation assessment. *Neurocase, 5*, 355–364.
Schnider, A. (2001). Spontaneous confabulation, reality monitoring, and the limbic system: A review. *Brain Research Reviews, 36*, 150–160.
Schnider, A., Gutbrod, K., Hess, C. W., & Schroth, G. (1996). Memory without context: Amnesia with confabulations after infarction of the right capsular genu. *Journal of Neurology, Neurosurgery, and Psychiatry, 61*, 186–193.
Séguin, J. R. (2004). Neurocognitive elements of antisocial behavior: Relevance of an orbitofrontal cortex account. *Brain and Cognition, 55*, 185–197.
Shamay-Tsoory, S. G., Tomer, R., Berger, B. D., & Aharon-Peretz, J. (2003). Characterization of empathy deficits following prefrontal brain damage: The role of the right ventromedial prefrontal cortex. *Journal of Cognitive Neuroscience, 15*, 324–337.
Siebert, M., Markowitsch, H. J., & Bartel, P. (2003). Amygdala, affect, and cognition. *Brain, 126*, 2627–2637.
Snitz, B. E., Hellinger, A., & Daum, I. (2002). Impaired processing of affective prosody in Korsakoff's syndrome. *Cortex, 38*, 797–803.
Sprengelmeyer, R., Rausch, M., Eysel, U. T., & Przuntek, H. (1998). Neural structures associated with recognition of facial expressions of basic emotions. *Proceedings of the Royal Society of London, 265*, 1927–1931.
Sprengelmeyer, R., Young, A. W., Schroeder, U., Grossenbacher, P. G., Federlein, J., Büttner, T., et al. (1999). Knowing no fear. *Proceedings of the Royal Society of London B, 266*, 2451–2456.
Stephan, H. (1975). *Allocortex. Handbuch der mikroskopischen Anatomie des Menschen* (Vol. 4, Part 9) [Allocortex: Handbook of microscopic human anatomy]. Berlin: Springer.
Stuss, D. T., Alexander, M. P., Floden, D., Binns, M. A., Levine, B., McIntosh, A. R., et al. (2002). Fractionation and localization of distinct frontal lobe processes: Evidence from focal lesions in humans. In D. T. Stuss, & R. T. Knight (Eds.), *Principles of frontal lobe function* (pp. 392–407). New York: Oxford University Press.

Sugiura, M., Shah, N. J., Zilles, K., & Fink, G. R. (2005). Cortical representations of personally familiar objects and places: Functional organization of the human posterior cingulate cortex. *Journal of Cognitive Neuroscience*, *17*, 183–198.

Swanson, L. W., & Petrovich, G. D. (1998). What is the amygdala? *Trends in Neuroscience*, *21*(8), 323–331.

Tranel, D., Bechara, A., & Denburg, N. L. (2002). Asymmetric functional roles of right and left ventromedial prefrontal cortices in social conduct, decision-making, and emotional processing. *Cortex*, *38*, 589–612.

Tranel, D., & Hyman, B. T. (1990). Neuropsychological correlates of bilateral amygdala damage. *Archives of Neurology*, *47*, 349–355.

Uekermann, J., Daum, I., Schlebusch, P., & Trenckmann, U. (2005). Processing of affective stimuli in alcoholism. *Cortex*, *41*, 189–194.

Victor, M., Adams, R. D., & Collins, G. H. (Eds.). (1989). *The Wernicke-Korsakoff syndrome and related neurologic disorders due to alcoholism and malnutrition* (2nd ed.). Philadelphia, PA: F. A. Davis Company.

Voegelin, H. (1897). Beitrag zur Kenntnis der Stirnhirn-Erkrankungen [Contribution to knowledge on frontal lobe disorders]. *Allgemeine Zeitschrift für Psychiatrie und ihre Grenzgebiete*, *54*, 588–599.

Vogt, B. A., Nimchinsky, E. A., Vogt, L. J., & Hof, P. R. (1995). Human cingulate cortex: Surface features, flat maps, and cytoarchitecture. *Journal of Comparative Neurology*, *359*, 490–506.

Welt, L. (1888). Ueber Charakterveränderungen des Menschen infolge von Läsionen des Stirnhirns [Changes in human character after frontal lobe lesions]. *Deutsches Archiv für klinische Medicin*, *42*, 339–390 (and 1 Table).

Wicker, B., Keysers, C., Plailly, J., Royet, J.-P., Gallese, V., & Rizzolatti, G. (2003). Both of us disgusted in my insula: The common neural basis of seeing and feeling disgust. *Neuron*, *40*, 655–664.

Wildgruber, D., Pihan, H., & Ackermann, H. (2002). Dynamic brain activation during processing of emotional intonation: Influence of acoustic parameters, emotional valence and sex. *NeuroImage*, *15*, 856–869.

Zald, D. H., & Pardo, J. V. (1997). Emotion, olfaction, and the human amygdala: Amygdala activation during aversive olfactory stimulation. *Proceedings of the National Academy of Sciences of the USA*, *94*, 4119–4124.

Milestones and Mechanisms of Emotional Development

Manfred Holodynski

Abstract This chapter describes central stages in the development of emotions and emotion regulation. A developmental theory is proposed that focuses on the complex interaction of emotions and social interactions. Expression signs for emotions in caregiver–child interaction are seen as an important mediating factor that serves as the critical means of communication, particularly during early ontogenesis, and through which culture enters emotion. The growing ability to regulate emotions *intra*personally becomes increasingly important for a socially coordinated and adequate regulation of actions. Based on recent empirical evidence, three of the five stages of emotional development are described: (1) The stereotypical precursor emotions of newborns are followed by sign-mediated emotion systems in the toddler that are based on caregiver–child interactions. These are mediated by expression signs modulated, and in part created, by the cultural context. Their purpose is to influence the caregiver's behavior in terms of caring for the child; that is, they serve an *inter*personal regulation function. (2) Starting at toddler's age, emotions begin to serve an *intra*personal regulation function; that is, they direct the child's behavior toward his or her own motives. Thus children actively learn to control their emotions. (3) During school age, the increasing internalization of emotional expression signs (making them "invisible" to an observer) is associated with adherence to cultural rules as well as with the possibility of deception. The ability to regulate emotions becomes more efficient owing to more flexible social coordination of motive satisfaction.

How do human emotions develop? Although this question seems so simple, a scientific answer calls for a highly complex approach. The first thing that has to be decided is what one wants to define as an emotion. It is then necessary to conceive of dimensions on which emotions can in any way develop and use them

M. Holodynski (✉)
Psychology and Sport Studies, University of Münster,
Münster, Germany
e-mail: manfred.holodynski@uni-muenster.de

B. Röttger-Rössler, H.J. Markowitsch (eds.), *Emotions as Bio-cultural Processes*,
DOI 10.1007/978-0-387-09546-2_7, © Springer Science+Business Media, LLC 2009

to describe emotional processes in infants and adults. Should these differ to a major extent—and this does seem to be the case—a theory is needed that can explain how infant emotions may develop through empirically confirmed steps into adult emotions and which mechanisms underlie this development. A variety of past theories on emotions differ greatly in the importance assigned to the biological anchoring of versus sociocultural influences on emotions. However, current theories on emotion have dropped this controversial "either–or" approach in favor of a complex synthesis of the two (see Campos, Kermoian, & Witherington, 1996; Frijda, 1986; Lazarus, 1991; Scherer, 2001; Sroufe, 1996).

In this chapter, I follow the approach described above and present an integrative, socioculturally oriented phase model as my theory: the internalization model of emotional development (see Holodynski & Friedlmeier, 2006). I name the central developmental tasks for each phase—the milestones—and describe the underlying mechanisms.

Definition of Emotion

An emotion is defined here as a functional psychological system involving the synchronic interplay of several components that serves to regulate the actions in the individual action system in line with that individual's motives and concerns (see also Frijda, 1986; Scherer, 2001).

Within this framework, an emotion is made up of four components (see Fig. 1): appraisal, expression, body regulation, and feeling. These components

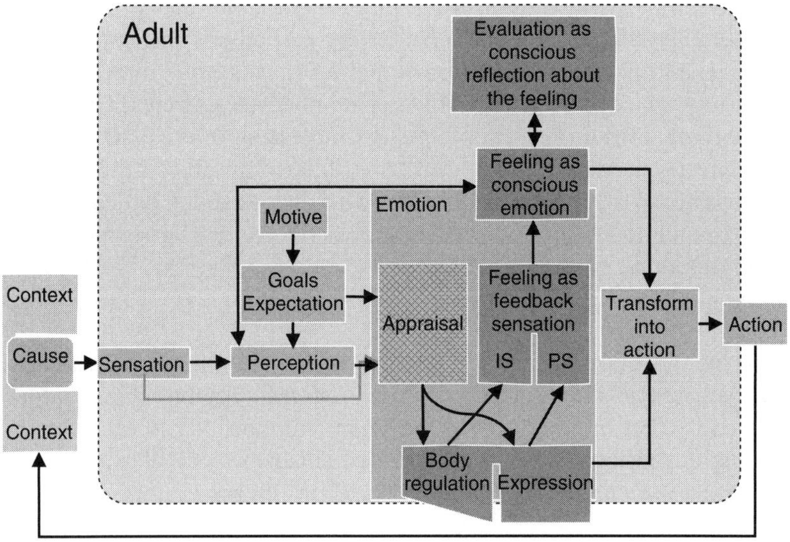

Fig. 1 Structure of emotion in an adult. *IS*, interoceptive body sensations; *PS*, proprioceptive body sensations

form a dynamic psychological system that takes the following prototypical course.

1. External (e.g., a birthday present) or internal (e.g., a mental projection) context-related triggers are appraised in terms of their significance for satisfying one's own motives.
2. This appraisal triggers adaptive expressive and body reactions.
3. Through body feedback, these reactions are experienced subjectively as bodily sensations that are related to the trigger of the emotion. It is precisely this that is experienced as a feeling.

The action readiness given objectively in expressive and body reactions and subjectively as a feeling triggers subsequent motive-serving actions either in the individual concerned or in an interaction partner—assuming that the individual does not suppress or modify them (Holodynski & Friedlmeier, 2006; see also Engelen et al., Emotions as Bio-cultural Processes). In the introductory chapter to this section of the book, Engelen et al. present a further distinction in the feeling component: the sensational experience of an emotional state and the conceptualized emotional experience. By the former, we mean the perception of bodily sensations themselves (e.g., experiencing tension in one's abdomen). In the latter, this bodily sensation is related to the trigger of the emotion and is thereby assigned what de Sousa (2003) called a "formal object" (see also the concept of somatic markers in Damasio, 1994, pp. 173–174). It is this that turns a bodily sensation into a feeling. This definition describes an emotion that is "fully functional" in terms of action regulation. In this sense, there is no difference between basic and complex emotions (see Engelen, Anger, Shame, and Justice). Furthermore, later in the chapter I show that this full functionability is not observed in neonates but is a product of development—not just for complex emotions but for basic emotions as well.

A typical feature of an emotion is that the initial *appraisal processes* are generally involuntary and not conscious. They have to be distinguished from any (subsequent) cognitions on the possible trigger of the emotion and its subjective significance because these are voluntary and conscious processes, which Engelen et al. (Emotions as Bio-cultural Processes) called "evaluation/reappraisal."

Regarding the action-regulating function of emotions, the four components of an emotion mentioned above interact systemically, with individuals using the appraisal component to assess how relevant the triggers they perceive are to their motives. Motive is defined initially as a state the individual desires to attain without linking it in advance to any specific source of this motivation or a specific level of consciousness or intentionality. For example, blocking an anticipated action goal triggers anger if the individual attributes this blockage to the intentional action of another person. Modern appraisal theories in the psychology of emotion have analyzed this component in detail (for an overview, see Scherer, Schorr, & Johnstone, 2001).

Because of their expressive and body components, emotions are not purely mental situation appraisals. They embody an active action readiness that sets a subsequent coping action in motion that should transform the current relation between the individual and the environment in line with personal motives and concerns. This second function is analyzed only marginally in appraisal theories even though it represents a major key to understanding the development of emotions, as is shown below.

When these (coping) actions are performed by the individual himself or herself, emotions are applied for *intra*personal regulation. However, motive-serving actions can also be performed vicariously by another individual, in which case emotions are being used for *inter*personal regulation. For example, sorrow may lead individuals to seek out somebody who can comfort and console them (interpersonal regulation). However, it may also lead them to turn away from others and to cry alone and comfort themselves (intrapersonal regulation). Hence, every emotion can be used both inter- and intrapersonally.

Dimensions of Emotional Development

The question regarding what actually develops during emotional development can be broken down along the dimensions described in the following sections.

Quality of an Emotion

It seems that new emotional qualities form during the course of human development. The adult has a number of emotions that a neonate does not yet have. If we look at Lazarus' (1991) list of emotions—shame, guilt, envy, jealousy, pride, relief, hope, empathy—they start to form only during the course of infancy and preschool age. Sroufe (1996) even assumed that other emotions (e.g., anger, fear, sadness, joy, affection) emerge only during the first year of life from initially unfocused, "precursor" emotions. A central question here is which specific features characterize an emotional quality and how far are social and cultural factors involved.

Regulative Function of Emotions

Emotions have the function of regulating actions in a way that serves motives. During infancy, this action-regulating function essentially occurs in the interaction between caregiver and child or, in other words, interpersonally. Caregivers perform all the actions necessary to satisfy the infant's motives because the infant is still unable to master them alone. Caregivers do it by interpreting the infant's expression signs as authentic signals regarding his or her current feeling and then acting according to the perceived appeal function of these expressive reactions. This gives expressive reactions a major mediating role (see below).

It is only among older children, adolescents, and adults that the action-regulating function of emotions becomes, in many cases, *intra*personal: Adults can carry out the actions to serve their emotional action readiness by themselves. The feeling component of the emotion performs the regulative function by signalizing the relevance of stimuli to the individual's motive (see Clore, 1994). Hence, when angry, one *feels* one's tensing muscles as strong arousal, one *feels* the impulse to engage in confrontation and go on the offensive. It is only this continuous self-regulation process that allows the emotion to function smoothly as part of a system. This is because neither the emotion-triggering action and context constellations nor the motive-serving actions are (with few exceptions) innate. They have been learned over the course of ontogenesis. Therefore, during each emotional episode, the trigger of the emotion, the expressive and bodily reactions triggered, and the available actions have to be represented simultaneously with the feeling if they are to become optimally attuned to each other.

From the perspective of developmental psychology, the dominant initial form of regulation is interpersonal. Fogel (1993) talked about "co-regulation" to emphasize the reciprocal interweaving of regulation processes between caregiver and infant. The ontogenetic course of development consists in a shift from *interpersonal* regulation to *intrapersonal* regulation. Sroufe (1996, p. 151) described this accurately when he stated that "one of the most significant aspects of socio-emotional development is the transition from the virtually complete dependency of the infant to the later autonomous functioning of the child."

If, at the beginning of ontogenesis, emotions have an essentially interpersonal regulation function, expressive reactions are one of the central mediators in childhood action regulation, and they perform this role in their *semiotic* function as signs for others. The quality of expression signs and the ability of caregivers to be impressed by the expressive signs of their children then become the focus of analysis.

Form of an Emotion: Expressive Reactions as a Medium of Emotional Development

In line with other syndrome theories in the psychology of emotions (e.g., Ekman, 1984; Izard & Malatesta, 1987; Meyer, Schützwohl, & Reisenzein, 1993, pp. 22–34; Scherer, 1990), an emotion is defined as a configuration of peripheral physiological body changes, forms of expression, and subjective feeling states that depends, in turn, on the appraisal of the emotion-triggering situation. The central question is how much the configuration of these forms of emotion changes over the course of development. There are reasons to assume that is particularly the expression component that changes in ontogenesis and that it takes on a major mediating function in emotional development within the emergence of culturally influenced emotions.

It has already been mentioned above that emotions predominantly serve interpersonal action regulation, particularly at the beginning of ontogenesis. If an interpersonal regulation is to function in any way, it requires a medium that other persons can perceive. This is provided by the expressive reactions of an emotion. The expression is not just facial; it also involves body movement and posture, gestures, tone of voice, eye behavior, personal space, and touch (see Collier, 1985). Expressive reactions consist of behaviors that establish or reinforce, weaken, or discontinue a specific form of contact with aspects of the environment or are intended to do this.

There are two ways in which expressive reactions can be used to change the relation between the individual and the environment (see Frijda, 1986, p. 13).

- *Instrumental use*. Expressive reactions change the relation between the individual and the environment *directly*. A prototypical example is the expression of disgust. This expressive reaction (retching, opening the mouth, pushing out the tongue, wrinkling the nose) reduces contact with an unpleasantly tasting foodstuff and leads to it being disgorged. A range of instrumental expressive reactions are already preprogrammed by protective reflexes, such as the gag reflex for the expression of disgust or the startle reflex for the expression of fear (see Fridlund, 1994, pp. 112–120).
- *Semiotic use*. Expressive reactions change the relation between the individual and the environment *indirectly* by influencing the behavior of an interaction partner so he or she changes the relationship in a way that serves the individual's motives. For example, a feeding caregiver can interpret a baby's expression of disgust as signalizing that he or she is no longer hungry and one should stop feeding. In this case, the expression becomes an expressive *sign* for others.

Using expressive reactions semiotically, that is, as communicative signs, extends the scope for interpersonal regulation enormously. Signs have an impact on the interaction partner as both a symptom and an appeal, as Bühler (1934/1984) noted in his organon model of sign usage (see also Scherer, 1992).

- As a *symptom*, an expressive sign signalizes the current feeling and the action readiness of the sender.
- As an *appeal*, it simultaneously creates a feeling in the receiver that he or she should act in a certain way.

Children who have reached preschool age—and adults even more so—have the ability to apply expressive reactions intentionally or use them deceptively. They then use them as a display (or, in Bühler's terminology, as a symbol). As a symbol or display, an expression sign represents feeling states in a conventionalized form. Children already do this in their role play, just like actors or any normal individual receiving a disappointing present who nonetheless smiles when thanking the giver. A sender who uses an expression sign as a symbol acts as if he or she is currently feeling the feeling expressed to elicit the same appeal effect in the receiver that an actually felt emotion would do.

This ability to use expression signs symbolically is a key mechanism in both culture-historical and ontogenetic terms. It marks the point at which expressive and emotional development leaves its biological cradle and becomes integrated into culture-historical symbol formation processes (e.g., Althoff, 2004). This makes it possible to create new expression signs culture-historically and ontogenetically and assign them a culture-specific meaning that represents corresponding culture-specific situation appraisals, feeling states, and action readiness, thereby allowing new culture-specific emotions to emerge (for more detail, see Holodynski & Friedlmeier, 2006).[1]

Relation of the Subfunction "Emotion" to Other Psychological Subfunctions in Action Regulation

If one wants to uncover the function of a psychological process, one needs a structural model of the complete system in which this subprocess is embedded. This complete psychological system is individual action regulation. At any time point in development, the single psychological subfunctions form a reciprocally coordinated system with an internal structure designed to permit adaptive regulation of action. A central question is how people learn over the course of ontogenesis not only to be guided by their emotions but also, vice versa, to control and regulate them according to consciously set goals. Research on emotion is currently studying this topic intensively under headings such as "emotion regulation" (see Campos, Frankel, & Camras, 2004; Cole, Martin, & Dennis, 2004; Denham, 1998; Friedlmeier, 1999a,b; Underwood, 1997; Walden & Smith, 1997) and "levels of processing" (van Reekum & Scherer, 1997).

Emotion regulation is the ability to modify emotions in terms of their quality, intensity, frequency, course, and expression. In this case, it is not actions that are being regulated by emotions, but the individual (or another person) is performing an action with the goal of modifying the emotion. If one is annoyed about having to wait far too long in a restaurant for one's dinner, one can let off steam by shouting at the waiter—with the goal of getting the food served more quickly (emotional action regulation). Alternatively, one could decide to reinterpret the situation, saying to oneself that the waiter is simply too busy and it is not his fault—with the goal of transforming one's anger into equanimity or sympathy and making the waiting easier to bear (emotion regulation).

Because these forms of regulation are mixed in real-life actions, current developmental research on emotions is increasingly using the term emotion regulation to describe all regulatory processes that emerge in the context of emotions—even those in which emotions trigger actions to serve motives without the emotions being regulated themselves. To some degree, this confusion of terms is understandable because a motive-serving action triggered by an emotion leads, in turn, to a change in the emotion. For example, fear triggers flight—and as a consequence fear is replaced by relief when the individual has successfully escaped danger. Nonetheless, labeling this process emotion regulation leads to the loss of the important conceptual distinction made above between the two complementary processes: emotions regulating actions compared with actions regulating emotions.

Such a confusion of terms can also be the outcome of an all too static approach to emotions in which an emotion simply "triggers" an action and then disappears. Detailed process analysis generally reveals that an emotion subsides only as a function of the success of the action triggered. Hence, the emotion persists alongside the triggered action, and it regulates this action. If being offended by another person triggers indignation, which leads the individual to engage in verbal abuse (as action), the indignation either increases or decreases depending on the impact of the verbal abuse on the offending person. This regulates the verbal abuse by modifying its intensity and direction. In this sense, an emotion regulates subsequent actions and does not just trigger them.

Ontogenetic Phases of Emotional Development

This section presents a developmental theory of emotions that tries to provide first answers to the questions sketched above (for details, see Holodynski & Friedlmeier, 2006). This internalization model divides emotional development into five major phases, of which only the first three are described here. Each phase is characterized by specific emotion-related developmental tasks-called milestones-that children have to master and by specific mechanisms that underlie emotional development (see Fig. 2). The term "phase of development" is applied in the sense that the developmental steps it describes first emerge in this age range.

Ontogenetic Starting Point: With What Are Neonates Equipped When They Enter Our World?

In terms of the above-described systemic characterization of emotions, one cannot, strictly speaking, find any emotions in neonates—only "precursor" emotions (Sroufe, 1996) with which interpersonal regulation can start. Precursor emotions are (1) triggered by absolute physical stimulus thresholds and not by acquired, meaning-related appraisals, and (2) their expressive and bodily reactions are still not coordinated with the situational trigger and context but are, in part, reflex-like (see Fig. 3).

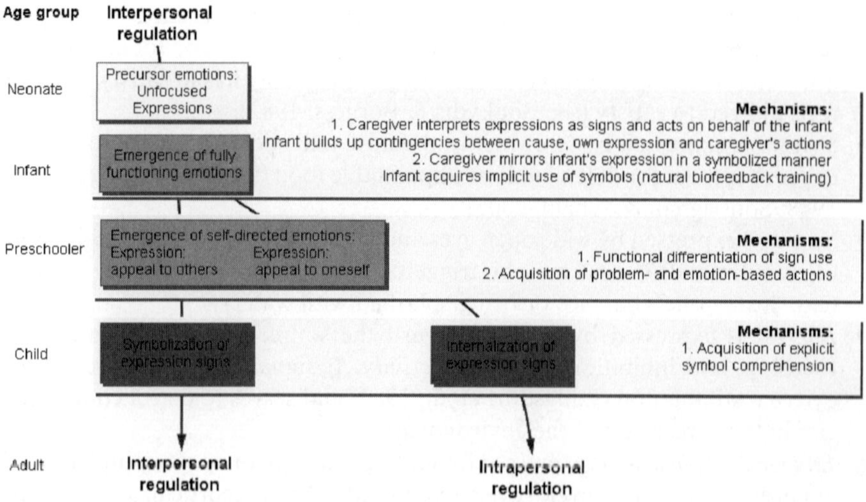

Fig. 2 Milestones and mechanisms of emotional development according to the internalization model

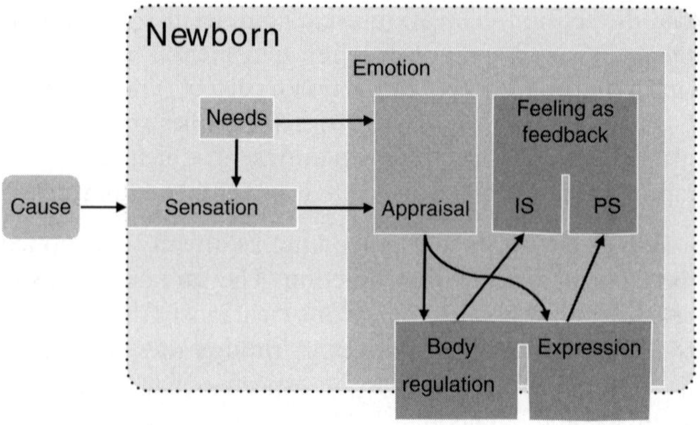

Fig. 3 Structure of an emotion in the neonate. *IS*, interoceptive body sensations, *PS*, proprioceptive body sensations

Research on the emotional reactions of neonates provides unanimous indications that they are able to react consistently to five discernible classes of trigger with five different patterns of expression (see Izard & Malatesta, 1987; Sroufe, 1996). This allows us to conclude that neonates have five precursor emotions at their disposal: distress, disgust, fright, interest, and endogenous pleasure. The main purpose of the first three precursor emotions is to signalize need-related deficit states or impairments of physical integrity, and the last two serve to build up psychological representations of the external environment and the internal body world (e.g., a feeling for tension and relaxation cycles during functional games such as rocking or swinging) (see Sroufe, 1996).

- *Distress* is expressed particularly through crying preceded by motor restlessness. This crying signalizes an urgent need (be it for food, warmth, body contact, or attention) that the caregiver not only has to satisfy but also feels obliged to satisfy (see Boukydis & Burgess, 1982).
- *Disgust* is expressed by screwing up the nose and sticking out the tongue in order to spit out food. It signalizes unpalatable food (see Rosenstein & Oster, 1988; Soussignan & Schaal, 2005).
- *Startle* is expressed by wide open eyes and body tension. It signalizes a threat of overstimulation that may be triggered by an abrupt and strong irritant (e.g., losing one's balance or being splashed with water).
- *Interest* is expressed by turning toward the source of stimulation, visual focusing, and inhibition of motor activity. It signalizes the novelty of an external stimulation (Langsdorf et al., 1983) and serves to detect contingencies in the perception of the environment.
- *Endogenous pleasure* is expressed by smiling that signalizes the completion of a tension–relaxation cycle triggered initially by subcortical stimulation. Nonetheless, over the first weeks of life, it is triggered increasingly when the baby recognizes contingencies between stimuli (e.g., repeatedly seeing the face of the caregiver). According to Sroufe's (1996) tension modulation hypothesis, the tension–relaxation cycle completed by smiling is designed to document the successful construction of a mental representation with a positive emotional marker the caregiver can perceive and toward which he or she direct further actions. By trying to make babies smile and laugh, caregivers intuitively lead them into situations in which they can construct mental representations of perceived environmental contingencies.

These precursor emotions in the neonate, as already mentioned, have an essentially interpersonal regulation function. They are designed so caregivers will interpret them as appeals to carry out vicariously those actions that are necessary to satisfy the infant's motives. Although these findings have been collected in Western cultures, it is to be expected that these five emotional patterns are universal to all neonates. They represent the biological cradle for emotional development. As a result, the precursor emotions are not comparable with the developed emotions of sorrow, disgust, fear, interest, and joy in adults.

Emergence of Sign-Mediated Emotion Systems During Infancy

The first phase of development during babyhood and infancy confronts a child with the following tasks.

- Start with the precursor emotions and build up a differentiated repertoire of emotions conveyed by expression signs
- Acquire a repertoire of actions with which to satisfy one's motives by oneself

In the following sections, we focus particularly on the first developmental task and describe the underlying developmental mechanism.

Developing Differentiated Emotions

Research on neonates and infants indicates that through interpersonal regulation with sensitive caregivers the following functional emotional systems emerge from the five precursor emotions (distress, disgust, fright, interest, endogenous pleasure): (1) frustration, anger, and defiance along with sorrow and sadness; (2) disgust and aversion; (3) fear and embarrassment; (4) interest and surprise; and (5) pleasure, joy, affection, and amusement.

This differentiation process is confirmed by studies on the development of smiling that track how the person- and effect-directed joy of a 6-month-old emerge from endogenous pleasure (see Sroufe, 1996, Chap. 5). Likewise, the cross-sectional study of Stenberg and Campos (1990) showed how the distress reaction of the neonate evolves into the frustration of the 4-month-old and finally the anger of the 7-month-old infant. The development of expressive reactions can be described as follows: The undirected, in part still unorganized expressive reactions of the neonate, which also require some time to "build up steam," turn into cause-directed, emotion-specific organized expression signs with an unequivocal appeal character. The latter follow the cause promptly, their timing and orientation are coordinated with the specific context, their effect is confirmed by appropriate bodily reactions, and they can purposefully trigger motive-serving reactions—generally in the caregiver.

Developmental Mechanism of Emotional Differentiation

Which developmental mechanism underlies this differentiation of fully functional emotions? According to the internalization model, the decisive mechanism is to be found in the interplay between two factors: (1) the caregiver's mirroring of the infant's emotional expression and his or her motive-serving response interacting with (2) the infant's motor mimicry of the caregiver's emotional expression and his or her learning from experience (see Gergely & Watson, 1999).

Infants do not just differentiate their emotions in physical space. They also differentiate them in a semantic space in which their emotional experiences are mediated by the interpretations of their caregivers. The infant's expression signs take on a major mediating role in the emergence of these interpretations—not just as instrumental adaptive reactions to the physical environment but also as signs that impress the caregiver (see Holodynski & Friedlmeier, 2006). Caregivers use the contingency between situational features, their knowledge of the infant, and the infant's current expressive and bodily reactions as a basis by which to deduce his or her emotions and intentions; and they react in line with this interpretation of infant expression. In turn, they deduce how successful or unsuccessful their actions have been based on the subsequent course of infant expression and bodily reactions.

Papoušek and Papoušek (1987, 1999) talk about intuitive parenting in this context. Parents intuitively adapt their communication to the limited perceptions of the infant by reducing the complexity and increasing the succinctness of their messages until they are able to elicit contingent reactions in the infant. They do not just interpret the infant's expression signs as an appeal directed toward them and respond with appropriate care. They additionally try to maintain an optimal level of arousal in the infant at which learning processes can succeed. They make it possible for the infant to experience temporal, sensory, and spatial contingencies between the emotional trigger, emotional expression, and the action that led to the construction of situation-dependent, emotion-specific appraisal patterns in the infant that are determined by the meaning assigned to them and no longer by absolute stimulus qualities.

In addition, caregivers use their own expression to mirror the infant's expression signs in a way that is not only succinct but also corresponds to social conventions. This mirroring enables the infant to experience contingencies between expression, feeling, and its action-regulating consequences, which leads to the emergence of the symbolic use of expression signs and the conscious perception of feelings (see Gergely & Watson, 1999). Stern (1985) called this affect-reflecting mirroring "affect attunement," and he illustrated it with an example.

> A 9-month-old boy bangs his hand on a soft toy, at first in some anger, but gradually with pleasure, exuberance, and humor. He sets up a steady rhythm. Mother falls into his rhythm and says "kaaaaa-*bam* kaaaaa-*bam*." The "*bam*" falling on the stroke and the "kaaaaa" riding with the preparatory upswing and the suspenseful holding of his arm aloft before it falls. (p. 140)

Malatesta and Haviland (1982) have shown that mothers respond selectively to emotion-specific expression signs when interacting with their 3- to 6-month-old infants and that they mirror them intuitively in their own expression. In a play episode and in a reunion episode after a brief separation, mothers responded to the expression of interest by their children with a stronger own expression of interest; to happiness, with increased happiness; and to surprise with stronger surprise—as measured in each case with Izard's (1979) MAX scale. The expression of negative emotions, such as sorrow and anger, was mirrored less frequently but nonetheless more often than chance. However, the expression of anger was at times mirrored only with a knitting of the eyebrows, and negative forms of expression were quickly replaced by more positive ones. In contrast, the expression of distress and simple knit brows were ignored. In the 6-month-olds compared with the 3-month-olds, there was a decline in those expressive reactions that were not mirrored by caregivers such as knit brows. Moreover, the expressive reactions changed far less in 6-month-olds compared with 3-month-olds. In contrast, there was an increased correlation between infant and maternal expression patterns. Hence, a synchronization of infant and maternal expression patterns occurs. Malatesta, Grigoryev, Lamb, Albin, and Culver (1986) also confirmed this developmental trend in a longitudinal study of infants when they were 2.5, 5.0, and 7.5 months old.

To summarize, infant precursor emotions develop into completely functional motive-serving emotions only when the caregiver appropriately interprets the still unfocused infant expression and body reactions, mirrors them in his or her own expression in the form of succinct expression symbols (or displays), and responds promptly with motive-serving actions. Hence, the infant emotion process is initially shared between child and caregiver; they function together as a co-regulated system. Starting with interpersonal regulation initiated by the caregiver, the infant develops increasingly autonomous regulation over the course of the second year of life—particularly by actively demanding the caregiver's support in regulation.

Acquisition of a Repertoire of Actions

Along with this differentiation of emotions, children learn a variety of motive-serving actions during the first 2 years of life, such as fetching things for themselves, handling everyday objects, and extending their range of mobility. As a consequence, by the age of two they can already carry out a number of their motive-serving actions by themselves, making them less completely dependent on vicarious regulation by their caregivers.

Emergence of Intrapersonal Regulation in Toddlers and Preschoolers

The second phase of development when children are toddlers and preschoolers sees the first emergence of *intra*personal regulation. The child becomes increasingly able to perform motive-serving actions alone without any social support and to coordinate his or her satisfying motives with the social environment and situational demands. The emergence of self-evaluative emotions such as pride, shame, and guilt as well as the emergence of symbolically conveyed emotion regulation strategies play a major role here.

During the first phase of development, caregivers make sure they react immediately to the emotional reactions of their infants and satisfy their accompanying motives promptly and appropriately. During the second phase of development, in contrast, they increasingly demand that their children regulate their own actions and emotions themselves. The following developmental tasks emerge for toddlers and preschoolers.

- Perform motive-serving actions by themselves
- Adopt social norms through the formation of the self-evaluative emotions shame and pride
- Acquire emotion regulation strategies

The first task is to *perform motive-serving actions by themselves*. Because children must learn to carry out actions to satisfy their motives by themselves, they are encouraged to use the expression signs and the actions acquired during *inter*personal regulation for their own *intra*personal regulation. Emotional expression should no longer be an appeal directed toward others but should now be understood as an appeal to the self to carry out the necessary actions alone.

The observation that infants do not want to remain alone but always seek the proximity of a familiar person can be explained in terms of the internalization model. Studies in attachment research have shown that separation from the mother in the Strange Situation Test (Ainsworth & Wittig, 1969) and being alone is a stress factor for infants that generally triggers fear of separation, thus motivating them to follow their mothers. In this way, they can ensure that their caregiver remains available for any potentially necessary interpersonal regulation (Spangler, 1999). It is only when they reach preschool age that children become able to remain alone and handle an emotional episode by themselves without immediately seeking another person with whom to share their emotions.

This was confirmed in a cross-sectional study of 4-, 5-, and 6-year-old children (one-half boys and one-half girls) (see Holodynski, 1997, Study V). The children were given a coin with which to purchase a candy packet from a slot machine. They were alone, and when they opened the packet they found that there was no candy in it. On a bipolar rating scale with the poles *joy* and *disappointment*, four-fifths of the children reported being disappointed. Interpersonal regulation (seeking the experimenter) declined from 47% in the 4-year-olds to 10% in the 6-year-olds. The children were given another coin for which they received a full packet of candy from the machine. All children reported joy. Interpersonal regulation declined from 79% in the 4-year-olds to 10% in the 6-year-olds. These findings could also be replicated in a longitudinal study of children aged 4 to 6 years for disappointment (Steinhoff & Holodynski, 2008) and for joy (Holodynski & Steinhoff, 2008).

The second task is to *develop the norm-oriented self-evaluative emotions shame and pride*. In the phase of development that takes place during young childhood, the child must learn that the current motive cannot always be satisfied immediately-that motive satisfaction has to be coordinated with the social environment. This requires the ability to rank motives in a hierarchy, delay their gratification, or drop them completely. Caregivers set behavioral standards and thereby demand that the child forms new motives directed toward maintaining them. The triggers for this development are episodes with caregivers in which the child gains the experience that motives can no longer be satisfied unconditionally and immediately but only when he or she takes the social context of his or her actions into account and orients them toward social norms. The beginning of this process can be seen when a child no longer reacts only with joy over a successful effect but also with pride over meeting a behavioral standard, and he or she no longer reacts just with anger or disappointment over unsuccessful effects but also with shame over failure to comply with a behavioral standard (Barrett, 1995; Holodynski, 1992; Stipek, Recchia, & McClintic, 1992). It should be noted that this emotional norm compliance is not the outcome of a purposeful decision based on conscious insight into the justification for the norm. The latter first emerges at late preschool age.

How does this transition take place? Stipek et al. (1992) and Holodynski (1992) independently developed models in which the social evaluations of childhood activity are assigned a major function in mediating the emergence of pride and shame. Whereas both models broadly agree in their conceptualization of the first two phases of development up to preschool age, their conceptualizations of the subsequent third phase differ regarding the status of the social context in the induction of pride and shame (see Holodynski & Friedlmeier, 2006).

- *First phase.* Up to the third year of life, children are exclusively effect-motivated; they display joy over self-elicited effects and disappointment and anger over failure to elicit successful effects but no self-evaluative reactions in the form of pride and shame. This is the phase in which they are learning to distinguish between self and other. It enables them to become aware of when they are the focus of attention of other persons, which manifests in the first reactions of embarrassment (see Asendorpf, 1990; Lewis, Sullivan, Stanger, & Weiss, 1989). Furthermore, they are learning that their actions do not generate effects just in the physical environment but simultaneously in the social environment. This occurs when caregivers start to apply standards to their children's actions and to praise them for norm-abiding behavior, blame them for norm-violating behavior, and even subject them to social exclusion for strong misbehavior. Because praise and blame also contain an affective component (Harter, 1978), it leads, via the mechanism of emotional contagion, to (1) socially triggered joy in the child after praise and (2) strong feelings of rejection after blame or social exclusion.
- *Second phase.* As already mentioned, in roughly the third year of life, children discover that they can trigger praise or blame in their caregivers through their actions. This discovery leads them to try to determine what elicits the esteem of another person (i.e., the social effect) in order to attain the "pleasure" of its positive affective consequences. This triggers what are the first pride reactions. In situations in which they are confronted with blame and threats of exclusion, they respond with social withdrawal and their first shame reactions.
- *Third phase.* After the third year of life, research by Stipek and other authors (see Belsky, Domitrovich, & Crnic, 1997; Lewis, Alessandri, & Sullivan, 1992) shows that children react with pride when they succeed on difficult tasks rather than easy ones and with shame when they fail on easy tasks rather than difficult ones—without any need for the adult to have previously performed a social evaluation. Stipek (and others such as Heckhausen, 1985)

concluded that this is the age at which children start to evaluate themselves with competence standards because they already react spontaneously with pride or shame.

However, a careful analysis of the experimental settings used in such research casts doubt on the idea that preschool-age children broadly display pride and shame independently from social evaluations and contexts. It is notable that Stipek (along with all other authors) used exclusively social contexts in their studies. In contrast, my own cross-sectional studies (Holodynski, 1992, 2006) have shown that preschool-age children performing achievement-related tasks displayed pride and shame almost exclusively in the presence of another person but not when they were alone. In solitary situations, they reacted predominantly with joy, anger, and disappointment. A follow-up experiment 2 years later gave comparable achievement-related tasks to the same children at elementary school age (Fleiter, 2007). They now also reacted with shame over failure when they were alone.

The findings from these studies can be interpreted as indicating that preschool-age children initially display the self-evaluative emotions pride and shame almost exclusively in the presence of other persons. Cultural standards do not yet seem to be sufficiently separated from direct interaction with an esteemed other. They still require the presence of an adult as a living representative of the standards they wish to demonstrate and are now able to meet. With the transition to elementary school, children seem to begin to internalize these evaluations and to assess their performance in terms of competence standards independently from external appraisal and the presence of esteemed others.

Another task is *acquisition of emotion regulation strategies*. The ability to engage in emotion regulation also emerges during the second phase of development. Children become increasingly able to suppress voluntarily an immediate emotional action impulse, not pursuing it in the here and now but postponing it until a later, more appropriate occasion. This ability to engage in emotion regulation is indispensable for the development of an adult form of motive satisfaction because most motives cannot always be satisfied ad hoc. It is necessary to seek out appropriate situations, wait for suitable occasions, and reach agreement with other persons who contribute to motive satisfaction. Situations demanding a delay in gratification for a child (see Patterson & Mischel, 1976) or in which two contradictory motives emerge are prototypical waiting and conflict situations. To regulate their own emotions, it is necessary for children to acquire and autonomously apply effective strategies so they can modify the intensity and quality of their emotions in line with social norms and situational demands without having to fall back on interpersonal regulation by their caregivers (see Friedlmeier, 1999a).

These are, on the one hand, behavior-related regulation strategies such as distracting or calming oneself (see Bridges & Grolnick, 1995; Friedlmeier & Trommsdorff, 2001) and, on the other hand, symbolically conveyed regulation strategies in which one reinterprets the situation and ranks competing motives

Table 1 Types of emotion regulation strategies

Strategy	Examples
Behavioral strategies	
Touch	Rocking, stroking, comforting mode of speech; body contact
Distracting attention	Shifting attention to another object
Flight, withdrawal	Caregiver removes child from the situation
Symbolic strategies	
Comforting, consoling	Verbal consoling and comforting
Distracting attention	Talking about something else
Reinterpreting (e.g., trivializing, downward comparison, rejection of guilt, denial)	Reinterpreting the emotion episode, giving a plausible explanation
Ranking motives in time hierarchy	Parents put off gratification of child's motive to later point in time
Antecedent strategies	
Approach	Providing positive emotion episodes
Avoidance	Caregiver protects child from potentially negative emotion episodes
Discourse over the regulation of emotions	Caregiver talks to child about emotions and their regulation

in a temporal hierarchy (see Table 1). This last-mentioned regulation strategy proves to be particularly successful, as Bischof-Köhler (2000) has ascertained in her cross-sectional study of 3- to 5-year-olds. Children had to wait for a present and also master a conflict of motives. In the latter, they could apparently choose between catching candies by hand as they came out of a machine at irregular intervals and eating them or going into the next room and watching a cartoon on television. They could also place a bowl underneath the candy machine, watch television in the next room, and then come back and empty the candies out of the bowl. Results showed that some children were already capable of engaging in mental time travel. These children were particularly able to master the conflict successfully. Mental time travel calls for an ability to switch cognitive reference systems and imagine satisfying a motive not now but in the future, allowing one to pursue another activity in the meantime. To do this, a child seems to have built up a theory of mind and a comprehension of time: Approximately three-fourths of the children who coped successfully with the conflict of motives had these two abilities at their disposal compared with only about one-fourth of the children who did not cope successfully.

Infants whose actions are still guided exclusively by emotions become children who, with increasing age, become incrementally better at understanding how to no longer be led by their emotions but to regulate them to satisfy a higher-ranking motive. The increase in reflective aspects of regulation over the course of development also explains the developmental trend toward a general decrease in the frequency and intensity of emotions during ontogenesis.

Interestingly, Shoda, Mischel, and Peake (1990) performed a longitudinal follow-up study on adolescents who had worked on a delayed gratification task at the age of 4 years. Parents of adolescents who themselves had been able to master the task when they were 4 years old rated their adolescents as being more tenacious, more balanced, and more efficient at emotion regulation than parents of those who themselves had been unable to perform the task without interpersonal support as young children.

Development of Expression Signs From Age 6 Onward

Use of Expression to Display Emotions in Interpersonal Regulation

Individuals can also use emotional expression to *suggest* to an interaction partner that they are currently experiencing a particular feeling. In this case, the expression is being used as an emotional display (or as a "symbol" in Bühler's organon model terminology). This possibility of shaping expression voluntarily represents an important extension to interpersonal regulation because simulated emotional displays have the same urgent appeal function for those addressed as the expression of actually felt emotions.

Acquisition of the ability to apply emotional displays is a major milestone in emotional development. It enables a child to influence interaction partners more effectively so they act in line with his or her motives. Second, a child can use this ability to adapt to whatever cultural display rules (Ekman, 1972) are valid and not step outside the given normative framework. Display rules are normative rules prescribing in which situations one can or should display which expression to whom (e.g., smiling and saying thank you for a disappointing present).

A host of studies have analyzed how children learn to comply with such display rules (see Saarni & Weber, 1999). They reveal that girls can mask negative emotions more effectively than boys, and they improve this ability markedly from the ages of 4 to 10 years, whereas boys do not. A study by Davis (1995), however, indicated that this gender effect seems to be due to a lack of motivation in boys rather than any lack in the ability to control expression.

How children learn to apply their expression as an effective means of communication with which they can influence other persons has been studied particularly frequently in babies. However, in older age groups, it has been examined only in relation to deliberate deception. There are still no systematic developmental analyses of the wide-ranging aspects of implicitly exerting influence through expression display as in, for example, defiant or "begging" behavior. The dominance of the display-rule approach has inhibited the formulation of theories here because this concept views expression predominantly as the symptom of an emotion and not as an appeal to an interaction partner. However, it is the appeal character of the expression sign that is at the heart of an independent nonverbal communication system that first grants verbal communication its personal meaning and can also be used for deliberate self-display (see Goffman, 1958, 1967; Laux & Weber, 1993). The latter becomes particularly significant during adolescence when, for example, boys wish to impress girls by displaying their "coolness" and girls by displaying their attractiveness, with the help of fashion articles.

Internalization of Expression Signs In Intrapersonal Regulation

During the third phase of development, from about the sixth year of life onward, the internalization model predicts internalization of the psychological means of regulation. This prediction is based on the observation that adults do not share their emotions with external observers as much as children do. Whereas one can read the emotions of young children from their expression like an open book, adults have a world of private feelings that are not always observable in their expressive reactions.

Therefore, it seems as if objective expression and subjective feeling become detached from each other during the course of ontogenesis—in Western cultures but also in other cultures. Malatesta and Haviland (1985) talk about the "desomatization" of emotions. This leads to the question of whether adults "suppress" the authentic expression of their feelings as the term "expression control" suggests or the emergence of this growing private world of feeling is based on further developmental mechanisms that relate to the increasing use of symbols (e.g., in the form of expression and speech signs and the emergence of a mental level of expression, speech, and action).

There is a great deal of empirical research supporting the latter premise (Fridlund, 1994; Holodynski & Friedlmeier, 2006). It has shown that when adults are alone and in no way need to be shy about expressing their emotions they display a much weaker emotional expression than in comparable situations in which familiar persons are present to whom they want to communicate their feelings.

This so-called miniaturization effect cannot yet be seen in preschool-age children (Holodynski & Steinhoff, 2008; Steinhoff & Holodynski, 2008). We induced joy and disappointment in 4- to 6-year-olds under two conditions: once when they were alone and once in the presence of a familiar experimenter (whom they trusted sufficiently to communicate their emotions). The children revealed a comparable intensity of expression in both conditions and for both emotions.

However, a cross-sectional study of 6- to 8-year-olds (Holodynski, 2004) using the same experimental setting confirmed a miniaturization of expression in solitary situations as a function of increasing age. Whereas the 6-year-olds still showed a comparably intensive emotional expression under both conditions, the 8-year-olds already showed weaker expression in the solitary condition than in the social condition, even though they reported experiencing a comparably intensive feeling of joy or disappointment in both.

For an external observer, this miniaturization of expression can proceed so far that in the extreme case no more expression sign can be perceived. However, does this mean that the expression disappears completely? Viewed from the subjective perspective of the actor, this does not seem to be true. Instead, it seems that expression signs become internalized, so—in the extreme case—their perception as expression and bodily sensations remains only subjective: An audible curse becomes an inner curse; a broad smile becomes an inner sensation of smiling.

A comparable phenomenon can be observed in the development of speech that is known as self-instruction. During the course of preschool age, children start to use speech not only for communication but also for self-regulation. They give themselves verbal instructions and still do it audibly (see Vygotsky, 1934/1987). During the course of elementary school age, this audible private speech turns into inner speech in which individuals talk to themselves in their thoughts without outsiders being able to hear them (Bivens & Berk, 1990). Hence, during elementary school age, a mental level of expression, speech, and action emerges—a private world of feelings and thoughts.

This mental level permits subjective feelings that seem no longer to relate to feedback from real expression and body reactions but to their somatosensitive representations instead (see Damasio, 1994), just like internal speech no longer requires any whispering lip movements. This may explain why in many adult emotional episodes an agreement can no longer be observed externally between the feeling reported by the individual and the overtly visible expression and body reactions. From the actor perspective, in contrast, the totality of emotional expression and body reactions seems to be retained because the individual experiences them subjectively as *mentally* expressive and with bodily sensations.

The first findings in support of this premise have been obtained from studies of adults working on an imagination exercise in which they reexperienced two prior events in their lives: the feeling of intensive joy at meeting someone they had not seen for a long time (joy at reunion) (Upmann, 2000) and an episode of pride (von Olberg, 1999). Those participants in whom outsiders could observe no emotional expression reported that they had felt expressive sensations such as smiling, cries of triumph, puffed-up chest, or the impulse to take the old friend in their arms. This may be interpreted as indicating that expressive reactions do not disappear but become internalized.

Summary and Outlook

It has been possible only to sketch the major basic assumptions of the internalization model of emotional development here, as lack of space prevents detailed derivations of the single assumptions and a broader account of empirical findings supporting them. One important task for future longitudinal research is to focus on differentiating single emotion qualities and their regulation in more detail and to pay particular attention to interindividual differences. Attachment research offers promising working hypotheses in this field (see Spangler, 1999). It is important to analyze interindividual differences to ascertain which developmental tasks a child has to master in which way and with which social support to become an adult capable of acting in an emotionally competent way. It will also be necessary to take cultural preferences into account—something that has not been addressed in this chapter.

The current description of ontogenesis is restricted exclusively to emotional development in Western cultures. The studies reported here are Anglo-American and German. Cross-cultural studies should examine how far the prototypical course of development sketched here is universal and how far the internalization model is able to explain possible culture-specific differences in the development of emotions and their regulation. Such culture-specific differences should particularly emerge when the patterns of interaction between caregivers and children deviate from those described here (see Holodynski & Friedlmeier, 2006, Chap. 5). The internalization model assumes that it will be possible to find the developmental mechanisms underlying the single phases, such as affect mirroring by caregivers or the increasing internalization of interpersonal regulation by children in all cultures—though with differences in degree.

Notes

[1] In line with Donald (1993) and Raeithel (1994), one can say that expression signs represent an *independent mimetic meaning system*. The child's adoption of culturally formed expression signs with their culture-specific meanings reveals a developmental mechanism by which culture-specific emotions may emerge that have not been generated by verbal meaning systems. An example of a culturally developed expression sign and the emotion it embodies is genuflection. This, and even more so prostration, express strong differences in social rank such as those between master and subject, and they embody the emotion of humility. In the days of absolute monarchs, this expression sign was part of the familiar expression system of European cultures. However, one can no longer find it in the modern egalitarian cultures of Europe, with their emphasis on citizens with equal rights. Nonetheless, it is still found in the context of religious practices in which the believer expresses humility before God (see Stollberg-Rilinger, 2004; Wierzbicka, 1995, 1999). More-detailed analyses of the expression signs used in a culture are still lacking.

References

Ainsworth, M. D. S., & Wittig, B. A. (1969). Attachment and the exploratory behavior of one-year-olds in a strange situation. In B. M. Foss (Ed.), *Determinants of infant behavior* (pp. 113–136). London: Methuen.

Althoff, G. (Ed.). (2004). *Zeichen—Rituale—Werte* [Signs, rituals, values]. Münster, Germany: Rhema-Verlag.

Asendorpf, J. (1990). The expression of shyness and embarrassment. In W. R. Crozier (Ed.), *Shyness and embarrassment. Perspectives from social psychology* (pp. 7–118). Cambridge, UK: Cambridge University Press.

Barrett, K. C. (1995). A functionalist approach to shame and guilt. In J. P. Tangney & K. W. Fischer (Eds.), *Self-conscious emotions: The psychology of shame, guilt, embarrassment, and pride* (pp. 25–63). New York: Guilford Press.

Belsky, J., Domitrovich, C., & Crnic, K. (1997). Temperament and parenting antecedents of individual differences in three-year-old boys' pride and shame reactions. *Child Development, 68*, 456–466.

Bischof-Köhler, D. (2000). *Kinder auf Zeitreise. Theory of Mind, Zeitverständnis und Handlungsorganisation* [Children on a journey through time: Theory of mind, time concept, and action organization]. Bern, Switzerland: Huber.

Bivens, J. A., & Berk, L. E. (1990). A longitudinal study of the development of elementary school children's private speech. *Merrill-Palmer Quarterly, 36*(4), 443–463.

Boukydis, C. F. Z., & Burgess, R. L. (1982). Adult physiological response to infant cries: Effects of temperament of infant, parental status, and gender. *Child Development, 13*, 1291–1298.

Bridges, L. J., & Grolnick, W. S. (1995). The development of emotional self-regulation in infancy and early childhood. In N. Eisenberg (Ed.), *Social development* (pp. 185–211). Thousand Oaks, CA: Sage.

Bühler, K. (1984). *Sprachtheorie* [Theory of language]. Jena, Germany: Fischer. (Original work published 1934).

Campos, J. J., Kermoian, R., & Witherington, D. (1996). An epigenetic perspective on emotional development. In R. Kavanaugh, B. Zimmerberg, & S. Fein (Eds.), *Emotion: Interdisciplinary perspectives* (pp. 119–138). Mahwah, NJ: Erlbaum.

Campos, J. J., Frankel, C. B., & Camras, L. (2004). On the nature of emotion regulation. *Child Development, 75*, 377–394.

Clore, G. L. (1994). Why emotions are felt. In P. Ekman & R. J. Davidson (Eds.), *The nature of emotion* (pp. 103–111). New York: Oxford University Press.

Cole, P. M., Martin, S. E., & Dennis, T.A. (2004). Emotion regulation as a scientific construct: Methodological challenges and directions for child development research. *Child Development, 75*, 317–333.

Collier, G. (1985). *Emotional expression*. Hillsdale, NJ: Erlbaum.

Damasio, A. R. (1994). *Descartes' error. Emotion, reason, and the human brain*. New York: Avon.

Davis, T. L. (1995). Gender differences in masking negative emotions: Ability or motivation? *Developmental Psychology, 31*, 660–667.

Denham, S. A. (1998). *Emotional development in young children*. New York: Guilford Press.

Donald, M. (1993). *Origins of the modern mind: Three stages in the evolution of culture and cognition*. Cambridge, MA: Harvard University Press.

Ekman, P. (1984). Expression and the nature of emotion. In K. R. Scherer & P. Ekman (Eds.), *Approaches to emotion* (pp. 319–343). Hillsdale, NJ: Erlbaum.

Ekman, P. (1972). Universals and cultural differences in facial expressions of emotion. In J. Cole (Ed.), *Nebraska Symposium on Motivation, 1971* (pp. 207–283). Lincoln, NE: University of Nebraska Press.

Fleiter, N. (2007). *Die Entwicklung selbstbewertender Emotionen im Vor- und Grundschulalter* [Development of self-evaluative emotions in preschool and elementary school age]. Unpublished diploma thesis, University of Bielefeld, Germany: Abteilung für Psychologie.

Fogel, A. (1993). *Developing through relationships: Origins of communication, self, and culture*. Chicago, IL: University of Chicago Press.

Fridlund, A. J. (1994). *Human facial expression: An evolutionary view*. San Diego, CA: Academic Press.

Friedlmeier, W. (1999a). Emotionsregulation in der Kindheit [Emotion regulation in childhood]. In W. Friedlmeier & M. Holodynski (Eds.), *Emotionale Entwicklung. Funktion,*

Regulation und soziokultureller Kontext von Emotionen (pp. 197–218). Heidelberg, Germany: Spektrum.
Friedlmeier, W. (1999b). Sozialisation der Emotionsregulation [Socialization of emotion regulation]. *Zeitschrift für Soziologie der Erziehung und Sozialisation, 19*, 35–51.
Friedlmeier, W., & Trommsdorff, G. (2001). Entwicklung der Emotionsregulation bei 2- und 3-jährigen Mädchen [Development of emotion regulation in 2- and 3-year-old girls]. *Zeitschrift für Entwicklungspsychologie und Pädagogische Psychologie, 33*, 204–214.
Frijda, N. H. (1986). *The emotions*. New York: Cambridge University Press.
Gergely, G., & Watson, J. S. (1999). Early socio-emotional development: Contingency perception and the social-biofeedback model. In P. Rochat (Ed.), *Early social cognition: Understanding others in the first months of life* (pp. 101–136). Mahwah, NJ: Erlbaum.
Goffman, E. (1958). *Presentation of self in everyday life*. Edinburgh: University of Edinburgh Press.
Goffman, E. (1967). *Interaction rituals. Essays on face-to-face behavior*. Garden City, NY: Anchor Books.
Harter, S. (1978). Effectance motivation reconsidered: Toward a developmental model. *Human Development, 2*, 34–64.
Heckhausen, H. (1985). Emotionen im Leistungsverhalten aus ontogenetischer Sicht [Emotions in achievement behavior from an ontogenetic perspective]. In C. Eggers (Ed.), *Emotionalität und Motivation im Kindes- und Jugendalter* (pp. 95–131). Frankfurt, Germany: Fachbuchhandlung für Psychologie.
Holodynski, M. (1992). *Leistungstätigkeit und soziale Interaktion. Ein tätigkeitstheoretisches Modell zur Entstehung der Leistungsmotivation* [Achievement action and social interaction: An action theory model on the origins of achievement motivation]. Heidelberg, Germany: Asanger.
Holodynski, M. (1997). *Ausdrucksminiaturisierung und die Entwicklung der Emotionsregulation* [The miniaturization of expression and the development of emotion regulation]. Unpublished postdoctoral thesis, University of Bielefeld, Germany.
Holodynski, M. (2004). The miniaturization of expression in the development of emotional self-regulation. *Developmental Psychology, 40*, 15–27.
Holodynski, M. (2006). Die Entwicklung der Leistungsmotivation im Vorschulalter. Soziale Bewertungen und ihre Auswirkung auf Stolz-, Scham- und Ausdauerreaktionen [The development of achievement motivation in preschool age: Social appraisals and their impact on reactions of pride, shame, and persistence]. *Zeitschrift für Entwicklungspsychologie und Pädagogische Psychologie, 38*, 2–17.
Holodynski, M., & Friedlmeier, W. (2006). *The development of emotions and emotion regulation* (J. E. Harrow, Trans.). New York: Springer.
Holodynski, M., & Steinhoff, C. (2008). *Preschool-age emotional development: Self-regulation and the expression of joy*. Manuscript submitted for publication.
Izard, C. E. (1979). *The maximally discriminative facial movement coding system (MAX)*. Newark, DE: Instructional Resources Center University of Delaware.
Izard, C. E., & Malatesta, C. Z. (1987). Perspectives on emotional development I: Differential emotions theory of early emotional development. In J. D. Osofsky (Ed.), *Handbook of infant development* (pp. 494–554). New York: Wiley.
Langsdorf, P., Izard, C. E., Rayias, M., & Hembree, E. A. (1983). Interest expression, visual fixation, and heart rate changes in 2- to 8- month-old infants. *Developmental Psychology, 19*, 418–426.
Laux, L., & Weber, H. (1993). *Emotionsbewältigung und Selbstdarstellung* [Handling emotions and self-display]. Stuttgart, Germany: Kohlhammer.
Lazarus, R. S. (1991). *Emotion and adaptation*. New York: Oxford University Press.
Lewis, M., Alessandri, S. M., & Sullivan, M. W. (1992). Differences in shame and pride as a function of children's gender and task difficulty. *Child Development, 63*, 630–638.

Lewis, M., Sullivan, M., Stanger, C., & Weiss, M. (1989). Self development and self-conscious emotions. *Child Development, 60*, 146–156.

Malatesta, C. Z., Grigoryev, P., Lamb, D., Albin, M., & Culver, C. (1986). Emotion socialization and expressive development in preterm and full-term infants. *Child Development, 57*, 316–330.

Malatesta, C. Z., & Haviland, J. M. (1982). Learning display rules: The socialization of emotion expression in infancy. *Child Development, 53*, 991–1003.

Malatesta, C. Z., & Haviland, J. M. (1985). Signals, symbols, and socialization: The modification of emotional expression in human development. In M. Lewis & C. Saarni (Eds.), *The socialization of affect* (pp. 89–116). New York: Plenum Press.

Meyer, W. U., Schützwohl, A., & Reisenzein, R. (1993). *Einführung in die Emotionspsychologie* [Introduction to the psychology of emotions]. Bern, Switzerland: Huber.

von Olberg, B. (1999). *Unterschiede im Ausdruck und Erleben von Stolz und Wiedersehensfreude. Eine experimentelle Trance-Studie* [Differences in the expression and experience of pride and joy at reunion: An experimental trance study]. Unpublished diploma thesis, University of Bielefeld, Germany: Abteilung für Psychologie.

Papoušek, H., & Papoušek, M. (1987). Intuitive parenting: A dialectic counterpart to the infant's integrative competence. In J. D. Osofsky (Ed.), *Handbook of infant development* (pp. 669–720). New York: Wiley.

Papoušek, H., & Papoušek, M. (1999). Symbolbildung, Emotionsregulation und soziale Interaktion [Symbol formation, emotion regulation, and social interaction]. In W. Friedlmeier & M. Holodynski (Eds.), *Emotionale Entwicklung. Funktion, Regulation und soziokultureller Kontext von Emotionen* (pp. 135–155). Heidelberg, Germany: Spektrum.

Patterson, G. R., & Mischel, W. (1976). Effects of temptation and task facilitating plans of self-control. *Journal of Personality and Social Psychology, 32*, 209–217.

Raeithel, A. (1994). Symbolic production of social coherence. *Mind, Culture, and Activity, 1*(1–2), 69–88.

van Reekum, C. M., & Scherer, K. R. (1997). Levels of processing in emotion-antecedent appraisal. In G. Matthews (Ed.), *Cognitive science perspectives on personality and emotion* (pp. 259–330). Amsterdam: Elsevier.

Rosenstein, D., & Oster, H. (1988). Differential facial responses to four basic tastes in newborns. *Child Development, 59*, 1555–1568.

Saarni, C., & Weber, H. (1999). Emotional displays and dissemblance in childhood: Implications for self-presentation. In P. Philippot, R. S. Feldman, & E. J. Coats (Eds.), *The social context of nonverbal behavior* (pp. 71–105). New York: Cambridge University Press.

Scherer, K. R. (1990). Theorien und aktuelle Probleme der Emotionspsychologie [Theories and current issues in the psychology of emotions]. In K. R. Scherer (Ed.), *Psychologie der Emotionen. Enzyklopädie der Psychologie* (pp. 1–38). Göttingen, Germany: Hogrefe.

Scherer, K. R. (1992). Vocal affect expression as symptom, symbol, and appeal. In H. Papoušek, U. Jürgens, & M. Papoušek (Eds.), *Nonverbal vocal communication: Comparative and developmental approaches* (pp. 43–60). New York: Cambridge University Press.

Scherer, K. R. (2001). Appraisal considered as a process of multilevel sequential checking. In K. R. Scherer, A. Schorr, & T. Johnstone (Eds.), *Appraisal process in emotion. Theory, methods, research* (pp. 92–120). New York: Oxford University Press.

Scherer, K. R., Schorr, A., & Johnstone, T. (Eds.). (2001). *Appraisal processes in emotion: Theory, methods, research*. Oxford, UK: Oxford University Press.

Shoda, Y., Mischel, W., & Peake, P. K. (1990). Predicting adolescent cognitive and self-regulatory competencies from preschool delay of gratification. *Developmental Psychology, 26*, 978–986.

Sousa, R. de (2003). Emotion. In E. N. Zalta (Ed.), *Stanford Encyclopedia of Philosophy* (3). Retrieved December 30, 2005, from http://plato.stanford.edu/archives/spr2003/entries/emotion.

Soussignan, R., & Schaal, B. (2005). Emotional processes in human newborns: A functionalist perspective. In J. Nadel & D. Muir (Eds.), *Emotional development: Recent research advances* (pp. 127–159). New York: Oxford University Press.
Spangler, G. (1999). Frühkindliche Bindungserfahrungen und Emotionsregulation [Early childhood attachment experiences and emotion regulation]. In W. Friedlmeier & M. Holodynski (Eds.), *Emotionale Entwicklung. Funktion, Regulation und soziokultureller Kontext von Emotionen* (pp. 176–196). Heidelberg, Germany: Spektrum.
Sroufe, L. A. (1996). *Emotional development: The organization of emotional life in the early years.* New York: Cambridge University Press.
Steinhoff, C., & Holodynski, M. (2008). *Emotionale Entwicklung im Vorschulalter: Selbstregulation und Ausdruck von Enttäuschung* [Emotional development during preschool age: Self-regulation and expression of disappointment]. Manuscript submitted for publication.
Stenberg, C. R., & Campos, J. J. (1990). The development of anger expressions in infancy. In N. L. Stein, B. Leventhal, & T. Trabasso (Eds.), *Psychological and biological approaches to emotion* (pp. 247–282). Hillsdale, NJ: Erlbaum.
Stern, D. (1985). *The interpersonal world of the infant. A view from psychoanalysis and developmental psychology.* New York: Basic Books.
Stollberg-Rilinger, B. (2004). *Knien vor Gott—Knien vor dem Kaiser. Zum Ritualwandel im Konfessionskonflikt* [Kneeling before God, kneeling before the Kaiser: Changing rituals in religious conflict]. In G. Althoff (Ed.), Zeichen—Rituale—Werte (pp. 501–534). Münster, Germany: Rhema-Verlag.
Stipek, D., Recchia, S., & McClintic, S. (1992). Self-evaluation in young children. *Monographs of the Society for Research in Child Development, 57*, 1–84.
Underwood, M. K. (1997). Top ten pressing questions about the development of emotion regulation. *Motivation and Emotion, 21*, 127–146.
Upmann, K. (2000). *Ausdruck und Erleben von Wiedersehensfreude. Eine experimentelle Trance-Studie.* [The expression and experience of joy at reunion: An experimental trance study]. Unpublished diploma thesis, University of Bielefeld, Germany: Abteilung für Psychologie.
Vygotsky, L. S. (1987). *The collected works of L. S. Vygotsky* (R. W. Rieber & A. S. Carton, Eds.) New York: Plenum Press.
Walden, T. A., & Smith, M. C. (1997). Emotion regulation. *Motivation and Emotion, 21*, 7–26.
Wierzbicka, A. (1995). Kisses, handshakes, bows: The semantics of nonverbal communication. *Semiotica, 103*(3/4), 207–252.
Wierzbicka, A. (1999). *Emotions across languages and cultures: Diversity and universals.* Cambridge, UK: Cambridge University Press.

Gravestones for Butterflies: Social Feeling Rules and Individual Experiences of Loss

Birgitt Röttger-Rössler

Abstract Both the quality and intensity of emotions change with age and according to one's age-specific pool of experience and knowledge. This is even more so because the different phases of life not only contain different productive and reproductive tasks that have to be solved in age-specific ways but are also the focus of specific social models of emotion. In particular, biological, psychic, and social turning points, as well as "critical" incidents, are connected with social expectations regarding which behavior and feeling are "suitable." Because the emotional models change during the life cycle, individuals are obliged to readjust their emotions constantly to deal with changed biological and social living conditions. It can be assumed that emotional adjustment to changed life circumstances always takes place within a social exchange, that is, within processes of interactive "meaning making." This chapter illuminates such processes of emotional meaning-making through the example of the German "star children movement" (*Sternenkinderbewegung*) set up a few years ago by parents who had suffered a pregnancy loss or stillbirth and wanted to create a social place for grief that is widely ignored by society.

Cultures expand the emotional capacities inherent to the human organism into complex social information and communication systems. Cultural and social codes specify at which times and in which manner which emotions are to be shown, emphasized, or subdued, and in which contexts which emotions should be felt by whom. In short, cultures formulate feeling rules (Hochschild, 1983) or "emotional imperatives" as well as appropriate forms of emotional expression, the "display rules." Therefore, one focus of interest in ethnological (social anthropological) research lies in unraveling the culture-specific feeling rules. Nonetheless, these rules cannot be conceived as homogeneous but as highly variable codes because the social feeling rules within each culture differ in manifold ways

B. Röttger-Rössler (✉)
Max Planck Institute for Social Anthropology, Department I – Integration and Conflict, Halle, Germany
e-mail: roettger@eth.mpg.de

B. Röttger-Rössler, H.J. Markowitsch (eds.), *Emotions as Bio-cultural Processes*,
DOI 10.1007/978-0-387-09546-2_8, © Springer Science+Business Media, LLC 2009

depending, inter alia, on aspects of sex, social status, and age. One important but widely neglected issue is that the different phases of the human life span are always connected with specific emotion models prescribing how individuals should emotionally and behaviorally meet the specific productive and reproductive challenges of particular life phases. Thus, any analysis of the interrelation between emotions and the life cycle must concentrate on the age-specific social feeling rules while simultaneously turning toward the question of how these emotional models are themselves modified in the context of macro-societal processes of change (see also Neckel, this volume, Emotion by Design).

Critical macro-social changes frequently confront individuals with life situations of such novelty that there are no socially tested, well defined emotional models with which they could categorize, interpret, and communicate their specific life experiences. Moreover, certain events that recur repeatedly in the human life cycle—such as birth and parenthood—have acquired a different social significance through processes of social change and can no longer be coped with appropriately on the basis of the given conventional feeling rules. In the following, I approach this question of a reformulation of culture-specific feeling rules through the example of one highly specific aspect of the "reproduction topic" that is predominantly typical of young adulthood-pregnancy loss. Stillbirths and miscarriages belong to the universal dimensions of experience in human existence, even though the cultural and social significance attributed to these phenomena varies across cultures and times. Along the lines of the "empty cradle" movements, which have recently spread in Germany, I investigate how important aspects of the existing rules for grief and mourning have attained a point of change.[1]

Over the last decade or so, parents having to cope with the experience of a stillbirth or miscarriage have been setting up support networks. Today, almost every major town has at least one "empty cradle" group. Although most have emanated from private initiatives, some have been established by churches, midwifes, or counseling centers specializing in grief support. The Internet offers another important networking possibility for parents of what they call "star" or "butterfly" children (*Sternen-* or *Schmetterlingskinder*). The existence of such groups and the considerable number of aggrieved parents belonging to them indicate that the social conventions for dealing with the loss of preterm infants are being perceived as increasingly problematic and stressful. Parents of butterfly children complain that the traditional social feeling rules do not allow them to feel intensive grief for their premature or stillborn babies. In contrast, the rules expect them to overcome these losses quickly. Mothers and fathers who come together in such support groups perceive themselves as being unable to obey the dominant feeling rules defining prolonged mourning and depression after the loss of a premature child as abnormal and pathological. These feeling rules are also reflected in the related psychological and psychiatric literature, which tends to evaluate emotional reactions of more than 6 months' duration with a persistence in feelings of loss, sadness, irritability, and depression as "prolonged reactions" indicating the emergence of "serious psychiatric disorders" (Yee, 1986, p. 122; see also Janssen, Cuisinier, & Hoodduin, 1996). As a consequence of these social norms, butterfly parents experience less public support and understanding for their grief and sorrow because the death of a yet-to-be-born child is not recognized as a socially significant, or "social," death (Malacrida, 1998, p. 6).[2] A preterm infant is socially salient only to parents and close kin. For others, he or she is socially not "real" because he or she died before existing in a social sense as the following quotation from such a mother illustrates.

> Neighbors, colleagues, families haven't seen the child; they haven't felt it, touched it, so it doesn't exist. We're not allowed to mourn. But even the children we can't "put on display," they're still our children! [1][3]

Background

On an institutional level, these implicit grieving rules can be seen in what until recently has been a complete lack of funeral possibilities for miscarriages and pregnancy losses. Until a few years ago, parents were allowed to bury stillbirths only from 1000 g upward—something that leads to definitional questions and related legal aspects.

In Germany, the law differentiates between miscarriages (pregnancy losses) and stillbirths. One speaks of the former when a pregnancy ends prematurely due to spontaneous or consciously initiated abortion of the fetus, which itself shows no signs of life (e.g., breathing, heartbeat, umbilical cord pulse) and weighs less than 500 g. If the abortion occurs up to the 12th week of pregnancy, it is called a miscarriage (*frühe Fehlgeburt*); if it occurs between the 13th and the 25th week, it is called a pregnancy loss (*späte Fehlgeburt*). All fetuses that are born dead later, which explicitly includes death in the uterus as well as during the process of birth, are classified as stillborn if they weigh more than 500 g. The weight for legally differentiating between pregnancy losses and stillbirths was 1000 g until 1994, when parents' initiatives achieved a change in the applicable laws regulating legal matters of births and deaths in Germany.

Stillbirths (> 500 g) are recorded at the civil registry office; first and family names of the stillborn can be listed in the register of births if the parents so wish. In former times, only the date of death and sex were registered. However, they have to be buried properly only when they weigh more than 1000 g in many federal states in Germany, even though it is possible to have a funeral for stillborn children weighing less than 1000 g if parents so wish.[4] Being able to have funerals for stillbirths weighing more than 500 or 1000 g (depending on the individual state) still does not mean that parents have to organize or finance the funeral themselves. They can leave this task to hospitals that usually collect the corpses and bury them anonymously in a common grave or cremate them. Stillbirths can no longer be disposed of as "medical waste."

Miscarriages and pregnancy losses (< 500 g) are not recorded in official registers or statistics; there is no right to a name, and no obligation for a funeral. According to the legal norm, such bodies have to be disposed of in a proper medical way (normally combustion) together with other human tissue such as amputated extremities, organs, or used blood bottles. In 2001, Bremen was the first federal state in Germany to implement a legal obligation to bury all dead fetuses older than 12 weeks. Since then, all states have established the parents' right to a funeral, even though parents are often unaware of this right. Moreover, it is quite common for authorities to refuse to allow a funeral at the local cemetery with reference to the law, thus blurring the difference between obligation and right.

Premature birth is defined as the birth of a living child up to the 37th week of pregnancy who weighs less than 2500 g. The decisive criterion here is that the fetus is born with unambiguous signs of life (e.g., breathing, heartbeat, umbilical cord pulse), even if it happens at a time and in such a fragile condition that extrauterine life is impossible and the neonate dies immediately after birth. These humans are born alive and died afterward, even though both incidents are close to each other in time. Thus, they count as social persons with a right to a name, and their dead bodies are officially recognized as corpses that have to be buried.

Looking at these regulations, one could philosophize at great length on the ties between medicine and law and the inherent power of this coalition to define decisive parameters of our being—such as the borders between life and death, between human being and organic waste—and to vary these definitions constantly in line with the biomedical state of the art. However, we are interested in emotional meanings here: the implicit social expectations and feeling rules that are related to such assertions and the practices connected with them. We are also interested in the subjective perceptions of these latent codes by affected individuals because their immediate feelings often appear to differ somewhat from the social norms.

Narrations of Pregnancy Loss

These tacit feeling rules become accessible in the self-reports and autobiographical narrations of persons who have experienced a pregnancy loss and found themselves confronted with a set of social norms and expectations prescribing how they should normally cope with such loss, both behaviorally and emotionally. I analyzed a large number of such self-reports in which butterfly parents described their struggles to meet the standards and the inner conflicts that were provoked by their felt inability to do so. All of the self-reports I investigated are written accounts recorded in the context of support groups—mostly as a therapeutic step—or postings at various Internet forums. What follows is a short synopsis of my findings.

All the narrations can be divided into four thematically distinct parts: (1) the onset, (2) the time together, (3) the experience of "giving death," and (4) the time of sorrow.

Onset

Usually, narrations start with some information on the parents' relationship and how strongly they wanted to have children.

> I [born 1966] have been together with Jörg [born 1957] since 1982. We knew right from the start that we wanted to have at least two children. (Conny, www.muschel.net) [2]
> My husband and I got married just before my 21st birthday in April 1983. Soon afterwards, I graduated from the university and became pregnant. We were so happy. Everything went just as we had planned it. (www.totgeburt.net/html/body_meine_geschichte.html) [3]

These introductions are immediately followed by a description of finding out that one is pregnant and the emotions it triggers. This in no way means only joy: The emotional reactions to the pregnancy depend on the individual history and personal circumstances. Most fathers and mothers without negative predisposition—that is, parents embarking on their first pregnancy or in which former pregnancies were successful and without complications—show effusive joy. Those who have already suffered pregnancy losses or in which the desire for a child has been fulfilled only after lengthy and stressful fertility treatment normally experience a sort of joy mixed with significant sorrow. Women or couples in very difficult or critical personal circumstances normally experience desperation or despondence because they can see no space for a child in their lives.

> On January 16th 2005, I had a positive pregnancy test in my hands. I had been suspecting it might have worked this time for a couple of days. I was jumping round in circles for joy; we were very happy. The delivery date was September 21, 2005. The first examination was on February 1, the little heart is beating already, everything's alright, according to the ultrasonic scan, the child is 4 days younger than I thought, even though I'm sure I know the exact date of the ovulation. Anyway, it doesn't matter; everything else is going well. I feel pretty pregnant, with hunger attacks but no morning sickness. Brilliant—in the good way only a pregnant woman can feel. Everything's just perfect! (Angela, www.muschel.net.de) [4]
>
> We had already been waiting 3 years for our baby. I went through three IVF treatments and all three of them were without success. After thinking about it for a long time, I took a pregnancy test on January 27th, 2005, and to our immense surprise it was positive.... We were sitting in Dr X's office the same evening, ... she made an ultrasonic right away and said quite soberly: Yes, you're pregnant at the moment, but I don't see any cardiac action. Come back on Wednesday. I'll have to be able to see something then! (Lissy, www.muschel.net.de) [5]
>
> I had very mixed feelings about this child. Christian and I had so much stress that we just couldn't imagine we'd have the necessary love and peace of mind to raise a child and also be able to pay for everything. We argued a lot and didn't get any support from our parents—I was really upset and even thought about not wanting to have the child. I also wasn't able to enjoy the first checkup. There was my little child's heart beating on the screen and I didn't even take a proper look. (Sara, www.muschel.net.de) [6]

Apart from the different emotional connotations, these examples show that the first ultrasonic examination is a highly significant event because it visualizes the new life through the embryo's cardiac action. The heartbeat, the most powerful metaphor for life, which can be perceived only much later in a "natural" acoustic manner, is visualized on the ultrasonic screen during the early weeks of pregnancy. Thus, it is no longer just abstract urine and blood tests or subjective pregnancy feelings in the woman (ravenous appetite, nausea, dragging pains in breast and abdomen) that emerge as a sign of growing life for expectant parents. Objective images highlight and serve as plain proof of what is happening within the woman's body. After this first ultrasonic examination, a pregnancy becomes truly real, which is the reason why this *topic* is not missing in any of the (early phase) narrations.[5]

Time Together

The topos also serves as transitory passage to the second part of the narrations describing the course of the pregnancy, which is in fact the only time that the mother (as well as the father) and the child spend *together*. Depending on the length and course of the individual pregnancy, these accounts have a more or less complex structure. What appears to be a meticulously kept pregnancy diary at first glance proves on closer inspection to be a sometimes eloquent description of the developing emotional bonds between mother and child as well as father and child. The reports can include touching passages of fathers getting the new child's room ready and stroking their partners' bellies, the joy of first heart sounds and child movements, grandparents buying romper suits, and so forth.

Of course, the ultrasonic examinations play a central role in these accounts. Therefore, descriptions of ultrasonic encounters with the child occupy much narrative space, and the ultrasonic images are often integrated into the self-reports presented in the various Internet forums. It can be assumed that the development of emotional bonds between unborn children and parents is highly intensified by these options of modern prenatal diagnostics and regular pregnancy checkups. This is particularly the case for men, who nearly all reported that it was the ultrasonic scans that first enabled them to grasp the new life in their partner's womb and that they were going to be fathers.[6] In summary, these accounts reveal the pregnancy as a socially and emotionally liminal or transitional phase in which everyone affected—parents, siblings, grandparents—prepare themselves internally and externally for the expected new relationship structures and life circumstances. The texts clearly demonstrate that the reporting mothers and fathers have begun to build an emotional relationship with the child from the very moment they became aware of the pregnancy. For them, the unborn already constitutes an interaction partner, a socially significant other, who plays an important part in their decision-making and everyday routines and thus occupies a great amount of social space. In other words, the unborn already "takes its place," takes a position in the family (see Lyon, this volume, Emotion, Embodiment, and Agency).

The following extract from a letter a mother wrote to her "angel born" vividly illustrates the social relevance of the unborn.

> We always wanted to have you so much!. . . I often stroked you through the skin on my belly and talked to you. I concentrated on every single one of your movements and often said, "Hey baby, did you wake up?" Sometimes your brothers came along and put their hands on my belly to feel you and they even tried to hear you. And your father was such a proud "expectant dad"! In short, we were all very happy and full of joyful anticipation. . . . We had your room decorated already and everything was waiting in the wings. . . . (www.hartmann-klaus.de) [7]

Experience of Giving "Death"

The third part of the narrations then addresses the end of pregnancy, the loss of the expected child. Accounts vary greatly in complexity depending on whether (1) the end came rather early and suddenly; (2) it was a long, difficult, risky pregnancy with a dramatic course vacillating between fear and hope; or (3) it had been a complete, fairly easy pregnancy with sudden death during birth. Women who have experienced a classic stillbirth are conceded a comparably large amount of grief, whereas the opposite is true for women who have had an early miscarriage. Late pregnancy losses can be placed somewhere between these two extreme poles.

For illustration, I have chosen an account of a loss during the 22nd week of pregnancy initiated by the premature breaking of the mother's waters, a rather common cause of pregnancy loss:

> Nearing the end of the 21st week my waters broke at night. It was Wednesday, September 18, 1991. The doctor tried to dash my hopes; but as the ultrasonic scan showed that my child was alive, I was not willing to waive the labor-inhibiting drugs they had offered me because of the slim chances. In spite of that, I was hoping for the 4% to 5% [chance] the doctors gave our baby.
>
> The next day (Thursday Sept. 19) I was in slight labor despite taking the drugs, but the CTG showed that our son's heart was beating in the morning as well as in the evening, and optimism was slowly spreading throughout the ward, "maybe there will be a happy ending after all!" There was a flurry of excitement especially in the morning: When a nurse came to search for heart sounds, she was very surprised that our child was still alive: "There are still heart sounds, I don't believe it, real heartbeats!". . . Jörg stayed with me the whole day. . . . Because there was no water now, we could actually see our child (his back) clearly on the right of my belly and we could see and feel him moving. That was a very strange feeling because I had only started to feel faint movements about 3 weeks before, and I had only been certain about them for 2 weeks. . . . I wasn't able to sleep well, and I asked my son—I was sure he was a son and called him by his name—to stay with us. I told him that we need and love him; that he shouldn't leave us.
>
> The next morning, Friday September 20, the first day of the 22nd week, I was examined, the mouth of the uterus was fully open, "birth is imminent now, we can't do anything anymore." . . . It was way too early for our baby to have any chances of survival outside my body—nobody wanted to check for heartbeats any longer; they did not want to make it even harder for me. (Conny, www.muschel.net.de) [8]

This report shows how women who lose the fetus at a late stage of pregnancy perceive this experience as an act of "giving death": In cases like this, delivering a baby means to kill it. Another woman phrased this shared experience as: "The worst thing was to still feel the baby kick and knowing that she was alive and that I'd killed her. Because that's what it felt like—to deliver her was to kill her."

These are retrospective interpretations. Only later, when reflecting on what happened, do the women start to interpret and describe their feelings during delivery as the "pain of giving death." Most women experienced the actual process of delivery in a sense of unreality, numbness, and disbelief. Many also report that they experienced the whole situation as something not really happening to them. Some stated that they had felt like they were acting in a film. While knowing intellectually that their baby was dead or would die soon, the experiential knowledge of the meaning of this death came only later. During the actual labor, they felt detached, a not-yet grief for a baby not-yet dead. For fathers, the sense of unreality and numbness seems to differ somewhat. They, too, described feelings of unreality, of not yet understanding the profundity of their loss. However, their primary focus was on their wives' health and mental well-being. They perceived themselves mainly as supporters of their wives, with their feelings being only secondary.[7] However, detachment is a typical, rather normal reaction to traumatic situations in which people tend to act and react in a more schematic, semiconscious way. A full, emotional understanding of a critical situation always seems to emerge with reflection (i.e., during the process of reviewing and ascribing meaning to the event).

Time of Sorrow

In the last part of the self-reports the narration turns to the experiences after the loss. I call it the "time of sorrow." These accounts allow several interesting insights into the complexity of grieving processes and emotion regulation in general, but because of the lack of space, I concentrate on the immediate and medium-term reactions to the loss.

The narrations revealed that it is of utmost importance for bereaved parents to see and touch the corpse of their baby after birth; that is, to gain sensory access to their child and, at the same time, to his or her death. This becomes evident in the self-reports of parents who had recently suffered a pregnancy loss. Thanks to the complete change of attitude in German hospitals, it was possible for these parents to see, touch, and hold their premature or stillborn child and peacefully say goodbye. All these parents said that the time spent with their dead child was extremely moving and bonding. They emphasized how important it had been for them to receive the child they had been waiting for, to be able to take it in with all their senses; and they reported that this experience made their loss and mourning easier to bear.

> At 19:15, our son Jonas Nikolaus entered this world in complete peacefulness and stillness. His little sick heart was no longer beating and he did not have to suffer. He looked so peaceful and liberated. Simply wonderful and a completely perfect, tiny little baby. He had amazingly long little fingers and toes and a mop of dark hair. One could

> see how he would look like Erwin. The baptism ceremony allowed us, very gently, to say goodbye to him. (www.schmetterlingskinder.de/Jonas/geschichte.htm) [9]

Parents who were denied a chance to see and touch their baby—still the dominant hospital practice only a decade ago—stated that it made the experience agonizing. The period of anticipation, hope, and looking forward to having a child along with the sometimes highly dramatic experience of miscarriage was followed by a sudden vacuum. The usual medical practice was to give the women general anesthesia after delivery and abrasion. When they came round, everything was over, the case was medically closed, and they were sent home with some medication. One woman recalls this experience in the following words:

> It was like a nightmare. Nothing remained that referred to my pregnancy, to the child who had been growing inside me. Nothing apart from the pain in my body and my memories that nobody wanted to hear.[8] [10]

She regretted that she did not insist on seeing and touching her son, and she is haunted by the thought that his body might have been disposed of as "medical waste." When trying to communicate these feelings to others, she experiences a complete lack of understanding: "What do you want to bury?" her own mother asked her. "You have had a miscarriage and did not bear a child."

After birth, bereaved parents have to face resistance from others in commemorating their loss. Mothers or close relatives who had planned to come and "help with the baby" end up canceling their visit "because you won't be needing me anymore." At best, butterfly parents are confronted with goodwill slogans from friends and family members aimed at minimizing their grief, such as: "You are young; you can still have another child." "It's God's way of doing things." "Things happen for a reason." At worst, they are confronted with comments challenging the legitimacy of their sorrow, such as: "Why are you so depressed? Your baby was never alive!" "You never saw it, you never got to know it; there's no reason to cry." "You should be relieved because there was probably something wrong with the baby." "Don't be sad, you already have living children."

In short, they run into a social vacuum with their feelings. In addition to their loss, they have to cope with the cultural feeling rules prescribing that one should overcome the pregnancy loss as soon as possible. The burden of this additional emotion work makes their grief particularly difficult.

A great many of the women stated that they felt ashamed and insufficient in a twofold sense: (1) for not being able to give birth to a healthy child (i.e., having failed in their reproductive role); and (2) for not being able to go on as usual (i.e., having failed in their emotion management). As a consequence, many of them lose self-confidence and begin to perceive themselves as bodily and psychologically incomplete and insufficient women.

Men also get caught up in a double bind. They have to cope with the loss of the child and the grief of their partner, whom they are expected to (and want to) support. Most men define themselves primarily as the supporter and comforter of their wives who they acknowledge as the "main sufferer" in the tragedy.

A man is expected to be inwardly calm and psychologically stable so he can act as a mainstay and relay confidence to his partner. However, this can lead to a dilemma: If a man wants to discuss his feelings openly with his partner, it may well be suggested to him, in a more or less subtle way, that it would upset her, and that, after all, his role at this time is to support her rather than to grieve with her. If he does not show his feelings, however, he may be perceived as uncaring (Puddifoot & Johnson, 1997, p. 844). Therefore, men have even less space than women to express their own feelings. Their grief is completely ignored by society.[9]

To sum up: After returning home from the hospital, bereaved parents must deal with the silence of a social environment that tends to belittle their loss. The social support and mourning rituals normally available to bereaved individuals are not available to them. In reaction to these powerful taboos, most parents withdraw and become alienated from others. On an emotional level, they react mainly with a mixture of anger, disappointment, and sorrow to the seeming disinterest of their social environment. Many state that well established friendships and family relations become weakened by the lack of commemoration. This distancing places additional burdens on butterfly parents, further increasing their isolation.

Discussion

The material presented here shows that bereaved parents often find their personal experiences to be at odds with the prevailing feeling rules on pregnancy losses/perinatal deaths. The parents see themselves placed in a position of having to justify their feelings in the face of denial and silence from a social environment that tends to evaluate intensive and prolonged grief in cases of perinatal loss as an abnormal mental reaction. The sharp discrepancy they perceive between the commonly held feeling rules and their own actual emotions causes (many of) them to seek opportunities to share their experiences with other bereaved parents and thus to organize themselves in support networks. Such empty cradle networks have now spread throughout Germany and are expanding continuously. By using these networks, parents set out to articulate their feelings and thus resist the dominant grieving rules. They have started to demand a social space and legitimacy in which to mourn their perinatal losses, and they have been quite successful. These initiatives have not only achieved a change in the relevant laws by readjusting weight regulations downward. They have also managed to codify the right to record a name in the birth registers and thus gain an official acknowledgement of the very existence of children who have never lived outside their mothers' wombs. Moreover, they are responsible for burial spaces being made available for pregnancy losses and stillbirths in many cemeteries and for many churches and undertakers having developed specific funeral rituals. They also use the Internet as a means to communicate and, even more importantly, to set up commemoration pages or virtual graves for their butterfly children.

Butterfly parents have succeeded in (1) legalizing their feelings, (2) providing social space for their grief and sorrow, and thus (3) transforming society's grieving rules. The motivation for their efforts obviously emerges from the discrepancy/tension between their subjective emotional experiences and the socially prescribed emotion and expression rules. It can be taken for granted that stillbirths and pregnancy losses have always been extremely painful experiences, especially for women, and that it has always meant hard emotional work to match the prevailing feeling rules that belittle these losses and do not admit grief for perinatal deaths. However, the question this leads to is: Why has this discrepancy, which must always have been present, become so unbearable in recent times?

It could be argued that perinatal loss has become more difficult in modern society owing to factors of macro-societal change. I mention only a few.

1. Lower birth rates (the emergence of the typical "two-kids family pattern") ascribe more importance to the particular child and hence pregnancy.
2. The increased availability of reproduction control means that women are now more likely to focus on choosing, rather than preventing, pregnancy. Pregnancies no longer just "happen" but are planned—often in a long-term perspective. Presumably, this results in less emotional ambivalence (or more pure joy) when women become pregnant. On the other hand, it becomes much more difficult to accept a loss.[10]
3. The significantly higher age of women at their first pregnancy narrows the biological chances of reproduction, thus increasing the importance of each single pregnancy. Numerous women report that the "ticking of the biological clock" made it even more difficult for them to accept their loss, and they consequently tried even harder to become pregnant again before they had completely come to terms with the trauma of the previous pregnancy.
4. New reproductive technologies such as ultrasonic scans facilitate parent–unborn child bonding at a very early stage by allowing visual bonds to the baby in utero, determining the sex of the child, and so forth.
5. Increasing medicalization of pregnancy and childbirth means that women/couples expect the pregnancies they actually do choose to have to end successfully. Modern reproductive and perinatal medicine fosters the belief that pregnancy is now typically safe and successful.
6. Women's health movements and natural birth movements encourage an ethic of individual responsibility—if one is only diligent and hard-working enough, each pregnancy will be healthy and each delivery successful.
7. The liberal ideology that women have the right and ability to control their fertility also seems to contribute to the implicit assumption that they may well be responsible for their pregnancy losses (Layne, 2000, p. 360).

Taken together, these factors form a modern concept of pregnancy as a selectable, manageable, predictable undertaking; and this, in turn, fosters unrealistic expectations of success in reproductive matters. As Layne (2000, p. 357) pointed out, pregnancy losses destroy the "narrations of linear progress" cultivated in Western societies as a consequence of the deep-rooted belief in the benefits of technological achievements coming from a deeply rooted belief in progress and technology. Layne (2000) stressed that the prominence and even the power of this belief makes it difficult to tell other stories, that is, stories that do not conform to the general expectations of linear progress and feasibility. Layne also pointed to another highly significant aspect: that the unpredictable and uncontrollable and that pain, suffering, and death are no longer daily narratives and rarely topics of public or medical discourse. Before modern obstetrics, in contrast, the possibility of a pregnancy not coming to term or even ending fatally for mother and child was anchored much more strongly in public awareness.[11] Although earlier social feeling rules did not permit intensive or long mourning of miscarriages or stillbirths, it can be assumed that such events did not affect the individual in such an unprepared way as today. It is only in relation to the modern technology of reproductive medicine and within the context of the general "we can do it" ideology that the complete "culture of silence" (Layne, 2000, p. 359) could develop that the parents of butterfly children are now beginning to break down.[12]

Conclusion

The empty cradle movement illustrates something that goes far beyond the subject of pregnancy loss and has general relevance for emotion theory. This relevance is the enormous importance of communication—of relaying and sharing experiences and feelings and of being able to regulate, classify, and manage them. In modern individual-oriented societies, people often find themselves in relatively few intense relationships, and they have fewer and fewer people with whom to share their stories, their joys, and their sorrows. Self-help networks such as the ones described here provide the social communication, the collective meaning making, necessary for a successful intrapersonal regulation of emotions especially in the context of critical life events. Moreover, the empty cradle movement demonstrates the importance of social rituals for expressing, communicating, and guiding feelings. Particularly for critical life transitions such as birth and death, rituals not only mark the passage from one life stage to another but also provide individuals with scripted ways of acting and feeling. Through the performance of rituals, changes in the life course become socially (interpersonally) visible and communicable as well as psychologically (intrapersonally) tangible. On the one hand, rituals articulate and "cognize" feelings; on the other hand, they "embody" them by intensifying physiological arousal and thus the bodily perception of the enacted emotions. The phenomenon of emotional contagion (Hatfield, Cacioppo, & Rapson, 1994)—that is, the human tendency to automatically mimic and synchronize facial expressions, vocalizations, posture, and movements with those of another person (which apparently constitutes a crucial neural mechanism with regard to affect sharing; see Singer, 2006)—also plays an important role in these processes. The effectiveness of rituals in evoking certain emotions in the participants—not just as "cold" thoughts but as "hot" bodily felt sensations—seems to be based on this biopsychological mechanism. *Rites de passage* constitute powerful means of emotional expression, regulation, and affect sharing; and they seem to operate at a crucial bio-cultural intersection and should thus receive more attention in emotion research.

Notes

1 I use the term *grief* here to refer to the direct subjective reactions to a loss and the term *mourning* to refer to intrapsychic and interpersonal processes that act to resolve the grief (including the public display of grief) (see also Rando, 1993, p. 23; Charmaz, 1980, p. 280; Malacrida, 1998, p. 12).

2 A social death refers to the loss of an individual to the community, to society, and to living others (Malacrida, 1998, p. 6; Mulkay, 1993;). It can be independent from a biological death, as when an ailing individual detaches more and more from his/her social group and thus his/her presence (and hence loss) becomes increasingly less salient to community members. Intensive, long-term grief in the case of the loss of an old-aged, ailing person is not supported socially either. Instead, mourners are encouraged to evaluate the loss as a relief.

3 All quotations are numbered so that readers can easily refer to the German originals in the Appendix.

4 In Germany, the annual number of stillbirths has remained quite stable at around 3000 children in recent years. For 2002, the Federal Statistics Office reported 2700. Despite enormous improvements in prenatal diagnostics, the reasons for stillbirths are still mostly unclear.

5 An interesting detail illustrating the power of images in our current media-savvy society is given by the narrations of some women who had already sensed physiologically that "something was not right" in their pregnancy, but they were not taken seriously because the ultrasonic images did not (yet) show any anomalies. In all cases, the women's apprehensions soon proved correct. Generally, the women referred to highly specific physical sensations such as "hardening of the abdomen, contractions, dragging pains"; and it can therefore be assumed that we are not dealing with purely rhetorical components here. In any case, if the diagnostic practices do not represent the women's physical perceptions, it is the images that determine the physicians' judgments.

6 This is also highlighted in the conversations that McCreight (2004, p. 334) has conducted with fathers of "butterfly children" (see also Johnson & Puddifoot, 1996; Puddifoot & Johnson, 1997).

7 See also McCreight (2004), Puddifoot & Johnson (1997, 1999), and Malacrida (1998, p. 17).

8 Personal conversation with Sabine S., who suffered a late pregnancy loss 13 years ago and was not allowed to bury her son.

9 According to Lasker and Toedter (1994), men are therefore at risk of developing a chronic grief response. See also McCreight (2004) and Puddifoot and Johnson (1997, 1999), who pointed in the same direction.

10 See Letherby (1993).

11 During the mid-1980s, it was still standard practice in Germany not to officially start documenting a pregnancy until the end of the third month; and, in general, couples informed their relatives about the pregnancy only after this deadline.

[12] This "culture of silence" can also be found in the scientific literature. For example, the topic of pregnancy loss receives little attention in either the sociology or ethnology fields, although both disciplines pay a great deal of attention to other aspects of reproduction. See Reinharz (1988, pp. 4–5) and Layne (2003), who have pointed to the conspicuous neglect of this topic among women's studies as well.

Appendix

1. Die Nachbarn, die Kollegen, die Familien haben das Kind nicht gesehen, sie haben es nicht gefühlt, nicht berührt, also existiert es nicht. Die Trauer wird uns abgesprochen. Dabei sind auch die Kinder, die wir nicht "vorzeigen" können, unsere Kinder!
2. Seit 1982 bin ich (Jahrgang 1966) mit Jörg (Jahrgang 1957) zusammen. Wir wussten von Anfang an, dass wir mindestens zwei Kinder haben wollen.
3. Kurz vor meinem 21. Lebensjahr, im April 1983, heirateten mein Mann und ich. Bald darauf beendete ich mein Studium und wurde schwanger. Wir waren glücklich. Alles verlief nach unseren Vorstellungen.
4. Am 16. Januar 2005 hielt ich einen positiven Schwangerschaftstest in der Hand, nachdem ich schon einige Tage lang ahnte, dass es geklappt haben könnte. Ich bin vor Glück im Viereck gehüpft, wir haben uns sehr gefreut. Am 21. September 2005 ist der Entbindungstermin, (...) Am 1.2.2005 war die erste Untersuchung. Das Herzlein schlägt schon, alles bestens, laut Ultraschall ist das Kind 4 Tage jünger als ich annahm, dabei bin ich mir sicher, den Eisprung auf den Tag genau zu kennen. Naja, egal, ist ja sonst alles im Lot und bestens. Ich fühle mich ziemlich schwanger, mit Heißhunger, aber völlig ohne Übelkeit. Klasse – so gut wie man sich als Schwangere nur fühlen kann. Alles ist einfach perfekt! (...).
5. Wir warteten bereits seit drei Jahren auf unser Baby. Drei Kinderwunschbehandlungen habe ich über mich ergehen lassen müssen und alle drei waren ohne Erfolg. Am 27.01.2005 machte ich nach langer Überlegung einen Schwangerschaftstest, der zu unserer riesigen Freude positiv ausfiel. (...) Am selben Abend saßen wir bei Frau Dr. X im Sprechzimmer, (...) sie hat dann sofort geschallt und meinte völlig nüchtern: "ja, im Moment sind sie schwanger, aber ich sehe keine Herzaktion. Kommen sie am Mittwoch wieder, dann muss ich was sehen!"
6. Ich hatte sehr zwiespältige Gefühle diesem Kind gegenüber. Christian und ich hatten so viel Stress, dass wir uns nicht vorstellen konnten, noch ein Kind mit der nötigen Liebe und Ruhe zu erziehen und auch finanziell alles abzusichern. Wir stritten viel und hatten keine Unterstützung von unseren Eltern – ich war richtig verzweifelt und dachte sogar darüber nach, dieses Kind nicht bekommen zu wollen. Auch die erste Vorsorgeuntersuchtung konnte ich nicht genießen. Da schlug das Herzchen meines kleinen Kindes und ich sah nicht einmal richtig hin.

7. Du warst unser absolutes Wunschkind! (...) Ich streichelte dich oft durch die Bauchdecke und sprach mit dir. Ich konzentrierte mich auf jede deiner Bewegungen und sagte oft: “Na, Kleiner, bist du aufgewacht?” Dann kamen manchmal deine Brüder und legten die Hände auf meinen Bauch, um dich zu spüren, sie versuchten sogar dich zu hören. Auch dein Papa war ein sehr stolzer “werdender Vater“! Kurzum: Wir waren alle sehr gluecklich und so voller Vorfreude. (...) Wir hatten dein Zimmer bereits eingerichtet und alles stand bereit ...
8. Ende der 21. SSW hatte ich nachts einen Blasensprung. Es war Mittwoch, der 18. September 1991. Der Arzt machte mir kaum Hoffnung, doch da der Ultraschall zeigte, dass mein Kind lebte, war ich nicht bereit, auf die wehenhemmenden Mittel zu verzichten – was mir aber aufgrund der geringen Chancen angeboten wurde. Dennoch hoffte ich auf die vier, fünf Prozent Chance, die der Arzt noch für unser Baby ausgerechnet hatte.

   Am nächsten Tag (Donnerstag, 19. September) hatte ich trotz der Medikamente leichte Wehen, aber das Herz unseres Sohnes schlug sowohl morgens als auch abends beim CTG, auf der gesamten Station breitete sich allmählich Optimismus aus, “vielleicht geht es ja doch noch gut!”. Besonders am Morgen herrschte helle Aufregung: Als eine Krankenschwester kam, um nach Herztönen zu suchen, war sie ganz aufgeregt, dass unser Kind noch lebte – womit offensichtlich niemand mehr gerechnet hatte: “Da sind ja noch Herztöne, das gibt’s doch nicht, das sind doch Herztöne!” (...) Jörg war den ganzen Tag bei mir, (...) Dadurch, dass das Fruchtwasser fehlte, konnten wir auf meiner rechten Bauchseite deutlich unser Kind (seinen Rücken) und seine Bewegungen sehen und spüren. Das war schon ein merkwürdiges Gefühl, denn ich hatte erst seit ca. drei Wochen zarte Kindsbewegungen gespürt, war mir ihrer erst seit knapp zwei Wochen ganz sicher gewesen. (...) Ich schlief schlecht und bat meinen Sohn – ich war mir nun sicher, dass es ein Junge ist und redete ihn mit seinem Namen an –, bei uns zu bleiben, erzählte ihm, dass wir ihn brauchen und lieben; und dass er uns nicht verlassen darf.

   Am nächsten Morgen, Freitag, 20. September 1991, dem ersten Tag der 22. SSW, wurde ich untersucht, der Muttermund war vollständig geöffnet, “die Geburt ist nicht mehr aufzuhalten, wir können nichts mehr tun.” (...) Für unser Baby war es viel zu früh, um außerhalb meines Körpers irgendwelche Überlebenschancen zu haben – nach Herztönen wollte niemand mehr suchen, um es mir nicht noch schwerer zu machen. (...)
9. Um 19.15 kam unser Sohn Jonas Nikolaus ganz friedlich und still zur Welt. Sein kleines krankes Herz hat nicht mehr geschlagen und er musste nicht leiden. Er sah so friedlich und erlöst aus. Einfach wunderschön und ein ganz perfektes, winzig kleines Baby. Er hatte unglaublich lange Fingerchen und Zehen und einen dunklen Flaum auf dem Kopf. Man konnte ahnen, dass er einmal Erwin ähnlich sieht. Wir konnten uns mit einer Taufe ganz in Ruhe von ihm verabschieden.

10. Es war wie ein Spuk, wie ein Alptraum. Es gab nichts mehr, was auf meine Schwangerschaft, auf das Kind, das in mir gewachsen war hindeutete. Nichts mehr außer meinen Erinnerungen und die wollte niemand hören.

References

Charmaz, K. (1980). *The social reality of death: Death in contemporary America*. Reading, MA: Addison-Wesley.

Hatfield, E., Cacioppo, J., & Rapson, R. (1994). *Emotional contagion*. New York: Cambridge University Press.

Hochschild, A. R. (1983). *The managed heart: Commercialization of human feeling*. Berkeley, CA: University of California Press.

Janssen, H. J., Cuisinier, M. C. J., & Hoodduin, K. A. L. (1996). A critical review of the concept of pathological grief following pregnancy loss. *Omega, 33*,121–142.

Johnson, M. P., & Puddifoot, J. E. (1996). The grief response in partners of women who miscarry. *British Journal of Medical Psychology, 69*, 313–327.

Lasker, J. N., & Toedter, L. J. (1994). Satisfaction with hospital care and interventions after pregnancy loss. *Death Studies, 18*(1), 41–63.

Layne, L. L. (2000). The cultural fix: An anthropological contribution to science and technology studies. *Science, Technology, & Human Values, 25*(3), 352–379.

Layne, L. L. (2003). Unhappy endings: A feminist reappraisal of women's health movement from the vantage point of pregnancy loss. *Social Science & Medicine, 56*, 1881–1891.

Letherby, G. (1993) The meanings of miscarriage. *Women's Studies International Forum, 16*(2), 165–180.

Malacrida, C. (1998) *Mourning the dreams: How parents create meaning from miscarriage, stillbirth and early infant death*. Edmonton, Alberta, Canada: Qual Institute Press.

McCreight, B. S. (2004). A grief ignored: Narratives of pregnancy loss from male perspective. *Sociology of Health & Illness, 26*(3), 326–350.

Mulkay, M. (1993). Social death in Britain. In D. Clark (Ed.), *The sociology of death: Theory, culture, practice* (pp. 31–50). Oxford, UK: Blackwell.

Puddifoot J. E., & Johnson, M. P. (1997). The legitimacy of grieving: The partner's experience at miscarriage. *Social Science and Medicine, 45*(6), 837–45.

Puddifoot J. E., & Johnson, M. P. (1999). Active grief, despair, and difficulty coping: Some measured characteristics of male response following their partner's miscarriage. *Journal of Reproductive and Infant Psychology, 17*(1), 89–93.

Rando, T. A. (1993). *Treatment of complicated mourning*. Champaign, IL: Research Press.

Reinharz, S. (1988). Controlling women's lives: A cross-cultural interpretation of miscarriage accounts. *Research in the Sociology of Health Care, 7*, 3–37.

Singer, T. (2006). The neuronal basis and ontogeny of empathy and mind reading: Review of literature and implications for future research. *Neuroscience and Biobehavioral Reviews, 30*, 855–863.

Yee, L. S. (1986). The bereaved mother of a stillborn. *Journal of Hong Kong Medical Association, 38*(3), 121–123.

Emotion by Design: Self-Management of Feelings as a Cultural Program

Sighard Neckel

Abstract In sociological theory, the social process of regulating emotions has been described as the proliferation of self-constraints and rationalization. In contrast, the loosening of emotional discipline during the 20th century represented itself as "informalization" of feeling rules. Current programs for emotional self-management, however, as found in current concepts of work and business, as well as of consultation, training, and therapy, point to the fact that in the meantime the opposition between discipline and informalization has begun to dissolve. In the wake of a modern market society, which finds its economic yardsticks in personal efficiency and financial success and that is culturally accompanied by processes of "subjectivation," programs of self-management dedicated primarily to the cognitive triggering and the strategic use of emotions are on the rise. Feelings do not thereby remain the object of subjective and social control alone. Rather, modern self-management aims at the "optimization" of emotional experience and performance, for which Daniel Goleman's popular concept of "emotional intelligence" is exemplary. Curiously, such programs of modern emotionalizing in society and economics have the paradoxical effect of leading precisely to the "affective neutrality" that they purport to confront.

From the perspective of sociology, it would be extremely limited to view emotions as only conditionally individual phenomena that are unable to reveal any social regularities. Emotional feelings are always embedded in an individual's social relationships; and these social relationships, in turn, exert a decisive influence on when, why, and in which way emotions arise and are displayed. Such "feeling rules" (Hochschild, 1983) become a key element of sociological analysis as soon as one goes beyond the internal psychological dimensions of emotions and also considers their social reality. This reality is shaped by the fact that emotions are subject to social regulation in a multitude

S. Neckel (✉)
University of Vienna, Institute of Sociology, Vienna, Austria
e-mail: sighard.neckel@univie.ac.at

B. Röttger-Rössler, H.J. Markowitsch (eds.), *Emotions as Bio-cultural Processes*,
DOI 10.1007/978-0-387-09546-2_9, © Springer Science+Business Media, LLC 2009

of ways that gratifies desired feelings, sanctions "inappropriate" ones, and generally determines the way in which individuals are "emotional" and models their feelings in each and every social context (see also Röttger-Rössler, Gravestones for Butterflies). Cultural norms and social institutions exert a major influence on which emotional behavior is expected in which situation. For example, the occupational sphere of modern societies acknowledges standards for the regulation of feelings that are different from those in the private domain; moreover, the cultural norms addressing socially desirable behavior of adults, men, or members of social elites imply feeling models that are different from those applied to children, women, or persons from the lower strata of society. Social feeling norms are also subject to continuous social change. Complex societies with long chains of action require strong emotional discipline; economic and political processes of change influence, in turn, the directions in which the everyday feeling world changes. Hence, as a result of modern capitalism, forms of handling one's own emotions in a rationalized and "calculating" way developed that were unknown to other societies. In addition, the expressive relationship to one's own emotions, which modern individuals claim as a personal right, is also accompanied by a political change in the history of society that has declared the freedom of the individual to be a normative maxim. It is only against this background that we can begin to understand why today's individuals embark on a search for their "authentic feelings."

This chapter uses the example of a contemporary change to address the sociology of social feeling regulation. Since the beginning of the modern age, the process of social emotion regulation has been characterized by the increasing dissemination of self-constraints and rationalization. The 20th century, in contrast, witnessed a loosening of emotional discipline that sociology describes as the "informalization" of emotion rules (Wouters, 1999). Nowadays, in contrast, we are witnessing a spread of "emotional self-control" right in the middle of the spheres of work and management and of counseling, training, and therapy programs, indicating that the contradiction between disciplinization and informalization in the control of social feeling patterns is beginning to break down. An example is the popular concept of "emotional intelligence" (Goleman, 1995), which does not focus only on the social control of emotions but strives to "optimize" emotional feeling and display. In the following sections, such modern feeling-regulation programs are subjected to a critical analysis, revealing that emotional self-management can have paradoxical effects and may well be contributing to the spread of those forms of emotional impoverishment that the programs are supposed to counter.

Emotions and Economic Action

In sociological theory, the social regulation of emotions has been described as the proliferation of self-constraints, as objectification and rationalization. In particular, the economic organization of modern society has been identified as a major force through which the emotional dimensions of experience and social actions have been kept in check. According to Norbert Elias (2000, pp. 374–375), the growing interdependencies in an increasingly more complex system of economic exchange have contributed to a tightening up of affect control. Georg Simmel pointed to the "leveling of emotional life" (Simmel, 1990, p. 432) as a characteristic of the modern lifestyle that results from the spreading of a monetized economy. Max Weber, on the other hand, considered "charisma"—the most emotion-based variant of deference to power—as a "necessarily noneconomic" phenomenon and "immediately endangered in its virulence when the interests of everyday economic life become predominant" (Weber, 1968, p. 1120), which is why the path of charisma in modern capitalism is destined to lead from a "turbulently emotional life that knows no economic rationality to a slow death by suffocation" (ibid.).

The assumption that the spheres of market and money, the inner life of modern economic organizations, and the world of work are emotion-free zones is present in the most negative social theory critiques of capitalism. The alienation critique developed by Horkheimer and Adorno in the *Dialectic of Enlightenment*, for example, posits that owing to the imperative of instrumental reason the most intimate human reactions in relation to oneself are so completely reified that "personality scarcely signifies anything more than shining white teeth and freedom from body odor and emotions" (Horkheimer & Adorno, 1977, p. 167).

In contrast, the modern sociology of emotion during the past two and a half decades has shown that economic organizations and their actors cannot abolish emotions from the workplace, nor can they afford to renounce the use of emotions as a means of scoring economic gains (cf. Fineman, 2000a; Flam, 1990; Schreyögg & Sydow, 2001). Rather than being characterized by "affective neutrality," as Talcott Parsons (Parsons & Shils, 1951, pp. 77–88) described the modern action orientation, economic processes are accompanied by specific forms of emotion management that shape the feelings of business leaders and employees, investors, customers, and service providers. "Objectivity" as an ideal in economic action disappeared long ago in modern market society, if indeed it ever played a predominant role. Products and sales transactions are intentionally charged with emotion, which is demonstrated, for example, by the role of "emotional design" in the shaping of modern consumer goods or by the euphoric presentations of brand images that can best be observed in any shopping mall or Nike store.

The economic strategy of marketing standard mass consumer goods and standardized services as purportedly authentic and unique products means that the workers in the consumer and service industries are expected to act as living "*gisements d'authenticité*" ("reserves of authenticity") (Boltanski & Chiapello, 1999, p. 535) by using their individual characteristics to reinforce the illusion of a "personal offer." In this context, feelings become the most genuine evidence of personal authenticity; and for this reason the emotionalization of both the products and contact with customers is an explicit strategy employed by management. Furthermore, in economic organizations today, human resources have shifted emphasis to the psychologization of management communication between superiors and subordinates (Pongratz, 2004), which means that emotional competencies are imparted in everyday internal business negotiations and simultaneously made obligatory.

From the perspective of the sociology of emotion, economic action does not represent a special case of social interaction. Like social practices in general, economic interactions are related to feelings insofar as corresponding events are emotionally evaluated by economic actors, who then express their feelings about them outwardly as they impart their assessment. Panic purchases are an example of this, as is the shame of economic bankruptcy and the elation and enthusiasm expressed in stock market rallies. As in all other social spheres, in the economic arena social institutions prescribe specific rules that govern feelings, leading the actors to experience and express their emotions in socially desired ways. Whenever it serves an economic purpose, "affective neutrality" may serve as a norm in business transactions. From the standpoint of the sociology of emotion, however, this norm only confirms the existence of rules that regulate emotion. Economic actors do not by any means simply follow their material interests without affect. "Feeling rules" are therefore a social necessity, and the subjective management of emotions is an economic prerequisite in all business practices.

Two Hypotheses in Sociological Research: Alienation Versus Informalization

Despite all concurrence within the sociology of emotion, there is broad disagreement as to the precise nature of emotion management. Arlie Hochschild's work, for example, represents the tradition of alienation critique that emphasizes the instrumentalization of emotions in modern capitalism. Her most well known book, *The Managed Heart* (Hochschild, 1983), offers a sociological critique of the commercialization of feelings in modern service industries. At the core of Hochschild's work is the idea that employees in the service sector are coerced in two ways to perform "mental self-manipulation" (Rastetter, 2001, p. 117). First, the norms of the modern "customer orientation" require that employees outwardly express feelings that they do not really have. In addition, stressful work situations evoke strategies of "deep acting," with which the actor must produce the required feelings. According to Hochschild, these requirements in emotion management result in a gap between the expression of emotions and the experience of them; in a strategic habit of emotional inauthenticity, it makes the emotional world of the individual external to the self. The market and the instrumental relationships it creates between its actors thus colonize their subjectivity to a deep emotional level.

Hochschild's work has elicited numerous debates and critiques, not only in research on the sociology of emotion but also in the sociology of work. More recent studies on the service industries have pointed to the fact that the management of emotions also includes the employees' personal strategies aimed at influencing customers as well as superiors and colleagues, which possibly scores them interactive power gains. The employees may experience these gains in power as a reaffirmation of their ability to have an effect on others, which may thereby contribute to their self-esteem (cf. Thoits, 2004; Voswinkel, 2004).

In contrast to this detail-oriented critique, the contemporary representatives of civilization theory have formulated more fundamental objections. They suggest that the alienation critique of emotion management evokes the false image of a purportedly authentic realm of emotions—a realm that they say is always already shaped by social patterns. In addition, they maintain that the informalization of feeling rules that emerged during the second half of the 20th century has brought a loosening up of emotional discipline—a change that is not reflected in the work issuing from alienation critique. Contemporary studies on the informalization of social norms that are engaged in critical dialogue with the work of Norbert Elias have noted that one of the most obvious changes in behavior is a general acceptance of expressive emotional patterns. This, of course, represents a development opposite to that posited by classic civilization theory-the modern trend toward an ever-increasing degree of control over the emotions. Even in the modern service industries—according to, for instance, Dutch sociologist Cas Wouters—the range, density, and rigidity of social control over the emotions is generally in decline, whereas emotion culture today is simultaneously moving in the direction of comparatively less obligatory and more flexible forms of self-control (Wouters, 1999, pp. 143–153).

Thus, two opposing views on social regulation of feelings have been put forth in the contemporary sociology of emotion. The hypothesis emphasizing discipline finds that the commercial exploitation of emotions leads to the conditioning of feelings, which results in social suffering and alienation. In contrast, the hypothesis that feeling rules have undergone a process of informalization points to an increase in personal autonomy in the shaping of emotional expression that is largely the result of a significant loosening up of affect control in the self and in modern society at large.

Common to these two opposing positions, however, is that they both explore a change that can be described as the "subjectivization" of emotion management. In the alienation critique, this subjectivization takes a strategic form. In her more recent work, Hochschild describes actors as learning to understand their feelings as "emotional capital" and learning to behave like "emotional entrepreneurs" who purposefully invest their feelings in the markets of work and relationships to increase their social capital and, when necessary, divest them (Hochschild, 1998, pp. 10–15). In contrast, the informalization hypothesis interprets subjectivization as an increasing self-reflexivity on the part of the individual concerning his or her emotional world. This interpretation is indebted to a general awareness that emotions are also social constructs and that there are increasing demands on the individual's emotional self-regulation (Wouters, 1999, pp. 61–66).

Emotional Self-Management in "Flexible Capitalism"

The common denominator in current debates on the sociology of emotion thus seems to be an image of the subject who may—or, alternatively, must—increasingly understand his or her emotions as a personal task and is hereby either able to access new freedoms or is simply obeying a changed set of social constraints. In formulating these two alternatives, the sociology of emotion enters a terrain that is not unfamiliar to contemporary sociological interpretations of our society. Many sociological interpretations of the present address the paradox that increasing liberties and increasing constraints are, in fact, correlatives and do not contradict one another (cf. Honneth, 2002). In particular, current analyses of modern market society posit that in "flexible capitalism" autonomy and control are conflated such that they have become indistinguishable. Subjectivization is understood here as the process by which individual attributes and needs are integrated into the functioning of the workplace and the market (Kocyba, 2000; Lohr, 2003). Insofar as workers are both expected to and indeed do strive to enjoy their work, entrepreneurial "visions" are supposed to elicit enthusiasm, various forms of empathy shape communication at the workplace, and employees want to and must motivate themselves. In modern work, a nexus of "emotionality and efficiency" (Pongratz, 2002) emerges that inseparably intertwines purposive rationality with emotional acts.

In their book on *Le Nouvel Esprit du Capitalisme* Luc Boltanski and Ève Chiapello (1999) interpreted this development as an expression of a new order of justification in social status distribution. They argued that today's "network capitalism" has begun to erode the borders between private life and the world of work, and it is now demanding that the individual mobilize personal competencies and emotional resources in the service of project goals set by himself or herself. Social advantages are gained by actors who interpret work as the development of their own personality; who demonstrate initiative, responsibility, sociability, reliability, and an authentic self at work; and who utilize all their mental abilities in doing so. Because this new "syncretism of economy and lifestyle" (cf. Neckel, 2003) represents not only a need but also a demand, there is an increased desire for, and necessity of, personally appropriating the activist ethos of new capitalism through "self-management."

Proper self-management has therefore become a horizon toward which today's economically leading concept of subjectivity is aimed. Given the transformations described above, it is no surprise that it is, above all, *emotional* self-management that is the focus of efforts to promote the flexible personality. One indicator of this is the inundation of advice books and popular nonfiction addressing the significance of feelings for everyday life and the modern workplace. In contrast to earlier waves of popular advice books, those of today do not just give instructions on how to rationalize one's own behavior and become maximally effective by following through on methodic work plans. Rather, the present-day "feeling engineers" (Bertolt Brecht) propagate techniques of emotional empowerment that offer the individual insight and tips for an appropriate emotional life. Some relevant German titles are:

- *Die Glücksformel—Wie die guten Gefühle entstehen* (Klein, 2003) [The Formula for Happiness: How Good Feelings Arise]
- *Die Kraft der positiven Gefühle—Mit neuen Mentaltechniken innerlich frei werden* (Schmidt, 2001) [The Power of Positive Feelings: Liberation from Within via New Mental Techniques]
- *Emotionales Management. Erfolgsfaktoren sozial kompetenter Führung* (Gonschorrek & Berg, 2002). [Emotion Management: Success Factors in Developing Socially Competent Leadership].

Characteristic of all these advice manuals is that they link instructions on how to control one's own emotions with the promise that the emotions of others can also be controlled effectively. Emotional self-management is offered as a recipe that yields a commodity: "transforming emotion into a marketable product" (Fineman, 2000b, p. 102). As a commodity, emotional advice products must demonstrate their usefulness, above all, in the areas of therapy and organizational management, where steering one's own emotions as well as those of others is considered to be a new blueprint for solving all manner of modern management problems related to efficiency. In both cases, emotions are not reflected on for their own sake but for their usefulness in realizing goals that are subject to the rational calculation of how to increase one's own skills, well-being, and effectiveness through a greater understanding of emotion.

Bringing together the postulates of self-realization ("liberation from within"), strategic tips on emotion regulation (the "success factor"), and the promise of subjective fulfillment ("good feelings"), the advice books on emotional self-management are typical for the body of management texts published since the 1990s. It is from this body of management texts that Boltanski and Chiapello reconstructed the principles of the new order of social evaluation in contemporary network capitalism. Characteristic of this evaluation order is that it has integrated the widespread critique of the emotional "coldness" of the old industrial capitalism and transformed it into a "*marchandisation de l'authentique*" ["economization of the authentic"] (Boltanski & Chiapello, 1999, p. 535). The most important indicator of authenticity is represented by the "unaffected" emotionality of a person, which purportedly demonstrates by virtue of a person's "natural" feelings that the realization of subjective needs and the functional ability to conform are not mutually contradictory.

If "*la grandeur se voit de plus en plus souvent appréciée en fonction de leur capacité d'autoréalisation*" [the "rating (of people)" is thus "increasingly measured according to their potential for self-realization"] (ibid., p. 516), their emotionality is granted a more central role than ever before. Today, the most valued characteristics when recruiting personnel are readily apparent communicability and openness to new contacts (which connotes an "easy-going" character), reliable ability to judge the feelings of others, and credible presentation of self-assured immediacy—all of which indicate that one is capable of participating in flexible networks and of bringing a fresh supply of enthusiasm to each new and ever-changing work situation (cf. ibid., p. 168). "Emotional work," the recipes for which are a standard offer in advice books today, imparts key competencies that are not only sought after in the service sector of the "smile industry" (Fineman, 2000b, p. 107), but also increasingly determine the assessment of employees in other spheres of modern corporate management.

The advice literature is, however, only one element of the current discourse on the social regulation of emotion that has a wide-ranging influence on not just the media and public sphere but also on work and management, consulting, training, and therapy. Numerous forms of knowledge aim at making emotion accessible for instrumental purposes. Usually, this popular knowledge is based on the idea that people can choose their own feelings if they acquire certain skills. According to this view, feelings are not to be sought within oneself, as recommended by the post-1968 culture of self-realization. Because our feelings can be chosen, goes the theory, they are also subject to personal self-management. Thus, the belief in the personal choice of our feelings forms the basis of many training programs and short-term courses of therapy. The most successful of these is currently "neurolinguistic programming" (NLP), a combination of behavioral therapy, hypnosis, and esotericism that is commonly found in contemporary consulting, coaching, and management theory. NLP considers emotions as optional "target states" and poses itself as a curriculum for developing these states. One of their training booklets (O'Connor & Seymour, 1994) thus declares:

> If you learn to choose your own emotional state, that is, your thoughts and feelings, then your talents will automatically flow forth, and you will be in the position to do the best job at all times with a minimum of effort.... And of course changing your emotional state is the easiest way to influence your audience and also change their emotional state. (p. 146)

Even many philosophical advice manuals on the art of living attempt to create an emotional suntan studio for the educated but disgruntled reader. Examples of this kind of wellness philosophizing are the bestsellers by the French philosopher Alain de Botton (2004), which offer instructions on how to transform modern status anxieties emotionally. These philosophical tips do not shy away from trivialities, recommending as a response to feelings of greed, for example, that one keep in mind the conciliatory idea that all rivals ultimately rest in equality in the grave.

Example of "Emotional Intelligence"

The most influential concept in the discourse on emotional self-management, however, is undoubtedly that of "emotional intelligence." This concept was first developed in 1990 by American psychologists Peter Salovey and John D. Mayer (cf., most recently, Salovey, Kokkonen, Lopes, & Mayer, 2004), who defined emotional intelligence "as the subset of social intelligence that involves the ability to monitor one's own and others' feelings and emotions, to discriminate among them and use this information to guide one's thinking and actions" (Salovey & Mayer, 1990, p. 189). As a cultural program that is widely noticed in public, "emotional intelligence" was made popular by American psychologist Daniel Goleman (1995), whose therapeutic version of emotional intelligence has since been rejected by its scientific founders because of its blurred outlines (cf. Salovey et al., 2004, p. 326). Goleman's concept shares many of the characteristics found in other mental training programs, especially as regards method. Among others, suggestions include techniques for autosuggestion and "reframing," in which painful events are to be transformed into motivational experiences and negative moods into positive energies.[1] The focus is on techniques for spurring charismatic self-enthusiasm that lead the individual to believe in himself or herself as an infinite source of personal potential. The central message is thus that one must tirelessly work toward improving one's true inner self, with the key word being "self-motivation." If the true self still fails to materialize, then feelings of personal inadequacy are to be countered with the self-enactment of stoic optimism (i.e., positive thinking).

What has helped establish the predominance of the "emotional intelligence" concept over the long run is the fact that it makes recourse to two frameworks of interpretation that play a key role in modern culture. On the one hand, it refers to purportedly established insights from the natural sciences, in particular, recent research on brain function (for a critique of this, see Sieben, 2001). On the other hand, "emotional intelligence" promises substantial gains in personal "success" and thus reinforces the overall guiding principle of social competition today (cf. Neckel, 2001, 2004): "The market forces that are reshaping our worklife are putting an unprecedented premium on emotional intelligence for on-the-job success" (Goleman, 1995, p. xiii).

By linking brain research and the drive to succeed, "emotional intelligence" leaves the impression that being successful is merely a matter of learning to manipulate brain anatomy properly. One of Goleman's texts (Goleman, Boyatzis, & McKee, 2002) devoted to business management thus explained:

> The left side of the prefrontal area . . . is part of a key circuit that inhibits neurons in the amygdale and so keeps a person from being captured by distress. This circuitry helps a leader to calm rocky emotions and maintain a confident, enthusiastic mood. (p. 45)

Emotional problems, on the other hand, are construed as problems originating in the emotions rather than in the events that trigger them. Whether worry, sadness, or fear may have real causes is not mentioned in the numerous examples of proper emotion management (e.g., Goleman, 1995, pp. 65–69). In fact, persons feel on the basis of their understanding of real situations (see Engelen et al., Emotions as Bio-cultural Processes), which is something that is completely neglected in Goleman's writings. Instead, responsibility for a problematic emotional state is placed in the hands of the individual, who must actively work to avoid emotional distress. The brain itself offers the key to accomplishing this, according to Goleman. Because of its plasticity, the brain is always open to change, such that the appropriate training can be used to obtain optimal neuronal connections (goes the theory). The individual is seemingly able to profit from the fact that the brain is itself an "emotion manager" (ibid., p. 24) and provides a "risk/benefit ratio" (ibid., p. 25) of all its reactions.

In this context, Goleman referred to a number of psychological experiments related to impulse control. One of them is the "marshmallow test," a long-term experiment applied to schoolchildren to measure their willingness to hold back on immediate gratification in favor of subsequent advantages. In the marshmallow test, 4-year-old children are offered the choice of immediately eating a marshmallow, or waiting 20 minutes, at which time they will be rewarded with two marshmallows. Those who were able to hold off on immediate gratification later proved, as 18-year-olds, to be "more socially competent: personally effective, self-assertive, and better able to cope with the frustrations of life" (ibid., p. 81). For the remaining one-third of the 4-year-olds who ate the marshmallow right away, a problematic development was noted later in life.

> They were more likely to be seen as shying away from social contacts; to be stubborn and indecisive; to be easily upset by frustrations ... to be mistrustful and resentful about not "getting enough"; to be prone to jealousy and envy; to overreact to irritations with a sharp temper, so provoking arguments and fights. (p. 82)

The impatient children also proved to be among the least accomplished students upon high school graduation, whereas the patient ones scored the best results on college entrance examinations.

In contrast, undesired feelings that still cannot be shut off despite the brain's presumed "risk/benefit ratio" by which the neocortex and the amygdale presumably interact, are declared pathological (ibid., p. 79). According to Goleman, these feelings represent an "emotional hijacking in which limbic surges capture the rest of the brain" (ibid., p. 92). In cases in which negative moods regularly hinder all possibilities of positive motivation, Goleman recommended "reeducating the emotional brain" (ibid., p. 208), for which, in addition to suggestive techniques such as "upbeat denial" (ibid., p. 75), psychotropic medication, and in severe cases electroshock treatment (cf. ibid., p. 73) are indicated.

A closer look shows that the concept of "emotional intelligence" is aimed at nothing less than a fundamental change in what modern culture has always understood by the term "feelings." Emotions—which are, in fact, "feelings" insofar as they also have a bodily and an involuntary affective component in addition to their cognitively based evaluative function—are not accepted in themselves as a medium that transmits information about the internal state of a person. When an emotion retreats from all attempts at conscious manipulation and cannot be used to attain the goals set by cognition, it is stigmatized as a psychopathological symptom.

Socially desired emotions are thus characterized as an internal reservoir of mental resources that can be mobilized at any time and instrumentalized for strategic purposes. The criterion that distinguishes normal from pathological emotions is thus solely the emotion's usefulness in achieving personal gains and success. According to Goleman, emotional intelligence has become the most important factor in attaining success in life, taking precedence over professional skills and cognitive intelligence (ibid., p. 34). For this reason, Goleman has developed a learning model that promises to raise our "success quotient" systematically via emotional self-optimization (Goleman, 1998). Specifically, this model is made up of five dimensions of emotional intelligence, among which 25 emotional competencies are divided up that are supposedly decisive for personal and professional success (cf. ibid., pp. 26–27). Among the intrapersonal forms of emotion management are the first three dimensions-self-awareness, self-regulation, motivation- which designate the recognition of one's own feelings, proper control over them, and ultimately the self-generation of useful emotional states. *Interpersonal* emotion management contains the dimensions "empathy" and "social skills," which refer to the ability to read the emotions of others and to trigger the desired emotions in them.

If these categories can in fact be understood as having something to do with emotional self-management, consideration of the numerous individual competencies subsumed under them shows that "emotional intelligence" has been employed as a generalized term to put forth a managerial concept of subjectivity. The intrapersonal dimensions of emotional intelligence include learning goals such as "conscientiousness," "accurate self-evaluation," and "drive to achievement," which have little to do with emotional competence. In the interpersonal dimension, qualities such as "service-oriented" and "leadership" count as emotional competence—yet these qualities can be understood just as well as wholly cognitive qualities. Even the "marshmallow test" represents a general behavioral concept that has long been known in sociology and social psychology as the "deferred gratification pattern" (Schneider & Lysgaard, 1953).

"Emotional intelligence"—a concept that lacks any definition of emotion itself—is thus just a fuzzy umbrella term that not only includes skills related to emotion that can purportedly be learned, it also covers a whole spectrum of desired attributes and personal dispositions as well as culturally preferred value patterns and morals. As a comprehensive means for making sense of the human world, emotional self-management here takes on a role that is otherwise usually occupied by religious beliefs and political ideologies: the generation of ideal images of humankind and the human order. Wide-reaching cosmologies do not resist their own implementation at the minute level; on the contrary, they need this to become comprehensible to those who believe in them. Therefore, like the conventional intelligence test, the model of "emotional intelligence" has taken shape as a standardized system of evaluation ("emotional competence inventory") with which a person's level of emotional intelligence can presumably be accurately measured. In business management, this model is now used worldwide for hiring purposes. It is licensed by the Emotional Intelligence Service, a consulting firm founded by Daniel Goleman himself.

Program of Authentic Self-Programming

In general, emotional self-management—exemplified by the idea of "emotional intelligence"—can be understood as a compact cultural program because it comprises organized patterns of interpretation for the purpose of understanding self as well as normative guidelines for behavior and concrete methods for regulating conduct. What is new about this cultural advice for emotional improvement is that it is devoted to the cognitive generation of emotions: "emotion by design." The objective is emotional self-programming that is meant to produce feelings appropriate to a given situation and to utilize these feelings according to what is required. The program for emotional self-management goes far beyond the known methods for attaining good performance and the strategic deployment of emotion. Older concepts for regulating emotions usually assumed the preexistence of certain feelings, which were then to be controlled using the appropriate techniques; the goal was to provide guidance in the interactive staging of feelings. A prime example is the early classic of modern advice literature, Dale Carnegie's *How to Win Friends and Influence People*, which first appeared in 1937 (1990); it attempts to teach the reader how to manipulate the feelings of others so they are unaware that they are being manipulated. Self-control and deceiving others are represented as belonging hand in hand, and they are promoted here with the goal of instrumentalizing others for one's own purposes by simulating affection.

The program of emotional self-management, in contrast, is only mildly interested in simulated emotions because it aims to change the very emotions themselves that are presumed to be given in the role scripts of emotional staging. It also brings into play cognitive dispositives that were previously unknown and that have been derived from brain research and neurobiology. These dispositives reinforce the belief that everyone has the capacity to intervene strategically in the making of their emotions. Modern self-management, in effect, strives to "optimize" emotional experiences—an endeavor that the subject is expected to undertake authentically on his or her own.

Feelings do not, thereby, merely remain the object of subjective and social control. Instead, the emotional habitus itself is to be shaped systematically, which also implies explicit encouragement for people to be emotional. The alienation critique[2] in the sociology of emotions, which has always objected to the forced discrepancy between emotional experience and its expression, is today in danger of missing that which is, in fact, objectionable in the program of emotional self-management. In the end, the alienation critique is trapped in a repressive model of emotions in which the distinction between "real" and "simulated" feelings is taken for granted, and "real" feelings are always found to be a disturbance in the functioning of modern organizations. However, the repression or changing of "real" feelings is not the only method of socially regulating emotions. In present capitalism, which expects the emotional engagement of workers, emotionality is increasingly called for, and each and every subject is asked to answer this call. They do so by invoking self-techniques for inducing feelings, whereby an already existing stock of authentic emotions can no longer be unproblematically assumed[3].

On the other hand, the self-management of feelings cannot be understood as a phenomenon that confirms the informalization theory. The new patterns of regulating emotion have little in common with an increase in emotional liberties and the loosening of affect control in society. Instead, emotional self-management emerges as a standardized demand that controls socially undesirable emotions and stipulates that the individual properly experience "good feelings." Those who engage in a critique of the alienation hypothesis must also admit that being emotionally authentic in a socially prescribed way has its own emotional costs. When emotional self-management serves as a general cultural program, and attaining the goals promoted by such programs is taken as proof of emotional autonomy, there is apparently no "weaker coercion coming from others" (Wouters, 1999, p. 62), as the informalization theory generally describes our era of civilization today. The informalization theory—like Elias' theory of civilization itself, to which it makes recourse in a critical way—is caught in a pneumatic theoretical model of emotional regulation. The relation between self-constraints and external constraints is represented as one in which an increase in the former leads to a decrease in the latter. Our present culture seems to be moving away from these mechanisms for emotional pressure balance. Today, a paradoxical effect can be noted in which increased autonomy corresponds to increased control, which points to a change different from that described by the informalization theory.

Paradoxes in the Modern Regulation of Emotion

The differences between conditioning and autonomy, instrumentalism and self-control, and alienation and informalization that currently divide the theoretical positions within the sociology of emotion therefore tend to dissolve in the cultural program of emotional self-management. The economization of emotions (and, vice versa, the emotionalization of the economy) seems to be able to anchor emotional constraints in the subject by shaping the emotionality of actors and incorporating their emotional needs. New approaches to emotion theory should thus first study the empirical consequences of the current patterns of emotion regulation. The attempt to turn actors into "reflexive co-players"

(Neckel, 2005, pp. 198–204) in self-programming of emotions has its own paradoxical effects and brings new subjective burdens that are, in fact, a result of these paradoxes in the first place. One such effect is disappointment. Because feelings are closely linked with the body, they can never be wholly induced by mental training. They also always maintain an unconscious dimension that cannot simply be shut off via cognitive efforts (see Engelen et al., Emotions as Bio-cultural Processes). The deliberate attempt to do so often brings unintended side effects, the most familiar of which is the emotional burnout syndrome, in which the emotional work required of the subject becomes so overwhelming that personal feelings temporarily shut down.

Feelings are—to use a phrase by Jon Elster (1983, p. 43)—"states that are essentially by-products": If they are consciously striven for, they do not appear; and training our emotions may even have an effect opposite to what it promises the subject. Research in the psychology of emotion has recognized the "ironic process" by which a deliberate attempt to control undesired feelings only leads to these feelings receiving even more attention from the subject and thus bringing about the negative moods they are meant to avoid (Leary, 2003, p. 782). Emotional self-management itself has emotional consequences that are revealed to the individual when feelings react to emotion management that ultimately cannot be managed. Emotion therapy thus touches off precisely those emotional disturbances it is intended to cure.

In turn, the pressure to have positive feelings leads us to perceive our negative feelings all the more as a source of personal failure. One consequence of this is susceptibility to depression, as French sociologist Alain Ehrenberg (1998) has shown in his study on "the exhausted self." Overwhelmed with the feeling that one is responsible for every last personal trait and frustrated that one has repeatedly failed to reach the ideal of becoming a happy and successful person, the notorious feeling of personal failure is transformed into a dark mood. Depression is thus described by Ehrenberg as the modern illness of always feeling wholly inadequate. It is expressed in feelings of sadness and futility and accompanied by exhaustion and a slowing down of thinking, acting, and deciding. In the end, the individual's emotions are "frozen" because nothing in experience can still reach the person's vital interests. This modern illness arises in a society that may have less rigid rules of conformity but which demands initiative and mental skills from the individual and thereby forces upon him or her a compulsory model of the autonomous self. In the words of Ehrenberg (1998):

> Si, comme le pensait Freud, "'l'homme devient névrosé parce qu'il ne peut supporter le degré de renoncement exigé par la société", il devient déprimé parce qu'il doit supporter l'illusion que tout lui est possible. [If, as Freud thought, a person becomes neurotic because he cannot bear the full extent of renunciation required by society, he becomes depressed because he must bear the illusion that he is capable of everything.] (p. 293)

It is this kind of illusion about one's own emotional world that can ultimately lead modern actors to the "affective neutrality" that sociological theory falsely concluded had always been characteristic of rationalized modernity. The "elimination of all purely personal ... and emotional elements," which Max Weber (1968, p. 975) described as unique to modern culture and "specifically [to] its technical and economic basis" (ibid.), would not be the result of a purportedly emotionless modernity but, instead, first developed with the modern emotionalization of the economy. In Kathrin Röggla's documentary novel *Wir Schlafen Nicht* (2004), a literary account of the emotional crises among professionals in the IT branch, a young key account manager says:

> You are and remain such a copy, everyone always told her, "a copy of yourself." Yes, a self-made copy, what else. She's really just a number, she was always told. But of what she couldn't remember. Of what was she a copy, of what a number?[4] (p. 205)

Notes

1 On the process of emotional self-regulation in general, see Leary (2003, pp. 781–782), who distinguished between the following methods: conforming to subjective expectations, choosing suitable social comparisons, and modification of attention. All of these methods are also found in the concept of "emotional intelligence"—for example, the technique of "upbeat denial" (Goleman, 1995, p. 75), the reference to "distraction" (ibid., p. 63), or the recommendation of "downward comparisons" (ibid., p. 74). In addition, however, "emotional intelligence" focuses on the reinterpretation of negative experiences ("reframing"), which emphasizes the claim that the concept creates whole new emotional worlds.

2 The opposition between emotion and alienation—in addition to that of feeling and reason—seems to be a second fundamental cultural dichotomy that has influenced the modern discourse on emotion in Western society, as the American emotion ethnologist Catherine Lutz (1988) posited. For a discussion of this idea, see Röttger-Rössler (2004, pp. 53–68).

3 In contrast, see Arlie Hochschild's definition of emotion management: "An act of emotion management, as I use this term, is an effort by any means, conscious or not, to change one's feeling or emotion. We can try to induce feelings that we don't at first feel, or to suppress feelings that we do. We can—and continually do—try to shape and reshape our feelings to fit our inner cultural guidelines" (Hochschild, 1998, p. 9). The view that emotion management is only about the modification of "real" feelings is also found in an approach to the theory of emotion that is quite opposite to that of Hochschild's "constructivism." The rather influential work of Paul Ekman posits that there are innate and therefore universal emotions that are only "secondarily" shaped by cultural "display rules." Here, it is also assumed that there are subjective means for presenting emotions that may change prior emotional states but cannot induce them (cf. Ekman, 1970, pp. 152–153).

4 "Du bist und bleibst so ein Exemplar," habe man immer zu ihr gesagt. "ein Exemplar deiner selbst." Ja, Selbstausgabe sei sie, was sonst auch. So eine Nummer sei sie, hat man ihr immer wieder gesagt. Nur sie erinnere sich nicht mehr von was. Von was sei sie die Ausgabe, von was die Nummer?

References

Boltanski, L., & Chiapello, È. (1999). *Le nouvel esprit du capitalisme* [The new spirit of capitalism]. Paris: Gallimard.

Botton, A. de (2004). *Status anxiety*. New York: Pantheon.

Carnegie, D. (1990). *How to win friends and influence people*. New York: Pocket Books/Simon and Schuster. (First published 1937)
Ehrenberg, A. (1998). *La fatigue d'être soi. Dépression et société* [The exhausted self: Depression and society]. Paris: Éditions Odile Jacob.
Ekman, P. (1970). Universal facial expression of emotions. *California Mental Health Research Digest, 8*, 151–158.
Elias, N. (2000). *The civilizing process: Sociogenetic and psychogenetic investigations* (Rev. ed.). Oxford: Blackwell. (First published 1939)
Elster, J. (1983). *Sour grapes: Studies in the subversion of rationality*. Cambridge, UK: Cambridge University Press.
Fineman, S. (Ed.). (2000a). *Emotion in organizations*. London: Sage.
Fineman, S. (2000b). Commodifying the emotionally intelligent. In S. Fineman (Ed.), *Emotion in organizations* (2nd ed., pp. 101–114). London: Sage.
Flam, H. (1990). Emotional man: Corporate actors as emotion-motivated emotion managers. *International Sociology, 5*, 225–234.
Goleman, D. (1995). *Emotional intelligence*. New York: Bantam.
Goleman, D. (1998). *Working with emotional intelligence*. New York: Bantam.
Goleman, D., Boyatzis, R., & McKee, A. (2002). *Primal leadership: Realizing the power of emotional intelligence*. Boston, MA: Harvard Business School Press.
Gonschorrek, U., & Berg, E. (2002). *Emotionales Management. Erfolgsfaktoren sozial kompetenter Führung* [Emotion management: Success factors in developing socially competent leadership]. Frankfurt, Germany: Frankfurter Allgemeine Buch.
Hochschild, A. R. (1983). *The managed heart: Commercialization of human feeling*. Berkeley, CA: University of California Press.
Hochschild, A. R. (1998). The sociology of emotion as a way of seeing. In G. Bendelow, & S. J. Williams (Eds.), *Emotions in social life: Critical themes and contemporary issues* (pp. 3–15). London: Routledge.
Honneth, A. (Ed.). (2002). *Befreiung aus der Mündigkeit. Paradoxien des gegenwärtigen Kapitalismus* [Emancipation from responsibility: Paradoxes of modern capitalism]. Frankfurt, Germany/New York: Campus.
Horkheimer, M., & Adorno, T. W. (1977). *Dialectic of enlightenment: Philosophical fragments*. New York: Seabury. (Original work published 1944)
Klein, S. (2003). *Die Glücksformel oder Wie die guten Gefühle entstehen* [The formula for happiness: How good feelings arise]. Reinbek bei Hamburg, Germany: Rowohlt.
Kocyba, H. (2000). Der Preis der Anerkennung. Von der tayloristischen Missachtung zur strategischen Instrumentalisierung der Subjektivität der Arbeitenden [The price of recognition: From the Taylorist disregard to the strategic instrumentalization of the subjectivity of the workers]. In U. Holtgrewe, S. Voswinkel, & G. Wagner (Eds.), *Anerkennung und Arbeit* (pp. 127–140). Konstanz, Germany: UVK.
Leary, M. R. (2003). The self and emotion: The role of self-reflection in the generation and regulation of affective experience. In R. J. Davidson, K. R. Scherer, & H. Hill Goldsmith (Eds.), *Handbook of affective sciences* (pp. 773–786). Oxford, UK: Oxford University Press.
Lohr, K. (2003). Subjektivierung von Arbeit. Ausgangspunkt einer Neuorientierung der Industrie- und Arbeitssoziologie [Subjectivization of work: Starting point for a new orientation in industrial sociology]? *Berliner Journal für Soziologie, 13*, 511–529.
Lutz, C. (1988). *Unnatural emotions: Everyday sentiments on a Micronesian atoll and their challenge to Western theory*. Chicago, IL: University of Chicago Press.
Neckel, S. (2001). 'Leistung' und 'Erfolg.' Die symbolische Ordnung der Marktgesellschaft ["Achievement" and "success": The symbolic order of the market society]. In E. Barlösius, H.-P. Müller, & S. Sigmund (Eds.), *Gesellschaftsbilder im Umbruch. Soziologische Perspektiven in Deutschland* (pp. 245–265). Opladen, Germany: Leske & Budrich.
Neckel, S. (2003). Die Marktgesellschaft als kultureller Kapitalismus. Zum neuen Synkretismus von Ökonomie und Lebensform [The market society as cultural capitalism: The new

syncretism of economics and lifestyle]. *Mitteilungen des Instituts für Sozialforschung, 14*, 7–21. Frankfurt, Germany: Institut für Sozialforschung.

Neckel, S. (2004). Erfolg [Success]. In U. Bröckling, S. Krasmann, & T. Lemke (Eds.), *Glossar der Gegenwart* (pp. 63–70). Frankfurt, Germany: Suhrkamp.

Neckel, S. (2005). Die Verwilderung der Selbstbehauptung. Adornos Soziologie: Veralten der Theorie—Erneuerung der Zeitdiagnose [The running wild of self-assertion, Adorno's sociology: Aging of theory—revival of time diagnosis]. In A. Honneth (Ed.), *Dialektik der Freiheit. Frankfurter Adorno-Konferenz 2003* (pp. 188–204). Frankfurt, Germany: Suhrkamp.

O'Connor, J., & Seymour, J. (1994). *Training with NLP: Skills for managers, trainers and communicators*. London: HarperCollins.

Parsons, T., & Shils, E. A. (Eds.). (1951). *Toward a general theory of action*. Cambridge, MA: Harvard University Press.

Pongratz, H. J. (2002). Emotionalität und Effizienz. Typen von Erwerbsorientierungen und Lebensführung im Vergleich [Emotionality and efficiency: A comparison of types of employment orientation and life-style]. In M. Weihrich, & G. Günter Voß (Eds.), *Tag für Tag. Alltag als Problem—Lebensführung als Lösung* (pp. 47–68). München/Mering, Germany: Rainer Hampp.

Pongratz, H. J. (2004). *Subordination. Inszenierungsformen von Personalführung in Deutschland seit 1933* [Subordination: Ways of staging personnel management in Germany since 1933]. München/Mering, Germany: Rainer Hampp.

Rastetter, D. (2001). Emotionsarbeit. Betriebliche Steuerung und individuelles Erleben [Emotion work: Company control and individual experience]. In G. Schreyögg, & J. Sydow (Eds.), *Emotionen und Management* (Managementforschung, 11, 111–134). Wiesbaden, Germany: Gabler.

Röggla, K. (2004). *Wir schlafen nicht* [We don't sleep]. Frankfurt, Germany: S. Fischer.

Röttger-Rössler, B. (2004). *Die kulturelle Modellierung des Gefühls. Ein Beitrag zur Theorie und Methodik ethnologischer Emotionsforschung anhand indonesischer Fallstudien* [The cultural modeling of feeling: A theoretical and methodological contribution to ethnological emotion research based on Indonesian case studies]. Münster, Germany: LIT.

Salovey, P., & Mayer, J. D. (1990). Emotional intelligence. *Imagination, Cognition and Personality, 9*, 185–211.

Salovey, P., Kokkonen, M., Lopes, P., & Mayer, J. D. (2004). Emotional intelligence: What do we know? In A. S. R. Manstead, N. Frijda, & A. Fischer (Eds.), *Feelings and emotions: The Amsterdam symposium* (pp. 321–340). Cambridge, UK: Cambridge University Press.

Schmidt, P. (2001). *Die Kraft der positiven Gefühle—Mit neuen Mentaltechniken innerlich frei werden* [The power of positive feelings: Liberation from within via new mental techniques]. München, Germany: DTV.

Schneider, L., & Lysgaard, S. (1953). The deferred gratification pattern: A preliminary study. *American Sociological Review, 18*, 142–149.

Schreyögg, G., & Sydow, J. (Eds.) (2001). *Emotionen und Management* [Emotions and management] (Managementforschung, 11). Wiesbaden, Germany: Gabler.

Sieben, B. (2001). Emotionale Intelligenz—Golemans Erfolgskonstrukt auf dem Prüfstand [Emotional intelligence: Testing Goleman's success construct]. In G. Schreyögg, & J. Sydow (Eds.), *Emotionen und Management* (Managementforschung, 11, 135–170). Wiesbaden, Germany: Gabler.

Simmel, G. (1990). *The philosophy of money* (edited by David Frisby). London: Routledge. (Original work published 1900)

Thoits, P. A. (2004). Emotion norms, emotion work, and social order. In A. S. R. Manstead, N. Frijda, & A. Fischer (Eds.), *Feelings and emotions: The Amsterdam symposium* (pp. 359–378). Cambridge, UK: Cambridge University Press.

Voswinkel, S. (with A. Korzekwa) (2004). *Dienstleistungsarbeit und Anerkennung. Arbeiten im Kundenkontakt und die Servicekulturdebatte* [Service sector work and recognition] (Forschungsbericht). Frankfurt, Germany: Institut für Sozialforschung.

Weber, M. (1968). *Economy and society* (edited by Guenther Roth & Claus Wittich). New York: Bedminster.

Wouters, C. (1999). *Informalisierung. Norbert Elias' Zivilisationstheorie und Zivilisationsprozesse im 20. Jahrhundert* [Informalization: Norbert Elias' civilization theory and civilization processes in the 20th century]. Wiesbaden, Germany: Westdeutscher Verlag.

Emotion, Embodiment, and Agency: The Place of a Social Emotions Perspective in the Cross-Disciplinary Understanding of Emotional Processes

Margot L. Lyon

Abstract A social approach to emotion as defined here makes possible a deeper understanding of emotion's role in the mediation of bodily and sociocultural domains. This is accomplished, firstly, through the fact that such an approach gives emphasis to the role of social structure in the ontology of emotion, and thus to the import of emotion in understanding social processes. Secondly, a social approach allows for the articulation of the place of emotion in understanding how social life comes to be embodied, that is, how social life is grounded in bodily processes that are fundamental in the constitution of the "somatic" dimensions of social being. Thirdly, in that the social emotions approach makes explicit how emotion has not only a social relational genesis but also social consequences, makes possible the understanding of the body as simultaneously object and agent in the social world, thus contributing to the delineation of the place of emotion in our understanding of action and agency, and of the relationship between agency and structure.

Introduction

The aim of the ZiF Research Group on Emotions as Bio-cultural Processes was to "build foundations for the development of an interdisciplinary model of emotions in which the *bio-cultural dialectics of emotional processes* receives special attention" (Markowitsch & Röttger-Rössler, 2003, p. 2; italics added). The focus on the question of the dialectic between the bodily and sociocultural dimensions of emotional processes rightly emphasizes the importance of addressing directly the nature of the relationship between social and bodily life. The term dialectics (*Dialektik*) suggests a necessary engagement with questions fundamental to contemporary emotions theory, for to take the example of Marxian theory, dialectics is concerned with the philosophy of internal

M.L. Lyon (✉)
School of Archaeology and Anthropology, The Australian National University, Canberra, ACT, Australia 0200
e-mail: margot.lyon@anu.edu.au

B. Röttger-Rössler, H.J. Markowitsch (eds.), *Emotions as Bio-cultural Processes*,
DOI 10.1007/978-0-387-09546-2_10,

relations i.e., the way in which the "whole is present through internal relations in each of its parts" (Ollman, 1993, p. 37).

Marx provides an apt referent here, too, in that the materialist conception of history requires acknowledgment of both the corporeal roots and the corporeal organization of social life. *The German Ideology* (Marx & Engels, 1947), for example, represents one of the earliest engagements with the body in classical sociological theory, seeing it as a starting point for a materialist conception of history, even if this dimension was never elaborated adequately by Marx himself. The idea of a dialectical relation between bodily and sociocultural life foregrounds the question of the importance of emotion in understanding the ways in which social-relational processes are embodied, for emotions clearly are relational just as they are also bodily. Thus, the term dialectics in its concern with whole-part relations suggests engagement with deeper issues in emotions theory, for example, how emotion in fact has a constitutive role in social-relational processes, and thus also a determinative and constitutive role in the embodiment of those processes.

The question of the interpenetration of social and bodily life is not a trivial one. It underlies the fundamental problematic of social theory, that is, how best to understand and represent the relation between complex social forms and individual life, including the question of agency. The argument here is that an explicitly social concept of emotion, at least as outlined in this chapter, provides a better means to conceptualize just how social processes come to be embodied and, in turn, provides a deeper understanding of emotion's role in theorizing action and agency.

It is thus worth "unpacking" some of the contributions that the social study of emotion can make in addressing these questions. Although these arguments cannot be fully developed here, this chapter is intended as a contribution to the attempt to integrate social, psychological, and biological domains in the study of emotion.

A Social Emotions Approach and its Implications

I have stated that an explicitly social emotions approach makes possible a deeper understanding of emotion's central place in the mediation of bodily and sociocultural domains. Such an approach is thus the starting point of this chapter. In this section, I briefly outline the key features of a social approach to emotion and provide an indication of the implications of this approach for understanding how emotional processes are actively engaged in the bridging of bodily and social domains.

The Social Ontology of Emotion

Firstly, a social approach to emotion emphasizes the role of social structure and social relations in the ontology of emotion, that is, that emotions and feelings always arise in a social context. It thus moves away from commonsense and psychological views of emotion that see it as primarily "located" in individual psyches, and also from purely cultural constructionist approaches that give primacy to meaning systems in the genesis of emotions. The social emotions perspective directs us toward a more sociological view that focuses on social structure and group organization, and on social processes as the ground of experience and thus of emotion and feeling. It does not, of course, deny a role for culture; rather, it sees cultural processes as a subset of, or as implicate within, social processes in the larger sense (Lyon, 1995). Culture, of course, has a role in shaping what emotions are experienced in any given context, how they are expressed, and the meanings given to them.

In a social approach, emotion in fact can be conceived of as a complex aspect or dimension of social processes themselves, and therefore also as constitutive of the field of subjectivity that *is* social life. However, we must go further and ask how we are to construe the relationship of social-emotional processes to this field of subjectivity and being. This requires the acknowledgement of the crucial role of the body.

The Body and Emotion

Both the experience and expression of emotion are grounded in bodily capabilities. An adequate approach to emotional processes must therefore give primacy to the bodily basis of emotion as well as its social ontology. Evidence from research on the evolutionary bases of emotion systems (see Casimir, also Daum, this volume; Eds.), as well as research from developmental psychology (see Holodynski, this volume; Eds.), clearly demonstrates that emotions become increasingly specialized for the mediation of social relationships. In evolutionary terms, emotions are less about private feeling than about bringing internal states into the public domain where they contribute to directing social behavior, and are thus part of the constitution of social action.

The understanding of emotion's role in mediating the bodily and social dimensions of lived existence is facilitated when we consider the fact that the capacities of the body necessarily include emotion. That is, the capacity to experience and respond in indeterminate and creative ways to the world *depends* on emotional processes. Emotional capacities might be seen, in a sense, to supervene on complex bodily capacities. This extends the notion of the emotional capacities of the organism beyond the more restricted notions of the bodily bases of emotion to include its interactive and social dimensions, for it is through emotional processes that social life comes to be experienced, enacted, and thus embodied.

Emotional capacities are therefore *part of* the somatic or bodily dimensions of lived existence, just as they are integral to the constitution of social and cultural life. They are a central aspect of our engagement with the social world, for emotional processes always involve the structuring of bodily relations within any given sociocultural context (Lyon, 1997). We thus move beyond seeing emotions as simply behavioral or feeling responses to social events, or primarily as drives or some other feature of a relatively stable organic substrate. This approach also, as already noted, moves us beyond purely social or cultural constructionist approaches that tend to address embodiment primarily in terms of representations of the body rather than the organism itself.

In sum, understanding how emotion has a social ontology, and its foundations in bodily being, is therefore crucial if we are to explore the question of how social processes are embodied. The question of the place of emotional processes in the embodiment of social forms, however, raises complex issues as to the conceptualization of "how" and "where" body and social world interpenetrate and how the whole is emergent in the interrelationship of these two domains.

Emotion and Social Structure

We have said that social emotional processes can be seen always to involve the structuring of bodily relations within a sociocultural context. In that emotions arise in, and indeed are always part of, the substance of social relations, they are variously experienced, felt, expressed, or acted on by individuals depending partly on how these individuals are "located" or positioned in particular social structures as well as on how they conceptualize these positions. This third aspect of the social emotions approach casts into relief the need for a framework that acknowledges the location of individuals and groups in any given social structural context and the implications of particular positions for social and bodily relations. This point is taken up in more detail in the following section.

The importance of social structure in reference to emotion has been widely treated in early studies on the sociology of emotion by scholars such as Kemper (e.g., 1978, 1984, 1990), Scheff (1988, 1990, 1994), and De Rivera (1977, 1992) as well as Collins (1984, 1990). Kemper, for example, demonstrated how the social environmental determinants of emotion can be given analytical status through explicitly relational concepts such as social class, hierarchy, power, and status, and how these affect and are at the root of an individual's or group's emotional experience in the context of particular social relational forms (Kemper, 1984, p. 370). It is important to note here that the relations entailed can be seen as properties of the group, not just of individuals, and that emotions that arise in structured interaction may act either to integrate individuals or groups, for example, the emotions of love, loyalty, and pride, or act to differentiate them, for example, envy, fear, and anger (Kemper, 1984, p. 374).

The social emotions approach, then, is concerned with the ways in which sociocultural forms, or "social facts" in Durkheim's terms, become and are in a continual process of becoming embodied via emotional processes themselves. This approach thus makes possible exploration of the interrelation of body and society in praxis, that is, how bodily and sociocultural being might be conceptualized as an ongoing dialectical process cohering within specific, embodied emotional processes. In addition, this perspective helps take us beyond the tendency to see emotional life as simply inhering in face-to-face interaction, or as characterizing the social world as static and intersubjective.

Further, the fact that emotion has a social ontology raises the issue of how to characterize the social field, how people variously "occupy" or are located within it, and how this determines social experience and thus emotion, and ultimately forms of social action. This positioning, that is, how emotions situate individuals and groups within larger social structural forms, and how position is fundamental in the structuring of emotional experience and the generation of feeling, has direct implications for the question of action. Thus, our fourth point is one that directs us to consider more closely the question of emotion's role in theories of agency.

Social Emotional Processes and Agency

Any discussion about the central place of emotion in the embodiment of social processes inevitably raises the question of agency, that is, how emotion is bound up with action and is thus agential in these processes. Only in this way can we acknowledge the central place of emotion not only in the phenomenological apprehension of the world but also in its making.

Emotion is, in fact, implicated in action; indeed, it can be conceptualized as an important dimension of action within social processes generally, whether understood at individual or group levels. The "somatic" dimensions of action, which include the embodied dimensions of social-emotional processes more generally, must therefore be seen as integral to any conception of agency. For the body is never simply the passive recipient of society's forces, but through emotion, contributes to the *making* of the social world through its own transformation and its transformative acts.

This position extends conventional notions of agency and, in turn, facilitates the understanding of social life and action as a dynamic process, permitting an open rather than an overly determined or closed model of the interrelationship between social forms and individual life. It can be argued that this position also makes possible the understanding of a wider, more complex range of behavior as agential. It further helps to free us from the limitations of models of agency grounded in intentionality and outcomes, and from the reification of the micro–macro divide in theories of structure and agency.

In sum, the social conception of emotion moves beyond conventional approaches in that it is neither concerned with emotion simply as reflecting internal states, nor primarily as a reaction to social events, but rather as an embodied, active phenomenon arising within and constituting an aspect of the social field itself. It is not bound to situationalist or interactionist views of social experience and action, but opens the way for exploring how larger social structural forces are embodied through experience and action. This, in turn, results in a dynamic view of emotional capacities as fundamental to agency and action in the context of social life.

Next Steps

The next step, then, is to examine how best to get at the particularities of the relationship between social forms and individual life, that is, how—through emotion—situatedness is actively embodied. At this point, it is informative to look at another, much earlier integrative approach to the nature of social and bodily life. In the following section, I briefly take up the example of philosophical anthropology in order to point to a convergence in core questions posed, as well as to suggest how the emotions field may contribute to furthering the pursuit of these questions.

The Quest of Philosophical Anthropology

Integrative approaches in the human sciences are hardly new. In this section, I draw a brief comparison with another approach to the interrelationship between biological and sociocultural domains to bring into further relief two issues that continue to be central in the quest for an integrative biosocial approach.

A path toward an integrative approach, one that was already well underway early in the first half of the 20th century in Weimar-period Germany, was the scientific and philosophical movement[1] of "philosophical anthropology", or "philosophical biology." Both terms have been applied, often interchangeably, to the same set of European scientist-philosophers, although the term philosophical anthropology tends to dominate, particularly in European social science.[2] The emphasis of this largely German anthropological tradition was on the question of the fundamental nature of humans and their relation to nature. It sought to integrate natural-scientific and philosophical approaches. Concerned as it was with human nature and the fundamental structures of life including its biological foundations, most of the key scholars in philosophical anthropology came to it from one or another of the empirical sciences (Grene, 1968, p. vii; see also 1970). Core figures were Adolf Portmann, Helmuth Plessner, F. J. J. Buytendijk, Max Scheler, and E. Minkowski, as well as Erwin W. Straus, Kurt Goldstein, and Arnold Gehlen.

When philosophical anthropology first emerged, philosophy and science were everywhere still largely one discipline, with the distinctions between them becoming more prominent later following the acceleration in the rate of scientific advances in biology, chemistry, and physics in the context of the expansion of universities and industry during the early decades of the 20th century.[3] The quest of philosophical anthropology was ultimately submerged by rapid growth in the biological sciences and by developments in social science outside Germany, as well as by developments in philosophy, particularly of existential philosophy, that combined to support the growing conceptual and intellectual divide between models of the physical and social worlds.

Unlike anthropology in Britain and the United States, which concerned itself with the ethnological study of indigenous cultures, philosophical anthropology, in keeping with both its philosophical and scientific roots, was concerned with fundamental questions about the nature of humans and their relationship to nature. Philosophical anthropology was always comparative and multidisciplinary in conception, and so sought to illuminate the relationship between the construction of knowledge in both the social and the natural sciences.

German philosophical anthropology clearly prefigures the more holistic or cross-disciplinary debates that are reemerging today in new areas, including contemporary emotions research. The growth of scientific knowledge in areas as diverse as neurobiology, immunology, and developmental psychology certainly supports further work at the "borders" or interface between biology and the sociocultural sciences—work that would have the social sciences take the body seriously. In social science, such work could include, for example, not only the implications of tactile-kinesthetic and other bodily based forms of knowledge (Sheets-Johnstone, 1990, pp. 320–321), but also both the bodily and the social dimensions of emotion. After all, the notions of touch and movement are central to our understanding of emotion and feeling, and motor engagement is fundamental to social engagement and to emotion.

Yet in a world in which much of social science, at least within English-speaking traditions, seems to have fallen into the embrace of radical subjectivism, attempts to reembody social and cultural theory have not gone much beyond what is more lip service to the import of the body. In the study of emotions, there is a growing need not only to move beyond subjectivist models but also to resist the present-day reductions of neo-Darwinism and the physicalist straitjacket of molecular biology. Counter forces to the contrary, there are good reasons for emotions research to intensify its attempt to engage with wider, interdisciplinary models that can help to illuminate processes occurring at the borders of existing intellectual domains. The cross-disciplinary study of emotions therefore, can be a primary arena for this work.

The questions posed by philosophical anthropology take us further than the logocentric and constructionist accounts that continue to dominate social science today. Honneth and Joas, commenting on the German anthropological tradition, point out a need for renewed engagement with the foundations of social, psychical, and bodily being. They see philosophical anthropology as providing an arena for "self-reflection of the social and cultural sciences on their biological foundations and on the normative content of their bodies of knowledge, considered in relation to determinate historical and political problems...." (1988, p. 9).

There are recent indications of a revival in philosophical anthropology, or at least a reengagement with its concerns with human nature, particularly in the face of advances in biotechnology and economic globalization. The announcement for a 2005 multidisciplinary conference entitled "Philosophical Anthropology Reviewed and Renewed: History, Theory, Synthesis & Normative Implications," stated that it aimed to bring together "the legacy of a German philosophical tradition with the theoretical and empirical work from leading investigators in the human sciences."[4]

In the following, I briefly draw on material from philosophical anthropology in order to foreground the importance of two core issues crucial to our task of understanding emotion's role in bridging bodily and social domains. These are firstly, the *active nature of the body*, that is, the active role of corporeal capacities in social processes, and secondly, the fact that the *body is always situated*, both socially and somatically, in reference to its environment. Each of these issues has direct implications for understanding the experience of the individual and group not only as subjects but as agents.

The Active, Constitutive Role of the Body in Society and Culture

One of the chief concerns of philosophical anthropology, as already noted, was precisely the incorporation of a natural science explanation in the understanding of society and human nature. It actively sought to clarify "the relationship between the natural and the socio-cultural sciences, not by means of definitional demarcations, as had been done previously, but through investigation of the subject matter of mediating scientific domains, such as biology" (Honneth & Joas, 1988, p. 41). Philosophical anthropology sought to move beyond the philosophical dualisms of mind/soul and body, dualisms that figured in earlier philosophical traditions including phenomenology, and that persist in one form or another in much of social science theory today.

In Anglo-American social science, the acknowledgment of the import of a bodily basis for experience is often credited to the work of the phenomenologist, Merleau-Ponty (e.g., 1962). In this tradition, bodily being is seen as the basis of world construction. In fact, however, Merleau-Ponty did little to engage with the body *qua* body, and although he made the point that the ground of bodily experience is in fact social, an important matter for us in emotions theory, he did not greatly develop this in his work.

In a critique of the way in which phenomenology typically sees the notion of "embodiment" to contain the solution to the interconnections between mental and physical domains, Sheets-Johnstone (1990, p. 303) points out that real embodiment requires more than just the conception of the self as somehow packaged in the flesh. She terms as a mere "grammatical union" the notion that "the body 'embodies'—presumably as the mind 'inspirits'" (ibid). Where this purely grammatical union is made, she states, causes us to lose view of the "empirical frame of reference," that is, just how the lived body actually is lived or comes to be so. She notes that "statements about 'our lived experience of being embodied' need to be cashed in for evidence that shows embodiment to be an experienced fact" (p. 304).

What is of import here is attention to what Sheets-Johnstone calls a "bodily logos" in the constitution of social life, that is, seeing social being as arising from the active capacities of the body itself. We need to ask, she says, "what, then, is the self or mind that is embodied? What is this act or fact of embodiment?" (1990, p. 304). Thus, we must consider the body first in terms of the body's evolved corporeal capacities, that is, its role and potentialities in the constitution of the nature of human society and meaning. These capacities are the starting point for social life and being.

The philosophical anthropology of Helmuth Plessner and others in this movement, such as Adolph Portmann and later Arnold Gehlen, commenced with such questions. Plessner (e.g., 1928/1975) was much concerned with the relationship of the body to the active or performative aspects of social life. He saw that humans stand in an active relationship with the world in which they find themselves. He draws a distinction between *being a body*, that is, how, like animals, we are centered in our bodies, and *having a body*, that is, how we are also aware of our place in reference to the social and natural environment and thus decentered. This distinction is, in a sense, parallel to George Herbert Mead's (1934) notion of the "I" and the "me."

A major contribution of Plessner is his notion of boundary. Plessner sees life to be lived at the boundary formed through the engagement of our bodies with the natural and social environment. This is not the physical boundary of the skin, but the domain formed through our active "production" of our world in interaction with it, such that our lived existence includes and incorporates this boundary. Furthermore, we are always *positioned* in reference to or in opposition to this boundary. This includes being what he terms *excentrically positioned*; that is, we are in relationhip with phenomena beyond the body as well as having a relationship with the body that is directed back within it. This boundary structure, including its relational dimensions, was termed by Plessner "positionality" (Grene, 1968, p. 78).

We are continually adapting to this boundary structure, incorporating or embodying dimensions of it. We are thus open to the world, excentrically positioned in reference to it in Plessner's terms. It is here at this border that we live and that we actively apprehend the world. It is here that, through human expressive and creative capacities, social life is realized. The display of positionality is what constitutes a living being, not in the static sense of location, but in the sense of the organism's relationship to its place in the world.

Plessner's conceptions have implications for theories of action and agency. As noted, any theory of social action must acknowledge the corporeal foundations of social life including the capacity for action. Moreover, the active and social-relational character of existence is crucial to arguments about the creativity of action and agency. In the opinion of Honneth and Joas (1988, p. 47), who have written most informatively on social action and the foundations of social theory, philosophical anthropology can be understood precisely as a theory of action.[5]

Once the embodied and active nature of human existence is acknowledged, along with its role in the constitution of the organism's relationship to the social and natural environment, the way is opened toward a deeper consideration of the affective horizons of social agency. From the perspective taken in this chapter, the active, corporeal capacities of the human organism, as already noted, include emotional capacities and these are always and everywhere relational.

In the following, I briefly use Plessner's notion of positionality to explore the relation of emotion to agential social processes and hence to social structure.

The Concept of Positionality and Its Implications in the Study of Emotion

Plessner's concept of positionality can lead us toward much more than simply the conceptualization of the active interrelationship of organism and environment. The concept was formed "in order to establish, in everyday, direct perception, a foundation for the whole study of living things from morphology to anthropology" (Grene, 1968, p. 120). For Plessner, an inanimate object simply fills space, whereas a living thing *takes its place*, for positionality means being alive. As Grene (1968, p. 75) notes, "it not only has a position in the coordinate system of space and time; it has *its* place." Furthermore, the inclusion of both spatial and temporal dimensions means that the concept of positionality includes not only the relational aspects of being but also the dynamic character of those relational processes, that is, how lived existence is constituted through this creative relationship between self and world as the individual simultaneously internalizes and opposes itself to it (see Grene, 1968, p. 76).

This double aspect of the relation between the organism and its environment helps overcome the shortcomings of dualist theory. As Grene (1968) states, "a body with this kind of boundary structure is not simply divisible into inner and outer; it is, through its relation to its boundary, *both* directed *out* beyond the body that it is *and* back *into* it again" (p. 78; italics in original). For Plessner, the active taking of a place meant that the boundary structure is part of itself. Thus, "the relation of the body to its boundary is a relation of *itself* to *itself*" (Grene, 1968, p. 77; italics in original). The person establishes that boundary and exists in relationship to it, and within that process embodies it. It is thus through this process of the embodiment of the boundary that the self is in relationship with the world in which it is situated.

For our purposes here, we now need to consider how a social emotions perspective in fact expands on Plessner's concept of positionality, and ultimately how this expanded perspective assists in understanding the mediation of social and bodily being.

Emotion as an Aspect of "Taking a Position"

It is my argument that emotion can be seen as an aspect of positionality itself; that is, emotions both arise within and are a constitutive part of the processes involved in Plessner's notion of the taking of a position. As emotion is an aspect of all action, and thus integral to the construction of human subjectivity, emotion is therefore a capacity that is clearly intertwined with our embodied subjectivity, as it is, by definition, about our engagement with the world.

Given that the conception of positionality also encompasses social relations and thus emotion, the social nature of emotion is therefore linked to the issue of how to characterize the social field and the ways in which people variously "occupy" or take their place within it. Further, in that emotions are always part of the substance of social relations, how they are experienced, expressed, or acted on depends on how individuals are "located," or positioned, in particular social structural contexts. Thus, a notion such as positionality can contribute to our understanding of how emotion is fundamental to the constitution of complex social relationships. Feeling states arise in reference to how one experiences the actions of others relative to the self in any given situation and the implications such actions may have in ongoing social circumstances.

The experience of positionality, however, is not only about microsociological or interactional processes. It is also about one's place—or the place of the group or groups with which one is affiliated—in the larger social milieu, that is, in reference to objective social structural forms such as those that determine economic standing or status. It is these forms that define the structure of opportunities that, in turn, affect the conditions under which we must live and experience our lives. The next step, then, is to consider more closely the interrelation between actively taking a position and the question of the embodiment of social structural forms.

Emotion, Action, and the Embodiment of Structure

Plessner tells us that the boundary created through the organism's engagement with the world is in fact *part of itself*. The constitution of this boundary, then, entails a process of its incorporation or its embodiment within the self. Thus, our relation to the world becomes an embodied aspect of the self. We could say that in taking a position the organism is always in a process of *becoming* something, this property of becoming also being a property of itself (Grene, 1968, p. 78).

The incorporation of this boundary that is entailed by the engagement between self and world raises the important question of how social structural forms come to be embodied. And, as we have seen, this question is closely tied to how we view agency, for the active engagement of bodies in social processes entails an essential relationship with reference to social structural forms.

"Where" in the body, then, is "structure"? More to the point, in what embodied processes is structure revealed? Any question about "where" structure lies entails also the question of the mode of apprehension of structure. As we have said, we know structure or position through how it "affects" us, through our own embodied, emotional apprehension of it in the context of interaction with the world in which we live. Structures affect us in ways that are an outcome of the particular relationship we have with our milieu through our active engagement with it, and this impact is independent of whether or not we have any self-reflective awareness of how those processes operate.

The emotional apprehension of the world can thus be seen to encompass relational processes that are both agential and that entail their incorporation or embodiment within the self. Action itself is thus about the production of social forms as well as about their incorporation and transformation. This perspective also permits consideration of how processes of embodiment come to be socially shaped, for example, through basic mechanisms such as conditioning and habit as well as more complex phenomena such as cultural influence. The result might be said to be the concept of a social body, thus returning us to the question of the dialectic between bodily and social life and emotion's place in its mediation.

Subjectivity, Action, Feeling, and Time

Areas of inquiry that can help to further our understanding of the social shaping of bodily life, and thus how the social "enters" or becomes "part" of the body, include the further exploration of the nature of subjectivity and the importance of the temporal dimension in emotional processes. It is clear that a major contribution of philosophical anthropology to the development of a theory of agency derives at least partly from its implications for a deeper understanding of subjectivity as arising from within processes of action, that is, from the interaction of the organism and its environment, rather than arising out of forms of conscious knowing (Buytendijk, 1974, p. 18; see also 1950). The social study of emotion contributes in that it explicates the role of emotion in the constitution of these relational processes of which subjectivity is a product. It is these processes that are foundational to the unity of the body as both object and actor.

The emotional dispositions that arise within social life are thus an integral aspect of both the foundations of action and the situatedness of individuals and groups in reference to the wider social and natural environment. Indeed, agency and emotion can be conceived of as logically, and ontologically, of a similar order. Each is dynamic and indeterminate; each is inseparable from context. As Aylwin (1985) notes in a study of the relationship between thought and feeling, "agents do not act without motivation and experiencers do not feel outside the context of action . . . even grief occurs against a background of action, in that it indicates the necessity to abandon plans for co-action" (pp. 151–152).

Further, the temporal dimension is crucial here if we are to avoid conventional, static approaches to embodiment. Both agency and emotion are also about our relationship to time, that is, about the projection of self into both future and past, and thus about the process of becoming in Allport's (1955) sense; that is, it is not about clock time but about feeling and action and the creative aspects of being (Aylwin, 1985, p. 137). We "become" through being moved, that is, through emotional processes (Lyon, 2003, p. 95). It is through action that "our present self creates or preserves the vital relationship with its future self, the self that it is planning to become" (Aylwin, 1985, p. 145). And, the realization of this self is precisely in our relationship with the world.

What is becoming, what is being created in these processes, is, in a sense, structure. That is, ultimately, embodied positionality is about our relation to structure and so the internalization of structural forms. Thus, the elaboration of the role of a social approach to emotion helps to ground the interpenetration of structural and social forms in human praxis, and so assist in making manifest the dialectic between bodily and social life.

Conclusion

The above has how core issues in a cross-disciplinary approach to emotion are cognate with directions of inquiry in a much earlier philosophical anthropology, and how an explicitly social perspective on emotion can advance that quest. Philosophical anthropology acknowledged early on the active and creative role of the body in the constitution of human social perception, experience, being, and action. In parallel with Plessner's notion of positionality, it is clear how emotion acts to situate individuals in social life and how social-emotional processes are both active and creative.

The social emotions approach thus has direct implications for how we conceptualize action and agency. In that emotion is about processes that both underlie and are part of our engagement with the world, it is thus both a constitutive and generative factor in social action. In turn, we have seen how this extended notion of agency opens the way for a deeper understanding of the larger sociological question of the relation between structure and agency. That is, such an approach reveals how emotional processes are fundamental in the active embodiment of social forms.

In sum, the argument here has been that the social study of the emotions makes a theoretical contribution in two areas: one is the further explication of the dynamic and relational character of social action; the second is how, through action, social forms or structures come to be given bodily form. This makes possible the explanation of a far greater range of behavior in a way that shows it's agential nature, while moving beyond a dependence on notions of efficacy or purpose that figure so heavily in conventional models of agency.

It therefore can contribute to the deeper analysis of phenomena such as social change and the constantly shifting character of social formations, as well as take theories of interest beyond the analysis of structural variables to include a dynamic role for the emotions. Further, the social emotions approach helps us to better understand the more inwardly directed forms of embodiment of social situatedness, such as the embodied dimensions of immiseration, suffering, and sickness.

Notes

[1] Strictly speaking, philosophical anthropology is less a movement than what in German was termed a circle (*Kreis*), or school, or more accurately a series of interconnected circles or schools.

[2] The term philosophical biology is perhaps less commonly used than philosophical anthropology. Philosophical biology tends to figure in works by authors whose focus was on organic models and the biological foundations of conceptual life. Grene (1968) uses philosophical biology rather than philosophical anthropology in her discussion of the work of Portman, Plessner, Buytendijk, Straus, and Goldstein.

[3] This inclusiveness is well reflected in the German term for science, *Wissenschaft*, that encompasses natural, experimental, and social sciences.

[4] The conference was held in the United States at the University of Notre Dame, Indiana, on May 6–9, 2005. Accessed at www.nd.edu/~lmoss/PAConfolder/Index.shtml/.

[5] For Honneth and Joas (1988, p. 47), the work of Helmuth Plessner and Arnold Gehlen constitute the "two major theories of philosophical anthropology."

References

Allport, G. W. (1955). *Becoming: Basic Considerations for a Psychology of Personality*. New Haven, CT: Yale University Press.

Aylwin, S. (1985). *Structure in Thought and Feeling*. London: Methuen.

Buytendijk, F. J. J. (1950). The phenomenological approach to the problem of feelings and emotions. In M. L. Reymert (Ed.), *Feelings and Emotions: The Mooseheart Symposium* (pp. 127–141). New York: McGraw Hill (in cooperation with the University of Chicago).

Buytendijk, F. J. J. (1974). *Prolegomena to an Anthropological Physiology*. Pittsburgh, PA: Duqesne University Press.

Collins, R. (1984). The role of emotion in social structure. In K. R. Scherer & P. Ekman (Eds.), *Approaches to Emotion* (pp. 385–396). Hillsdale, NJ: Erlbaum.

Collins, R. (1990). Stratification, emotional energy, and the transient emotions. In T. D. Kemper (Ed.), *Research Agendas in the Sociology of Emotion* (pp. 27–57). Albany, NY: SUNY Press.

De Rivera, J. (1977). *A Structural Theory of the Emotions*. New York: International Universities Press.
De Rivera, J. (1992). Emotional climate: Social structure and emotional dynamics. In K. T. Strongman (Ed.), *International Review of Studies on Emotion* (pp. 199–218). New York: Wiley.
Grene, M. (1968). *Approaches to a Philosophical Biology*. New York: Basic Books.
Grene, M. (1970). Foreword. In H. Plessner, *Laughing and Crying: A study of the Limits of Human Behavior* (J. S. Churchill & M. Grene Trans.). Evanston, IL: Northwestern University Press.
Honneth, A., & Joas, H. (1988). *Social Action and Human Nature* (R. Meyer, Trans.). New York: Cambridge University Press. (Original work published 1980)
Kemper, T. D. (1978). *A Social Interactional Theory of Emotions*. New York: Wiley.
Kemper, T. D. (1984). Power, status, and emotions: A sociological contribution to a psychophysiological domain. In K. R. Scherer & P. Ekman (Eds.), *Approaches to Emotion* (pp. 369–383). Hillsdale, NJ: Erlbaum.
Kemper, T. D. (1990). Social relations and emotions: A structural approach. In T. D. Kemper (Ed.), *Research Agendas in the Sociology of Emotions* (pp. 207–237). Albany, NY: State University of New York Press.
Lyon, M. L. (1995). Missing emotion: The limitations of cultural constructionism in the study of emotion. *Cultural Anthropology, 10*(2), 244–263.
Lyon, M. L. (1997). The material body, social processes, and emotion: "Techniques of the Body" revisited. *Body and Society, 3*(1), 83–101.
Lyon, M. L. (2003). "Immune" to emotion: The relative absence of emotion in PNI, and its centrality to everything else. In J. Wilce (Ed.), *Social and Cultural Lives of Immune Systems* (pp. 82–104). London: Routledge.
Markowitsch, H. J., & Röttger-Rössler, B. (2003). *Research Outline: Emotions as Bio-cultural Processes*. Bielefeld, Germany: Zentrum für interdisziplinäre Forschung (ZiF): ZiF Research Group 2004/2005.
Marx, K., & Engels, F. (1947). *The German Ideology*. New York: International Publishers. (Original work published 1846)
Mead, G. H. (1934). *Mind, Self and Society from the Standpoint of a Social Behaviourist*. Chicago, IL: University of Chicago Press.
Merleau-Ponty, M. (1962). *Phenomenology of Perception* (C. Smith, Trans.). New York: Humanities Press. (Original work published 1945)
Ollman, B. (1993). *Dialectical Investigations*. New York: Routledge.
Plessner, H. (1975). *Die Stufen des Organischen und der Mensch* [The Stages of the Organic and the Human Being]. Berlin: de Gruyter. (Original work published 1928)
Scheff, T. (1988). Shame and conformity: The deference-emotion system. *American Sociological Review, 53*, 395–406.
Scheff, T. (1990). *Microsociology: Discourse, Emotion and Social Structure*. Chicago, IL: University of Chicago Press.
Scheff, T. (1994). *Bloody Revenge: Emotions, Nationalism, and War*. Boulder, CO: Westview Press.
Sheets-Johnstone, M. (1990). *The Roots of Thinking*. Philadelphia, PA: Temple University Press.

On the Nature of Artificial Feelings

Achim Stephan

Abstract Several fictitious scenarios provide us with questions about the nature of artificial and natural feelings. It turns out that, traditionally, three features are relevant for the attribution of an emotion to humans: the functional role it typically has; the phenomenal quality that typically accompanies it; and the neurophysiological basis that brings about the phenomenal state. On the basis of these features I discuss several cases: artificially generated feelings, feelings in artificial systems, and unfelt emotional processes in psychopathology.

Introduction

In philosophy, we often gain insight into how we conceive of things by using thought experiments to extend our thoughts from real entities, events, and situations to fictitious ones. Fictitious events and situations help to test both the content of our concepts and to state what we take to be the essential constituents of the things in question. Thus, thinking about what we would claim about fictitious artificial feelings of various types should help us gain insight into the nature of feelings in general. Let us start with some examples.

Could you have artificial feelings? Suppose you feel downcast and dejected; you go to the pharmacy and ask for some antidepressants. You take a pill, and after a short while your despondency has gone, you feel better, the whole world looks different. Do you have an *artificial* feeling?

Your girlfriend does not believe in pills. She goes to her therapist and talks to him about her hardships and desires. He induces some relaxation and uses slightly hypnotic techniques to suggest that her depression will fade away and she will soon feel better—she feels better shortly after. Is your girl friend's new feeling of comfort *artificial*?

A. Stephan (✉)
Institute of Cognitive Science, University of Osnabrück, Osnabrück, Germany
e-mail: acstepha@uos.de

B. Röttger-Rössler, H.J. Markowitsch (eds.), *Emotions as Bio-cultural Processes*,
DOI 10.1007/978-0-387-09546-2_11, © Springer Science+Business Media, LLC 2009

Let us change the situation. Some science fiction may be permissible. Three of your colleagues are engaged in research. The first is a chemical engineer in pharmaceuticals. All the time, he has been dreaming about inventing *new* feelings and moods. He now claims to have succeeded. You try one of his newest pills, and you really feel strange; you cannot tell exactly: You feel ashamed in a very pleasant way, superimposed by a touch of easygoing melancholy. Is this an *artificial* feeling?

The second colleague works as a cultural anthropologist. He always wanted to know what it is like to be Japanese, particularly what it is like to experience *amae*. According to the Japanese psychoanalyst Takeo Doi (1973, 1986), this peculiar feeling may be compared with the childhood experience of loving parents—the feeling of passive love in the sense of being cared for and looked after lovingly by others. Unlike in Japan, this form of (infantile) attachment behavior is not cultivated in relationships among adults in Western culture. We do not even have a word for *amae* in our European languages (see Coulmas, 1993, pp. 33–37). Now, suppose that joint research with colleagues from the neurosciences has led to the discovery of the neural correlates of *amae* in the Japanese. Suppose further that neuroscientists succeed in stimulating the very same neural processes in your colleague's brain that are active in the Japanese while experiencing *amae*. Would he then experience *amae*? Would it be an artificial feeling? Would your colleague know what it is like to be Japanese?

The third colleague likes to report news on his robots. He says that the latest one is behaving like no robot before. Yesterday, it foamed at the mouth, he tells us, did everything wrong, scattered all its things over the room, and refused to tidy up afterward. Does the robot have feelings? Was it in a bad mood?

I guess it is time to sort things out a bit. The first two cases obviously are cases of feelings being "artificially"*induced.*[1] The feelings themselves, however, are thoroughly natural. Different life circumstances would have allowed their bearers, the two persons, to experience feelings of the same kind as those generated by the pharmacological or hypnotic treatment, but they would hardly have appeared by themselves in you or your girlfriend's specific situation. Pharmaceutical advances have made it possible to modify neurochemical processes in such a way that more agreeable moods can replace unpleasant ones. The same holds true for hypnosis. The better feeling is artificially induced in both cases, although the techniques used are common mood-regulating practices in our culture.

Up to now, most medication has been developed to correct sorrowful basic moods and counter physical pain. As far as I know, there are no pills on the market for (or against) shame, jealousy, and anger. More complex feelings as discussed under the label of emotions in a stronger sense—which include intentionality (i.e., a directedness toward some specific state of affairs or some object and that are accessible to rational evaluation)—are usually not generated by medication. This does not mean that, in principle, emotions in this stronger sense could not be influenced pharmaceutically. It only shows that we have no medical need for the artificial release of specific emotions. Anger, shame, and so forth are, by their very nature, much more short-lived (ephemerally) than long-lasting basic moods that may cast a shadow on all of our doings and therefore give more reason for therapeutic intervention.

Let us consider the more interesting cases now. The chemist has synthesized a *new* feeling—a feeling that nobody has experienced in this specific way before. Not only was it generated artificially—this is what it has in common with the first two cases—it also has some new artificial quality. It feels different from ordinary feelings—"easygoing melancholia." We seem able to have such experiences. Our nature allows us to have such strange artificial feelings, although—seen from an evolutionary perspective—there has been no need in the past for such feelings to be released by normal situations. Many drugs seem to elicit artificial feelings of such a kind.

What about the cultural anthropologist? He seems to experience those bodily sensations that Japanese people experience when they are in the emotional state of *amae*, certainly a new feeling for him—without doubt, artificially triggered. It is also artificial in the sense that it would not have occurred to him in everyday life, not even in Japan. For him to be able to feel *amae*, he would have to have been raised in Japan and educated in a Japanese way. On the other hand, feeling*amae* is not artificial for humankind in general. It is deeply rooted in the Japanese culture and plays a major role in Japanese social life. Should we therefore speak of "natural" and "artificial" feelings relative to certain cultures? Would that make sense?

What about the robot that behaves as if it has acquired feelings—an artificial system with natural feelings? Does it have them? Can it have any natural feelings at all?

Before considering these questions in more detail, we need to do some preliminary work. First, the heterogeneous group of mental states that, loosely speaking, are called feelings or emotions might be subdivided into felt bodily sensations (e.g., pain, pins and needles, numb limb), moods (e.g., euphoria, melancholia), undirected feelings (e.g., anxiety, delight), or directed complex emotions (e.g., shame, anger, jealousy). Now, the question at issue is whether, and if so under what circumstances, we could say of some of these states that they are *artificial* feelings.

Sometimes, however, it is better to turn the tables around and start with the opposite question, asking what makes a feeling a natural one? Furthermore, what is essential for legitimately claiming of some system that it has feelings?

To answer these questions, it is still fascinating to take a look at Aristotle's writings. In *De Anima*, he is concerned with all the affections of the soul: passion, gentleness, fear, pity, confidence, and joy as well as both loving and hating. For Aristotle, there is no doubt that all the affections involve matter (i.e., our bodies). Hence, an example of the definition is "being angry is a particular movement of a body of such and such a kind, or a part . . . of it, as a result of this thing and for the sake of that" (403a). The student of nature and the dialectician, however, would define each of these differently. For example, they would differ in their definitions of anger: "the latter would define it as a desire for retaliation or something of the sort, the former as the boiling of the blood and hot stuff round the heart. Of these, the one gives the matter, the other the form and principle" (*De Anima* 403a). In his *Rhetoric*, Aristotle added that "Anger may be defined as an impulse, accompanied by pain, to a conspicuous revenge for a conspicuous slight directed without justification towards what concerns oneself or towards what concerns one's friends ... It must be always attended by a certain pleasure—that which arises from the expectation of revenge.... Hence, it has been well said about wrath" (1378a). Here Aristotle referred to Homer's *Iliad* (cf. 1378 b):

> ...which rises up in the soul of a man like smoke, and the taste thereof is sweeter than drops of honey. (*Iliad*, book xviii)

Aristotle mentioned nearly all the aspects we take to be essential for the occurrence of natural emotions. Some of these features are externally observable; others are accessible only to those who have the particular emotion.

Externally observable is what Aristotle called "a particular movement of a body of such and such a kind or part of it, as a result of this thing and for the sake of that." Couched in modern philosophical vocabulary, this amounts to the specification of an emotion via its *causal* or *functional* role:[2] To be in a state of anger means to be in a state triggered typically by certain situations underlying an evaluation (e.g., conspicuous slights) that go along with both typical bodily reactions (e.g., rise in blood pressure, release of hormones) and other mental states (e.g., thoughts such as, "That S.O.B., I'll pay him out in his own coin") and that often end in certain behaviors (e.g., angry words, brawls).[3] Except for the accompanying thoughts, everything else is externally observable.

Whereas painful bodily sensations and directed emotions such as shame, anger, or jealousy typically are associated with specific triggering causes, the onset of certain moods is less bound to specific antecedent life events. This is the main reason why moods easily evade convincing functional specifications.

Another aspect already considered by Aristotle has to do with the sensational experiences that go along with specific emotions. Some of these seem to represent the emotional state itself in a characteristic way: It feels different to be angry than to feel ashamed or afraid. Others—specific bodily sensations—correspond to the bodily changes and states that typically accompany our emotional states: It feels different when our "blood boils around our heart" than when we have "collywobbles" or a "lump in our throat." Both types of sensation are not externally observable. They are phenomenal qualities accessible only to the emotionally excited person. According to some philosophers and psychologists, most notably William James, the phenomenal aspect of an emotion is nothing but the felt bodily sensation. As James (1890/1983) said:

> If we fancy some strong emotion and then try to abstract from our consciousness of it all feelings of its bodily symptoms, we find we have nothing left behind, no "mind-stuff" out of which the emotion can be constituted, and that a cold and neutral state of intellectual perception is all that remains. (p. 451)

We can add that feelings actually experienced are based on certain processes in specific brain areas that seem to realize them in humans and other animals, or they at least covary with those phenomenal states. The brain processes that are correlates of the felt feelings are, once again, overtly accessible at least in principle; they are even open to manipulations by specific techniques.

Hence, we should bear in mind three parameters for the individuation of some specific emotion. Accordingly, a specific emotion can be determined by the following.

1. The functional role it typically plays[4]
2. The phenomenal quality that typically accompanies it—what it is like for someone to be, for example, angry
3. The neurophysiological basis that brings about the phenomenal states

Let us return to the earlier examples. We are now in a better position to classify them and to distinguish them from each other.

The first two cases obviously deviate from the "natural" situations in which such feelings arise. There was no cheerful atmosphere, no visit by friends, and no other joyful event that contributed to the end of the melancholic mood. Instead, chemical or hypnotic interventions triggered change. The causal chain that eventually led to better feelings did not start with an ordinary life situation but with an intervention in the complex human organism that directly produced the desired feeling.

Transferred to the example of anger, this means that it was not an insult that triggered rage but perhaps some stimulation of the amygdala, a part of the limbic system. The sensational experience of the artificially induced emotion, however, would not differ from the one that accompanies "naturally generated" anger. Mark Solms (1996, p. 514), to whom I am referring here, remarked that stimulation of specific parts of the amygdala leads to typical somatic phenomena accompanying aggression and attack behavior in animals such as teeth baring, snarling, hissing, ruffling up, and so forth. I take it for granted that the human case is analogous. That is, in such a case, Features 2 and 3 are fulfilled, although the ordinary functional embedment is incomplete-the typical triggering situation is missing. The *trigger* is artificial. That is why we speak of artificially engendered feelings. However, the two other parts of the functional specification-the somatic reactions and the readiness to react aggressively-are present in the typical (natural) way. If we were able to monitor in detail the neurophysiological pathways proceeding from an initial perception of an insult to our readiness to react in wrath, we could see at which downstream location in this complex process we intervened to engender reactions of anger artificially when there has been no insult. It seems true, however, that artificially released feelings are genuine feelings in all respects apart from the fact that they are *triggered* artificially. They might be compared to situations in which relaxants bring the sleep we long for and without which we would have sleepless nights before us. Although generated artificially, it is still genuine sleep.

Now look at the novel feeling the chemist created: "easygoing melancholia." This feeling does not even have a "job description"—it is an unnatural, a synthetic feeling. Neither the sensations nor the bodily reactions that go along with it fit any functional specification that refers to ordinary life circumstances. This is what makes it artificial through and through. Even if you try to lump together environmental and social factors in such a way that their common occurrence would lead to such a blended feeling, this situation would be downright artificial as well.

The case of the inquiring anthropologist is different again. Although there exists a functional specification of the artificially created state of *amae*, it does not exist within the frame of our culture. Likewise, the anthropologist does not have the essential cognitive states that typically accompany the feeling of *amae* in the Japanese. He might be engaged in meta-reflections about his current sensations: "This seems to be how it feels for a Japanese to be in the state of *amae*." However, he does not seem to be in a genuine state of *amae*; rather, it is a sensation of weird somatic processes that do not fit into any established category.

Let us now focus on the potential feelings of an artificial system. What could be meant, and how would it make sense to speak of feelings—artificial feelings—in such cases?

What is *not* meant, obviously, is that for such a system to be treated as a feeling system it must have "bodily states" of the same type as humans or other organisms. Nor is it necessary for its emotional sensations to be realized in the same way as ours. We do not demand that artificial organs or joints be made of flesh and blood; what we want is that they do their job appropriately. In other words, the artificial components should do what their natural counterparts do if they are functioning well. The former replace the latter if they lose the capacity to do what they used to do. For artificial feelings, this means that they should take care of tasks that are normally done by natural feelings. However-and this is important-they do not perform these tasks in us but in artificial systems by providing them with what is necessary for them to become autonomous agents.[5]

To address this point, let us go back to the three parameters we extracted above. The specification of an emotion by the first feature, its functional role, does not in principle seem to be an obstacle for artificial systems. Because neural networks are good at pattern recognition at this stage, it should not be an insurmountable problem in the future to train them regarding situations that are emotionally important to us. It should also be possible to equip them with a set of adequate reactions. Nonetheless, it is impossible for artificial systems to come into being in body states such as ours. It is not to be expected. It would indeed be very narrow-minded if we were to bind the potential of having feelings to our organic structure (i.e., to Feature 3). This would imply that no inhabitant of this universe with another bodily constitution could have emotional states. Last, but not least, considerations of this kind led many philosophers to withdraw from the identity theory during the late 1960s. The identity theory had claimed that having certain mental states is type-identical with being in certain bodily states. Since then, several versions of functionalism have been favored in which mental states can be individuated by their *functional* or *causal* role.

However, this approach confronts us immediately with all the objections that were raised against functionalism in general during the last three decades. Prominently, does the occupation of a certain functional role suffice to guarantee having a certain feeling (or sensation)? If we believe that the key aspect for having a genuine feeling is that we experience it in some way or other, the plain occupation of a certain functional role by some states of a system does not guarantee that this system experiences certain phenomenal qualities or genuine feelings. If things are such, the putative feelings of artificial systems might turn out to be mere "pseudo-feelings"—nothing but bogus simulations of emotional states.

Katrin Hille, however, a former coworker of Dietrich Dörner, would disagree. In Dörner's group, the modeling of our mind has been a research topic for many years. In 1997, Hille published a book whose title translates as *The "Artificial' Soul"* in which she emphasized that she is not interested in mere simulations of emotions but, rather, in their modeling. She presupposed that because the substrata of mental processes are irrelevant their simulations are themselves mental processes (see Hille, 1997, p. 22). She proposed that successful computer simulations of mental processes (e.g., gaining an insight or having an emotion) are thereby models of those processes. Hence, the simulation of psychic processes differs in important ways from the simulation of some other natural processes (e.g., simulation of a hurricane). If we simulate a hurricane, we do not have to fear that thunderstorms will break out in our notebook or that microchips will start swirling around (see Dennett, 1978, pp. 191–192).

Hille and Dörner believed that emotions should be considered modulations of cognitive processes that prepare and control behavior. Modulation can be characterized by four parameters: *activation* (the speed of information processing or the energy invested in a certain task), *selection threshold* (the tendency to concentrate on the actual intention), *resolution level* (the accuracy with which environment, planning, and decision-making are looked at), and *updating* (the attentiveness with which we monitor changes in the environment). By now it should be clear that Hille's modeling of emotions encompasses only the first feature, the functional role of emotions. She and Dörner did not care about the subjective experiences typically accompanying emotions. As little as we need to fear roaring hurricanes in my notebook, so little do we need to fear that Hille's computer will suffer when she models pains in it. After all, we know that her PC has no phenomenal states; it is just in various electromagnetic states that represent the parameters of modulation.

Let us elaborate a bit further. Suppose the "artificial soul" not only models emotional human behavior in a computer simulation, but it instantiates such a theory by controlling the highly complex behavior of a so-called autonomous agent in a real-life situation. We are on the way to embedded cognition. Now, our robot really does "exhibit" emotionally dyed behavior. It can turn crimson, tear its antennas, pace around agitatedly, and so forth; and it always does this in the appropriate circumstances. Does it have feelings, then? In this case, we certainly would have to concede that it has internal states controlling its behavior in a way that emotions control ours. However, does it feel anything through being in these states?

This question leads us straight to a notorious problem within the philosophy of mind—the so-called qualia problem: Phenomenal qualities (sensations or sensational experiences that accompany emotions) seem to resist reductive explanations in principle (see Stephan 2006, pp. 488–491). If they prove to do so, in fact, we would not have any base for a well founded judgment about the occurrence of conscious feelings in highly complex systems such as robots that differ manifestly from (human) organisms. How can we go further here?

Maybe it is not so important to experience emotions. Would it not be enough to attribute feelings to a robot by virtue of its emotionally dyed behavior? Genuine feelings? To an artificial system? Do we not, at times, attribute feelings to some of our conspecifics, although they say that they do not experience feelings? Particularly from psychoanalytical case studies, we know of patients who are not able to perceive their feelings—if it can be said that they have any. Analysts then often speak of unconscious affects (e.g., unconscious shame, unconscious fear, unconscious aggression). I quote Ulrich Moser (1978, pp. 236–237, as cited in Thomä & Kächele, 1987):

> These affects [vexation, anger, rage, hate, etc.] are employed as internal signals in the same way as anxiety, given that affective experience has at all reached the developmental level of an internal reporting system (signal system). In many neurotic developments (e.g., in neurotic depressions, compulsion neuroses, neurotic character disturbances) the aggressive signal system is completely stunted or poorly developed. These are patients who do not notice their aggressive impulses, consequently do not recognize them, and cannot classify them in a situational context. (p. 108)

Moser stressed two consequences: Some patients exhibit aggressive behavior without being able to recognize it and without being able to acknowledge it retrospectively. Others, though reacting in an emotionally excited way to environmental stimuli that are apt to elicit aggressions, interpret them differently (e.g., as signals of fear). Even more interesting for our topic is a case study on a heart neurosis reported by Hans Carl Leuner (1985, pp. 183–184). His patient did not feel his aggressive impulses, neither did he react aggressively, nor did he interpret the triggering situation in another way. Instead, he somatized, he developed a cardiac neurosis, a psychosomatic disease in a situation that was apt to elicit violent aggression in others.

Diseases of that kind are explained by the assumption that, in a certain sense, our body reacts adequately in a situation that could justify aggressive behavior. Because the aggressive impulse is not recognized (as no phenomenal experience of anger or wrath goes along with the bodily changes), no adequate action is released. However, the bodily excitation persists and this can lead to chronic disease.

In these cases, to what extent can we speak in any way of feelings—even though unconscious? Let us take another look at the aberrances from our model by the emotionally controlled robot and the patients with unconscious feelings.

The robot reacts adequately in a situation that is apt to elicit aggression. It exhibits aggressive behavior. When asked, it states that it is angry and is waiting for an apology. We apologize to it. It accepts it and calms down. The neurotic, however, does not feel aggression in a similar situation; he does not feel the conspicuous slight-no wrath whose taste is sweeter than drops of honey rises up in his soul like smoke. There is no aggressive attack, but tachycardia occurs; his blood is "boiling around the heart" so intensely as to be agonizing for the self.

In contrast to the robot, the neurotic does not react adequately; moreover, he lacks privately accessible feelings and bodily sensations that typically go along with anger. Instead, he has either no or completely different sensations such as tachycardia.

What has led us to the assumption of unconscious anger is a theory. It is the idea that our body provides us with what is necessary for aggressive behavior. In fact, aggressive behavior would be released if the aggressive impulses had not been inhibited so severely that even the perception of the situation becomes distorted. Moreover, experience has shown that given the right therapeutic treatment previously unfelt aggressions become noticeable to patients—often hand in hand with fading of the somatic symptoms. That is, we attribute unconscious feelings to creatures that are capable of having conscious feelings too. Per contra, it may seem weird to attribute unconscious feelings to a system that is not even able to have conscious feelings.

Could it not be that the robot has true feelings, and we just do not know? I cannot exclude this possibility. Admittedly, this is the point at which we reach the cloud of the "Ignoramus" in recent philosophy of mind and cognition. In a nutshell, this leaves us with the following picture.

Among the three features I proposed as characteristic for feelings, it is the third—the neurophysiological basis of our qualitative feeling states—that is least significant. Its presence should not be taken as necessary for the existence of feelings. Nonetheless, it may serve to classify a state that is taken, for other reasons, to be a genuine feeling state as a state of an *artificial system* and to do this when the realization basis of the feeling is not a natural one.

What is decisive for whether a specific state in an artificial or natural system can in any way be a feeling state is the second feature: the phenomenal quality that actually accompanies that state, or at least (as in the case of unconscious feelings) could accompany it. In contrast, the first feature, the functional role, cannot be viewed as either sufficient or necessary for the presence of a genuine feeling state. If the sensation aspect (the second feature) is principally lacking, adequate functional embedment is not enough—as in, for example, the modeling of behavior in artificial systems—to enable us to attribute these systems with having feelings.

On the other hand, we do not hesitate to call *artificially generated* feelings real feelings, even when they show deficits in their functional embedment because the natural triggering situation is missing. It is only when all the behavioral and mental reactions that specify the functional role of a specific feeling are missing that we no longer talk about genuine feelings.

One problem, however, which we can ascertain objectively in artificial systems (in particular) is whether they have the characteristic phenomenal sensations for feeling states. In these cases, arguments by analogy that—as in the attribution of common feelings among human conspecifics—can fall back on a shared neural constitution simply do not work. The only solution would be a theory that could reductively explain phenomenal states. Until we have such a theory-and the outlook is not promising-we can neither demonstrate that artificial systems have feelings nor show that they have none.

Notes

[1] I call feelings or moods "artificially induced" or "artificially generated" if they are the result of actions performed explicitly to generate those moods, instead of being reactions to "normal life events." Artificial induction, thus, also differs from the emotional regulation that occurs when we reappraise an emotionally significant episode.

[2] Functionalism (in the philosophy of mind) characterizes mental states in terms of their "causal" (or "functional") roles: Pain, for example, is typically caused by bodily injury (input). It often produces anxiety, the belief that something is wrong with the body, and the desire to be out of that state (connection to other mental states); and it typically causes wincing or moaning (output).

[3] A similar analysis of anger was given by Descartes (1649/1985) in § 199 of his Passions of the Soul: "Anger is also a kind of hatred or aversion that we have towards those who have done some evil or who have tried to harm not just anyone they happen to meet but us in particular. Thus it has the same content as indignation, and the more so in that it is based on an action which affects us and for which we have a desire to avenge ourselves. For this desire nearly always accompanies it, and it is directly opposed to gratitude, as indignation is to favor. But it is incomparably more violent than these other three passions, because the desire to ward off harmful things and to avenge oneself is the most compelling of all desires. It is desire, joined to self-love, which makes anger involve as much agitation of the blood as courage and boldness can bring about; and hatred causes this agitation to affect primarily the bilious blood coming from the spleen and the small veins of the liver. This blood enters into the heart and there, because of its abundance and the nature of the bile with which it is mingled, it produces a heat more extreme and more intense than any that may be produced by love or joy."

[4] The functional role a specific emotion typically possesses comprises several features that are usually listed separately; for example, facial expressions, gestures, action readiness, and appraisal (see Engelen et al., Emotions as Bio-cultural Processes, pp. xxxxxx). In this context, however, it suffices to group these features under one label: the "functional role an emotion typically possesses."

[5] Although we cannot transplant feelings, we may speculate about whether it could be possible, in principle, to build artificial evaluation devices that would help people who have suffered severe injury to their prefrontal cortex and lost the ability to monitor and evaluate emotionally the consequences of their decisions and behavior.

References

Aristotle. *On the Soul (de anima)* (D. W. Hamlyn, Trans.). Oxford, UK: Clarendon Press, 1968.

Aristotle. *Rhetoric* (W. R. Roberts, Trans.). Retrieved July 19, 2006 from http://classics.mit.edu/Aristotle/rhetoric.html

Coulmas, F. (1993). *Das Land der rituellen Harmonie. Japan: Gesellschaft mit beschränkter Haftung* [The land of ritual harmony. Japan: Society with limited liability]. Frankfurt, Germany: Campus.
Dennett, D. (1978). Why you can't make a computer that feels pain. In D. Dennett (Ed.), *Brainstorms* (pp. 190–229). Brighton, UK: Harvester Press.
Descartes, R. (1649). The passions of the soul (Les Passions de L'Ame). In: *The Philosophical Writings of Descartes* (J. Cottingham, R. Stoothoff, & D. Murdoch, Trans.) Vol. 1. Cambridge, UK: Cambridge University Press, 1985.
Doi, T. (1973). *The anatomy of dependency*. Tokyo: Kodansha International.
Doi, T. (1986). *The anatomy of self: Self versus society*. Tokyo: Kodansha International.
Engelen, E.-M., Markowitsch, H. J., von Scheve, C., Röttger-Rössler, B., Stephan, A., Holodynski, M., et al. (2008). Emotions as Bio-cultural Processes: Disciplinary Debates and an Interdisciplinary Outlook. In H. J. Markowitsch & B. Röttger-Rössler (Eds.), *Emotions as Bio-cultural Processes*. New York: Springer.
Hille, K. (1997). *Die ‚künstliche Seele'. Analyse einer Theorie* [The "artificial soul"]. Wiesbaden, Germany: Deutscher Universitätsverlag.
Homer. *The Iliad* (S. Butler, Trans.). Retrieved July 19, 2006 from www.abcd-classics.com/homer/theiliad/the_iliad.html
James, W. (1983).*The principles of psychology* (with an introduction by G. A. Miller). Boston, MA: Harvard University Press. (Original work published 1890)
Leuner, H. (1985). *Lehrbuch des Katathymen Bilderlebens* [Textbook of catathymic reverie]. Bern, Switzerland: Huber.
Moser, U. (1978). Affektsignal und aggressives Verhalten. Zwei verbal formulierte Modelle der Aggression [Affect signal and aggressive behavior: Two verbally formulated models of aggression]. *Psyche*, *32*, 229–258.
Solms, M. (1996). Was sind Affekte [What are affects?]? *Psyche*, *50*, 485–522.
Stephan, A. (2006). The dual role of 'emergence' in the philosophy of mind and in cognitive science. *Synthese*, *151*, 485–498.
Thomä, H., & Kächele, H. (1987). *Psychoanalytic Practice. Vol. 1 Principles*. Berlin: Springer.

Part II
Empirical Studies—Shame and Pride: Prototypical Emotions Between Biology and Culture

“Honor and Dishonor”: Connotations of a Socio-symbolic Category in Cross-Cultural Perspective

Michael J. Casimir and Susanne Jung

Abstract In this contribution we describe the complex social and symbolic category “honour and dishonour” and show how this “pair” relates to values and norms in various societies. We then discuss the similarities and differences of these norms and values in societies in which honour and dishonour are positioned at the apex of the social fabric. We show that “honour and dishonour” in most but not all societies relate mainly to men and to prescriptions in the realm of women’s behaviour in the sexual sphere. However, individual male attributes such as wealth and bravery, but also spirituality and wisdom, can be important for honour being attained or attributed. For women, next to the maintenance of chastity norms, culture-specific female capacities and qualities lead to more or less honour. Among both men and women the trespassing of behavioural rules and the nonfulfilment of given norms can lead to losing honour with often dramatic consequences.

Introduction

> Honour is the value of a person in his own eyes but also in the eyes of his society. It is his estimation of his own worth, his *claim* to pride, but it is also the acknowledgement of the claim, his excellence recognized by society, his *right* to pride. (Julian Pitt-Rivers, 1966, p. 21)

It was 137 years after Prosper Mérimée (1803–1870) published his famous short story, “Mateo Falcone” that J. G. Peristiany (1966) edited *Honour and Shame: The Values of Mediterranean Society*. In Mateo Falcone, Mérimée described in exemplary fashion the terrible dilemma and pain of a Corsican father who, to maintain his honour, must kill his only son. The honourable Corsican landlord, Mateo Falcone, had granted refuge and hospitality to the bandit Gianetto. However, his young son, seduced by the officer Gamba, who

M.J. Casimir (✉)
Department of Social and Cultural Anthropology, University of Cologne, Cologne, Germany
e-mail: michael.casimir@uni-koeln.de

B. Röttger-Rössler, H.J. Markowitsch (eds.), *Emotions as Bio-cultural Processes*,
DOI 10.1007/978-0-387-09546-2_12, © Springer Science+Business Media, LLC 2009

offered him a much desired watch, had revealed Gianetto's hideout, and to maintain his honour Mateo Falcone had to kill his son. This story is prototypical of many accounts and legends told by people in regions where "honour" is said to be the most important quality of a person and the core of one's masculine or feminine integrity; even today, "honour" and the consequences of lost honour are the central topic in works such as Ismail Kadare's (1980/2005) novel on a blood feud in Albania or Ioanna Karystiani's (2001/2005) novel staged in Crete.

In this chapter, we try to systematise the meaning of the categories "honour" and/or "being honourable" and "dishonour" and "being dishonoured." We start by using a sample of various societies as a basis to analyse the distribution of the "honour and shame complex," investigate the various culture-specific concepts underlying the connotations of honour and shame (dishonour), and describe the specific situations or behaviours that are appraised as relevant for these attributes.

As explained later in the chapter, we prefer the term "dishonour" to the term "shame" for the socio-symbolic category so as not to confuse the former with the meaning of the latter in the sense of, for example, "being ashamed" signifying an emotion.

Honor and Dishonor: In Search of a Category

As with all categories, that of honour also reflects the problem of rigorously dividing the world into two basically different types of society or group: (1) those in which honour and shame (dishonour) are the "prime movers" related to most or all norms and values and thus largely determining social structure, and (2) those in which they are of only minor importance or even no importance at all (see Kressel, 1992, p. 34; Pina-Cabral, 1989). Also, as Twinam (1999; see also Johnson & Lipsett-Rivera, 1998) has shown so lucidly, in some societies honour cannot be understood as being related to a distinct cluster of individuals including only some while excluding others once and forever. As examples taken from her analysis of colonial Spanish America show, honour, first claimed only by the dominating white population, became more and more negotiable through the increasing mixture with the black population.

Since Peristiany's (1966) trail-breaking volume, numerous articles and books have been published on the phenomenon of honour; and the terminology "honour and shame societies" has become established in social anthropology to characterise and denote cultures in the Mediterranean world. However, especially after the publication of Gilmore's (1987a) edited volume, controversies arose over whether the notion of honour and shame (dishonour) is specifically important in this region and if it legitimises denoting the region as a specific "cultural area." This problem was taken up again by Peristiany and

Pitt-Rivers in 1992 in the introduction to their volume *Honor and Grace in Anthropology* in which they explained that they had never intended to designate the Mediterranean as a cultural area. They wrote:

> Our aim in treating the Mediterranean as a whole was epistemological only and we never attempted to define it geographically. Thus when mention is made of "Mediterranean concept of honor" we recognize that it indicates a tendency to associate masculine honor with female sexual purity only rather vaguely, for there are areas near the Mediterranean where this connection is not made at all, for example certain areas in northern Spain or the Mzab or Ouled Naïl of Algeria, and that in any case there is considerable variation within what is loosely termed so. (p. 6; see also Boissevain, 1979; Davis, 1977, pp. 5–10; Pina-Cabral, 1989)

Many investigators have analysed and shown in detail that honour and shame (dishonour) are important psychosocial and symbolic categories (cf. Blok, 1981; Herzfeld, 1984) and that they regulate, or regulated, an individual's social conduct and determine the social fabric in many societies.

Another problem relates to terminology. Kressel (1988, p. 167) questioned "the use of the term *shame* as an antonym to the term *honour*" and showed that "honour and shame ... are not completely antipodean, the poles of one-and-the-same spectrum of social evaluation." He understood "*honour* as an elementary property of human beings, as long as they follow the prescriptions of moral behaviour; that is honour is there to begin with but can be depleted by improper conduct of moral affairs." In the same vain, Unni Wikan (1984, p. 636) wrote: "Whereas honour is an aspect of the person, shame applies to an act only" (see also Wikan, 1988, p. 170). Such problems led Herzfeld (1980, p. 349) to ask whether this terminology is in any way analytically useful and perhaps even counterproductive; but Delaney (1987, p. 35) rightly warned us that to dispose of them altogether when they appear to encapsulate something of existential importance is equivalent to throwing the proverbial baby out with the bathwater (for more recent critical discussions, see Giordano, 2001; Horden & Purcell, 2002, pp. 488–523).

When discussing the "contestable pair" honour and shame (Wikan, 1984), we often see some confusion due to the double meaning of the term "shame" in the English language (see Cohen, 1992, p. 599). On the one hand, its meaning is synonymous with that of the term "dishonour" (e.g., "He brings shame upon his family"); on the other hand, it can describe and stand for the specific emotion/feeling situation in which someone has been ashamed. Thus, the English term shame stands for an enduring situation in which an individual or a family finds itself dishonoured and has "to live in shame," but in another context it describes only a short emotional episode. Particularly in the German scientific literature, this has often led to fatal misunderstandings-such as when Peristian's title *Honour and Shame* was rendered into *Ehre und Scham* instead of *Ehre und Schande* (e.g., Berrenberg, 2002, p. 82; see also Möwe, 1998, p. 496).

This problem and this distinction were already made clear by Gilmore (1987b) when he entitled his introduction to *Honor and Shame and the Unity of the Mediterranean* "The Shame of Dishonour." Peristiany and Pitt-Rivers (1992) also noticed this possible misunderstanding and dealt with it in the introduction to their second book, *Honor and Grace in Anthropology*, in which they wrote:

> We might have perhaps have done better to entitle the book "Honor and Infamy" rather than "Honor and Shame" in order to guard against this misapprehension, but this would have impoverished the theme since, unlike honor, infamy refers uniquely to reputation and not to sentiments. While admitting all the interest that a study of psychology of shame may have, especially in relation to [the] physiology of blushing and other psycho-physiological phenomena, we were content to limit ourselves strictly to the field of social anthropology and confine our investigation to the role of concepts of honor and shame in ordering society rather than confront the ill-defined problems of the personality of Mediterranean peoples. (p. 6)

Steward (1994) pointed our attention to the same misunderstanding. When discussing Wikan's (1984) thesis and Kressel's (1992) reply, he noted that honour is not the opposite of shame. As he rightly remarked:

> Shame is generally looked at as an emotion, whereas honor is not usually regarded as an emotion, and an emotion can scarcely be the exact opposite of something that is not an emotion. The obvious choice for an opposite of shame is pride. (p. 129)

From the bulk of literature dealing with honour and shame, it is obvious that as the opposite of honour the term shame was used only in the sense of being "dishonoured" or with a slightly different meaning, "falling from grace." For our purpose and to avoid confusing terminology, in the following sections we use the term "dishonour" when referring to this specific, more or less enduring state of mind. The term "shame" is used only when the short episodic negative emotional experience is meant (see chapter 13, Casimir, "Honor and Dishonor" and the Quest for Emotional Equivalents, this volume). For our endeavour here and for reasons of clarity, it seemed appropriate to us to reformulate the "contestable pair," to paraphrase Wikan (1984), into the noncontestable pair "honour and dishonour."

In Search of a Typology

Honour as "inner honour" and equated with "dignity" was understood by Aristotle and Thomas Aquinas and especially by the Renaissance philosopher Pico della Mirandola as a basic and intrinsic attribute of all humans. In the Christian tradition of the Middle Ages, however, honour should belong to God alone; and blasphemy, the violation of His honour, was related to the arch sin of human pride and arrogance and punished severely (see Schwerthoff, 1995). On the other hand, it was also proclaimed that "His Grace" provided honour and status to the ruling elite because of their virtues, and it can be seen that honour and dignity were always distributed unevenly in complex societies. They had social value (Weinrich, 1971, p. 341) and were linked to power and economics. From the early Middle Ages onward, the "honourable" nobility were always the owners of large estates in most parts of Europe. The royal families, as owners of the whole country, were the most honourable ones; and the lower ranks of nobility acquired their land holdings, usually granted to them by the king, as a reward for military services and heroic deeds in war.

Apart from this basic principle, it must also be clear that the connotation of honour and the way in which to acquire honour differ from region to region and from time to time. Two examples from the European past should suffice here.

During the Italian Renaissance, other than the mentioned Pico della Mirandola, various authors discussed the "point of honour" and arrived at different explanations of the means of acquiring that state, ranging from "inborn qualities" as a result of noble descent to the honour that could be acquired through bravery and/or good deeds. The conception that nature is in an uncorrupted state and a sign and symbol of God's glory also led to the idea that "honor is an uncorrupted state of nature" (Robertson Bryson, 1933/35, p. 5). This then led to Vieri's (1580, as cited in Robertson Bryson, 1933/35, p. 5) assumption that the

> bodies of the men who most desire honor are better "tempered" than those of others; that is, they have a better mixture of heat, cold, dryness, and moisture. As a result, their flesh is more delicate, their "humors" more refined, and their "spirits" more subtle.

In sum, honour was mainly to be expected in men of high-ranking families, either of noble descent or among the wealthy (because being rich was understood as a God-given reward for being virtuous). The amalgamation of such qualities and capacities to "produce" honour was nowhere better expressed than in Rabelais' *Gargantua* (I, 57, as cited in Burckhardt, 1877/78/1928, p. 433), in which he wrote: "Free people, of good birth, of good education, associating together in good society, have by nature an instinct and incentive which always impels them to virtuous deeds and withdraws them from vice: this (impulse) they call honor."

To gain an understanding of the connotations of honour and dishonour in postrevolutionary France, Reddy (1997) noted in his brilliant analysis of honour and sentiment that the

> sense of the word *honneur* implied a single state, rather than a multitude of ranks. In this sense, honor was something one preserved from taint; if one failed, one fell into an opposite state of dishonor (*déshonneur*) or shame (*honte*). It was in that sense that one "honored" (*honorer*) one's commitments, whether they were contractual obligations, debts, or the obligation to show courage on the field of battle or to defend one's name from insult. Perhaps the most frequent usage in this sense was the phrase "*ma parole d'honneur*" (my word of honor). (p. 21)

Thus, apart from the understanding in which honour is "given by God/nature," it also is understood as embedded in the social context and prescribed by others. Here the individual's or group's specific honour results from the appraised prestige and reputation (outer honour). The individual's or group's capacities, conduct, and actions are judged against the culture- or group-specific values, norms, and connotations of virtue (see Gilmore, 1987a, p. 5; MEL, 1980; Miller, 1993, pp. 116–117; Ortner & Whitehead, 1981, pp. 14–15; Pope, 1955, pp. 771–772; Weinrich, 1971).

Horizontal Versus Vertical Honour

Steward (1994) postulated two main typological differences for analysing the codes of honour in different societies or groups today or in the recent past: "horizontal" versus "vertical" honour and "individual" versus "collective" honour. According to Steward (1994, pp. 54–63), the first type, horizontal honour, is supposed to be more or less synonymous with "personal honour" or "inner honour" and equivalent in meaning to "dignity." It denotes the individual's right to the respect due to an equal. This is something that can be lost. To retain it, one must follow certain rules; and to maintain it, one has to follow the standards, the "code of honour," of the society or group to which one belongs. "Vertical honour," Steward denoted, is "the right to special respect enjoyed by those who are superior, whether by virtue of their abilities, their rank, their service to the community, their sex, kin relations, office" (p. 59). The individual's honour can be augmented by deeds and enterprises that are evaluated positively in the eyes of his or her community or group according to their "honour code." The factors and/or the behaviour through which a man's individual honour can be increased are, in principle: (1) successful economic enterprises and augmenting wealth leading to a growth in power and prestige; (2) virtues in a religious or a general moral sense, which, however, often go hand in hand with wealth; and (3) last, but not least, the conduct of the female members of the household group. These points show the lopsided concentration on man's honour—something that is an outcome not only of accounts being written by male ethnographers but also to the fact that in most societies in which "honour" plays a dominant role women are said to have no honour on their own (but see the section on women below; see also Dane, 2005; Farès, 1932, p. 44).

Steward noted that "vertical and horizontal honor are of course compatible with each other; but are not necessarily so" (p. 61). Communities employing a "pure" horizontal honour, as Steward described for certain Bedouin groups, seem to be extremely rare and, from the theoretical point of view, can only be expected in acephalous societies. However, his description and analysis can be questioned on the basis of the bulk of the literature on many other Bedouin tribes reporting that honour always relates to competition between men for leadership. Quoting Laffin (1975, p. 84), Giordano (2001, p. 46) wrote: "From top to bottom, Arab society is permeated by a system of rival relationships. It is fed by the simple fact that in the Arab value system a major attribute of prestige is the ability to dominate others" (see also Black-Michaud, 1975, pp. 143–160; for the Kabyle society, see Bourdieu, 1966, 1977).

Individual Versus Collective Honour

When discussing the honour code in Mediterranean societies, authors from a range of disciplines (e.g., Baroja, 1966; Kuzkaya, 2001; Pitt-Rivers, 1966) distinguish between individual and collective honour.

The term *individual honour* refers to an individual's self-estimate and self-esteem, which, last but not least, emerges through a positive evaluation by others. It relates to his or her prestige and rank in a given society or group,[1] either "given by birth," as in the case of nobility, and/or through the individual attainment of high-ranking cultural goals. Accordingly, the term individual honour refers to the fact that people can exalt their own personal esteem and prestige through deeds that, if positively evaluated by the members of their society or group, increase their honour within their community (see Kuzkaya, 2001, pp. 20–24). Ambition, capacity, capability and independence are often mentioned as being employed by people to cut out other individuals in the continuous competition for social and economic status and prestige (Rodriguez Mosquera, Mansteadt, & Fischer, 2000, p. 835). However, not every member of a given society can reach the same level of honour; access to honour is differentiated according to cultural determinants such as different age classes, sex/gender division, more or less prestigious professions, and differences in wealth.

In some societies in which an honour code was and is less strongly elaborated, a man's honour relates "traditionally" to him (alone) as the head of the household; to his right to respect, autonomy, and privacy; and to his position as the founder of a lineage. However, in societies in which a girl's lack of virginity and premarital birth are not dishonouring, as described by Johnson-Hanks (2006, pp. 40, 75, 162, 164) for the Beti society in southern Cameroon, honour (especially in women) relates mainly (if not solely) to individual respectability and dignity; and especially in women it has undergone a remarkable change over time. Currently, their (but also men's) honour, dignity, and pride relate mainly to their formal education and to Catholicism (Johnson-Hanks, 2006, pp. 40, 58–88).

The term *collective honour* refers to differential high esteem and honour of a whole, more or less well defined and institutionalised corporate social group (the "honor group") (Steward, 1994, p. 54), a lineage or clan, or even to a whole society, state, or country/nation as a whole (national honour). This collective honour, as Pitt-Rivers (1966) pointed out, can in principle be found in groups of any size around the world.

> Social groups possess a collective honour in which their members participate: the dishonourable conduct reflects upon the honour of all, while a member shares in the honour of his group "I am who I am" subsumes "who I am associated with." (p. 35)

Here the individual's honour is also drawn from his or her high self-esteem but is based mainly on the knowledge that one is a member of a high-ranking, prestigious group. However, the group's prestige and thus its collective honour also depends on its members' achievements and moral performances. In feuding societies, it is often related to the group's defence of their territory and their resources.

> In feuding societies honour and power are synonymous. The one implies the other. The group's defence of its honour is thus in a very real sense the defence of its right to live in a given area and to exploit its birthright of natural resources.... For an individual, on the other hand, defence of his own honour and that of his group provides an opportunity for self-aggrandizement and the acquisition of prestige. In an economically very homogeneous society a man's prestige ultimately summarizes all those qualities which differentiate him from other members of the same society and together constitute his qualification for success in the competition for leadership. (Black-Michaud, 1975, p. 178; see also Marcus, 1987)

The group's reputation and honour grows with the number of positively evaluated deeds performed by its members. Honour, therefore, can be "both a personal attribute, in the sense of the individual's own integrity or honesty, and a collective attribute, in the sense that honour is shared with others" (Fischer, Manstead, & Rodriguez Mosquera, 1999, p. 151; for the Old Norse cultures, see Miller, 1993, pp. 93–124). As Pitt-Rivers (1977) stated:

> There is a near-paradox in the fact that while honour is a collective attribute shared by the nuclear family it is also personal and dependent upon the will of the individual; individual honour derives from individual conduct but produces consequences for others who share collective honour with this individual. (p. 78)

Thus the factors determining individual and collective honour are not mutually exclusive, and horizontal and vertical honour usually are found to be simultaneously present in most, if not every, society with a "code of honour." A group can profit from the honour gained by one of its members, and the honour of individual members also results from being associated with the group (see Al-Khayyat, 1990, pp. 21–26; Black-Michaud, 1975, p. 178; Dresch, 1989, pp. 38–47). For the Sarakatsani of Greece, Campbell (1964) noted:

> The honour of a group is opposed to the honour of another if only for the reason that there is an implicit comparison between different honours in reference to a pattern of ideal attributes. But honour also reflects on the correct status relations between individuals or groups. When two groups are in communication the behaviour of the persons representing them implies, on either side, a certain evaluation of the other group. If a man suffers treatment that is less than his due, his honour, and the honour of the group he represents, are diminished. (p. 316)

The following describes the code of honour in societies and groups in which it has, or recently had, a predominant function in structuring their social and political fabric along with some other societies and groups in which parts or aspects of the code still are, or used to be, found. It should also be mentioned here that the importance of a "honour and dishonour code," once so elaborated among the upper classes in most central European countries, has faded away since the French Revolution and has lost its power and meaning. This is not to say that the terms "honour" and "dishonour" are no longer used; they are in fact still widely used but their connotation has shifted away from the ritualised and aggressive "duel cultures" of the past.[2]

Code of Honor: Examples of Cultural and Regional Similarities and Differences

Mediterranean World

Spain

Spanish society as a whole has no homogeneous conception of honour, as Julian Pitt-Rivers (1966, 1968) pointed out during the 1960s. First, the concept of honour shows regional variations that are pronounced between rural and urban areas (see Gilmore, 1987c; see also Brandes, 1981).

In some rural areas, honour has been described as a general regulating principle of all kinds of relations (economic, political, moral, social) that are personally negotiated in small face-to-face village communities with their highly effective social control (Pitt-Rivers, 1966, p. 61). As Nisbett and Cohen (1996, p. xvi) remarked, "A person sits in the proper pew or not; and his daughter marries well or badly, depending on his honor," and this is evaluated by the other inhabitants of the village.

Often, honour is especially related to the hierarchically organised status of a person in Spanish society:

> The concept of honour presents itself in a different contextual framework to the individual according to his place in the social structure, and the differing value attached to it can be explained by this. Its relation to economic and political power is not seen in the same light by those who possess such power and by those who do not. (Pitt-Rivers, 1966, p. 61)

In all of these cases, however, honour relates to the different prescriptions for appropriate behaviour/conduct for a honourable man and the behaviour/conduct for a honourable woman not only in private but also, particularly, in the public sphere. Here Pitt-Rivers (1966, p. 42) drew a distinction between men's "masculinity," men's strength (see also Brandes, 1981, p. 2247), and the defence of the family reputation on the one hand and women's "timidity" to secure their sexual purity on the other. Again, though, regional differences are striking, and various connotations of the different terms in use can be observed. In most contexts, as described by Pitt-Rivers, *honor* is used as a term for honour in the broadest sense and refers to the individual attributes of a man who embraces a whole gamut of virtues. Lison-Tolosana (1966, pp. 314–331, 350–351), for instance, has shown that in a small community in Aragon the term *honor* is rarely used and is related only to noblemen and understood as "bookish and too elegant for ordinary use" (p. 314). There, *honra/honradez* is used and understood as one component of *vergüenza* (shame); in other parts of Spain, the latter term often relates only to the "essence of womanhood." Today, in large cities such as Malaga the situation is reversed; the term *honor* is used to denote a whole spectrum of an individual's capacities and qualities, whereas *honra* is understood as old-fashioned, being used only in old texts and literature

(Angela Brachetti, personal communication). In general, it seems that in the large cities the gender-specific patterns Pitt-Rivers discovered during the 1960s have faded. Fischer et al. (1999) confirmed this for Sevilla by asking college students to answer a questionnaire to identify honour-related values. Even on the Iberian Peninsula as a whole, great differences seem to exist. Whereas the honour and dishonour code was, or still is, important in many regions and communities in Spain, this does not seem to be the case in Portugal. In her careful analysis of a peasant community in northern Portugal, Pina-Cabral (1986) did not mention honour and dishonour at all, and it seems that the code is of no great importance or even of no importance at all (see also Cutileiro, 1971).

Italy

In the hierarchical and status-oriented societies of Sicily and Sardinia, the honour and dishonour code are complex and important, and these terms are used by people to classify each other. Honour is retained or gained, and an individual is "honourable" if he or she has complied with value-related cultural norms. Consequently, "dishonour" corresponds to the individual's divergence from these norms (Di Bella, 1992; Schmidt, 1994; see also Bell, 1979). In this context, the emotion shame is said to play an important role because it indicates the personal sensitivity for one's reputation, which is understood as essential for functioning of the honour and dishonour complex (Schmidt, 1994, p. 194). In both regions, what is most important for a man's reputation, and thus for his honour, is his *abilitá*, which relates to his labour capacity and economic success (Di Bella, 1992, p. 114; Schmidt, 1994, p. 196). In the Sardinian countryside, a man's reputation and honour is also enhanced through the successful theft of livestock (*la bardana*), which can be understood as an inter-male competition for courage and bravery. In general, honour is related to quick success, and the title *omine balente* is ascribed to a man who knows how to react quickly and does, on the one hand, not hesitate to obtain resources (e.g., livestock) from others while, on the other hand, successfully guarding his own animals (Schmidt, 1994, p. 199). According to the complementary working spheres of men and women, *abilitá*—and thus respect and honour—depend on the gender-specific success in mastering work. Thus for women, who are responsible for the private domain of the household,*abilitá* comprises working indefatigably in house and garden, successfully rearing children, and bargaining at the market and consequently being thrifty (Schmidt, 1994, p. 197). Furthermore, for Sicily, Di Bella (1992, p. 120) described gossip as a female duty to support the reputation of her husband and family by casting light on the behavioural inadequacy of others in the public sphere.

For women, morality-related venerability is most important (Schmidt, 1994, p. 197). Thus, married women behave honourably if their conduct is modest (*sa brigungia*) and if they are loyal to their husbands. For unmarried women, virginity is important, although an illegitimate pregnancy leads to dishonour and shame for a girl and her family only if she does not marry the father of her yet unborn child (Schmidt, 1994, p. 200). For the Sardinian community, Schmidt (1994, pp. 199–200) pointed out that, as for women, extramarital relations are disapproved of for men, but a term for male chastity does not exist.

In Sardinia, both sexes try to accumulate prestige for the nuclear family through their proper conduct because the household is understood as the centre and focal point of honour (Schmidt, 1994, p. 196) that can be jeopardised at any time by the slander and insult of envious neighbours. In such a case, it is a man's duty to defend the reputation of his household and family, and he is expected to avenge insult. As in Sicily, men have different ways of avenging (*vinditta*) the insult or attack, but avenging is only possible between men of the same social status (Schmidt, 1994, p. 194). If someone's honour is violated, the dishonoured one usually tries to pay back with the same coin, or, if that is not possible, by stealing or destroying the offender's possessions. It is only in rare cases that such quarrels and disputes escalate and blood is shed. However, when a man has been killed, his male relatives are obligated to avenge the murder and take the blood of the murderer or one of his male relatives—only then is the honourable reputation of the family regained (pp. 203–204).

With the exception of the honour concepts of the Mafia and related organisations, little has been published on Italy. Horden and Purcell (2002, p. 503), for instance, when quoting Davis, reported that central Italy "has not produced reports of honour." Therefore, we have to recall what holds true for many other regions in which the honour and dishonour code seems important and be careful not to extend the findings in single reports on single regions to a larger region or a whole country.

Greece

In general, as Safilios-Rothschild (1969) has noted, the Greek concept of *philótimo* (ethymologically: love of honour) clarifies the connection between honour and shame and determines whether any action must be taken to restore the damaged honour. "It is the possession of *philótimo* that sensitises a Greek to public opinion and obliges him (her) to conform to the traditional norms of conduct" (p. 205).

For the Sarakatsani, until recently a mainly transhumant society in south-eastern Greece, it is said that with the exception of the lowest lineages all members of the community have honour "by nature." However, some leading families have more honour than others. This inherent honour (*timé*) must be defended, and rivalry is greatest between those families, the majority of the society, who show few differences in wealth, courage, and honour (Campbell, 1964, pp. 266–67). Among the Sarakatsani, the interrelatedness of prestige, wealth, and honour is especially pronounced. Prestige and honour are two sides of a coin, whereby prestige can be gained not only through wealth, especially property in large herds of sheep and goats, but also through the number of sons; it may also be augmented through marriage alliances.

> Self-regard is a subjective and personal sentiment. At the same time the situations which provoke it are socially defined. All those elements of prestige, whether of the individual or the family, affect it and are sanctioned by it. A man's self-regard leads him to conserve his honour, to act honourably, to strive after wealth, to act proudly and arrogantly and so on. (p. 309)

It is suspected that being poor is the result of some moral shortcomings that go hand in hand with a lack of honour (pp. 273, 297–300). Men's honour (and thus the honour of the family and the household) is related to the virtues of manliness: A man must have a regular physiognomy, be strong in body and *barbatos* (well endowed with testicles), and be courageous and fearless (see also Lazaridis, 1995). However, this "physiological basis" of manly honour becomes true manliness only when it is disciplined and spiritualised. On the women's side, honour is related to sexual shame, to the virginity of girls and the chastity of women who "must remain virginal in thought and expression," so the manliness of men is not dishonoured (pp. 270, 287–288). A woman is said to be "above all cunning, especially in the sense that her cunning involves the corruption of another, that is the man. She is a constant threat to his honour" (p. 277). A man's or a household's honour can be violated through homicide, the drawing of blood, verbal insult, seduction, rape, or broken betrothal (pp. 268–269). In such cases,

> [if an] attack is made on the family's honour [it] demands an immediate response whereby as also in Montenegro and northern Albania the notion of chivalrous conduct is absent. An honour killing is accomplished without warning, by a bullet fired from behind cover, or a knife in the back . . . the accent is on effective action, the achievement of success, the avoidance of failure. Ends matters more than means. (p. 318).

Failure to respond fatally damages the prestige of the outraged group and all its members (p. 273).

For the Sarakatsani, shame, like self-regard, is a sanction for all those elements that are relevant for the prestige of the family or an individual.

> Anything which leads to, or is the basis of, low prestige is a matter for shame. Whatever may be the underlying psychological character of shame, its cultural definition amongst the Sarakatsani is the sense or fear of failure. . . . When a man acts disgracefully he hurts himself. . . . And the sense of shame, an essentially internal sanction of action, is related to the external threat of social abandonment, the fear that the community will judge him to be "lost." (p. 310, see also pp. 311–312).

Balkans

Montenegro and Northern Albania

In both Montenegro and Albania, two of the classic feuding societies, all norms, values, and the code of conduct revolve around honour and dishonour. Violating or even questioning the honour of an individual brings dishonour not only to him (or her) but also to the whole household, the extended family, and the clan. Christopher Boehm (1984) noted that:

> The moral system and its operation in Montenegro presents a portrait of a people who were extremely sensitive in the matter of honor. This means that their lives and behavior were shaped very effectively by tribal public opinion simply because they were so vulnerable to that opinion. This concern of Montenegrins with their personal and clan reputation was the basis of feuding, in that the taking of blood vengeance was not merely morally justifiable but was morally necessary if one's reputation was to remain unblemished. (p. 85)
>
> Two words for honor were used very widely in Montenegro: *čast* and *obraz*. *Čast* means much the same thing as the English word "honor"; it also designated the hospitality that was offered to a guest. *Obraz*, however, was a different kind of word, in that it was figurative. Literally, *obraz* meant "the cheek on your face." Figuratively, it was used in a special sense which was very important in Montenegro. *Obraz* stood for your moral reputation, your ability to hold your head up in the company of other tribesmen, to look them straight in the eye, to associate freely with people because you carried no major moral blemish that would make them view or treat you as a person who was socially unacceptable. (p. 78)

Here, as in so many of the typical honour and dishonour societies, gossip "served as the major indirect mechanism of social control, even though gossiping was not done with any such intention" (pp. 81–84; see also Fonseca, 2004, pp. 104–108). If, during a quarrel, the honour of one or both opponents was questioned, blood vengeance might start. Duels were seldom fought in such cases, as was the usual practice in western Europe (see Boehm, 1984, pp. 117–118), and killings did not usually take place in the heat of the moment. "The insulted man might brood about things for a time and then simply shoot his enemy down in what we would call cold blood" (pp. 88–89; see also Denich, 1974).

In neighbouring Albania, especially in the northern, mountainous part of the country, male honour is related to manliness and strength. According to the traditional code of honour (the *kanun*), murder is one of the most common and most serious affronts against the honour of a family. The murderer puts the family of the killed one in a temporary state of dishonour until "blood has been taken again," and the most honourable way to do this is by killing the murderer or a male member of his family. This often then leads to century-long blood feuds (see Anderson, 2000; Hasluck, 1967; Schwandner-Sievers, 1996, 1999). The complex term *besa* signifies many of the duties obliging the "house" to protect the honour of the householder and his family. As Schwandner-Sievers (1996, pp. 116–17) explained, the term comprises a multitude of meanings and is related to, for instance, honour in general, the given "word of honour," alliances, loyalty, or trustworthiness. The *besa* can be broken by having not protected a guest, betraying a friend, or rape, which are are some of the most severe cases in which honour is lost. Honour, then, has to be reinstalled by killing the offender, the one who has "blackened the face" of the dishonoured one, his family, and the household. As in many other areas in which the code of honour is at the apex of the social structure, the one who has lost his honour, and with him the members of his family, are socially dead. The only path that can lead him and the members of his household back into the social life of the community is that of regaining honour by "taking blood."

Arabic World

The ideal married woman is a mother, but one who is virginal in mind and feelings. (Al-Khayyat, 1990, p. 26)

Since the earliest times in the Arabic world, honour and dishonour have been one of the main themes in literature and poetry, and it seems that little has changed between pre-Islamic times and the present day (Farès, 1932). A good example is the tale of Laylā and Majnun, which is well known from Turkey to India in various versions. It tells of the hopeless love between Laylā and Qays of the Amir tribe living on the desert plateau of Najd. Laylā's father is not willing to give his daughter to Qays because the latter has openly declared his love for Laylā. As Yamanaka (2001) wrote:

But Laylā's father refused to give his daughter's hand to a "majnun," [a madman] especially since the boy had revealed his devotion for Laylā in his poems, thus disgracing Laylā and her family's honor in public. (p. 147)

Aḥaywāt and Awlāt Ali Bedouin of Egypt

Regarding the Aḥaywāt Bedouin of the Sinai, Steward (1994) argued that:

The fact that honor among the Bedouin is not connected with class differences is perhaps reflected in their vocabulary. In literary Arabic there are two words that are commonly translated "honor," *'ird* and *sharāf*. The word *sharāf*, both in classical and modern literary language, has not only the sense of "honor" but also the sense of "elevation, eminence, high rank"; it resembles the words for honor in the major modern European languages in that it often relates to both vertical and horizontal honor [see also Abu-Zaid, 1966, pp. 245–247].

'Ird, in contrast, carries no suggestion of vertical honor. In many dialects both words are used, often in somewhat different ways. It is noteworthy that *sharāf* and related words from the same root are rarely used by the Aḥaywāt in any sense to do with honor or rank; and when they are so used, it is I suspect the result of outside influence. The absence of the word *sharāf* may reflect the fact that the Bedouin are in many ways markedly egalitarian, and that the most prominent kind of honor among the Bedouin is horizontal rather than vertical. (pp. 132–133)

Steward continued:

It is only sexual offences against a man's ward that involve his *'ird*. If someone hits or insults a man's sister or daughter it is, of course, an offence against him, but not an offence against his *'ird*.... A sexual offence against a man's ward ... or the violation of a man's protection ... always constitutes a primary impugnment of a man's *'ird*. (pp. 134–135)

Abu-Zaid (1966, p. 247) also made clear that among the Awlād Ali Bedouin of Egypt the term *'ird* is exclusive and "is used only in connection with female chastity, prudence and continence." Sexual offences, however slight they may be, are offences against that particular and more specific kind of honour that is called *'ird*. As already stated, *'ird* is affected only by the conduct of the woman and in this respect it differs from the more general concept of *sharāf*. *'Ird* differs also from *sharāf* in that *sharāf* can be acquired and augmented through right behaviour and great achievements, whereas *'ird* "is linked only with sexual conduct" (Al-Khayyat, 1990, p. 21).

It is important to note that the distinction by which honour is related solely to men and shame (as women's honour) only to women is a simplified generalisation (see Antoun, 1968). In Arabic societies, and in most parts of Asia as well (see also Paulhus, Duncan, & Yik, 2002), the prescriptions of shameful conduct, in terms of decent behaviour and shyness, relate to men just as much as to women. Abu-Lughod (1990), after having quoted Peters (1952), who had described an incident in which all the younger men abruptly fled the tent when she brought up the topic of marriage or women, even leaving their shoes behind in their haste, stated:

> This avoidance is said to be motivated by a sentiment, called *ḥasham*, which can be translated as "modesty," "embarrassment," or "shame." *Ḥasham* refers both to what we might think of as an internal state of shyness, embarrassment, or shame and to a set of behaviors associated with these "feelings," although the Awlad 'Ali do not make that distinction. The cultural repertoire of such behaviors includes dressing modestly for both sexes (which means covering the hair, arms to the wrists, and legs to the ankles) and respect of demeanor such as downcast eyes, formal posture, and refraining from eating, smoking, talking, laughing, and joking. It is also marked, for married women, by veiling in certain circumstances. Very importantly, as I have described, it involves sexual propriety. What is clear is that *ḥasham* is *the* moral sentiment. The person with social sense, the good person—*taḥashshams* —feels shy and acts modestly in the appropriate situations. Children, idiots, and the insane don't. Nor do bad people. (p. 32; see also Abu-Lughod, 1993, especially Chap. 5)

Ghiyata of Eastern Morocco

Among the Ghiyata, a peasant and merchant community in eastern Morocco, Marcus (1987) has shown that the protection and defence of their land and the control of women's conduct are the main honour-related realms. Not being able to protect the land or control women dishonours a man. Before the times of French colonialism,

> Ghiyatan also developed ideologies of egalitarianism and generosity as other concomitants to the perception of "goodness" as a scarce resource.... These ideologies express the pacifist side of honor: men who are considered honorable by virtue of wealth (one of Mediterranean honor's "three vectors of competition," along with status and respect; Gilmore, 1982, p. 191), that is, those who possess ... are obliged to share their bounty with those who have little or nothing. This dictum applied to the treatment of non-Ghiyata as well, as in the case of other tribespeople occasionally finding refuge among them. But when Ghiyata state emphatically that "all men are not equal in value" (*quima*), they refer to a sense of general social worth that is not reckoned in material or monetary terms alone. The "egalitarianism" of the Ghiyata is analogous to what Herzfeld (1980, p. 342) has argued is its characteristic form throughout the Mediterranean: "a *nominal* equality of access to moral resources." (p. 54)

However, with the drastic socioeconomic and political changes that took place during the colonial period, the land-related honour ideology lost its meaning, and: "As tribesmen are increasingly proletarianized, previously solidarity local groups fall apart. What is the fate of honour, when *siba*, feudal-like relations of production, and much of the basis for tribal social organization have disappeared?" (p. 55). In contrast to David Hart (1976, p. 94), who studied the Rifian Aith Waryaghar in the same region, Marcus (1987) was not of the opinion that labour migration to Europe replaced the importance and social function of feuding over honour:

> Can these leave-takings, like the mobility and exploits of the horsemen of the past, be considered pathways to the achievement of honor? I do not believe so, although it is true that a worker's accumulation of earnings provides him with a certain measure of personal autonomy.... I do not believe that Ghiyata see honor as obtainable in this way. Wealth earned abroad may indeed be put to the service of such traditional ends as buying land, building new houses, getting married, giving feasts, and the like. These goals are within reach, but status and respect—which are moral, not material, resources—are not easily come by; they cannot be purchased with money. (p. 55)

Kabyle Society of Algeria

No one has analysed the complex structured network of social relations organised around a honour and dishonour paradigm more carefully than Pierre Bourdieu (1966, 1977) in his description of the Kabyle society of Algeria. He reported that the Kabyles differentiate between honour *ḥurma*, "honour, that entirety of which is *h'aram*, that is to say all that is prohibited under the penalty of committing sin, or is sacred" (1966, p. 216) and *nif*, self-esteem or point of honour. In analogy to Marcel Mauss's (1954) "gift," honour (*nif, ḥurma*) in Kabyle society is organised within the framework of a complex, often ritualised display of giving and taking in which the manifestation of honour and rank order occur. The *qanun* (see the *kanun* of Albania)-the rules for competitive verbal display, giving of gifts, and the often violent patterns of revenge-taking including blood vengeance (*thamgart*)-are regulated on the basis of what is frequently a village-specific code. As in many other societies of the region, a man's honour is related to his manliness, bravery, and the respect (*laḥya*) he can expect from others. A man's honour is thus related to "one's house, one's women, one's rifles" (1966, p. 219), which is comparable to the "gold, women, and soil" that the Pashtuns of Afghanistan use to denote the courageous protection of a man's possessions in the broadest sense.

West and Central Asia

Turkey

According to Hüseyin Kuzkaya (2001) and Andrea Petersen (1985), who examined the code in a rural area of Turkey, two main concepts of honour (*seref* vs. *namus*) regulate the public and private sphere of society.

Seref, as a specific type of honour, has been translated as an amalgam of dignity, prestige, and esteem (see Kuzkaya, 2001, p. 21; Petersen, 1985, p. 67). It is one of the major principles next to respect (*saygi*) that determine the hierarchical order in the public sphere of society, and it is said that only men have access to it. Furthermore, *seref* has a quantitative component and can be accumulated through deeds that require certain modes of conduct to exalt the personal status of a man within his age group. Attributes such as courage, power, generosity, hospitality, and wealth as well as religious education enlarge individual prestige and esteem, whereas stinginess, timidity, and lack of success reduce the prestige and esteem of a man in the public sphere (see Kuzkaya, 2001, p. 21).

The other principle of honour termed *namus* refers to the private sphere of the household and the family, which is dominated by the female members of society but is represented in public by men. The honour of women, in the first place, has to do with sexual purity and depends, secondly, on the marital status of the individual. If unmarried, the *namus* of a daughter that corresponds to the honour of her father depends on her virginity. The *namus* of a wife is defined by chastity and loyalty to her husband. The appropriate conduct comprises physiological and psychological weakness; fainting and shame (in the sense of shyness and bashfulness) indicate either virginity or sexual chastity (Kuzkaya, 2001, p. 22; see also Petersen, 1985, p. 11). *Namus* is translated by Kuzkaya (2001, p. 22) as "*sexuelle Ehre*" [sexual honour], and it refers not just to the woman itself but to all male members of her family. The defiance of *namus* can even lead to the loss of the collective honour of a whole village, which is represented to the outside world by the male inhabitants.

In comparison to *seref*, *namus* consists of qualitative components that are innate. *Namus* has to be defended throughout the life of a woman because damage to *namus* cannot be repaired; and if lost, dishonour is brought to the collective the woman belongs to (see Kuzkaya, 2001, p. 22). Women protect their *namus* by avoiding the company with unrelated men; and in the public sphere, young women in particular join the company of other women to defend their honour, which can easily be transformed into dishonour by rumours (Petersen, 1985, p. 11). Men who are dependent on the sexual honour of the female members of their family have the duty to defend and secure the high-valued *namus* because it reflects on their honour, which in the case of defiance is lost once and forever (see also Petersen, 1985, pp. 20, 29–32).

In the area of Aydin in western Turkey, Möwe (1998) described how the meaning and use of the term *namus* has changed. Among the peasants in the region, it is still associated with wealth, capital, power, and strength; but now, mainly among the educated urban middle class, *namus* has shifted away from these "traditional" connotations and is now mostly related to the good upbringing of children and especially to a good education.

Afghanistan (Pashtuns)

Among the Pashtuns, mainly in eastern Afghanistan, honour is the central theme of the *pashtunwal*' the customary law that defines, as a code of conduct, the behavioural prescriptions of a "good Pashtun." Central to this code are the protection of "women, gold, and land" (*san, sar, samin*).

> Here the inviolability of women and land is closely interconnected or ideologically considered as practically identical. A common saying is: . . . "He who cannot protect the integrity of his family cannot protect anything, anyone is free to snatch away from him what he wants, his possessions, his land." (Glatzer, 1996a, p. 5)

Especially related to manliness is the term *nang*, standing for honour, dignity, courage, and bravery. As Glatzer (1996a) wrote: the one who has *nang*, a *nangialay*,

> brings honour and fame to his tribe. To be called *benanga* ("shameless," "undignified") is the worst possible insult in Pashtu and a deadly threat to the social position of the insulted. Killing the insulter is an accepted way of regaining one's *nang* and thus of one's social status. (p. 4)

Directly related to the idea of *nang* are the terms *sharm* and *namus*. The former, as in many languages from Turkey to northern India, relates to shame in the sense of modesty, bashfulness, and decent behaviour. *Sharm* relates to clothing, ways of eating, behaviour towards elders, and so forth but mainly to the conduct of women who represent the honour of men, the household, and even that of the whole clan. The latter term, *namus*, also relates more specifically to women's conduct[3]—as Glatzer (1996a) wrote:

> It means privacy and the protection of its sanctity. In the narrower sense namus relates to the integrity, modesty and respectability of women and to the absolute duty of men to protect them . . . in the widest sense it is the Afghan home land to be protected . . . in general men consider young women to be less able to think and act rationally, to have less self-control and to be more inclined to sexual activities, in short they are believed to be an easy prey to any seducer who comes along. Thus men feel obliged to fight for maintaining their namus, i.e., first of all to keep the women of their families under tight control, and to protect the women from their own "weaknesses."
>
> Even more feared than the actual behaviour of women is the neighbours' gossip, that is what erodes namus most effectively and what is most difficult to control. Better do not let anybody see the women. (pp. 4–5)

The term *tura* (the sword) also relates to honour but primarily to the individual man's honour, autonomy, and equality to demonstrate one's refusal to bow before any arbitrary power. Secondarily, *tura* is related to the honour of a man's family and clan (see also Berrenberg, 2002; Glatzer, 1996b, 2000; Janata & Hassas, 1975, Kieffer, 1972; Lindholm, 1982, pp. 188–189, 209–238; Mahdi, 1986; Steul, 1981).

These specific connotations of the "honour complex" as formulated in the *pashtunwali* are to be found mainly in the eastern parts of the country. In the western areas, for example among the Durrani Pashtuns, a more general concept of *pahtu* is used. Informants among the Nurzai and Milarzai often explained that "the real Pahtuns" (who really know the *pashtunwali*) are those living in the eastern part of the country (Casimir & Glatzer, unpublished data). For the Maduzai Durrani, Tapper (1991) gave the following description.

> A man's reputation and that of his household are constructed in terms of the idiom of honour and shame. From the extensive vocabulary, the most widely used terms are *sharaf* (nobility, goodness), *gheyrat* (pride, self-respect), *nang* (honour), *izzat* (respect), *sharm* and *haya* (shame in both opposed senses), and *namus* (a man's honour derived from the morality of his womenfolk). There is a considerable overlap between these terms; in essence they refer to the control of fertility (see also Janata & Hassas, 1975, p. 86). The concept may also be subsumed in the more general notion of *num* (reputation, literally name, the big name or good name of a big man). (pp. 106–107)

The extreme preoccupation of women in Afghanistan with honour, dishonour, and shame related to their body becomes evident when in today's civil-war-like situation, women at the eve of elections describe their main fear.

> The women say they do not fear death. They fear the shame a public death would bring their families. "My biggest fear is that if something happens at the election day, the whole town will talk afterward," said Farida, who is 23 and unmarried.... "There is already a general rumor that women who work outside the home are prostitutes to Americans or foreigners, that women who work outside the home lose their honour." There is a saying in the culture, Farida said: For a woman, a death in the home—with purdah ... is a death of honour; a death outside the home is a death with dishonour. "I just don't want to die on the street," Farida said.
>
> Roshana, about 30 and the mother of a 14-year-old son, agreed. She said she envisioned lying in the street missing the head or a limb, being viewed by strange men. It would be an insoluble stain on her family's reputation. (Waldman, 2004, p. 2)

South Asia

The notion of honour and dishonour is nowhere as pronounced as in many South Asian societies. The importance of the hierarchical ordering of castes or ethnic groups with the central connotation and importance of ritual "purity and pollution" goes hand in hand with the connotation of men's honour. Manliness and the "protection" of women, which leads to their more or less strict seclusion (*parda*), guarantees honour and high esteem for men, the whole family, and even the whole group. Women's chastity and thus their purity relates directly to men's honour and is therefore one of the main concerns in men's attitudes and behaviour. A wife's or daughter's misbehaviour brings dishonour especially over all the menfolk of the family and often over the whole caste, subcaste (*gōt*), clan, or lineage. In this respect, there is no principal difference between South Asia and other countries or regions in which the code of honour plays an important role. Compared with many other societies or regions, it seems, however, to have overwhelming importance here with the consequence that dishonouring the family or group more often leads to extreme punishments (see the reference to honour killings, below). For the situation in Pakistan, where the situation is especially severe, we read:

> Women are seen to embody the honour of the men to whom they "belong" [and] as such they must guard their virginity and chastity. By being perceived to enter an "illicit" sexual relationship, a woman defiles the honour of her guardian and his family. She becomes *kari* [black] and forfeits the right to live.... In most communities there is no other punishment for a *kari* but death. A man's ability to protect his honour is judged by his family and neighbours. He must publicly demonstrate his power to safeguard his honour by killing those who damaged it and thereby restore it. "Honour killings" consequently are often performed openly.... The perception of what defiles honour has become very loose. Male control extends not just to a woman's body and her sexual behaviour, but to all of her behaviour, including her movements and language. In any of these areas, defiance by women translates into undermining male honour. Severe punishments are reported for bringing food late, for answering back, for undertaking forbidden family visits. Standards of honour and chastity are not applied equally to men and women, even though they are supposed to. Surveys conducted in the North West Frontier Provinces and in Balochistan found that men often go unpunished for "illicit" relationships whereas women are killed on the merest rumour of "impropriety." (AI, 1999, p. xx; see also AIUSA, n.d.).

This is certainly true for many of the northern castes and tribes of the subcontinent with their positive attitude toward violence (for a comprehensive analysis of the honour and dishonour concept of the Baluch of western Pakistan, which is quite similar to that of the Pashtuns described above, see Orywal, 2002, pp. 342–352). This positive view was used by the British to justify extending their power and their sphere of influence: In 1860, they developed a political concept that continues to have consequences until today. Central to this concept is the term "martial races," referring to the idea of "belligerent, martially good fighting races." The conjunction of readiness to fight with political fidelity led to more and more recruitment of members of these "martial" groups (e.g., Sikh, Gurkha, Dogra, Pashtuns, Jat) whose code of honour and dishonour is of overarching importance. These groups were particularly useful soldiers for the British colonial army and thought to be, "by nature," more manly and belligerent and therefore more honourable than others, and they were also "encouraged ... to see themselves as 'martial races'" (McLeod, 1989, p. 749; see also Rao, 1996).

Even today, these castes still look down on the "lower ones" (as European nobility used to do toward, for example, peasants or itinerant peoples), insisting that only they have an exclusive bravery-linked right to honour.

> During an attack on the Indian parliament on December 13, 2001, five security personal were killed in a gunfight with the militants. While the nation honoured the assistant police sub-inspector Nanak Chand with a *Kirti Chakra* (an army medal of honour), a village council (*panchayat*) in the province of Haryana denied his wife the right to construct a memorial in his honour. The high caste Jat community members turned down her wish with the argument that Nanak Chand was a Dalit (member of a "low caste"). Their argument was, that "... Dalits cannot be brave. Bravery is only for the upper castes." (Kumar, 2002).

Here, of course, a word of caution is necessary because sweeping statements and generalisations about "South Asia" will give the wrong impression. The values and norms and the related connotations and behavioural patterns described above differ in their importance for the hundreds and thousands of castes and groups (e.g., "tribal groups" or *adivasi*) for which such a code of honour plays only a marginal or no role at all.

Southeast Asia

In many Southeast Asian Societies, especially Malay-speaking ones, the cultural emphasis is not so much on honour but on shame. In everyday routines and interactions, all kinds of improper conduct—from the slightest offences against good manners up to serious violations of moral standards—are stressed as shameful events. The Malay and Indonesian term *malu*, usually translated as shame, shyness, embarrassment (Boucher & Brandt, 1981; Collins & Bahar, 2000; Heider, 1991, pp. 84–86, 292–311) signifies a powerful concept that plays a prominent role in a wide range of social realms. Honour, on the other hand, constitutes a more implicit category. It is seen as an elementary property of humans that becomes visible only when affected through acts of misbehaviour. Each act of misconduct evokes feelings of shame (*malu*)—not only in the ones who have misbehaved but also in the ones who have witnessed the failure or who are directly affected by it. If, for example, a person attends a feast unintentionally in everyday clothes, he or she feels shame for being inadequately clad, and the host feels humiliated or embarrassed by the disrespectfully dressed guest. Thus, normally, persons who are unable to meet the demands of a certain dress code do not attend the respective social event to avoid embarrassing their hosts and disgracing themselves.

A wide variety of behaviours result from the desire to avoid experiencing shame or provoking shameful situations. Shame becomes evident here as a fundamentally social emotion that motivates conformity with shared social standards while simultaneously displaying a person's acceptance of group standards. An important aspect is that shame feelings are caused not only by failure of some sort but also by hierarchical distances between persons. Individuals of inferior social rank usually feel *malu* in the presence of superiors, even though they have done nothing wrong. This experience is so salient that the status of high-ranking individuals is often described not in structural terms but with reference to their capacity to elicit *malu* in others (see Fessler, 1999, p. 77, 2004; Röttger-Rössler, 2004, pp. 246–252).

Thus, in Southeast Asian societies, especially in Malaysia and Indonesia, shame (*malu*) constitutes a "hypercognised emotion" (Levy, 1984) that plays an important role in everyday behaviour and is closely connected with social hierarchy. An intersection between hierarchy, gender, and shame is given through the social rule that a woman should never marry below the social status of her mother. This prescription turns every love relationship between a low-ranking man and a higher ranking woman into a serious affront to the integrity of the respective woman's family, thereby evoking intense feelings of embarrassment in the women's kin, leading them to engage in acts of compensation. Depending on the individual society, these acts range from killing the couple, to lifelong banishment of the daughter and erasing her name from the family's genealogy, to temporarily limited exclusion of the couple from the social community (e.g., Pelras, 1996; Röttger-Rössler, 1989, 2004, pp. 108–113). Nonetheless, although there is a clear connection between the reputation of a family and the conduct of their women, especially their daughters, this is not emphasized with the same rigour as, for example, in the Arabic or (former) Mediterranean world (see above).

East Asia

China

In China, as Hu (1944) reported, there are two sets of criteria distinguished by two words that both, on the physical side, mean "face." One of them, *mien-tžu*, stands for the kind of prestige that is emphasised in the country: a reputation achieved through getting on in life, through success and ostentation. This is prestige that is accumulated by means of personal effort or clever manoeuvring. For this kind of recognition, ego is dependent at all times on the external environment. The other kind of "face," *lien*, is also known to Americans without being accorded formal recognition. It is the respect of the group for a man with a good moral reputation: the man who fulfils his obligations regardless of the hardship involved, who under all circumstances shows himself a decent human being. It represents the confidence of society in the integrity of ego's moral character, the loss of which makes it impossible for him to function properly within the community. *Lien* is both a social sanction for enforcing moral standards and an internalised sanction. (p. 45).

If we compare the situations appraised in the Mediterranean world as leading to dishonour with those described by Hu (1944), we note that none of the 21 situations she described (pp. 55–69), which are expressed by various phrases containing, or words connected with, the terms *mien* or *lien* connoting honour or dishonour, relate to women in general or their chastity. They invariably deal only with men's virtues, prestige, and reputation. As she pointed out:

> The main criterion for *lien* consists of the virtues of a decent man. A single lapse is punishable by ridicule and comments on "loss of *lien*"; repeated offences arouse strong disapproval and cause the withdrawal, psychologically speaking, of the community from ego. The consciousness that "loss of *lien*" means that the confidence of society in his character is impaired, and places him in danger of being despised and isolated, usually acts as a strong deterrent on the individual. (pp. 54–55)

The traditional Confucian connotations of honour, however, became amalgamated and underwent a degree of transformation with the emergence of the dominant ideology of the Communist system. Nowadays, as Jankowiak (1993, pp. 60–96) has described, fulfilling one's cadre-related duties in the hierarchical system of the Communist political organisations determines an individual's prestige and honour.

Japan

Honour, as Asano-Tamanoi (1987, p. 113) pointed out, is much less related to the individual; it is always related to the household. She continued:

> We have seen that the abstract concept of shame can be coupled with the notion of *na*, which refers to the ideal state of household continuity. We have also seen that *na* is at the same time manipulable. Japanese has various expressions regarding na: "*na o ageru*" (to raise one's name), "*na o kegasu*" (to pollute one's name), ... and so forth. All these *na* forms refer to the family name or names of groups one belongs to .... And if the quality of *na* can change, the quality of household continuity expressed by *na* can also change. Such qualities depend upon the moral conduct of men and women who constitute the household. Thus, "*rippana na*" or "*meiyo-aru na*" (honorable or honored name) refers to the state of household continuity that has been realized through honorable conduct of its members. Honor is subsumed under the notion of *na* but makes its appearance only when people, through gossip, evaluate men and women's conduct in terms of their respective obligations as household members. Honor, then, like shame, is conferred upon both men and women, as they integrally constitute the household .... Honor is given to those men and women who do fulfil such obligations, leading to the "honorable name" of the household. (p. 116)

Honour and dishonour/shame in Japan are primarily in the eyes of the society but "women are the main evaluators of honor and shame through their powerful gossip" (p. 116; see also Al-Khayyat, 1990, p. 23; Bachnik, 1992; De Vos, 1986; Kuwayama, 1992; Lebra 1992, Zíková, 2006, pp. 72–82). This describes the meaning of honour only in the civic and agrarian sections of Japanese society.

Different from the connotation of honour in the civic society in the past (and in the memory of many still today as well as related also to the bravery of soldiers in World War II) was the *point d'honneur* of the warrior "caste" of the Samurai. This comprises a typical canon of manliness, bravery, honour, and pride as well as the related possibility of being dishonoured. Originating about the 9th century, these military specialists were the protectors of nobility, great landlords, and later Kyoto's princely household. In about 1600, they then mainly became important bureaucrats in towns and fortresses until the institution of the samurai was abolished with the restoration of the Meiji in 1668.

When Saikaku (1642–1693) published his famous *Tales of Samurai Honour* in 1688, he was describing an institution that was already slowly on its way down. The institution of the samurai with its extremely elaborated code of honour (*bushidō*, the ways of the warrior) can be traced back to the 12th century when the warrior's stipend during the time of the wars between the Genji and the Heike clans was paid for real military service. It was mainly in the succeeding centuries that, under the influence of Zen Buddhism, the code of honour (*meiyo, giri*) (for the complexity of the meanings of *giri*, see Bin, 1995, p. 31) acquired its philosophical and aesthetic connotations. The main virtues of this manliness warrior code of honour comprised duty, obligation, justice, and social courtesy including bravery, making the right and honourable decisions, respect, and loyalty to one's lord. These virtues were coupled with major behavioural challenges (*dojokun*), such as modesty, bravery, fighting spirit, cold-bloodedness, patience and endurance, simplicity, and purity, to name just the most important ones.

> A samurai was ... obliged to keep his reputation unsullied, and this required him to avoid disgrace by observing the due proprieties and to clean his name of any real or imagined insults. In this sense, the concept of *giri* in Saikaku's days came close to that of pride and self-respect. Just as the great fulfilment of giri was the sacrifice of life itself in its name, so the greatest disgrace was to die badly.... A samurai therefore had to be spiritually prepared to meet death bravely and fittingly at any time.... *Giri* was the keystone of *bushidō*, it set the samurai apart from the commoners and justified their position at the apex of the social hierarchy. (Callahan, 1981, pp. 10–11)

Maintaining these virtues and behaving accordingly comprised the honour of the samurai. This was gained by dying honourably in battle but also by killing themselves (*seppuku*) should they have infringed on one of the above-mentioned codes/rules. There was an extremely elaborated code for duelling to clear a samurai's name of any disgrace.

New Guinea

In many New Guinea societies, emotions, especially pride and shame, are of great importance. However, as Hallpike (1977, pp. 245–249) has stated, they are often not connected directly to honour or dishonour, as in the case of the Tauade who live in the southeastern part of the island. In her comparative analysis of *The Experience of Shame in Melanesia*, Epstein (1984) stated both explicitly and generally that:

> In the dynamic and highly individualistic world of New Guinea, where a man is encouraged to be combative and self-assertive, shame is clearly coupled with pride. By contrast, in more static societies, where there is much concern with matters of personal status, shame is more appropriately paired with the concept of honour. (p. 49)

Eves (1998) deduced from his findings that the feelings of shame are related to the category dishonour only for the Lele, in whom both of these feelings relate to either the breaching of exogamy rules or the discovery of illicit sexual relations.

> People who breach the rules of exogamy, like dogs, are considered to lack a sense of shame.... Like other illicit liaisons in pre-colonial times, if people were discovered to have engaged in incest, the couple were either killed or given ropes with which to hang themselves.
>
> A similar situation arises in relation to women's sexual relations, which at all times must be concealed from their clansmen.... If women's premarital and extramarital relations become publicly known, shame is brought to the clan and women may

> attempt suicide if those which whom they are in avoidance relationships learn of their sexual relations.
>
> In the past, the divulgence of a female clan member's sexual relation brought great shame to the clan, shame which could only be removed by her death.... The man (a male clan member) would then go and tell the woman to hang herself, and after she had done so, he would go to the central area of the hamlet and beat a slit gong to mark her death. Then the members of the women's clan would seek the death of the man involved, in reciprocation. If this happened to be an important man, as a magician or a man who had hosted many feasts, he could be fortunate and escape death by substituting a man with less power for himself. There was not, however, the possibility of replacing the woman because, as a man put it, "women have not got much power." (pp. 134–135)

Here, however, compared with other regions in which blood feuds often follow such killings (e.g., the Balkans) (see Boehm, 1983, pp. 65–72, 1984; or among the Baluch, see Orywal, 1996, pp. 61–72), further retaliations are prevented by ritual exchange of goods between the two clans to retain good relations. The practice of killing the violators of the rule of clan exogamy or in the case of a extramarital sexual relation has now disappeared; today, such "breaches of kin etiquette require the 'buying' or removal of the shame with shell valuables and/or the killing of a pig" (p. 135).

Northern Africa (Fulbe)

The Fulbe (also termed Peul, Fula, and Fulani, among others) of whom a large proportion are nomadic animal husbanders, comprise a cluster of different ethnic groups living in most parts of the Sahel belt. As Elisabeth Boesen (2000) has explained, the general code of conduct of the Fulbe of North Benin, *pulaaku*, can be translated as "being or doing Fulbe." This code is based on the three columns, *munyal* (patience), *hakkillo* (reason), and *senteene* (dishonour); the latter term is also related to *dimaaku*, which also includes the connotations of pride and dignity. This general code comprises mainly three behavioural rules: Do not be scared/frightened (*wata a hula*); do not lie (*wata a fena*); and, here of special interest, *wata a hersa*, meaning that you should not bring shame on yourself. Shameful behaviour is mainly connected to the violation of an elder's dignity—something that should be respected. Young people have to avoid elders and if they meet them should not look at them. Here, as in many other African and also Australian societies, expressions we may render into "I am ashamed in someone's presence" are equivalent to "I honour someone."

Among the Fulbe, rumours (in which, however, names are never mentioned) and the fear of rumours are the most effective means of regulating the social network. However, rumours alone do not dishonour people. This can only happen in the rare case when young men singing songs name and blame someone who has trespassed against given norms and rules in public. Even then, however, ostracism is not practiced in this society.

East Africa (Pokot)[1]

The patrilineally organised pastoral nomadic Pokot number about 220,000 people and live mainly in Kenya's West Pokot District, East Pokot Subdistrict, and across the Kenyan-Ugandan border on Ugandan territory (for details, see Bollig, 1992).

Resion is the Pokot term for the concept most similar to honour. Equally important is *konyit*, which can be translated as "to honour somebody." The term *arasï* corresponds both to dishonour and shame depending on the specific situational context. In the truest sense of the word, dishonour and shame coincide owing to the fact that in most situations causing dishonour the affected persons also feel ashamed.

The highest honour (*resion*) for a Pokot man is to be killed by enemies while trying to raid animals from them. He is remembered as a hero and a warrior, and the other men tell stories about his outstanding courage and his heroic deeds. They say about him: *Kemeghchu kelio tich*! (He died in the footsteps of cattle!). It is a matter of fame and honour for a man to be initiated into the social status of a killer (*kolin*). The passage to this status is performed ritually, and the newly acquired social position is marked by ornamental scars (*kola*) on the upper arm, chest, and shoulder of the initiate and by a new name—the "killer's name" (Bollig, 1992, pp. 293–300). The other men honour a *kolin* by assigning him a leading position when they go for a raid. In peace negotiations, he is given the honour of speaking in the presence of the enemy.

Misconduct and the violation of norms and values are almost universally accompanied by *arasï* (dishonour/shame) in Pokot society. The most important examples for *arasï* in the sense of dishonour are as follows.

It is a great dishonour for a man if nobody wants to marry his daughters and/or if his sons perform poorly in the management of animals. Coming home from a raid without a single looted animal or being noticed for extraordinarily cautious behaviour during a raid is almost as big a dishonour for a Pokot man as being looked upon as a coward. He is accused of *Imitenyi kelio muron!* (Walking only in other men's footprints).

Dishonour of the worst category is associated with a man who stays at home when the other men go off on a raid. He is called *yakor* (coward), and his wives tell other people that there is no man in their homestead, only women. Other men taunt him: *Imungenyi ngo? Mo korkengunyiny ongut?* (You are not able to beat anybody except your wife!). His wife/wives are ridiculed and encounter snide comments such as *Kipkinyi korka*! (You are married to a woman!).

A girl brings great dishonour on herself and her entire family if she screams or even cries during her genital circumcision. This is performed in the context of an initiation ritual that turns girls into young women who can be married

[1] This section was kindly provided by Mathias Österle, Department of Social and Cultural Anthropology, University of Cologne.

afterward. The immediate sanction for this grave violation of a cultural norm is exclusion from the group of initiates. The girl has to undergo the rest of her initiation process separately, and satirical shaming songs about her malpractice can be composed and performed in public, for example, in the context of future rituals.

Pregnancy while still going to school or an affair with a married man also bring dishonour for a girl and her family.

A woman who is known for her careless attitude in domestic affairs and/or who is said to be lazy, slatternly, and filthy is called *sosa* (slob, rag bag). She is a source of dishonour for her husband. The female offspring of a *sosa* are burdened with their mother's bad reputation, and even a very beautiful, decent girl is reproached with the fact that she is "the daughter of her mother." It is *arasi* for a mother if her daughter is unable to find a husband and she is therefore left without a son-in-law, if she gives birth only to children of the same sex (girls are worse than boys), or if she delivers a disabled child.

A Pokot woman feels *aras*? in the sense of being shame if she is caught with a lover during intercourse and if she is seen naked—and the buttocks and vagina are particularly shameful. In contrast, a man's nakedness is generally not connected with shame. This circumstance becomes eminently manifest when men of all ages bathe in one of the rivers on a market day and in doing so display their naked bodies in public. Even the presence of women has no affect on their behaviour.

"Old American South"

One of the most pronounced and elaborated codes of honour, as described in a brilliant analysis by Wyatt-Brown (1982), developed in the American South between 1800 and 1860 and was carried to an extreme in the years of the Civil War with the North. Here, honour was applied to all classes of "southern whites," but "gentility" was a more specialised and sophisticated form of the code in which uprightness was coupled with high social position. In 18th century Virginia and South Carolina, planters had established close-knit marital alliances that restricted the circle of gentility to the very wealthiest and well-born families (Wyatt-Brown, 1982, p. 89). The honour code of a Southern gentleman comprised all the typical factors of manliness (defined by Wyatt-Brown as "primal honours"), such as personal courage and bravery, family protectiveness, and defence of kinsmen as well as bellicosity.

> In its most fundamental form, honour was a state of grace linking mind, body, blood, hand, voice, head, eyes, and even genitalia. The blood of self-regarding nobility transmitted the appropriate qualities. The heart held the intention that had to be open and honest towards friends and superiors and closed and implacable toward the honourless. The right hand gave the signal of respect in friendship, revenge in enmity. The eyes witnessed honor and looked down in defence or shame. Thus a steady gaze from a slave signalled impudence. (Wyatt-Brown, 1982, p. 49)

Here, as in all places where an extreme male-oriented code of honour exists, male bodily appearance was of utmost importance; and poor health, small stature, or any other physical defect carried special opprobrium in the Old South. The genitalia were the most sacred and the most vulnerable aspect of a man's body, and "sexual honour" was a central theme of the code. Again, as in all places where the code is important, moral purity and the chastity of women and their "protection" were central to the code; and women's salient duty was to act commensurately with male prestige and the maintenance of their honour. Thus, women's powers were formidable because they could destroy male reputation. Therefore, "the origin of male anxiety ... resided in two elements and complementary sources: male physical dread of what seemed alien in a woman's biological functions, and male fear of woman's ability to shame him before other men" (p. 52).

Not astonishingly, the typical two-faced morality could be found with young men seeking to prove their manhood by seducing women. This led to pronounced challenging of the authority of the older generation and mandatory fierce retaliation when a daughter or wife had been dishonoured—commonly involving retaliation by duelling. George Fenwick Jones (as quoted in Wyatt-Brown, 1982) summarised the typical interplay of wealth power and the code of honour in the "Old South" by reformulating the Sermon on the Mount (Matthew 5: 2–11):

> Blessed are the rich, for they possess the earth and its glory.
> Blessed are the strong, for they can conquer kingdoms.
> Blessed are they with strong kinsmen, for they shall find help.
> Blessed are the warlike, for they shall win wealth and renown.
> Blessed are they who keep their faith, for they shall be honored.
> Blessed are the open-handed, for they shall have friends and fame.
> Blessed are they who wreak vengeance, for they shall be offended no more, and they shall have honor and glory all the days of their life and eternal fame in ages to come. (p. 60)

It's a Man's World but What About Women?

In most societies in which the concept of "honour" together with the corresponding "code of honour" takes the predominant role in structuring social life, "manliness" plays a central role. The concept of manliness relates to the more or less aggressive defence of property and kin, and especially to "femininity" understood as the virginity and chastity of consanguinally but also affinally related women. In most if not all of these societies, we also find an asymmetrical distribution of "honour and dishonour" with double standards related to the transgression of sexual behavioural norms. Peristiany's (1992) analysis, based on his observations in a Cypriot mountain village community, can, to a certain extent, be generalised.

Sex outside the wedlock results in honor gained and honor lost, man's gain being woman's loss. This is particularly true when social distance is markedly wide, as man, ever sensitive to the dictates of honor, adds a social dimension to his good fortune when he overcomes a woman of higher rank, while feminine sexual motivation, being mainly conditioned by physiology and sentiment, is less sensitive to the social evaluation of her lover. In terms of this masculine logic the sexual act is, for woman, an almost asocial fulfillment of nature while, for man, the blend of physical and social achievement is measured by the qualities he has ravished: virginity, youth, beauty, and social position figuring among his trophies. The masculine imagery of sex is that of a hostile act: a battering-ram scattering the defence of a castle, the impaling of an enemy, the planting of a flag on conquered territory. The subduing of modesty also forms a man's strategy, so that each concession seems as the infliction of a humiliation, marks a new victory.... The behavior of the lover, a natural braggart, was inspired by the belief that men want to seduce virgins while young woman wish to seduce seducers. He therefore paraded his experiences freely, the stories becoming more scabrous with each telling. (p. 123)

It must be clear that in all societies in which the code exists the utmost importance of women's chastity and daughters' virginity are embodied in both sexes. The conduct of female kin is of equal importance to both men and women and is essential for the honour and dishonour of both. It is therefore interesting to ask whether some "code of honour" can be found among women that is more or less independent from that of men. In their introduction to a collection of essays dealing with honour codes in colonial Latin America, Johnson and Lipsett-Rivera (1998) remarked that some of the essays

> overturn the notion of a passive feminine participation in the culture of honor. As the traditional literature on honor points out, the behavior of women, particularly in terms of their sexuality, was a central concern to the honor of their fathers, husbands, and brothers. But women valued their own and their family's reputation independently as well. Women did not necessarily wait for their fathers, brothers, or other males to defend their honor. Instead individual women or women acting with kinswomen or friends mobilized to protect their reputation through the legal system or, on occasion, with the use of violence. (p. 12)

The double standard, however, as mentioned by Peristiany (see above), concerns men's sexual behaviour. Men, and particularly young men, are comprehensively exempted from the strict rules that apply to women's conduct. A man's fame is, to a certain extent, also related to his capacity to seduce other men's wives and daughters and can be understood as one aspect of the daring behavioural complex that is part and parcel of what is thought typical for a "real man." Moreover, in colonial Latin America in general, the birth of a illegitimate child did not dishonour the father but brought shame upon the mother (Potthast, 2003, p. 98; but see Findlay, 2005). As Horden and Purcell (2002, p. 501) noted for the Mediterranean region: "A seduced women is always shamed, her seducer may well gain honour." Nonetheless, it should be recalled that this double standard is not a characteristic found exclusively in "honour and dishonour societies" in the strict sense, as the example of many societies in Polynesia (Ortner, 1981, pp. 371–378, see also Shankman, 2006) and that of the American South (see above) shows.

However, in most of the case studies presented, we have been informed about only half of the society—the culture-specific differences in "women's honour" have been largely neglected (but see Petersen, 1985; Wikan, 1984). Women's honour was simply subsumed under that of men whose honour is threatened and endangered by women's misbehaviour. It is often said that a woman is the "guardian of her family's honour"; but once again this finally mainly reflects her duty to protect the honour of the head of her household and that of the males of her family of origin (and her natal family). In most studies, as Gilmore (1982, p. 180) has noted, "Women are said to be private creatures who are inactive economically. Yet there is constant evidence of the importance of female contribution to the domestic economy." He continued (p. 194): "Almost every anthropologist who has worked in the area speaks of an unbridgeable gulf between a male 'public' and a female 'private' sphere." Thus, "a somewhat distorted male-oriented image of both worlds has emerged." It was only in Muslim studies that this picture was corrected (for details, see pp. 195–196).

Matri-centred socioeconomic units have long existed in many Muslim and non-Muslim agricultural and herding communities—e.g., in Rajasthan (India) and Sind (Pakistan) and in some nomadic groups in western Afghanistan—in which men entrust the cash earned for safe-keeping to mothers and wives. However, among most traditional Muslims, Hindus, and Sikhs, direct female participation in production processes outside the precincts of the household economy depends on and is an indicator of family wealth and social status and the concept of (male) honour. The less the visibility of such participation, the higher is the status, especially in urban areas (Jeffery, 1979; Mandelbaum, 1988; Vreede-de Stuers, 1968) but also in many rural settings (Kotalová, 1993; Naveed-i-Rahat, 1990).

As in the Old Norse, as already mentioned, in the cases of Japan and China the relation between men's honour and the virginity and chastity of the related women play no or only a minor role. Maintaining high-ranking moral virtues, such as honesty and the right conduct of behaviour, the prosperity of the household and especially the continuity of the household over many generations are of overwhelming importance, leading to high prestige and honour.

As Dane (2005, pp. 69–74) has shown for central Europe, the earliest law text that had a general validity for the whole country (*Reich*), the Carolina, enacted at the Reichstag von Regensburg in 1532 as well as the later Codex Bavarici Criminalis (1751) took women's honour explicitly into account. Cases of rape were understood as an attack on women's honour demanding the death penalty (it should, however, be mentioned, that rapists were executed with the sword (being the honourable way of execution), whereas murderers and robbers were put to death by hanging (for a discussion and details, see Dane, 2005, p. 70; see also Knott, 2006).

An independent women's code of honour typically can be found only where women are relatively independent from men's governance, and this can be expected only in the highest or in the lowest sectors of a society. According to Elizabeth S. Cohen (1992, p. 623), who analysed the honour code in early modern Rome, aggression against outsiders was no concern of women; using the example of the prostitutes of Rome in the 16th and early 17th century, however, she showed well how women even of the lowest strata of the society defended their honour.

> Ironically, the secular ritual of house-scorning, [by smearing excrement on the house or door] which revenged damaged honour entangled inextricably with the milieu of those archetypically "bad," that is, shamed women, the courtesans. Most of the people who went to court seeking redress for such affronts against their honor were, indeed, women who should have none. Furthermore, in practicing house-scorning, the male assailants implied that their victims had enough honor that some could be stolen from them. The courts in taking the prostitutes' accusation seriously corroborated that view. (Cohen, 1992, p. 624)

As already mentioned, it has been mainly male anthropologists who have analysed the honour and dishonour code in different societies. They never (even when it would have been possible) discussed this aspect with the women themselves.

Generally, however, it can be said that successfully caring for all members of the domestic unit and managing everything that is under their control contributes to a woman's good reputation and thus to her honour. Her honour is also related to the number of children—in patriarchal and patrilineal societies, usually with special stress on the number of sons—she has raised successfully (for a detailed description for Montenegro, see Boehm, 1984, pp. 70–71; for the Sarakatsani of Greece, see Campbell, 1964, p. 289; for the Kabyles, see Bourdieu, 1966, p. 223; for Brazil, see Fonseca, 2004, pp. 99–100).

In this context, the historian Reddy (1997), discussing France between 1814 and 1848, differentiated men's honour as described above in a way similar to that for women when he stated:

> This aspect of honour was largely a male concern; women were, however, expected to comport themselves[3]—in terms of dress, household management, social relations, consumption, conversation[3]—in a manner appropriate to the rank of their husband or male relations. (p. 21; see also Gilmore, 1987a, p. 14)

In this sense, the honours of both sexes are ideally related to each other and mirrored by the attributes, virtues, and capacities of the respective partner. A man's honour also relates to that of his wife, and similarly a woman's honour may well relate to that of her husband (see also Reddy, 1997, Chap. 3, particularly p. 67). A "quantitative" equilibrium between the success of deeds and behaviours in accordance with the culture- or group-specific norms, values, and virtues enhances the prestige and the good reputation; and, in sum total, they make up a honourable household or family, as we saw in the case of Japan. By and large, however, it seems that the more important the honour and dishonour code and the *point d'honneur* in a society is, the more women play only the part of contributing to or supposedly endangering a men's honour, status, and prestige. It is only in societies such as the Beti of southern Cameroon—where men's domination over women was and is not extreme, where men and women's honour was "traditionally" not focussed on virginity and chastity, and where honour was always mainly individualised-that women were able, after the colonial period, to gain and augment their honour in terms of dignity, self-esteem, and pride through formal education and Catholicism (Johnson-Hanks, 2006).

When in rare cases honour was granted to a women outside the domestic sphere, it occurred only when they had embodied the typical attributes ascribed to male heroes such as courage, bravery, and especially willingness to sacrifice their lives when freeing the country from foreign occupation. The typical examples of such heroines are the virgin (!) Jeanne d'Arc (c. 1412–1431) and Laskarina Bouboulina (1771–1825) who is honoured in Greece as *Kapetanissa* or *Megali Kyra* and fought to liberate Greece from the Turkish occupation as the first and only admiral.

Honor Lost— Honor Restored

Honor Lost

As we have seen, the violation or transgression of one or several of the faculties of the honour code and often even an attack on one or more of a person's qualities and capacities related to the code by blackening (factual or nonfactual) can lead to the loss of honour.

In many parts of the world in which the code is taken seriously, being banned from the community (social death) is the usual punishment for a person who has failed to meet the standards of the code and has thus lost honour. If the disgraced person has not been ostracised from the village or the group's territory, he or she is usually forbidden to eat and drink with the other members of the community. This, for instance, is expressed in most languages in eastern Afghanistan, Pakistan. and northern India, where it is said that someone is banned from the communal water-pipe smoking and water drinking (e.g., Hindi: *hukka pani band hai*). Such a principle is often not followed strictly, however. For instance, among the Bedouins studied by Steward (1994, p. 116), it was *said* that no one would pay attention to such a person "having no value," and "a rug would not be spread on the ground for him to sit on . . . and so on." In practice, however, in the cases Steward had documented, the blackened persons were still treated like the other members of the group.

Until about the beginning of the 20th century, in many parts of Europe the dishonoured person often had to leave her social environment, and not a few women then committed suicide (particularly when they became pregnant outside wedlock). Today, although ostracism in this form is not mandatory in Europe, many people leave their immediate environment voluntarily and move to another city, for example, if they have to face "social death" in their community or neighbourhood. In a more symbolic way, depending on the type and severity of the crime, persons can also be deprived of their civil rights (German: *bürgerliche Ehrenrechte*) by a court of law, meaning that they can no longer serve as a witness, vote in elections, or stand for public office.

In the institutionalised form in which persons are stigmatised because of, for instance, their despicable profession, they always were spatially separated or set apart from the "normal citizen." In central Europe, the executioner, for instance, always had his own separate table in a corner of the inn where nobody joined him, and the "gypsies" always had to camp relatively far away from settlements.

To dishonour persons who violated given norms or who dishonoured others, they were exposed to public shaming by being locked into "stocks," being soiled in public, or being forced to parade through the village carrying a dead animal. Women often had their hair cut off. This procedure was still used to shame women in Nazi Germany who had entered a sexual relationship with a Jew; in other countries occupied by the Germans, women or girls who had fallen in love with the occupying German soldiers suffered the same fate after liberation.

Honor Restored

The codes of honour, together with the *point d'honneur* in various societies and groups, also determine how lost honour can be restored and how those who have dishonoured someone or a whole social group have to be punished.

In Japan before about 1600, an attack on a samurai's honour rarely led to individual duels. One's honour was restored through the already mentioned institution of *seppuko,* ritual suicide. In later times of peace, when these warriors were no longer needed, the only way in which a samurai could display his martial prowess to restore someone's honour was to engage in a "vendetta" (*katakiuchi*). *Katakiuchi* was the slaying of a person who had killed or caused the death of a relative; alternatively, someone closely connected to the avenger (e.g., a friend, teacher, master) could do the deed. For whom and under which circumstances a possible avenger could obtain the necessary official permission from the appropriate governmental office to carry out the "vendetta" was strictly regulated. Trespassing against these regulations by carrying out a non-officially registered duel was, if discovered, punished severely (for details, see, e.g., Callahan, 1981, pp. 15–16).

In the central European context, mortal duels were carried out when knightly honour was violated (e.g., Zmora, 1995) or when high-ranking men were insulted by having been cuckolded or slandered by a member of their own class until about the beginning of the 20th century. It has often been overlooked that, particularly during the Middle Ages, duels and feuds were avoided through the intervention of mediators chosen to avoid casualties (Althoff, 1995). To carry out a duel with a member of the lower classes was impossible because they, deprived of (equal) honour, could not insult an honourable member of the upper ranks of the society. In Germany, it was said that such a person was not *satisfaktionsfähig* (for the situation of black people in Kabyle society-who are supposed to be without honour—see Bourdieu, 1966, p. 200). It must be clear, however, that also among the so-called lower classes men (who, according to the upper classes, were supposed to have no honour) also fought each other to maintain or restore their honour (for the situation in colonial Mesoamerica, see Boyer, 1998; Landerdale, 1998; Lipsett-Rivera, 1998). At the end of the 19th century, there was still much scientific dispute in favour of and against the duel, and duelling was legally abolished in Germany only at the beginning of the 20th century (for a comprehensive analysis, see Frevert, 1991).

"Honor Crimes" and "Honor Killings"

> "We have killed him on purpose." said Pedro Vicario "but we are innocent." "Maybe before God," said Padre Amador. "Before God and mankind," said Pablo Vicario. "It was an affair of honour." (Gabriel García Márquez, 1981/1995, our translation)

The extreme forms of revenge aimed at restoring lost honour by "taking blood" from the violator or his kin, which in some areas lead to feuds and in some societies may last for generations, are the central theme in many narratives and legends (e.g., Dresch, 1989, Gilsenan, 1996). Such events are also a central topic of many anthropological reports dealing with "honour and dishonour societies." This can lead to the assumption that such deeds are common and hence "normal" in these societies, and we have to be careful not to generalise and overestimate their frequency. In most if not all of these societies, there are many ways out of a situation that can bring misery or tribulation to the families involved, and it is often the case that bloodshed becomes mandatory only when there is no other way to restore honour.

Moreover, the rules and means for restoring lost honour are quite different from culture to culture and from region to region. Different from the Turkmen of northern Iran, where blood feuds are practiced (Irons 1975, pp. 61–65), the Turkish Shahsevan nomads (Irons, 1979, pp. 127–131), practise neither blood vengeance nor feuds-if the honour of an individual or the lineage is violated, the problem is solved without bloodshed. Even if a girl's or woman's honour (*namus*) is violated, it is only in rare cases that her guardians kill the culprit(s). We also find major differences when comparing the traditional laws of the various Bedouin tribes. In some cases, and under specific circumstances, a payment of "blood money" can settle the case; in others, it is necessary and expected that the offender will kill the one who has violated his or his family's honour (e.g., Steward, 1994, pp. 86–98). Usually, though, in the case of an offence against a girl's or a woman's sexual integrity, the father (or brother) of the girl—and in the case of adultery the husband and/or the next male relative of the woman—must kill the seducer or, more often than not, both. In the Balkans, particularly in Montenegro and Albania, taking blood in honour-related feuds is common, but only men are allowed to kill each other; to kill a woman dishonours the killer and is permitted only under rare special circumstances. In other parts of the world, mainly in some areas of northern Africa, in western Asia, and in some parts of central Asia (Afghanistan, Pakistan) as well as in northern India and Bangladesh, it is mainly women who become the victims if they have threatened men's honour by violating the rules of chastity.

In the present time with its increasing discussion on violence in the name of honour, we have to bear in mind the need to differentiate between the multitude of *crimes of honour* directed against members of a society or group and the special cases of so-called *honour killings*, although they are both committed overwhelmingly against women (for the methodological problems in collecting and analysing field data, see Makris, 1992; Safilios-Rothschild, 1969).

In its 1999 Report, the UN Special Rapporteur on violence against women used information on honour crimes in Lebanon as a basis to define honour

> in terms of women's assigned sexual and familial roles as dictated by traditional family ideology. Thus, adultery, premarital relationships (which may or may not include sexual relations), rape and falling in love with an "inappropriate" person may constitute violation of family honour. (Cited in Welchman & Hossain, 2005, p. 5)

In the name of this honour, women in many societies are humiliated, beaten up, shut away, and even killed when they have (or have been thought to have), according to the group's code of honour, destroyed an individual's honour and thus usually also the family's or group's honour.

Kressel's (1981) analysis (mainly from newspaper sources) of cases of honour killings started a heated controversy (e.g., Joseph, 1981; Khazanov, 1981). Many of his critics thought that his generalisations focussed too much on such killings in the Arabic and Islamic world when, for instance, he wrote: "The special moral code seems ... to be intertwined with the combination of Arabism and Islam" (p. 143). Again, it must be clear that we have to differentiate between "crimes against women" occurring in so many patriarchal societies all over the world and the usually well planned "honour killings"—crimes committed to restore the individual's and thus also the family's and the group's honour. Kressel (1981, p. 151) may have been wrong when he wrote that in the case of honour killings murderers gain honour. In agreement with Ginath (1981, p. 153), it can be argued that "the concept of *'ird* is such that although it can be lost or detracted from through a female's misbehaviour it cannot be added to. By killing a woman an individual does not *gain* honour, but restores it" (but see Tellenbach, 2003, p. 5).

Reading the relevant literature often gives the impression that honour killings are ubiquitous in the Islamic and Arabic countries and that they are part and parcel of their hegemonic masculine ideology. However, the many facets and different connotations of masculinity in the Islamic world, as described by

Ouzgane (2006) and his co-authors, are usually neglected. Furthermore, such honour killings are neither typically Islamic nor typically Arabic; they seems to be a "relict" from more ancient socio-moral values and norms that are still to be found today in many societies (see Welchman & Hossain, 2005; Wehler-Schöck, 2007) in which the transformation to more democratic governance has not taken place (see, also, Ortner, 1978). Conditions in South Asian are quite revealing here. As Uma Chakravarti (2005) writes:

> Violation of marriage codes is regarded as an attack upon *izzat* ("honour" or "prestige"), a wide-ranging masculine concept underpinning patriarchal practices in India across all castes. Action to uphold *izzat* is always a male prerogative: women can only "incite" action; since violence is sanctioned to uphold *izzat* the use of the term masks its real meaning for those who experience the violence. As the case studies . . . demonstrate the concept of "honour" in punishing "defilers" is essentially a means of maintaining the material structure of "social" power and social dominance. "Honour" is one of the most valued ideals in the subcontinental patriarchies, whether Hindus, Sikh or Muslim—with most communities seeking to gain and maintain "honour." (p. 309)

Typical examples of honour killings that are related to neither the Arabic World nor specifically to Islam are the following cases in which social boundaries (here caste boundaries) were violated: On October 8, 2003, Shazia Khaskheli, a bank officer's daughter and her husband, Mohammad Hassan Solangi, originally from the lowly fisherman (*Machi*) caste, were tortured and murdered in the presence of thousands. It was one more case of honour killings (*karo kari* = masculine and feminine form of "the black one") in Sindh, Pakistan, where 132 women were murdered during the first 3 months of 1999 and 176 during the first 9 months of 2003 (along with dozens of men); similarly, 286 women were killed in the Punjab in 1999 (HRCPS, 2003). The murdered along with hundreds of forcibly divorced women had soiled the honour of their families and communities by flouting social norms (Shazia had married not only beyond her tribe but also a lower caste man). Among many communities in Pakistan and Azad Kashmir, marriage entails transfer of all rights over the woman from her natal to her conjugal family, and these include that of killing her, often on the slightest suspicion of marital infidelity. Such infidelity constitutes an attack on the husband's honour, and he must retaliate by killing the woman and her presumed lover (e.g., Ahmed & Zeenat, 1981). Her natal family has the right of revenge by killing a kinsman of the murderer or by demanding a young girl of his family as marital compensation. If the infidelity is "genuine," the murdered woman's family gains in status by forgiving the murderer. The Pakistani law of *qisās* and *diyat* (physical injury, manslaughter and murder) permits the victim's heirs to decide the fate of the murderer, thus accepting women being murdered and/or used as objects of compensation. The December 2003 court ruling in Multan (Pakistan) ordering a man's public blinding and imprisonment for having blinded his fiancé with acid—an increasingly frequent occurrence in both Pakistan and Bangladesh—also indicates such tacit approval of gender-related "custom." Official statistics presented before the Pakistani state in July 2004 put the total number of lives lost through such killings between 1998 and 2004 at 4,000 (see, for detailed reports and analyses, AI, 1999).

Shalinsky (1986, pp. 336–337) has described an event, narrated to her in Northern Afghanistan, in which among the Uzbeks, a brother (the "guardian," to use Steward's, 1994, pp. 144 terminology, see, also, Steward, 1991), as the protector of his sisters (his wards) and in order to protect his family honour, killed his younger sister and the husband of his elder sister because they had been engaged in an illicit sexual relationship.

The Gujarat genocide of 2002 (IIJG, 2003) showed how central sexual violence is to the ideology of the state-sponsored Hindutva project and its constructed notions of Hindu honour and men's virility. Even women Members of Parliament from extreme right-wing parties in India have abetted young Hindu men to attack Muslims and their places of worship, spurring them on in the name of "male honour" and "national pride."

Honour killings occur more often when the transgression involves the wife or daughter of a high-ranking member of the society who has had a relationship with a man of lower status. Here, both transgressors are often killed in order to compensate for the dishonour the wrongdoers have brought upon the high-ranking family. The ranking can comprise the status defined by either wealth and/or power, by hierarchically differentiated lineages or clans or by the caste system. However, when the relationship is reversed, and a high-ranking powerful man has seduced or even raped a women from the lower strata of a society, there will often be no revenge, due to fear of the, for example, mighty landlord.

Such honour killings are not restricted to countries like those named above (see, for an excellent recent overview and analysis, Welchman & Hossain, 2005). With the growing number of people originating from countries in which the code of honour predominantly structures the social fabric, the rate of honour killings has also become a major problem in Europe. The 2002 Report of the Council of Europe (CE, 2002) has estimated that there were 22 honour killings in the UK between 1997 and 2002 (see, for a comprehensive report and overview, CHANGE, 2004; also, Wilson, 2006). In recent times, such killings, mostly involving immigrants from eastern Turkey, have become quite frequent in Germany. Under the pressure of an often hostile and racist environment, members of such communities may even cling more to such honour-based values, norms and behaviours than their counterparts in their countries of origin. Thus, CHANGE (2004, quoting Akbar Ahmad, as cited in Alam, 2004) writes:

> Cultures are never static—although communities that are feeling confronted or insecure in some way often try to resurrect and rigidify historic conventions and traditions to restore their confidence. They may develop "hyper-honour" in which they hold onto traditional practices even more fiercely than in their countries of origin. (p. 7)

Most analyses dealing with the moral justifications brought forward by perpetrators of gruesome violent acts, be they in Nazi Germany, in the Vietnam War or in acts of terrorism in the name of religion, freedom fighting or patriotism, address the psychological mechanisms of moral disengagement. Bandura (1990, 1999) has explained that:

> One set of moral disengagement practices operates on the cognitive reconstruction of behavior itself. People do not ordinarily engage in harmful conduct until they have justified to themselves the morality of their actions. In this process of moral justification, detrimental conduct is made personally and socially acceptable by portraying it as serving socially worthy or moral purposes. People then can act on a moral imperative and preserve their view of themselves as a moral agent while inflicting harm on others. Regional variations in the social sanctioning and use of violent means are predictable from moral justifications rooted in a subcultural code of honor. (Bandura, 1999, p. 195)

This analysis might be correct when the perpetrators belong to a "subculture" and are aware of the contradiction between their moral point of view and those of the majority of the wider society. However, if honour killings are part of the moral and behavioural imperative of the majority of people in a country, it is questionable whether their perpetrators have to morally disengage themselves from their deeds. As the different laws in the various countries in which honour killings are common show, public opinion about honour, and specially about sexually defined male honour, is more or less in agreement with the law (see Rumpf, 2003, for Turkey; Tellenbach, 2003, for many countries in the Arabic World). In cases of adultery, for instance, jurisdiction is lopsided. With very few exceptions, the penalty is much less or even suspended when a women and her lover are caught red handed and killed by the husband, and often even when only the suspicion of a women's or girl's adultery was the reason for a husband or a male relative to kill them. To avoid penalty under the stricter new laws in Turkey, honour killings are now "avoided," specially in East Anatolia by forcing the victim to commit suicide by "offering disgraced daughters poison, a rope or a gun" (Bilefsky, 2006, p. 2).

Some Generalisations

From the multitude of examples given above, it seems that the connotations and meanings of honour, and thus also those of dishonour, differ to a certain extent from country to country and from one social group to the other while also changing over time. Even if many aspects can be understood as key symbols (Ortner, 1975) that structure the social fabric and regulate behaviour in the societies concerned, prominent differences can be found between the various populations and ethnic groups as pointed out by Pina-Cabral (1989) and, in the same vein, Cohen (1992) who remarked:

> Concerning the notion of a culture of honor, there is risk of overgeneralizing and reifying a convenient idea by transplanting concepts too casually from one society to another. Careful study of linguistic usage reveals that groups may distinguish between "honor," "reputation," and "respect," and between "dishonor" and "shame" .... To understand honor, it is important to distinguish region from region, urban from rural, elite from popular, male from female, and one era from the next ... clear honor culture

> may appear in the scholar's theoretical construction, its application in social practice is ridden with ambiguity. (pp. 599–600)

Herzfeld (1980) was also well aware of this fact, and with particular reference to the Mediterranean area, he remarked:

> The notion of honor and shame are not uniform and constant throughout the Mediterranean area. The use of the English gloss, "honor and shame," tends to fix them as if they were stable and unalterable, when in fact they cover a variety of terms, meanings and practices. (p. 349)

Today, it seems to be less the question whether we can view honour and dishonour as a key variable for specifically understanding the cultures around the Mediterranean Sea but rather what do we mean when we talk about honour and dishonour, and how, if at all, can we compare the meanings and social functioning as well as the related behavioural prescriptions in different cultures when we translate the multitude of their terms with the two Anglo-American terms honour or shame. Uni Wikan (1984, p. 649) has rightly remarked that "unless careful attention is paid," it is easy to forget that "the value of a person in her or his own eyes but also in the eyes of her or his society is a matter of greater complexity than has been acknowledged in the literature on honour and shame."

Bearing all these warnings in mind, we have to be very careful when translating or rendering the culture specific concepts in which we are interested here into our Western concepts of honour and dishonour. Nonetheless, we think that there is strong basis for inferring (see our sample) that the central meanings and rules of conduct *described* and the overlapping central connotations found allow comparisons and some general statements, while still being able to describe some of the differences as well.

"Honour," Black-Michaud (1975, p. 184) has pointed out, "is a blanket term which subsumes all the qualities required of a leader. Honour is required in the successful prosecution of feud, that is 'struggle,' in conditions of 'total scarcity,' over values and claims to scarce status, power and resources. " In most "honour groups," all these attributes are more or less equally important to constitute the individual's and/or the group's honour. However, in most societies and, as Black-Michaud (1975) has noted, specially in feuding societies:

> There are few hard and fast rules as to which actions are honourable and which are not. Individuals interpret the notion very much as they please and as circumstances permit, manipulating it in furtherance of their own political [and it can be added, economic] ends. (p. 179)

Thus becoming a "big man" in the New Guinea Highlands can be interpreted as symbolic capital (Bourdieu, 1984) that can be turned into "real" capital, as Meggitt (1977, pp. 8–9) explains for the Mae Enga:

> It would be a mistake to assume that success in the *Te* [a complex exchange system] is the ultimate value in Mae culture. The Mae do not compete for prestige for its own sake. Prestige achieved through prestations help a clan maintain its territorial

> boundaries by attracting military allies, as well as wives who will produce future warriors and workers. (p. 9)

It finally seems that it all boils down to the competition for highly valued materialistic goals intertwined with the goal of gaining leadership. All these, however, are often moulded and internalised as culture- or group-specific "non-materialistic goals" and schemas of virtue that can, however, in line with Bourdieu (1977, specially pp. 171–83), be understood as a form of "gift" (see Mauss, 1954, p. 35), and as exchangeable symbolic capital. The exchange of such gifts is then taken to an extreme in the often inter-generational continuations of the blood feuds between, for instance, the Marri and the Bugti clans of the Baluch in western Pakistan (Orywal, 1996, 2002, pp. 324–334), the Montenegrins (Boehm, 1984), the Albanians (Hasluck, 1967) or among the Swat Pashtuns in Pakistan (Lindholm, 1982, pp. 76–77).

Davis (1977) has noted:

> The essential characteristics of honour are first that it is a system of stratification: it describes the distribution of wealth in a social idiom, and prescribes appropriate behaviour for people at the various points in the hierarchy; it entails acceptance of super-ordination and subordination. (p. 98)

Or, quoting Schneider, "honour is an ideology of defence: it is associated with the defence of patrimony in states without government" (p. 100).

Back in 1982, Gilmore (pp. 191–192) had already analysed and identified the different honour concepts of the Mediterranean area. He found three separate vectors of competition: wealth, identified as an honour of position and related to class and power; status in the sense of a discrete moral category devolving from achievement of reputation among social peers; and masculinity defined narrowly as virility and strongly related to the feminine virtues of chastity and virginity. Gilmore (1982, p. 191–198) also pointed out that, in many rural areas, those who own land and are free from despised manual work are seen as "men of honour" because, as he noted, "honor and leisure are inseparable" and, quoting Gilsenan (1977, p. 169), "work and honor are opposed."

Alongside the importance of—and often an obsession with—women's chastity and virginity that influences the status, reputation and thus honourableness of men, other factors also play a role to a greater or lesser degree. Honour can be attributed to a man who belongs to a privileged class (nobility or "old family," see Peristiany, 1992), or it can be obtained through economic success, which is part and parcel of protecting and preserving his family's and household's well-being. We shall label these honour-related, often aggressive capacities and qualities, which are primarily directed towards the outer world, "centrifugal" (see, also, Petersen, 1985, pp. 57–59). Last but not least, honour can also be gained and augmented by being wise and living a virtuous and religious life dedicated to the well-being of the community as in the example of the wise *sopron* of the Cypriot highlands (Peristiany, 1992). This type of ascribed honour is also indicated by the use of the term *honra* in early Spanish culture and literature and in colonial Latin America (see Johnson &

Lipsett-Rivera, 1998, p. 3; Lipsett-Rivera, 1998, pp. 180–181, 196–197). It is also a quality prescribed to the *mukaddam*, the highly respected leader among the pastoral Bakkarwal in the Western Himalayas (Casimir & Rao, 1995; Rao, 1998, pp. 282–286).

Nonetheless, the few examples given so far suggest to us that in all societies or groups in which the institution of honour and dishonour plays a central role in the moral and socio-psychological framework determining the conduct of their members, we can isolate and describe some major factors by which (mainly men's) honour is said to be maintained and/or obtained:

1. Masculinity, good health and bravery, which, again, are related to the capacity to defend wealth and kin or a leadership position (see Black-Michaud, 1975, p. 176), and also usually correlate positively with greater wealth compared with the "average tribesmen" (Black-Michaud, 1975, p. 183).
2. Controlling women's conduct.
3. Defending a group's territory or individual wealth in land or income, ensuring the continuation of a household or a large clan or lineage, which usually again relates to the economy of the group. And/or:
4. Moral and/or religious virtues that can, in line with Bourdieu (1977), be interpreted as symbolic capital, which not infrequently also pays out directly (see Black-Michaud, 1975, p. 180; Casimir & Rao, 1995; Röttger-Rössler, 1989, 2004).
5. Finally, many of these societies usually reveal an interrelatedness between men's and women's honour (involving their families, often also their ancestors and their clan or lineage) and a strict observance of women's virginity and chastity. These factors together with strict marriage rules (which are again related to socio-economic variables, prestige and wealth) more often than not boil down to a preoccupation, often even an "obsession," with the concept of the "purity of blood." In neo-Darwinian theories, this would be understood as the struggle to enhance individual and/or group fitness.

Status, and thus the respect and honour related to a person, can rely on two different, though sometimes also combined, individual qualities and capacities. Because they are all related to the society's values and norms, the amount of respect and honour also relies on the culture-specific rank order of these qualities and capacities. In a society that assigns a high rank to "being a good human being"—according to, for example, given religious prescriptions—a poor but pious and empathetic person may have more prestige and be more honoured and praised than a rich one (and vice versa). However, it can be assumed that if both types (the pious and the rich one) are high ranking, respect and honour can be "blended" differently with different emotions emerging in group members. In the first case, it may be love; in the second, fear. Thus, in the first case, praising and honouring the person is "true," whereas, in the second case, it sometimes can be "false," because praise is often showered on the rich for opportunistic reasons (see Casimir & Rao, 1995).

Putting together the central aspects and connotations of the phenomena we have linked to the categories honour and dishonour on the basis of the described concepts in the different societies and their analysis, we may now give the following definition:

Honour and dishonour comprise (internalised) social and symbolic categories that are linked to each other. They are related to certain culture-specific values and idealised norms attributed to the bearer (e.g., virtues related to religion, ideologies of manliness and femininity and the expected appropriate conduct; and rank-related to economic success, "innate" status such as nobility etc.). An individual's conduct and/or behaviours are evaluated and acknowledged by or disapproved of by the members of his or her society or group. Fulfilling these norms augments the individual's honour; violating norms or trespassing against rules dishonours the individual and often the whole family, group or community.

As mentioned at the beginning, we cannot equate honour and dishonour with, or even call them, emotions, but it seems obvious that there is a strong link between some specific emotions and this socio-symbolic category and that this may emerge under certain conditions (see chapter 13, Casimir, "Honor and Dishonor" and the Quest for Emotional Equivalents, this volume).

Notes

[1] Kahl (1957, p. 8) related "individual prestige" to "respect" and to "honour" in his definition: "An individual has a high prestige when his neighbours, in general, have an attitude of respect towards him. Another word that is often used for this attitude is deference, or the granting of social honour." He also distinguishes between "prestige" and "esteem" when stating that "the behavior of a man in a given role leads to esteem in the eyes of the others, but the importance of the role itself is the source of his prestige" (p. 20). Hence, we may argue that self-esteem relates to the fulfilment of an individual's role expectation in his or her own eyes—influenced, of course, by the judgment of the members of his or her reference group.

[2] On the difference between the Mediterranean type of "code of honour" and the one of the Old Norse in which "little premium was placed on a woman's virginity or a child's legitimacy," see Miller (1993, pp. 118–119). For an analysis of the history of the "code of honour" in central Europe, see Dane (2005), Knott 2006, Montaigne (1580/1962, Chap. VII, p. 421), Pitt-Rivers (1991, p. 26), Schreiner and Schwerthoff (1995), and Zmora (1995). On the situation of the "lower classes" with "dishonourable professions" (prostitutes, thieves, executioners, scavengers, undertakers, and all itinerant populations such as "gypsies," tinkers, etc. who are said to have no honour), see Dane (2005), Danckert (1963), Girtler (1994), Jütte (1995), and Weinrich (1971, p. 342); see also Rao (1987, pp. 8–11, 2004, p. 284). For the meaning and connotations of "honour" in German villages during the 17th and 18th centuries, see Cohen (1992), Crocker and Major (1989), Frank (1995), Jütte (1995). For the changing significance of the code in France, specially related to the "duel culture," see Nye (1991, 1993), Reddy (1997, p. 63); and for the history of the duel in Germany, see Frevert (1991). A comprehensive analysis of the honour code and its transformations in colonial Latin America is provided by Johnson and Lipsett-Riviera (1998; see also Caulfield, Chambers, & Putnam, 2005; Potthast, 2003, pp. 91–110). For a discussion on the fate of the code of honour in central Europe, see Blok (1981, p. 436), Luhmann (1998, pp. 183–185), Steward (1994, p. 9), Weinrich (1971). The situation today in which individuals

are honoured for outstanding deeds in the arts or public services and the importance of paraphernalia, symbols, and signs has been described by Vogt 1997, Vogt & Zingerle (1994a,b); for the importance of symbols related to honour in colonial Latin America, see Burkholder (1998, pp. 30–34). Best (1982) has analysed the transformation of the "honour complex" after the French Revolution, during which, with growing nationalism and chauvinism, the focus shifted from nobility and especially the monarch to the fatherland and the country. Individual honour was transformed into "national honour." Wyatt-Brown (1982) has analysed the amalgamation of personal honour of the individual with the honour of a whole collective for the case of the Civil War in the "Old American South." There, individual honour and pride are still important, and the rate of "crimes of honour" is much higher compared with other parts of the United States (Cohen & Nisbett, 1994). For the projection of honour on even larger units under the influence of certain ideologies such as socialism in which the "honour of the working class" became central, see Best (1982).

References

Abu-Lughod, L. (1990). Shifting politics in Bedouin love poetry. In C. A. Lutz & L. Abu-Lughod (Eds.), *Language and the politics of emotion* (pp. 24–45). Cambridge, UK: Cambridge University Press.

Abu-Lughod, L. (1993). *Writing women's worlds. Bedouin stories*. Berkeley, CA: University of California Press.

Abu-Zaid, A. (1966). Honour and shame among the Bedouins of Egypt. In J. G. Peristiany (Ed.), *Honour and shame: The values of Mediterranean society* (pp. 245–259). Chicago, IL: University of Chicago Press.

Ahmed, A. S., & Zeenat A. (1981). "Mor" and "Tor": Binary and opposing meanings of Pakhtun womanhood. In T. S. Epstein & R. A. Watts (Eds.), *The endless day: Some case material on Asian rural women* (pp. 31–46). New York: Pergamon Press.

AI (1999). *Amnesty International*. AI Index: ASA 33/018/1999.

AIUSA (n.d.). *Pakistan: Violence against woman*. (http://amnestyusa.org/our-countries/Pakistan/index.do).

Alam, F. (2004, July 6). Take the honour out of killing: Domestic violence in minority communities must be tackled with understanding—and not used as an excuse for Islamophobia. *The Guardian*.

Al-Khayyat, S. (1990). *Honour and shame. Women in modern Iraq*. London: Saqi Books.

Althoff, G. (1995). Compositio: Wiederherstellung verletzter Ehre im Rahmen gütlicher Konfliktbereinigung [Reestablishing injured honour in material conflict resolutions]. In K. Schreiner & G. Schwerhoff (Eds.), *Verletzte Ehre: Ehrkonflikte in Gesellschaften des Mittelalters und der frühen Neuzeit* (pp. 63–76). Cologne, Germany: Böhlau Verlag.

Anderson, S. (2000). Ein mörderischer Kreis [A circle of murder]. *Geo*, *9*, 104–124.

Antoun, R. T. (1968). On the modesty of women in Arabic Muslim villages: A study in the accomodation of traditions. *American Anthropologist*, *70*, 671–697.

Asano-Tamanoi, M. (1987). Shame, family, and state in Catalonia and Japan. In D. D. Gilmore (Ed.), *Honor and shame and the unity of the Mediterranean*. Washington, DC: A special publication of the American Anthropological Association, No. 22, 104–120.

Bachnik, J. (1992). Kejime: Defining a shifting self in multiple organisational modes. In N. R. Rosenberg (Ed.), *Japanese sense of self* (pp. 152–172). Cambridge, UK: Cambridge University Press.

Bandura, A. (1990). Mechanisms of moral disengagement. In W. Reich (Ed.) *Origins of terrorism: Psychologies, ideologies, theologies, states of mind* (pp. 161–191). Cambridge, UK: Cambridge University Press.

Bandura, A. (1999). Moral disengagement in the perpetration of inhumanities. *Personality and Social Psychology Review* (Special Issue on Evil and Violence), *3*, 193–209.
Baroja, C. J. (1966). Honour and shame: A historical account of several conflicts. In J. P. Peristiany (Ed.), *Honor and shame: The values of Mediterranean society* (pp. 79–137). Chicago, IL: University of Chicago Press.
Bell, R. M. (1979). *Fate and honour, family and village: Demographic and cultural change in rural Italy since 1800*. Chicago, IL: University of Chicago Press.
Berrenberg, J. (2002). *Eine Sache der Ehre. Über die Grundlagen sozialer Prozesse bei den Pashtunen Pakistans und Afghanistans anhand der Heiratsformen* [A matter of honour: The foundations of social processes in the Pashtuns of Pakistan and Afghanistan as revealed in forms of marriage]. Berlin: Peter Lang.
Best, G. (1982). *Honour among men and nations: Transformations of an idea*. Toronto, Canada: University of Toronto Press.
Bilefsky, D. (2006, July 24). How to avoid honor killing in Turkey? Try honor suicide. *The New York Times* (reprinted in the *Süddeutsche Zeitung*).
Bin, K. (1995). *Zwischen Mensch und Mensch. Strukturen japanischer Subjektivität* [Person to person: Structures of Japanese subjectivity]. Darmstadt, Germany: Wissenschaftliche Buchgesellschaft.
Black-Michaud, J. (1975). *Cohesive forces. Feud in the Mediterranean and the Middle East*. Oxford, UK: Basil Blackwell.
Blok, A. (1981). Rams and billy-goats: A key to the Mediterranean code of honour. *Man, 16*, 427–440.
Boehm, C. (1983). *Montenegrin social organization and values: Political ethnography of a refuge area tribal adaptation*. New York: AMS Press.
Boehm, C. (1984). *Blood revenge: The anthropology of feuding in Montenegro and other tribal societies*. Lawrence, KS: University Press of Kansas.
Boesen, E. (2000). *Scham und Schönheit. Über Identität und Selbstvergewisserung bei den Fulbe Nordbenins* [Shame and beauty: Identity and being certain about the self among the Fulbe of North Benin]. *Beiträge zur Afrikaforschung*, Vol. 14. Münster, Germany: LIT Verlag.
Boissevain, J. (1979). Towards a social anthropology of the Mediterranean. *Current Anthropology, 20*(1), 81–93.
Bollig, M. (1992). *Die Krieger der gelben Gewehre: Intra- und interethnische Konfliktaustragung bei den Pokot Nordwestkenias* [The warriers of the yellow rifles: Intra-and interethnic conflict resolution among the Pokot of North-West Kenya]. Münster, Germany: Lit Verlag.
Boucher, J. D., & Brandt, M. E. (1981) Judgment of emotion: American and Malay antecedents. *Journal of Cross-Cultural Psychology, 12*(3), 272–283.
Bourdieu, P. (1966). The sentiment of honour in Kabyle society. In J. G. Peristiany (Ed.), *Honour and shame: The values of Mediterranean society* (pp. 193–241). Chicago, IL: University of Chicago Press.
Bourdieu, P. (1977). *Outline of a theory of practice*. Cambridge, UK: Cambridge University Press.
Bourdieu, P. (1984). *Distinction: A social critique of judgement of taste*. London: Routledge.
Boyer, R. (1998). Honor among plebeians: Mala sangre and social reputation. In L. L. Johnson & S. Lipsett-Riviera (Eds.), *The faces of honor: Sex, shame, and violence in colonial Latin America* (pp. 152–178). Albuquerque, NM: University of New Mexico Press.
Brandes, S. (1981). Like wounded stags: Male sexual ideology in an Andalusian town. In S. B. Ortner & H. Whitehead (Eds.) *Sexual meanings: The cultural construction of gender and sexuality* (pp. 216– 239). Cambridge, UK: Cambridge University Press.
Burckhardt, J. (1928). *The civilization of the renaissance in Italy*. London. (Original work published as *Die Cultur der Renaissance in Italien*, Leipzig, 1877–78)
Burkholder, M. A. (1998). Honor and honors in colonial Spanish America. In L .L. Johnson & S. Lipsett-Riviera (Eds.),*The faces of honor: Sex, shame, and violence in colonial Latin America* (pp. 18–44). Albuquerque, NM: University of New Mexico Press.

Callahan, C. A. (1981). Introduction to Ihara Saikaku's '*Tailes of Samurai Honor*'(pp. 1–23). Tokyo: Monumenta Nipponoca.

Campbell, J. K. (1964). *Honour, family and patronage: A study of institutions and moral values in a Greek mountain community*. Oxford, UK: Oxford University Press.

Casimir, M. J., & Rao, A. (1995). Prestige, possessions and progeny: Cultural goals and reproductive success among the Bakkarwal. *Human Nature, 6*(3), 241–272.

Caulfield, S. Chambers, S. C., & Putnam, L. (Eds.). (2005). *Honor, status, and law in modern Latin America*. London, Duke University Press.

CE (2002). *Council of Europe* (Crimes of Honour 2002, Section 3.46).

Chakravarti, U. (2005). From fathers to husbands: Of love, death and marriage in North India. In L.Welchman & S. Hossain (Eds.), *"Honour": Crimes, paradigms, and violence against women* (pp. 308–31). London: Zed Books.

CHANGE (2004). *Honour-Based Violence in the UK*. Document prepared for the Kvinnoforum Shehrezad Project 2004.

Cohen, D., & Nisbett, R. E. (1994). Self-protection and the culture of honor: Explaining southern violence. *Personality and Social Psychology Bulletin* (Special Issue: The Self and the Collective), *20*, 551–567.

Cohen, E. S. (1992). Honor and gender in the streets of early modern Rome. *Journal of Interdisciplinary History, 22*(4), 597–625.

Collins, E. F. & Bahar, E. (2000). *To know shame: Malu and its uses in Malay societies*. Crossroads *14*(1), 35–69.

Crocker, J., & Major, B. (1989). Social stigma and self-esteem: The self-protective properties of stigma. *Psychological Review, 96*(4), 608–630.

Cutileiro, J. (1971). *A Portuguese rural society*. Oxford, UK: Clarendon Press.

Danckert, W. (1963). *Unehrliche Leute* [Dishonourable people]. Bern, Switzerland: Francke.

Dane, G. (2005). *"Zeter und Mordio". Vergewaltigung in Literatur und Recht* [Rape in literature and law]. Göttingen, Germany: Wallstein Verlag.

Davis, J. (1977). *People of the Mediterranean: An essay in comparative social anthropology*. London: Routledge & Kegan Paul.

Delaney, C. (1987). Seeds of honor, fields of shame. In D. D. Gilmore (Ed.), *Honor and shame and the unity of the Mediterranean* (pp. 35–48). Washington, DC: A Special Publication of the American Anthropological Association, No. 22.

Denich, B. S. (1974). Sex and power in the Balkans. In M. Z. Rosaldo & L. Lamphere (Eds.), *Women, culture and society* (pp. 243–262). Stanford, CA: Stanford University Press.

De Vos, G. (1986). The relation of guilt toward parents to achievement and arranged marriage among the Japanese. In T. S. Lebra & W. P. Lebra (Eds.), *Japanese culture and behavior* (pp. 80–101). Honolulu, HI: University of Hawaii Press.

Di Bella, M.P. (1992). Name, blood, and miracles: The clams to renown in traditional Sicily. In J. G. Peristiany & J. Pitt-Rivers (Eds.), *Honor and grace in anthropology* (pp. 151–166). Cambridge, UK: Cambridge University Press.

Dresch, P. (1989). *Tribes, gouvernment, and history in Yemen*. Oxford, UK: Clarendon Press.

Epstein, A. L. (1984). *The experience of shame in Melanesia: An essay in the anthropology of affect*. Royal Anthropological Institute of Great Britain and Ireland, Occasional Paper No. 40.

Eves, R. (1998). *The magical body: Power, fame and meaning in a Melanesian society*. Amsterdam: Harwood Academic Publishers.

Farès, B. (1932). *L'honneur chez les arabes avant l'Islam* [Honour among Arabs before Islam]. Paris: Librairie d'Amérique et d'Orient.

Fessler, D. M. T. (1999). Toward an understanding of the universality of second order emotions. In A. L. Hinton (Ed.), *Biocultural approaches to the emotions* (pp. 75–116). New York: Cambridge University Press.

Findlay, E. J. (2005). Courtroom tales of sex and honor: Rapto and rape in late-nineteenth century Puerto Rico. In S. Caulfield, S. C. Chambers, & L. Putnam (Eds.), *Honor, status, and law in modern Latin America* (pp. 201–222). London: Duke University Press.

Fischer, A., Manstead, A. S., & Rodriguez Mosquera, P. M. (1999). The role of honour-related versus individualistic values in conceptualizing pride, shame and anger: Spanish and Dutch cultural prototypes. *Cognition and Emotion*, *13*, 149–79.

Fonseca, C. (2004). Honor and violence in a Brazilian slum: Gendered checks and balance in the politics of everyday life. In M. Anderson (Ed.), *Cultural shaping of violence. Victimization, escalation, response* (pp. 95–109). West Lafayette, Indiana: Purdue University Press.

Frank, M. (1995). Ehre und Gewalt im Dorf der frühen Neuzeit. Das Beispiel Heiden (Grafschaft Lippe) im 17. und 18. Jahrhundert [Village honour and violence in the early modern era]. In K. Schreiner & G. Schwerhoff (Eds.), *Verletzte Ehre. Ehrkonflikte in Gesellschaften des Mittelalters und der frühen Neuzeit* (pp. 191–214). Cologne, Germany: Böhlau Verlag.

Frevert, U. (1991). *Ehrenmänner: das Duell in der bürgerlichen Gesellschaft* [Men of honour: The duel in bourgeois society]. Munich, Germany: C. H. Beck.

Gilmore, D. D. (1982). Anthropology of the Mediterranean area. *Annual Review of Anthropology, 11*, 175–205.

Gilmore, D. D. (Ed.) (1987a). *Honor and shame and the unity of the Mediterranean.* Washington, DC: A Special Publication of the American Anthropological Association, No. 22.

Gilmore, D. D. (1987b). Introduction: The shame of dishonour. In D. D. Gilmore (Ed.), *Honor and shame and the unity of the Mediterranean* (pp. 2–21). Washington, DC: A Special Publication of the American Anthropological Association, No. 22.

Gilmore, D. D. (1987c). Honor, honesty, shame: Male status in contemporary Andalusia. In D. D. Gilmore (Ed.). *Honor and shame and the unity of the Mediterranean* (pp. 90–103). Washington, DC: A Special Publication of the American Anthropological Association, No. 22.

Gilsenan, M. (1977). Against patron-client relations. In E. Gellner & J. Waterbury (Eds.), *Patrons and clients in Mediterranean societies* (pp. 167–183). London: Duckworth.

Gilsenan, M. (1996). *Lords of the Lebanese Marches: Violence and narrative in an Arab society.* Berkeley, CA: University of California Press.

Ginath, J. (1981). Comment on: Kressel Gideon M. 1981.Soricide/Filiacide: Homicide for Family Honour. *Current Anthropology, 22*(2), 153.

Giordano, C. (2001). Mediterranean honour reconsidered: Anthropological fiction or actual action strategy? *Anthropological Journal on European Cultures, 10*, 39–58.

Girtler, R. (1994). "Ehre" bei Vaganten, Ganoven, Häftlingen, Dirnen und Schmugglern ["Honour" among vagrants, crooks, convicts, prostitutes and smugglers]. In L. Voght & A. Zingerle (Eds.), *Ehre: Archaische Momente in der Moderne* (pp. 212–229). Frankfurt am Main, Germany: Suhrkamp.

Glatzer, B. (1996a). *Sword and reason among Pashtuns: Notion of individual honour and social responsibility in Afghanistan.* Revised ms. version of a paper presented at the 14th European Conference on Modern South Asian Studies in Copenhagen, August 1996.

Glatzer, B. (1996b). Schwert und Verantwortung: Männlichkeitsideale in Afghanistan [Sword and reason: Masculine ideals in Afghanistan]. In E. Orywal, A. Rao, & M. Bollig (Eds.), *Krieg und Kampf: Die Gewalt in unseren Köpfen* (pp. 107–120). Wiesbaden, Germany: Franz Steiner Verlag.

Glatzer, B. (2000). Zum Pashtunwali als ethnisches Selbstportrait [The Pashtunwali as an ethnic self-portrait]. In G. Best und R. Kößler (Eds.), *Subjekt und Systeme: Soziologische und anthropologische Annäherungen* (pp. 93–102). Festschrift für Christian Sigrist zum 65. Geburtstag. Frankfurt am Main, Germany: IKO-Verlag.

Hallpike, C. R. (1977). *Bloodshed and vengeance in the Papuan mountains: The generation of conflict in Tauade society*. Oxford, UK: Clarendon Press.

Hart, D. M. (1976). *The Aith Waryaghar of the Moroccan Rift*. Tucson, AZ: University of Arizona Press.

Hasluck, M. (1967). The Albanian blood feud. In P. Bohanan (Ed.), *Law and warfare: Studies in the anthropology of conflict* (pp. 381–408). Garden City, NJ: The Natural History Press.
Heider, K. (1991). *Landscapes of emotion: Mapping three cultures of emotion in Indonesia.* Cambridge, UK: Cambridge University Press.
Herzfeld, M. (1980). Honour and shame: Problems in the comparative analysis of moral statements. *Man* (N.S.), *15*, 339–351.
Herzfeld, M. (1984). The horns of the Mediterraneanist dilemma. *American Ethnologist, 11*, 439–454.
Horden, P., & Purcell, N. (2002). *The corrupting sea: A study of Mediterranean history.* Oxford, UK: Blackwell.
Hu, C. H. (1944). The Chinese concept of "face". *American Anthropologist*(N.S), *46*(1), 45–64.
HRCPS (2003). *Human Rights Commission, Pakistan and Sind Graduates Association.* Retrieved.(www.amnestyusa.org/countries/Pakistan/reports/honour/overview.html).
IIJG (2003). *Threatened existence: A feminist analysis of the genocide in Gujarat: Redressing violence against women committed by state and non-state agencies.* Bombay: International Initiative for Justice in Gujarat.
Irons, W. (1975). *The Yomut Turkmen: A study of social organisation among a central Asian turcik-speaking population.* Ann Arbor: The University of Michigan Press.
Irons, W. (1979). Political stratification among pastoral nomads. In Pastoral production and Society (Ed.), *L'Équipe écologie et anthropologie des sociétés pastorals* (pp. 361–374). Cambridge: Cambridge University Press.
Janata, A., & Hassas, R. (1975). Gheiratman—der gute Paschtune: Exkurs über die Grundlagen des Paschtunwali [Gheiratman—the good Pashtun: Excurse over the basics of Paschtunwali]. *Afghanistan Journal, 2*(3), 83–97.
Jankowiak, W. R. (1993). *Sex, death, and in a Chinese city. An anthropological account.* New York: Columbia University Press.
Jeffery, P. (1979). *Frogs in a well: Indian women in purdah.* Delhi: Vikas.
Johnson, L. L., & Lipsett-Riviera, S. (1998). *The faces of honor: Sex,shame, and violence in colonial Latin America.* Albuquerque, NM: University of New Mexico Press.
Johnson-Hanks, J. (2006). *Uncertain honour: Modern motherhood in an African crisis.* Chicago, IL: University of Chicago Press.
Joseph, R. (1981). Comment on: Kressel Gideon M. 1981. Soricide/Filiacide: Homicide for Family Honour. *Current Anthropology, 22*(2), 153–154.
Jütte, R. (1995). Ehre und Ehrverlust im Spätmittelalter und Frühneuzeitlichen Judentum [Honour and loss of honour in Judaism in the middle ages and early modern era]. In K. Schreiner & G. Schwerhoff (Eds.), *Verletzte Ehre: Ehrkonflikte in Gesellschaften des Mittelalters und der frühen Neuzeit* (pp. 144–165). Cologne, Germany: Böhlau Verlag.
Kadare, I. (1980/2005). *Prilli I thyer* (*Der zerrissene April*) [Strife-torn April]. Tirana, Albania: Naim Frashëri; Frankfurt am Main, Germany: S. Fischer.
Kahl, J. A. (1957). *The American class structure.* New York: Holt, Rinehart and Winston.
Karystiani, I. (2001/2005). *Koustoumi sto choma* (*Schattenhochzeit*) [Shadow marriage]. Athens: Kastaniotis; Frankfurt am Main, Germany: Suhrkamp.
Khazanov, A. M. (1981). Comment on: Kressel Gideon M. 1981. Soricide/Filiacide: Homicide for Family Honour. *Current Anthropology, 22*(2), 154.
Kieffer, C.M. (1972). Über das Volk der Pashtunen und sein Pashtunwali [On the Pashtun people and their Pashtunwali]. *Mitteilungen des Instituts für Orientforschung, XVII*(4), 614–624.
Knott, S. (2006). *Bei der Ehre gepackt! Die Ehrenstrafe in Bayern seit 1700* [To appeal to someones honour! The honour penalty in Bavaria since 1700]. Regensburg: Pustet.
Kotalová, J. (1993). *Belonging to others: Cultural construction of womanhood among Muslims in a village in Bangladesh.* Uppsala: Acta Universitatis Upsaliensis.
Kressel G. M. (1981). Soricide/Filiacide: Homicide for family honour. *Current Anthropology, 22*(2), 141–158.

Kressel G. M. (1988). More on honour and shame. *Man, 23*, 167–9.
Kressel G. M. (1992). Shame and gender. *Anthropological Quarterly, 65*(1), 34–46.
Kumar, R. (2002). *Martyr's memorial incomplete: Caste gets in the way*. Retrieved December 13, 2002 from NDTV.com\martyr-hero-caste-NDTV_com.htm.
Kuwayama, T. (1992). The reference of other orientation. In N. R. Rosenberg (Ed.), *Japanese sense of self* (pp. 121–151). Cambridge, UK: Cambridge University Press.
Kuzkaya, H. (2001). *Ehre und Scham in der türkischen Sprache*: Prototypische Weltkonstruktion einer traditionell ländlichen Gesellschaft [Honour and shame in the Turkish language: Prototypical construction of the world in a traditional rural society]. Unpublished doctoral dissertation, University of Hamburg, Germany.
Laffin, J. (1975). *Rhetoric and reality: The Arab mind considered.* New York: Taplinger Publishing Company.
Landerdale, G. (1998). Honor among slaves. In L. L. Johnson & S. Lipsett-Rivera (Eds.), *The faces of honor: Sex, shame, and violence in colonial Latin America* (pp. 201–228). Albuquerque, NM: University of New Mexico Press.
Lazaridis, G. (1995). Sexuality and its cultural construction in rural Greece. *Journal of Gender Studies, 4*(3), 281–295.
Lebra, T. S. (1992). Self in Japanese culture. In N. R. Rosenberg (Ed.), *Japanese sense of self* (pp. 105–120). Cambridge, UK: Cambridge University Press.
Levy, R. (1984). Emotion, knowing, and culture. In R. A. Shweder & R. A. LeVine (Eds.), *Culture theory: Essays on mind, self, and emotions* (pp. 214–237). Cambridge, UK: Cambridge University Press.
Lindholm, C. (1982). *Generosity and jealousy: The Swat Pakhtun of Northern Pakistan.* New York: Columbia University Press.
Lipsett-Rivera, S. (1998). A slap in the face of honor: Social transgression and women in late-colonial Mexico. In L. L. Johnson & S. Lipsett-Rivera (Eds.), *The faces of honor: Sex, shame, and violence in colonial Latin America* (pp. 179–200). Albuquerque, NM: University of New Mexico Press.
Lison-Tolosana, C. (1966). *Belmonte de los Caballeros. A sociological study of a Spanish town.* Oxford, UK: Clarendon Press.
Luhmann, N. (1998). Gesellschaftsstruktur und Semantik [Social structure and semantics]. *Studien zur Wissenssoziologie der modernen Gesellschaft* (Vol. 3). Frankfurt am Main, Germany: Suhrkamp.
McLeod, W. H. (1989). *Way of a Sikh.* Oxford, UK: Nelson Tornes Ltd.
Mahdi, N. Q. (1986). Pukhtunwali: Ostracism and honor among the Pathan hill tribes. *Ethology and Sociobiology, 7*, 295–304.
Makris, J. (1992). Ethnography, history and collective representations: Studying vendetta in Crete. In J. de Pina-Cabral & J. Campbell (Eds.), *Europe observed* (pp. 56–72). London: Macmillan.
Mandelbaum, D. G. (1988). *Women's seclusion and men's honor: Sex roles in North India, Bangladesh, and Pakistan.* Tucson, AZ: University of Arizona Press.
Marcus, M. A. (1987). Horsemen are the fence of the land: Honor and history among the Ghiayata of Easterm Morocco. In D. D. Gilmore (Ed.), *Honor and shame and the unity of the Mediterranean* (pp. 49–60). Washington, DC: A Special Publication of the American Anthropological Association, No. 22.
Márquez, G. G. (1981/1995). *Crónica de una muerte annunciada* [Chronicle of a death foretold]. Barcelona: Plaza & Janes Editores, S.A.
Mauss, M. (1954). *The gift: Forms and functions of exchange in archaic societies.* London: Cohen & West.
Meggitt, M. (1977). *Blood is their argument: Warfare among the Mae Enga tribesmen of the New Guinea highlands.* Palo Alto, CA: Mayfield Publishing Company.
MEL (1980). *Meyers Enzyklopädisches Lexikon* [Meyers encyclopedia] (Vol 7, pp. 456–457). Mannheim, Germany: Bibliographisches Institut.

Miller W. I. (1993). *Humiliation and other essays on honor, social discomfort, and violence.* New York: Cornell University Press.
Modigliani, A. (1971). Embarrassment, facework, and eye contact. *Journal of Personality and Social Psychology, 17*(1), 15–24.
Montaigne, M. de (1580/1962). *Essais* [Essays] (Vol. I.) Paris: Éditions Garnier Frères. (original work published 1580).
Möwe, I. (1998). Der Wert der Ehre [The value of honour]. *Asiatische Studien/Études Asiatiques, LH, 2* 495–530.
Naveed-i-Rahat (1990). *Male outmigration and matri-weighted households: A case study of a Punjabi village in Pakistan.* Delhi: Hindustan Publ. Corp.
Nisbett, R. E., & Cohen, D. (1996) *Culture of honor: The psychology of violence in the South.* Boulder, Co: Westview Press.
Nye, R. A. (1991). Honor codes in modern France. *Ethnologia Europaea, 21*, 5–17.
Nye, R. A. (1993). *Masculinity and male codes of honor in modern France.* New York: Oxford University Press.
Ortner, S. B. (1975). On key symbols. *Americam Anthropologist, 75*(5), 1338–1346.
Ortner, S. B. (1978). The virgin and the state. *Feminist Studies, 4*(3), 19–35.
Ortner, S. B. (1981). Gender and sexuality in hierarchical societies: The case of Polynesia and some comparative implications. In S. B. Ortner & H. Whitehead (Eds.), *Sexual meanings: The cultural construction of gender and sexuality* (pp. 359–409). Cambridge, UK: Cambridge University Press.
Ortner, S. B., & Whitehead, H. (1981). Introduction: Accounting for sexual meaning. In S. B. Ortner & H. Whitehead (Eds.), *Sexual meanings: The cultural construction of gender and sexuality* (pp. 1–27). Cambridge, UK: Cambridge University Press.
Orywal, E. (1996). Die Ehre der Gewalt: Recht und Rache in Baluchistan [The honour of violence: Law and revenge in Baluchistan]. In E. Orywal, A. Rao, & M. Bollig (Eds.), *Krieg und Kampf: Die Gewalt in unseren Köpfen* (pp. 61–71). Berlin: Reimer Verlag.
Orywal, E. (2002). *Krieg oder Frieden: Eine vergleichende Untersuchung kulturspezifischer Ideale—der Bürgerkrieg in Baluchistan/Pakistan* [War or peace: A comparative study of culture-specific ideals—the civil war in Baluchistan/Pakistan]. *Kölner Ethnologische Mitteilungen* (Vol. 13). Berlin: D. Reimer Verlag.
Ouzgane, L. (Ed.). (2006). *Islamic masculinities.* London: Zed Books.
Paulhus, D. L., Duncan, J. H., & Yik, M. S. M. (2002). Patterns of shyness in East-Asian and European-heritage students. *Journal of Research in Personality, 36*, 442–462.
Pelras, C. (1996). *The Bugis.* Oxford, UK: Blackwell.
Peristiany, J. G. (1966). *Honour and shame: The values of Mediterranean society.* Chicago, IL: University of Chicago Press.
Peristiany, J. G. (1992). The *Sophron*—A secular saint? Wisdom and the wise in a Cypriot community. In J. G. Peristiany& J. Pitt-Rivers (Eds.), *Honor and grace in anthropology* (pp. 103–127). Cambridge, UK: Cambridge University Press.
Peristiany, J. G., & Pitt-Rivers, J. (1992). Introduction. In J. G. Peristiany & J. Pitt-Rivers (Eds.), *Honor and grace in anthropology* (pp. 1–17). Cambridge, UK: Cambridge University Press.
Peters, S. (1952) *The Bedouin Bait.* Unpublished B. Lit. Thesis. Oxford University.
Petersen, A. (1985). *Ehre und Scham: Das Verhältnis der Geschlechter in der Türkei* [Honour and shame: Gender relations in Turkey]. Berlin: Express Edition
Pina-Cabral, J. de (1986). *Sons of Adam, daughters of Eve: The peasant worldview of the Alto Minho.* Oxford, UK: Clarendon Press.
Pina-Cabral, J. de (1989). The Mediterranean as a category of regional comparison: A critical view. *Current Anthropology, 30*(3), 399–406.
Pitt-Rivers, J. (1966). Honour and social status. In J. G. Peristiany (Ed.), *Honour and shame: The values of Mediterranean society* (pp. 19–77). Chicago, IL: University of Chicago Press.

Pitt-Rivers, J. (1968). Honor. *Encyclopedia of the Social Sciences* (Vol. 6, pp. 503–511). New York: Macmillan.

Pitt-Rivers, J. (1977). *The fate of the Sechem, or the politics of sex: Essays in the anthropology of the Mediterranean.* Cambridge, UK: Cambridge University Press.

Pitt-Rivers, J. (1970/1992). La maladie de l'honneur. In M. Gautheron (Ed.), *L'honneur: image de soi ou don de soi un idéal équivoque.* Paris: Edition Autrement (Séries Morales 3). (On the Obsolescence of the Concept of Honor). *Archives européennes de sociologie, XI*(2), 20–36; 1970)

Pope, R. M. (1955). Honour. In J. Hastings (Ed.), *Encyclopedia of religion and ethics* (3rd ed., Vol. VI). Edinburgh: T.& T. Clark.

Potthast, B. (2003). *Von Müttern und Machos: Eine Geschichte der Frauen Lateinamerikas* [Mothers and machos: A history of Latin American women]. Wuppertal, Germany: Hammer Verlag.

Rao. A. (Ed.) (1987). *The others nomads: Peripatetic Minorities in cross-cultural perspective.* Cologne: Böhlau Verlag.

Rao, A. (1996). Die Konstruktion der Schande [The construction of shame]. In E. A. Orywal, A. Rao, & M. Bollig (Eds.), *Krieg und Kampf: Die Gewalt in unseren Köpfen* (pp. 91–105). Berlin: Reimer Verlag.

Rao, A. (1998). *Autonomy: Life cycle, gender and status among Himalayan pastoralists.* Oxford, UK: Berhahn Books.

Rao, A. (2004). Strangers and liminal beings: Some thoughts on peripatetics, insiders, and outsiders in Southwest Asia. In J. C. Berland & A. Rao (Eds.), *Customary Strangers. New Perspectives on peripatetic peoples in the Middle East Africa, and Asia.* (pp. 269–298). London: Praeger.

Reddy, W. M. (1997). *The invisible code: Honor and sentiment in postrevolutionary France 1814–1848.* Berkeley: University of California Press.

Robertson Bryson, F. (1935). *The point of honor in sixteenth-century Italy: An aspect of the life of a gentleman.* Chicago, IL: Private Edition, Distributed by the University of Chicago Libraries.

Rodriguez Mosquera, P. M., Mansteadt, A. S., & Fischer A. H. (2000). The role of honor-related values in the elicitation, experience, and communication of pride, shame, and anger: Spain and the Netherlands compared. *Personality and Social Psychology Bulletin, 26*(7), 833–844.

Röttger-Rössler, B. (1989). *Rang und Ansehen bei den Makassar von Gowa, Süd-Sulawesi/ Indonesien* [Rank and prestige in the Makassar of Gowa, South Sulawesi, Indonesia]. Berlin: Reimer.

Röttger-Rössler, B. (2004). *Die kulturelle Modellierung des Gefühls. Ein Beitrag zur Theorie und Methodik ethnologischer Emotionsforschung anhand indonesischer Fallstudien* [The cultural modelling of feeling: A theoretical and methodological contribution to ethnological emotion research based on Indonesian case studies]. Münster, Germany: LIT.

Rumpf, C. (2003). *Die Ehre im türkischen Strafrecht.* (www.tuerkei-recht.de).

Safilios-Rothschild, C. (1969). 'Honour' crimes in contemporary Greece. *British Journal of Sociology, 20*(2), 205–18.

Saikaku, I. (1688/1981). *Tales of Samurai Honor. Buke Giri Monogateri* (C. A. Callahan, Trans.). Monumenta Nipponica. Tokyo: Sophia University.

Schmidt, A. (1994). "Wo die Männer sind, gibt es Streit". Ehre und Ehrgefühl im ländlichen Sardinien ["Where the men are is dispute": Honour and the feeling of honour in rural Sardinia]. In L.Voght & A. Zingerle (Eds.), *Ehre: Archaische Momente in der Moderne* (pp. 193–211). Frankfurt am Main, Germany: Suhrkamp.

Schreiner, K., & Schwerhoff, G. (Eds.) (1995). *Verletzte Ehre: Ehrkonflikte in Gesellschaften des Mittelalters und der frühen Neuzeit* [Offended honour: Honour conflicts in societies of the middle ages and early modern era]. Cologne, Germany: Böhlau Verlag

Schwandner-Sievers, S. (1996). Zur Logik der Blutrache in Nordalbanien. Ehre, Symbolik und Gewaltlegitimation [The logic of blood feuds in northern Albania: Honour, symbolism, and the legitimation of violence]. *Sociologus, 46*, 109–29.

Schwandner-Sievers, S. (1999). Humiliation and reconciliation in Northern Albania: The logic of feuding in symbolic and diachronic perspective. In G. Elwert, S. Feuchtwang, & D. Neubert (Eds.), *The dynamics of collective violence: Processes of escalation and de-escalation in violent group conflicts*. Supplements to *Sociologus, 1*, 133–152.

Schwerthoff, G. (1995). *Blasphemare, dehonestare et maledicere Deum*. Über die Verletzung der göttlichen Ehre im Spätmittelalter [Offending God's honour in the late middle ages]. In K. Schreiner & G. Schwerhoff (Eds.), *Verletzte Ehre: Ehrkonflikte in Gesellschaften des Mittelalters und der frühen Neuzeit* (pp. 252–278). Cologne, Germany: Böhlau Verlag.

Shalinsky, A. C. (1986). Reason, desire, and sexuality: The meaning of gender in Northern Afghanistan. *Ethos, 14*(4), 323–343.

Shankman, P. (2006). Virginity and varacity: Regarding historical sources in the Mead-Freeman controversy. *Ethnohistory, 53*(3), 479–505.

Steul, W. (1981). *Paschtunwali: Ein Ehrenkodex und seine rechtliche Relevanz* (Pashtunwali: A code of honour and its legal relevance]. Wiesbaden: Steiner Verlag.

Steward, F. H. (1991). The woman: Her guardian, and her husband in the law of the Sinai Bedouin. *Arabica, 38*, 102–29.

Steward, F. H. (1994). *Honor*. Chicago, IL: University of Chicago Press.

Tapper, N. (1991). *Bartered brides: Politics, gender and marriage in an Afghan tribal society*. Cambridge, UK: Cambridge University Press.

Tellenbach, S. (2003). Ehrenmorde an Frauen in der arabischen Welt. Anmerkungen zu Jordanien und anderen Ländern [Honour killings of women in the Arab world: Comments on Jordan and other countries]. *Wuqûf—Beiträge zur Entwicklung von Staat und Gesellschaft in Nordafrika, 13*, 74–86. (cf. www.gair.de)

Twinam, A. (1999). *Public lives, private secrets: Gender, honor, sexuality, and illigitimacy in colonial Spanish America*. Stanford, CA: Stanford University Press.

Vieri, F. (1580). *Trattato della lode, dell'honore, della fama, et della gloria* [Treatise on praise, honour, reputation and fame]. Florence.

Vogt, L. (1997). *Zur Logik der Ehre in der Gegenwartsgesellschaft: Differenzierung, Macht, Integration* [The logic of honour in contemporary society: Differntiation, power, intergration]. Frankfurt am Main, Germany: Suhrkamp.

Vogt, L., & Zingerle, A. (Eds.). (1994a). *Ehre: Archaische Momente in der Moderne* [Honour: Archaic elements in modern times]. Frankfurt am Main, Germany: Suhrkamp.

Vogt, L., & Zingerle, A. (1994b). Zur Aktualität des Themas Ehre und zu seinem Stellenwert in der Theorie [The topicality of honour and its status in theory]. In L. Vogt & A. Zingerle (Eds.), *Ehre: Archaische Momente in der Moderne* (pp. 9–34). Frankfurt am Main, Germany: Suhrkamp.

Vreede-de Stuers, C. (1968). *Pardā: A study of Muslim women's life in Northern India*. Assen, NL: Van Gorcum & Co.

Waldman, A. (2004, October 6). Afghan woman dread shame if they vote. *International Herald Tribune*, p. 2.

Wehler-Schöck, A. (2007). *Ehrenmorde in Jordanien. Ursachen und mögliche Gegenstrategien.* [Honour killings in Jordan. Causes and possible counterstrategies.] Berlin: Peter Lang.

Weinrich, H. (1971). Mythologie der Ehre [Mythology of honour]. In M. Fuhrmann (Ed.), *Terror und Spiel* (pp. 341–356). Munich, Germany: Wilhelm Fink Verlag.

Welchman, L., & Hossain, S. (2005) *'Honour': Crimes, paradigms, and violence against women*. London: Zed Books.

Wikan, U. (1984). Shame and honour: A contestable pair. *Man, 19*, 635–652.

Wikan, U. (1988). An answer to Kressel. *Man, 23*, 170.

Wilson, A. (2006). *Dreams, questions, struggles: South Asian Women in Britain*. London: Pluto.

Wyatt-Brown, B. (1982). *Southern honor: Ethics and behavior in the Old South*. New York: Oxford University Press.

Yamanaka Y. (2001). The desert as a realm of unbound passion: Love and madness in the tale of Layla and Majnun. *Senri Ethnological Studies, 55*, 147–152.

Zíková, M. (2006). *Die kulturspezifische Formung des Gefühls. Japan im interkulturellen Vergleich* [The culture-specific formation of feeling: Japan in an intercultural comparison]. In M. J. Casimir (Ed.), *Kölner Ethnologische Beiträge, 19*.

Zmora, H. (1995). Adlige Ehre und Ritterliche Fehde: Franken im Spätmittelalter [Aristocratic honour and knightly feuds: Franconia in the late middle ages]. In K. Schreiner & G. Schwerhoff (Eds.), *Verletzte Ehre: Ehrkonflikte in Gesellschaften des Mittelalters und der frühen Neuzeit* (pp. 92–109). Cologne, Germany: Böhlau Verlag.

"Honor and Dishonor" and the Quest for Emotional Equivalents

Michael J. Casimir

Abstract In this chapter I describe how the moral and/or socioeconomic attributes of honour define an individual's hierarchical positioning within societies and groups and contribute to the individual's self-esteem. The relation between the honour of individuals and the honour of the whole group, class, or society is discussed. If emotions are defined as relatively short-term, bodily felt, expressed experiences, surely the "state" of being honourable or living in dishonour cannot be understood as an emotion. When, however, an individual is honoured or dishonoured because of his or her behaviour, the reactions of his or her group elicit emotions—bodily felt and expressed—that are understood and recognised as the social emotions of "pride" or "shame," respectively. I thus ask whether, and if so how, honour is related to the feeling and emotion of pride and dishonour to those of shame. This leads to a general discussion of shame and pride, their ontogenetic embodiment, and their culture-specific elicitations in later life. Some ideas about the phylogeny of pride and shame in the light of the evolution of social animals who are organised according to sex and age classes are discussed at the end of the chapter.

Introduction

One of the problems associated with emotion research concerns the question of whether and how specific internalised social and symbolic categories such as "nostalgia," *Gemuetlichkeit*, "being blue," or even "patriotism"—and, in our case, "honour" and "dishonour"-are related to the social or even the so—called basic emotions. The categories honour and dishonour are often found at the apex of a social system determining and structuring the relations and interactions of the majority of the members of a given society or group (see chapter 12, Casimir and Jung, "Honor and Dishonor": Connotations of a

M.J. Casimir (✉)
Department of Social and Cultural Anthropology, University of Cologne, Cologne, Germany
e-mail: michael.casimir@uni-koeln.de

B. Röttger-Rössler, H.J. Markowitsch (eds.), *Emotions as Bio-cultural Processes*, DOI 10.1007/978-0-387-09546-2_13,

Socio-symbolic Category in Cross-Cultural Perspective, this volume). Here the question arises of how such long-term enduring states as "being an honourable person or family" and "being dishonoured" relate to the emotions of the individuals concerned. I thus tackle the question of whether honour and dishonour can be understood as emotions, or if they cannot, which feelings and emotions might have a close relation to these categories.

It seems plausible that the self-conscious emotions of "pride" and "shame" are closely linked to honour and dishonour; thus, the ways in which they may be connected are described. The interrelated psychodynamic factors of self-worth, self-esteem, and well-being then lead us to discuss the embodiment, social embeddedness, and social functioning of pride and shame. I then try to answer the question of whether the "honour and dishonour complex" is a more or less pronounced but differentially elaborated universal phenomenon. Finally, employing a narrow category within a bio-cultural approach, I link some theoretical aspects of evolutionary psychology to the emergence of human social structure(s) and examine the functioning of the "honour and dishonour code" in the framework of human cultural history.

Honour, Dishonour, and the Emotions Pride and Shame

> By nature, men are alike. Through practice, they have become far apart. [Confucius, Lun Yü (Analects)]

In his famous account of a "honour and dishonour system," Bourdieu (1966, 1977) analysed *The Sentiment of Honour in Kabyle Society*. However, in his structuralist approach, he did not discuss the inherent problem of how "honour," as a complex socio-symbolic institution, is linked to a "sentiment" that is part of the "psycho-emotional complex." It is obvious that an institution itself cannot be an emotion—and even during the 1990s it was still being disputed whether or how emotions are linked to honour when Steward (1994, p. 33) doubted Pitt-Rivers' claim that "honor in one of its facets, is a sentiment" asserting that it "is certainly closely linked with a sentiment, just as it is closely linked with moral worth."

As a starting point for our analysis, it is important to note that the social structure of all societies and groups is related to norms and values, and that the related notion of "right and wrong" is employed by fellow group members to evaluate an individual's behaviour. Honour and dishonour are directly connected to the actor's reputation based on his or her deeds, achievements, and status as a member of a more or less hierarchically structured group or society. It can be assumed further that the evaluation of a person's behaviour by group members leads to transmission of positive or negative signals toward the actor, to more or less outspoken praise or blame or humiliation that, in turn, has a positive or negative effect on the actor's emotional condition. Honour and dishonour themselves cannot be emotions because, as already stated, they are understood as enduring socio-symbolic states ascribed to an individual by others and, of course, known by the individual himself or herself. However, under certain conditions and in specific situations related to these states, certain emotions may emerge. Of the sum total of possible emotions we can think of being strongly connected to honour and dishonour, pride and shame seem to be the most important ones.

In situations in which a person is honoured and praised, blamed, or blackened and dishonoured, he or she experiences the relatively short-term emotions[1] pride or shame that, of course, can be mixed or followed by the feelings of anger/rage often described as the shame-anger/rage spiral (e.g., Casimir & Schnegg, 2002; Mariauzouls, 1996; Retzinger 1987, Rodriguez Mosquera, Mansteadt, & Fischer, 2000; Scheff, 1987; Strathern, 1993; Tangney, 2002, pp. 103–104). Obviously, nobody can constantly feel either pride or shame (in contrast to guilt) over a long period of time. It can, however, be expected that a "honourable person" will feel pride repeatedly in situations in which someone shows respect, and a dishonoured person will feel shame repeatedly when members of his or her group show disrespect or contempt.

To analyse how pride and shame are related to the socially embedded status of being honourable or being dishonoured, we first have to clarify what we mean by "pride" or "being proud" and "shame" or "being ashamed."

Pride and Shame as "Self-Conscious Emotions"

> Pride is the self-regarding version of respect for others. (Casey, 1990, p. 46)

Nowadays, the emotions pride and shame are usually classified among the "higher," "social," or "ethically relevant" emotions. They "involve, as a central feature, some form of self-reflection and self-evaluation" (Tangney, 1999, p. 541)[2] and are related to ego's self-esteem and self-worth, as is discussed later in detail. They are not "innate" like some "basic" emotions that emerge very early in life, and it is only at about the age of 3 years that feelings of pride and shame emerge under the influence of the inculcated culture-specific values and norms and the related codes of conduct.

For our endeavour we may define

> pride and shame as emotions, different from, for example, "moods," as relatively short-term bodily felt and expressed experiences. These emotions emerge in the individual through his or her awareness of a positive or negative evaluation of and the related reaction to his or her conduct and behaviour by the members of his or her society or group. These evaluations are based on certain culture-specific norms and values.

When discussing the standards underlying such evaluations, especially those of an individual's moral conduct, within the European philosophical tradition, Shaver (1985, pp. 72–78) noted that whether:

> the precondition for a judgment of moral accountability is thought to be a causal connection or merely a social need to hold some person responsible for the occurrence of harm, what actually constitutes harm—and what should be done about it—must be determined by reference to some general standards. (p. 77)

However, he also noted the following.

> "Truth" about causality, responsibility, and culpability cannot be known apart from the intellectual tradition in which the questions have been asked. This conclusion has quite different implications for an analysis of blame, depending on whether the theory of blame to be constructed is a philosophical or a psychological theory. (p. 5)

Kant claimed that all feelings, even the most primitive, have a cognitive component, and that they all, even the most basic ones, relate to pleasure and displeasure and have a moral significance. In his *Tugendlehre*, he specifically pointed out that "moral feelings" have to be differentiated from all others. They are the ones directly responsive to the recognition of moral law, related to affective dispositions or predispositions (*Gemütslagen*), the love for one's neighbour, and self-respect (for a comprehensive discussion, see Cagle, 2005).

Viewing pride and shame in this way, we first have to understand the reference group's moral point of view that is so significant for the attributions of causality, responsibility, and culpability. The antecedents of an event that lead to blaming the actor by his or her reference group and eliciting the emotions mentioned are related to the standards of a culture's or group's specific moral code that, in turn, correspond with their more or less specific worldview. Lindholm's (2005, pp. 39–40) description of specific emotions as "felt-thoughts" is in accordance with the ideas of Kant; they all have in common that they are much stronger than the "basic" ones; they are influenced by cognitions, transformed and regulated by the social environment, and thus mainly concerned with interpersonal relations. As De Sousa (1987) noted:

> A vast array of very specific emotions concerned with personal relations may have their origins in certain kinds of social conventions and in the paradigm scenarios associated with participating in such conventions. Apart from trust and its cognates—the reluctance to cheat, the feeling of being betrayed, loyalty—we might also want to include diffidence, pride in the achievements of one's friends, and also "negative" emotions like envy, jealousy, shame, and resentment. All of these should figure in an expanded list of ethically relevant emotions. (p. 313)

We suspect that the emotions pride and shame are pan-human (see Fessler, 1999, 2002), meaning that we find them in all human cultures or groups. To make the terminological distinction between "basic emotions" and "pan-human emotions" clear, it can be said that all basic emotions are also pan-human ones, but that not all pan-human emotions are basic.

In some cultures, the sociopsychological importance of the emotions pride and shame, together with the connotation of honour and dishonour, are more developed and elaborated; they are hypercognisised, as Heelas (1986) and Levy (1973) explained. However, it is important to note that in societies in which the principles of honour and dishonour play an important role in structuring and maintaining the society's sociopolitical fabric, the situation in which an individual is praised or blamed (and thus proud or ashamed) is, to a large extent, culture-specific in line with the given culture's values and norms (see Steward, 1994).

Pride

As Fisher (1992) has shown in his outstanding *Study in the Values of Honour and Shame in Ancient Greece*, the relation between honour and dishonour and the emotions pride and shame were discussed widely and were the topic of many classic philosophical and literary texts. Aristotle, for instance, in his *Ethics*, said that honour is thought to be related to fortune on the one hand and to superiority on the other: "Men who are well-born are thought worthy of honour, and so are those who enjoy power or wealth: for they are in a superior position, and everything that has superiority in something good is held in greater honour." However, he also said, somewhat equivocally, "But in reality only the good man ought to be honoured, although he that has both virtue and fortune is esteemed still more worthy of honour" (as cited in Casey, 1990, p. 202). However, as honour and pride are closely connected or often lead to extreme self-centred pride (overweening pride) among the ruling class and the rich and powerful (Fisher, 1992, p. 497), hubris became a central theme because it was seen as a threat to social harmony and political stability. As Fisher (1992) wrote:

> At all times ... because hybristic behaviour can constitute a serious attack on the honour of the individual or group affected ... it is constantly seen as a major crime, endangering the cohesion of the community as well as the essential self-esteem and identity of the individual. (p. 493)

Therefore, Solon (ca. 640–559 AD), Athenian statesman and lawgiver, "carefully graduated 'honour' and privilege to the different classes of citizens, and also established rights to a basic 'honour' for all citizens and their dependants [*sic*], and imposed a very severe sanction for those who infringed it" (Fisher, 1992, p. 494). Here as well, as in many other societies and communities, honour was mainly if not exclusively understood as a male quality, as Fisher (1992) wrote:

> The law of *hybris* asserts for all male members of the community the value of the inviolable honour located in a person, or the body, of the individual or of his dependent women and children. The conception of the state's role in protecting the honour of the individual male citizen may be seen perhaps as another case of the "democratic" extension of aristocratic values of honour and shame to all male members of the community. (p. 495)

In the Judeo-Christian era then, especially in the Augustinian tradition, an individual's pride was always understood as dangerous and as hubris related to a fundamental and pervasive "original sin." Pride was understood as a primary human problem because it relates to self-centredness, self-love, and God replacement and as such is a form of idolatry. Finally, then, this original sin, symbolised in the biblical Fall, led to "original guilt." The sin of pride was understood as the false belief that humans can, by their own efforts, make themselves god-like (see Nussbaum, 2001, pp. 527–528; for a comprehensive discussion, see Cooper, 2003).

As a definition of pride for Western countries today, Mascolo and Bhatia (2002) suggested

> that the experience of *pride* involves appraisals that the self is responsible for producing a valued outcome, a phenomenal experience of the body as high, stronger, or on top of the world; and action tendencies to show one's worthy outcome to others. (p. 73)

To show one's worthy outcome to others is the sine qua non for climbing up in a group's ranking system. As Webster, Duvall, Gaines, and Smith (2003) showed, the public aspect of a performance, together with the superior standing suggested by any praise accomplishing this publicity, is important in the experience of pride. It is now up to the individual, and to his or her capacity of emotional management, to decide how strongly pride should be displayed. Again, how intensely the individual should display pride is determined and accepted or rejected by culture- or group-specific norms and values (e.g., Stipek, 1998). However, there is always a limit to the extent to which it should be shown. Between a "British understatement," which may be coupled with the indirect hope of receiving praise by "fishing for compliments," and the expected exaggerated behaviours displayed in the so-called "boasting speeches" practiced in some native American cultures (see chapter 12, Casimir and Jung, "Honor and Dishonor": Connotatious of a Socio-symbolic Category in Cross-Cultural Perspective, this volume), there is a wide range of what is expected and accepted in different groups and societies under specific circumstances.

To show that pride (in Western cultures) is adaptive, whereas exaggerated and especially unwarranted pride (arrogance) is maladaptive, Barkow (1997) noted:

> Feelings of pride would presumably have been adaptive when associated with self-esteem and with a sense of group membership (i.e., pride in the group). Overbearing pride, however, is by definition arrogance, the verbal and nonverbal communication to others that one is so much their superior that ordinary norms of social interaction do not apply. This assumption of superiority, even when not contested, rubs the noses of those around one in their relative inferiority and thereby risks alienating them; the arrogant may therefore find that they have forfeited their relationship of reciprocal altruism. Excessive pride, therefore, has been maladaptive. (p. 407)

A special type of arrogance, termed "cognitive arrogance" by Cook (1992), can be understood as a specific coping strategy related to the emotional management of the individual under stress. This cognitive arrogance, as he pointed out,

> is marked by a belief in the superiority of cognitive abilities, a self-directed orientation and a need for control.... The MCA [measure of cognitive arrogance] was found to be significantly correlated with measures of narcissism, need for social power and self-esteem [and] arrogance was found to be negatively correlated with traits of anxiety. (pp. iv–v).

Shame

All human societies dispose of conventions and "obligations that are based on cultural consensus" (Eckensberger, 1994, p. 72). They manifest in behavioural rules whose violation is punishable to varying degrees. A person who notices that he or she has disregarded such conventions, has trespassed against the related rules, and thinks or realises that he or she has been observed by others (see Leary & Meadows, 1991; Modigliani, 1971; Mulkens, de Joung, Dobbelaar, & Bögels, 1999) is likely to experience relatively similar emotions and bodily sensations in all cultures.

Miller (1993) gave one of the best descriptions of the relation between honour, shame, and envy[3] when he wrote:

> Honor is above all the keen sensitivity to the experience of humiliation and shame, a sensitivity manifested by the desire to be envied by others and the propensity to envy the success of others. To simplify greatly, honor is the disposition which makes one act to shame others who greatly have shamed oneself, to humiliate others who have humiliated oneself. The honorable person is one whose self-esteem and social standing is intimately dependent on the esteem or the envy he or she actually elicits in others. (p. 84).

Embodiment of Pride and Shame and the Related Pan-Human Behavioural Code

> The wishes and opinions of the members of the same community . . . either form the sole guides of our conduct, or greatly reinforce the social instincts; such opinions, however, have sometimes a tendency directly opposed to these instincts. The latter fact is well exemplified by the *Law of Honour*, which is the law of opinion of our equals, and not of all our countrymen. The breach of this law, even when the breach is known to be strictly accordant with true morality, has caused many a man more agony than a real crime. We recognise the same influence in the burning sense of shame which most of us have felt, even after the interval of years, when calling to mind some accidental breach of a trifling, though fixed rule of etiquette. (Darwin 1871/1896, p. 121)

Acting in the world and interacting and communicating with the social environment take place with and through the body. Information provided by an actor is perceived and embodied by the "other." Among this information, there are many signs and signals through which the "sender" displays his or her emotional state willingly but also indicates it subconsciously or unwillingly (e.g., when trying to suppress one's feelings, according to the rules of emotional management in the specific culture). Nancy Sheper-Hughes (1994, p. 235) wrote "People *everywhere*, men as well as women, and people of *all* classes, employ their bodies in expressing complicated, contradictory, and hostile sentiments." In our context, we are not dealing with the complex and far-reaching connotations of "embodiment" as presented by, for example, Merleau-Ponty or Csordas (for a comprehensive overview, see Wolputte, 2004); our focus is much less fastidious and therefore we employ only Goffman's (1963) definition.

> The information that an individual provides, whether he sends it or exudes it, may be *embodied or disembodied.* A frown, a spoken word, or a kick is a message that a sender conveys by means of his own *current* bodily activity, the transmission occurring only during the time that his body is present to sustain this activity. Disembodied messages, such as the ones we receive from letters and mailed gifts.... (p. 14)

When emotional states are communicated, we always have to distinguish between the basic biologically "innate" part and the learned culture- or group-specifically coded behavioural component(s). When more or less "pure basic emotions" are transmitted through facial expressions and/or body postures, the innate component is usually quite strong and behavioural signals relatively uniform, whereby the probability of a correct pan-human interpretation of the sender's emotional state is high—as Ekman and his coworkers have shown again and again when describing and analysing the functioning and meaning of facial expressions. Appadurai (1990), discussing "embodied experience," advised us to take both aspects, the "discursive public form" and the "biological substrate" into account when he wrote:

> Yet, it ... seems that emotions, unlike other phenomena, appear to have a basis in embodied experience, thus inclining us to see them as rooted in some elementary biophysical repertoire that is both limited and universal. To ignore this second aspect of emotion is to run the risk of deconstructing emotion altogether as a distinctive phenomenon to be investigated.... We need to deepen our understanding ... that emotions are discursive public forms whose special power does indeed draw on embodied experience, without implying any parsimoniously describable universal biological substrate. (pp. 92–93)

Goffman's (1967) notion of "face" ties up particularly with the emotions embarrassment, being humiliated, and "losing face." As a result, "face" has to be watched and controlled carefully if cohesion and harmony in a group are to be maintained (see Harris, 2006; see also Koutlaki, 2002). As Brown and Levinson (1992) explained:

> Face is something that is emotionally invested, and that can be lost, maintained, or enhanced, and must be constantly attended to in interaction. In general, people cooperate (and assume each other's cooperation) in maintaining face in interaction, such cooperation being based on the mutual vulnerability of face. That is, normally everyone's face depends on everyone else's face being maintained and since people can be expected to defend their faces if threatened, and in defending their own to threaten other's faces, it is generally in every participant's best interest to maintain each other's face, that is, to act in ways that assure the other participants that the agent is heedful of the assumptions concerning face. (p. 61)

Many of the facial expressions and gestures that can be subsumed under the notion of face are culture-specific and can be understood only when the specific cultural code is known. In the case of the emotions pride and shame, in which the specific social/cultural influence strongly determines whether and under which circumstances a corresponding behaviour should be displayed, it seems that if they are expressed they are mainly displayed in the same way in all cultures and societies.

Western expressions denote the bodily behaviours of someone who is ashamed, embarrassed, or shy as "with a lowered gaze" or "shying away." Persons describe their intention when facing a shameful situation by saying: "I wish the earth would swallow me up." These are common examples in English but can be found in many other languages as well—e.g., in one of the languages of West Queensland, Australia (Evans, 1992, p. 328) in which these behaviours also connote respect, shyness, and fear. The term "blushing," which denotes the physiological phenomenon of flushing in the social context (see Gerlach, Gruber, Roth, & Wilhelm, 2001; Gerlach, Wilhelm, & Roth, 2003), is used most frequently to describe a person who is ashamed, embarrassed, or shy or who suddenly sees himself or herself as the focus of attention (Shearn, 1992). Casimir and Schnegg (2002) have shown that the various metaphors and/or metonyms related to blushing in some 125 languages around the world indicate that this physiological reaction (although not always visible) occurs in all humans.

Both pride and the exaggerated feeling of pride (i.e., arrogance) are expressed by an erect body posture (Stepper, 1992; Stepper & Strack, 1993; Weisfeld, 1997, p. 437), the head slightly tilted backward (nose in the air),[4] and protrusion of the chest (puffing oneself up) as well as raising arms. In three experiments, Tracy and Robins (2004) showed that undergraduate students in the United States recognised such postures as pride expressions correctly and were able to differentiate them from bodily signs of happiness.

Nye (1993, p. 223) cited Ludovic Dugas who in the early 20th century advised French men on how to (re)gain manliness and courage and "the attitude and allure of decision and energy" so the individual would be able "to raise up his head, throw out his chest, look his interlocutor squarely in the eye and speak in a strong and sonorous voice" (for the Sarakatsani of Greece, see Campbell, 1964, pp. 304–305). Although little information is available on such pride expressions in non-Western cultures, Lindholm's (1982) description of the Swat Pashtuns of Pakistan was similar to that of Bourdieu (1966, p. 232) regarding the Kabyle men of Algeria and Nye's description, quoted above, when he wrote:

> Only pride, courage, and an implacable belief in one's own honour enables a man to continue the eternal and usually fruitless battles of ordinary life. A man without bravery and pride is soon destroyed, as there is no room for the weak-willed in Swat.... Pride is demonstrated in the ordinary bearing of the men, who carry themselves erect, walk with a swagger, and look one another straight in the eye. (p. 218)

It seems that the bodily expressions of the two self-reflexive emotions pride and shame are opposite to each other. Whilst feelings of shame are often shown by bending forward, tilting the head downward, and lowering gaze, those of pride are expressed by standing upright and raising the head combined with a gaze that openly screens the environment. In these behavioural patterns, we can recognise the connection to the basic emotion fear—in the case of shame understood as "social fear" and in the case of the more aggressive emotion pride the link is to the basic emotion anger or rage. The tendencies for flight or attack are also embodied in both.

Self-Evaluation, Self-Esteem, and the Reference Group

Pride and shame as emotional episodes relate directly to and influence the ego's self-esteem and self-worth. In situations in which an actor is proud, self-esteem is influenced positively and raised; in situations in which ego feels shame, it is lowered. The individual's self-esteem and self-worth, as Tyler and Blader (2002) showed, are influenced not only by the ego's judging the characteristics and the status of his or her reference group (autonomous status evaluation) but also by the ego's assessment of the status in the group (comparative status evaluation). The latter approach to status implies competition, in which, in terms of a zero-sum game, if there is a winner there also must be a loser. If competition for status and rank in the group are based on comparative status evaluation, hostile feelings such as jealousy and aggression between members of the group are the unavoidable consequences—as Lindholm (1982) showed for the Swat Pashtuns in Pakistan, for whom aggression and jealousy are the leitmotiv in the status-enhancing rivalries between the male members of society.

Conflicting situations, however, as Simmel (1955/1971) explained, also have group-binding qualities and provide individuals or "subgroups" with new opportunities.

> Hostility not only prevents boundaries within the group from gradually disappearing, so that these hostilities are often consciously cultivated to guarantee existing conditions. Beyond this, they also are of direct sociological fertility: often they provide classes and individuals with reciprocal positions which they would not find, or would not find in the same way, if the causes of hostility were not accompanied by the *feeling* and the expression of hostility—even if the same objective causes of hostility were in operation. (p. 75)

In many Western societies, however, such comparative status evaluations seem to play a secondary role in self-evaluation and maintaining and enhancing self-worth. As indicated by Tyler and Blader's (2002) results, within groups, "people are influenced primarily by autonomous assessments of status based on their internal standards, which develop from the status associated with prototypical characteristics linked to inclusion in a group" (p. 813).

People with high self-esteem also "showed superior performance, were quite effective at setting appropriate goals and living up to them, thereby maximising their outcomes." It has also been shown that high self-esteem "carries the risk of making commitments that exceed capabilities, thus leading to failure" (Baumeister, Heatherton, & Tice, 1993, pp. 141, 154; see also NASA-National Association for Self-Esteem, 2005). The higher individuals climb in a hierarchy, the more they have to guard and defend their position; but if they are successful, the stress related to constantly defending a position is counterbalanced by the positive effects of high self-value and strong self-esteem. As is discussed below, the relation between the various aspects of the self, self-evaluation, self-esteem, and self-worth is still a matter of controversy. Whereas many experiments have shown that self-evaluation determines self-esteem, others now point to the fact that self-esteem strongly influences self-evaluation (Brown, Dutton, & Cook, 2001). Comparing the relevant literature, and weighing the findings and arguments for and against each other, I can only conclude that all of these factors are more or less interdependent; they require and influence each other.

Pride, Shame, and the Pain of Being Excluded

> How selfish soever man may be supposed, there are evidently some principles in his nature, which interests him in the fortune of others, and render their happiness necessary to him, though he derives nothing from it except the pleasure of seeing it. (Adam Smith, 1759, p. 3)

As early as the 1940s and 1950s, Maslow (e.g., 1943, 1954) and later Alderfer (1972), in an endeavour to rank human needs hierarchically, discussed the importance to humans of belonging to a group, experiencing the social acceptance of conspecifics, and experiencing love and empathy and how these factors are related to the ego's self-esteem. Attachment among humans (and many other higher social vertebrates) to other members of the species and belonging to a social group, as well as loss and deprivation of this bonding and social exclusion, leading to loneliness, insecurity, anxiety, fear and depression (Allen & Badcock, 2003; Baumeister & Tice, 1990; Buss, 1990; Greenberg et al., 1992; Leary, 1990; Leary & Downs, 1995) are among the strongest feelings governing social behavioural patterns. Many have supported the view that a strong or weak early attachment, particularly to the primary caretaker(s), influences social capacities and the development of "normal" self-esteem in later life.[5]

Behaviours that tighten the socio-emotional bonds between the group members and secure the individual's membership in the group not only lead to positive emotions and mood states ("characterised by their persistence and by their loose connection to particular events"—Kahneman, Diener, & Schwarz, 1999a, p. x) but also guarantee the group's coalition and stability (Collins, 1984).

The neurophysiological correlates of fear of social loss and the pain of being socially excluded have recently been analysed by Eisenberg, Lieberman, Kipling, & Williams (2003) using neuroimaging methods. When discussing these important findings, Panksepp (2003) stated:

> The psychological pain of social loss is reflected in the neural circuitry of the human brain ... functional magnetic resonance imaging (fMRI) ... [showed] that certain human brain areas that "light up" during physical pain are also activated during emotional pain induced by social exclusion.... These results are consistent with the idea that aversive feelings of social exclusion and physical pain arise in part, from the same brain region. (pp. 237–239)

Figure 1 shows an idealised connection between an event (the individual's behaviour), the appraisal of the event by his or her reference group members, the resulting emotional episode that emerges in the actor, and the possible effects of being still included in the group or being excluded from group membership.

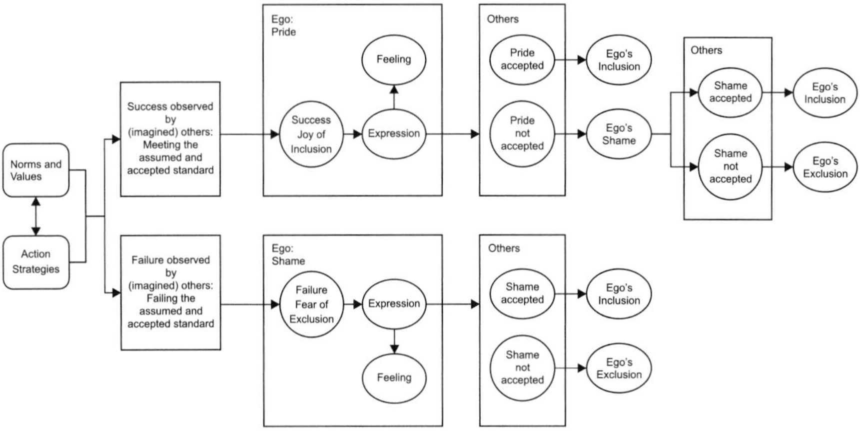

Fig. 1 Idealised connection between an event/action, the appraisal and reaction of the actor's group members, the possible resulting emotions of the actor, and the possible consequences. (*see* the text for futher information)

If the ego's conduct and behaviour meet the normative standards and are approved by the group members, his or her membership in the group is consolidated, he or she experiences feelings of joy, and expressions and feelings of pride are legitimate. Signs of pride, especially if they are institutionalised, are indeed expected and welcomed by the other members of the group. In general, however, opposite to joy, communicating exaggerated pride, triumph, and self-satisfaction are deemphasised (see Zammuner, 1996) and semanticised as conceit or arrogance. Group members then blame and put the actor to shame, as in the case of the Greek Sarakatsani among whom men are expected to show their pride and modesty is understood as a sign of weakness, but "care must be taken not to make a boast which can be proved to be empty. The boaster whose bluff has been called is despised" (Campbell, 1964, p. 284).

Signs of shame (lowered gaze, turning away, blushing) can be accepted by the group as signs of remorse, and the prior haughtiness is forgiven. If under certain conditions and in specific extreme cases remorseful behaviour is not signalled, the person may be punished and excluded from the group. In the second case, if actors notice that group members have observed that they had not attained the goal, they experience shame and express it as described in the first episode. Again, as in the first case, group members may decide that the displayed negative shame emotion is enough "punishment" for the actor; or they may decide to blame and thus shame the actor even more, and, eventually—if the deed seriously violated group norms and values—even expel him or her from the group. The emotional management of such and other emotions or moods[6] not only concerns the individual but also the other group members who, though they may well feel empathy, nonetheless have to decide whether ego's misbehaviour should be forgiven or punished. As Levenson (2003, p. 363) noted: "We become emotional in the presence of others who are emotional, sometimes as part of group processes of alerting and calming and sometimes in the more intimate realms of interpersonal empathy . . . we are feeling things in response to their feelings."[7]

This mechanism guarantees that a line is drawn between those violators who have trespassed against the group's code of conduct severely (endangering the group's coalition and therefore having to be excluded) from those who have violated the norms only marginally and who show the pains of knowing they have misbehaved. In the latter case, empathetic reactions of group members lead to forgiveness and to the consolation of the actor, who then loses the fear of being excluded. Thus, empathy and forgiving serve as mechanisms that strengthen the bond between individuals, also by forming microcoalitions among group members that then also balance and smooth out extreme forms of domination by high-ranking members (for an evolutionary approach to empathy, see Preston & de Waal, 2002; for experimental analysis of emotional contagion and the possibility of empathy in animals, see Langford et al., 2006; Miller, 2006). Such feelings of empathy are related to one's own experiences of physical or emotional pain, as has been shown by Singer et al. (2004a): Empathy pain experienced by a person who observes somebody else's physical or psychological pain activates those regions of the brain that would be active when a person himself or herself were to be in pain. If empathetic pain is experienced, however, the components of the "pain area" indicating the sensory qualities of pain are not active. Emotional empathy is also related to fairness. Trespassing against the group's behavioural norms and failing in an enterprise may elicit *Schadenfreude* in the observers. As Singer et al. (2004b) showed using fMRT methods, observing the punishment of an unfair "player" activates the nucleus accumbens in the male brain region that normally is active when a person experiences a reward. Brain activity in this "reward region" is less pronounced in women; here also, the regions indicating empathy show some activity.

Because of the importance of cognitive and emotional conformity among group members (Darell, 2008), an individual's competitive behaviour, his or her success or failure, have for the individual (e.g., Hochschild, 1979) decisive impact on the cohesion and persistence of the whole group, with the consequence that the group then also rises or falls in relation to other competing groups (see Neckel, 1991, pp. 59–80, 193–234). Thus, emotional management plays a major role. The individual always has to decide how to balance the emotional impulse to compete with other group members against the possibility of endangering the group's cohesion by his or her actions—something that may lead to the deterioration and decline of the group's standing against other rival groups.

Self-Esteem, Pride, Shame, and Well-Being

> Lord, you who alone dominate over others without pride, for you are the sole true God.
> (St. Augustine, *The Pride of Life* (Book 10, Chap. 36 [59], p. 267)

Contradicting Augustine, Cooper (2003) has argued that we have a need for "self-acceptance" and "self-love," surely related to self-esteem and self-worth because without these sentiments, we cannot experience compassion and are unable to love others. As he wrote:

> Many of us have also experienced problems with low self esteem or deep-rooted feelings of inadequacy. These problems don't quite match the Augustinian pride portrait. Out of negative feelings about ourselves, we may have consulted the helping professions, which are often highly influenced by humanistic psychotherapies. We've been told that far from having a problem with pride, we are struggling with self-hatred and a need for self-acceptance. Surely the Augustinian emphasis on pride [as the most basic problem] is wrong. Our major problem is low self-esteem or even self-contempt. Destructive, hurtful behavior towards others stem from this negative view of ourselves. (pp.. 7–8)

Robins, Trzesniewski, Tracy, Gossling, and Potter (2002) argued that the universal human urge for high self-esteem has a "baseline" level and is, in principle, independent from gender, socioeconomic status, ethnicity, and nationality. According to their cross-cultural analysis, self-esteem is generally high during childhood, drops during adolescence, rises again gradually throughout adulthood, and declines sharply in old age. Relative to this generalised and averaged ontogenetic fate of self-esteem, the individual's self-esteem and "felt" self-value, at a given moment of time, is related to the personally appraised relation to the assumed standing of the other members of his or her hierarchically organised reference group.

Barkow's (1980, p. 325) definition of self-esteem as "a goal-state maintained as long as the self can evaluate itself as higher than at least some others" is useful. Referring to the findings of various authors, he summarised:

1. Self-esteem is a prerequisite for mental health, in general, and for appropriate esteem of others in particular.
2. A low level of self-esteem leads to mental pathology, in general, and to negative attitudes (hostility, distrust, contempt) towards others in particular.
3. Low levels of unconscious self-esteem lead to the use of one or more distortions of information concerning the self that maintain the minimum of conscious self-esteem required for nonpsychotic functioning in most interpersonal environments. (p. 325)

He suggested three additional (and more problematic) assumptions:

4. Socialization experiences interact with the individual's genetic given to establish the minimum level of self-esteem necessary for the individual to function without pathology.
5. The major strategy for the maintenance of self-esteem is the pursuit of prestige.
6. Socialization determines the major strategies the individual will utilize in seeking prestige. (p. 325)

He has also stated that to climb up in the ranking system, "striving for the respect and approval of those whom one is associated with is the simplest and perhaps the most powerful of all prestige strategies" (p. 327) and that attaining prestige then strengthens or even enhances the ego's self-esteem and self-worth. If in a hierarchical social system the individual tries to evaluate himself or herself as higher than at least some others, and if high self-esteem and self-value are related to rank, striving for dominance is the sine qua non. The individual's aspiration to obtain rewarding high self-esteem can be fulfilled only when a rank-related highly valued goal of the reference group is attained, although under the constraints of certain norms and behavioural rules.

Steffenhagen and Burns (1987, p. 28) drew on Adler's early work and understood "self-esteem" as "the totality of the individual's constructs of the self: self concept (mental), self-image (physical), and the social concept (cultural). These perceptions exist only in the immediate milieu of a broader culture."

The "quality of the self" is related to the individual's self-esteem and self-worth; and these, in turn, are related to certain emotions that occur during the interaction with members of a reference group. However, high or low self-esteem and "feelings" of self-worth are not emotions in the strict sense of the term; they are more similar to "moods" that are dependent on and constructed and reconstructed through interactions with members of the relevant social group. During the course of such interactions, short emotional episodes of pride and shame can emerge in the actor. As described above, their emergence may depend on the individual's knowledge or presumption that an aspired goal has been attained successfully or whether he or she has failed, but it mainly depends on the approving or disapproving reactions of group members. Thus, the reaction of the ego's group members in the form of either praising or blaming is decisive for whether the ego's self-esteem and self-value grows or diminishes. Negotiating and evaluating the ego's behaviour takes place among the relevant persons of the group in a more or less ritualised process. In that context, Appadurai (1990) wrote:

> In particular I shall argue that praise is *not* a matter of *direct* communication between the "inner" states of the relevant persons, but involves the public negotiation of certain gestures and responses. When such negotiation is successful, it creates a "*community of sentiment*," involving the emotional participation of praiser, the one who is praised, and the audience of the act of praise. Praise is therefore that set of regulated, improvisatory practices that is one route to the creation of communities of sentiment.... (pp. 93–94)

Rational Actor Theory, Well-Being, and Worrying

> It is fair to say that there are two predominant methods of defining rationality of behaviour in mainline economic theory. One is to see rationality as internal *consistency* of choice, and the other is to identify rationality with maximization of *self-interest*. (Amartya Sen, 1990, p. 12)

The predominant rational actor theory assumes that individual behaviour is strategically directed at optimising well-being, and it has been presumed that well-being can be understood as a sociopsychological "master value" (Wolf,

2003). From a proximate perspective, the motivation for action generally lies in the wish to enhance physical and/or psychological well-being. Many bodily felt morphological/physiological and psychological basic needs—those of curbing hunger, fulfilling sexual desires, and so forth—although fundamentally related to innate structures, are transformed and refined by cultural values and norms. The enhancement of an individual's proximate desires or her or his well-being is, of course, an optimising process that consists in maximising the desired effects under given environmental and/or sociocultural constraints. The results of such actions are either in accordance with the values and norms of a society/ social group, or they are in conflict with them. As already argued, an essential component of well-being is feeling secure, and an important part of that feeling relates to strong positive ties to other members of the society, particularly to a group to which one belongs.

Reducing uncertainty "that source and archetype of all fear" (Bauman, 1993, p. 7) has always been the driving force behind the desire to learn about the future, and strategies are developed to reduce concern and anxiety. Rosen (1978, p. 155) asked why this desire "is one of the most ancient human cravings," and suggested that it is

> so that we shall be able to decide what to do *now*. Perhaps the preponderance of conscious human behavior is the execution of *plans*; and the making of plans always requires some information pertaining to the future. For this reason, forecasting has always been a central human activity. (p. 155; see also Sjöberg, 1998, p. 91)

The gathering and processing of information itself, independent of direct material benefits or utility, often seems to have an emotional, pleasure or pain, component, as Loewenstein (2006) stated when discussing the findings of Bern et al. (2006). Such emotions emerging together with an information can be related to the utility derived from anticipating future outcomes, and "utility derived from self-image—that is, from information about one's value as a person—can have diverse ramifications, including encouraging prosocial behavior" (Loewenstein, 2006, p. 705). Information coupled with negative emotions can lead to feelings of uncertainty and worrying, understood in line with Lindholm (2005, pp. 39–40) as "felt-thoughts." Worrying is always about the future and is a bodily experience insofar as, in the Heideggerian sense of "being in the world," the world can be experienced only through the embodied self (see Csordas, 1994; Lyon, 1999; Ramachandran & Blakeslee, 1999, p. 247). Reducing uncertainty also means reducing the pain of sorrow and worrying we experience when unfavourable circumstances are expected and the situation is thought to be deteriorating. Worrying is an unpleasant psychological experience because it involves "preoccupation with thoughts about uncertain and unpleasant events" as a response to a "perceived level of risk [that] calls for a more intellectual judgement and worry [that] tends to refer to emotional reactions" (Sjöberg, 1998, p. 85). Worry may be related to bodily pain and/or psychological stress, pain in the near future, or punishment in the long term—even in the "next life," or "afterlife." The fear that basic physical, mental/

psychological, or spiritual needs or wants may not be fulfilled if some action is not taken are the prime movers behind actions that involve taking risk (see also Casimir, 2007, p. 29–31).

The emergence of worry, anxiety, and fear related to probable risk and the danger of "loss" must be understood in relation to not only the different hierarchical structures of culture-specific values but also individual circumstances (Rohrman, 1994). As Yates and Stone (1992) observed, in risk-taking situations and in risk evaluation we tend to synthesise the various risks involved into an "overall risk appraisal"—not only on the basis of our current situation, past experiences, and specific emotions but also according to our present culture-specific values, norms, needs, and wants.

All of these factors then dictate the risk-taker's choice of an appropriate coping strategy and behaviour vis-à-vis risk. However, any behaviour appraised by the members of his or her society or group also bears the risk of being appraised negatively by these members. The violator of given social norms or the trespasser against conventions is then blamed and put to shame, thereby potentially losing prestige and social bonding. This may lead to low self-esteem and may diminish well-being (Fig. 2).

However, fulfilling social norms and attaining the society- or group-specific high-ranking goals (Strauss, 1992a, 1992b) may result in being praised and honoured, thus eliciting the emotion of pride in the actor. His or her self-esteem

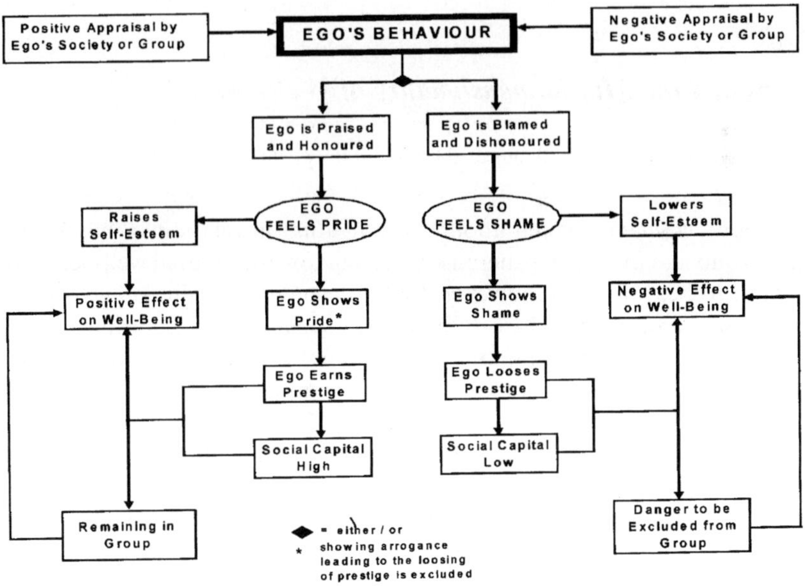

Fig. 2 Relation between an individual's behaviour under the threat of being excluded from the group of reference, the actor's group's appraisal and reactions, the related feelings, emerge in the actor that and the effect on the actor's self-esteem and well-being

grows, buffers anxiety, and promotes, protects, and restores feelings of self-worth (Brown et al., 2001; Greenberg et al., 1992; see also Baumeister, Campbell, Krueger, & Vohs, 2005) and thus has a positive influence on the ego's well-being. Here, however, as so often, we are confronted with an interdependent phenomenon. As Sapolsky (2004, p. 409) summarised in his findings: "In theory, health can both influence and be influenced by SES [socioeconomic status]. Although there is evidence for poor health causing a downward spiral, prospective studies have amply documented that SES can precede health status and be highly predictive of it."

The prestige gained, understood as symbolic or cultural capital (Bourdieu, 1977), can then be used; and with high probability it helps the actor approach and eventually reach new social-cum-economic goals.

In sum, it can be said that the feelings of pride and shame resulting from the society's or group's positive or negative evaluation of an ego's behaviour are a strong mechanism for either fastening or loosening social ties. The resulting high or low self-esteem then amplifies or lowers the ego's well-being in the future and, as already discussed, may raise the prestige of the whole group and thus of each of its members. It has, however, been noted that the self-esteem system, understood as a "sociometer," seems to function lopsidedly; there is some good evidence that it responds primarily to exclusion rather than to inclusion (Leary & Dows, 1995, pp. 33–34). This again is a good indicator that worrying and the fear of being excluded—losing the support of the reference group—are the main motive governing an individual's actions.

Emotions and the Multidimensionality of Well-Being

> The coolly rational types may fill our textbooks, but the world is richer. (Amartya Sen, 1990, p. 11)

Up to now, we have spoken about an individual in relation to his or her reference group and his or her generalised striving toward optimal well-being. It is important to bear in mind, however, that an aspired set-value of well-being shifts over time and is embodied differently in social terms according to the different values of different groupings (Worthman, 1999). Group memberships, however, do not just change ontogenetically; the adult individual is normally also a member of various groups and coalitions. He or she can be associated simultaneously with a group of people practising the same religion, belong to a group of professionals, and be a member of a group of political activists as well as a group of stamp collectors. All of these groups have more or less different, sometimes also overlapping, creeds and "high values." Accordingly, the individual has to adapt more or less frequently to different social situations, requiring differential management of emotions and the organisation of behavioural strategies in line with the particular psychosocial constitution of the relevant group and its members. Therefore, we are dealing here not only with the abstract and generalised phenomenon of "well-being" but also with different and ever-changing individual set-points that are embodied through the socially defined values and goals of the specific group and the different sociopsychological composition of its members. To avoid being scandalised and thus at risk of losing membership, individuals have to manage their emotions in such a way that the behavioural strategies applied are attuned to the specific group members' expectations, particularly to those of high rank. To avoid moral dilemmas, the strategies applied in line with the particular circumstances should not contradict the inculcated overarching moral norms and values of the actor himself or herself that are relevant for acceptance in the broader society. These overarching norms and values may include, for example, his or her specific religious creeds and/or the idea of "human rights." As we see below, in extremely conflicting situations "moral disengagement" may take place so the individual's self-respect and self-worth are not overly devastated and may, to a certain extent, be attuned to the moral standards of the wider society.

Thus, "well-being" has to be understood situationally and processually (see Hinton, 1999) and covers an enormous range of individual subjective desires, emotional needs, and goals—as has been shown by the contributors to Kahneman, Diener, and Schwarz' (1999b) ground-breaking volume. Furthermore:

> There are serious doubts on the hypothesised empirical connection between choice satisfaction and well-being on which the welfarist case for preference utilitarianism must ultimately rest. It has shown that people constantly make choices in a fashion that violates fundamental canons of economic rationality. (Kelman, 2005, p. 392)

There are, as Kelman (2005) discussed, serious theoretical and methodological problems in the field of a hedonic psychology—particularly with its relation to welfare that he more or less equated with well-being. In this chapter, however, we are not dealing with Bentham's simplistic equation in which the sensations of pleasure and pain are generally equated with the welfare/well-being of a whole community or state. We are dealing only with the ephemeral individual's psychic and/or physical well-being related to and caused by episodes of positive or negative emotions of pride and shame. However, if such feelings accumulate over time, an individual's self-esteem and self-value rise; and, all other factors excluded, the individual enjoys a (relatively) high level of well-being and self-esteem that may then also condense into a longer-lasting positive mood. A word of caution is necessary here as well: Although most authors agree on the positive and negative influence of affects on health (see Allen & Badcock, 2003; Sapolsky, 2004), it seems difficult to *prove* that enduring positive moods exert a positive influence on health (Pressman & Cohen, 2005). Despite all these difficulties, we believe that especially in societies in which the honour and dishonour code is the most important social prime mover the disposition of an embodied knowledge of "honour" or, in the opposite case, "dishonour" has a strong influence on the individual's well-being in all its facets.

Is Honor to Pride What Dishonor is to Shame?

> Suffice to say that if the Vikings or any Other are not just like us, and they are not, they are not centipedes either.... I now doubt interpretations that claim to demonstrate difference almost (the qualifier is important) as much as I have heretofore questioned the complacency of our willingness to see sameness. If we choose to locate sameness in the eye of the beholder, then difference belongs there too. (Miller, 1993, p. 13)

Based on what has been said so far, it can be supposed that, in specific situations, feelings of pride or shame can emerge in all humans. However, apart from the historical analysis based mainly on documents and literature, the occurrence of shame and especially that of pride is not well documented outside the Western world. Some examples are now given that seem to indicate that these emotions are not necessarily related to the "honour/dishonour code."

Meyer (2005, pp. 228–247; see also Todd Romero, 2006, pp. 309–313) analysed the "boasting speeches" (German term used by the author: *Prahlreden*) of Native Americans and noted that, in most cases, boasting about the speaker's own extraordinary qualities and/or those of his tribe or clan goes hand in hand with the denigration and shaming of his opponents. In many Native American societies, Meyer analysed such or similar boasting rhetoric that is applied either to enhance the own status vis-à-vis other members of the group or as, in the case of the Yanomami, to warn possible aggressors coming from neighbouring groups. When analysing his sample, Meyer (2005, p. 245) concluded that in all cases loud, proud boasting demonstrates the value of the own person and represents a method to elevate and revaluate oneself socially.

In the Melanesian "big men societies," the competition for status and political power, obtained through the distribution of gifts, engaged in by the members of the ego's kin group and his followers, is often combined with the shaming of competitors (e.g., Godelier & Strathern, 1991; Meggitt, 1967, 1974, 1977; Rubel & Rosman, 1978; Sahlins, 1963; Strathern, 1971). "Shame" and "shaming" are mentioned in this and many other contexts (e.g., Epstein, 1984; Lipset, 1997, pp. 153, 288) throughout the literature we have consulted on Melanesian "big-men societies," and they are described as one of the major factors structuring the sociopolitical fabric. But honour is mentioned only rarely in this literature, one of the few exceptions being Trompf (1994, p. 402; see also Mauss, 1954) who, in a sweeping statement, called Melanesian societies "shame/honour cultures" without, however, providing us with descriptions or examples.[8]

As early as 1954, Mauss (p. 35) had pointed to the relation between honour, property, transactions expenditure, and prestige among the Native Americans of the northwestern coast of the United States.[9] For the Kwakiutl, Meyer (2005, p. 231, translated) concluded from the literature that: "The speaker utters anger and rage and the willingness to evoke shame and dishonour in the addressees (see also Drucker & Heizer, 1967, pp. 118–124; Rosman & Rubel, 1971, pp. 176–180) and that the expression of rage "is a means of raising his own status over that of the others." Benedict (1956, pp. 160–205), who gave one of the best descriptions of honour and shame in these U.S. northwestern coast groups. He also reported that every trespass against given norms and even an individual's misfortune brings shame and dishonour to the whole group. Only a specific ritual and sometimes even only a suicide can wash the stain from the individual's and the group's dishonour. Here, "shame" and "shaming" are related to "dishonour," but pride and honour are not mentioned directly. In none of these societies or in those described by Whitehead (1981) in North America and by Ortner and Shore (1981) for Polynesia, "does male prestige depend heavily upon women's activities and/or men's relations with women, and notions of female pollution, disruptiveness and threat are not developed" (Ortner & Whitehead, 1981, p. 20).

In other societies, as we have seen, honour and dishonour, next to prestige (deriving from rank, status, and wealth), are mainly dependent on the women's conduct and behaviour in line with strictly prescribed gender relations.

To draw some final conclusions on the basis of these and other scattered reports is difficult. Looking at the bulk of the literature we have consulted, we can, however, state that shame is a pan-human emotion (see Casimir & Schnegg, 2002), and this can be used to infer that it seems highly improbable for societies or groups to exist in which the opposite experience of pride never emerges. That pride is rarely reported might have the following reason: We know that displaying and talking about one's pride as related to arrogance receives negative approval in many (but not all) cultures and has to be suppressed, even if felt, through emotional management.

To answer the question of how the emotions pride and shame are related to the socio-symbolic category of honour and dishonour, it can finally be deduced that striving for high self-esteem and self-worth and also the related feelings of pride and shame are pan-human psychological universals. However, these feelings/emotions are not necessarily linked to a socio-symbolic code of honour and dishonour found in only some cultures. However, when this socio-symbolic code is central to the social setup of a society, feelings of pride are also of paramount importance, and those of shame are feared immensely.

Based on this conclusion, we can seek an answer to the final question tackling the riddle of how these emotions have evolved as well as how, when, and under what circumstances the specific "honour and dishonour code" has been related to, added to, or merged with in some cultures—but not all.

On the Origin of the Honor-Dishonor Code

Hierarchies, Dominance, and Feelings: Evolutionary Perspective

> The cortex is a neuro-cultural "playground" where the more ancient gifts and curses of our animal nature can be moulded into the many subtle feelings that are distinctly human. (Panksepp, 2003, p. 60)

From the evolutionary point of view, intraspecific competition, based on the differential capacities and needs of individuals, is part and parcel of hierarchical structures in social, group-living animals. Being dominant raises the individual's access to scarce resources such as food, sexual partners, or shelter. Striving for dominance emerged early in the evolution of social animals and can be understood as one of the proximate means for individual fitness maximisation. As Washburn and Hamburg stated in 1968:

> Being dominant appears to be its own reward—to be highly satisfying and to be sought, regardless of whether it is accomplished by advantage in food, sex, or grooming. In the long run, position guarantees reward, but in the short run, position itself is the reward.... (p. 473, as cited in Weisfeld, 1980, pp. 273–274)

Aggressive behaviour on the one hand and submission on the other are the principal strategies of the individual who govern his or her positioning in rank order systems. Violating sociobehavioural rules leads to punishment by dominant group members, and successful support of a group member against an aggressor can lead (well documented in, for example, chimpanzee groups) to "obligations" and "gratitude" of those who have been supported. In terms of "delayed reciprocity," those who have once been helped will support the past helper in future struggles.

Motivational processes—such as social arousal, differentiated into approach-avoidance, reward, stress/anxiety, and dominance-rank-related agonistic behaviours such as rage or fear—can be observed in many relatively simple hierarchically organised animal societies (see Goodson, Evans, Lindberg, & Allen, 2005). It can be assumed that even the anthropomorphic behavioural equivalents of pride can be seen—as Konrad Lorenz described for geese, among whom the winner of a fight displays an extreme upright posture, raises the head, stretches out the wings, and utters what Lorenz called *Triumphgeschrei* (cry of triumph). In such social groups, an individual must be capable of recognising the behavioural intentions of other group members so his or her own goal-oriented motivations can be organised and transformed into adequate actions. Even in lower vertebrates, patterns such as sex-specific markers, acoustic signals, and specific body postures are the main stimuli/signals that are "understood" by social partners and on which the individual reacts. With this true for some lower vertebrates, we can expect that the related bodily "felt" physiological changes (e.g., fear and rage) have been moulded at a very early state of primate evolution (Mellers, 2002, p. 265; Öhman, 1986) and are homologous to the equivalent human experience. They emerge (and can be measured) in comparable conflicting and dangerous situations; are observed with the same senses and passed on by the same afferent neuro-pathways (e.g., Barkow, 1980; Bernstein, 1980; Omark, 1980; Weisfeld, 1980); and finally lead to comparable similar behavioural reactions. In nonhuman primates and humans, this also forms the basis for the capacity of "mind reading" in which the individual, by observing the Other, is able to anticipate his or her intention (Emery, 2000; see also Byrne, 1995; Byrne &

Whitten, 1988). This can even been done by, for instance, following and "analysing" the direction of the Other's gaze.

It can also be assumed that the equivalent emotional episodes we call "pride" arise in the individual when a successful behavioural enterprise raises his or her rank in the group, and that the equivalent feeling of "shame" (defined as social fear, especially that of being excluded from the group) emerges when punishment for trespassing against sociobehavioural rules can be expected (see Weisfeld, 1997).

With the emergence of "advanced" hominids and the rise of group-specific cultural traits, group-specific norms and more complex codes of behavioural conduct developed as well. The tighter the interdependent cultural and behavioural network based on such norms are knit, the more does inclusion or exclusion of the individual determine the individual's survival. Climbing up the social ladder and reaching a higher social position in the group enhances "well-being" and thus fitness, whereas losing a position leads to the opposite situation. At the very episodic moment in which the individual has noticed the success or the failure of an enterprise, when he or she has been displaced from his or her position in this zero-sum game of hierarchical dynamics, either positive or negative feelings emerge that we may equate with "joy" or "happiness" (see Barkow, 1997; Washburn & Hamburg, 1968) on the one hand or "fear" and "panic" on the other. Then, either "pride" or "shame" is "felt."

Human Cultural History and the Emergence of the Honor/Dishonor Code

> The art of war shows no signs of decay, but has evolved with the general evolution of society. Lastly, there is no biological ground for supposing that the warlike strain in our breed is being gradually eliminated. Yet, though the animal and impulsive basis of human character tends to be constant, a system of moral education can do much to bring our warlike and peaceful propensities into harmony. (Marett, 1920, p. 28)

During the past decades, anthropologists and historians have developed various hypotheses to explain the emergence and functions of the honour and dishonour code. As early as 1971, Jane Schneider, but later also Wyatt-Brown (1982), attempted to show that the code was originally linked to the pastoral mode of production. In their analyses, the nomad's competition with the agricultural communities in the area for land and water was understood as the basis for the code's emergence. Honour, related to the appropriation of property and wealth and thus understood as family honour and, in extension, as lineage honour was then projected onto women, a process by which "woman are reduced to currency" (Schneider, 1971, p. 37):

> The repository of family or lineage honor, the focus of common interest among the men of the family or lineage, is women. A woman's status defines the status of all the men who are related to her in determinate ways. These men share the consequence of what happens to her, and share therefore the commitment to protect her virtue. (p. 18)

Later, she argued that "honour" as well as "shame" fulfill the same function because: "As with honor, the idea of shame serves both to defend or enhance the patrimonies of families and to define the family as a corporate group" (p. 21), and she further explained:

> Although she [the woman] is drawn toward the new family for which she will bear children, she does not sever her attachment to her father and brothers. They are still the guardians of her honor, and she of theirs.... In a sense there is a division of labor between virginity and shame. The first is central to the solidarity of the family of origin, and to the honor of the patrimonial group (and it is perhaps more pronounced on the North African side). The second shores up the family of procreation and the honor of its head—a form more appropriate to European organization. The two concepts, however, are by no means mutually exclusive, for the virgin feels shame and the married woman feels chaste. (p. 21)

These qualities and capacities were then subjected to public evaluation, which leads to more or less prestige and to a good or bad reputation of a person, thus building the cornerstones of a person's honour.

In his analysis based on psychology and symbolism, Blok (1981, p. 436) also understood "honour as part of an originally pastoral code, predicated upon virginity but also on men's physical strength." Here, honour was understood as being reciprocal to shame (see Schneider, 1971, p. 2) and related to men's virility and women's chastity. His analysis understood the relation of the deceived husband to the symbol of "horns" (see Cohen, 1992, pp. 603, 604–605) and the opposition of "rams and billy-goats" (see Campbell, 1964, pp. 31–32) as key symbols (see Ortner, 1975; see also Pitt-Rivers, 1966, pp. 45–46) for understanding the Mediterranean code of honour. His proposal of such psychological explanations and particularly those posited by Gilmore (1987) for whom the "code of honour [is] predicated upon virility and physical strength" led to heated controversy (e.g., the criticism of Pina-Cabral, 1989 and the reply by Gilmore, 1990; see also Kaufman, 1997).

Apart from the idea of a relationship between pastoralism and the code of honour, Pitt-Rivers, as early as 1966 and 1968, mainly stressed the intimate relation between honour and the physical person. He linked the two "in terms of the symbolic functions attached to the body: to the blood, the heart, the hand, the head, and the genitalia," and noted that "any form of physical affront implies an affront to honour" and "the ultimate vindication of honour lies in physical violence" (Pitt-Rivers, 1966, pp. 25–29; Pitt-Rivers, 1968, pp. 505–506; see also Wyatt-Brown, 1982, p. 49). Comparing all the data at hand, comprising not only the Western but also the non-Western areas in which the code is important, it seems that, as Nye (1993) lucidly argued in his summarising chapter, the body and especially the male body and male "courage" must be understood as the main factors around which the code always revolves. As he noted:

> The link these studies forged between shame and fear, and the physiological status they accorded to shameful emotions helped provide a modern scientific discourse for the historic honour/shame binary. As ... argued, men bedevilled by timidity or fearfulness

> were proportionately enfeebled in their sentiments of personal dignity and masculine honor, which corresponds to the opinion they have of themselves and that others have of them. That is why men are so angered at the appearance of an emotion that robs them of their force, lessening them in their own eyes and weakening them against their rivals in the struggle for life and in sexual conquest. The irony of fear . . . is that it leads to more not less conflict, and therefore to greater "discouragement" and "impotence." (p. 223)

Sherry Ortner (1978), rejecting most current explanations, argued that:

> With the exception of the psychoanalytic argument (e.g., Blok, 1981), all . . . share a common functionalist orientation: the purity of the women is seen as adaptive for the social coherence, economic viability, or cultural reputation of the group, regardless of whether the group is a caste, lineage, or family. When the theorists try to explain why women in particular should represent the coherence and integrity of the group, rather than, say, a totemic bird or a sacred flute, the answers are more variable—in terms of women's natural childbearing abilities, women's physical structure (internal pollution), women's function as tokens of alliance, or women's symbolic roles in the family. None of these answers is very satisfactory; all use as explanations the very things that need explaining. We are still left with the paradox that male-defined structures represent themselves and conceptualise their unity and status through the purity of their women. (p. 22)

In a comparative analysis, she went on to develop her own hypothesis on the origin of the honour and dishonour code, postulating that:

> No pre-state societies, as far as I have been able to ascertain, evince the sort of pattern I am concerned with here—the ideological linkage of female virginity and chastity and the social honor of the group, such chastity being secured by the exertion of direct control over women's mobility to the point of lifetime seclusion and/or through severe socialization of fear and shame concerning sex. What I am suggesting, then, is that this sort of concern with the purity of women was part of, and somehow structurally, functionally, and symbolically bound up with, the historical emergence of systematically stratified state-type structures, in the evolution of human society. (p. 23)

To describe the great ideological shift in women's status and situation brought about by the emergence of such stratified state type-like sociopolitical structures, she wrote:

> Before they [women] were dangerous, but now they are said to be in danger, justifying male protection and guardianship. Before they were polluting, and this had to be defended against, but now they are said to be pure, and to need defending. (p. 26; see also Bruck, 1996)

Most of the various, more or less monocausal approaches applied to solve the problem of the origin of the code are not convincing. As our small cross-cultural sample has shown, neither a purely economic (i.e., pastoral) nor a purely historical/political approach related to state formation can explain the emergence of the honour and dishonour code in different societies and regions. If we align contemporary societies along a continuum, at one pole we would find those with highly elaborated institutions of a honour and dishonour code positioned at the apex of the sociopolitical structure (e.g., northern Albania or Pakistan); in the middle range are those in which honour and dishonour are relatively less important (e.g., the Beti of southern Cameroon); and at the other pole are societies in which such an institution is not to be found (e.g., modern central Europe). We can also observe a process of transformation in which prestige status and honour, which had been tied, for instance, to nobility, male bravery, and/or wealth, are now linked in some sections of society to good upbringing and good education (see the case of western Turkey mentioned above or the situation in parts of Latin America, described in, for example, Putnam, Chambers, & Caulfield, 2005).

As already argued, if the code is highly elaborated, the individual's sensitivity to the emotions pride and shame is also highly developed. However, if shame and shaming are highly significant in a society or group, it does not imply that the code can also be found. The same is true for the emotion of pride and its display.

Conclusion

As we have seen, the socio-symbolic category and the related institutions of "honour and dishonour" are connected to the biopsychological complex of the emotions pride and shame; and these, in turn, are related to the effort to maintain or enhance self-esteem to buffer anxiety and possibly secure a higher position in the reference group. This interconnected emotional, social, and behavioural complex is grounded in the early evolution of our species, and it can be assumed that it emerged homologously with our nearest relatives, the higher nonhuman primates. It can be supposed that early hominids were already organised hierarchically, with strong males dominating the group. When more complex sociocultural patterns emerged in these bands, they were linked to specific norms and behavioural rules. In such early, relatively small hunting and gathering bands, group-specific cultural differentiations can be imagined, whereby some, especially under the optimal environmental conditions that supported larger populations, remained hierarchical. Others, especially small-band societies in marginal environments, developed a more egalitarian ethos in which those individuals who tried to dominate and strive for power and rule were subjected to restraints, as can still be observed today in some of the remaining hunter-gatherer societies.

With the coming of the Neolithic age and the domestication of plants and animals in various parts of the world, larger and stratified societies with different modes of production and different patterns of ownership, dependencies, and obligations came into being. In these agrarian societies, more complex hierarchies—related to differences in wealth and ownership and patron–client relations—evolved, and, with these, different cultural norms, values, and codes of conduct came into being. It then became necessary for an "elite" to defend property and kin against the envious aggression of the poorer and lower ranking members of the society, and it became necessary to defend the whole territory of the group against competing outsiders. In both situations, the land (the means of production) and women (the means of reproduction) had to be protected. This then became a central theme and ethos in *some* of these societies whenever the livelihood of kin was endangered either by internal groupings or by aggressive outsiders. When force was the means chosen and applied to defend kin, group, and territory, it was courage and bodily power—ascribed mainly to men—that were paramount, an ethos of courage and self-sacrifice, the ethos of the warrior, emerged. This then led to hypercognisised manliness, bravery, and the ethos of heroism; and together with the emotions of the pride of the hero and victor and the shame of the coward and loser, a "code of honour and dishonour" was constructed. In *some* of these societies, this code then took a central place in the group's ideology and stood at the apex of the whole sociopolitical structure. In others, it came to be the central creed and ethos of a specific warrior caste or class (e.g., the Ksatriya/Rajput in India, the *boshido* in Japan, and of course the knights in parts of Europe during the Middle Ages) (see Tuchman, 1978, pp. 62–69). In the case of armed conflict, the courageous defender's hope of proudly gaining honour and his fear of shameful scorn became psychological driving forces that went hand in hand with the socio-symbolic category "honour and dishonour." Such "honour and dishonour societies" can be understood as special cases of a "hegemonic masculinity" complex (Connell, 1987, 2002; Cornwall & Lindisfarne, 1994; Lindisfarne, 1994, as cited in Horden & Purcell, 2002, p. 522; Dinges, 2005).

In short, pride as an emotion/feeling emerging in the individual who has successfully reached a positive-evaluated goal and shame as an emotion/feeling arising from failure in the actor's own and other's eyes are phylogenetically old substrates. However, over time, with the evolution of hominid culture(s), these feelings became modulated and adjusted to the changing norms and values of a given group or society.

Such hypothetical explanations based on evolutionary-cum-prehistoric thinking and socioecological theories may shed *some* light on the biopsychological preconditions that may have *facilitated* the emergence of codes of honour and dishonour in *some* cultures. However, the question remains how and under which *specific* circumstances in only *some* societies the highly elaborated code has emerged in which (next to men's strength and bravery) women's conduct, especially their chastity and fidelity and the virginity of girls, are of utmost importance.

Notes

1 For a psychoanalytic approach, see Wurmser (1981).

2 Only then can children experience and show pride and shame in, for example, an experimental situation in which they have to overcome task difficulties and successfully solve the problem or fail (e.g., Belsky, Domitrovich, & Crnic, 1997; Lewis, Alessandri, & Sullivan, 1992). For a detailed analysis of the ontogeny of basic and "higher" emotions, see Holodynski (this volume); Holodynski and Friedlmeier (2006); see also Panksepp (1994, p. 117).

[3] On envy and symbolic behaviour, see Foster (1972).

[4] The observation that a proud/arrogant person often raises his head and tilts it slightly backward, so in an extreme case the eyes and the nose form a horizontal line (nose in the air) has led people to the anthropomorphic supposition that the camel is an arrogant animal. In the Arabic World, the following well known legend is told: When Mohammed had to flee from Mecca to Medina and the enemy came closer and closer, he revealed to his camel the hundredth name of God, which no one else knows and of course the grateful animal doubled his speed and secured the Prophet. Humans only know the 99 names of Allah and everyone can see the pride in the camel's face that it is the only creature on earth that knows them all.

[5] For details, see Ainsworth (1972, 1989); Bowlby (1969, 1973); Coopersmith (1967, pp. 223–234); Magai, Distel, and Liker (1995); Rohner (1975); for a comprehensive and critical discussion, see Barkow (1980, pp. 325–332), Capitano (1992, pp. 512–513), Kraemer (1992).

[6] To be differentiated from moods, affecting phenomena of longer duration, see Harrison (2001); Mellers et al. (2002, p. 265); see also Harrison (2004).

[7] For the development of empathy in children, see Bischof-Köhler (1995).

[8] Tuzin (1982) used both terms, "honour" and "pride" (without informing us about the indigenous terms to which he was referring) when he described the feelings of an Ilahita Arapesh man (Papua New Guinea) who had beaten up a fellow villager for attacking his wife:

> On the face of it, this was simply a matter of a man defending his *own* honor by attacking his wife's assailant. Nevertheless, prompted by the circumstances and personalities involved, I asked Falipen why he had fought Akotan. "I would not have done it," he replied, his voice and lips quivering, "but *he made her* cry." However much his own pride had been involved, it was Falipen's feeling for his wife that had precipitated his action. (pp. 331-332).

[9] Summarising his findings on Polynesia, Melanesia, and the Native Americans of the U.S. northwest coast, Mauss (1954) wrote:

> We see, then, that the notion of honour, strong in Polynesia, and present in Melanesia, is exceptionally marked here (Northwest Coast Native Americans).... The notion of honour is no more foreign to these civilisations than the notion of magic. Polynesian *mana* itself symbolizes not only the magical power of the person but also his honour, and one of the best translations of the word is "authority" and "wealth." The Tlingit and Haida *potlatch* consists in considering mutual services as honours.... Men could pledge their honour long before they could sign their names. (p. 36).

References

Ainsworth, M. D. S. (1972). Attachment and dependency: A comparison. In J. L. Gewirtz (Ed.), *Attachment and dependency* (pp. 97–137). Washington, DC: V.H. Winston.

Ainsworth, M. D. S. (1989). Attachments beyond infancy. *American Psychologist*, *44*, 709–716.

Alderfer, C. (1972). *Existence, relatedness, and growth*. New York: Free Press.

Allen, N. B., & Badcock, P. B. T. (2003). The social risk hypothesis of depressed mood: Evolutionary, psychosocial, and neurobiological perspectives. *Psychological Bulletin*, *129*(6), 887–913.

Appadurai, A. (1990). Topographies of the self: Praise and emotion in Hindu India. In C. A. Lutz & L. Abu-Lughod (Eds.), *Language and the politics of emotion* (pp. 92–112). Cambridge, UK: Cambridge University Press.

Barkow, J. H. (1997). Happiness in evolutionary perspective. In N. L. Sega, G. E. Weisfeld, & C. C. Weisfeld (Eds.), *Uniting psychology and biology: Integrative perspectives on human development* (pp. 397–418). Washington, DC: American Psychological Association.

Barkow, J.H. (1980). Prestige and self-esteem: A biosocial interpretation. In D. R. Omark, F. F. Strayer, & D. G. Freedman (Eds.), *Dominance relations: An ethological view of human conflict and social interaction* (pp. 319–332). New York: Garland STPM Press.

Bauman, Z. (1993). *Modernity and ambivalence*. Cambridge, UK: Polity Press.

Baumeister, R. F., & Tice, D. M. (1990). Anxiety and social exclusion. *Journal of Social and Clinical Psychology*, *9*(2), 165–195.

Baumeister, R. F., Heatherton T. F., & Tice, D. M. (1993). When ego threats lead to self-regulation failure: Negative consequences of high self-esteem. *Journal of Personality and Social Psychology*, *64*(1), 141–156.

Baumeister, R. F., Campbell, J. D., Krueger, J. I., & Vohs, K. D. (2005). Exploding the self-esteem myth. *Scientific American, 292*(1), 70–77.

Belsky, J., Domitrovich, C., & Crnic, K. (1997). Temperament and parenting antecedents of individual differences in three-year-old boys' pride and shame reactions. *Child Development*, *68*(3), 456–466.

Benedict, R. (1956). *Patterns of culture*. New York: Mentor Book.

Bernstein, I. S. (1980). Dominance: A theoretical perspective for ethologists. In D. R. Omark, F. F. Strayer, & D. G. Freedman (Eds.), *Dominance relations: An ethological view of human conflict and social interaction* (pp. 71–84). New York: Garland STPM Press.

Bischof-Köhler, D. (1995). The development of empathy in infants. In M. E. Lamb & H. Keller (Eds.), *Infant development: Perspectives from German-speaking countries* (pp. 1–33). Hillsdale, NJ: Erlbaum.

Blok, A. (1981). Rams and billy-goats: A key to the Mediterranean code of honour. *Man, 16*, 427–440.

Bourdieu, P. (1966). The sentiment of honour in Kabyle society. In J. G. Peristiany (Ed.), *Honour and shame: The values of Mediterranean society* (pp. 193–241). Chicago, IL: University of Chicago Press.

Bourdieu, P. (1977). *Outline of a theory of practice*. Cambridge, UK: Cambridge University Press.

Bowlby, J. (1969). *Attachment 1: Attachment and separation*. New York: Basic Books.

Bowlby, J. (1973). *Separation: Anxiety and anger, Vol. 2: Attachment and loss*. New York: Basic Books.

Brown, J. D., Dutton, K. A., & Cook, K. E. (2001). From the top down: Self-esteem and self-evaluation. *Cognition and Emotion*, *15*(5), 615–631.

Brown, P., & Levinson, S. C. (1992). *Politeness: Some universals in language use*. Cambridge, UK: Cambridge University Press.

Bruck, G. von (1996). Being worthy of protection: The dialectics of gender attributes in Yemen. *Social Anthropology*, *4*(2), 145–162.

Buss, D. M. (1990). The evolution of anxiety and social exclusion. *Journal of Social and Clinical Psychology*, *9*(2), 196–201.

Byrne, R. (1995). *The thinking ape: Evolutionary origins of intelligence*. Oxford, UK: Oxford University Press.

Byrne, R., & Whitten, A. (1988). *Machiavellian intelligence: Social expertise and the evolution of intellect in monkeys, apes and humans*. Oxford, UK: Clarendon Press.

Cagle, R. (2005). Becoming a virtuous agent: Kant and the cultivation of feelings and emotions. *Kant-Studien*, *96*(4), 452–467.

Campbell, J. K. (1964). *Honour, family and patronage: A study of institutions and moral values in a Greek mountain community*. Oxford, UK: Oxford University Press.

Capitano, J. P. (1992). What do attachment objects afford? Commentary to Kraemer, Gary W., A Psychobiological Theory of Attachment. *Behavioral and Brain Sciences, 15*, 493–541.
Casey, J. (1990). *Pagan virtue: An essay on ethics*. Oxford, UK: Clarendon Press.
Casimir M. J., & Schnegg, M. (2002). Shame across cultures: The evolution, ontogeny and function of a "Moral Emotion." In H. Keller, Y. Poortinga, & A. Schölmerich (Eds.), *Between biology and culture: Perspectives on ontogenetic development* (pp. 270–300). Cambridge, UK: Cambridge University Press.
Casimir, M. J. (2007). The mutual dynamics of cultural and environmental change: An introductory essay. In M. Casimir (Ed.), *Culture and the changing environment: Uncertainty, cognition and risk management in cross-cultural perspective* (pp. 1–62). Oxford: Berghahn Books.
Cohen, E. S. (1992). Honor and gender in the streets of early modern Rome. *Journal of Interdisciplinary History, 22*(4), 597–625.
Collins, R. (1984). The role of emotion in social structure. In K. R. Scherer & P. Ekman (Eds.), *Approaches to emotion* (pp. 385–396). London: Lawrence Erlbaum.
Connell, R. W. (1987). *Gender and power*. Sydney: Allen & Unwin.
Connell, R. W. (2002). Hegemoniac masculinity. In S. Jackson & S. Scott (Eds.), *Gender. A sociological reader*. (pp. 60–63). London: Routledge.
Cook, J. R. (1992). *An empirical investigation of cognitive arrogance as a coping style*. Unpublished doctoral dissertation, Auburn University, Alabama.
Cooper, T. D. (2003). *Sin, pride & self-acceptance*. Downers Grove, IL: InterVarsity Press.
Coopersmith, S. (1967). *The antecedents of self-esteem*. San Francisco: W. H. Freeman.
Cornwall, A., & Lindisfarne, N. (1994). Dislocating masculinity: Gender, power and anthropology. In A. Cornwall & N. Lindisfarne (Eds.), *Dislocating masculinity* (pp. 11–47). London: Routledge.
Csordas, T. (1994). *Embodiment and experience: The existential ground of culture and self*. Cambridge, UK: Cambridge University Press.
Darwin, C. (1871/1896). *The descent of man and selection in relation to sex*. New York: Appleton.
Denrell. J. (2008). Indirect social influence *Science, 321*, 47–48.
De Sousa, R. (1987). *The rationality of emotions*. Cambridge, MA: MIT Press.
Dinges, M. (Ed.) (2005). *Männer-Macht-Körper. Hegemoniale Männlichkeiten vom Mittelalter bis heute* [Men-power-body: Hegemonial masculinity from the middle ages to today]. Frankfurt am Main, Germany: Campus Verlag.
Drucker, P., & Heizer, R. F. (1967). *To make my name good: A reexamination of Southern Kwakiutl Potlatch*. Berkeley, CA: University of California Press.
Eckensberger, L. H. (1994). Moral development and its measurement across cultures. In W. J. Lonner & P. Malpass (Eds.), *Psychology and culture* (pp. 71–78). London: Allyn and Bacon.
Eisenberg, N., Lieberman, I., Kipling, M. D., & Williams, D. (2003). Does rejection hurt? An fMRI study of social exclusion. *Science, 302*, 290–292.
Emery, N. J. (2000). The eyes have it: The neuroethology, function and evolution of social gaze. *Neuroscience and Behavioral Reviews, 24*, 581–604.
Epstein, A. L. (1984). *The experience of shame in Melanesia: An essay in the anthropology of affect*. Royal Anthropological Institute of Great Britain and Ireland, Occasional Paper No. 40.
Evans, N. (1992). *Kayardild dictionary and thesaurus. A vocabulary of the language of the Bentinck Islanders, North-West Queensland*. Melbourne: Department of Linguistics and Language Studies.
Fessler, D. M. T. (1999). Toward an understanding of the universality of second order emotions. In A. L. Hinton (Ed.), *Biocultural approaches to the emotions* (pp. 75–116). New York: Cambridge University Press.

Fessler, D. M. T. (2002). Emotions and cost-benefit assessment: The role of shame and self-esteem in risk taking. In G. Gigerenzer & R. Selten (Eds.), *Bounded rationality: The adaptive toolbox* (pp. 191–214). Cambridge, MA: MIT Press.
Fisher, N. R. (1992). *Hybris: A study in the values of honour and shame in Ancient Greece*. Warminster, UK: Aris & Phillips.
Foster, G. M. (1972). The anatomy of envy: A study in symbolic behavior. *Current Anthropology, 13*(2), 165–202.
Gerlach, A. L., Gruber, K., Roth, W. T., & Wilhelm, F. H. (2001) Blushing and physiological arousability in social phobia. *Journal of Abnormal Psychology, 110*(2), 247–258.
Gerlach, A. L., Wilhelm, F. H., & Roth, W. T. (2003). Embarrassment and social phobia: The role of parasympathetic activation. *Anxiety Disorders, 17*, 197–210.
Gilmore, D. D. (1987). Introduction: The shame of dishonour. In D. D. Gilmore (Ed.), *Honor and shame and the unity of the Mediterranean* (pp. 2–21). Washington, DC: A Special Publication of the American Anthropological Association, No. 22.
Gilmore, D. D. (1990). On Mediterranean studies. *Current Anthropology, 31*(4), 359–396.
Goodson, J. L., Evans, A. K., Lindberg, L., & Allen, C. D. (2005). Neuro-evolutionary patterning of sociality. *Proceedings Biological Sciences, 272*(1560), 227–235.
Godelier, M., & Strathern, M. (1991). *Big men and great men*. Cambridge, UK: Cambridge University Press.
Goffman, E. (1963). *Behavior in public places: Notes on the social organization of gatherings*. London: Collier Macmillan.
Goffman, E. (1967). *Interactional ritual: Essays on face to face behavior*. Garden City, NJ: Doubleday.
Greenberg, J., Solomon, S., Pyszczynski, T., Rosenblatt, A., Burling, J., Lyon, D., Simon L. and Pinel, E. (1992). Why do people need self-esteem? Converging evidence that self-esteem serves an anxiety-buffering function. *Journal of Personality and Social Psychology, 63*(6), 913–922.
Harris, C. R. (2006). Embarrassment: A form of social pain. *American Scientist, 94*, 524–533.
Harrison, S. (2001). Smoke rising from the villages of the dead: Seasonal patterns of mood in a Papua New Guinea society. *Journal of the Royal Anthropological Society* (*Incorporating Man*), *7*(2), 255–274.
Harrison, S. (2004). Emotional climates: Ritual, seasonality and affective disorders. *Journal of the Royal Anthropological Institute* (N.S.), *10*, 583–602.
Heelas, P. (1986). Emotion talk across cultures. In R. M. Harré (Ed.), *The social construction of emotions* (pp. 234–266). Oxford, UK: Oxford University Press.
Hinton, A. L. (1999). Outline of a bioculturally based, "processual" approach to the emotions. In A. L. Hinton (Ed.), *Biocultural approaches to the emotions* (pp. 299–328). Cambridge, UK: Cambridge University Press.
Hochschild, A. R. (1979). Emotion work, feeling rules, and social structure. *American Journal of Sociology, 85*(3), 551–75.
Holodynski, M., & Friedlmeier, W. (2006). *Development of Emotions and Emotion Regulation* (J. Harrow, Trans.). New York: Springer.
Horden, P., & Purcell, N. (2002). *The corrupting sea: A study of Mediterranean history*. Oxford, UK: Blackwell.
Kahneman, D., Diener, E., & Schwarz, N. (1999a). Preface. In D. Kahneman, E. Diener, & N. Schwarz (Eds.), *Well-being: The foundations of hedonic psychology* (pp. ix–xii). New York: Russell Sage Foundation.
Kahneman, D., Diener, E., & Schwarz, N. (1999b). *Well-being: The foundations of hedonic psychology*. New York: Russell Sage Foundation.
Kaufman, M. (1997). The construction of masculinity and the triad of men's violence, in gender violence. In L. L. O'Toole & J. R. Schiffman (Eds.), *Interdisciplinary perspectives*. New York: New York University Press.

Kelman, M. (2005). Hedonic psychology and ambiguities of "welfare." *Philosophy & Public Affairs*, *33*(4), 391–412.
Koutlaki, S. A. (2002). Offers and expressions of thanks as face enhancing acts: tæ'arof in Persian. *Journal of Pragmatics*, *34*, 1733–1756.
Kraemer, G. W. (1992). A psychobiological theory of attachment. *Behavioral and Brain Sciences*, *15*, 493–541.
Langford, D. J., Crager, S. E., Shehzad, Z., Smith, S. B., Sotocinal, S. G., Levenstadt, J. S., Chanda, M. L., Levitin, D. J. & Mogil, J. S. (2006). Social modulation of pain as evidence of empathy in mice. *Science*, *312*(5782), 1967–1970.
Leary, M. R. (1990). Responses to social exclusion: Social anxiety, jealousy, loneliness, depression, and low self-esteem. *Journal of Social and Clinical Psychology*, *9*(2), 221–229.
Leary, M. R., & Meadows, S. (1991). Predictors, elicitors and concomitants of social blushing. *Journal of Personality and Social Psychology*, *60*, 254–262.
Leary, M. R., & Downs, D. L. (1995). Interpersonal functions of the self-esteem motive: The self-esteem system as a sociometer. In M. H. Kernis (Ed.), *Efficacy, agency, and self-esteem* (pp. 123–44). New York: Plenum Press.
Levenson, R. W. (2003). Blood, sweat and fears: The autonomic architecture of emotion. *Annual New York Academy of Sciences*, *1000*, 348–366.
Levy, R. I. (1973), *Tahitians: Mind and experience in the Society Islands*. Chicago, IL: University of Chicago Press.
Lewis, M., Alessandri, S. M., & Sullivan, M. W. (1992). Differences in shame and pride as a function of children's gender and task difficulty. *Child Development*, *63*(2), 630–638.
Lindholm, C. (1982). *Generosity and jealousy: The Swat Pakhtun of Northern Pakistan*. New York: Columbia University Press.
Lindholm, C. (2005). An anthropology of emotion. In C. Casey & R. B. Edgerton (Eds.), *A compendion to psychological anthropology: Modernity and psychocultural change* (pp. 30–47). Oxford, UK: Blackwell Publishing.
Lindisfarne, N. (1994). Variant masculinity, variant virginities: Rethinking "honour and shame." In A. Cornwall & N. Lindisfarne (Eds.), *Dislocating masculinity: Comparative ethnographies* (pp. 23–55). London: Routledge.
Lipset, D. (1997). *Mangrove man: Dialogics of culture in the Sepic Estuary*. Cambridge, UK: Cambridge University Press.
Loewenstein, G. (2006). The pleasures and pains of information. *Science*, *312*(5774), 704–706.
Lyon, M. L. (1999). Emotion and embodiment: The respiratory mediation of somatic and social processes. In A. L. Hinton (Ed.), *Biocultural approaches to the emotions* (pp. 182–212). Cambridge, UK: Cambridge University Press.
Magai, C., Distel, N., & Liker, R. (1995). Emotion socialisation, attachment, and patterns of adult emotional traits. *Cognition and Emotion*, *9*(5), 461–481.
Marett, R. R. (1920). *Psychology and folk-lore*. London: Methuen.
Mariauzouls, C. (1996). *Psychophysiologie von Scham und Erröten* [The psychophysiology of shame and blushing]. Unpublished doctoral dissertation, University of Munich, Germany.
Mascolo, M. F., & Bhatia, S. (2002). The dynamic construction of culture, self and social relations. *Psychology and Developing Societies*, *14*(1), 55–89.
Maslow, A. (1943). A theory of human motivation. *Psychological Review*, *50*, 370–396.
Maslow, A. (1954). *Motivation and personality*. New York: Harper.
Mauss, M. (1954). *The gift: Forms and functions of exchange in archaic societies*. London: Cohen & West.
Meggitt, M. J. (1967). The patterns of leadership among the Mae-Enga of New Guinea. *Anthropological Forum*, *II*(1), 20–35.
Meggitt, M. J. (1974). "Pigs are our hearts!" The Te exchange cycle among the Mae Enga of New Guinea. *Oceania*, *XLIV*(3), 165–203.
Meggitt, M. (1977). *Blood is their argument: Warfare among the Mae Enga tribesmen of the New Guinea highlands*. Palo Alto, CA: Mayfield Publishing Company.

Mellers, B. A., (2002). Group report: Effects of emotions and social processes on bounded rationality. In G. Gigerenzer & R. Selten (Eds.), *Bounded rationality: The adaptive toolbox* (pp. 263–279). Cambridge, MA: MIT Press.
Meyer, C. (2005). *"Mahnen, Prahlen, Drohen...". Rhetorik und politische Organisation amerikanischer Indianer* [Warn, boast, threaten: Rhetoric and political organization among American Indians]. Frankfurt am Main, Germany: IKO-Verlag für Interkulturelle Kommunikation.
Miller, G. (2006). Signs of empathy seen in mice. *Science, 312*(5782), 1860–1861.
Miller W. I. (1993). *Humiliation and other essays on honor, social discomfort, and violence*. New York: Cornell University Press.
Modigliani, A. (1971). Embarrassment, facework, and eye contact. *Journal of Personality and Social Psychology, 17*(1), 15–24.
Mulkens, S., de Joung, P. T., Dobbelaar, A., & Bögels, S. M. (1999). Fear of blushing: Fearful preoccupation irrespective of facial coloration. *Behaviour Research and Therapy, 37*, 119–1128.
NASA (2005). *Review of self-esteem research: National Association for Self Esteem*. Retrieved March 19, 2007from http://www.self-esteem-nase.org/research.shtml
Neckel, S. (1991). *Status und Scham. Zur symbolischen Reproduktion sozialer Ungleichheit* [Status and shame: The symbolic reproduction of social inequality]. Frankfurt am Main, Germany: Campus.
Nussbaum, M. C. (2001). *Upheavals of thought: The intelligence of emotions*. Cambridge, UK: Cambridge University Press.
Nye, R. A. (1993). *Masculinity and male codes of honor in modern France*. New York: Oxford University Press.
Öhman, A. (1986). Face the beast and fear the face: Animal and social fears as prototypes for evolutionary analyses of emotions. *Psychophysiology, 23*(2), 123–145.
Omark, D. R. (1980). The group: A factor or an epiphenomenon in evolution. In D. R. Omark, F. F. Strayer, & D. G. Freedman (Eds.), *Dominance relations: An ethological view of human conflict and social interaction* (pp. 21–67). New York: Garland STPM Press.
Ortner, S. B. (1975). On key symbols. *American Anthropologist, 75*(5), 1338–1346.
Ortner, S. B. (1978). The virgin and the state. *Feminist Studies, 4*(3), 19–35.
Ortner, S. B. (1981). Gender and sexuality in hierarchical societies: The case of Polynesia and some comparative implications. In S. B.Ortner & H. Whitehead (Eds.), *Sexual meanings: The cultural construction of gender and sexuality* (pp. 359–409). Cambridge, UK: Cambridge University Press.
Ortner, S. B., & Whitehead, H. (1981). Introduction: Accounting for sexual meaning. In S. B. Ortner & H. Whitehead (Eds.), *Sexual meanings: The cultural construction of gender and sexuality* (pp. 1–27). Cambridge, UK: Cambridge University Press.
Panksepp, J. (1994). The role of brain emotional systems in the construction of social systems. *Politics and the Life Sciences, 13*(1), 116–119.
Panksepp, J. (2003.) The archaeology of mind: The ancestral sources of human feelings. *Soundings: An Interdisciplinary Journal, LXXXVI*(1–2), 41–69.
Pina-Cabral, J. de (1989). The Mediterranean as a category of regional comparison: A critical view. *Current Anthropology, 30*(3), 399–406.
Pitt-Rivers, J. (1966). Honour and social status. In J. G. Peristiany (Ed.), *Honour and shame: The values of Mediterranean society* (pp. 19–77). Chicago, IL: University of Chicago Press.
Pitt-Rivers, J. (1968). Honor. *Encyclopedia of the Social Sciences* (Vol. 6, pp. 503–511). New York: Macmillan.
Preston, S. D., & de Waal, F. B. M. (2002). Empathy: Its ultimate and proximate bases. *Behavioral and Brain Sciences, 25*(1), 1–72.
Pressman, S. D., & Cohen, S. (2005). Does positive affect influence health? *Psychological Bulletin, 131*(6), 925–971.

Putnam, L., Chambers, S. C., & Caulfield, S. (2005). Introduction: Transformations in honor, status, and law over the long nineteenth century. In S. Caulfield, S. C. Chambers, & L. Putnam (Eds.), *Honor, status, and law in modern Latin America* (pp. 1–24). London: Duke University Press.

Ramachandran, V. S., & Blakeslee, S. (1999). *Phantoms in the brain: Human nature and the architecture of the mind.* London: Fourth Estate.

Retzinger, S. M. (1987). Resentment and laughter: Video studies of the shame-rage spiral. In H. B. Lewis (Ed.), *The role of shame in symptom formation* (pp. 151–81). Hillsdale, NJ: Erlbaum.

Robins, R. W., Trzesniewski, K. H., Tracy, J. L., Gossling, S. D., & Potter, J. (2002). Global self-esteem across the life span. *Psychology and Aging, 17*(3), 423–434.

Rodriguez Mosquera, P. M., Mansteadt, A. S., & Fischer, A. H. (2000). The role of honor-related values in the elicitation, experience, and communication of pride, shame, and anger: Spain and the Netherlands compared. *Personality and Social Psychology Bulletin, 26*(7), 833–844.

Rohner, R. P. (1975). *They love me, they love me not: A worldwide study of the effects of parental acceptance and rejection.* New Haven, CT: HRAF Press.

Rohrman, B. (1994). Risk perception of different societal groups: Australian findings and crossnational comparisons. *Australian Journal of Psychology, 46*(3), 150–163.

Rosen, R. (1978). On anticipatory systems: I. When can a system contain a predictive model of another? *Journal of Social and Biological Structures, 1*, 155–162.

Rosman, A., & Rubel, P. (1971). *Feasting with mine enemy: Rank and exchange among Northwest Coast societies.* New York: Columbia University Press.

Rubel, P., & Rosman, A. (1978). *Your pigs you may not eat.* Chicago, IL: University of Chicago Press.

Sahlins, M. D. (1963). Poor man, rich man, big man, chief. *Comparative Studies in Society and History, 5*, 285–303.

Sapolsky, R. M. (2004). Social status and health in humans and other animals. *Annual Review of Anthropology, 33*, 393–418.

Scheff, T. J. (1987). The shame-rage spiral: A case study of an interminable quarrel. In H. B. Lewis (Ed.), *The role of shame in symptom formation* (pp. 109–49). Hillsdale, NJ: Erlbaum.

Schneider, J. (1971). Of vigilance and virgins: Honour, shame and access to resources in Mediterranean societies. *Ethnology, 10*(1), 1–24.

Sen, A. (1990). *On ethics and economics.* Delhi: Oxford University Press.

Shaver, K. G. (1985). *The attribution of blame: Causality, responsibility, and blameworthiness.* New York: Springer.

Shearn, D. (1992). Blushing as a function of audience size. *Psychophysiology, 29*(4), 431–436.

Sheper-Hughes, N. (1994). Embodied knowledge: Thinking with the body in critical medical anthropology. In R. Borowsky (Ed.), *Assessing cultural anthropology* (pp. 229–242). New York: McGraw-Hill.

Shore, B. (1981). Sexuality and gender in Samoa: Conceptions and missed conceptions. In S. B. Ortner & H. Whitehead (Eds.), *Sexual meanings: The cultural construction of gender and sexuality* (pp. 192–215). Cambridge, UK: Cambridge University Press

Simmel, G. (1955/1971). Conflict. In D. N. Levine (Ed.), *Georg Simmel: On individuality and social forms* (pp. 70–95). Chicago, IL: University of Chicago Press. (Reprint from *Conflict and the Web of Group-Affiliation*, pp. 13–28, 35–48 Glencoe, Ill.: Free Press, 1955; original work published as "Der Streit" in *Soziologie* (Munich and Leipzig: Duncker & Humblot, 1908).

Singer, T., Seymour, B., O'Doherty, J. P., Kaube, H., Dolan, R. J., & Frith, C. D. (2004a). Empathy for pain involves the affective but not sensory component of pain. *Science, 303*, 1157–1162.

Singer, T., Seymour, B., O'Doherty, J. P., Stephan, K. E., Dolan, R. J., & Frith, C. D. (2004b). Empathic neural responses are modulated by the perceived fairness of others. *Nature Advance Online Publication*. Retrieved January 18, 2006 from 18.1.2006 (doi: 10.1038/nature04271).
Sjöberg, L. (1998). Worry and risk perception. *Risk Analysis*, *18*(1), 85–93.
Smith, A. (1759). *The theory of moral sentiments*. London: A. Miller.
Steffenhagen, R. A., & Burns, J. D. (1987). *The social dynamics of self-esteem: Theory to therapy*. New York: Praeger.
Stepper, S. (1992). *Der Einfluss der Körperhaltung auf die Emotion "Stolz"* [The influence of posture on the emotion "pride"] Unpublished doctoral dissertation, University of Mannheim, Germany.
Stepper, S., & Strack, F. (1993). Proprioceptive determinants of emotional nonemotional feelings. *Journal of Personality and Social Personality*, *64*(2), 211–220.
Steward, F. H. (1994). *Honor*. Chicago, IL: University of Chicago Press.
Stipek., D. (1998). Differences between Americans and Chinese in the circumstances evoking pride, shame, and guilt. *Journal of Cross-Cultural Psychology*, *29*(5), 616–629.
Strathern, A. (1971). *The rope of Moka: Big-men and ceremonial exchange in Mount Hagen* New Guinea. Cambridge, UK: Cambridge University Press.
Strathern, A. (1993). *Voices of conflict. Ethnology Monographs* 14. Pittsburgh, PA: Department of Anthropology, University of Pittsburgh.
Strauss, C. (1992a). Models and motives. In R. D'Andrade & C. Strauss (Eds.), *Human motives and cultural models* (pp. 1–20). Cambridge, UK: Cambridge University Press.
Strauss, C. (1992b). What makes Tony run? Schemas as motives reconsidered. In R. D'Andrade & C. Strauss (Eds.) *Human motives and cultural models* (pp. 191–224). Cambridge, UK: Cambridge University Press.
Tangney, J. P. (1999). The self-conscious emotions: Shame, guilt, embarrassment and pride. In T. Dalgleish & M. J. Power (Eds.), *Handbook of cognition and emotion* (pp. 541–568). New York: Wiley.
Tangney, J. P. (2002). Self-conscious emotions: The self as a moral guide. In A. Tesser (Ed.), *Self and motivation: Emerging psychological perspectives* (pp. 97–117). Washington, DC: American Psychological Association.
Tood Romero, R. (2006) "Ranging foresters" and "women-like men": Physical accomplishment, spiritual power, and Indian masculinity in early-seventeenth-century New England. *Ethnohistory*, *53*(2), 281–329.
Tracy, J. L., & Robins, R. W. (2004). Show your pride: Evidence for a discrete emotion expression. *American Psychological Society*, *15*(3), 194–197.
Trompf, G. W. (1994). *Payback. The logic of redistribution in Melanesian regions*. Cambridge: Cambridge University Press.
Tuckman, B. (1978). *A distant mirror. The calamitous 14th century*. New york: Ballantine Books.
Tuzin, D. F. (1982). Ritual violence among the Ilahita Arapesh: The dynamics of moral and religious uncertainty. In G. H. Herdt & R. M. Keesing (Eds.), *Rituals of manhood: Male initiation in Papua New Guinea* (pp. 312–355). Berkeley, CA: University of California Press.
Tyler, T. R., & Blazer, S. L. (2002). Autonomous vs. comparative status: Must we be better than others to feel good about ourselves? *Organizational Behavior and Human Decision Processes*, *89*, 813–838.
Washburn, S. L. & Hamburg, D. A. (1968). Aggressive behaviour in Old World monkeys and apes. In P. Jay (Ed.), *Primates: Studies in adaptation and variability (pp. 458–478)*. New york: Holt, Rinehart & Winston.
Webster, J. M., Duvall, J., Gaines, L. M., & Smith, R. H. (2003). The roles of praise and social comparison information in the experience of pride. *Journal of Social Psychology*, *143*(2), 209–232.

Weisfeld, G. E. (1980). Social dominance and human motivation. In D. R. Omark, F. F. Strayer, & D. G. Freedman (Eds.), *Dominance relations: An ethological view of human conflict and social interaction* (pp. 273–286). New York: Garland STPM Press.

Weisfeld, G. E. (1997). Discrete emotions theory with specific reference to pride and shame. In N. L. Sega, G. E. Weisfeld, & C. C. Weisfeld (Eds.), *Uniting psychology and biology: Integrative perspectives on human development* (pp. 429–443). Washington, DC: American Psychological Association.

Whitehead, H. (1981). The bow and the burden strap: A new look at institutionalized homosexuality in native North America. In S. B. Ortner & H. Whitehead (Eds.), *Sexual meanings: The cultural construction of gender and sexuality* (pp. 80–115). Cambridge, UK: Cambridge University Press.

Wolf, J. (2003). Scanlon on well-being. *Ratio* (New Series), *XVI*(4), 332–345.

Wolputte, S. van (2004). Hang on to your self: Of bodies, embodiment, and selves. *Annual Review of Anthropology*, *33*, 251–269.

Worthman, C. M. (1999). Emotions: You can feel the difference. In A. L. Hinton (Ed.), *Biocultural approaches to the emotions* (pp. 41–74). Cambridge, UK: Cambridge University Press.

Wurmser, L. (1981). *The mask of shame*. Baltimore, MD: John Hopkins University Press.

Wyatt-Brown, B. (1982). *Southern honor: Ethics and behavior in the Old South*. New York: Oxford University Press.

Yates, J. F., & Stone, E. R. (1992). Risk appraisal. In J. F.Yates (Ed.), *Risk-taking behavior* (pp. 49–85). New York: Wiley.

Zammuner, V. L. (1996). Felt emotions and verbally communicated emotions: The case of pride. *European Journal of Social Psychology*, *26*, 233–245.

End of Honor? Emotion, Gender, and Social Change in an Indonesian Society

Birgitt Röttger-Rössler

Abstract The intention of this chapter is twofold: (1) to present a general insight into the code of honor and shame in an Indonesian society, using the anthropological means of a "thick description" to illustrate some of the theoretical issues raised by Casimir and Jung in the introductory chapter to this part and (2) to analyze the relation between social and emotional processes of change. Two general questions are particularly relevant for this last point: What role do emotions play within the context of innovative individual acts that initiate or process social change? How are cultural models of emotions (and thereby emotions themselves) transformed within the context of changing conditions in society?

I tackle these issues on the micro level with an empirical case study illustrating what can be called "change in the making." I present a social drama in which individuals involved in a social conflict give up their conventional normative behavior for emotional motives and by doing so inaugurate significant processes of social change. This also reveals how I approach my research methodologically. I take an actor-centered approach and try to discover how macrostructural phenomena are generated (i.e., simultaneously activated and modified) in daily social interactions. This demands a strong focus on individual life courses and life episodes leading to a stronger emphasis on idiosyncratic, individual-psychological aspects and their role in social processes.

One way to tap the role of emotions in social interactions is to perform systematic observation, documentation, and analysis of complex "social dramas" (Garbett, 1970; Turner, 1957, 1974; van Velsen, 1967). Although emotional phenomena are associated with each and every social event, they tend to remain latent within the normal routine interactions of daily life, making them difficult for an external observer to examine. In contrast, they can be accessed more easily during

---

B. Röttger-Rössler (✉)
Max Planck Institute for Social Anthropology, Department I – Integration and Conflict, Halle, Germany
e-mail: roettger@eth.mpg.de

B. Röttger-Rössler, H.J. Markowitsch (eds.), *Emotions as Bio-cultural Processes*,
DOI 10.1007/978-0-387-09546-2_14, © Springer Science+Business Media, LLC 2008

social conflicts or other exceptional events because participation in dramatic incidents also intensifies emotional involvement, generally making it more visible. Moreover, *emotional displays* serve as a central communication medium in social conflicts. This is why I have focused primarily on assessing cases of social conflict. I present only one of the more than 100 major and minor social dramas that I have been able to document during the course of my research.[1]

Ethnographic Context

Understanding the following social drama requires some ethnographic background information, albeit in a highly compressed form. Most of my research in Indonesia has been carried out with the Makassar, an approximately two million strong people living along the southern coast and in the mountainous interior of the island of Sulawesi. Whereas fishing and trade play a central role along the coast, the economy of the highland Makassar is based on wet rice cultivation. Most Makassar practice Islam. However, although the coastal regions converted to Islam at the beginning of the 17th century, this religion only started to gain a weak foothold in the highlands at the beginning of the 20th century (Rössler 1997).

Makassar society is characterized by a strict hierarchical organization that can be viewed as feudal. In precolonial times, the Makassar had formed a powerful kingdom that controlled, at the peak of its power in the 17th century, a region extending from the Philippines to North Australia. This powerful, rigidly organized kingdom successfully resisted Dutch colonial expansion, and the Dutch managed to gain a foothold on Makassar territory only at the beginning of the 20th century. The old noble families continue to play an important role in this extremely status-oriented society, which is organized into a great variety of strata and substrata. Social status is based on individual descent, with the rank assigned to an individual being determined on the basis of the bilateral system of relatives—of both matrilateral and patrilateral origins. The single social strata are—at least theoretically—separated from each other along the lines of rank endogamy, with the norm being that a woman should never marry below her rank, significantly linking the two aspects of hierarchy and gender. This also offers some explanation for the strict rule of gender separation characterizing this society. It is applied particularly rigidly to young men and women of marriageable age to minimize the risk that they will form socially unacceptable intimate relationships. Marriages are arranged by the families, and the families generally try to marry their daughters to men of higher or at least equal rank. Violations of this norm are considered extremely shameful events, deeply affecting the reputation and honor of the respective woman's family. In Makassar society, as well in other Indonesian societies (Boelstorff & Lindquist, 2004; Collins & Bahar, 2000; Goddard, 1996), honor constitutes a mainly implicit category that becomes visible only through acts of improper conduct that elicit feelings of shame in the one(s) who have misbehaved and feelings of "being ashamed" in the ones affected by the respective event. Honor is viewed as a quality that is basically available to everyone and that can be weakened or forfeited only by one's own misbehavior. What is significant is that individuals can show that they are "persons with no sense of shame" in both an active and a passive way. In the former, individuals directly violate social standards and behavioral prescriptions themselves; in the latter, they fail to react appropriately to norm violations perpetrated upon them by others—another way to display a lack of any sense of shame. It is these two sides that make the Indonesian concept of shame such a particularly effective social control mechanism.

Case Study: Badiah's Marriage

Dramatis Personae

The drama presented here focuses on Badiah, who was 17 years old in 1993 when the events described below took place. I have known Badiah personally since my first field trip to the highlands of south Sulawesi in 1984/1985 when she was 8 years old. On my second 1-year field trip in 1990/1991, Badiah lived in our household and helped look after our own two children. Badiah had lost both her parents when she was very young, and she and her three siblings (two sisters and a brother) were raised by relatives. When her oldest sister Mariamah got married, the three younger siblings moved into her new home. After completing his schooling, her brother Mangambi had entered a military career and was now living in Jakarta, from where he nonetheless continued to take an interest in the fate of his siblings in Sulawesi. He felt particularly responsible for his two still unmarried sisters and fetched them both to Jakarta in 1991 to find them husbands there. However, both were very unhappy on the main island of Java and returned to Sulawesi after only a few months. Other important relatives along with these three siblings are Badiah's aunt Nuri (mother-sister, MZ), her cousin (mother-sister-daughter, MZD) Tati, and two maternal uncles, Mawang and Majid. Two important outsiders are, first, the subdistrict head, the so-called *Kades* (*kepala desa*), who presides over the various villages and community leaders (*kepala dusun*). The presiding *Kades* is not just the most powerful person on a subdistrict level because of his office within the modern Indonesian administration but also because of his high rank within the local nobility. The second important outsider is the *Camat*, Karaeng Masiki (Prince Masiki), an uncle of the *Kades*, who served as district head (*Camat)* for many years. Under the traditional political system of the highland Makassar, Karaeng Masiki would have been the ruler of the entire highland. A major proportion of the respect extended to this man and the power he is granted is based on this traditional claim to leadership.

Badiah's Marriage

In August 1993, I returned to Sulawesi for another field trip. Within a few days of my arrival, I met Badiah again in her cousin Tati's house in the village of Bontolowe. Badiah seemed changed completely; she looked dejected, miserable, and sick. I found out that she was 4 months pregnant by Ngai, the son of a trading family from the next village whom she had been meeting secretly for quite some time. Only a few close female relatives knew about her condition. They included Tati and Tati's mother Nampa as well as Mariamah (Badiah's older sister) and her aunt Nuri. These women were now considering what could be done to avert a catastrophe. They decided to get in touch with Ngai's mother immediately and make here aware of the situation. She should then put pressure on her family to officially ask for Badiah's hand as quickly as possible.

However, 2 days before the planned announcement of this official courtship secretly arranged by the women, Badiah's brother Mangambi turned up unexpectedly from Jakarta. He had been sent on military exercises to Sulawesi and had asked for a few days leave to visit his family. When his older sister Mariamah told him that Ngai's family was about to propose to Badiah, Mangambi made it very clear that Ngai was unacceptable. He said he would not even think about agreeing to a marriage between his sister and a man with such a bad reputation who was generally viewed as a good for nothing. In any case, his plan was to take Badiah back to Jakarta again and marry her there. Badiah burst into tears and threatened to kill herself if her brother insisted on taking her to Jakarta. The other women also tried to persuade Mangambi to give up his plan. They argued that there was no sense in taking Badiah back to Jakarta against her will; she would only be unhappy there. It would be better to accept the planned proposal because Badiah wanted to marry Ngai. Rejecting it would only lead to a risk of her eloping in order to get her own way. Mangambi was not very impressed by these arguments or by Badiah bursting into tears. He countered that there was no need to fear a marriage by elopement. He would set out for Jakarta with Badiah in 1 week, and until then they would simply keep her in the house and guard her carefully.

One night later, with the active assistance of her sister Mariamah, Badiah fled to the house of a distant cousin in southeast Sulawesi. The next morning, when Mangambi found out what had happened, he knew straight away that Badiah would never have been able to flee without help from within the family. He shouted at his sister Mariamah, calling her a person without *siri'* (honor, shame) and saying that by helping Badiah to flee she had brought dishonor upon the entire family. Mariamah then explained that Badiah was pregnant and needed to get married as quickly as possible, but that Mangambi, despite all the hints he had been given, apparently did not want to understand this. This admission triggered a fit of rage in Mangambi. He went on a rampage in his sister's house, smashing windowpanes and dashing chickens against the wall so violently that he broke their necks. Attracted by all the noise, the whole family and the neighbors gathered round. But Mangambi carried on raging and not even his older uncle was able to calm him. In the meanwhile, the women decided to take the initiative: Tati and her mother went to the village head, and asked him to act as arbitrator. He took the women straight to see his uncle the subdistrict head (*Kades*), who presided in the neighboring village where Ngai's family lived. The *Kades* immediately summoned Ngai's family. After assuring himself that they were willing for their son to marry Badiah and to announce a proposal, the official used the authority of his office to act on behalf of the bride's family, specify the size of the bride wealth, and set a data for the marriage ceremony (*nikka*). Then, the village head took the two women back to Bontolowe and the house of Badiah's sister. They announced the decision of the subdistrict head to a still extremely aroused Mangambi and the others. No longer able to oppose a marriage proclaimed by the highest local authority, Mangambi calmed down, and his anger gave way to strong dejection. In the night, Mariamah told me later, she had heard Mangambi crying. The next day, he left the village. Badiah was fetched back and was married to Ngai within the week. The marriage ceremony was kept simple, with only a few guests and no marriage feast. Instead of her brother Mangambi, Badiah's uncle Mawang, the father of Tati and husband of Nampa, signed the marriage contract.

Interpretation

In my subsequent discussions of this case with the women involved, all emphasized that their compassion (*pacce*) with Badiah had motivated them to help her; that is, to keep her illegitimate pregnancy secret and arrange things so that the men in the family would be unable to react to this flagrant norm violation. To grasp the significance of this case, it is necessary to understand that illegitimate pregnancies belong to the category of so-called *siri' lompo* incidents; that is, they represent a particularly drastic violation of the honor, the *siri'*, of the girl's family. Even as late as the 1970s, such an offence to family honor could only be assuaged by killing the pregnant girl—assuming she had not been raped—along with the man responsible.

In general, illegitimate pregnancies are rare, and illegitimate births are almost nonexistent. This is due to the institution of *erangkale ri imang*, which, translated literally, means "presenting oneself to the Imam." It is a special form of marriage by elopement in which women who have become pregnant outside of marriage flee to the Imam, admit their condition to him, and name the purported father. The Imam then immediately marries these women either to the father of the unborn child or—should this be impossible for whatever reason—another man. There are always enough impoverished men willing to enter into such a marriage because they would never be able to raise the necessary bride wealth to marry normally. Such a marriage is subject to the usual norms governing marriages by elopement. The couple has to hide from the girl's family until they permit their readmittance (*ammotere' baji'*). Because of the severity of the *siri'* violation in such cases, this generally takes several years. During my field research during the second half of the 1980s, such women were still ostracized by the village community and not invited to any communal activities or feasts despite readmission to their families.

Two questions emerge from this context: (1) What led the women in Badiah's family to develop such compassion for her that they were prepared to cover up what still continues to be a major norm violation? (2) Why did Badiah not use the traditional means of fleeing to the Imam or eloping with Ngai to assert her interests?

We start with the first question. Insight into the women's motives for supporting Badiah can be gained from the history leading up to the event. I present this here in the form reported to me by Badiah's aunt (MS) Nuri.

> Poor Badiah! She was never any trouble; she was always obedient and willing to help. Once, 2 years ago, she had a *pacar* [admirer, boyfriend] from Sironjong. He really wanted to marry her, but his mother didn't approve; she didn't want Badiah as her daughter-in-law. He then asked Badiah to elope with him, but Badiah refused. She did not want to cause her family any grief. Last year, Ngai started to become interested in her, and she liked him as well (*cinna-cini'*). Ngai begged his parents to ask for Badiah's hand. But our men didn't want to know about it. Ngai was a good for nothing, they said, he was not capable of doing a day's work, and so on. But what young man is not a good for nothing before he gets married?... For months and months, I tried to persuade my brothers to accept a proposal from Ngai's family. But they had let their heads be turned by Mangambi's letters and all his talk about having a rich Javanese friend who was so keen to marry Badiah. But Badiah didn't want to marry anybody from Java and have to go and live in Jakarta. Why should she be forced to? I felt sorry for her (*paccengku ri Badiah*). Badiah should already have been married to Ngai a year ago, and then all this wouldn't have happened. Another thing: She hadn't been happy about living in her sister's house for a long time either (*kodi pa'mai'na*).

Nuri starts by considering Badiah's original irreproachability, namely, her rejection of a proposed marriage by elopement for the sake of family honor. (It is not unusual for Nuri to know about this intention to elope. It is mostly older female relatives who are involved in such incidents as accessories and assistants.) When, after a time, a new prospect emerged, somebody from a thoroughly acceptable family whom Badiah also wished to marry, the female elders in Badiah's family were immediately willing to support this plan. Another contributory factor was that the women, as Nuri's words reveal, also sympathized with Badiah's growing desire to be independent and raise her own family. Likewise, they could appreciate her reluctance to submit to her brother's plans and marry away from home. The women sent out informal feelers to see if Ngai's family would be willing to ask for Badiah's hand. Ngai's family confirmed that they would, expecting, in turn, an assurance that their official proposal would be accepted. Official marriage proposals are always preceded by such informal female "agency" to ensure a positive response because rejection of an official marriage proposal always represents a major loss of face for the family of a potential bridegroom. In Badiah's case, the women acting as agents were unable to give the desired assurance because the men in the family—predominantly Badiah's two uncles (mother-brother, MB) Majid and Mawang—were not prepared to accept Ngai as a suitor, which, in the women's opinion, was attributable to the influence of Badiah's brother Mangambi. Put briefly: Badiah's pregnancy and subsequent flight was preceded by several months of internal family dispute over the potential marriage of Badiah and Ngai. In the women's opinion, it was predominantly lack of male insight into Badiah's situation that finally led her to be so intimate with Ngai that she became pregnant. For example, Nampa, the wife of Badiah's oldest uncle Mawang, commented:

> It's obvious that desire will eventually awaken in two people who have been a couple (*pacaran)* for so long. If they had both been married straight away, this would never have happened. It was the men's fault; believing Mangambi and all his letters about rich Javanese suitors.

Badiah's older married cousins also thought she was not to blame. When talking to me, they stressed that Badiah had found it increasingly hard to live with her sister as the last unmarried girl in the house and to have to look after Mariamah's children and home.

However, we still have to ask why Badiah did not fall back on the traditional and much used means of marriage by elopement or at least—after becoming pregnant—*flight to the Imam* to assert her interests against those of her uncles and her brother. I posed this question to Badiah personally at a later time. She answered me in two short phrases: "I didn't want to; that [*flight to the Imam*] is an old-fashioned rule. The daughter of Bara' was also pregnant when she got married."

In this statement, Badiah evaluated flight to the Imam as an inappropriate move in modern times, and she rejected the attendant *siri' c*omponents as being no longer appropriate feelings. She justifies this by referring to a celebrated case about a year before of a pregnant young woman who also got married with a normal marriage ceremony. Interestingly, this was a high-ranking member of the local nobility: one of the daughters of the highly respected Prince *Karaeng* Masiki and his likewise highly noble wife who were both exceptionally popular throughout the highlands. They were viewed as model personalities, as persons with a strong sense of honor who know how to maintain tradition while simultaneously setting the tone for conduct in the modern world. This prominent couple, of all people, had married one of their daughters at a late stage of pregnancy with a normal *nikka* —not quietly and discretely but with a lavish marriage feast. What motivated such unusual behavior in this noble couple? It was certainly the outcome of various social antagonisms and constraints to which Prince Masiki and his family were subject. Makassar nobility also has to function and find its place within the contradictions between local ethnic conventions or hierarchies and the values of the modern Indonesian state. In his position as a former *Camat*, that is, as an administrative representative of the Indonesian government, Prince Masiki was bound by national doctrines and directives, even when they clash head on with the normative standards of his people. Because representatives of the government are directed to do all they can to contain or prevent *siri'* conflicts on regional levels, Masiki was unable to react to the illegitimate pregnancy of his daughter in the traditional way by declaring her dead (expulsion) or even killing her.

Let us leave the regional and national sphere and return to the local level of the village. In the opinion of the village inhabitants, a precedent for their own case has been given on the highest level (i.e., by persons who function as models for others to look up to in this hierarchically oriented society). Others can now justify their actions by referring to it. In relation to this incident, it should also be noted that the village head and the subdistrict head (*Kades*), whom the women called on to intervene in the Badiah conflict, were immediately prepared to arrange a *nikka* for Badiah and Ngai. Regardless of what they may have believed personally, these two holders of office were not in a position to act otherwise. If they had rejected the petition by the women from Badiah's family and thus approved and activated traditional *siri'* rules, this would have been equivalent to compromising the high-ranking Prince Masiki who had set a clear, directive sign with the public marriage of his pregnant daughter. The precedent was particularly powerful because overt opposition to those of higher rank is unacceptable in this hierarchical society, and any attempts to do this would be evaluated as offending the honor (*siri'*) of one's superiors. This is what made it impossible for Badiah's male relatives to rebel against the ruling of the *Kades*. The women's initiative took the solution of the conflict out of their hands by referring it to higher authorities. The traditional rules on how to react to illegitimate pregnancies with schemas of "feeling dishonored" and anger (*siri'—larro*) on the emotional level accompanied by expulsion or killing of the guilty persons on the action level were officially annulled by the ruling of the *Kades*, who, in turn, was complying with national state doctrine. If Badiah's male relatives were to have insisted on this emotional and behavioral code, they would have been in direct revolt against the authority of the subdistrict head and thus guilty of *sala siri'* (i.e., a false sense of honor). To deny Badiah a legitimate marriage would have been not only to cast doubt on the legitimacy of the marriage of the Prince's daughter but also to oppose the doctrines of the national state.

How did these men cope personally with this situation? Did they find it difficult to suppress their suddenly forbidden feelings of dishonor and anger? Badiah's brother Mangambi, who had gone back to Java, later managed to reconcile himself with his sister by writing her a letter. Because he left the village immediately after failing to enforce his will, it is not clear whether he found the necessary emotion regulation particularly long lasting and difficult. This also made it impossible to see how far his drastic fit of anger was staged or felt deeply. This is in no way an irrelevant question because staging anger is a common means of demonstrating one's own feeling of honor in the Makassar context, without even considering that such an act can help evoke the socially expected feelings. In the present case, there are essentially four arguments indicating that Mangambi's anger probably was "authentic:" (1) his red-rimmed eyes, darkened face, and strained breathing—all indicators of strong physiological arousal; (2) his destruction of significantly valuable property (furniture, window panes, chickens); (3) the fact that he was not just concerned with the dishonorable behavior of his sister but also, to a major extent, upset by the setback to his own plans and status aspirations in the capital city that hinged on marrying Badiah to a wealthy gold trader; and (4) the extreme tension and concentration to be seen in the body language and facial expressions of the other persons present, granting the entire scenario a threatening connotation that is difficult to put into words.

It seems that Badiah's older uncle Mawang had to perform some hard work on his emotions. Initially, he was highly aroused and angry, and he retired by himself for several days to a hut in his rice paddy. After his return, however, he was completely calm and interacted peacefully with everybody, including Badiah. Her other uncle Majid, in contrast, did not seem to need to carry out any hard "emotion work." In a personal talk about what had happened, he told me that the exaggerated reactions of his nephew Mangambi to Badiah's illegitimate pregnancy had initially prevented him from feeling any great anger himself. His main task had been to calm Mangambi and make sure he did not start assaulting anyone. When I asked directly whether the incident had made him *siri'* (dishonored), he answered:

> I'm not allowed to be *siri'*. The *Kades* has ordered this. It also has its good side. In the old days, we would have had to kill Badiah or banish her. Who wants something like that? Nonetheless, I am shamed (*siri' - siri'*) because we were unable to marry Badiah in the same way as her sister Mariamah with a proper big feast.

This statement reveals the cultural feeling rules that specify the social contexts in which individuals may feel dishonored and react accordingly. Which events do and do not have the potential to violate honor is not something that the individual can decide on the basis of personal standards. The appropriate triggers are defined normatively. The events described here show that some of the behaviors in the domain of gender relations that function as triggers of *siri'* are undergoing a marked change. Within 6 months of Badiah's wedding, another girl in Bontolowe got married when she was pregnant, and up to 1997—that is, over a period of about 4 years—a total of six more girls in the village did the same. Since then, this number has grown even higher, and nowadays such incidents are no longer evaluated as a great scandal. Just as Badiah drew on the marriage of Karaeng Masiki's daughter to justify her own decision, her example went on to serve as a precedent in the village. The prince's daughter, in turn, had most certainly been reacting to events in the far more cosmopolitan university circles of Jakarta and the biographical decisions of persons with whom she had come into contact there, or perhaps she was only drawing on other earlier precedents within the nobility. Such case studies cast light on the complex biographical references unfolding along social networks that generate processes of change in society.

Discussion

How can we explain the relatively undramatic acceptance of this sudden rejection by the highest local authorities of a scenario that previously had been accepted as a critical trigger of *siri'* feelings and actions? In my opinion, two factors are particularly responsible for the apparent ease with which these not inconsiderable changes in the domain of gender relations are accepted. The first is that *siri'* refers primarily to aspects of norm conformity and the social hierarchy and relates only indirectly to gender relations. If certain social events are defined by the appropriate authorities as no longer being legal triggers for *siri'* reactions (in both an emotional and a behavioral sense), it is precisely the *siri'* doctrine that obliges individuals to no longer allow themselves to be provoked by them. An insistence on traditional values in which an illegitimate pregnancy has to be viewed and avenged as a particularly drastic violation of family honor now becomes an act of opposition to the norm-defining authorities, represented here by the local nobility, and thereby a *sala siri'*, a reaction based on a "false sense of honor." The *siri'* complex as such is not affected directly here; initially, there is just a modification in the domain of *siri'* triggers. However, we have to ask when will the emotion model itself be modified or eliminated by changes in the antecedents? If the trigger factors, the antecedents, are conceived as a constituent element of the emotion process, the feelings triggered through the scenarios should also disappear or undergo major qualitative change—at least from a more long-term perspective. It probably makes a significant difference on a subjective level if the relatives of an unmarried pregnant girl perceive the situation as only shameful, unfortunate, and rather undesirable, but no longer have to fear the social exclusion, ostracism, and disgrace of an event that is evaluated as a flagrant norm violation requiring sanction. If the norms and values of society change from explicit behavioral rules to implicit behavioral expectations, it is always followed by marked modifications to the corresponding feeling models. It seems as if a process is taking place here that can be described as a gradual privatization of honor/shame (see also Scheff, 1988, 1990). Individual relatives of illegitimately pregnant girls will certainly continue to feel "dishonored" and "shamed" in the future and react with the corresponding anger toward the particular "delinquent." However, they will no longer be able to translate these feelings into the conventional compensatory acts of expelling, declaring dead, or even killing this delinquent. These action impulses triggered by incidents of *siri' lompo* have lost their legitimization. It is also worth considering the legal aspects here as well: According to customary law (*adat*), compensatory actions in response to *siri' lompo* violations (e.g., death or expulsion) are necessary and legitimate measures; but according to modern Indonesian criminal law, such actions are illegal and punishable. Nonetheless, charges and legal proceedings are rarely brought in *siri'* cases; and because of their status in customary law, punishment is comparatively mild, with offenders receiving 1 to 2 years of incarceration.[2] These changing conditions lead to a need for alternative forms of emotion regulation. One can almost say that conditions invert: Just as in the old days some people used to find it difficult to "build up" their arousal and really feel the anger expected of them, nowadays others find it necessary to "tone it down."

Another aspect that might be responsible for the ease with which these changes to the social feeling rules have become accepted is that being forced to expel or even kill persons one felt close to was always a cause of great suffering for those performing the culturally prescribed behaviors in such cases. Hence, it is conceivable that the men (who are more strongly obliged to protect family honor than women) also view the abrupt change in the law abolishing *siri'* offenses quite simply as emancipation from the compulsion to act in a way they often perceived to be harsh. This reveals the relevance of a thesis presented by the historian William Reddy (1997). He proposed that human creativity results from the discrepancy between the subjective perception of a situation and societal "feeling rules." He claimed that although cultural codes shape the management of emotional experience as well as the communication of emotions they never completely form the emotional experience itself. This discrepancy generates the necessary tension from which the creative power to shape reality in humans emerges: their ability to change the world in which they live and the emotional codes that shape them (see also Röttger-Rössler, this volume, p. 165–180).

Conclusion

In the case study presented here, two indigenous emotion models are particularly apparent: *siri'* and *pacce*—honor and compassion. *Siri'* appears as an extremely complex emotion model encompassing to an equal extent the aspects of honor and disgrace, of shame and shaming. It is oriented directly toward compliance with social conventions and norms—thus specifically promoting social conformity. *Pacce*, in contrast, emerges on the performative level as an emotional scheme oriented primarily toward maintaining and strengthening interpersonal relations—hence promoting social cohesion. Compassion and sympathy establish or also express social closeness and motivate acts of solidarity that may be diametrically opposed to the *siri'* dictate of norm conformity. *Pacce* appears as an emotional force that often takes the sting out of the behavioral dictates of a strict social hierarchy, smoothing their rough edges and softening their blow. In the conflict presented here, *pacce* even led some of the female actors to support the deviant behavior of the main protagonist Badiah by boycotting maintenance of the social reputation and actions based on honor by other members of her family. It is interesting to see that it is women who have more strongly internalized the *pacce* model and the related behaviors of deescalating conflicts and strengthening social relations in their actual interactions, whereas men are more committed to the *siri'* model and thereby—for the sake of social conformity—the shaping of conflicts as well as the threat of social disintegration.[3] The case of Badiah's marriage is prototypical in this respect. Through this gender-specific emotionality, men and women in this society seem to adopt different but mutually complementary roles in maintaining but also modifying the social system. Nonetheless, turning briefly away from these gender-specific aspects, it also seems generally more promising from the perspective of a theory of emotions to pay closer attention to socially binding emotions such as empathy and sympathy when studying human conflicts. These emotions are crucial for acts of solidarity and often motivate behaviors that run counter to social norms. As a result, one significant issue in future conflict research will be to trace how far antagonistic tensions between social conformity and social cohesion in all cases and at all times provoke processes that change not only social structures but also their emotional codings.

Notes

[1] The empirical material reported in this chapter was gathered during the course of several field trips, mostly in the years 1989, 1990–1991, 1993, and 1997.

[2] For more information on the coexistence of national law, local customary law, and religious law in Indonesia, see, for example, von Benda-Beckmann and von Benda-Beckmann (2005); on the concept of legal pluralism in general, see von Benda-Beckmann (1994).

[3] For a more detailed analysis of the *siri'* and *pacce* model, see Röttger-Rössler (2004).

References

Benda-Beckmann, F. von, & Benda-Beckmann, K. von (2005). Adat, Islam und Rechtspluralismus in Indonesien [Adat, Islam, and legal pluralism in Indonesia]. In M. Kemper & M. Reinkowski (Eds.), *Rechtspluralismus in der islamischen Welt* (pp. 89–104). Berlin: de Gruyter.

Benda-Beckmann, F. von, (1994). Rechtspluralismus: Analytische Begriffsbildung oder politisch-ideologisches Programm [Legal pluralism: Analytical concept or political and ideological program]. *Zeitschrift für Ethnologie*, *119*, 1–16.

Boelstorff, T., & Lindquist, J. (2004). Bodies of emotion: Rethinking culture and emotion through Southeast Asia. *Ethnos*, *69*(4), 437–444.

Collins, E. F., & Bahar, E. (2000). "To know shame". Malu and its uses in Malay Societies. *Crossroads: An Interdisciplinary Journal of Southeast Asian Studies*, *14*(I), 35–69.

Garbett, K. G. (1970). The analysis of social situations. *Man*, *5*(2), 214–227.

Goddard, C. (1996). The "social emotions" of Malay (Bahasa melayu). *Ethos*, *24*(3), 426–464.

Rössler, M. (1997). Facets of Islamization and the reshaping of identities in rural South Sulawesi. In R. W. Hefner & P. Horvatich (Eds.), *Islam in an era of nation-states: Politics and religious renewal in Muslim Southeast Asia* (pp. 275–308). Honololu, HI: University of Hawai'i Press.

Röttger-Rössler, B. (2004). *Die kulturelle Modellierung des Gefühls. Ein Beitrag zur Theorie und Methodik ethnologischer Emotionsforschung anhand indonesischer Fallstudien* [The cultural modeling of feeling: A theoretical and methodological contribution to ethnological emotion research based on Indonesian case studies]. Münster, Germany: LIT.

Scheff, T. (1988). Shame and conformity: The deference/emotion system. *American Sociological Review*, *53*, 395–406.

Scheff, T. (1990). Socialization of emotions: Pride and shame as causal agents. In T. Kemper (Ed.), *Research agendas in the sociology of emotions* (pp. 281–304). New York: State University Press.

Turner, V. (1957). *Schism and continuity in an African society*. Manchester, UK: Manchester University Press.

Turner, V. (1974). *Dramas, fields, metaphors*. Ithaca, NY: Cornell University.

Velsen, J. van (1967). The extended-case method and situational analysis. In A. L. Epstein (Ed.), *The craft of social anthropology* (pp. 129–149). London: Tavistock.

"Beggars" and "Kings": Emotional Regulation of Shame Among Street Youths in a Javanese City in Indonesia

Thomas Stodulka

Abstract Officially, street youths are as nonexistent as street children in Indonesia. Stigmatized by the media and most of their social environment and excluded from the "Indonesian national family" by the government, it seems almost impossible for these youngsters to develop any degree of self-confidence or emotional well-being on the streets. This chapter deals with the (sub-)cultural strategies of male street youths in a Javanese city of about one million inhabitants that enable them not only to cope with their hardships on the streets but also to create a collective identity-the "*tekyan*" identity. *Tekyan* means "a little, but enough," and expresses the youths' pride in being able to live independently. Without neglecting the physical and psychological suppression they experience in their numerous encounters on the city's streets, I focus on the collective strategies of emotional regulation that transform initial individual shame in being a society dropout into a collective pride in being a *tekyan*, a street youth.

Introduction

"Street children" and "street youths" can serve as powerful catchwords for both social welfare organizations and social scientists. With their powerful media images, they are easy to activate as a politicized category to raise money or gain attention instead of being used to describe a specific, extraordinary way of life and the motivations or emotions of "real humans" (Adick, 1997; De Moura, 2002). In view of the universalized street child image and the numbers of children and youths living on the streets documented by international welfare organizations, Panter-Brick (2002, p. 153) argued that

> very large estimates of the number of children in the street are produced to draw attention to the need for the agency's work. At best, these estimates rest upon largely elastic and nebulous definitions of homeless and working children. At worst they are made up.

T. Stodulka (✉)
PhD candidate in social anthropology, Germany
e-mail: tstodulka@hotmail.com

B. Röttger-Rössler, H.J. Markowitsch (eds.), *Emotions as Bio-cultural Processes*,
DOI 10.1007/978-0-387-09546-2_15, © Springer Science+Business Media, LLC 2009

I consider the mutual influence of fiction, media, and scientific discourses to be a crucial aspect (Moore, 1994), and that it is particularly necessary to stress this interrelationship in the case of street children whose powerful media image of both victimization and criminalization seems to exert such a strong influence in the social sciences (Hermanny, 1997; LeRoux, 1998; Liebel, 2005).

Moreover, when the media or social sciences focus on street youths in Southeast Asia, they mainly pay no attention to cultural differences and reduce them to stereotypes strongly resembling those in Latin America, Africa, or eastern Europe. Up to now, the scientific literature on street children and youths has rarely addressed issues such as their motivation for living on the street or whether it is their only option for survival; nor has the exploration gone beyond their economic strategies to secure daily survival or examined the sociopsychological strategies they apply to establish psychological and emotional well-being—an aspect that also has to take into account the importance of different cultural contexts. However, if we fail to address cultural and local specifics along with the strategies youths use to establish a degree of emotional well-being to survive, we will never understand their sometimes "irrational" social and economic behavior.

Here I focus on the collective strategies of a group of about 30 male street youths[1] that allow them to establish a positive collective identity in a social environment that is hostile to their very existence. I concentrate strongly on the process of an emotion-regulation strategy that transforms an initial individual shame at living on the streets into a collectively initiated pride in being a street youth. In other words, the two central questions triggering my scientific curiosity are the following: How is it possible for street youths to change their behavior and outer appearances so quickly once they become integrated into a community of others who share their 'fate'? And is it possible that they no longer *feel* like 'beggars' but more like 'street kings' once they no longer try to hide their stigmatized identity as society dropouts and publicly define themselves as street youths?

Regulation of Emotions

Being well aware of the theoretical dangers and traps involved in defining the transformation from shame to pride as a strategy of emotion regulation, let me clarify my motivation for doing this. The academic roots of the recent and intensive discussions on the concept of emotion regulation date back more than a century (if not back to when philosophers first reasoned about human actions and the motives behind them). The persisting interest in the regulation of emotions has been the focus of two psychological traditions. Whereas the psychoanalytical tradition concentrated on anxiety regulation (see Gross, 1999), the stress and coping research provided the groundwork for the contemporary study of emotion regulation by directing attention toward the "cognitive and behavioral efforts to manage a troubled person–environment relationship" (Folkman & Lazarus, 1985, p. 152).

Cole, Martin, and Dennis (2004, p. 317) argued that the "concept has been applied to such a range of diverse phenomena that its utility as a construct has been questioned." Both the application of the concept in diverse scientific contexts and the current debate can be viewed as a consequence of the lack of consensus on the definition of emotion itself (Campos, Frankel, & Camras, 2004; Cole, 2004; Cole et al., 2004). The difficulty of defining emotions is not just bound to psychological research; it also represents challenges to the interdisciplinary canon of emotion research. One vivid example is the long-lasting debate over the last two decades in the anthropology of emotions between relativists and universalists on whether emotions should be conceptualized as being culturally constructed or can be reduced ultimately to certain universal basic emotions (Abu-Lughod, 1986; Ekman & Heider, 1988; Levy, 1984; Lutz & White, 1986). Just as, nowadays, this debate can be regarded as a fruitful discussion that led to a rewarding compromise between two opposing approaches, the tough contemporary discussion about the concept of emotion regulation needs to be viewed as a necessary stage on the path toward a better understanding of emotions and their regulation.

The two opposing traditions in the research on the regulation of emotions are a consequence of the debate on whether it is possible to define a certain emotion and then be able to regulate it (two-factor approach) (see Cole, 2004; Cole et al., 2004; Gross, 1999, 2001, 2002) or the regulation of an emotion is itself part of the process of emotion generation (one-factor approach) (see Campos et al., 2004; Greenberg, 2002, 2004). Greenberg (2004) stated that the two-factor approach is the result of the current dominance of cognitive views in psychology, and that although it seems theoretically and analytically convenient it runs the risk of oversimplifying a complex phenomenon. The same argument is the core of Campos et al.'s (2004) understanding. They found that this

> canonical approach is too simple. In the first place, we argue that there is no "pure" emotion, if by that is meant an emotion that ever exists in an unregulated manner. If so, there is no first factor to account for in a two-factor theory. (p. 378)

Without denying these various facets of emotion regulation in the discourses within different scientific disciplines, I want to follow the tradition of two-factor approaches for two reasons. First, when taking an anthropological perspective focusing primarily on collective strategies, group phenomena, and cultural rather than individual differences, it is difficult to work with such an approach as the one-factor one whose great strength lies in concentrating on individual differences in emotion regulation. Although Campos et al. (2004, p. 379) argued that their approach also has to separate "emotions" from their "regulation" analytically, it is difficult to apply it from an anthropological perspective that concentrates primarily on cultural similarities and differences. How can we compare the emotional experience *and* its regulation not only between different cultures but also within a cultural setting when we cannot define an initial emotional process that needs to be up- or down-regulated in relation to the specific feeling rules of a given cultural context? Also, how is it possible then to distinguish between the various emotional regulation strategies of certain social or subcultural groups in relation to a prevalent and dominant cultural model of emotional experience and display?

The second consideration concerns an interdisciplinary approach to the concept. Without ignoring the multidimensionality of "emotion regulation," it seems favorable to narrow the focus to avoid further "fuzzification" of the concepts of emotion generation and their regulation. Let me sketch this briefly.

There are three major challenges to the concept that both one-factor and two-factor approaches need to handle: (1) Emotions are inherently regulative; (2) they regulate (our memories and attention) and influence interpersonal processes; and (3) they need to be regulated to interact with others (Cole et al., 2004). By stressing that both individuals themselves (emotional self-regulation) and interacting partners (mutual regulation) are able to regulate an individual's emotions, I argue that the concept unfolds strongest when we concentrate on that last notion (3) and define it as "emotion regulation".

Taking these assumptions as the theoretical basis of the concept, I combine two different process models to grasp the collective emotion regulation strategies of street youths in the Javanese city theoretically: (1) Gross's (1999, 2001, 2002) well discussed process model of emotion regulation (see Fig. 1) and (2) Britt and Heise's (2000) process model of a shame-to-pride transformation in social movements (see Fig. 2).

Gross (2002) defines emotion regulation as "the processes by which we influence which emotions we have, when we have them, and how we experience and express them" (p. 282). His process model shows how specific regulation strategies can be differentiated along the timeline of unfolding emotional

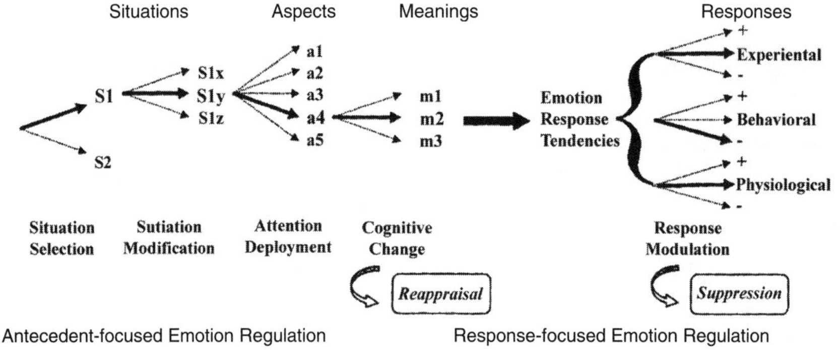

Fig. 1 Gross's (2001, p. 215) process model of emotion regulation. Emotion may be regulated at five points: situation selection; situation modification; attentional deployment; cognitive change; and modulation of experiential, behavioral, or psychological responses. The first four of these processes are antecedent-focused; the fifth is response-focused

responses to emotionally challenging situations. On the broadest level, he distinguished between antecedent-focused and response-focused strategies. Antecedent-focused strategies "refer to things we do before emotion response tendencies have become fully activated and have changed our behavior and peripheral physiological responding" (2002, p. 282). To illustrate these assumptions, he gave the example of a job interview that can be cognitively interpreted in different ways. To avoid experiencing fear or anxiety, one can reappraise the interview situation as a possibility of learning for the future instead of attaching all one's hopes for the future to it. Response-focused strategies are, in contrast, the things we do once an emotion is already underway and after the response tendencies to a certain situation have been generated.

Rather than presenting all the strategies of emotion regulation in Gross' controversially discussed model (Röttger-Rössler, 2004; Westphal & Bonano, 2004), I focus on two strategies for down-regulating emotions: cognitive *reappraisal* and expressive *suppression* (see Fig. 1). As an antecedent-focused emotion regulation, reappraisal comes early in the emotion-generative process and is described as a type of cognitive change. It consists in changing the way a situation is construed to decrease its emotional impact on the individual. Suppression, in contrast, comes later in the process of emotion generation and consists in inhibiting the outward signs of inner feelings. Gross (2002, p. 283) defined it as "inhibiting ongoing emotion-expressive behavior" once contextually negatively evaluated emotions are already about to be expressed by the individual.[2]

Taking these assumptions as the groundwork of my focus on "emotion regulation," I argue that the street youths' practices of transforming individual shame at living on the streets into a collective pride in being a street youth should be considered a form of collective reappraisal of their harsh living situation. Instead of feeling ashamed of being society dropouts, they develop a distinctive subcultural lifestyle that allows them to be proud of a collective identity they themselves call *tekyan*, which means "a little, but enough" in their own street slang. This strategy of emotion regulation is not only a precondition for the street youths' psychological well-being, it is crucial for their physical survival on the streets. To capture these transformation processes analytically, I generalize Britt and Heise's (2000) transformation model of social movements to the case of the street youths. Before I can focus on the transformation from individual shame to collective pride, however, it is necessary to consider the functions of the social emotions themselves.

Social Emotions of Shame and Pride

From among the many research perspectives devoted to the emotion of shame (although less to pride), I choose to take that of identity politics and examine shame and pride more closely as crucial social emotions. These emotions are perceived as human universals. This means they are known in all societies throughout the world (Casimir, 2002). They represent the individual perception of social exclusion and inclusion in the context of society because their relevance and functions are connected strongly to the norms and values of specific social and cultural systems. I want to show how individual participation in different forms of collective action converts shame and loneliness into collective pride.

Shame and pride are categorized as social emotions because they arise from viewing the self from the standpoint of others, be these real or imagined (Casimir, 2002; Lewis, 1998; Scheff, 1988; Tangney, 1999). The view of the observer is always oriented toward the specific norms and values of the society to which the person belongs. Thus, norms and values function as internalized guidelines for adequate behavior within the community and build up the foundation for evaluation. According to these considerations, the expression and feeling of shame occur if an actor has noticed that group members have observed a failure to meet the assumed and accepted behavioral standards of the group. The observed failure by oneself and others results in negative evaluations, which evoke the feeling of shame. Observable signs of shame are hiding behaviors, which include blushing, lowering one's gaze, averting one's eyes, or turning away from the other person (Casimir, 2002; Tangney, 1999). When the other members of the social group accept these signs of remorse, the substandard behavior is forgiven. If the deed has seriously violated group or (from a greater perspective) society's norms and values, the signs of remorse may be rejected by the others. In this case, the other members of the group may decide to exclude or even expel the actor as punishment. Therefore, the feeling of shame can be defined as a fear of social exclusion (Holodynski, Casimir, Jung, & Kronast, 2004).

Pride is defined as an emotion antagonistic to shame (Holodynski et al., 2004; Tangney, 1999). If an actor is successful and meets group standards, she or he is able to experience joy. However, pride contains more than an evaluation of the self; it is reflected in a manner of interacting with others. Through the observation of others and their positive evaluation of the deed, the actor gains acknowledgment as a respected member of the group. Therefore, it is possible to define pride as the joy of acknowledged membership or felt inclusion within a social group. Expressions and feelings of pride are then legitimate. Prideful behavior involves public display, which means a clear, powerful public discourse. Proud people like to talk about their achievements. Other signs of this positively evaluated emotion are a steady gaze and erect posture. However, if pride behavior is exaggerated and turns into arrogance, group members do not accept this and blame the actor. This kind of punishment may then evoke the negative emotion of shame when the actor realizes that his or her behavior is evaluated negatively by other members of the group or society (Holodynski et al., 2004).

In summary, shame and pride can be seen as important social communicators of societal integration. In fact, these emotions generate the desire for conformity among members of a community (Lewis, 1998; Scheff, 1988) that is essential for maintaining its social structure. Through shame and pride, individual action strategies and goals usually adapt to the predominant norms and value systems. This means that they are not only social emotions but also crucial for social exclusion and inclusion.

Cultural Differences: Shame and Malu

Because my perspective is anthropological, I want to focus on another important phenomenon before I attend to the transformation process from individual shame to collective pride in the context of street youths.

From a cross-cultural perspective, it is important to pay attention to similarities and variations in the meaning, use, and functions of emotional vocabulary and expression among cultures. Without focusing further on the simplifying dichotomy of so-called individualistic versus collectivistic cultures, I must stress the great importance of shame or shame-like emotions in Indonesian cultures. The Indonesian concept of shame—*malu*—plays a major role in daily social encounters. According to Goddard (1996, p. 432), there "is perhaps no better term than *malu* from which to begin a survey of traditional Malay culture through the prism of its emotional lexicon." Most authors who have analyzed the different facets of shame in Indonesian cultures agree that *malu* is a "moral affect" (Rosaldo, 1983, p. 136) that positions the individual within a social order. Fessler (2004), Goddard (1996), Lindquist (2004), and Peletz (1995) translated *malu* approximately as shame, shyness, embarrassment, and restraint and propriety.[3] In the Javanese context, *malu* is not always evaluated negatively as the socially crippled or the "dark side" of pride but as playing a central role in almost every social interaction and definition of a person's social status. For example, Collins and Bahar (2000, p. 39) considered *malu* in encounters with a socially higher ranked person as a positive sentiment, perhaps best understood as "appropriate shyness or deference." Keeler (1983) claimed that learning *isin*, the Javanese concept of *malu*, is crucial in the emotional development of children and closely connected with learning complicated forms of linguistic and social status. As young Javanese persons mature, they are supposed to learn the importance of status in every social interaction and to see that receiving deference matters just as much as giving it; that controlling others' behavior is just as significant as controlling one's own. They come to appreciate, therefore, how interaction defines them and how socially inappropriate behavior—either their own or others'–induces *isin*. Status in Java is fluid and largely situational. "Gestures and language matter so much and can, if applied improperly, give rise to vivid feelings of *isin* because they do not simply reflect status but also affect it" (Keeler, 1983, p. 159).

To avoid further confusing the reader with different local connotations and ethno-theoretical concepts of shame, I shift attention away from the traditional

Javanese concept of *isin* and focus on *malu*, which is an expression in the pan-Indonesian language Bahasa Indonesia. There are two major reasons for this.

First, unlike the classic studies of shame and embarrassment in Southeast Asia (Geertz, 1973; Rosaldo, 1983), the street youths' everyday life is constituted within the framework of the nation rather than exclusively within the context of a local community in which culture, place, and language appear to easily correspond. Focusing on *malu* therefore opens up an important field of analysis that poses questions about the anxieties that emerge in the shadows of the Indonesian project of development and why socially undesirable people such as street youths are officially excluded from the national Indonesian family by even being denied identity cards. In this context, *malu* appears—in addition to its positively evaluated meanings in a ritualized social interaction with a socially higher-ranked person—as an emotion that describes the "failures" of the stigmatized to live up to the ideals of the nation.

The second reason is quite simple but even more convincing: Although most of the youths come from Java and have been socialized by learning about the concept of *isin*, they themselves use the expression *malu* on the streets.

In this regard, I argue that whereas *isin* (Java), *lek* (Bali), and other related emotional tropes have remained bound to a particular ethnic group and language, *malu* travels and becomes the politicized link between the street and the *kampung* (a village or village-like social unit in cities), between the stigmatized and the nation.

Malu and Stigma

In what way have street youths "failed" to live up to the ideals of the Indonesian nation and their social environment? How do stigma and shame/*malu* interrelate? And how can these youths develop a certain pride over a fiercely stigmatized identity in an environment that is hostile to their very existence?

As mentioned above, learning about *malu* is one of the most important developmental tasks for Javanese children. Alongside its connotation as a negatively evaluated emotional experience by oneself and others (due to failure to adhere to common social interaction norms and cultural standards), the enactment—not the experience—of *malu* is a kind of interaction guideline or cultural feeling rule that, when enacted properly, reflects the social status of the interaction partners. Thus, it is a strong force in conserving both social interaction and the social structure of a given social context.

People who seem to ignore *malu* are not recognized as "grown-up" members of society (Mulder, 1990, 1996). Youths become acknowledged adults as soon as they are able to show that they understand the concept of *malu* in a more or less ritualized social interaction. If adults behave in a social encounter as if they do not know this hypercognitive and hyperexpressive cultural concept, their own social prestige as well as that of their interaction partner is diminished. The proper enactment of *malu* in public consists of the use of certain facial expressions, gestures, and a refined, almost ritualized speech that are based on knowledge of one's own status. Because street youths seem to ignore these appropriate forms of social interaction in various social encounters and induce yhe experience of *malu* in themselves and others, they are excluded not only officially from the Indonesian nation but also from their immediate urban environment. Their social environment stigmatizes them because of their nonconformist physical appearance and unpredictable behavior, and the Indonesian state excludes street youths by declaring them officially nonexistent because they fail to represent the propagated development and progress of the nation. Hence, their mere existence or physical appearance is already enough to trigger stigmatization by the state and its authorities.

The association between *malu* and stigma appears obvious. Both refer to a "damaged self" (Lewis, 1998, p. 126). In this context, *malu* can be understood as an intense negative emotion involving the self in relation to standards, responsibility, and attributions of self-failure. Hence, stigma, as a public mark that can be noticed by others and that involves, as Goffman (1963) said, a "spoiled identity," is a cause of *malu*. From the point of view of conformity and social standards, it is clear that the stigma possessed by an individual represents a deviation from the accepted standards of the society. This deviation may be in appearance or conduct. The person is stigmatized by having characteristics that do not match publicly acknowledged standards. These can, of course, vary with time and culture, "but such standards always exist and individuals whose appearance and behavior deviate from them can be said to suffer from a stigma" (Lewis, 1998, p. 127).

Holding oneself responsible is a critical feature of stigma and the generation of *malu* because violation of standards is not enough to elicit *malu* unless responsibility can be placed on the self. Stigma may differ from other elicitors of *malu* because it requires a social appearance factor. The degree to which a stigma is socially apparent is the degree to which one must negotiate the issue of blame, not only for oneself but also between oneself and others who witness the stigma. Therefore, stigmatization is a much more powerful elicitor of the experience of *malu* because it requires a negotiation between oneself and one's attributions as well as between oneself and the attribution of others. Much of the intense emotional experience of *malu* associated with stigma is due to it representing the individual. Thus, the whole self becomes defined by the stigma (Lewis, 1998, p. 128). In addition to a street youth's behavior, it concerns his bodily appearance. This makes it comparable to examples of ethnic difference (or racism) and physical disability. Their "spoiled identity" can hardly be hidden because of their "bizarre" bodily appearance compared with "normal" youths. In addition, the stigmatized adolescents—in clear contrast to children living on the streets—are mostly blamed themselves for their exclusion from their families, the urban community, and the nation.

Transformation from Shame to Pride

I now turn to Britt and Heise's (2000) transformation model formulated by analyzing the "coming-out" situation of homosexuals in North America. I start with a short description of what it means to be a "newcomer" to the streets in the city and then describe the transformation model by pointing to the differences in this case that result from not only the different cultural context but also the youths' extremely marginal socioeconomic position within their urban social environment.

Youths who decide to break away from their family and turn to the streets (although this is more of a process than a sudden breakup, there is nonetheless a specific moment when they have to decide to leave or try to leave home) are easy to recognize because of their "dirty look." As a consequence, they are easily identified as *gembel* (beggar, scum), *tuna* (rag picker, tramp), or *preman* (criminal, gangster) and reduced to the stigmatized identity of a society dropout. Thus, the initial emotional experiences on the streets are dominated in almost every social encounter by *malu.* Most of the youths experience *malu* because they feel unable to fulfill even the minimal ascribed social standards—staying with their parents and attending school—and they are suddenly reduced by their social environment to a socially deviant identity: that of a street youth.

Compared with other stigmatized groups (e.g., gay and lesbian people in Britt and Heise's model, 2000, or in chapter 12, "Honor and Dishonor": Connotations of a socio-symbolic category in cross-cultural perspective, M. J. Casimir, S. Jung, this volume), these youths do not have time to evaluate the pros and cons of coming out as a street youth because as soon as they interact in public space they are already labeled as such. Public space is more or less the home of people living on the streets, so there is hardly any way to hide their "spoiled identity." Another big difference is not only the heightened socio-emotional pressure compelling youths to join a community of others who share their stigma but also a simple economic one: the satisfaction of basic human needs—eating, drinking, bodily comfort, safety, and shelter to survive. Thus, it is not only an emotional pressure to avoid *malu* that makes the youths create communities but also an economic one. I use the word "also" here, because to explain the collective strategies of street youths research seems primarily to emphasize economic motivations and neglect the importance of a street youth's emotional well-being. To put it the other way round, the creation of communities represents not only an economic survival strategy but also an emotional one to establish a positively evaluated collective identity that strengthens both the adolescent's self-esteem and his agency or action readiness in various social encounters. The intensity of both the socioemotional and economic pressures to join a community can be grasped most clearly through the initiation rituals to which every *anak baru* (new child) on the streets has to submit: An *anak baru* can be beaten up, robbed of his possessions, or sexually abused by an older street youth only to be incorporated into the group afterward. As a sign of solidarity, he is looked after and served with food and shelter until he is streetwise enough to earn his own share and contribute to the group.

As Britt and Heise (2000) argued in their model, participation in different kinds of collective action offers social support in terms of shared and legitimized feelings within the stigmatized minority group. The shared feeling is what motivates participation in a social movement, whereas participation itself may transform individual feeling so it mirrors the shared affect of other members (Thoits, 1990, 2004). In general, this process of identity formation is not just accompanied by different sequences of emotion. It is emotions that play the fundamental role of motivators in activating the individual action in this kind of self-searching process. Through solidarity, the negative emotions of shame and loneliness can be replaced by the positive emotion of collective pride.

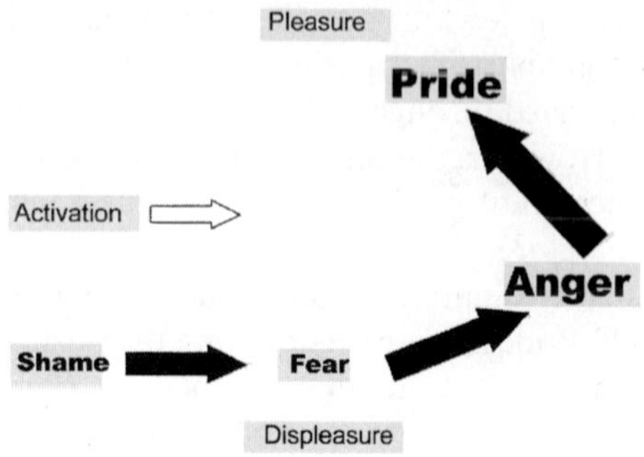

Fig. 2 Britt and Heise's (2000, p. 265) process model of emotion transformations in identity politics

Social movements engaging in identity politics deal with people who initially are ashamed, and isolated. The negative emotion of shame is unpleasant, makes one vulnerable, and implies a low activity level (MacKinnon & Keating, 1989; Morgan & Heise, 1988). The realization that other individuals share the same stigma represents an enormous improvement for the individual development of a collective identity, but it does not automatically remove the feeling of shame.

To be able to act and become a self-conscious social agent, the feeling of shame has to be transformed into another sequence of emotion: that of fear. Fear activates people. The negative consequence of fear is that it leaves them in the stage of feeling jeopardized, so they may decide to run away and hide instead of actively trying to overcome their marginal position. Therefore, another emotional transformation process is necessary. For the activated individuals to join a community as participants, Britt and Heise (2000, p. 256) argued that fear also has to be transformed into a further sequence of emotion: that of anger.

In the case of the *tekyan*, the feeling of fear can be transformed into a feeling of anger by participating in collective activities with other street youths who share the same stigma. Anger is a powerful emotion that motivates individual action. Stigmatized individuals do not just feel angry because their "fate" is unjust but because they have been made to feel ashamed by their social environment. Britt and Heise (2000, p. 258) stated that the emotional potential of anger is, by itself, not sufficient to ensure collective action. They argued that once their example of homosexual men and women have become angry they still need to be brought together to join public demonstrations to escape what Scheff (1990) called the "shame–anger spiral." Friends play a fundamental role as motivators here because personal contacts support people who are ready to participate in collective action. Another possibility for transforming individuals into active participants in collective movement activities is emotional contagion. Public demonstrations by people who are displaying pride might recruit other people through the tendency to mimic another person's emotional experience and expression and thus experience and express the same emotions oneself (Lyon, 1999). The result can be described with the German term *Wir-Gefühl* (we-feeling) that participants in collective actions evaluate positively because it overcomes the vulnerable feeling of loneliness. By observing other participants in collective action and their positive reaction toward the self, an individual feels acknowledged as a member of a community. This positive evaluation by others can induce the emotion of pride generated through collective actions (Britt & Heise, 2000, p. 263).

However, the emotional transformation process does not end with pride. The emotion of pride has to be seen as a temporary contextual state of transition. Therefore, we can assume that pride may be regenerated repeatedly through collective public display, but it does not represent a lifelong condition for the self. Pride requires actions and the positive evaluation of these actions by others and oneself-it cannot be defined as a permanent emotional experience. Through the repeated elicitation of collective pride, an individual may ultimately overcome an earlier feeling of shame and therefore come to accept the stigmatized identity as another component of the self. The emotion of pride can then be understood as a "prerequisite to the integration of the identity into the positive self and the threshold to the identity's deemotionalization" (Britt & Heise, 2000, p. 266). To clarify this assumption, I apply it to the concrete case of street youths by focusing on two examples of emotionally challenging social encounters.

In contrast to Britt and Heise's (2000) and especially elaborated example described in chapter 12, "Honor and Dishonor": Connotations of a socio-symbolic category in cross-cultural perspective, M. J. Casimir, S. Jung, this volume of homosexuals, street youths experience a fear that might be defined as being far more direct than the fear homosexuals experience when they hear or read about aggression or violent acts against other homosexuals. A street youth does not have to read or hear about police violence or aggressive acts by passing strangers; he experiences them on an almost daily basis as soon as he turns to the street. Thus, the anger directed against the state, the police, or other potential "enemies" does not have to be induced by publications, publicity campaigns, or organized public demonstrations. It must be considered as a daily emotional experience and a fixed spot in the emotional landscape of youths living on the street. Anger is further intensified through group-internal narratives based on emphasizing their differences to the dominant society and "normal" youths through self-elevation and a heightened *Wir-Gefühl*, thus enforcing the transition to *bangga*-pride in their collective identity.

Ethnic Pride

What is this collective identity that helps street youths express and fill their selves with pride? It is what they themselves call *tekyan*, "a little, but enough." This term is not just an emic expression for male youths living on the streets, it also reflects a collective philosophy and lifestyle that correlates with certain rules of conduct, norms, values, and outer appearances (see also Beazley, 2000).

The *tekyan* pride consists mainly in actions emphasizing the differences to nonstreet youths whom the *tekyan* call *cilik*, meaning "small." In their encounters on the streets and at traffic lights, they express the advantages of being a *tekyan*: their independence through earning their own money, adventurous journeys in and between cities, public consumption of alcohol and drugs, and *sex bebas* (free sex). They define themselves as more masculine and adult and claim to be more streetwise than "normal" adolescents. Once a youth is an initiated member of the *tekyan*, he changes his name. Mohammed, for example, prefers to be called Bob (Marley) on the streets, because the name Mohammed is too holy for a street kid, and he himself considers it to be inappropriate for when he is acting "dirty" on the streets. The bodily enactment of their collective *tekyan* identity and pride is presented through tattoos, piercing, and extravagant haircuts or long hair. To further distance themselves from the dominant social and cultural expectations of "normal" youths, they even develop their own language or slang that they call *bahasa senang*—the happy language. It is an ever-changing mixture of low-class Javanese, Indonesian, English, and self-created neologisms. Their gatherings on the streets often include swearing contests in which one *tekyan* tries to shout down another with vulgar expressions. This is one of the most "sinful" behaviors in a cultural context in which refined speech, reserve, and devotion are the dominant way of interacting in public. Why do the *tekyan* invest in an identity that further stigmatizes them from the viewpoint of conformist behavior and bodily appearance?

To explain this emphasis and creation of collective identity, I introduce the concept of ethnic pride. I consider this to be a special kind of collective pride usually used to describe pride and solidarity in ethnic minority groups (Beer, 2002). Without trying to enforce or even advocate an unreflected eclecticism, the use of a well established and elaborated anthropological concept can help sharpen our focus on "the neglected sibling" (Tangney, 1999, p. 557) of shame, embarrassment, and guilt from an interdisciplinary perspective.

I do not want to discuss the concept of "ethnic identity" in depth but stress its central importance within cultural anthropology. "Ethnicity" or "ethnic identity" refers to an ethnic group's collective similarities: descent, language, a shared system of norms and values, belief systems, and last but not least a collective feeling of belonging in contrast or relation to other ethnic groups (see Barth, 1969).

These theoretical considerations have already been integrated successfully into interdisciplinary research on ethnic minorities, subcultures, and social movements by emphasizing that individuals do not necessarily refer to common descent, locality, or physical appearance to form communities but stress their shared differences or their use of common symbols. The subversion of stigmatized identities plays a central role in the theoretical constructions of many feminist scientists (Butler, 1991; Hauser-Schäublin & Röttger-Rössler, 1997; Ong, 1995; Schlehe, 2000) and so-called cultural studies (Clarke, Hall, Jefferson, & Roberts, 1976; Hall, 1996, 1999; Woodward, 1997). These stress that marginalized or stigmatized individuals are able to convert negative attributions within a dominant discourse into a positively evaluated identity, and this identity is expressed publicly by emphasizing their shared differences and creating alternative communities.

From an almost neofunctionalist perspective, research then focused almost explicitly on the sharing of common symbols, common social practices, and the social construction of (subcultural) conformity without paying attention to the most important motivator of these actions, the individuals' emotions underlying marginalization, stigmatization, and creation of alternative communities, subcultures, or whatever term with which they may be decorated. My aim is not to introduce the concept of "ethnic identity" to the interdisciplinary canon of emotion research, but that of "ethnic pride"—the pride in one's ethnicity—to shift attention to the emotional meaning of subcultural, countercultural, or other collective strategies and their consequences for an individual's emotional well-being.

As Kulis, Napoli, and Marsiglia (2002) noted when discussing the positive outcomes of rediscovering and stressing a shared marginal ethnic identity among Native American adolescents:

> [S]ome evidence suggests that being embedded in traditional values and practices provides protection against social, psychological, and health problems by offering opportunities to integrate core traditional values and teachings about contemporary life. Cultural embeddedness also may protect American Indian youths by enhancing pride, self-esteem, interpersonal skills, and positive ethnic identity. . . . Ethnic pride is linked to an attitude of self-empowerment as opposed to a feeling of victimization or self-denigration and is associated with higher self-esteem. (p. 102)

Although the cultural, social, and economic settings are completely different here, I argue that these principles of focusing on shared differences from a dominant social or cultural environment-and thus inducing collective pride-are observable to the same degree within the *tekyan* community.

The answer to the question of why the *tekyan* publicly display their pride over an identity that further stigmatizes them is based on these assumptions taken from the "ethnic/collective pride" concept. Although it may initially appear "irrational," they invest in an "othered" identity because it secures them not only physical survival but also emotional well-being and the possibility of a positive self-evaluation. Even though this further nourishes their own stigmatization, they enact their pride over an alternative way of life, appearance, and behavior because it seems to be the only way to both relieve emotional pressures and fight economic ones to survive.

From "Beggars" to "Kings:" A Metamorphosis?

Is it possible to define the display of prideful behavior in the youth's subculturally positively evaluated actions such as swearing, drinking, or singing publicly and the resulting integration of a stigmatized identity into a street youth's self-concept as a "metamorphosis?" If metamorphosis signifies a transformation in which the final condition of the process is permanent and stable, leaving previous problems and emotional difficulties behind, like slipping into a new coat, the answer has to be a resolute "no."

As already mentioned, the emotional transformation does not end with pride, although pride is a prerequisite to incorporating the *tekyan* identity into a youth's self-concept. Let me sketch this briefly with two examples of social encounters. In my opinion, a focus on social encounters seems promising for two reasons.

First, stigma and shame or *malu* relate the self to others' views. Although the feelings of being stigmatized may occur in the absence of other people, the associated feelings come about through one's anticipation of interactions with them.

Second, focusing on social encounters can be an effective strategy within scientific discourse itself to avoid adding a scientific "objectification" or victimization (by creating scientifically convenient coherent pictures of individuals and their culture) to the stigmatization the people are already experiencing in reality. According to Norwegian anthropologist Fredrik Barth (1993), it cannot be preferable to reduce complex human personalities and identities to coherent cultural representations. It is necessary to accept the contradictions and incoherencies of human life in scientific research. Thus, it might be more honest and fair to the street youths to argue against their reduction to intellectually convenient representations and, instead, highlight the heterogeneity of their lives and identities (and thus accept contradictions) by focusing on their various encounters in public space.

"King" Encounters: Tekyan and Rendan

In their encounters with girls living on the streets, the *tekyan* intensively stress and reproduce their collective identity through prideful behavior. When they interact with girls in their nightly *tithikans* (their expression for socializing in a certain place on the main street in the city center), they perform their elaborated swearing contests, stress their sometimes exaggerated sense of masculinity by drinking excessively, recount their "heroic" deeds on the streets (e.g., beating up a member of another group), tell stories of sexual encounters with adult women, or display their new tattoos and piercings. To increase their self-esteem, they emphasize the differences between themselves and the girls. The creation of a social boundary is also accentuated linguistically: They call the girls *rendan*. This is a *bahasa senang* abbreviation of the Javanese *kere berdandan*—"vagrants wearing makeup" (Beazley, 2002, p. 1665). In a certain way, they reproduce a dominant discourse of power and suppression that they themselves reject. By basing their othering of street girls on paternalism and masculinity, they subvert their own marginalization into dominance over an even more marginalized group. They marginalize the girls by emphasizing the dominant politicized cultural ideal that the streets are—even less than for the boys—in no way a space for girls or women to live. However, the interrelations between pride, social status, and power seem even more obvious when we turn to the encounter of a *tekyan* with his parents.

Encounters with Their Parents: "Beggars" Again?

To establish culturally highly esteemed conformist and harmonious social relationships, the regulation of negative emotions is the dominant aim in the socialization of Javanese children and youths. Conflicts with parents are considered sacrilegious; and even when they cannot be avoided, their existence is usually denied. They are labeled as socially shameful and destructive to one's personality (Mulder, 1996).

When a *tekyan* returns to his parents' village to visit them or to try to reintegrate into his family, he is faced with a variety of problems. The most difficult one seems to be the negotiation of his newly achieved (and, in other social encounters on the streets, proudly enacted) *tekyan* identity. Most try to hide or even deny their *tekyan* identity and invent stories about their daily living and earnings because they are afraid of being labeled *gelandangan* (rag picker or beggar) and thus experiencing *malu*. This is particularly true if they come home looking poor and disheveled.

Let me quote 16-year-old Bagus,[4] who has been living on the streets for about 5 years.

> When I went back to the village for my mother's death ceremony last year, my old school friends were passing by our house in the rice fields. I told them I am sometimes in City X and sometimes in City Y. When they asked me: "Are you working there?" I just lied to them. "I am working as a bus driver for a big company in City Y." I would feel *malu* if I were to tell them I still live on the streets. I told the same lie to my father.

In contrast to their encounters with street girls, they try to meet their parents' demands by acting respectfully, politely, reservedly, and answering in a low voice. Tattoos, piercings, long hair, or extravagant haircuts are hidden. They deny their otherwise proudly worn symbols of *tekyan* identity and feel deeply *malu* when their parents, siblings, or other villagers uncover their life stories as a lie. Masculinity, the demonstration of independence and freedom, public swearing, or the use of their vulgar slang are abandoned in favor of socially accepted behavior and outer appearance. Through the display of appropriate interaction-regulative *malu* in their encounters with their socially higher-ranked parents, family, and neighbors, they appease them and show their subordination to them and the dominant sociocultural standards of social interaction.

Conclusion

Finally, I want to refer to the initial question on whether youths are able to change their initially experienced shameful emotion on the streets induced by being identified as "beggars" into a more positive emotion by identifying themselves as little "street kings." The transformation from individual shame to collective pride described here is not a metamorphosis in the sense of a completely new coat that can be worn in every time, space, and social context. However, if we consider a metamorphosis as less absolute than, for example, the famous biblical transformation of Saul to Paul, we can even observe two metamorphoses.

First, from a life span perspective the transformation is more of a "biographical metamorphosis" in the sense of the process of integrating a new identity into one's self-concept. Second, the very fact that the individual is able to enact this newly achieved identity through a public display of pride or hide it shamefully in different social contexts, can—at the same time—be defined as more of a "situational metamorphosis."

Collective actions that induce the pleasant emotion of pride are considered as a prerequisite for the collective creation of a positively evaluated self-identity. Without trying to oversimplify an individual's clashing motivations in situations and encounters in a complex social reality that calls for permanent negotiation of identities, I argue that a *tekyan*'s conscious decision when to stress certain aspects of his identities is not only the result of intense emotional pressures; it relates closely to economic considerations. Taking these reflections into account, I define the various emotional, social, and economic considerations of the *tekyan* as a "socioemotional economy." The psychosocial strategies that street youths use to create a distinctive collective identity are obviously not only a "context-dependent socioemotional metamorphosis" but also the individual's insight into the need to handle economic pressures to survive both psychologically and physically. Like other humans, a street youth consciously reflects on the situation, time, and context in which he is able to invest in the display of pride or, on the contrary, the enactment of shame or *malu*.

Notes

1 The youths I am writing about are between 15 and 22 years old. To ensure their anonymity and safety, I do not describe their locations within the city. For the same reason, and because I consider this chapter to have a primarily theoretical focus, I do not describe their subcultural practices and initiation rituals on the streets in any more detail than necessary.

2 Gross focused mainly on the affective, behavioral, and social consequences of the two strategies and stated that suppression decreases negative and positive emotion-expressive behavior and has little impact on negative emotion experience, while decreasing positive emotion experience. Furthermore, he assumed that expressive suppression consumes cognitive resources by impairing memory for information presented during the emotion regulation period and defined it as "bad" in the social domain: By suppressing emotional

experience, individuals share less of their positive and negative emotions. The result is then supposed to be weakening of social support due to being less well liked. Reappraisal, in contrast, is believed to decrease negative emotion experience and expression while increasing positive emotion experience and expression. No negative cognitive consequences are assumed (Gross, 2002, p. 289). From a cross-cultural perspective, however, these assumptions have been neither verified nor falsified and seem highly questionable (see Röttger-Rössler, 2004).

[3] Fessler (2004) used an evolutionary approach to analyze in detail the well elaborated emotional shame, or *malu*, cluster in another Indonesian context. He not only showed the different notions of shame in southern California and *malu* in Bengkulu/Sumatra but also developed an elaborated argumentation for defining Indonesian cultures as shame cultures and North American ones as guilt cultures. By clarifying the sometimes overlapping meanings and social evaluations of shame and guilt, he demonstrated from a cross-cultural perspective why research on shame in a shame culture is more rewarding than research on shame in a guilt culture such as ours.

[4] As with the following names of the cities of which he spoke, I have changed his name to protect his identity.

Acknowledgments I thank the *tekyan* in the Javanese City, Ebby, Jonathan Harrow, and the members of the ZiF Research Group *Emotions as Bio-cultural Processes*, especially Susanne Jung, Birgitt Röttger-Rössler, Stefanie Kronast, Manfred Holodynski, Michael Casimir, and Daniel Fessler for their great emotional and intellectual assistance.

References

Abu-Lughod, L. (1986). *Veiled sentiments: Honor and poetry in a Bedouin society*. Berkeley, CA: University of California Press.

Adick, C. (1997). “Straßenkinder” in Entwicklungs- und Industrieländern: Definitionen, Erklärungskonzepte und pädagogische Maßnahmen im Vergleich. In C. Adick (Ed.), *Straßenkinder und Kinderarbeit: Sozialisationstheoretische, historische und kulturvergleichende Studien* (pp. 7–28). Frankfurt am Main, Germany: IKO.

Barth, F. (1969). *Ethnic groups and boundaries*. Bergen, Norway: Universitetsforlaget Allen & Unwin.

Barth, F. (1993). *Balinese worlds*. Chicago, IL: University of Chicago Press.

Beazley, H. (2000). Street boys in Yogyakarta: Social and spatial exclusion in the public spaces of the city. In G. Bridge & S. Watson (Eds.), *A companion to the city* (pp. 472–488). Oxford, UK: Blackwell.

Beazley, H. (2002). “Vagrants wearing make-up:” Negotiating spaces on the streets of Yogyakarta, Indonesia. *Urban Studies, 39*(9), 1665–1683.

Beer, B. (2002). *Körperkonzepte, interethnische Beziehungen, Rassismustheorien: Eine kulturvergleichende Untersuchung*. Berlin: Dietrich Reimer Verlag.

Britt, L., & Heise, D. (2000). From shame to pride in identity politics. In S. Stryker, T. Owens, & R. White (Eds.), *Self, identity, and social movements* (pp. 252–268). Minneapolis, MN: University of Minnesota Press.

Butler, J. P. (1991). *Das Unbehagen der Geschlechter*. Frankfurt am Main, Germany: Suhrkamp.

Campos, J. J., Frankel, C. B., & Camras, L. (2004). On the nature of emotion regulation. *Child Development, 75*(2), 377–394.

Casimir, M. (2002). Shame across cultures: The evolution, ontogeny and function of a “moral emotion.” In H. Keller, Y. I. Poortinga, & A. Schölmerich (Eds.), *Between culture and biology: Perspectives on ontogenetic development* (pp. 270–300). Cambridge, UK: Cambridge University Press.

Clarke, J., Hall, S., Jefferson, T., & Roberts, B. (1976). Subcultures, cultures and class. In S. Hall & T. Jefferson (Eds.), *Resistance through rituals: Youth subcultures in post-war Britain* (pp. 9–74). London: Harper Collins Academic.

Cole, P. M. (2004, December). *Emotion regulation: A developmental pychopathology perspective*. Paper presented at the ZiF Workshop on Emotion Regulation, Bielefeld, Germany.

Cole, P. M., Martin, S. E., & Dennis, T. A. (2004). Emotion regulation as a scientific construct: Methodological challenges and directions for child development research. *Child Development, 75*(2), 317–333.

Collins, E., & Bahar, E. (2000). To know shame: Malu and its uses in Malay society. *Crossroads: An Interdisciplinary Journal of Southeast Asia Studies, 14*(1), 35–69.

De Moura, S. L. (2002). The social construction of street children: Configuration and implications. *British Journal of Social Work, 32*(3), 353–368.

Ekman, P., & Heider, K. G. (1988). The universality of a contempt expression: A replication. *Motivation and Emotion, 12*(4), 303–308.

Fessler, D. M. T. (2004). Shame in two cultures: Implications for evolutionary approaches. *Journal of Cognition and Culture, 4*(2), 207–262.

Folkman, S., & Lazarus, R. S. (1985). If it changes it must be a process: Study of emotion and coping during three stages of a college examination. *Journal of Personality and Social Psychology, 48*, 150–170.

Geertz, C. (1973) *The interpretation of cultures*. New York: Basic Books.

Goddard, C. (1996). The "social emotions" of Malay (Bahasa Melayu). *Ethos, 24*(3), 426–464.

Goffman, E. (1963). *Stigma: Notes on the management of a spoiled identity*. Englewood Cliffs, NJ: Prentice Hall.

Greenberg, L. S. (2002). *Emotion-focused therapy: Coaching clients to work through their feelings*. Washington, DC: American Psychological Association.

Greenberg, L. S. (2004, December). *Emotion regulation*. Paper presented at the ZiF Workshop on Emotion Regulation, Bielefeld, Germany.

Gross, J. (1999). Emotion regulation: Past, present and future. *Cognition and Emotion, 13*(5), 551–573.

Gross, J. (2001). Emotion regulation in adulthood: Timing is everything. *Current Directions in Psychological Science, 10*(6), 214–219.

Gross, J. (2002). Emotion regulation: Affective, cognitive, and social consequences. *Psychophysiology, 39*, 281–291.

Hall, S. (1996). Who needs "identity?" In S. Hall & P. DuGay (Eds.), *Questions of cultural identity* (pp. 1–17). London: Sage.

Hall, S. (1999). Encoding, decoding. In S. During (Ed.), *The cultural studies reader* (pp. 507–517). London: Routledge.

Hauser-Schäublin, B., & Röttger-Rössler, B. (1997). Differenz und Geschlecht: Eine Einleitung. In B. Hauser-Schäublin & B. Röttger-Rössler (Eds.), *Differenz und Geschlecht: Neue Ansätze in der ethnologischen Forschung* (pp. 7–22). Berlin: Reimer.

Hermanny, C. (1997). Straßenkinder brauchen Spenden: Wie international operierende Hilfswerke in Deutschland über "Straßenkinder" informieren. In C. Adick (Ed.), *Straßenkinder und Kinderarbeit: Sozialisationstheoretische, historische und kulturvergleichende Studien* (pp. 141–165). Frankfurt am Main, Germany: IKO.

Holodynski, M., Casimir, M., Jung, S., & Kronast, S. (2004). *The social emotions shame and pride*. Working Paper, ZiF Bielefeld, Germany.

Keeler, W. (1983). Shame and stage fright in Java. *Ethos, 11*(3), 152–165.

Kulis, S., Napoli, M., & Marsiglia, F. F. (2002). Ethnic pride, biculturalism, and drug use norms of urban American Indian adolescents. *Social Work Research, 26*(2), 101–112.

Levy, R. I. (1984). Emotion, knowing and culture. In R. A. Shweder & R. A. LeVine (Eds.), *Culture theory: Essays on mind, self, and emotion* (pp. 214–237). Cambridge, UK: Cambridge University Press.

LeRoux, J. (1998). Public perceptions of, and reactions to, street children. *Adolescence: An International Quarterly, 33*(132), 901–913.

Lewis, M. (1998). Shame and stigma. In P. Gilbert & B. Andrews (Eds.), *Shame: Interpersonal behavior, psychopathology, and culture* (pp. 126–140). New York: Oxford University Press.

Liebel, M. (2005). *Kinder im Abseits—Kindheit und Jugend in fremden Kulturen*. Weinheim, Germany: Juventa-Verlag.

Lindquist, J. (2004). Veils and ecstasy: Negotiating shame in the Indonesian borderlands. *Ethos, 96*(4), 485–508.

Lutz, C., & White, G. M. (1986). The anthropology of emotions. *Annual Review of Anthropology, 15*, 405–436.

Lyon, M. (1999). Emotion and embodiment: The respiratory mediation of bodily and social processes. In A. L. Hinton (Ed.), *Biocultural approaches to the emotions* (pp. 182–212). New York: Cambridge University Press.

MacKinnon, N., & Keating, L. (1989). The structure of emotion: A review of the problem and a cross-cultural analysis. *Social Psychology Quarterly, 52*, 70–83.

Moore, H. L. (1994). *A passion for difference: Essays in anthropology and gender*. Cambridge, UK: Polity Press.

Morgan, R. L., & Heise, D. (1988). Structure of emotions. *Social Psychology Quarterly, 51*(1), 19–31.

Mulder, N. (1990). *Individuum und Gesellschaft in Java: Eine Untersuchung zur kulturellen Dynamik*. Saarbrücken, Germany: Breitenbach.

Mulder, N. (1996). *Inside Indonesian society: Cultural change in Java*. Amsterdam: Pepin Press.

Ong, A. (1995). State versus Islam: Malay families, women's bodies, and the body politic in Malaysia. In A. Ong & M. Peletz (Eds.), *Bewitching women, pious men: Gender and body politics in Southeast Asia* (pp. 159–194). Berkeley, CA: University of California Press.

Panter-Brick, C. (2002). Street children, human rights, and public health: A critique of further directions. *Annual Review of Anthropology, 31*, 147–171.

Peletz, M. G. (1995). Neither reasonable nor responsible: Contrasting representations of masculinity in a Malay society. In A. Ong & M. Peletz (Eds.), *Bewitching women, pious men: Gender and body politics in Southeast Asia* (pp. 76–123). Berkeley, CA: University of California Press.

Rosaldo, M. (1983). The shame of headhunters and the autonomy of self. *Ethos, 11*(3), 135–151.

Röttger-Rössler, B. (2004, December). *Emotion regulation: Some thoughts and questions from a social anthropological perspective*. Paper presented at the ZiF Workshop on Emotion Regulation, Bielefeld, Germany.

Scheff, T. J. (1988). Shame and conformity: The deference-emotion system. *American Sociological Review, 53*(3), 395–406.

Scheff, T. J. (1990). Socialization of emotions: Pride and shame as causal agents. In T. D. Kemper (Ed.), *Research agendas in the sociology of emotions* (pp. 281–304). Albany, NY: State University of New York Press.

Schlehe, J. (2000). Globalisierung und Gender in neuen Begegnungsräumen. In S. Hess & R. Lenz (Eds.), *Geschlecht und Globalisierung: Ein kulturwissenschaftlicher Streifzug durch transnationale Räume* (pp. 78–100). Königstein, Germany: Ulrike Helmer Verlag.

Tangney, J. P. (1999). The self-conscious emotions: Shame, guilt, embarrassment and pride. In T. Dalgleish & M. J. Power (Eds.), *Handbook of cognition and emotion* (pp. 541–568). Chichester, UK: Wiley.

Thoits, P. A. (1990). Emotional deviance: Research agenda. In T. D. Kemper (Ed.), *Research agendas in the sociology of emotions*. Albany, NY: State University of New York.

Thoits, P. A. (2004). Emotion norms, emotion work, and social order. In A. S. R. Manstead, N. Frijda, & A. Fischer (Eds.), *Feelings and emotions: The Amsterdam symposium* (pp. 359–378). Cambridge, UK: Cambridge University Press.

Westphal, M., & Bonano, G. A. (2004). Emotion self-regulation. In M. Beauregard (Ed.), *Consciousness, emotional self-regulation and the brain* (pp. 1–33). Amsterdam: John Benjamins Publishing Company.

Woodward, K. (1997). *Identity and difference*. London: Sage.

The Search for Style and the Urge for Fame: Emotion Regulation and Hip-Hop Culture

Sven Ismer

Abstract The aim of this chapter is to draw a line between the development of emotions and emotion regulation during adolescence and the creation or adoption of a youth culture using the example of today's most popular style: hip-hop. During the human life-span, Adolescence is commonly seen as a period where fundamental changes take place. Youngsters have to face new challenges, and their social focus shifts from family to school and peer relationships. This is sometimes especially difficult for the children of marginalized urban groups. They have to learn the "code of the street" (Anderson 1994) to handle themselves in a street-orientated environment. Basic emotional needs such as feeling safe in the neighbourhood, being part of a group, and being proud of yourself are difficult to reach for many. A popular way of dealing with these emotional problems leads to the formation of often violent youth gangs. Another, more peaceful and creative way of regulating these emotional problems can be seen in the creation of hip-hop groups. To help analyse this process, a brief overview on the literature on emotion development during adolescence is given. While the traditional view on adolescent development has described this phase in life as a painful and forced adaption to the rules and standards of society, later tendencies in research on youth put a stronger bias on agency. Socialisation is seen as an active process of dealing with the given opportunities in which the individual not only reacts to the society but is able to create a space of his own. A broad concept of emotion regulation is proposed that enables us to see the connection between individual emotional development and the genesis of new cultural styles. The chapter furthermore analyses the socio-cultural background of hip-hop in the past and today to show the reasons for the enormous popularity hip-hop enjoys with teenagers all over the world.

Introduction

> You got wealth, good health and you're stuck / on yourself / let me tell you that you're better than no body else / 'cause you got no self-esteem, so I'm richer / and when you

---

S. Ismer (✉)
Department of Movement Science, University of Hamburg, Hamburg, Germany
e-mail: sven.ismer@uni-hamburg.de

B. Röttger-Rössler, H.J. Markowitsch (eds.), *Emotions as Bio-cultural Processes*,
DOI 10.1007/978-0-387-09546-2_16, © Springer Science+Business Media, LLC 2009

> leave this earth you can't / take money witcha / so play your dumb game, call me out / my name, but there's nothing / you can do that could make me feel shame / we're all created equal we live and we / die, so when you try to bring / me down I keep my head up high / don't judge a book by it's cover 'cause / It's never what it seems / now I know what I'm sayin' and I feel / I gotta scream / that I am somebody / like you are somebody / he is somebody / like I am someone / so be yourself, huh!!! (Excerpt from the rap song *I Am Somebody*: Grandmaster Flash, 1987)

Contemporary discussions on youth cultures—mainly in fields of sociology, education science, and cultural studies—focus on their historical development, their internal structure, and their relation to the cultural mainstream. The emergence of youth cultures is generally understood as an outcome of transformations in society. The somewhat earlier idea that new youth cultural styles function as a "magical solution" (Clarke, 1979) to problems in various domains (family, school, work, unemployment) seems to have been forgotten. This chapter aims to reintegrate this older tradition into current theory by analyzing a process of cultural change and the genesis of a new cultural style as an outcome of collective emotion regulation. It uses today's most popular style, hip-hop, to illustrate how the problems related to the development of emotions and emotion regulation during adolescence—especially those arising in an environment that restricts the opportunities available to its youth—are connected to the creation or adoption of a youth culture.

The chapter starts with a brief overview of recent research on emotional development during adolescence and of related parts of the discussion on emotion regulation. It then goes on to trace the history and the present state of hip-hop as well as its internal structure.

Socialization as an Active Process in a Changing Environment

Adolescence is commonly seen as a period of fundamental changes in the human life-span. Often, these are accompanied by times of crisis for the individual. Developing teenagers have to face difficult challenges as their social focus shifts from family to school and peer relationships.[1] Their bodies change quickly, and various new experiences and identity processes lead to new emotions as well as a rising need for emotion regulation and control.

Whereas the traditional view on adolescent development describes this phase in life as a painful, forced adaptation to the rules and standards of society, more recent trends in research on adolescence place a stronger focus on agency. Parts of the discussion are now tending to abandon the concept of socialization and prefer the idea of lifelong development (Elder, 1994); others, in contrast, are focusing on the term "self-socialization." Socialization in this sense is viewed as an active process of dealing with the given opportunities in which individuals not only react to society but create a space of their own (Ferchhoff & Neubauer, 1997). The developing teenager is no longer seen as a passive receptor of socialization messages but as an active participant in a process that changes both the individual and his or her environment. This means that children and adolescents give meaning to themselves and to their environment. They construct their own goals and reasons for their actions (Zinnecker, 2000). This process enables the formation of a specific youth space consisting of meanings and explanations that are not necessarily similar to those of adult society. I believe that more attention should be paid to this tendency in future research on adolescent emotion development. The specific cultural standards for dealing with emotions, for expressing or suppressing them, and the attitudes toward certain feelings are subject to constant and fluent changes. Most of these changes occur first among the younger generation of a society who adjust their emotions to the requirements of a changing environment.[2]

Development of Emotions and Emotion Regulation During Adolescence

The development of emotions and emotion regulation are intimately connected to the developmental tasks societies impose on their younger generations. The reorganization of social relations is not just an important task in Western societies alone. Although its meaning differs across cultures, teenagers are generally expected to gain autonomy, reorganize their relationship to their parents, and establish a network of peers as well as heterosexual relationships (Fend, 1998, 2000; Offer, Ostrov, Howard, & Atkinson, 1988; Youniss & Smollar, 1989). Furthermore, they have to deal with rapidly increasing demands at school, the pressures of integration into working life, bodily changes, and the problems of a developing identity.

Leaving the security of the family and attempting to find friends can lead to negative emotions tied to feelings of insecurity about one's identity and the restructuring of one's self-concept. Sometimes teenage development contains stages of egocentrism or even a period of narcissistic retraction (Goossens, Seiffge-Krenke, & Marcoen, 1992; Seiffge-Krenke, 2002). However, developing peer relationships also demands that juveniles learn emotional competence quickly. This developing identity is sustained and reinforced within the peer group. Several studies illustrate the increasing importance of peer relationships and the decreasing relevance of the family (Fend, 1998; Parker & Gottman, 1989; Seiffge-Krenke, 1995). Research on this growing significance of peer groups has shown that they are the most important sources of intimacy for today's teenagers, and they have now taken on a number of the functions previously assumed by families. Indeed, searching for solutions within a friendship or a peer group is now the most common coping strategy for Western youth (Seiffge-Krenke, 1992, 1995). Peer groups are the dominant space for experiencing intense positive and negative emotions and the prevalent resource for the social regulation of emotions (Lempers & Clark-Lempers, 1992; Zimmermann, 1999, 2001). Social regulation of emotion among youngsters means that they mutually validate not only their experiences, pressures, and strains but also their interests and points of view. The peer group also fulfills an important function for initiating romantic relationships by forming a network that helps teenagers to communicate across gender borders and avoid direct rejection (Nieder & Seiffge-Krenke, 2001). Adolescents have to develop strong empathy skills quickly to be able to back each other up. This high level of empathy is also connected to a serious concern about how others view one's own personality (Seiffge-Krenke, 2002).

Attainment of Self-Esteem

Another important aspect of youth development is the attainment of self-esteem. This seems to be especially true for the North American context in which self-esteem is described as a central concern (Mesquita & Markus, 2004, p. 342). The emotions shame and pride are central for this part of identity construction. Although this is not the place to present in detail an academic discussion on the development of self (for an overview, see Lambrich, 1987), it is obvious that daily experiences of success or failure exert a strong influence on the developing self-image and self-conception through their connection with feelings of shame and pride.

Usually, two conditions are necessary for the experience of shame. Individuals feel shame in the first place because they either violate cultural norms (Holodynski & Friedlmeier, 2006) or feel unable to fulfill them. The second condition for shame is the individual's awareness of the fact that someone else knows about the inadequacy. Conformity to cultural norms is a requirement for membership in a society; shame can be seen as fear of exclusion, and the expression of shame is the way of communicating the knowledge of norms and the wish for reaffiliation (Scheff, 1988). In addition to their function for the social structure and social relationships within a society (Scheff & Retzinger, 2000), the emotions shame and pride are also important for the development of personality and identity. Repeated experiences of failure or of racial or social discrimination are constant sources of shame that can lead to depression, aggression, and a negative self-image (Auchter & Hilgers, 1994; Fend, 1997; see also Holodynski & Kronast, this volume). The impact of these emotions on the processes of identity construction has been examined quite thoroughly in psychology, sociology, and psychotherapy (Barrett, 1995; Gilbert, 1998; Lewis, 1992; Neckel, 1991; Retzinger, 1998; Scheff, 1998, 2003; Schore, 1998; Tagney, 1995). These studies agree that shame is an intense negative experience that has a strong impact on individuals' actions. The anticipation of shame leads to the avoidance of situations, and the anticipation of pride can be an important source of motivation for efforts to construct a specific setting. This chapter aims to show that a youth culture such as hip-hop can be seen as such a setting and as an outcome or way of coping with unsatisfying life situations.

These various strings of development can be summarized as follows: An adolescent is confronted with the goal of attaining an emotionally balanced personality. This goal implies the development of strategies of emotion regulation on several levels. The development of emotion regulation means that children learn which of the possible emotional reactions is suitable for attaining current goals and for acting according to social norms and rules (Friedlmeier, 1999). A discrepancy between the subjective view of the self and imposed developmental goals can arouse severe negative feelings. Zimmermann (1999, p. 230) remarked that adolescents tend toward emphasized self-representation to regulate these feelings and use music or fashion as a symbolic addition to their concept of self. This remark is one of the few hints in the literature on the relation between emotion regulation and the genesis of a new cultural style.

Toward a Broad View of Emotion Regulation

During the past three decades, emotion regulation has become a central topic of discussion and research in various disciplines. It is generally defined as "the selection and implementation of emotion responses and emotion-related action strategies" (Kitayama, Karasawa, & Mesquita, 2004, p. 252). In this volume, emotions are seen primarily as functional bio-cultural processes that organize and motivate human actions and reactions to events in the environment. Nevertheless, they have to be controlled or regulated constantly by the individual. Uncontrolled emotions or emotional expressions often do not conform to social rules and can, for this or other reasons, obstruct personal long- and short-term goals. The emotions of shame and pride are important in this context because they are deeply connected to the values and standards of society. Of course, emotion regulation is not only a task for the individual but is also a social phenomenon; it takes place not only within but between persons.

Furthermore, human emotions go along with specific pleasant or unpleasant feelings. Motivated by the anticipation of social reactions, individuals regulate emotions and actions, for example, to avoid feelings of shame and attain a positive self-image through feelings of pride. To prolong a positive feeling or to reach a more pleasant one, individuals can therefore try to regulate their emotions or avoid situations that evoke negative emotions and seek situations known to elicit positive ones. This difference in the focus of regulation was pointed out by Lazarus (1991), who called the two basic strategies "emotion-focused regulation" and "problem-focused regulation." The case of youth and hip-hop, which is discussed in more detail later, is an example of problem-focused regulation.

The discussion on emotion regulation in teenagers frequently emphasizes the styles of coping with the problems of adolescence (Hauser & Bowlds, 1990). The definition of coping, as Seiffge-Krenke and others use it, is based on the writing of Lazarus, Averill, and Opton (1974), who saw it as "problem-solving efforts made by an individual when the demands he/she faces are highly relevant ... and tax his/her adaptive resources" (p. 29).

Although sociology has added some important thoughts to the discussion—for example, on the question of emotion work (Hochschild, 1983)—the interplay between emotion regulation and the culture of a society has not been examined thoroughly up to now. Few anthropologists have examined the differing styles of emotion regulation in different cultures. Exceptions are Douglas Hollan's (1988) work on anger regulation among the Toraja in Sulawesi, Indonesia and the writings of Jean Briggs (1970) and Unni Wikan (1990). Kitayama et al. (2004) have also pointed to cultural differences in emotion regulation. They demonstrated empirically that socially disengaging emotions, such as anger and pride, are tolerated much more or even reinforced in the United States compared with the same emotions in Japan. Japanese society, in contrast, favors and promotes engaging emotions such as shame.

Most of the discussion on emotion regulation has been in the fields of psychology and developmental physiology. The main focus on the individual in these disciplines is a consequence of their areas of research. Constant feelings of frustration, humiliation, and hopelessness can lead to pathological developments in the individual. They can also be the reason for collective praxis, such as the creation of new cultural spaces that permit the development of a more positive self-image and daily experiences of related emotions such as pride. This interplay between emotion regulation and processes of cultural change or the genesis of new cultural styles has received little academic attention in the past. It is only in recent years that attempts have been made to link cultural coping resources and adolescents' identity processes. One example is the work of Spencer, Fegley, and Harpalani (2003) on identity construction among African American youth showing how it is a resource for coping with the restrictions of life in a poor black neighborhood. Another example is the work of Clay (2003), who considered how African American youth use hip-hop as a form of cultural capital in everyday settings to form a positive identity.

Hip-Hop: Arena for Emotion Regulation Through Identity Construction

The following section provides an insight into the sociocultural origins and the internal structure of hip-hop, and it shows the reasons for its enormous popularity among teenagers all over the world. This popularity is grounded in hip-hop's ability to fulfil a number of emotional needs and regulate long-term emotional deficits.

Invented in the Urban Jungle

Hip-hop is a term[3] for a global youth culture[4] that consists of rap music, break-dancing, and graffiti writing. Hip-hop was invented in the New York Bronx during the 1970s.[5] At that time, the Bronx enjoyed the ill fame of being a symbol of urban decline (Rose, 1997, p. 148). Burned-out buildings were a favored setting for movie productions about urban violence or even about a rapid breakdown of civilization (e.g., Fort Apache, Wolfen, Koyaanisqatsi—see Filmography). One of the first major rap hits describes the situation in the Bronx:

> Broken glass everywhere / people pissing on the stairs, you know they just don't care / I can't take the smell, I can't take the noise / Got no money to move out, I guess I got no choice / Rats in the front room, roaches in the back / Junkie's in the alley with a baseball bat / I tried to get away, but I couldn't get far / Cause the man with the tow-truck repossessed my car / Don't push me, cause I'm close to the edge / I'm trying not to lose my head / It's like a jungle sometimes, it makes me wonder; How I keep from going under (Excerpt from the rap song "The Message": Grandmaster Flash & the Furious Five, 1982).

At that time, no one would have thought that the Bronx, of all places, would give birth to a new cultural phenomenon that would go on to conquer young people's minds all over the world during the following three decades. However, the postindustrial urban ghetto can be seen as a necessary and central general framework for the development of hip-hop culture. As Rose (1994) stated:

> Hip hop is a cultural form that attempts to negotiate the experiences of marginalization, brutally truncated opportunity, and oppression within the cultural imperatives of African-American and Caribbean history, identity, and community. It is the tension between the cultural fractures produced by post-industrial oppression and the binding ties of black cultural expressivity that sets the critical frame for the development of hip hop. (p. 21)

Those who grew up in this environment had to face a huge gap between developing ideas about a possible individual future and the opportunities offered by society. They had to survive what was called the urban jungle. The character of the Bronx as a ghetto in the urban environment of New York City has molded hip-hop culture from its early days until its glamorous present.[6] The location of hip-hop origins in this setting gives it a deep-seated symbolism of urbanity. Its adaptation can, however, be seen as way to create an urban identity or a link to urbanity even outside any real urban life setting (Klein & Friedrich, 2003, p. 100). It can therefore satisfy desires for participation in the global culture even in the most remote parts of the world. Another important function of this inherent urbanity was worked out by Stokes (1994), who showed that "the identification with urban genres provides the means by which rural-urban migrants can transform themselves from peripheralized proletarians to urbanites" (p. 4).

The feeling of participation in a vivid and mainly positive cultural force can give the individual great satisfaction, which can, in turn, serve as a compensation for other problematic parts of daily life. In the case of hip-hop, the symbolism of an urban ghetto style is also a symbolism of (male)[7] strength and success. Those who survive in the "urban jungle" demonstrate their toughness and their cleverness.

Hip-hop's early protagonists were mostly youth with African American or Hispanic family backgrounds (Lipsitz, 1999; Mitchell, 1996; Toop, 1992). They hold a position in society once described as "structural outsiderism" (Kaya, 2001, p. 48)—another important factor for hip-hop's rise to global popularity. Hip-hop created a "new definition of cool" (Loh & Güngör, 2002, p. 23) that supported a positive identification with primordial attributes previously experienced as a stigma, such as a nonwhite skin color or a social background in an urban ghetto. Hip-hop became a space for those who felt constricted by the circumstances of their lives.

Internal Structure of Hip-Hop

It is not just the sociocultural and historical background of hip-hop that contributed to its success. The internal structure underlying rap music, breakdancing, and graffiti writing are also central to understanding the global phenomenon and its potential to solve problems arising from the specific settings in which adolescents grow up. This can be demonstrated through two main pillars of hip-hop: the artistic principles of sampling, which can be seen as bricolage, and the social principle of battle.

Sampling as a Tool for the Bricolage of an Identity

An important task for developing adolescents is the acquisition of identity. Identity should be seen a constant process, a constant change defining "Who am I?" and, of course, "Where do I belong?" for the individual. It is not only a matter of individual self-esteem but of finding a cultural identity. This can be difficult, especially for children of migrant families or other minority groups. They have to try to combine aspects of the cultural meaning systems that are different from those in which they grow up.

The first hip-hop disk jockeys (DJs)—Kool DJ Herc, Grandmaster Flash, Africa Bambaataa—invented most of the techniques that made hip-hop the perfect arena for construction of the multidimensional identity it is today. They organized block parties in their Bronx neighborhood and introduced the techniques of cutting and sampling to pop music. Cutting is the basis for the so-called break-beats, later becoming the rhythmic fundament of a large part of pop music during the last three decades. The DJ uses only selected rhythmic parts of a record that he or she can extend by playing the same record on a second turntable. This fundamental beat was enriched by short vocal or other acoustic pieces, so-called samples. These samples are either taken from other records or recorded on the street (e.g., a police siren). DJs started to combine different styles of music and therefore created something completely new. They became musicians and authors. Music became a material with which they could make new music. In this new music, the old song was negated, conserved, and elevated (Poschardt, 1997, p. 168).[8]

Hip-Hop Battle as a Source of Respect

The MC (Master of Ceremony) builds on this newly constructed music for his or her rap. In the early days of rap music, raps consisted mostly of rhymes calling on the crowd to dance. These rhymes soon became more elaborate, and MCs started to rap all kinds of stories from their lives. In the words of Chuck D, a member of the rap group Public Enemy, rap became the CNN of the black ghetto.

Owing to the explicit content of many rap lyrics, hip-hop is often associated with the glorification of violence and criminal behavior. Interpersonal violence was and still is one of the biggest problems in the Bronx and other poor inner-city communities whose members have to learn the "code of the street" (Anderson, 1994) to handle themselves in a street-oriented environment. This code is a set of rules dealing with the distribution of an important resource in this context: respect. In the social structure of urban ghettos, the feeling of being respected and the connected emotion of pride about one's own abilities are highly valued. Those who are not respected and who are not able to respond in a proper way to the often violent challenges on the street continuously have a hard time in their daily lives. The constant struggle for the commodity that is "hard-won but easily lost" (Anderson, 1994, p. 82) is often a violent one. The teenagers who have to face it are confronted with feelings of fear, despair, and hopelessness.

"Being respected" in this context implies a feeling of safety, something that is needed in a neighborhood in which the police are perceived as an enemy. Respect becomes a matter of successfully facing violent challenges on the street or of challenging others. It is also often connected to having expensive clothes or jewelry. Of course, this kind of respect is precarious because possessions make their owner a potential victim of others who want to gain respect by attaining trophies. A pair of sneakers can have a high symbolic value and be the reason for serious fights (Anderson, 1994, p. 88).

The demonstration of material wealth is also an important part of hip-hop. However, the competition for respect also found a new arena within hip-hop culture that helped to reduce violent conflicts. In the early days of hip-hop, the MCs and DJs, as well as the breakers and writers, began to compete against each other with their skills. The hip-hop battle was invented and developed its own rules. DJ and producer Africa Bambaataa is sometimes called the "father of hip-hop culture" because he appealed to the youth of his neighborhood to battle each other in the artistic disciplines of hip-hop and to put away the weapons of gang warfare. Hip-hop crews formed that recruited their members from existing street gangs. They provided a new kind of social support to the youth of the Bronx. Hip-hop can thus be seen as a space in which street youths find a creative way of dealing with the frustrations and handicaps of their situation and coping with the emotions of hopelessness, shame, fear, and lack of self-esteem. The hip-hop battle became a way to gain respect in a peaceful way because hip-hop kids are respected for their skills and their style. They were able to train skills they could be proud of within their peer group without constantly risking their life to earn respect.

A writer earns respect and becomes famous on the streets by demonstrating an elaborated artistic style when painting graffiti pieces in highly visible spaces that are difficult and dangerous to reach. A DJ sways the crowd with his well selected material and mixing skills. A rapper needs flow and rhetorical talent. A rap battle is about boasting and "dissing" at the highest possible rhetoric level:

> I used to guzzle 40's, and own a beat up Caddy / Since the hood still love me, I'll turn the heat up daddy / I went from mackin' fly honies on the train / to straight relaxin' on the beach, countin' money getting' brain / Soon as you rappers get a chance you wanna floss a lot / You buy a iced out watch because it cost a lot / Then you in the club, stylin' with dough / Profilin' with hoes that we boned, a while ago /You rookies haven't done enough laps around the track / You had one hot single, but then your album sounds wack / Son you bore me with your war stories / You ain't even do that shit, so that's just more stories / How you expect us to take you seriously? / The look in my eye punk, has got you scared of me / I'm blastin' your sons, I'm snatchin' your funds / You catch a royal ass-whoopin, you've been askin' for one (Excerpt from the rap song "Battle Lyrics": Gang Starr, 2002).

Local Adaptations of a Global Phenomenon

Over the last three decades, hip-hop has conquered the minds of adolescents all over the world. Although this is often described as the product of a U.S. cultural imperialism,[9] this position becomes unconvincing when the local specification and variation of hip-hop are examined carefully. The rhythmic fundament of today's rap music is often an artistic link between an individual or group history and its imagined future, between local identity and global belonging; it is an easy way of expressing multidimensional cultural identity. Kaya (2001) showed this in his impressive work on Turkish hip-hop youth in Berlin. Turkish youth can use their ethnicity as a strategic instrument to demonstrate authenticity and construct an identity that combines their different worlds. Kaya identifies several emotional problems and paradoxes that hip-hop helps solve or regulate. Whereas youth have a strong desire for autonomy from the traditional world of their parents, they also have a need for collectivity. They want to participate in global urban culture, but, at the same time they want be proud of their (ethnic) roots. They may experience a nostalgic feeling toward the history of their families in Turkey as well as an anxious desire to be connected to a yet undetected future. The rap music of these German-Turkish groups often contains samples of traditional Turkish "Arabesk" music expressing a: "dialogue between past and future, between homeland and country of residence, between different worlds of meaning, between various life-worlds, between global winds and local resistance, between 'roots' and 'routes,' between here and there" (Kaya, 2001, p. 174).

Another example is found in Amsterdam, where children of Surinamese immigrants use rap music and hip-hop culture to redefine their cultural identity in a "complicated process of evaluation and reinterpretation of one's culture and traditions" (Sansone, 1995, p. 127). They use hip-hop to perceive themselves not only as a part of a marginalized, poor migrant population in a country that confronts them with racism and few opportunities but also as members of a successful global urban style in which "being black" means "being cool." Other impressive examples were given by Mitchell (1999), who saw global rap as a "resistance vernacular" used to construct local cultural identity and articulate it in a global style. This seems to be true in a number of places, ranging from Greenland, where the rap band Nuuk Posse raps in the Inuit language to protest the Danish domination in Greenland; to French rappers using the Verlan slang of the suburbs for their critique of racism; to Maori youth, whose most important reason to learn the Maori language is to be able to rap in Maori.

Graffiti and Break-Dancing: Control of Space and Body

In addition to rap music, break-dancing and graffiti writing comprise important parts of hip-hop culture. The roots of contemporary street graffiti can be seen in the name tags street gangs used to mark their territory. During the 1970s, graffiti in the Bronx emancipated itself from this role and became something new (see Cross, 1993; Toop, 1992). Graffiti writers began to roam the streets at night to paint walls and subway trains beyond their original neighborhoods. Their writings were no longer connected to gang activities; hip-hop writers wanted to spread their own name tags (and those of their crews) over town. Their writings became more elaborated and colorful; style became the central issue. Today, a global graffiti underground exists with some writers being well known everywhere. Most graffiti activities are illegal and sometimes prosecuted fiercely. This may well be one of the reasons why one of the biggest art movements at the end of the 20th century still receives little commercial and even less academic attention.

Among the rare scientific works on graffiti, two studies have examined the function of graffiti as a creative means for youth to cope with the collective trauma of Yitzhak Rabin's assassination in Israel (Klingman, Shalev, & Pearlman, 2000; Luzzatto & Jacobson, 2001). Klingman et al. (2000) regarded graffiti as "a mode of communication with others that allows personal expression while behaving in an unconventional way and changing the environment while conducting a negotiation with it; thus, exercising some mastery/control" (p. 300). Of course these—mostly politically motivated—writings differ greatly from the hip-hop graffiti that mostly features the name of the writer or of his or her crew. However, it may be regarded as similar in one of its core motivators: It is also about changing or even conquering public space. Hip-hop graffiti reflects the desire to control and form an environment that actually does control and shape the life of the individual. The battle principle of hip-hop is also present in graffiti; but battles in graffiti are not as central as in rapping or breaking. The distribution of respect and fame—as writers call it—inside the graffiti scene follows different rules. A writer gains fame mostly by being active for a long time and constantly developing his or her personal style. Alongside the quality, it is also the quantity of work and the token risk that are important.

The case of break-dancing is somewhat different. It is not control of the environment for which the breaker strives but control of his or her own body. In daily training, breakers develop highly artistic bodily skills. Competition in a battle is a regular event for many breakers.

German youth research has pointed out that the breakers, who are mainly of migrant origin, do not just gain control of their body. Break dancing also forms a "third sphere" alongside the "inner sphere" of traditional family life and the "outer sphere" of German society's rules and standards (Nohl, 2003). Teenagers use this space for a process of intercultural learning while avoiding some of the most disturbing cultural expectations from both their families and the surrounding society. It is a space for action, for body experience, and even for experimental biographical options for the most ambitious dancers.

Summary: Rise of a Youth Culture as a Way of Creating a Space for Positive Emotion Experiences

Emotions help individuals find orientation in the world. If these emotions about the world and one's own position within it constantly evoke negative feelings such as fear or shame, they may lead to attempts to alter one's situation. Basic emotional needs such as feeling safe in one's neighborhood, feeling part of a group that cares, or developing self-esteem are difficult to fulfill for many ghetto youth. Their marginalized position within society and experiences of discrimination can be a constant source of feelings of shame, contributing to a negative self-image. A popular way of dealing with these emotional deficits is the formation of violent youth gangs. Another, more peaceful and creative manner of regulating these emotional problems can be seen in the creation of hip-hop groups. In this chapter, I have tried to show that these groups offer a space that satisfies various emotional demands. Within hip-hop, teenagers construct a positive identity via a process that can be viewed as a "real-time coping response" (Spencer et al., 2003, p. 183) to the constraints of their environment. The history and the internal structure of hip-hop turn this youth culture into an ideal space for the experience of positive emotions.

Although hip-hop has remained especially popular among the adolescents of marginalized groups of various societies, during the last three decades it has also become the largest mainstream pop culture. It has developed into a highly complex multidimensional phenomenon with different subgenres attractive to different target groups.[10] Therefore, hip-hop today offers a space that is used for various, sometimes contrasting, purposes. Some use it to escape the urban ghetto in which they live and others to produce urbanity and a global life style in a rural setting. However, most hip-hop youths are unified in their feelings of powerlessness against which they fight in the performance of their youth culture.

The innovative element in hip-hop can be found on two levels: The first is the principle of *sampling* invented by the early hip-hop DJs. This became a tool for multilevel identity constructions on a musical level and was/is used by teenagers to connect the various influences in their environment. Sampling constructs spaces in which the tensions between an urge for local authenticity and the desire for participation in a global cultural interaction can be released. In these spaces, an identity can be constructed allowing teenagers to be proud of their cultural origins while simultaneously escaping the restrictions they impose. The structure of rap music makes it possible to tell the individual and local story in a global "language" accompanied by a "glocal" beat. The beat is "glocal" because it connects the global hip-hop youth culture with local traditions and history.

Second is the *hip-hop battle*-the way of competing with artistic styles and skills. Central to the hip-hop battle is the possibility of gaining respect for the individual and the individual's peer group. It is a way to experience feelings of pride and, for many youngsters, nearly the only way to do so. The importance of the hip-hop battle points to the significance of artistic performance in this youth culture. Only by performing is it possible to gain respect in hip-hop. The central rule is: "You are what you're doing." By developing a specific style, individuals develop identity and define a border separating them from those who only consume and imitate (bite) the style: "denn es geht nicht um Hip-Kleidung, Hop-Konsum; der Kaufmonsum zerstört mein HipHop-Heiligtum" (excerpt from the rap song "Fenster zum Hof": Stieber Twins, 1997).[11]

Hip-hop was invented by youths who must have been seriously dissatisfied with their daily life and their opportunities for the future. Confronted with social and racial discrimination, they had to deal with feelings of shame and anger. At the same time, these youngsters must have been looking for fun and opportunities to develop their talents and be proud of them. They created a youth culture that went on to conquer the world because it was adopted by thousands of teenagers sharing the same desires.

This chapter has tried to show that youth not only use the culturally available means for these identity processes but also construct new ones to find an arena for the development of self-esteem.

Notes

1 Dealing with these challenges is sometimes especially difficult for the children of marginalized urban groups, as is shown later in the chapter.

2 Röttger-Rössler (this volume) provides a good example of such changes.

3 For the history and origins of the term, see Dorsey (2000, p. 327) and Poschardt (1996, p. 154).

[4] A first overview on the global significance of hip-hop was given by Mitchell (2001a).

[5] Toop (1992) gave a detailed account of hip-hop history and its sources in African American culture.

[6] See Verlan (2003, pp. 104–109) for a breakdown on the major influence of the ghetto-culture image on the adoption of hip-hop in France and Germany.

[7] Hip-hop has been a mostly male phenomenon, although there are many female rappers, writers, and dancers. For the influence of women in hip-hop's early years, see Guevara (1996).

[8] A similar structure can be observed in break-dancing, a dance developed at the early block parties in the Bronx. Break-dancing borrows from elements of African and African American dances as well as from East Asian martial arts and the Brazilian "dance-fight" capoeira (George, 1998, pp. 14–16; Guevara, 1996, p. 50; Mitchell, 2001b, p. 7).

[9] For a critical summary of this position, see Androutsopoulos and Scholz (1999) or Klein and Friedrich (2003).

[10] For the historical development of various genres in rap music, see Krims (2000) or Kage (2002).

[11] Rough translation: It's not hip gear; it's not hip consume. The consume monsoon; it's destroying my hip-hop sanctum. [AU: Is the word "consume" correct here (in two places)? Please verify.

Glossary of Terms

Afrika Bambaataa	Central person in hip-hop history. The New Yorker is a DJ, a producer, and the founder of the Zulu Nation.
Battle	Term for the hip-hop competition. It should not be viewed as a kind of sport played for its own sake. The battle is about facing a challenge-not losing face but earning respect and fame. Quality in a battle is a question of skills and style.
Battleraps	Rap lyrics consisting of highly elaborated insults (dissing) directed toward the opponent rapper or his crew and also swaggering about one's own skills (boasting).
Beats	background music forming the fundament for the rap lyrics. On stage, these are often produced by a DJ who combines selected sequences of different records on his turntables. They are also called break-beats because in the old days of hip-hop only the instrumental sequences (breaks) between the vocal parts of a song were used by the DJs.
Biting	Term for copying someone else's style, which is not popular in the rap and graffiti scene.
Boasting	Praising one's own neighborhood or city, the crew, or one's own style or skills.
Breaking	Term for the break-dance. Breaking is just one of three main break-dance styles-the other two are popping and locking. Today, breaking is most popular, although dancers frequently use elements of the other styles (Klein & Friedrich, 2003, p. 33).
Crew	Hip-hop group of peers.
Cutting	Term for the combination and repetition of short rhythmic or vocal parts of a record, attained with the help of a *mixer*.
Dissing	Short for disrespecting somebody.

Fame	Gaining fame is a central motivation in hip-hop.
Flow	Alongside style and skills, flow is a central aesthetic criterion in hip-hop. The flow of a writer is the fluent and harmonic transition between one letter and the next; the rappers' flow is the speed, intonation, and structure of the rhymes. There is a smooth transition between style and flow; flow is more a term for the technical part of the art, whereas style refers to the personal long-term development.
Freestyle rap	The art of rapping spontaneous improvisational rhymes.
Gangsta rap	Genre of rap music often criticized for glorifying violence and the use of explicit language.
Grandmaster Flash	One of the first hip-hop DJs who played a central role in the development of DJ techniques.
Human beat-boxing	Vocal production of a beat as a background for the rapper that the artist uses to replace the DJ or the electronic beat. Human beat-boxing is often used for rapping in schoolyards or on the street.
King	A writer who has been active for a very long time and who is famous for the quantity and quality of his graffiti pieces (see van Treeck, 2001, p. 180).
Kool DJ Herc	A famous DJ, sometimes the called the "father of hip-hop" because he organized the first hip-hop block parties in the Bronx.
MC	Master of Ceremony: a rapper presenting a good show on stage. A lot of rappers have made this token a part of their stage name (e.g., MC Lyte from the United States, MC Solaar from France, and the German MC Rene).
Party rap	Genre of rap music.
Piece	Writer language for a big multicolor mural, mostly the name of the writer or his or her crew.
Posse	Another word for crew but with a wider significance. The membership in a crew is more clearly defined.
Rap battle	Competition between two MCs regarding their spontaneous rhyming skills. Usually the crowd decides who is better through loud cheering.
Rapping	The verb "to rap" has been known since the 17th century in the African American language with changing meanings. Since the 19th century, it has been used for a special way of speaking. At the beginning of the 20th century, a rapper was a police informer. Later, the term came to be used for rhythmic speaking with or without music (Dorsey, 2000, pp. 326–327; Poschardt, 1997, p. 154).
Respect	To attain the respect of others is an important source of motivation for many youths in hip-hop. Respect can be gained mainly by the quality of a performance (although quantity can also be important for writers). Individuals who have been active in hip-hop for a long time are also respected.
Sample	Short piece of a song that is isolated and used within another song. Samples are also taken from movies or speeches.
Sampler	Technical device used for sampling. A lot of modern DJ mixers have integrated samplers, allowing them to sample "on the fly."
Sampling	The use of short pieces of existing music, recorded sounds, or acoustic parts of a movie for a new composition. Sampling is electronic citation.
Scratching	Isolating sound elements and creating rhythm by manual front and back spinning of a record. Grandwizard Theodore, a friend of Grandmaster Flash, seems to be the inventor of this technique (Werner, 2002, p. 58). Scratching has evolved into a complex discipline over the last three decades, and there are now world championships in "turntableism." Some DJ crews create music that consists only of scratching and cutting sounds from a number of turntables.

Style	Central criteria of the hip-hop aesthetic. For a rapper, a DJ, a breaker, or a writer, the development and improvement of a unique style is the most important thing.
Tag	Unicolored, graphically designed signature of a writer or a crew. Tags are the prototype of graffiti. Graffiti history once started with tags, and even today the first steps of a writer are usually easy tags before he or she tries to paint big pieces.
Toy	Writer term for a beginner or an untalented sprayer. The term is also used for other performances that are seen as bad or "unreal" (e.g., toy rap).
Westcoast	Usually means rap from Los Angeles. Typical westcoast genres are gangsta rap and player rap. Of course, these genres can also be found elsewhere.
Wholecar	Writer term for a piece covering a whole railway car (for detailed information, (see van Treeck, 2001, p. 408).
Writing	Term for spraying and painting graffiti.
Zulu Nation	Globally organized union of hip-hop that changed from a street gang dedicated to using hip-hop as an alternative way of life to a huge organization that developed a strong link to religious movements.

References

Anderson, E. (1994). The code of the streets. *The Atlantic Monthly*, *5*, 81–94.

Androutsopoulos, J., & Scholz, A. (1999). On the recontextualisation of hip hop in European speech communities. Retrieved April 30, 2005 from http://www.archetype.de/hiphop/ascona.html

Auchter, T., & Hilgers, M. (1994). Delinquenz und Schamgefühl: Zur Bedeutung von Stolz und Scham bei Straftätern [Delinquency and feeling ashamed: The role of pride and shame in offenders]. *Monatszeitschrift für Kriminologie und Strafrechtsreform*, *77*(2), 102–113.

Barrett, K. C. (1995). A functionalist approach to shame and guilt. In J. P. Tagney & K. W. Fischer (Eds.), *Self-conscious emotions. The psychology of shame, guilt, embarrassment, and pride* (pp. 25–63). New York: The Guilford Press.

Briggs, J. (1970). *Never in anger*. Cambridge MA: Harvard University Press.

Clarke, J. (1979): Stil [Style]. In H. Berger, A. Honneth, R. Lindner, U. Maas, J. Paech, & R. Paris (Eds.), *Jugendkultur als Widerstand. Milieus, Rituale, Provokationen*. Frankfurt am Main, Germany: Syndikat Autoren und Verlagswerkstatt.

Clay, A. (2003): Keepin' it real: Black youth, hip-hop culture, and black identity. *American Behavioral Scientist*, *46*(10), 1346–1358.

Cross, B. (1993): *It's not about a salary... Rap, race, and resistance in Los Angeles*. London, New York: Verso.

Dorsey, B. (2000). *Spirituality, sensuality, literality. Blues, jazz, and rap as music and poetry*. Vienna: Wilhelm Braumüller Verlag.

Elder, G. (1994). Time, human agency, and social change: Perspectives on the life course. *Social Psychology Quarterly*, *57*(1), 4–15.

Fend, H. (1997). Der Umgang mit Schule in der Adoleszenz. Aufbau und Verlust von Lernmotivation, Selbstachtung und Empathie [Handling school in adolescence: Formation and loss of learning motivation, self-esteem, and empathy].*Entwicklungspsychologie der Adoleszenz in der Moderne* (Vol. 4). Bern, Switzerland: Huber.

Fend, H. (1998). Eltern und Freunde. Soziale Entwicklung im Jugendalter [Parents and friends: Social development in adolescence].*Entwicklungspsychologie der Adoleszenz in der Moderne* (Vol. 5). Bern, Switzerland: Huber.

Fend, H. (2000): *Entwicklungspsychologie des Jugendalters. Ein Lehrbuch für pädagogische und psychologische Berufe* [Adolescent developmental psychology: A textbook for educational and psychological professions]. Opladen, Germany: Leske + Budrich.
Ferchhoff, W., & Neubauer, G. (1997). *Patchwork-Jugend: Eine Einführung in postmoderne Sichtweisen* [Patchwork youth: An introduction to postmodern perspectives]. Opladen, Germany: Leske + Budrich.
Friedlmeier, W. (1999). Sozialisation der Emotionsregulation [Socialization of emotion regulation]. *Zeitschrift für Soziologie der Erziehung, 19*(1), 35–51.
George, N. (1998). *Hip hop America*. New York: Penguin.
Gilbert, (1998). What is shame? Some core issues and controversies. In P. Gilbert (Ed.), *Shame. Interpersonal behavior, psychopathology, and culture* (pp. 3–38). New York: Oxford University Press.
Goossens, L, Seiffge-Krenke, I., & Marcoen, A. (1992). The many faces of adolescent egocentrism: Two European replications. *Journal of Adolescent Research, 7*(1), 43–58.
Guevara, N. (1996). Women writin' rappin' breakin'. In W. E. Perkins (Ed.), *Droppin' science: Critical essays on rap music and hip hop culture* (pp. 49–62). Philadelphia, PA: Temple University Press.
Hauser, S. T., & Bowlds, M. K. (1990). Stress, coping, and adaptation. In S. S Feldman & G. R. Elliot (Eds.), *At the threshold: The developing adolescent* (pp. 388–413). Cambridge, MA: Harvard University Press.
Hochschild, A. (1983). *The managed heart*. Berkeley, CA: University of California Press.
Hollan, D. (1988). Staying "cool" in Toraja: Informal strategies for the management of anger and hostility in a nonviolent society. *Ethos, 16*, 52–72.
Holodynski, M., & Friedlmeier, W. (2006). *Development of emotions and emotion regulation*. Boston, MA: Kluwer Academic.
Kage, J. (2002). *American rap: Explicit lyrics—US-HipHop und Identität* [US hip-hop and identity]. Mainz, Germany: Ventil.
Kaya, A. (2001). *"Sicher in Kreuzberg." Constructing diasporas: Turkish hip-hop youth in Berlin*. Bielefeld, Germany: Transcript.
Kitayama, S., Karasawa, M., & Mesquita, B. (2004). Collective and personal processes in regulating emotions: Emotion and self in Japan and the United States. In P. Phillipot & R. S. Feldman (Eds.), *The regulation of emotion* (pp. 251–273). Mahwah, NJ: Lawrence Erlbaum.
Klein, G., & Friedrich, M. (2003). *Is this real? Die Kultur des HipHop* [The culture of hip-hop]. Frankfurt am Main, Germany: Suhrkamp.
Klingman, A., Shalev, R., & Perlman, A. (2000). Graffiti: A creative means of youth coping with collective trauma. *The Arts in Psychotherapy, 27*(5), 299–307.
Krims, A. (2000). *Rap music and the poetics of identity*. Cambridge, England: Cambridge University Press.
Lambrich, H.-J. (1987). *Schulleistung, Selbstkonzeption und Unterrichtsverhalten. Eine qualitative Untersuchung zur Situation "schlechter" Schüler* [Academic achievement, self-concept, and teaching behavior: A qualitative study of the situation of "poor" students]. Weinheim, Germany: Deutscher Studien Verlag.
Lazarus, R. S. (1991). *Emotion and adaptation*. New York: Oxford University Press.
Lazarus, R. S., Averill, J., & Opton, E. M. (1974). The psychology of coping. In G. V. Coelho, D. A. Hamburg, & J. E. Adams (Eds.), *Coping and adaptation* (pp. 249–315). New York: Basic Books.
Lempers, J. D., & Clark-Lempers, D. S. (1992). Young, middle, and late adolescents' comparisions of the functional importance of five significant relationships. *Journal of Youth and Adolescence, 21*(1), 53–98.
Lewis, M. (1992). *Shame: The exposed self*. New York: Free Press.
Lipsitz, G. (1999). *Dangerous Crossroads: Popmusik, Postmoderne und die Poesie des Lokalen* [Pop music, the postmodern, and the poetry of the local]. St. Andrä-Wördern, Austria: Hannibal.

Loh, H., & Güngör, M. (2002). *Fear of a Kanak Planet. HipHop zwischen Weltkultur und Nazirap* [Hip-hop between world culture and Nazi rap]. Höfen, Austria: Hannibal.
Luzzatto, D., & Jacobson, Y. (2001). Youth graffiti as an existential coping device: The case of Rabin's assassination. *Journal of Youth Studies, 4*(3), 351–365.
Mesquita, B., & Markus, H. R. (2004). Culture and emotion: Models of agency as sources of cultural variation in emotion. In A. S. R. Manstead, N. Frijda, & A. Fischer (Eds.), *Feelings and emotions. The Amsterdam Symposium* (pp. 341–358). Cambridge, England: Cambridge University Press.
Mitchell, T. (1996). *Popular music and local identity. Rock, pop and rap in Europe and Oceania. London*. New York: Leicester University Press.
Mitchell, T. (1999). Doin' damage in my native language: The use of "resistance vernaculars" in hip hop in France, Italy and Aotearoa/New Zealand. Retrieved June 10, 2005 from http://www.international.activism.uts.edu.au/conferences/protglob/p_mitchell.html
Mitchell, T. (2001a). *Global noise. Rap and hip-hop outside the USA*. Middletown, CT: Wesleyan University Press.
Mitchell, T. (2001b). Another root—Hip-hop outside the USA. In T. Mitchell (Ed.), *Global noise. Rap and hip-hop outside the USA* (pp. 1–38). Middletown, CT: Wesleyan University Press.
Neckel, S. (1991). *Status und Scham. Zur symbolischen Reproduktion sozialer Ungleichheiten* [Status and shame: The symbolic reproduction of social inequalities]. Frankfurt am Main, Germany: Campus.
Nieder, T., & Seiffge-Krenke, I. (2001). Coping with stress in different phases of romantic development. *Journal of Adolescence, 24*, 297–311.
Nohl, A.-M. (2003). Interkulturelle Bildungsprozesse im Breakdance [Intercultural education processes in break-dancing]. In J. Androutsopoulos (Ed.), *HipHop: Globale Kultur – lokale Praktiken* (pp. 297–320). Bielefeld, Germany: Transcript Verlag.
Offer, D., Ostrov, E. J. D.. Howard, K. I., & Atkinson, R. (1988). *The teenage world: Adolescents' self-image in ten countries*. New York, London: Plenum Medical Book Company.
Parker, J. G., & Gottman, J. M. (1989). Social and emotional development in a relational context: Friendship interaction from early childhood to adolescence. In T. J. Berndt & G. W. Ladd (Eds.), *Peer relationships in child development* (pp. 95–131). New York: Wiley-Interscience Publication.
Poschardt, U. (1997). *DJ-Culture. Diskjockeys und Popkultur* [Disk jockeys and pop culture]. Hamburg, Germany: Rowohlt.
Retzinger, S. M. (1998). Shame in the therapeutic relationship. In P. Gilbert (Ed.), *Shame. Interpersonal behavior, psychopathology, and culture* (pp. 206–224). New York, Oxford: Oxford University Press.
Rose, T. (1994). *Black noise: Rap music and black culture in contemporary America*. Hanover, NH: University Press of New England.
Rose, T. (1997). Ein Stil mit dem keiner klar kommt: HipHop in der postindustriellen Stadt [A style nobody can handle: Hip-hop in the postindustrial city]. In Arbeitsgruppe für Symbolische Politik, Kultur und Kommunikation (Ed.), *Kursbuch Jugendkultur: Stile, Szenen und Identitäten vor der Jahrtausendwende* (pp. 142–156). Mannheim, Germany: Bollmann.
Sansone, L. (1995). The making of a black youth culture. Lower-class young men of Surinamese origin in Amsterdam. In V. Amit-Talai & H. Wulff (Eds.), *Youth cultures: A cross-cultural perspective* (pp. 114–143). London, New York: Routledge.
Scheff, T. J. (1988): Shame and conformity: The deference-emotion system. *American Sociological Review, 52*, 395–406.
Scheff, T. J. (1998). Shame in the labeling of mental illness. In P. Gilbert (Ed.), *Shame. Interpersonal behavior, psychopathology, and culture* (pp. 191–205). New York, Oxford: Oxford University Press.
Scheff, T. (2003). Shame in self and society. *Symbolic Interaction, 26*(2), 239–262.

Scheff, T. J., & Retzinger, S. M. (2000). Shame as the master emotion of everyday life. *Journal of Mundane Behavior*. Retrieved July 14, 2005 from http://www.mundanebehavior.org/index.htm

Schore, A. N. (1998). Early shame experiences and infant brain development. In P. Gilbert (Ed.), *Shame. Interpersonal behavior, psychopathology, and culture* (pp. 57–97). New York, Oxford: Oxford University Press.

Seiffge-Krenke, I. (1992). Coping behavior of Finish adolescents: Remarks on cross-cultural comparison. *Scandinavian Journal of Psychology*, *33*, 301–314.

Seiffge-Krenke, I. (1995). *Stress, coping, and relationships in adolescence*. Mahwah, NJ: Lawrence Erlbaum.

Seiffge-Krenke, I. (2002). Emotionale Kompetenz im Jugendalter: Ressourcen und Gefährdungen [Emotional competence in adolescence: Resources and threats]. In M. Von Salisch (Ed.), *Emotionale Kompetenz entwickeln: Grundlagen in Kindheit und Jugend* (pp. 51–72). Stuttgart, Germany: Kohlhammer.

Spencer, M. B.; Fegley, S. G., & Harpalani, V. (2003). A theoretical and empirical examination of identity as coping: Linking coping resources to the self processes of African American youth. *Applied Developmental Science*, *7*(3), 181–188.

Stokes, M. (1994). *Ethnicity, identity and music: The musical construction of place*. Oxford, England: Berg.

Tagney, J. P. (1995). Shame and guilt in interpersonal relationships. In J. P. Tagney & K. W. Fischer (Eds.), *Self-conscious emotions. The psychology of shame, guilt, embarrassment, and pride* (pp. 114–142). New York: The Guilford Press.

Toop, D. (1992). *Rap Attack. African Jive bis Global HipHop* [From African jive to global hip-hop]. Höfen, Austria: Hannibal.

van Treeck, B. (2001). *Das große Graffiti-Lexikon* [The big graffiti dictionary]. Berlin: Schwarzkopf & Schwarzkopf.

Verlan, S. (2003). *French Connection. HipHop-Dialoge zwischen Frankreich und Deutschland* [Hip-hop dialogue between France and Germany]. Höfen, Austria: Hannibal.

Werner, G. (2002). Grandmaster Flash: The Darth Vader of the slide fader is back. *Juice*, *3*, 58–64.

Wikan, U. (1990). *Managing turbulent hearts: A Balinese formula for living*. Chicago, IL: University of Chicago Press.

Youniss, J., & Smollar, J. (1989). Adolescents' interpersonal relationships in social context. In T. J. Berndt & G. W. Ladd (Eds.), *Peer relationships in child development* (pp. 300–316). New York: Wiley-Interscience Publication.

Zimmermann, P. (1999). Emotionsregulation im Jugendalter [Emotion regulation in adolescence]. In W. Friedlmeier & M. Holodynski (Eds.), *Emotionale Entwicklung* (pp. 219–240). Heidelberg, Germany: Spektrum der Wissenschaft.

Zimmermann, P. (2001). Gleichaltrigengruppe und Jugendkultur [Perr group and youth culture]. In H. Lukesch (Ed.), *Erziehung, Bildung und Sozialisation in Deutschland* (pp. 335–346). Regensburg, Germany: Roderer.

Zinnecker, J. (2000): Selbstsozialisation—Essay über ein aktuelles Konzept [Self-socialization: Essay on a topical concept]. *Zeitschrift für Sozialisationsforschung und Erziehungssoziologie*, *20*(3), 272–290.

Discography

Dukes, L, Glover, N., & Saddler, J. (1987). I am somebody [recorded by Grandmaster Flash & The Furious Five]. On *Ba-Dop-Boom-Bang* [LP]. New York: Elektra Entertainment Music.

Elam, K. (2002). Battle lyrics [recorded by Gang Starr]. On *8 Mile Soundtrack* [LP]. Santa Monica, CA: Interscope Records (Universal Music Group).

Fletcher, E., Glover, M, Robinson, S., & Chase, J. (1982). The message [recorded by Grandmaster Flash & The Furious Five]. On *The Message* [LP]. New York: Sugarhill Records Ltd.
Stieber, M., & Stieber, C. (1997). Fenster zum Hof [Backyard window] [recorded by Stieber Twins] on *Fenster zum Hof* [LP]. Munich, Germany: Arabella Musikverlag GmbH (BMG UFA Musikverlage).

Filmography

Hitzig, R. (Producer), & Wadleigh, M. (Director). (1981). *Wolfen* [Motion picture]. United States: Orion Pictures.
Reggio, G. (Producer & Director). (1983). *Koyaanisqatsi* [Motion picture]. United States: IRE (Institute for Regional Education).
Richards, M. (Producer), & Petrie, D. (Director). (1981). *Fort Apache, the Bronx* [Motion picture]. United States: Time-Life/Motion Picture Division.

Shame and Pride: Invisible Emotions in Classroom Research

Manfred Holodynski and Stefanie Kronast

Abstract This chapter deals with the role of shame and pride in school learning and achievement situations. It discusses the proposition that these emotions are ubiquitous in academic learning, although they seem surprisingly "invisible"—not only for their protagonists, the students and teachers, but in the scientific literature on teaching and learning at school. On the one hand, it can be clearly shown that the institution of school generates a great variety of opportunities for students to experience shame and pride not only while performing its societal tasks of qualification, allocation, and socialization but also because it provides students with a peer group. On the other hand, what the sociologist Thomas Scheff called the "invisibility" of shame in Western cultures can also be shown: Shame in particular has not been a part of public and scientific discourses on academic learning. To fill this gap, we examine how far well established scientific concepts such as the academic self-concept, self-esteem, and achievement motivation, which are so relevant in the school context, are linked to experiences of pride and shame, and why it would be a worthwhile endeavor to analyze them from the perspective of a psychology of emotions.

Introduction

> In our Western, achievement-oriented societies, school plays a central role in socialization throughout childhood and adolescence. As a major part of the child-rearing and education system, it does not just impart socially relevant knowledge but also the central norms and values of the specific culture. School also plays a decisive role in the later career track of students. Young persons with no school-leaving qualifications have to face exclusion from adult social life right from the start (Nyssen, 1995).

Hence, students do not experience school just as a location of learning but also as one in which they experience social inclusion and exclusion. Before these

M. Holodynski (✉)
Psychology and Sport Studies, University of Münster, Münster, Germany
e-mail: manfred.holodynski@psy.uni-muenster.de

B. Röttger-Rössler, H.J. Markowitsch (eds.), *Emotions as Bio-cultural Processes*,
DOI 10.1007/978-0-387-09546-2_17, © Springer Science+Business Media, LLC 2009

experiences undergo any cognitive reflection, they are perceived and processed emotionally: as pride over academic success signalizing that one is well regarded and belongs to the social group, and as anxiety (about tests) and shame over academic failures signalizing inferiority and social exclusion (see Barret, 1995; Scheff, 1988, 2003; Schultheiss, 1997). Because academic successes and failures are distributed unequally across students, it can be assumed that imbalances in emotional experience accumulate over the long term and have differential effects on personality development.

In this chapter, we discuss the proposition that shame and pride, as both socially evaluative and self-evaluative emotions, have a far more important role in the institution of the school than any current overview of the literature in educational psychology suggests (see Bibby, 2002; Pekrun, Götz, Titz, & Perry, 2002; Turner, Husman & Schallert, 2002). We start by describing how emotional experiences of shame and pride affect the acquisition of cultural norms and values during adolescence. In a second step, we show that the institution of school generates a great variety of opportunities for students to experience shame and pride not only while performing its societal tasks of qualification, allocation, and socialization but also by providing them with a peer group (see Faulstich-Wieland, 2002; Fend, 1997, 2000; Pekrun, 1994; Tillmann, 2000). In our third step, we examine the current state of research in educational psychology on the role of emotions in school learning and achievement situations and consider why the analysis of pride and shame has received so little attention up to now in the school context. This brings us to the sociologist Thomas Scheff's premise on the "invisibility" of shame in Western cultures. Finally, in the fourth step, we examine how far the academic self-concept, self-esteem, and achievement motivation, which are so relevant in the school context, are linked to experiences of pride and shame, and why it would be a worthwhile endeavor to analyze them from the perspective of a psychology of emotions.

Function of Shame and Pride in Conveying Cultural Norms

Living in a social community confronts individuals with the task of coordinating the satisfaction of their various personal motives and goals in a socially acceptable manner. This coordination functions with the help of the norms and values in the specific reference group toward which individual action regulation is oriented. In some situations, however, these norms and values may well run counter to the satisfaction of personal motives. How is it possible that norm-compliant behavior is still exhibited in these cases, and that persons comply with norms, even when they run counter to their actual motives in the here and now?

Psychological theories (e.g., Barret, 1995; Buss, 1980; Holodynski & Friedlmeier, 2006; Lewis, 1992; Stipek, 1995) and sociological theories (e.g., Scheff, 1988; Schultheiss, 1997) propose that two mechanisms are particularly responsible for the emergence of norm-compliant behavior. One is the punishment or material sanctioning of behavior that is norm-inconsistent. However, this mechanism is of limited impact because continuous external controls are needed to punish a norm violation and not just threaten to do so. The second mechanism is the experience of being either held in esteem by the social reference group for norm-compliant behavior or poorly regarded and threatened with exclusion from it for norm-violating behavior. This second mechanism seems to be more effective for the internalization of social norms because it permits emotional self-control of norm compliance by means of the emotions pride and shame.

External Evaluation and Self-Evaluation as Triggers of Pride and Shame

Sociologically oriented theories focus on experiences of social exclusion, stigmatization, and loss of the desired attachment to the relevant reference group as conditions triggering the emotion of shame, and they describe this process as being constitutive for compliance with norms (see Goffman, 1967; Scheff, 1988; Schultheiss, 1997; Simmel, 1983). Whereas a negative social evaluation is associated with weakening or disrupting the desired attachment to the reference person or group, a positive social evaluation is perceived as reinforcing or confirming it. This is why sociologists also talk about "socially evaluative" emotions.

Whereas the above-mentioned studies focus on the *social* evaluation of individual actions on the basis of prevailing norms, psychologically oriented theories consider the central element in triggering the emotions shame and pride to be the evaluation of the action by the individual himself or herself (self-evaluation). As a result, they call them "self-evaluative" emotions (Barret, 1995; Lewis, 1992). It is only when individuals evaluate their actions on the basis of the norms and values they have accepted that they feel pride over compliance with them and shame over their violation (see Barrett, 1995; Fessler, 1999; Holodynski, 2006).

These sociological and psychological perspectives are not mutually exclusive. It is far more the case that experiencing real social exclusion can be characterized as a precondition for the emergence of shame. This is the way in which individuals learn to evaluate their own actions on the basis of the norms that are valid in their reference group. Like Casimir and Jung ("Honor and Dishonor"), we view the pain of exclusion from the relevant reference group as constitutive for the emergence of norm-abiding behavior-that is, for the acceptance that personal motives may be satisfied only so long as they comply with the norms prevailing in the specific reference group. Individuals who display pride or shame over their own behavior are simultaneously signalizing that they have adopted the norms and values of their reference group. They guarantee that their individual actions and life plans remain embedded within the broader coordination of the social group and do not develop in opposition to it (see Holodynski & Friedlmeier, 2006).

Motivating Impact of Feeling Shame or Pride

A number of authors consider that the reason shame has such a particularly strong motivating power is because of the extremely intensive and physically observable way in which this emotion is felt. Smith (1982, p. 20) talked about the "internal sanction" and the threat of "horrors of shame and repentance" that deter individuals from norm violations. Authors from different disciplines share this opinion. Turner et al. (2002, p. 80) described the feeling of shame as being an "intensely disturbing and motivationally disruptive, acutely painful, potentially devastating emotion." Bibby (2002, p. 706; see also Giddens, 1991) stated that "shame depends on the feeling of personal insufficiency," and Jacoby (1997, p. 19; see also Nathanson, 1992; Scheff, 2003; Schultheiss, 1997) talked about a "painful hurt feeling." Hence, even as a physical feeling, shame seems to be so negative that individuals will do everything in their power to avoid it in the future. Pride, in contrast, is described as a positive emotion—both as a feeling and in terms of its effects on self-esteem and self-concept (Allesandri & Lewis, 1996; Hambly, 2003; Kövecses, 1990).

Pekrun et al. (2002) also classified pride and shame as *activating* emotions in the sense that they lead individuals to engage in active coping behavior. For shame, this means that although it can be viewed as negative in terms of an individual's subjective feeling, it may have a positive effect on future motivation. As a result, in terms of the activity triggered, shame can lead to either withdrawal and turning away from the task at hand or to greater effort to avoid renewed failure and thereby counteract any further experience of shame in the future. Nonetheless, this greater effort seems to be invested only when the shame-triggering situation cannot be avoided simply and the individual must counter it through greater exertion. It is only when individuals experience shame repeatedly in the situation in question-despite all personal effort-that hopelessness emerges. In achievement situations, this can lead to extreme forms of fear of failure and even go so far as internal rejection of the prevailing norm, making individuals eventually indifferent about compliance or about making an effort in achievement situations. Particularly at school, low-achieving students are frequently and repeatedly exposed to situations in which they must suffer failure despite making an effort (see below).

Pekrun et al. (2002) likewise characterize the *positively activating* emotion of pride as being "ambivalent" in terms of its effect on motivation. Whereas in the short term pride may impair effort, in the long term it encourages the motivation to invest in effort. These findings are supported by the studies of Turner et al. (2002) on the incidence rates and effects of the emotion of shame among American students.

These observations underline the conclusion that experiences of belonging to one's own reference group, and thereby episodes of pride, play a dominant role in imparting social norms and values. However, when there is a predominance of experiences of exclusion, and thereby episodes of shame, it may well lead to major impairment of the internalization of norms.

Institutionally Determined Episodes of Pride and Shame in Daily School Life

Nowadays, most children and adolescents attend school for at least 9 years (Fend 1991). This raises two questions: (1) What role does this institution with its relevant reference groups (the community of the class and the teachers) adopt in the life of students? (2) Which emotions can potentially be triggered within this context?

As an institution, the school has a legal framework (a constitution, laws, regulations) and an external structure (location, temporal duration, population, its own professional group). Its task is to use set methods and media to provide goal-directed, planned learning and teaching that impart sociocultural knowledge and attitudes to the young generation, thereby promoting the further development not only of society and culture but also of personality (Faulstich-Wieland, 2002; Tillmann, 2000). Four institutional tasks particularly generate a priori situations that may trigger pride or shame in students: qualification, allocation, socialization, and provision of a peer group.

Qualification and Allocation as Sources of Pride and Shame Experiences

The first task of the school, that of qualification, is to equip children and adolescents for later careers and thereby make it possible for them to participate in sharing the benefits of society. Schools should impart basic cultural techniques such as reading, writing, and arithmetic; a body of general knowledge in selected subject areas; and the ability to engage in self-directed lifelong learning. In this sense, schools are a location of learning and education.

They have a second task that is linked inseparably to qualification: the allocation of students to specific further opportunities in training, career, and life in general. Which students gain a right of access to further training options that are, in turn, oriented toward guidelines set by the state? Which students can move on to the next school grade, further education, or a career start? It is the teaching profession that decides these issues on the basis of the individual achievements that reflect the relevant qualifications, and these decisions are documented in the form of grades, annual reports, and school-leaving certificates. This makes the evaluation of individual student achievement the central instrument of qualification and allocation in the institution of the school. The question is, however: How does the application of such instruments contribute to the generation of episodes of pride and shame?

Whether individual student achievement should be rated as a success or failure is not decided by the task itself but only in relation to whatever specific reference norm is being applied. In line with the idea of the qualification task, the school ideally uses a reference norm based on a sequence of competence stages. Because most school curricula are not based on such models, teachers are unable to evaluate achievement on such a basis. In practice, two other, less optimal reference norms are applied instead: the individual and the social reference norm (see Rheinberg, 1987).

When applying an individual reference norm, a student's present achievements are compared with past ones; that is, one looks to see whether there has been any individual increase in learning. The disadvantage of assessing achievement on this basis is that it does not necessarily reveal anything about the attainment of specific areas of competence. Despite a clear improvement in performance, an individual may still not have attained the necessary minimum standard. This way of assessing achievement, however, also has advantages: Because all students learn more over time—particularly when they make an effort—it becomes possible for them to experience that such an effort can improve their performance continually—an experience that triggers pride and confidence in success and, in the long term, leads to a preponderance of feelings of pride over shame. Hence, the use of an individual reference norm promotes what is called a learning goal orientation in students; that is, it orients them toward increasing their individual areas of competence. Therefore, the use of an individual reference norm would be the preferable procedure for the school task of qualification.

Numerous studies have confirmed the positive relation between a student's learning goal orientation and learning and achievement. Students whose learning is goal-oriented tend to attribute their performance to their own effort rather than to their abilities, and this explanation is particularly advantageous in the case of failure (Ames & Ames, 1984). Furthermore, students with a learning goal orientation associate comparatively more positive emotions with learning and achievement tasks (Nicholls, Patashnick, & Nolen, 1985).

Examining individual student achievements from the perspective of the school allocation task makes the individual reference norm seem unfair because two students—one a weak achiever and the other a strong achiever—who have improved by exactly the same amount are evaluated as being equally good despite their differences in performance. This is why there is another reference norm for the task of allocating admission to restricted career tracks: the social reference norm. This norm compares the achievements of the single student with those of the class—or an even larger group of students. Measuring the achievements of all students in a class with an identical pool of tasks reveals the current achievement differences between them. The advantage of this method is that even without a reliable competence stage model it is still possible to rank student achievements as a basis for different career and academic allocations. The disadvantage of assessing student achievement purely with the social reference norm is that in the long term it can lead to stabilization of the relative performance differences among students. This is because the experiences of success and pride that are so helpful for learning are available only to strong achievers, whereas low achievers are exposed to repeated failure and shame through single performance tests, through having to repeat the school year (*Sitzenbleiben*), or finally through entering adult life with no school-leaving qualifications. Hence, a social reference norm has contradictory long-term consequences for the stronger versus the weaker achievers in a class.

In a study on how students with a "low achievement status" perceive and cope with their situation, Lambrich (1987) revealed the dire consequences of negative social achievement evaluation for their self-concept. He summarized his findings by quoting Thomason: "The sense of own stupidity becomes universal. As a result, the victims never know whether or not carrying out some action plan might make them look ridiculous" (Lambrich, 1987, p. 236, translated).

A longitudinal study by Rheinberg (1993) is extremely revealing in this context. He examined students attending German basic secondary school (*Hauptschule*) at the beginning and end of the fifth grade. Results showed that teachers were not obliged to impose a strict social reference norm orientation but could introduce more scope for an individual reference norm. Moreover, it was precisely an individual reference norm orientation that could remotivate low achievers and reduce their accumulated fear of failure (see Fig. 1). Unfortunately, he did not study which emotional experiences of pride and shame the students had been exposed to during this school year as a function of the different reference norm orientations. We return to this aspect of the role of pride and shame experiences in the development of achievement motivation later in the chapter.

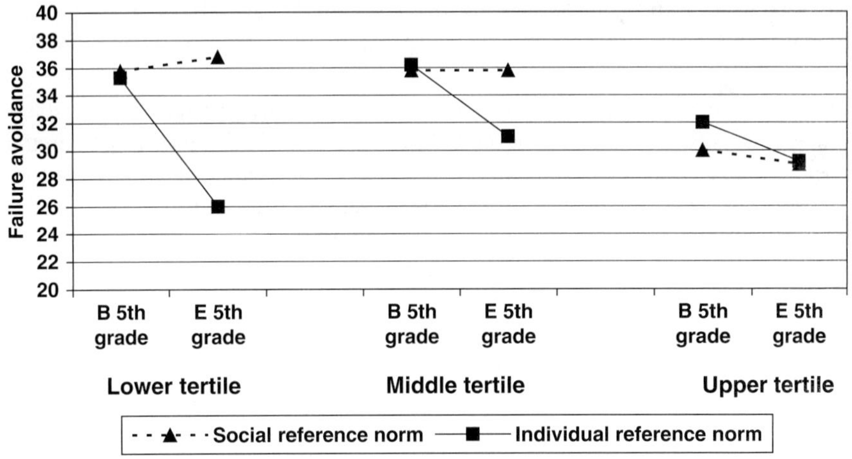

Fig. 1 Trends in failure avoidance during 5th-grade *Hauptschule* as a function of child's intelligence quotient and teacher's reference norm orientation.
Note. B 5th grade (Beginning of 5th grade), E 5th grade (End of 5th grade). IQ scores were used to divide the students in each class into three groups (lower, middle, and upper tertile). Adapted from Rheinberg (1980, p. 148).

School Socialization as Internalization of the Achievement Principle

Schools should impart not only subject knowledge in the form of abilities to prepare for careers but also socially desired attitudes and values. One of these socially desired values is that students should not just *accept* having their abilities evaluated according to external standards but also actively *embrace* this practice. They should develop a strong achievement motivation; that is, they should be motivated to attain the school's achievement standards. They will then attribute their successes in doing this to personal competence. The other side of the coin is that students also have to take responsibility for failures and process them personally—with the consequence that unsuccessful students predominantly attribute their failure in the necessary school selection processes to their own person rather than regarding it as also being an inevitable consequence of the need to distribute limited social resources (Oelerich, 1998). The desired emergence of a personality structure containing a strong achievement motive makes students "susceptible" not only to pride over successes but also shame over their failures. Although much research has focused on the cognitive and motivational aspects of achievement motivation, the intervening emotional processes and the consequences for development have yet to be studied in sufficient detail. We deal with this aspect later.

Empirical research confirms that students actually do adopt the socially desired achievement orientation as an internalized value. In a survey in the German state of Mecklenburg-Western Pommerania, Prüß et al. (2000) found that nearly all students (96%) reported that their own academic performance was important; and more than two-thirds noted that their parents were only interested in good academic grades and successful school graduation. In a study of seventh-grade students in a German school by Engel and Hurrelmann (1993), 87% reported that their goal was to leave school with university entrance qualifications (*Abitur*). Hence, academic success has strong subjective importance for most children and adolescents, with additional achievement pressure being built up through parents' expectations.

The claim that students adopting an achievement orientation are exposed to pride and shame situations can be demonstrated by examining their apprehensions and reactions to impending examinations, class tests, and decisions on whether they have to repeat the school year. As daily diary and interview studies have shown impressively over the last two decades (Czerwenka, 1990; Fend, 1997; Helmke, 1992; Lambrich, 1987), fear of shame and disgrace is predominant for most students. They fear that they will not be able to satisfy social demands and will thereby experience a feeling of failure.

Fend (1997), for example, performed a longitudinal study of approximately 2000 children and adolescents from 1979 to 1983, assessing them once a year in their sixth- to tenth-grade classes. One aspect studied was test anxiety. Results showed that fear of shame seemed omnipresent, as illustrated by the words of one student.

> The fear and the oppressive feeling that it might be "one's turn" at the front of the class the next day always cast a terrible shadow over the classroom. Trembling voices, weak knees, and sweaty palms were completely normal among us students. It was embarrassing if you couldn't recite the text to be learned without any mistakes. Blame and exposure were the consequences. The only time I was able to breathe more easily was when it was somebody else's turn. (Fend 1997, p. 71, translated)

It would be difficult to find a clearer description of shame reactions or the fear of being shamed. What is surprising is that neither the students surveyed nor the authors of the studies ever, or only marginally, associated these descriptions with the accompanying emotion of shame, even though this association is obvious from the perspective of the psychology of emotions. We deal with this later when discussing the invisibility of shame in more detail.

In sum, we can see that a proportion of those "failing" students who are at risk of having to repeat the school year, actually do so, or even have to change the type of school they attend do not fundamentally reject achievement demands and their legitimacy. They attribute their failures predominantly to themselves, thereby reacting with fear of potential disgrace and shame.

There are also other ways of reacting to repeated experiences of failure and shame. Students can belittle the importance of academic effort and develop sophisticated skills with which to avoid effort and work. The central goal then becomes the least possible work investment, with issues such as learning successfully or increasing one's learning losing almost all further relevance (see Spinath & Schöne, 2003). These students turn to extracurricular risk-taking behavior to satisfy their search for belongingness and experiences of pride. We view this turning away from the academic achievement motive as one feasible strategy for counteracting the threat of shame (see also Ismer, The Search for Style and the Urge for Fame, this volume).

The Class as a Source of Pride and Shame Experiences

Because schools organize learning in same-aged classroom groups, the class becomes a relevant social reference group for students. It has an internal social structure and also its own norms and values (Pekrun, 1994). This creates a further socialization agency in which a student is rated according to the norms of the peer group and exposed here as well to experiences of exclusion and belongingness and thereby shame and pride (see also Harrist & Bradley, 2002).

The norms of the peer group conflict to some extent with the norms of the teacher. As a result, students have to develop a specific emotional competence in regulating how they express their pride and shame: If a student feels proud because his or her achievements are praised by the teacher, an overt expression of this pride might be understood by other members of the class as indicating disdain for them because students displaying pride place themselves above the social group. This could provoke a counterreaction by peers who call a boastful student a "swot" or "teacher's pet" and exclude him or her from the social community. This demonstration of disdain from the class could trigger shame in the boastful student, and the expression of this shame signalizes the desire for reacceptance within the class community. Hence, during the course of a school career, every student learns that he or she can be proud of his or her achievements but should not display this openly within the class (see Banerjee, 2000; see also Casimir & Jung, “Honor and Dishonor”, this volume) (Fig. 1).

Students also develop competence in regulating the overt expression of shame. Shame over bad grades is also something that cannot simply be displayed in the class because classmates interpret it as a sign that the student accepts the norms represented by the teacher and recognizes good academic grades as a legitimate goal. The student may then be viewed as a “failed swot” who will suffer social exclusion from the class and be subjected to, for example, malicious joy and ridicule. Hence, during the course of a school career, students have to develop the ability to regulate and conceal the expression of not just feelings of pride over academic success but also of shame over failure. Up to now, little research has addressed this topic (but see Banerjee, 2000; Zammuner, 1996).

Shame and Pride in the School Context: The State of Research

The analysis so far should have made it clear that the emotions of pride and shame are particularly central phenomena that both accompany and determine school learning and achievement. As a result, they should be viewed as an important topic of research. Although this is something that has been called for repeatedly in recent years (Hofmann & Pekrun, 1999; Pekrun, 1992, 1998; Pekrun et al., 2002; Standop, 2001; Turner et al., 2002), research on this topic (with the exception of the emotion of test anxiety) is still only just starting.

Jeannine Turner has studied the emotion of shame in various learning- and achievement-related contexts over the last decade. She has focused particularly on the individual value that students attribute to an achievement and how it relates to their own self-esteem and their emotion-related control beliefs (Turner et al., 2002; Turner & Schallert, 1996, 2001; Turner, Thorpe, & Meyer, 1998).

Another decisive starting point for any analysis of emotions in the school context is the work of Pekrun and colleagues (Hofmann & Pekrun, 1999; Pekrun, 1992, 1998, 2000). Hofmann and Pekrun (1999) asked a sample of 56 higher secondary school students in Germany (*Oberstufenschülern*) to report their feelings in different situations (being in class, studying outside of class, taking tests and examinations). Among the 994 emotional episodes reported by the students, fear was the most frequently named emotion (16.1%) followed by relief (14.4%) and anger (9.4%). Nonetheless, the breadth of felt and anticipated emotions was far greater. Shame and pride episodes, in contrast, were named relatively infrequently (1.2% and 4.0%, respectively) among all the reported emotional episodes.

At first glance, these data seem to contradict our initial premise regarding the central significance of pride and shame in the school context. However, Hofmann and Pekrun's (1999) findings do not necessarily reflect their actual incidence and the impact they have on school learning and achieving.

"Invisibility" of Pride and Shame in Western Cultures

Support for such discrepancies can be found in the sociological and psychotherapeutic literature. In his major research on "Shame in Self and Society," Thomas J. Scheff (1988, 2003) analyzed not only the central role of shame and pride for norm-compliant behavior and personality development but also the minimal use of shame and pride concepts in the daily language of modern Western societies. This led him to pose his hypothesis on the "low-visibility" of pride and shame. However, he did not view the scarce attention paid to these emotions in the speech of Western cultures as a sign that they are less important in social interactions. He derived support for his hypothesis from studies in psychotherapy. For example, Helen B. Lewis (1971) documented and analyzed the "low visibility" of the emotion of shame in hundreds of clinical interviews by applying the Gottschalk-Gleser method of transcript analysis (Gottschalk-Gleser, 1969). With the help of this method, which contains numerous key words that can be correlated with specific emotions, she uncovered the central importance of the emotion of shame during therapeutic consultations while also documenting that the clients were unaware of their shame or did not communicate it overtly.

In line with Scheff and numerous other authors (Fessler, 1999; Kaufmann & Lev, 1984), we assume that the "low visibility" of shame reported in therapeutic contexts also generalizes to everyday interactions, and that this must be taken into account when assessing Hofmann and Pekrun's (1999) findings that students in semistructured interviews report having experienced only very few episodes of shame. It may well be that they either did not want to report their true frequency or that they did not classify shame episodes as such.

Test Anxiety as an Unrecognized Shame Anxiety

It can be shown that the emotion experienced most frequently by students (i.e., "test anxiety") (see Hofmann & Pekrun, 1999), is, on closer inspection, a fear of failure and can therefore be classified as a fear of shame. Shame as an anticipated and feared emotion would accordingly play a greater role in the daily school life of students than their self-reports initially suggest.

This conclusion can be supported by analyzing the instruments used to assess the feelings of test anxiety. These are generally standardized questionnaires. The first such questionnaire tests focused on tapping general features of anxiety, such as the feeling-of-tension dimension (covering restlessness, tension, and physiological arousal) and the worry dimension (covering general thoughts about not passing a test and what consequences it may have). However, they failed to address any specific threats or worries. Covington, Omelich, and Schwarzer (1986) criticized this limitation and broadened the analysis by asking which effects test anxiety has on an individual's self-image and self-efficacy. Their results showed that the best way to describe test anxiety is as a fear of being socially derogated and isolated by fellow students after failing an examination (see also Bamber, 1977; Schopler & Mathews, 1965).

More recent instruments for assessing test anxiety take these aspects explicitly into account. For example, the *Friedben-Test zur Prüfungsangst für Siebt- bis Zwölfklässler* (Friedman & Bendas-Jacob, 1997) contains fear of social derogation as one of three specific components of test anxiety in seventh- to twelfth-grade students. This component cannot be reduced to the other two components, worry and tension. Friedman and Bendas-Jacob tried to specify the particular threats and worries involved in test anxiety. They took a two-stage approach: First, they gave 80 students in eleventh grade (aged 17 years) the following four questions requiring unstructured answers: (1) What does a student whom you would define as suffering from test anxiety think and feel? (2) How would a student suffering from test anxiety behave before, (3) during, and (4) after a test? The answers were classified into five categories: 35% of the students described tension and unrest; 27% had nonspecific fears and worries (e.g., not passing the test or not being able to recall knowledge); 33% described threats to their self-image or self-efficacy elicited by anticipating failure; and 5% referred to threats to a student's social status should the failure to pass the test be made public.

The authors compressed the students' statements into 33 items and gave them to a 1925 seventh- to twelfth-grade students. Factor analysis resulted in three factors with 23 items meeting the simple structure criterion. The first factor could be identified unequivocally as social derogation: "the fear of degradation in one's self-image and sense of self-efficacy when anticipated negative social feedback makes it clear that one's social and academic status seem inferior" (p. 1041). This confirmed Friedman and Bendas-Jacob's (1997) suspicion that school learning with its examinations also has major social consequences for students. A test always elicits threats to social status if failure is possible and may be witnessed by significant others (classmates, teachers, parents). This is why tests are also always a threat or a challenge to perceived self-efficacy and thereby able to induce fear of shame. This is less the case for academically strong students but, in contrast, all the more so for the weak ones.

These conclusions have been confirmed in a study of worry cognitions (failure outcome expectations) in 14- and 15-year-old children from the Czech Republic (Hagtvet, Man, & Sharma, 2001). Results showed clearly that students focused less on self-related worries and far more on worries related to others, such as: "What will my parents, teachers, classmates (siblings) think about me if I do badly?"

Consequences of Excessive Experiences of Shame

Scheff (1988, 2003) emphasized that, despite the low visibility of shame, its functions—and those of pride—are still retained in both social interaction and identity formation. The fact that these emotions have become taboo in modern Western societies is no indication of any loss of function, only that they are less present in conscious communication. Future research needs to address these issues and take them into account when selecting appropriate assessment instruments.

Earlier research in educational psychology reported in the previous section examined the impact of experiences of failure within the context of the school (Fend, 1997; Lambrich, 1987). Analyses of daily diaries repeatedly described the fear of derision or of being shown up in public as decisive experiences. However, research has yet to focus directly on analyzing the incidence and impact of the emotion of fear of shame hiding behind these descriptions.

Interesting ideas on this topic can be found in sociological, psychological, and psychotherapeutic research showing that shame is linked closely to other emotions such as fear and anger (see also Casimir & Jung, "Honor and Dishonor", this volume). Helen B. Lewis (1971) described how the intrapersonal process of "shame over one's own shame" can lead to various forms of anger. Scheff (1988) has taken up this research and plotted the "shame–anger spiral" that may proceed both intra- and interpersonally and contains a transformation of shame into aggression and anger.

Jacoby (1991, 1997) described the relation between the emotions of fear and shame. Shame emerges during ontogenesis from the fear of being excluded from the attachment to one's reference person or group. This fear of exclusion is retained and grants shame its conformity-promoting function (see Casimir & Jung, "Honor and Dishonor", this volume; see also Holodynski, Milestones and Mechanisms of Emotional Development, this volume). However, excessive fear of shame, which can result from persistent experiences of failure at school, among others, may lead to pathological personality development.

In educational psychology, this opens up a new perspective for research on schools. The development of test anxiety can be viewed as a fear of shame. The development of aggression and violence can be viewed as possible self-protective reactions to personal failures and the accompanying experience of the low opinion of others that is interpreted as a threat to personal self-esteem. Aggressions directed toward those who shame should compensate for the felt shaming.

Impact of Shame and Pride on the Self-Concept, Self-Esteem, and Achievement Motivation

The following sections look at three psychological concepts central to student learning and achievement situations: the development of the academic self-concept; the development of self-esteem; and the development of achievement motivation. A closer analysis will reveal how decisively their development is influenced by experiences of pride and shame. Up to now, research has addressed this context only marginally.

Personality Development, Self-Concept, and Self-Esteem

Developing a personality means, on the one hand, evolving an appraisal of one's own traits and areas of competence that agrees with that made by the social environment while, on the other hand, distinguishing oneself from other persons as being a unique individual. Personality development involves the processing of self-related information that is then integrated into one's own self-concept and self-esteem (Faulstich-Wieland, 2000; Filipp, 1985; Mummendey, 1990; Trautner & Lohaus, 1985).

Process-oriented conceptions of personality development view the self-concept as being built up by processing information from both the social environment and one's own behavior. It includes not only descriptions of the self such as "I'm a clever person" but also evaluations of one's own person (Lambrich, 1987). The self-*concept* can accordingly be defined as the cognitive representation of the own person (Petermann & Petermann, 1989). In contrast, self-*esteem* can be understood as accumulated emotional experience that is conveyed to a decisive extent by episodes of pride and shame in which individuals experience their social and personal status.

Filipp (1985) proposed that three sources of self-related knowledge are available to the individual (see also Allport, 1937; Mummendey, 1990): (1) the social environment (comparisons with other groups); (2) observation of one's own behavior; and (3) self-reflection. From the perspective of emotion theory, self-reflection over one's own behavior and its evaluation in relation to social norms are, in turn, conditions that trigger the emotions of pride and shame (Barrett, 1995; Stipek, 1995; Tangney, 1995; Tomkins, 1987). Hence, developing a concept of the self-that is, becoming aware of which traits, behaviors, and areas of competence characterize one's own person-takes place within a socially evaluative and self-evaluative process that is also always linked to experiences of pride and shame (Hewitt, 1979; Shibutani, 1961; Wells & Marwell, 1976).

This means that the processes that can be taken to be fundamental for the formation of a self-concept are, to some extent, identical with those assumed to be fundamental for triggering shame and pride. Shame and pride are not experienced as one-off events but are emotions that individuals experience with varying frequency and intensity, leading to cumulative effects on the development of their self-concept and self-esteem (Jacoby, 1997; Lewis, 1992; Scheff, 2003). Hence, pride and shame are not just significant for the immediate origins of individual action regulation in social relations; they influence the ontogenesis of the self-concept. This idea has been accepted by authors from various disciplines, although not all of them conceptualize self- or self-esteem-related feelings in terms of shame and pride (Goffman, 1967; Lambrich, 1987; Shibutani, 1961; Simmel, 1983).

Whereas there are only a few scattered studies confirming the role of pride in the development of self-esteem and the self-concept (Allesandri & Lewis, 1996; Hambly, 2003; Kövecses, 1990), numerous publications from a great variety of disciplines have confirmed the negative effect of frequent experiences of shame on personality development (Gilbert, 1998; Jacoby, 1997; Lewis, 1992; Retzinger, 1998; Scheff, 1998; Schore, 1998; Tangney & Dearing, 2002). In an analysis of the stigmatization of social groups, Goffman (1967) described the individual experience of dropping out of the framework of social norm concepts as a shame experience, stating that one can view one's person and the pertaining attribute, which one conceives as something disreputable, as a cause to feel ashamed of oneself. Similarly, Simmel (1983) described how knowledge of one's own inadequacy, which additionally gains public attention, triggers shame and becomes a permanent element of one's own "life feeling."

The role of school in the process of personality development can be explained through the public evaluation of individual student performances based on social comparisons. Students understand these as statements on their own abilities and traits and, hence, as part of their academic self-concept. Defined broadly, the academic self-concept can be viewed as the totality of ideas about one's own abilities in academic achievement situations (Meyer, 1984; see also Pekrun, 1983). Schone et al. (2003) clearly distinguished the academic self-concept from the concept of self-esteem. All representations are divided into *affective* ("I'm ashamed") and *cognitive* ("of the fact that I am not clever") components. Affective representations are viewed as being constitutive for self-esteem and distinguished clearly from cognitive contents referring to one's own abilities. Given chronic failure, one can assume the negative development of not only the academic self-concept but also of the related dimensions of self-esteem, self-efficacy beliefs, action control, test anxiety, and self-acceptance (Fend, 1997).

Nonetheless, it should not be forgotten that children and adolescents are not just passive recipients of prevailing norms but also relate to them actively. For example, permanent experiences of failure can lead a student to turn away completely from the accepted achievement norms (see Ismer, The Search for Style and the Urge for Fame, this volume).

Shame and Pride and Their Influence on the Development of Achievement Motivation

We have already considered the important role of the achievement motive in academic learning. In the following, we want to show how pride and shame contribute to the development of achievement motivation or to alternative motive and goal orientations.

Back in 1966, Atkinson assigned a central incentive function for achievement motivation to the emotions shame and pride in his expectancy–value theory. Heckhausen (1975; Brunstein & Heckhausen, 2006) also assigned pride and shame a central mediating function for the self-evaluation of own achievements in his elaborated self-evaluation model, although he did not perform any empirical analysis of these emotional aspects of achievement motivation. Therefore, we try here, almost in retrospect, to work out the mediating function of pride and shame in Heckhausen's self-evaluation model for the formation of different types of motive in achievement motivation.

Self-Evaluation Model of Achievement Motivation

Heckhausen's self-evaluation model of achievement motivation (Heckhausen, 1975, 1977) integrates Atkinson's (1966) and Weiner's (1985) theories. It views the achievement motive as being composed of two complementary components.

1. A *hope-for-success motive component* in which an individual is driven to address a task by the anticipated feeling of pride over success
2. A *fear-of-failure motive component* in which an individual is driven to avoid a task by the anticipated feeling of shame over failure

Nonetheless, motive analyses based on Schmalt's (2005) achievement motive grid have shown that the failure motive takes two forms: (1) active, action-oriented failure avoidance that accompanies a low academic self-concept; and (2) passive, state-oriented fear of failure focusing predominantly on the (potential) social consequences of failure. The focus of this fear is on the threat of exclusion or the apprehension of not being held in esteem by significant reference persons (teachers) and reference groups (classmates). From a developmental perspective, the achievement motive is the outcome of achievement-related experiences that manifest during late childhood as a habitual disposition to engage in behavior directed toward either anticipating success or avoiding failure (Heckhausen & Heckhausen, 2006).

Two other factors along with the strength of the achievement motive must be considered before it can become an action-initiating motivation. These come from Atkinson's (1966) expectancy–value theory: (1) the individual's expectancy of actually being successful in the given situation; and (2) the value assigned to this success.

Finally, the self-evaluation model contains the assumption from Weiner's (1985) attribution theory that the causal explanation of achievement outcomes influences the development and stabilization of a dominant form of motivation. It proposes that achievements can be explained by either internal-stable (through ability), internal-variable (through effort), external-stable (through task difficulty), or external-variable causes (through good or bad luck).

Heckhausen's self-evaluation model can explain how experiences of success and failure acquired during ontogenesis may lead to the formation of a more

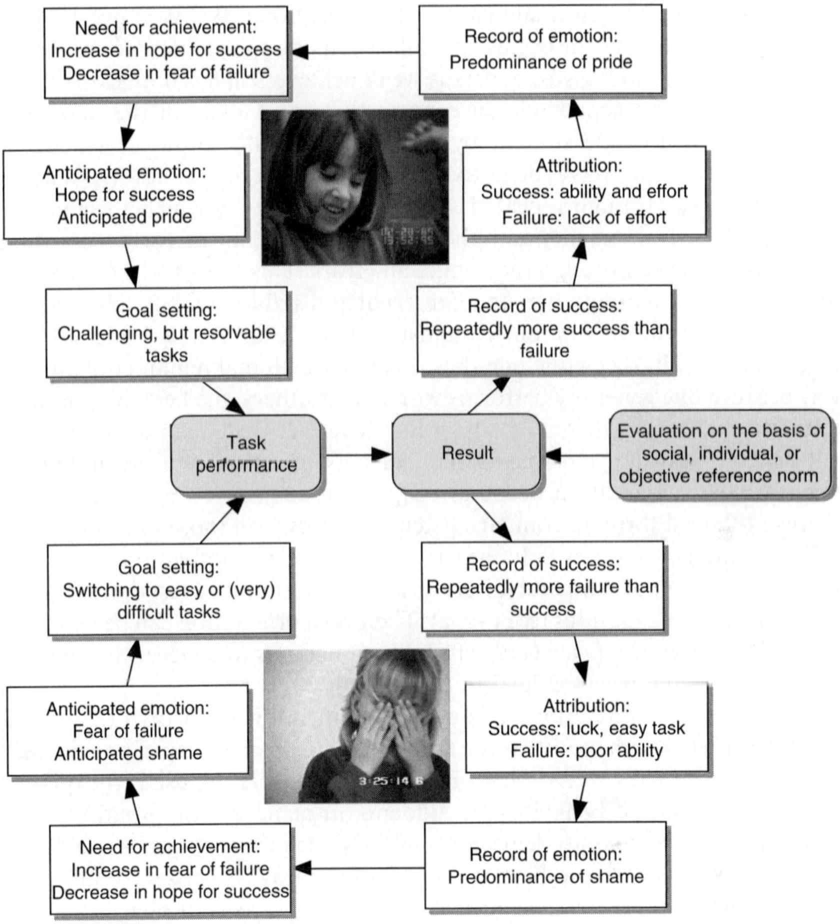

Fig. 2 Hope-for-success and fear-of-failure achievement motivation as a self-evaluation system with the mediating function of pride and shame.

success-anticipating or failure-avoiding action tendency (see Fig. 2), with pride and shame taking on a guiding intermediate function that is explained below.

Setting Reference Norms and Their Affective and Motivational Consequences

The parental home and school confront the young generation with continuous evaluations of their achievements and abilities. As mentioned above, the appraisal of one's own achievement as either a success or failure is not just a product of the task itself but is always performed in relation to an accepted reference norm. The reference norms prevailing in the school context have become decisive for the development of achievement motivation. They are the individual and the social reference norms described above that the school needs as instruments to fulfill its qualification and allocation tasks. We now show the opposing consequences the exclusive application of a social reference norm can have in the long term for strong versus weak achievers in a school class.

Application of a social reference norm-that is, evaluating the individual achievement of a single student by comparing it with the achievements of classroom peers-can have demotivating consequences on development in weak achievers. Through repeated social comparisons in which their performance is below average, they gain the experience that they perform worse than their classmates even though they make an effort. This leads them to attribute failures to a lack of ability (i.e., to an internal and stable cause of achievement) and successes more to random circumstances (i.e., an external and variable cause). As a result, they conclude that it is not worth making an effort; moreover, because one generally performs worse than others, the best thing to do is to avoid achievement demands altogether. The fact that weak achievers generally exhibit learning increments (i.e., success) in relation to an individual reference norm orientation becomes eclipsed in subjective experience by the failures perceived through comparing achievements with those of others.

These students develop failure-fearing achievement motivation dominated by the anticipation of shameful failures. As a result, they do everything to avoid such achievement situations (see Fig. 2). Their goal orientation can be described as an *achievement avoidance goal.* The main concern is to conceal the assumed deficits in their abilities (see Spinath & Schöne, 2003).

Covington (1992) described this development in his self-worth theory. He postulated a self-worth motive as the desire to build up and retain a positive self-image and respect for one's self-worth. This theory can be used to explain a number of avoidance behaviors by students in achievement situations. Our school system confronts students continuously with competition and achievement comparisons that also harbor the risk of failure. This poses a continuous threat to self-worth. Over the course of their school careers, it obliges students to turn increasingly to strategies that protect them from such threats. One of these strategies is to avoid effort when learning. With this strategy, one can still feel basically competent; one has simply not made enough effort. As a result, one can attribute a failure to lack of effort rather than lack of ability. In contrast, failure despite making an effort can only be attributed to a lack of ability, and this would lower self-worth even further.

In contrast to the academic learning and achievement experiences of weak achievers, when comparatively strong achievers are assessed with the social reference norm they find that they repeatedly do better than others. This leads them to attribute successes to their ability (an internal, stable cause) and failures more to bad luck or lack of effort (an external, variable cause) (see Fig. 2). Their strategy in achievement situations can be described as a performance goal orientation predominantly concerned with demonstrating and confirming their own knowledge and ability to themselves and others (see Spinath & Schöne, 2003).

There is a clear, empirically confirmed relation between the reference norm orientation of teachers and the achievement motivation of their students

(Rheinberg, 1987). Students whose teachers apply an individual reference norm orientation have a stronger success motive, whereas students whose teachers apply a social reference norm orientation are more failure-oriented. These reference norm orientations of teachers also have long-term effects on the self-image of students. A social reference norm applied over several years has a negative effect on the academic self-concept and the generalized self-concept of weak achievers (see Rheinberg & Krug, 1999; Stiensmeier-Pelster & Rheinberg, 2003, Chap. 4).

Rheinberg (1993) also analyzed the behavior of teachers who use different reference norm orientations. Results showed that teachers also apply pride- and shame-inducing tactics in the form of praise and blame and that the way they do this depends on their reference norm orientation: Teachers with a social reference norm gave more praise to above-average students even when their performance declined. Teachers with an individual reference norm, in contrast, criticized such students. Only teachers with an individual reference norm recognized and praised students with below-average achievements, and they were already doing this while work was in progress. Teachers with a social reference norm, in contrast, praised and blamed only after work had been completed; that is, they evaluated the outcome rather than the process. Although Rheinberg (1993) did not assess which emotional reactions differences in teachers' praise and blame behavior elicited in their students, one could posit that students subjected to an individual reference norm orientation have more experiences of pride than shame, whereas those exposed to a social reference norm orientation have diametrically opposing experiences depending on whether they are high or low achievers. Nonetheless, such potential hypotheses need to be examined and confirmed empirically.

Accordingly, empirical research on the impact of pride and shame on learning and achievement situations should focus particularly on analyzing the ways in which the development of learning and achievement behavior are motivated by external incentives.

Summary and Outlook

Our analyses have shown how far the development of the individual academic self-concept, self-esteem, and achievement motivation are related to experiences of pride and shame. At the same time, we have analyzed how the school systematically generates situations containing a multitude of intensive pride- and shame-relevant elements—not only when performing its institutional tasks of qualification and allocation but also through the accompanying long-term use of social reference norms in overt classroom achievement assessments. Moreover, we have shown clearly that the application of social reference norms leads to different proportions of pride and shame experiences in strong versus weak achievers. The opposing developmental spirals in the two achievement groups can lead students who are weak achievers at the beginning of their school careers to give up learning completely and drop out of the school system. This is not just a theoretical premise; it addresses an urgent contemporary problem with serious consequences for education systems throughout the world. As yet, the relations depicted here have been confirmed in only isolated studies. Research in educational psychology needs to augment these findings with large-scale and thorough research programs.

When academic successes or failures with self-esteem-relevant valencies are linked to a social comparison element that makes learning success a central condition for social recognition and belonging to the reference group, they seem to contain numerous, intensive shame- and pride-relevant events for students that require greater attention from future research in educational psychology.

References

Allesandri, S. M., & Lewis, M. (1996). Differences in pride and shame in maltreated and nonmaltreated preschoolers. *Child Development, 67*, 1857–1869.

Allport, G. W. (1937). *Personality: A psychological interpretation.* New York: Holt.

Ames, A., & Ames, R.C. (1984). Goal structures and motivation. *The Elementary School Journal*, 85(I), 40–52.

Atkinson, J. W. (1966). Motivational determinants of risk taking behavior. In J. W. Atkinson & N. T. Feather (Eds.), *A theory of achievement motivation* (pp. 11–31). New York: Wiley.

Bamber, J. H. (1977). The factorial structure of adolescent responses to a fear survey schedule. *Journal of Genetic Psychology, 130*, 229–238.

Banerjee, R. (2000). The development of an understanding of modesty. *British Journal of Developmental Psychology, 18*, 499–517.

Barrett, K. C. (1995). A functionalist approach to shame and guilt. In J. P. Tangney & K. W. Fischer (Eds.), *Self-conscious emotions. The psychology of shame, guilt, embarrassment, and pride* (pp. 25–63). New York: Guilford Press.

Bibby, T. (2002). Shame: An emotional response to doing mathematics as an adult and a teacher. *British Educational Research Journal, 28*, 705–721.

Brunstein, J., & Heckhausen, H. (2006). Leistungsmotivation [Achievement motivation]. In J. Heckhausen & H. Heckhausen (Eds.), *Motivation und Handeln* (pp. 143–192). Berlin: Springer.

Buss, A. H. (1980). *Self-consciousness and social anxiety.* San Francisco, CA: Freeman.

Covington, M. V. (1992). *Making the grade: A self-worth perspective on motivation and school reform.* Cambridge, UK: Cambridge University Press.

Covington, M. V., Omelich, C. L., & Schwarzer, R. (1986). Anxiety, aspirations, and self-concept in the achievement process: A longitudinal model with latent variables. *Motivation and Emotion, 10*, 71–88.

Czerwenka, K. (1990). *Schülerurteile über die Schule: Bericht über die internationale Untersuchung* [Student ratings of school: Report on the international study]. Frankfurt am Main, Germany: Lang.

Engel, U., & Hurrelmann, K. (1993). *Was Jugendliche wagen. Eine Längsschnittstudie über Drogenkonsum, Streßreaktionen und Delinquenz im Jugendalter* [The risks young people take: A longitudinal study of drug use, stress reactions, and delinquency in youth]. Munich, Germany: Juventa.

Faulstich-Wieland, H. (2000). *Individuum und Gesellschaft. Sozialisationstheorien und Sozialisationsforschung* [Individual and society: Socialization theories and socialization research]. Munich, Germany: Oldenbourg Wissenschaftsverlag.
Faulstich-Wieland, H. (2002). *Sozialisation in Schule und Unterricht* [Socialization in school and class]. Neuwied, Germany: Luchterhand.
Fend, H. (1991). *Identitätsentwicklung in der Adoleszenz. Lebensentwürfe, Selbstfindung und Weltaneignung in beruflichen, familiären und politisch-weltanschaulichen Bereichen* [Adolescent identity formation: Life plans, self-orientation, and entering adult life in work, family, and political domains]. Bern, Switzerland: Huber.
Fend, H. (1997). *Der Umgang mit Schule in der Adoleszenz. Aufbau und Verlust von Lernmotivation, Selbstachtung und Empathie* [Handling school in adolescence: Gain and loss of learning motivation, self-respect, and empathy]. Bern, Switzerland: Huber.
Fend, H. (2000). *Entwicklungspsychologie des Jugendalters. Ein Lehrbuch für pädagogische und psychologische Berufe* [Adolescent developmental psychology: A textbook for teachers and psychologists]. Opladen, Germany: Leske + Budrich.
Fessler, D. M. T. (1999). Toward an understanding of the universality of second order emotions. In A. L. Hinton (Ed.), *Biocultural approaches to the emotions* (pp. 75–116). New York: Cambridge University Press.
Filipp, S.-H. (1985). Selbstkonzept [The self-concept]. In T. Herrmann & E.-D. Lantermann (Eds.), *Persönlichkeitspsychologie. Ein Handbuch in Schlüsselbegriffen* (pp. 347–353). Munich, Germany: Urban & Schwarzenberg.
Friedman, I. A., & Bendas-Jacob, J. O. (1997). Measuring perceived test anxiety in adolescents: A self-report scale. *Educational and Psychological Measurement*, *57*, 1035–1046.
Giddens, A. (1991). *Modernity and self-identity*. Cambridge, UK: Polity Press.
Gilbert, P. (1998). What is shame? Some core issues and controversies. In P. Gilbert (Ed.), *Shame: Interpersonal behavior, psychopathology, and culture* (pp. 3–38). New York: Oxford University Press.
Goffman, E. (1967). *Stigma*. Frankfurt, Germany: Suhrkamp.
Gottschalk, L., & Gleser, G. C. (1969). *Manual of instruction for using the Gottschalk-Gleser content analysis scales*. Berkeley, CA: University of California Press.
Hagtvet, K. A., Man, F., & Sharma, S. (2001). Generalizability of self-related cognitions in test anxiety. *Personality and Individual Differences*, *31*, 1147–1171.
Hambly, K. (2003). *Mit erhobenem Kopf* [Head held high]. Zürich, Switzerland: Oesch.
Harrist, A. W., & Bradley, K. D. (2002). Social exclusion in the classroom: Teachers and students as agents of change. In J. Aronson (Ed.), *Improving academic achievement: Impact of psychological factors on education* (pp. 364–384). Amsterdam, Netherlands: Academic Press.
Heckhausen, H. (1975). Fear of failure as a self-reinforcing motive system. In I. G. Sarason & C. Spielberger (Eds.), *Stress and anxiety* (Vol. II, pp. 117–128). Washington, DC: Hemisphere.
Heckhausen, H. (1977). Achievement motivation and its constructs: A cognitive model. *Motivation and Emotion*, *1*, 283–329.
Heckhausen, J., & Heckhausen, H. (2006). Motivation und Entwicklung [Motivation and development]. In J. Heckhausen & H. Heckhausen (Eds.), *Motivation und Handeln* (pp. 393–454). Berlin: Springer.
Helmke, A. (1992). *Selbstvertrauen und schulische Leistungen* [Self-confidence and academic achievement]. Göttingen, Germany: Hogrefe.
Hewitt, J. P. (1979). *Self and society: A symbolic interactionist social psychology*. Boston, MA: Allyn and Bacon.
Hofmann, H., & Pekrun, R. (1999). Lern- und Leistungsthematische Emotionen [Emotions involved in learning and achievement]. In W. Friedlmeier & M. Holodynski (Eds.), *Emotionale Entwicklung. Funktionen, Regulation und soziokultureller Kontext von Emotionen* (pp. 114–134). Heidelberg, Germany: Spektrum.

Holodynski, M. (2006). Die Entwicklung der Leistungsmotivation im Vorschulalter. Soziale Bewertungen und ihre Auswirkung auf Stolz-, Scham- und Ausdauerreaktionen [The development of achievement motivation at preschool age: Social evaluations and their effect on pride, shame, and perseverance reactions]. *Zeitschrift für Entwicklungspsychologie und Pädagogische Psychologie*, *38*, 2–17.

Holodynski, M., & Friedlmeier, W. (2006). *Development of emotions and emotion regulation*. New York: Springer.

Jacoby, M. (1991). *Scham-Angst und Selbstwertgefühl. Ihre Bedeutung in der Psychotherapie* [Fear of shame and self-esteem: Their role in psychotherapy]. Freiburg, Germany: Walter.

Jacoby, M. (1997). Scham-Angst und Selbstwertgefühl [Fear of shame and self-esteem]. In R. Kühn, M. Raub, & M. Titze (Eds.), *Scham—ein menschliches Gefühl. Kulturelle, pychologische und philosophische Perspektiven* (pp. 159–158). Opladen, Germany: Westdeutscher Verlag.

Kaufmann, G., & Lev, R. (1984). Shame as taboo in American culture. In R. Browne (Ed.), *Forbidden fruits: Taboos and tabooism in culture* (pp. 57–64). Bowling Green, OH: Bowling Green University Press.

Kövecses, Z. (1990). *Emotion concepts*. New York: Springer-Verlag.

Lambrich, H.-J. (1987). *Schulleistung, Selbstkonzeption und Unterrichtsverhalten. Eine qualitative Untersuchung zur Situation "schlechter" Schüler* [Academic achievement, self-concept, and classroom behavior: A qualitative study of the situation of "bad" students]. Weinheim, Germany: Deutscher Studien Verlag.

Lewis, H. B. (1971). *Shame and guilt in neurosis*. New York: International University Press.

Lewis, M. (1992). *Shame. The exposed self*. New York: Free Press.

Meyer, W. U. 1984. *Das Konzept von der eigenen Begabung* [The concept of own ability]. Bern, Switzerland: Huber.

Mummendey, H. D. (1990). Selbstkonzept-Änderungen nach kritischen Lebensereignissen [Changes to self-concept following critical life-events]. In S.-H. Filipp (Ed.), *Kritische Lebensereignisse* (2nd ed., pp. 252–269). Munich, Germany: Urban & Schwarzenberg.

Nathanson, D. (1992). *Shame and pride: Affect, sex, and the birth of the self*. New York: Norton.

Nicholls, J., Patashnick, M., & Nolen, S. B. (1985). Adolescents' theories of education. *Journal of Educational Psychology*, *77*, 683–692.

Nyssen, E. (1995). Schule als Institution: Bildung für alle [The institution of school: Education for all?]? In E. Nyssen & B. Schön (Eds.), *Perspektiven für pädagogisches Handeln. Eine Einführung in Erziehungswissenschaft und Schulpädagogik* (pp. 01–154). Weinheim and Munich, Germany: Beltz.

Oelerich, G. (1998). *Zum Verhältnis der Jugendhilfe zur Schule. Systematische Rekonstruierung und empirische Analyse inter-institutioneller Beziehungen* [The relation of youth services to school: Systematic reconstruction and empirical analysis of inter-institutional relations]. Unpublished doctoral dissertation, University of Heidelberg, Germany.

Pekrun, R. (1983). *Schulische Persönlichkeitsentwicklung: Theorieentwicklung und empirische Erhebung zur Persönlichkeitsentwicklung von Schülern der 5. bis 10. Klassenstufe* [Personality development at school: Theoretical analysis and empirical assessment of personality development in 5th- to 10th-grade students]. Frankfurt am Main, Germany: Lang.

Pekrun, R. (1992). The impact of emotions on learning and achievement: Towards a theory of cognitive/motivational mediators. *Applied Psychology*, *41*, 359–376.

Pekrun, R. (1994). Schule als Sozialisationsinstanz [School as a socialization agency]. In K. A. Schneewind (Ed.), *Psychologie der Erziehung und Sozialisation* (pp. 465–494). Göttingen, Germany: Hogrefe.

Pekrun, R. (1998). Schüleremotionen und ihre Förderung: Ein blinder Fleck der Unterrichtsforschung [Student emotions and their promotion: A blind spot in classroom research]. *Psychologie in Erziehung und Unterricht*, *45*, 230–248.

Pekrun, R. (2000). A social cognitive, control-value theory of achievement emotions. In J. Heckhausen (Ed.), *Motivational psychology of human development* (pp. 143–163). Oxford, UK: Elsevier.

Pekrun, R., Goetz, T., Titz, W., & Perry, R. (2002). Academic emotions in students' self-regulated learning and achievement: A program of qualitative and quantitative research. *Educational Psychologist*, *37*, 2, 91–105.

Petermann, U., & Petermann, F. (1989). *Training mit sozial unsicheren Kindern* [Training socially at-risk children] (pp. 359–372). Munich, Germany: PVU.

Prüß, F., Bettmer, F., Hartnuß, B., & Maykus, S. (2000). *Forschungsbericht "Entwicklung der Kooperation von Jugendhilfe und Schule in Mecklenburg-Vorpommern"* [Research report: "Trends in cooperation between youth services and school in Mecklenburg-Western Pommerania"]. Greifswald, Germany: Universität Greifswald.

Retzinger, S. M. (1998). Shame in the therapeutic relationship. In P. Gilbert (Ed.), *Shame. interpersonal behavior, psychopathology, and culture* (pp. 206–222). New York: Oxford University Press.

Rheinberg, F. (1980). *Leistungsbewertung und Lernmotivation* [Achievement assessment and learning motivation]. Göttingen, Germany: Hogrefe.

Rheinberg, F. (1987). Soziale versus individuelle Leistungsvergleiche und ihre motivationalen Folgen [Social versus individual comparisons of achievement and their motivational consequences]. In R. Olechowski & E. Persy (Eds.), *Fördernde Leistungsbeurteilungen* (pp. 80–115). Vienna: Jugend und Volk.

Rheinberg, F. (1993). Bezugsnorm und Wahrnehmung eigener Tüchtigkeit [Reference norm and perception of own capability]. In S. H. Filipp (Ed.), *Selbstkonzeptforschung: Probleme, Befunde, Perspektiven* (pp. 237–252). Stuttgart, Germany: Klett.

Rheinberg, F., & Krug, S. (1999). *Motivationsförderung im Schulalltag* [Promoting motivation in daily school life]. Göttingen, Germany: Hogrefe.

Scheff, T. J. (1988). Shame and conformity: The deference-emotion system. *American Sociological Review*, *53*, 395–406.

Scheff, T. J. (1998). Shame in the labeling of mental illness. In P. Gilbert (Ed.), *Shame. interpersonal behavior, psychopathology, and culture* (pp. 191–205). New York: Oxford University Press.

Scheff, T. J. (2003). Shame in self and society. *Symbolic Interaction*, *26*, 239–262.

Shibutani, T. (1961). *Society and personality*. Englewood Cliffs, NJ: Prentice-Hall.

Schmalt, H.-D. (2005). Validity of a short form of the Achievement Motive Grid (AMG-S): Evidence for the three-factor structure emphasizing active and passive forms of fear of failure. *Journal of Personality Assessment*, *84*, 172–184.

Schöne, C. et al. (2003). Das Fähigkeitsselbstkonzept und seine Erfassung [The academic self-concept and its assessment]. In J. Stiensmeier-Pelster & F. Rheinberg (Eds.), *Diagnostik von Motivation und Selbstkonzept* (pp. 3–14). Göttingen, Germany: Hogrefe.

Schopler, J., & Matthews, M. W. (1965). The influence of the perceived causal locus of partner's dependence on the use of interpersonal power. *Journal of Personality and Social Psychology*, *2*, 609–612.

Schore, A. N. (1998). Early shame experience and infant brain development. In P. Gilbert (Ed.), *Shame, interpersonal behavior, psychopathology, and culture* (pp. 57–97). New York: Oxford University Press.

Schultheiss, C. (1997). Scham und Normen—Überlegungen aus sozialwissenschaftlicher und analytisch-philosophischer Sicht [Shame and norms from the perspective of social science and analytical philosophy]. In R. Kühn, M. Raub, & M. Titze (Eds.), *Scham—ein menschliches Gefühl* (pp. 97–110). Opladen, Germany: Westdeutscher Verlag.

Simmel, G. (1983). Zur Psychologie der Scham [On the psychology of shame]. In G. Simmel (Ed.), *Soziologische Schriften* (pp. 140–150). Frankfurt am Main, Germany: Suhrkamp.

Smith, A. (1982). *A theory of moral sentiments*. Indianapolis, IN: Liberty Press.

Spinath, B., & Schöne, C. (2003). Ziele als Bedingungen von Motivation am Beispiel der Skalen zur Erfassung der Lern- und Leistungsmotivation (SELLMO) [Goals as conditions for motivation illustrated with scales for assessing learning and achievement motivation]. In J. Stiensmeier-Pelster & F. Rheinberg (Eds.), *Diagnostik von Motivation und Selbstkonzept* (pp. 29–40). Göttingen, Germany: Hogrefe.

Standop, J. (2001). *Emotionen und kognitives schulisches Lernen aus interdisziplinärer Perspektive. Emotionspsychologische, neurobiologische und schulpädagogische Zusammenhänge—ihre Berücksichtigung im schulischen Bildungsauftrag wie den Forschungen zum Unterrichtsklima der Klassenführung* [Emotions and cognitive academic learning from an interdisciplinary perspective]. Frankfurt am Main, Germany: Lang.

Stiensmeier-Pelster, J., & Rheinberg, F. (Eds.). (2003). *Diagnostik von Motivation und Selbstkonzept* [Diagnosing motivation and the self-concept]. Göttingen, Germany: Hogrefe.

Stipek, D. (1995). The development of pride and shame in toddlers. In J. P. Tangney & K. W. Fischer (Eds.), *Self-conscious emotions. The psychology of shame, guilt, embarrassment, and pride* (pp. 237–254). New York: Guilford Press.

Tangney, J. P. (1995). Shame and guilt in interpersonal relationships. In J. P. Tangney & K. W. Fischer (Eds.), *Self-conscious emotions. The psychology of shame, guilt, embarrassment, and pride* (pp. 114–142). New York: Guilford Press.

Tangney, J. P., & Dearing, R. L. (2002). *Shame and guilt*. New York: Guilford Press.

Tillmann, H.-J. (2000). *Sozialisationstheorien. Eine Einführung in den Zusammenhang von Gesellschaft, Institution und Subjektwerdung* [Socialization theories: An introduction to relations between society, institution, and personality development]. Reinbek, Germany: Rowohlt.

Tomkins, S. (1987). Shame. In D. L. Nathanson (Ed.), *The many faces of shame* (pp. 133–161). New York: Norton.

Trautner, H.-M. & Lohaus, A. (1985). Entwicklung der Persönlichkeit [Personality development]. In F.-R. Herrmann & U. Lantermann (Eds.), *Persönlichkeitspsychologie* (pp. 387–395). Munich, Germany: Urban & Schwarzenberg.

Turner, J. C., Husman, J., & Schallert, D. L. (2002). The importance of students' goals in their emotional experience of academic failure: Investigating the precursors and consequences of shame. *Educational Psychologist, 37*(2), 79–89.

Turner, J. C., & Schallert, D. L. (1996). *Motivational and situational predictors of real-time shame reactions to an important academic evaluation.* Paper presented at the annual meeting of the International Psychology Conference, Montreal, Quebec, Canada.

Turner, J. C., & Schallert, D. L. (2001). Expectancy-value relationships of shame reactions and shame resiliency. *Journal of Educational Psychology, 93*, 320–329.

Turner, J. C., Thorpe, P. K., & Meyer, D. K. (1998). Students' reports of motivation and negative affect: A theoretical and empirical analysis. *Journal of Educational Psychology, 90*, 758–771.

Weiner, B. (1985). An attributional theory of achievement motivation and emotion. *Psychological Review, 92*, 548–573.

Wells, L. E., & Marwell, G. (1976). *Self-esteem: Its conceptualization and measurement.* Beverly Hills, CA: Sage Publications.

Zammuner, V. L. (1996). Felt emotions, and verbally communicated emotions: The case of pride. *European Journal of Social Psychology, 26*, 233–245.

Anger, Shame, and Justice: Regulative and Evaluative Function of Emotions in the Ancient and Modern Worlds

Eva-Maria Engelen

Abstract* Analyzing the ancient Greek point of view concerning anger, shame, and justice and a very modern one, one can see that anger has a regulative function, but shame does as well. Anger puts the other in his place, thereby regulating hierarchies. Shame regulates the social relations of recognition. Both emotions also have an evaluative function because anger evaluates a situation with regard to a humiliation and shame with regard to a misdemeanor. In addition, attention must be paid to the correct molding of these emotions and the correct ways of using them during rearing one to be good or just (i.e., in personality formation).

Introduction

"Anger" is the first word in Western literature. Homer's *Iliad* starts with "mênin" (anger),[1] emphasizing that Achilles' anger is the central theme of the first and powerful epic in our civilization.[2] Achilles seems to recognize no natural end to his anger, his rage, or his revenge—something that the classic epic makes very clear. Outbreaks of anger prolonged until their bitter end and an insatiable thirst for revenge were fatal for complete communities, bringing disaster to entire generations of uninvolved bystanders.

This indicates that the emotion of an individual can be a concern for the entire community. The present chapter focuses on two questions: (1) Which functions do emotions possess for the individual in a social context? (2) Which functions do emotions have for regulating social life and the recognition of rules? For the ancient world, the emotions anger and shame (predominantly

*This paper is a shortened and for this volume revised version of Eva-Maria Engelen (2008) in "Archiv für Begriffsgeschichte", 50.

E.-M. Engelen (✉)
Department of Philosophy, Faculty of Philosophy, University of Konstanz, Konstanz, Germany
e-mail: eva-maria.engelen@uni-konstanz.de

B. Röttger-Rössler, H.J. Markowitsch (eds.), *Emotions as Bio-cultural Processes*, 395
DOI 10.1007/978-0-387-09546-2_18, © Springer Science+Business Media, LLC 2009

in Aristotle) are singled out for this purpose. For modern times, this chapter analyzes only shame (in Kertész, 2002).

Myles Burnyeat (2002) has pointed out correctly that in Greek antiquity, anger was not just a legitimate emotion for men (in contrast to women) but a necessary one.[3] Aristotle, for example, says that a man who does not get angry when he or his friend has been insulted has a slavish character.[4] Such a man is unlikely to defend himself (NE IV 11, 1126a 3–9), even though it is wrong to endure being insulted (NE VII 7; 1149a 32-34). Hence, for Aristotle, lack of anger is not to be praised but to be blamed because one should not be without anger but should rage when necessary to defend from insult.

Therefore, according to Aristotle, the "good-tempered" man who remains unperturbed is also the man who can apply his anger in a controlled way to avenge the pain of insult. He knows how to be angry at the right things and with the right people and as long as he ought. Therefore, the virtuous man is the man who possesses the necessary degree of angry behavior and not he who is without anger (NE IV, 11; 1125b32-34). This may well make the angry man capable of ruling others (NE IV, 11; 1126b2-3). Anger, well apportioned, also helps the brave to be virtuous (NE III 11; 116b31-32). Aristotle even goes so far as to assume a link between anger and reason. For he who is unperturbed, the good-tempered man, combines anger with reason. The former is even ruled by the latter (NE IV, 11; 1125b33-35) because one is not deaf to reason in a state of anger (NE VII 7; 1149a25-27). Aristotle explains this by stating that the affect takes over the task revealed by the conclusions of reason: When reason judges that one has been insulted, the emotion of anger arises immediately as an outcome of the thought that one must defend oneself (NE VII 7; 1149a33-35). Hence, the emotion is finally an element that decides on and triggers actions; that helps determine order in the community.

That the practice of such laudable and valiant behavior is not just desirable for the individual but also benefits the general well-being of the community and the state is already suggested in the introduction to the *Nicomachean Ethics* (NE I 1; 1094b7-8). The Good is equal for the individual and the community.

Because individuals largely had to be self-reliant when asserting their own interests and rights as well as those of their dependents, they also had to learn how to assert themselves. In this context, Myles Burnyeat (2002) pointed out that there was no state monopoly on the use of force in antique states and no public prosecution service to pursue misdemeanors or crimes officially. Injured parties or their relatives had to bring charges before the court themselves. Naturally, this does not just apply to antique states, but they serve as an example disclosing more clearly how the exercise of force, the control of force, emotionality, and norms are interwoven.

Excessive anger, representing one pole on the dimension of being good-tempered or unperturbed (the other pole being a lack of anger) had to be avoided. The head of a household, for example, could beat his slaves or even his son or his wife to death, for this right pertained to his role of maintaining order in his miniature community. In such a society, punishment and revenge, as Burnyeat

(2002) pointed out, cannot be separated completely. Greek and Latin each use identical words for punishment and revenge: *timôréô* in Greek and *ulciscor* in Latin. He who (within appropriate limits) has to take revenge because he has been insulted and humiliated (a situation disturbing order in the community) and who additionally can and is obliged to punish others to maintain order in the community must be able to exercise appropriate control over his emotions. In a society lacking control over the use of force, but simultaneously having a binding code of honor, the control of anger or rage becomes particularly significant. Anger and shame also play a major role in some so-called face-to-face communities that have no written legal code but only a verbal common law based on customary rights. These emotions are accompanied by social exclusion, the threat of and occasional enactment of which being one of the mechanisms making people behave according to rules. Major legal infringements are followed by social death. Persons have to leave their community; and their honor, self-esteem, and pride are taken from them (see Casimir & Jung, this volume, section on "Pride, Shame, and the Pain of Being Excluded").

Hence, even seemingly purely destructive emotions such as anger or rage have a regulative function for a community, the destructive element being launched when a person does not know how to control these emotions. However, the ethic of self-restraint is a relatively late development in Greek antiquity. In Homer, one initially finds just a heroic ideal of self-assertion: The virtuous man always has to show that he is braver and more courageous than all the others with whom he is competing for primacy. Virtuous deeds are therefore matters of rivalry between men, but they also depend on fateful events over which the individual has no influence—even though they may suffice to shame him. For the individual, acquiring virtue-and that means predominantly courage-is therefore not only a question of struggling for dominance among all the other virtuous men who are striving for the same; it also requires the favor of the gods. The resulting combination of morals, shame, and honor is also called the Homeric culture of shame in the literature. A morality of self-restraint directed toward avoiding excess and striving more toward justice than valor becomes recognizable only 200 years after Homer in the work of Hesiod (Canto-Sperber, 2000, pp. 118–123).

Nonetheless, even the Homeric culture of shame, as Bernard Williams (1993) has pointed out, cannot be reduced to witnessed infringements of conventional standards and the accompanying disruption of order. It is also the case that shame discloses the social status of actors, their emotional well-being, and even their character. Hence, the Homeric concept of shame already displays several features that modern culture would subsume under the heading of guilt, although we are unable to say whether a concept of guilt was already present in Homer or in antiquity.

To characterize shame in Homer, Williams (1993) analyzed how he associated the following features with it: timidity, embarrassment, and shyness. Such associations are not unknown to us; we are familiar with them in our own as well as in other cultures (Röttger-Rössler, 2004, p. 153). What, in contrast, we may well find unfamiliar is the way in which the Greek word for shame (*aidós*) also serves as a kind of battle cry. In Homer, for example, an appeal to *aidós* on the battlefield is a frequently given motive for entering the fight; he who does not fight must later feel shame for having been ineffective.

Aidós, when combined with anger or indignation (*némesis*), is a social emotion. When humans have a sense of shame or an awareness of the borders to shame, not only do certain actions become taboo but also, and above all, they have a sense of the shame and honor of others (or at least those others they recognize as equals). They respond sensitively to violations of honor with indignation and anger.

Nonetheless, Williams (1993, p. 81) warns us against believing that the only object of Homeric shame was success or failure in individual competition, and that it involved only an adaptation to the prejudices of the community. Because the reaction of shame does not just depend on violations being detected, being seen, it cannot just be an adaptation to social standards. An *imagined* observer suffices; one does not actually have to be witnessed. This is important when we look at the development of social shame in humans in which this imaginary observer becomes internalized as a third party. This internalization is already found in Homer (Williams, 1993, p. 83; Casimir & Jung, this volume, section "Pride and Shame as 'Self-Conscious Emotions").

Williams shows clearly that these processes do not just involve the internalization of an imagined observer in the following.

> [T]here has to be something for these interlinked attitudes to be about . . . some kinds of behaviour are admired, others accepted, others despised, and it is those attitudes that are internalised, not simply the prospect of hostile reactions. If that were not so, there would be, once more, no shame *culture*, no shared ethical attitudes at all. (pp. 83–84)

and

> [T]he motivations of shame would not be internalised at all. No one would have a character, in effect, and, moreover, the very idea of there being a shame *culture*, a coherent system for the regulation of conduct, would be unintelligible. (pp. 81–82)

With the motive of shame, Williams is addressing the norms representing shared ethical attitudes. Basically, it does not really matter whether this is primarily an internalized attitude or an internalized and thereby acknowledged norm that is part of the ethics of the individual who feels shame. The internalized attitude is itself part of a normative behavior and, as an experienced attitude toward others, it also has, in turn, a normative character.

As Rapp (2002) points out, this relation can also be found in Aristotle.

> Insofar . . . as it is argued from 1384a23 onward [in *Rhetoric*] that one particularly feels shame in the presence of those persons to whom one attributes importance, it becomes clear that one's own evaluations are also reflected in the feared contempt of others; then by feeling shame in the presence of those whose opinion is important to one, shame also has something to do indirectly with the fact that one has failed to live up to one's own standards. (p. 632, translated)

The position of the "naturalistically" oriented sophists of the 5th century recalls the ethic of self-assertion but not the Homeric culture of shame.

Nonetheless, we have no direct source on this stance and can only reconstruct its essence from the Platonic Dialogues (*Gorgias, Politeia*). It proposes a naturalism countering existing laws with a morality based on nature according to which power and wealth should go to the strongest. The concept of honor, in direct contrast to Homer, is of no significance. In these writings, legitimacy is no longer established by an individual excelling in martial valor and proving his honor but is illustrated by the behavior of wild animals in which the stronger assert themselves. The issue of natural endowments and natural strengths and the associated success is already discussed here explicitly for ethics, whereas the nonnaturalistically oriented sophists assume that not only moral but also legal norms come from the conventionally fixed *nomos* and the agreement on it, thus making them teachable. We shall see that Aristotle has his own answer to the question whether there is a natural disposition for ethical behavior or whether it can be taught and should be a part of education.

That the issue of honor and of anger was also discussed during Plato's times can be seen in a definition of justice that Glaucon, acting as *advocatus diaboli*, proposed in Plato's *Politeia*: "an intermediate one between the best, namely being unjust and unpunished and the worst, namely, the inability to avenge oneself when suffering injustice" (359a). For Plato, sentiments, affects, and desires should also be subjected to rational judgment that is oriented toward the Good in order to act in harmony with justice. However, in Plato, we can also find, predominantly in the *Politeia*, approaches viewing virtue as a combination of thought, emotionality, and desire. Plato also associates rationality with a soul concept that includes desire and the affective domain. Nonetheless, he tries to transform ethics in the Socratic tradition into a pursuit of knowledge. This unresolved tension in Plato's works does not repeat itself in the Aristotelian conception of virtue (Canto-Sperber, 2000, p. 129).

Aristotle refuses to reduce virtue to knowledge. For him, it is not the *knowledge* of the Good that is crucial but the considerations on how to become virtuous and lead a virtuous life that can be put into practice. We have already seen that the virtuous is not free from emotions but feels them when they are appropriate and in the strength in which they are appropriate (EN 1106b21-24). In addition, even an emotion such as anger is not without reference to *logos* and does not emerge without reference to the conclusions of reason.

We have already seen that anger follows on from the idea[5] that one has been dishonored and must defend oneself. By reestablishing order in the social community through the interplay of what are perceived to be valid principles and the subsequently correct dosage of emotion, emotions also serve to impose norms. Emotions, even one such as anger, therefore have a regulative function in a community (for other ethnic groups, see chapter 12, Casimir & Jung, "Honour and Dishonour": Connotations of a Socio-symbolic Category in Cross-Cultural Perspective, this volume).

Anger, as we have seen, has a regulative function, but shame does as well. Anger puts the other in his place, thereby regulating hierarchies. Shame regulates the social relations of recognition: Whom do I respect; whose judgment is valuable to me? Both emotions also have an evaluative function because anger evaluates a situation with regard to humiliation[6] and shame with regard to a misdemeanor. In addition, attention must be paid to the correct molding of these emotions and the correct ways to use them in rearing to be good or just (i.e., in personality formation). According to Most (2003), Achilles' personality also reveals a development in terms of his emotionality. In the *Iliad*, Achilles changes from one who lives out his anger and his revenge on the battlefields to a character who feels sympathy for others. The role of emotionality in the development of personality or character is accordingly not limited to shame (Most, 2003, pp. 72–75). These regulative and evaluative functions are joined by *motivational functions* for the action readiness that Aristotle also mentions when he writes that anger emerges when humiliation is ascertained and persists until retaliation.

Uncontrolled emotion, in contrast, destroys the social order; and because it is not subject to any natural constraints, it requires a social or an internalized control. Viewed systematically, one can conceive of not only explicit or implicit norms in a society but also self-control (or autonomy) as being responsible for the establishment and maintenance of such a control. In his deliberations on ethics, Aristotle considers both forms of control: not only laws but also a control that becomes self-control through habitualization.

For Aristotle, affect or emotion is everything that has to do with pleasure or pain (NE 1105b),[7] and feeling pleasure or pain (NE 1104b) over the suitable is something that one has to be habitualized to know from infancy. It is necessary to practice the right *habitus* because virtue is a *habitus* (NE 1106a), an act of self-determination that is learned and practiced.

According to Aristotle, much is required to become good and noble. First, it is necessary to have the right disposition, which expresses itself in, among others, a certain shamefacedness that is not available to all and indeed is given to only a few. For Aristotle, shamefacedness displays a feeling for noble behavior. Boys with a sense of shame therefore indicate a good disposition for becoming good and just men (NE IV, 15; 1128b15-16; 1179b7-13). Education can build on this natural shamefacedness because it means a turning toward the beautiful and the Good that can be built up into a power of judgment through education so that those reared in this way will apply it by habit in later life. This is also necessary, according to Aristotle, because emotions, in their emergence and their impact, are always related to opinions, judgments, and beliefs (Rapp, 2002, pp. 554–555). Hence, one feels anger because one considers that one has been humiliated or shamed; and one feels shame because one believes that one has not lived up to a demand or a norm. However, this also implies a relation between the development of emotionality in a mature personal character and the development of judgment ability in this person. This is because Aristotle explains the emergence of emotions on the basis of physiological changes in the body and on the basis of character dispositions, which are actually dispositions toward a certain emotional reaction (Aristotle, *Rhetoric* 1356a1-20; see also Rapp, 2002, pp. 567–568).

Aristotle expressly treats the issue of whether there is a natural disposition to virtue—whether we become virtuous or good through habit or it can be taught. Finally, he offers us what in some ways is a mixture of the three named aspects. He says that there cannot be a natural disposition toward this because otherwise everybody would have to be virtuous by nature, which is not the case. Instead, virtue comes to few, and not by the power of nature but by the favor of the gods who nonetheless grant a *feeling* for the morally beautiful and good that is related to virtue (NE 1179b30-31).[8] Moreover, only those who possess a character akin to it, to such a feeling, are also receptive to talk and *teaching* if they have additionally been *habituated* to the Good and the beautiful through their upbringing. In other words, the teaching, the talk, the argument, the conclusion bear fruit to the fullest extent only in those who have a feeling or disposition for the Good and have additionally experienced habituation in this direction based on an upbringing directed toward wanting the Good and doing it.

For such habitualization to occur, it is necessary to anchor norms in society. Aristotle speaks of laws that prepare the way for habitualization.

> But it is hard for someone to get the correct guidance towards excellence, from childhood on, if he has not been brought up under *laws that aim at that effect*; for a moderate and resistant way of life is not pleasant for most people, especially when they are young. So their upbringing and patterns of behavior must be ordered by the laws; for these ways will not be painful to them if they have become used to them. (NE 1179b 31-35)

Hence, it is only when it has become second nature to recognize virtue and act in this sense that one has learned to be virtuous. But Logos and reason, which one tries to impart through upbringing, can only be heard by those who are shameful, and such persons are few and far between (NE 179b11-13). Shamefacedness is the fertile soil in which the habituation to virtue may grow. He who is ashamed of something has also recognized that the deed or the attitude for which he feels shame was incorrect. The virtuous person does not desist from doing something because he will be punished for it but because he feels shame (NE 1179b11-13).

"Shame," however, is not a virtue for Aristotle but an emotion (NE IV 15, 1128b10ff.).[9] More than two and a half decades ago, Myles Burnyeat (1980) pointed out that Aristotle, following Plato, described the state of moving from shamefacedness to virtue and to the just as a state similar to that following on closely from anger (NE 1135b28-29).[10] What shame and anger have in common is the orientation toward the just and the honor that one has to defend and demand for oneself and others.[11] Because the habitualization to virtue starts at an early age (Aristotle, NE 1104b10-13), but is only available to a small Greek elite, the other citizens of the *polis* have to be guided by laws and the threat of punishment—something that is not necessary for those habitualized in virtue (NE 1179b11-13).

Even though in some places Aristotle seems to assume that anger and shame as evaluative responses to processes in the world are reactions guided by judgments, in other places it is clear that these reactions are guided by the sensation of pleasure or pain, which is why one has to be reared from childhood onward to delight in or be distressed by the things one should (NE 1104b10-14) and to the right degree.

We do not first come to the conclusion that the behavior of the other should be interpreted as an insult to the person and then develop anger. We also do not reflect on the humiliation that has been done to us or that we do to others and then develop the feeling of shame. It is far more the case that the emotional reactions of shame and anger are mostly immediate responses to the situation itself or to our recall of the corresponding situations. This is not to imply that these emotional reactions proceed without the involvement of concepts and thoughts, but that the latter do not have to play the initial role (on the relation between emotions, thoughts, cognitive aspects, and the formal object, see DeSousa, 1997, pp. 204–207; on Aristotle in particular, see Rapp, 2002, p. 547). One indication for this is that shame for an act cannot be made to disappear simply by being told that we could not have acted in any other way. Even anger fades only slowly when we ascertain that the other did not act in the way he or she did to humiliate us.

In this sense, shame functions in an essentially different way than guilt. On the one hand, shame points us toward the social sphere and its regulations and on the other hand toward the person as an autonomous being: "What we have discovered about the Greeks' understanding of these reactions, that they can transcend both an assertive egoism and a conventional concern for public opinion, applies equally well to what we recognize in our own world as shame" (Williams, 1993, p. 88). Because shame, when we feel it, forces us to take the perspective of the other and not just to accept our guilt, it possibly relates us simultaneously to our self *and* to the other. Accepting our guilt, in contrast, places us in a far more intellectual relationship to the other than does the shame we feel toward the other. Although we also "feel" "guilty," this "feeling guilty" is more of a delayed insight regarding the event that is based on the guilt rather than any immediate emotional reaction that places oneself in a close relationship with the other.

Because emotional arousal does not disappear merely as result of argument, the reflected influence requires means in addition to the argument alone. This is why Aristotle worked out his ideas on the habitualization of virtue. This virtue has to be habitualized through upbringing in such a way that it becomes second nature to the individual. Virtuous, good behavior can therefore also not be taught. We cannot acquire it by listening to a lecture but only through being reared to it in practice. Shame acquires a special role here according to Aristotle because feeling shame prevents young men from the errors they would otherwise commit under the influence of sensations of pleasure and pain.[12] Those who have a sense of shame and have been brought up well have nonetheless learned to feel pleasure over just deeds and pain over unjust ones. Those who do not have this sense of shame, in contrast, as mentioned above, can be made to act correctly only through being threatened with punishment. The process of rearing one to the correct feeling of pleasure for the just deed, which begins with the disposition to sense shame, is the habitualization to virtue that is attained completely when the Good, as such, is perceived to be that which brings pleasure (NE 11537-15).

In the work of Imre Kertész (1990, 2004), we can find a discussion on shame in his *Kaddisch for an unborn child* that runs counter to those presented above but nonetheless cannot be understood without them.

> [W]illingly or not, I can do nothing else: if I write, I remember, I have to remember, though I don't know why I have to remember, obviously for the sake of knowing, remembering is knowing, we live in order to remember what we know, because we cannot forget what we know, don't worry, children, not out of some kind of "moral duty," no, come off it, it's simply *not at our discretion*, we are not *able*, to forget, that is the way we are created, we live in order to know and to remember, and perhaps, indeed probably, indeed with almost total certainty, the reason why we know and remember is in order that somebody should feel shame on our account if he has gone so far as to create us, yes, we remember for the one who either is or isn't, it doesn't matter, because either he is or he isn't: in the end it comes down to the same thing, the essential point is that we should remember, know and remember, that somebody—anybody—should feel shame on our account and (possibly) for us.[13] . . . And after that a gentle drizzle of surprise, daily renewed that, would you believe it, I leapt up and so to say concealed again after all, *ich sprang doch auf*, indeed I'm still here, though I don't know why, unless it was pure chance, the way I was born, I'm just as much an accomplice to my sticking around as I was to my coming into this world—all right, I concede, a grain more shame attaches to hanging around, especially if one has done one's utmost to hang around, but that's all, nothing more: I wasn't willing to be taken in like other suckers by the general passion and breast-beating claptrap about sticking around, God help us! and *in any case you're always partly to blame*, that's all there is to it, I have stuck around . . .. (pp. 26–28)

Kertész was reflecting on the shame of the concentration camp survivor, and we must take a closer look at what the function of this shame is. However, he is also reflecting on the shame of the adolescent regarding his cowardice at boarding school. In the perspective of the first-person narrator, the time spent at boarding school was decisively not used for what Aristotle would call the desired upbringing to virtue but solely to attain compliance with norms imposed from above. These passages also reveal that shame does not just refer to remembered situations, but that an immediate reaction to the event emerges in the remembering itself.

> I now know what sort of ritual it was that I witnessed in that paternalistic, father-usurping institution: I witnessed a *public castration* staged for purposes of our intimidation, *with our cooperation*; in other words, with our cooperation they castrated one of our pals *in order to intimidate us*, or in other words, through the very ceremony itself they turned us into the ultimately perverted accomplices of an ultimately perverted act, and it makes not the slightest difference, I said to my wife, whether they did this quite deliberately or merely out of habit, out of sheer *educational habit*, the pernicious habit of a pernicious education. (p. 106)

And later:

> Domination is unchallengeable, unchallengeable the laws by which we must live, though we can never fully live up to these laws: we are always sinners before our father and God, I said to my wife. After all, my father likewise only equipped me for the same thing, the same *culture*, as the school. . ..[14] (p. 111)

The culture that is being judged here is the education to obedience, which is precisely not an education to autonomy—to freedom—but to compliance with laws. That which he is denied in this upbringing, namely the attainment of freedom and autonomy, the first-person narrator has to acquire later at the concentration camp, where he experiences a living example of such behavior.

> During those years I also became aware of the true nature of my work, which in essence is nothing other than to dig, dig further and to the end, the grave that others started to dig for me in the clouds,[15] the winds, the nothingness. During those years I dreamed anew the task and secret hope that had been dreamed before, and now I know it was a dream based on "Teacher's" example. During these years I became aware of my life, on the one hand as fact, on the other as a *cerebral mode of existence*, to be more precise, a certain mode of existence that would no longer survive, did not wish to survive, indeed probably was not even capable of surviving survival, a life which nevertheless has its own demand, namely, that it *be formed*, like a rounded, rock-hard object, in order that it should *persist*, after all, no matter why, no matter for whom—*for everybody and nobody*, for whoever it is or isn't, it's all the same, for whoever will feel shame on our account and (possibly) for us; which I shall put an end to and liquidate, however, as *fact*, as the mere fact of survival, even if, and truly only if, that fact happens to be me. (p. 119)

The choice of vocabulary comes from Paul Celan's *Todesfuge* (Death Fugue). But in Kertész, it is not the one who orders graves to be dug and who sets his pack on the inmate who is dreaming but the one who has to do the digging. Kertész's first-person narrator adopts the role of the one giving the order to dig the graves. This change of roles reveals the total tragedy of survival. The survivor believes that he has helped to dig the others' graves: "God help us! and *in any case you're always partly to blame*, that's all there is to it, I have stuck around.... " (pp. 27–28). By adopting the role of the dreamer, the first-person narrator suggests that obeying orders is more than obedience. The identification with the murderer of the Jews in Celan's poem also manifests in the fact that both are writing. The murderer in Celan's poem writes letters to Germany, and his victim who identifies with him in Kertész's narrative, writes to be freed from having to obey orders. However, he can only gain this freedom when he is dead. Hence, digging one's own grave by writing, and that means by remembering, and the resulting knowledge of the conditions of freedom, is performed to follow the other dead ones whose grave he believes to have helped to dig. That the writing is a means to find personal freedom finally makes it possible for the first-person narrator to keep the tragedy of survival within bearable limits. For the reader, this suggests an unsuspected sense that the reader is nonetheless unable to pursue.

This sense is extended with the following sentences:

> [N]ow pay attention, what is truly irrational and genuinely inexplicable is not evil but, on the contrary, good. That is precisely why ... for a long time now I have been interested solely in the lives of saints,[16] because they are what I find interesting and incomprehensible, they are what I am unable to find merely rational explanations for; and even in this respect Auschwitz ... proved a fruitful enterprise, so ... I will tell you a story, and then you explain it to me, if you can. As I'm sitting in front of a roomful of old hands, I shall be brief, and if I say no more than *Lager*, and winter, and a hospital transport, and cattle wagons, and a single issue of cold food rations, when the journey will last for who knows how many days and the rations are doled out in tenths, and, lying on the wooden contraption that passed for my stretcher, I could not take my

> dog-eyes off a man, or rather skeleton, who, I have no idea why, was only ever referred to as "Teacher" and who had picked up my ration too, and then the entrainment, and of course, time after time, the roll call doesn't tally, and a yelling and commotion and a kick, then I feel myself being snatched up and dumped in front of the next wagon, and it's a long, long while since I saw either "Teacher" or my ration ... there was still a chance of staying alive. Except that with the ration gone this all at once looked extremely dubious, while on the other hand, and I clarified this cold-bloodedly to myself, my ration would precisely double "Teacher's" chances .... Yet what should I see a few minutes later? Calling out and looking frantically all around, "Teacher" was staggering towards me, a single issue of cold rations in his hand, and when he glimpses me on the stretcher he quickly places it on my stomach; I am about to say something, and it seems that astonishment must be written all over my face because he, though already scurrying back—if they don't find him in his place they will simply beat him to death.... "Teacher" ... did what he did in order I should stay alive ... he himself was plainly guided by something else, plainly it was primarily to preserve his own life that he did what he did, only incidentally to preserve my life too. And the question here, and find me an answer to it if you can, is why he did that.... Yes, and in my opinion *this* is what there is no explanation for, since it is not rational as compared with the tangible rationality of an issue of food rations, which in the extreme situation called a concentration camp might serve to avoid the ultimate end.... (pp. 41–44)

Later:

> I rejoined that that concept was, in my opinion, freedom, and freedom primarily because "Teacher" did not do what he *ought* to have done, that is, what he *ought* to have done according to rational calculations of hunger, the survival instinct and madness, and the blood compact that the dominating power had entered into with hunger, the survival instinct and madness, but instead, repudiating all that, he did something else, something that he *ought not* to have done and that no rationally minded person would expect from anybody. (p. 46)

Kertész suggests that "Teacher" did what he did because he can only live as a free person, and it is only when he does what he does—free from the constraint of human beings and nature—that he is free. "Teacher" stands out in a characteristic way from a mutual process of social recognition (see above). Perhaps Nietzsche's (1882/1930) saying, "*Was ist das Siegel der erreichten Freiheit?—Sich nicht mehr vor sich selber schämen*" [What is the sign that freedom has been achieved?—No longer having to feel shame when looking at oneself] applies to him.[17] The first-person narrator has to follow "Teacher's" path to the end, has to follow his example, so that somebody, who either is or is not, should feel shame on our behalf. In Aristotelian terms, we can say that "Teacher" has fulfilled his *ergon* as a human being by acting in freedom because being free belongs to the human *ergon*.[18]

What is he, who either is or is not, ashamed about when he feels shame in Kertész's pioneering story? This is the decisive question in the present context of shame and justice. It is necessary to go back further when trying to answer it. In the earlier examples from the ancient world in which shame took on a central role, the emergence of shame pointed to the failure to comply with a social norm or rule. That the reason for an exposure that leads to loss of honor and shame is a violation of a norm that has to be complied with as part of the self-image is a common definition (Neckel, 1993. p. 247). However, it is the noncompliance or the infringement of the forbidden that also indirectly reveals the existence of a norm in the first place. Kertész turns all this upside down. The shame of he who is or is not does not relate to noncompliance with norms but to compliance with norms and social and biological necessities. It is the shame of he who is or is not over the creature who obeys the rules in every case (i.e., slavishly) thereby participating in the destruction of the other; and it is the shame of the son before a father who approves of the boarding school rules. However, only the one who neither complies with the imposed social conventions of the concentration camp nor follows his biological instinct or the rational directives of rationality is free from the constraints that impose on him to do wrong. It is only on his behalf that no one (who either is or is not) needs to be ashamed.

This is why "Teacher" is also presented as an example for the life of a saint—because he evades all these necessities. Following the Jewish tradition, one can call him one of the just men whose life and deeds set examples for others. Kertész says he does not know why everyone in the camp called the man "Teacher." Disregarding the question of whether the story is true and whether there actually was a person in the camp called "Teacher," there is a Jewish tradition of the just teaching others what is good and just through the example of their own behavior.

For the first-person narrator, any attempt to copy the life of the just-of "Teacher"—means to continue to dig the grave in the breezes that he should dig according to the will of the murderers in the extension of his life because he can no longer follow the usual social norms. The incomprehensible in the implication of shame in Kertész's story is that the first-person narrator enters this path voluntarily in a search for freedom because he is shamed by his survival. He is ashamed of having complied with the norms of the concentration camp in order to survive. At the end of the day, he cannot live with this shame. Here, the shame once again reports with its accompanying logic the violation of a norm that becomes visible only through the shame: You should not have obeyed the rules of the concentration camp. Both Kertész and the first-person narrator know that this is impossible; it is only possible for the just and for God. Hence, he consciously distanced this way of being from that which was humanly possible. That there is another norm of justice, even though we are unable to pursue it, is finally disclosed once again by the shame[19]-the shame of one for his creature that either is or is not. This points to moral shame as an internal commandment that goes beyond external social constraints. Sighard Neckel (1993) comments on this as follows: "Moral shame accompanies guilt and is premised on action, responsibility, and damage to other. Social shame does not require this. It draws on the 'appearance,' the 'neglect,' one's own injury as a trigger for debasement and deficient self-evaluation" (p. 250, translated). Why Kertész told the story in the form of a prayer to the dead now becomes clear in one aspect. In the end, one prays for the one who has reached the end of the journey to freedom.

There is another aspect that can make it easier to understand one facet of the shame of the survivor over his own survival. This aspect can be found in a report on the life and survival of a young woman forced into prostitution: "The shame over that which other people have done to her is great" (Lembke, 2006, translated). Why do people feel shame who have been forced to do something that they would never have done voluntarily,[20] having only bowed to the law of the instinct for survival? It is not only because they have bowed to it but also because something was done to them that *should* never have been done to them, because it is so shameful that no person *should* have to bear it. Shame as an evaluative feeling shows that one has been humiliated, that it has left traces in one's own awareness of self-worth because one devalues oneself, loses self-respect (Neckel, 1993, pp. 245–246). This casts doubt on the whole person, one loses self-esteem and one's place in society. When one becomes the humiliated tool of this violation, the self, as Bernhard Williams (1993) shows in his analysis of shame in the ancient world, is not unaffected. "Shame looks to what I am" (Williams, 1993, p. 93)—and, we have to add, to what I am through the deeds of others that my ego has to remember—regardless of whether it wants to. It is like an injury to the self that robs the individual of the possibility of self-respect and of gaining the respect of others (see also Neckel, 1993, pp. 244, 253).

Shame that does not just relate to social conventions and norms but points beyond them also seems to point to an absolute freedom and autonomy of the individual. That the individual can never be completely autonomous is indicated by sentences such as, "The shame over that which other people have done to her is great" as well as Kertész's reference to the dimension of the saintly and godly. The abused person cannot disregard the humiliated status to which he or she has been assigned by the other. This also relates to what Bernard Williams (1993) says in his analysis of the relation between blame and shame:

> The most primitive experiences of shame are connected with sight and being seen ... and the expression of shame [is also] the desire to disappear, not to be there .. . . the wish that the space occupied by me should be instantaneously empty. With guilt, it is not like this; I am more dominated by the thought that even if I disappeared, it would come with me. (p. 89)[21]

Kertész, in contrast, assigned just deeds to the just and the grave to those who emulate him. The absolutely free and just person is alone in his shame over the lack of freedom in humanity, but the shame nonetheless remains a social emotion. Accordingly, the Good, the just, can be recognized when the social community is excluded, but on the other hand it cannot. As Williams (1993) put it:

> [Guilt] can direct one towards those who have been wronged or damaged, and demand reparation in the name, simply, of what has happened to them. But it cannot by itself help one to understand one's relations to those happenings, or to rebuild the self that has done these things and the world in which that self has to live. Only shame can do that, because it embodies conceptions of what one is and of how one is related to others. (p. 94)

We can read these sentences from Bernhard Williams as a commentary on Kertész's ideas on shame, even though they are written at the end of his analyses on the culture of shame in the ancient world. One of the bases for his treatment of this aspect is his analysis of the description of shame in Euripides' Hippolytos, which presents a literary discussion of the relation between private and public, the self and the imposed social opinion, the personal shame and the shame that follows loss of prestige (Segal, 1970, p. 287).

Even the just man in Kertész does not step outside the framework of the twofold conception of shame that Bernard Williams already ascertained among the Greeks at the end of the 5th century BC: between a shame that follows public opinion or public social rules and a shame that expresses an inner conviction that has formed autonomously (Williams, 1993, p. 95).

At the beginning of this chapter, I pointed out that Plato was primarily concerned with recognizing the Good and less with how the good lives. Plato symbolized this statement in a thought experiment in which he banishes the just into complete social isolation by making him seem to always be an unjust person although he is really always just. He did this to make it plausible that the just person who knows what is just leads a better life than those who do not know it, even when the just is not recognized as such by his fellows. Because the just person cannot recognize and decide what is just on the basis of the support or rejection of his fellows, he has to draw his knowledge from himself. Having to rely only on himself, no social emotion such as shame can provide any indications, only his intellect (*Politeia*, 361c-d; see Williams, 1993, pp. 98, 100–101). Aristotle, in contrast, had a different conception of the relation of the individual to justice. He considered that one has to be reared to be good, and that social emotions such as shame may well play a decisive role in this upbringing.

Kertész's account of the saint for which "Teacher" as a just man gave an example of just and correct deeds, suggesting that this is exactly the same figure as the just person in Plato's cave who acts as he acts without considering what is commanded and how people are behaving around him. "Teacher" does what he does without considering the social or biological constraints. However, according to the accounts of the time at boarding school and the accompanying judgment over the father, being reared to autonomy, to freedom, could mean that the narrator would have acted other than he did even though it would have cost him his life. This section in Kertész and the circumstance that "Teacher" is not depicted as a knowledge-seeking recluse but as one who does what he thinks is right as a matter of habit indicates that an upbringing in the sense of an Aristotelian upbringing to be good (i.e., habitualization of just behavior) would have been an upbringing directed toward freedom. An upbringing directed toward acting autonomously would have been none other than an upbringing to act justly, which would have meant certain death for the narrator.

The narrator first has to find the path toward such a freedom, such an autonomy, and, for him, this is the same as a path to death. That is why he says that he has to dig further until the end.

Accordingly, Kertész's comments revealed two conceptions of shame: one resulting from one's own humiliation and the other resulting from not having complied with norms. Nonetheless, the narrator recognizes these norms only retrospectively, in remembrance (both shame conceptions are usually also presented and distinguished in the literature on this emotion).

The image portrayed by Kertész is not one in which shame points us to the rule of justice or morality to which we gain insight through our understanding or through enlightenment by the saint. By pointing to the shame and not the guilt, he emphasized that the self is not only obliged to accept or reject a law but to behave in an autonomous and free way, thereby finding a path whose direction is determined not only by concern for the self but also by a turning toward others.

Personally, I consider this to be the true difference between shame and guilt. It is not true that the difference is predominantly that the guilt in our minds disappears earlier than the shame, which has also been described as the momentary loss of the world that accompanies this feeling (Williams, 1993, pp. 89–90; Neckel, 1993, p. 244; Casimir & Jung, this volume, section "Embodiment of Pride and Shame and the Related Pan-Human Behavioural Code"). Instead, shame points far beyond guilt and beyond the admission of guilt, to the wish to have acted differently, to have been different, to have experienced differently. It thereby contains an element of the utopian with regard to the past. In addition, it lacks the Christian element of the forgiveness of guilt. Shame remains-it cannot be forgiven, and it cannot be taken away.

Notes

[1] From *hê mênis*: anger, wrath. This term is applied particularly in poetic language, whereas philosophical literature always uses *hê orgê* or *ho thymós* for anger.

[2] Myles Burnyeat (2002) pointed this out in his review of *Restraining Rage: The Ideology of Anger Control in Classical Antiquity* by William Harris. Glenn Most (2003), in contrast, showed that pity is just as central to the *Iliad* as anger: "For when we feel distress at someone else's real or threatened undeserved suffering, we can focus either upon the dimension of the person who experiences that suffering or upon that of the person who causes it: in the former case we feel Homeric pity, in the latter case, Homeric anger" (p. 61; but see also pp. 54, 74). Most showed how Achilles' personality develops in the *Iliad* from that of an angry person to one able to feel pity. More on this later.

[3] Ethnologists also report how men may need to display anger or rage because their social status requires it. Birgitt Röttger-Rössler (2004) described such behavior in the Makassar, a moderately Islamized people living in Indonesia: "Particularly with minor irritations, a high-ranking individual has to display anger, annoyance, or indignation in order to demonstrate rank and social position" (p. 160, translated). For an account of the stabilizing function of so-called hostile feelings or emotions, see also Casimir and Jung (this volume, section on "Self-Evaluation, Self-Esteem, and the Reference Group").

[4] In *Rhetoric* 1378a31–1378a33, Aristotle defined anger as an impulse, accompanied by pain, to a conspicuous revenge for a conspicuous slight. See also Rapp (2002, p. 569).

[5] Christof Rapp (2002, p. 582) went even further, seeing the connection to *logos* in the fact that the emotion follows a principle. The principle that anger follows is accordingly that in which retaliation or revenge has to be undertaken for a humiliation or slight.

[6] So long as one does not follow the Aristotelian theory of a dissociation between the cognitive evaluation and the emotional reaction to it. In modern emotion theories, it is widely accepted that emotions have an evaluative function extending into the cognitive domain. On the question whether Aristotle proposed a cognitive theory of the emotions, see Rapp (2002, pp. 570–575).

[7] Rapp (2002) analyzed Aristotle's definition of emotion for the example of anger (*Rhetoric* II 1):

> [I]nstead, an emotion is defined through a general formal object as in anger through the "humiliation of some one who does not deserve it," from which three elements can be derived: If the general formal object is defined, then this results in, first, the (appropriate) object of, for example, anger; second, the (appropriate) target person; and, third, there are at least necessary preconditions for the state in which one feels the accompanying emotions .... (p. 547, translated)

Anger as a so-called mixed definition reveals both pain and pleasure elements (Aristotle, *Rhetoric* 1370b19-25): pain elements because of the humiliation suffered and pleasure elements because of the anticipated revenge. Apart from these systematic distinctions, even Aristotle already pointed to the physiological elements occurring with the emotion "anger" (see Rapp, 2002, p. 551; see also Konstan, 2003, pp. 101, 102, 112–113, 119–120, who, nonetheless does not go beyond Rapp's analysis).

[8] Myles Burnyeat (1980, p. 86) interpreted the state of those who are happy as also being a state of nature (as first nature) on which the so-called second nature is based and develops through upbringing and habitualization. John McDowell (1994) drew strongly on Myles Burnyeat for his own conception of first and second nature in *Mind and World*.

[9] Aristotle determined that shame is more of an emotion than a disposition through the fact that being ashamed makes one blush, and that this automatically occurring physiological change is appropriate for an emotion but not for habitualization (NE 1128b13–15).

[10] On the relation between shame and anger in Plato and Aristotle, see also Burnyeat (1980, p. 79) and Rapp (2002, p. 585). In the *Topik*, Aristotle stated: "Then the shame is in the thinking part of the soul ... the anger, in contrast, in the valiant part." Konstan (2003, p. 115) also pointed out that both anger and shame are a reaction to the low opinion that others have of us. The only difference being that in the case of shame this relates to our own behavior and in the case of anger not. On Homer, see Williams (1993, p. 93).

[11] Konstan (2003, p. 115) set a somewhat different accent, pointing out that both anger and shame are a reaction to the poor opinion that others have of us. This, however, does not cover the fact that we also shame ourselves when we are ashamed of our own deeds that do not live up to our own standards. Burnyeat's (1980) weighting of the direction toward the just and dignity, in contrast, can cover this circumstance.

[12] Other ethnic groups have also assumed that emotional experience is subject to a developmental process and is not equally strong in all phases of life. See, for example, the reports on the Makasser people in Röttger-Rössler (2004, p. 166).

[13] The philosopher László Földényj (2005) has interpreted this concept of God in Kertész correctly, in my opinion, when he stated:

> Should God, therefore, be the ultimate direction in which one would have to give witness—and naturally its origin? Possibly. However, this is not the God that Kertész repeatedly equates with Auschwitz, but another, distant, unknown God. Whom one could even equate with the inmost core of personality that is such a persistently reoccurring motive in Kertész's writings. This God is the most personal one; He is so close to humanity that He can even usurp humanity's ego from its throne: "In my

opinion, we cannot talk about God; God is neither a person nor an object; I fear we are confronted with a language problem. I talk about how human beings in certain situations have to think God or perhaps think about God—this is simply a witness, a '*documentum humanum*,' nothing more" (Kertész, Ich—ein anderer, 2002, pp. 68–69). (p. 45, translated)

The comment that this God is so close to humans is significant in the present context because shame is a social emotion that has an impact in a social grouping for which a "godlike" God would be too distant.

14 After his parents divorced in 1934, the 5-year-old Imre Kertész was placed in a boarding school for boys, where he completed his 4 years of elementary education. In an essay formulated as an interview with himself, Kertész tells us: "I was placed in a boarding school for boys, as a boarder." Question: "Can we recognize this boarding school in your *Kaddisch* novel" Answer: "With some effort, certainly" (Kertész, 2005, pp. 57–58). However, on page 61, when discussing the passage "we are always sinners before our father and God . . ." and, further: "Auschwitz appears before me in the image of the father; indeed the words father and Auschwitz generate the same echo in me. . . ." He stated: "Enough, enough! Don't forget you're quoting from a novel in which everything is exaggerated."

15 Black milk of daybreak we drink it at sundown
we drink it at noon in the morning we drink it at night
we drink and we drink it
we dig a grave in the breezes there one lies unconfined
A man lives in the house he plays with the serpents he *writes*
he *writes* when dusk falls to Germany your golden hair Margarete
he *writes* it . . .
. . .
he whistles his Jews out in earth has them dig for a grave
. . .
your ashen hair Shulamith we dig a grave in the breezes there one lies unconfined
. . .
he calls out more darkly now stroke your strings then as smoke you will rise in the air
then a grave you will have in the clouds there one lies unconfined
. . .
he sets his pack on to us he grants us a grave in the air
he plays with the serpents and *daydreams* death is a master from Germany
your golden hair Margarete
your ashen hair Shulamith
(Paul Celan,1952/1995, pp. 62–65, Death Fugue. Italics added).

16 Unfortunately, I am unable to check whether the original Hungarian text uses "saint" or perhaps more likely "just." In the Jewish tradition, there are no saints because only God is holy. However, there are the just whose lives and deeds serve as models.

17 F. Nietzsche, *Die Fröhliche Wissenschaft*, Drittes Buch, Nr. 273; Imre Kertész has also translated Friedrich Nietzsche's works into Hungarian.

18 *Ergon* (work, performance). For Aristotle, every thing and being differed according to its performance or its wealth. See the entry for "*ergon*" in Höffe (2005, pp. 208–210, specifically, p. 209).

19 Bernard Williams (1993) gave a similar interpretation of Sophocles' Antigone:

It might be thought that the heroic figure in Sophocles who stands in the greatest contrast to Ajax, whose consciousness is most obviously directed to a demand that transcends mere social esteem, and, even more, reaches beyond self-assertion, is Antigone.... Indeed, she does call, very famously (454–55) on the "unwritten, solid, laws of the gods" as opposed to Creon's "instructions"; and her last words appeal to a value of piety. (pp. 85–86)

[20] In his *Rhetoric* (1384a–1384a22), Aristotle pointed out that one also feels shame for things that one has suffered involuntarily.

[21] See also Casimir and Jung (this volume, section "The Embodiment of Pride and Shame and the Related Pan-Human Behavioural Code") when reporting how Australian aborigines talk about wishing that the earth would open up and swallow them.

References

Aristotle (2000). *Nicomachean Ethics* (R. Crisp, Trans. & Ed.). Cambridge, UK: Cambridge University Press.

Burnyeat, M. F. (1980). Aristotle on learning to be good. In A. Oksenberg Rorty (Ed.), *Essays on Aristotle's Ethics* (pp. 69–92). Berkeley, CA: University of California Press.

Burnyeat, M. F. (2002, October 17). Excuses for madness. *London Review of Books, 24*(20).

Canto-Sperber, M. (2000). Die Ethik. In J. Brunschwig & G. Lloyd (Eds.), *Das Wissen der Griechen: Eine Enzyklopädie* (pp. 116–139) [Le savoir grec. Dictionnaire critique]. Munich, Germany: W. Fink. (Original work published 1996)

Celan, P. (1996). *Paul Celan: Selected Poems* (M. Hamburger, Trans.). London: Penguin. (Original work published 1952)

DeSousa, R. (1997). *Die Rationalität des Gefühls* [The rationality of emotion]. Frankfurt am Main, Germany: Suhrkamp. (Original work published 1987)

Földényj, L. (2005). Der Identitätslose und sein Ich. Wie es Wilhelm Meister in Auschwitz erging. Zehn Begriffe für ein Kertész-Wörterbuch [He without identity and his ego. How Wilhelm Meister fared in Auschwitz. Ten terms for a Kertész dictionary]. *"du"—Zeitschrift für Kultur, 757, Imre Kertész. Der Fremde*, 42–45.

Höffe, O. (2005). (Ed.), *Aristoteles-Lexikon* [Aristotle dictionary]. Stuttgart, Germany: Kröner Verlag.

Kertész, I. (2002). *Ich—ein anderer* [I, an other]. Reinbek bei Hamburg, Germany: Rowohlt.

Kertész, I. (2004). *Kaddish for an unborn child* (T. Wilkinson, Trans.). New York: Random House. (Original work published 1990)

Kertész, I. (2005). Dossier K. Eine Ermittlung [Dossier K: An investigation]. *"du"—Zeitschrift für Kultur, 757, Imre Kertész. Der Fremde*, 52–62.

Konstan, D. (2003). Aristotle on anger and the emotions. In S. Braund & G. Most (Eds.), *Ancient anger: Perspectives from Homer to Galen* (pp. 99–120). Cambridge, UK: Cambridge University Press.

Lembke, J. (2006, January 11). Gefangen mitten in Berlin; Wie eine junge Frau aus Rumänien in Deutschland zur Prostitution gezwungen wurde [Held prisoner in the middle of Berlin: How a young woman from Romania was forced into prostitution in Germany]. *Frankfurter Allgemeine Zeitung*. Retrieved February 26, 2007 from http://www.faz.net/IN/INtemplates/faznet

Most, G. (2003). Anger and pity in Homer's Iliad. In S. Braund & G. Most (Eds.), *Ancient anger: Perspectives from Homer to Galen* (pp. 50–75). Cambridge, UK: Cambridge University Press.

Neckel, S. (1993). Achtungsverlust und Scham. Die soziale Gestalt eines existentiellen Gefühls [Loss of respect and shame: The social form of an existential feeling]. In H. Fink-Eitel & G. Lohmann (Eds.), *Zur Philosophie der Gefühle* (pp. 244–265). Frankfurt, Germany: Suhrkamp.

Nietzsche, F. (1930). *Die Fröhliche Wissenschaft* [The gay science]. Leipzig, Germany: Kröner Verlag. (Original work published 1882)
Rapp, C. (2002). *Die Emotionen. Vorbemerkung zu Kap. II2-11* [The emotions: Preface to Chap. II2–11]. In C. Rapp (Ed. & Trans.), *Aristoteles, Rhetorik* (pp. 543–583). Darmstadt, Germany: Wissenschaftliche Buchgesellschaft.
Röttger-Rössler, B. (2004). *Die kulturelle Modellierung des Gefühls. Ein Beitrag zur Theorie und Methodik ethnologischer Emotionsforschung anhand indonesischer Fallstudien* [The cultural modeling of feeling: A theoretical and methodological contribution to ethnological emotion research based on Indonesian case studies]. Münster, Germany: LIT Verlag.
Segal, C. (1970). Shame and purity in Euripides' Hippolytus. *Hermes, 98*, 278–299.
Williams, B. (1993). *Shame and necessity*. Berkeley, CA: University of California Press.

Index

Printed in the United States of America